NEW WORKS
IN ACCOUNTING
HISTORY

Richard P. Brief, *Series Editor*

Leonard N. Stern School of Business
New York University

A Garland Series

A HISTORY OF
CANADIAN ACCOUNTING
THOUGHT AND PRACTICE

Edited by
George J. Murphy

Garland Publishing, Inc.
New York and London 1993

Introduction copyright © 1993 by George J. Murphy

Library of Congress Cataloging-in-Publication Data

A history of Canadian accounting thought and practice / edited by George J.
Murphy.
p.cm.—(New works in accounting history)
Includes bibliographical references and index.
ISBN 0-8153-1248–2
1. Accounting—Canada—History. 2. Accountants—Canada. 3. Account-
ing—Standards—Canada—History. 4. Accounting—Law and legislation—
Canada—History. 5. Accounting—Canada—Chronology.
I. Murphy, George J. (George Joseph). II. Series.
HF5616.C2H57   1993   93–9763
657'.0971—dc20

All volumes printed on acid-free, 250-year-life paper.
Manufactured in the United States of America.

Design by Marisel Tavarez

To Angela . . .

CONTENTS

Acknowledgments   xi
Introduction   1
Authors   15
A map of Canada with selected historical statistics.   16

I: Early Records

1.   Mann, H., "Accounting for Les Forges De Saint-Maurice
      1730-1736," The Accounting Historians Journal, (The Academy of
      Accounting Historians), Spring 1979, pp. 63–82   23

2.   Felton, S. and Mann, H., "Accounting for a Brewery at Louisbourg,"
      Contemporary Accounting Research, Fall, 1990, pp. 261–277   43

3.   "A Complete System of Bookkeeping by Double Entry," Accounting
      Primer of Robin, Jones and Whitman, pp. 1–17   61

4.   Mann, H., "The Companies Reviewed", "The Financial Statements:
      Form and Format" and "Footnotes", The Evolution of Accounting
      in Canada, 1972, pp. 7–22, pp. 53–63 and p. 77 respectively   79

II: The Profession

1.   Parton, J., "Fifty Years Ago," Canadian Chartered Accountant,
      July 1961, pp. 94–96   108

2.   Gordon, H.D.L., "Fifty Years Ago," Canadian Chartered
      Accountant, July 1961, pp. 96–98   110

3. Edwards, H.P., "Three Score Years," <u>Canadian Chartered Accountant</u>, Feb. 1940, pp. 76–93   114

4. Creighton, P., "George Edwards, the Great Organizer," <u>A Sum of Yesterdays –Being a History of the First One Hundred Years of The Institute of Chartered Accountants of Ontario</u>, 1984, pp. 130–135133

5. Skinner, R.M., "Research Contributions to Canadian Standards: A Retrospective", <u>Research in Accounting Regulation</u>, (ed) G.J. Previts, Vol. 3, 1989, JAI Press, pp. 197–217   139

6. Murphy, G.J., "Early Canadian Financial Statement Disclosure Legislation," <u>The Accounting Historians Journal</u>, (The Academy of Accounting Historians), Fall, 1984, pp. 39–59   161

7. Richardson, A.J., "Professionalization and Intra-professional Competition in the Canadian Accounting Profession," <u>Work and Occupations</u>, Nov. 1987, pp. 591–615   183

8. Richardson, A.J., "Who Audits? The Emergence of Hegemony in the Ontario Accountancy Profession," Queens University Conference on Behavioural and Social Accounting, Kingston, July, 1986, pp. 1–37   209

9. Richardson, A.J., "Canada's Accounting Elite: 1880–1930," <u>The Accounting Historians Journal</u>, (The Academy of Accounting Historians), June 1989, pp. 1–21   251

III: Standard Setting

1. Ontario Provincial Statues, Financial Statement Disclosure Requirements, "The Ontario Companies Act, 1907," 7 Edn. VII, Ch. 34   274

2. Gray, J.C., "Standardization of Shareholders' Accounts and Auditors' Reports and Certificates," <u>Canadian Chartered Accountant</u>, January, 1919, pp. 193–206   275

3. Zeff, S.A., "Canada," Ch. IV of <u>Forging Accounting Principles in Five Countries: A History and Analysis of Trends</u>, Stipes Publishing Company, Illinois, 1971, pp. 269–305   289

4.   Waterhouse, J.H., "A Descriptive Analysis of Selected Aspects of the Canadian Accounting Standard-Setting Process" together with "Discussants Comments" by D.G. Ward and A.W. Hopkins in Research to Support Standard Setting: A Canadian Perspective, ed. by S. Basu and J.A. Milburn, The Clarkson Gordon Foundation, 1982, pp. 95–151   327

5.   Stamp, E., "Accounting Standard Setting... A New Beginning: Evolution Not Revolution," CA Magazine, September 1980, pp. 38–43   385

6.   Amernic, J.H., and Lemon, W.M., "Do We Need A Canadian Conceptual Framework," CA Magazine, July, 1984, pp. 22–27   401

7.   Accounting Standards Committee, "Financial Statement Concepts," The Canadian Institute of Chartered Accountants, Dec. 1988, Sec. 1000, pp. 101–111   423

IV: Legislation, Inquiries and Regulation

1.   Murphy, G.J., "Financial Statement Disclosure and Corporate Law: The Canadian Experience," International Journal of Accounting, Spring 1980, pp. 87–99   437

2.   Smails, R.G.H., "Directors' Reports – A Criticism and Suggestion," The Canadian Chartered Accountant, Sept. 1931, pp. 100–106   450

3.   Crandall, R.H., "Government Intervention - The PIP Grant Accounting Controversy," Cost and Management, Sept./Oct. 1983, pp. 55–59   457

4.   Beck, S.M., and Cherry, P.G., "How the Regulators See Us," CA Magazine, Oct. 1987, pp. 40–44.   463

5.   The Canadian Institute of Chartered accountants, "Report of the Commission To Study the Public's Expectation of Audits: Executive Summary," June 1988, pp. 1–22   473

6.   Lew, B. and Richardson, A.J., "Institutional Responses to Bank Failure: A Comparative Case Study of the Home Bank (1923) and Canadian Commercial Bank (1985) Failures," Critical Perspectives on Accounting, Vol. 3, No. 2, 1992, pp. 1–21   495

V: Chronologies

1.   Murphy, G.J., "A Chronology of the Development of Corporate
Financial Reporting in Canada," The Accounting Historians Journal,
(The Academy of Accounting Historians), Spring, 1986, pp. 31–62   519

2.   Richardson, A.J., "An Interpretive Chronology of the
       Development of Accounting Associations in Canada: 1879–1979,"
       1992, pp. 1–75   551

Index   629

Acknowledgments

The editor and publisher are grateful to the journals, publishers and authors listed in the contents for permission to reprint copyright material in this volume. Any further reproduction of this matter is prohibited without the permission of the copyright holders.

Much of the data in Professor Richardson's article on "Who Audits? The Emergence of Hegemony in the Ontario Accountancy Profession," a paper given at the Queen's University Conference on Behavioural and Social Accounting in 1986, was subsequently reformulated in terms of the concept of corporatism and published in *Accounting, Organizations and Society*, Vol. 14, No. 5/6, pp. 415–431.

The article by R.H. Crandall is reprinted from *Cost and Management*, September/October 1983, by permission of the Society of Management Accountants of Canada.

Special thanks are given to Margaret Forbes of Lakehead University for her help with the index and to Alister Mason of Deloitte and Touche for his encouragement of, and interest in, things historical over many years.

A HISTORY OF CANADIAN ACCOUNTING THOUGHT AND PRACTICE

INTRODUCTION

Canada's federal nature serves to complicate the jurisdictional authority for accounting matters. The Canadian constitution empowers the ten provinces to regulate educational concerns -- which includes the training and certification of accountants; and each province shares with the federal government the entitlement to incorporate organizations and associations. As a consequence of this division and overlay of responsibilities, a great deal of effort in Canada has been expended by accounting bodies on jurisdictional disputes and in the coordination of educational activities (see Richardson's articles herein on "Professionalization..." and "An Interpretive Chronology...").

Despite these problems, Canada's contribution to accounting thought and practice is both interesting and instructive. This anthology will focus largely on the evolution of accounting institutions, practices and standard-setting. Canadian accounting literature and the academic setting are not touched on. (For reviews of this literature, the reader is referred to Mattessich and to Richardson and Williams which are noted in the References).

The collection is divided under five headings: Early Records, The Profession, Standard-Setting, Legislation, Inquiries and Regulation; and Chronologies. These introductory comments provide some interpretive background.

1

EARLY RECORDS

The first enduring European settlements on present-day mainland Canada arose in the sixteenth century by the French. Some two hundred years later Britain conquered New France in 1759. Relatively few accounting records survive from those early times, or indeed from periods prior to the mid-nineteenth century.

Two commentaries from those earliest dates are provided by Professors Mann and Felton. Accounting for Les Forges Saint Maurice 1730-36 is an interesting reconstruction of the financing and building of a large capital project during the French regime, involving capital and operating budgets not dissimilar to their present-day counterparts. The accounts relating to the brewery at Louisbourg are of particular North-American colonial interest for this period because they represent the introduction of a financial statement with recognizable classifications and accruals, quite separate from the accounts themselves.

The National Archives of Canada houses a fairly extensive collection of the accounting records of Robin Jones and Whitman. This firm, head-officed in the Channel Islands, engaged in the fishing, processing and exporting of cod in the late eighteenth century off Canada's eastern coast. Among its records is a primer on A Complete System of Bookkeeping by Double Entry (dated 1788 on its informal leather binding) that is quite likely the earliest extant version of its kind in Canada. However, rather than it being the product of native minds, the editor has found that it is a close copy of Benjamin's Donn's The Accountant and of Daniel Dowling's The Universal Accountant, both of 1765. A set of illustrative wastebook/journals and ledgers detailing typical eighteenth century transatlantic trading activities forms part of the primer.

In the next article, Mann provides information on six prominent Canadian companies from the middle of the nineteenth century to the early part of this century. These doctoral thesis extracts include background information together with illustrations and commentary on their financial statements. It should be noted that,consistent with British practice, the specific incorporating disclosure legislation relating to banks, telephone and railway companies was from earliest times far more demanding than for general commercial and industrial companies.

The examination of pre twentieth century Canadian accounting records is in a very early state. The National Archives in Ottawa does have a small collection of nineteenth and late eighteenth century records--the most notable of which is Molson Breweries dating from 1783, which unfortunately, has not been examined for its accounting significance. One large work, not represented in this collection, is Professor C. McWatters' recent doctoral thesis (1991) which investigates the use and response of accounting records to changes in business enterprise for the nineteenth century Calvin timber company. The editor is unaware of any Canadian accounting examination of the long-lived English/Canadian Hudson Bay Company.

Similarly, little comprehensive and representative information about actual financial statement and corporate reporting practices is available for the early part of the twentieth century. Fortunately, however, there exists an annual anthology of Canadian corporate financial statements running from 1900 to 1940 which is available to form the base for a representative and accessible documentation of that period. The Annual Financial Review; Canadian edited by W. R. Houston, an Assistant Secretary of the Toronto Stock Exchange faithfully reflects the form and content of the vast majority of financial statements of those companies listed on the Montreal and Toronto stock exchanges for that period.

THE PROFESSION

Some of the flavour of the early days in the development of the public accounting profession is provided in the personal reminiscences of J. Parton, H. D. Lockhart Gordon, and H.P. Edwards. The latter's father, George Edwards, in a brief biographical extract from Creighton's excellent history of the Institute of Chartered Accountants of Ontario (ICAO), is viewed as the individual that supplied the firm foundation to that Institute--the leading provincial public accounting association in Canada since its formation in 1879. Both Parton and Gordon were, from the early part of the century, outstanding public practitioners and became very prominent in Institute affairs. Skinner's article provides an insider's view of the workings of a prominent researcher/ practitioner throughout the latter part of this century in one of the country's leading public accounting firms.

The editor's own article attempts to demonstrate the significance of the accounting profession in shaping the early corporate financial statement disclosure regulations. Those regulations--the Ontario Companies Acts of 1897 and 1907--were at the forefront of international legislated accounting disclosure requirements in the latter part of the nineteenth and early part of the twentieth centuries.

Three selections by Professor A. Richardson follow. They are pieces of research that are not in the general investigative, pattern-finding mould of traditional historical work. Rather, they bring to the inquiry, models from the social sciences which they use to explain certain aspects of the evolution or the existence of particular features of accounting events or institutions. These studies are particularly enriching of historical inquiry when they are able to provide generalizations on the evolution of competing institutional groupings and across differing professional fields. Richardson's first two articles outline the struggles of competing accounting associations to mark out their territory and achieve societal recognition by the adoption of the traditional symbolic attributes of professionalism. The much earlier organization of the

Chartered Accountants and their identification with the mandated audit legislation of corporate affairs gave that body a commanding lead in the pecking order--a lead which seems to have increased by the versatility of the Ontario Institute's activity in co-opting over time the values and even the leaders of challenging associations. Canada may rival Britain in the diversity of its accounting organizations.

Richardson's third contribution shows how quickly Canada's accounting elite took on religious (Anglican), political (Conservative) and country of origin (British) characteristics. However, this paper does not address a related and important question which has yet to be seriously studied: that is, how indigenously inspired and staffed was the formation of the late nineteenth century accounting associations in Canada? The editor is unaware of any British firms setting up offices in Canada as happened in America; and certainly such leading and influential individuals as E.R.C. Clarkson and George Edwards were both home-grown and educated Canadians. As with the documentation of a representative set of early Canadian accounting practices, knowledge of the origins of nineteenth century accounting in Canada is somewhat of an untended garden. Firm commissioned histories (see the bibliography of Richardson's "An Interpretive Chronology ..." herein) will prove helpful in this regard.

STANDARD SETTING

In the early years of Canadian financial reporting and well into the fourth decade of this century, the concern for accounting standards related to disclosure and only rarely to measurement. Prior to official standards recommendations for members of the Institute of Chartered Accountants (CICA) commencing in 1946, incorporating statutes outlined only minimal disclosure requirements.

The 1907 disclosure requirements of the Ontario's Companies Act is provided in the first selection. It represents path-breaking legislation in Canada and well ahead of its British counterpart for the period. It faithfully represents the recommendations of the Council of the ICAO of a year earlier. These requirements remained in force despite the requests of a British committee to obtain uniformity in Commonwealth company law which would have had the effect for Ontario of reducing annual disclosure requirements to British standards (the Province of British Columbia complied in 1910). This Ontario legislation was copied at the federal level some ten years later in 1917.

Gray's article provides some illustrative formats for financial statement presentation which were common to the second decade of this century. This format goes well beyond legislative requirements, reflecting very likely, the informal standards of public accounting practitioners, the normative accounting literature and the expectations of shareholders and creditors with regard to financial statement disclosure. Gray's illustrative set fall somewhat below the disclosure level implicit in the American Institute of Accountants UNIFORM ACCOUNTING of 1917.

Professor Zeff's article is invaluable in providing external and international comparative commentary on the formation of and influences on Canadian standard setting up to 1970. Shortly after Zeff's study the Canadian Business Corporations Act in 1975 effectively delegated responsibility to the CICA by requiring that financial statements, prepared as a consequence of its incorporating powers, be in conformity with the CICA Handbook. This delegation (unrequested!) of authority and responsibility to the profession may be unique among English speaking communities. By the mid 1970s, Waterhouse et. al. are pointing out the problems, both real and perceived, that have continued to face CICA standard setting since 1975. These concerns relate to the narrowness in background of committee membership (mostly Chartered Accountants!), processes that are not sufficiently open to the public, the lack of a conceptual framework which would legitimize standard setting, and a lack of concern for the political and economic consequences of standard setting. Changes in 1991 reduced the CICA-appointed voting members of the standard setting committee to eight (of thirteen).

In response to the long time charge that a conceptual foundation was needed, the CICA commissioned Professor Edward Stamp a naturalized Canadian to remedy this deficiency. This study elaborates the users, their needs and the criteria by which to assess standards and accountability. It sets forth the reasons, many of them historical and political, for a Canadian framework to differ from that of the American. Stamp's study CORPORATE REPORTING; ITS FUTURE EVOLUTION did not find acceptance in Canada--some of the reasons for which are put forward by Professors Amernic and Lemon. In 1988 the CICA incorporated into its Handbook a mini-framework, "Financial Statement Concepts", mirroring many of the FASB concepts, with the injunction that standard setters are to bear these concepts in mind when establishing accounting standards.

LEGISLATION, INQUIRIES AND REGULATION

Canadian legislation with respect to annual financial statement disclosure had been in early times at the international forefront of disclosure regulation. The Province of Ontario was in the vanguard with the 1897 and 1907 statutes requiring income and expenditure statements and audited balance sheets, and again in 1953 with a massive increase in disclosure--largely by way of footnotes. Federal legislation in 1917 and 1965 copied these provisions word for word. In Ontario the ICAO had provided the recommending drafts for this legislation. It is really only since the 1950s that the impetus for, and organization of standard setting has shifted from the Ontario provincial to the federal scene. In the mid 1970s incorporating and securities setting jurisdictions formally transferred authority for financial statement disclosure to the CICA and its Handbook, as outlined in the previous section.

Professor Smails' article is included because for three decades from the mid-1920s, together with Professors Ashley and Smythe, he lead the way in pointing out the shortcomings in financial statement reporting. This small piece is typical of his forthright style. Though he did not look for legislation to improve reporting practices, it was indeed the 1934 legislation that required and secured the disclosure of asset valuation bases and better income and surplus reporting--the latter prompted by the seeming deficiencies which the British RMSP case revealed.

In 1981, within six years of the delegation of authority to the Handbook, a startling challenge to the CICA emerged. The very federal jurisdiction that had initiated this delegation insisted that particular government investment incentive grants be viewed as a reduction of income rather than of assets. Professor Crandall outlines this dramatic confrontation. The CICA stood firm in its position and with the help of the Ontario Securities Commission (OSC), through its control of the Toronto Stock Exchange, forced federal authorities to back down. The question now arises whether the autonomy of the standard setting process in Canada has been confirmed by this event, or whether the CICA authority is now very much beholden to the OSC. Certainly the latter organization has in the last decade become much more active in attempting to influence the standard setting agenda, in requiring a Management and Discussion Analysis and Accounting Information Form and since 1988, in undertaking and circulating an annual review of the financial statements of Toronto Stock Exchange listed companies. Beck and Cherry, the Chairman and Chief Accountant of the OSC in 1987 demonstrate their forthrightness in the need for improved reporting. Their successors, Eprile and Sanford (1991), keep the pressure on.

The powers of the Ontario Securities Commission are not dissimilar to those of the SEC, and it is likely that this agency will increasingly mirror the activity and energy of its American counterpart.

Scandals have played an equivocal role in the history of accounting change in Canada: some banking failures in the early part of the century were the occasion to strengthen audit provisions, and similarly, some concern for financial reporting inadequacies led to changes in mid 1930 federal statutes. However, neither the path-breaking legislation in Ontario of 1907 nor of 1953 was occasioned by corporate failures or defalcations. And again, the changes in the federal legislation of 1964-65 were well underway prior to the first famous Canadian scandal involving the Atlantic Acceptance Corporation broke across the international headlines. Throughout the 1980s there has been a series of corporate scandals and failures relating to financial institutions. However, not until the failures of the relatively small provincially-based Northlands Bank and Canadian Commercial Bank in Alberta, were accounting and auditing standards and practices called into question. The Lew and Richardson article draws interesting parallels between two bank failures some sixty years apart. Judge W.Z. Estey's Royal Commission of 1986 dealt so harshly with then-existing bank accounting and auditing practices that the CICA commissioned a blue-ribbon committee of independent citizens to report on THE PUBLIC'S EXPECTATIONS OF AUDITS. The summary of this document presented here has served to set the agenda for standard setting since 1988.

The inquiries that corporate failures have given rise to during the 1980s have not served to dislodge the authority of the CICA in its standard setting role. A variety of reasons may account for the CICA's good fortune: the quick response of the CICA in setting up the Macdonald inquiry; the century old prestige of the leading Canadian accounting organization; the dominance of Chartered Accountant members in accounting and financial positions throughout Canadian institutions; and possibly the fact that of late, financial failures are seen to be internationally endemic to the excesses of the 1980s and not merely confined to Canada. It is also quite apparent that the Institute takes its role very seriously and has proved responsive in adjusting to changing circumstances. Similarly, the increased activity and reporting requirements of the Ontario Securities Commission has the effect not simply of encouraging and supporting the CICA's efforts, but also of somewhat diffusing responsibility. The CICA's role in future standard setting is very likely to be marked by increasing government surveillance particularly through the agency of the Ontario Securities Commission.

CHRONOLOGIES

Two chronologies are offered--the editor's own work relating to corporate reporting practices up to 1983, and that of Professor Richardson's outline of the first one hundred years of the birth, growth, death and merger of the many Canadian accounting and auditing associations and institutes. Richardson's chronology has not been previously published. It serves--together with his two articles under professionalism--to acknowledge and place in perspective the several bodies across the ten provinces that have contributed to the Canadian professional accounting and auditing scene.

The extensive bibliographies in the articles by Richardson and Murphy are brought to the reader's attention. They cover off a good proportion of the literature relevant to the topics considered in this collection.

REFERENCES

Eprile, B., and Sanford, D., "Beyond the Numbers: Improving Normative Financial Reporting in Canada", CMA Magazine, March 1991, pp.7-14.

Houston, W.R., The Annual Financial Review: Canadian, Houston's Standard Publications, Toronto, 1901-1941.

Mattessich, R.V., Academic Research Accounting and MIS in Canada: Evolution, Achievements and Institutional Environment, forthcoming, 1993.

McWatters, C., Accounting Change in Historical Context: The Case of the Calvin Company, 1839-1915, 1991, Doctoral dissertation, Queen's University.

Richardson, A.J. and Williams, J.J., "Canadian Academic Accountant's Productivity: A Survey of 10 Refereed Publications, 1976-1989", Contemporary Accounting Research, Fall, 1990, pp. 278-294.

Authors

Amernic, J.H., Professor, University of Toronto.

Beck, S.M., former Chairman, Ontario Securities Commission.

Cherry, P.G. former Chief Accountant, Ontario Securities Commission.

Crandall, R.H., (retired), Professor, Queen's University.

Creighton, P., private practitioner and historian.

Edwards, H. (deceased), partner at Edwards Morgan.

Felton, S., Professor, Brock University.

Gordon, H.D. Lockhart, (deceased), partner of Clarkson Gordon & Co., President of the Institute of Chartered Accountants of Ontario, 1933.

Gray, J.D., (deceased), practitioner.

Hopkins, A.W., consultant, formerly Professor, University of Regina,

Lemon, W.M., Professor, University of Waterloo.

Lew, B., Doctoral Student, Queen's University.

Mann, H., Professor, Brock University.

Murphy, G.J., Professor, University of Saskatchewan; Adjunct Professor of Management, University of Lethbridge.

Parton, J. (deceased), partner of George A. Touche and Co., President of the Canadian Institute of Chartered Accountants, 1918.

Richardson, A.J. Professor, Queen's University.

Skinner, R.M., (retired), partner of Clarkson Gordon & Co. (Ernst Young).

Smails, R.G.H. (deceased), Professor, Queen's University.

Stamp, E., (deceased), Professor, University of Lancaster.

Ward, D.G., practitioner.

Waterhouse, J.H., Professor, University of Waterloo.

Zeff, S.A., Herbert S. Autrey Professor of Accounting, Rice University.

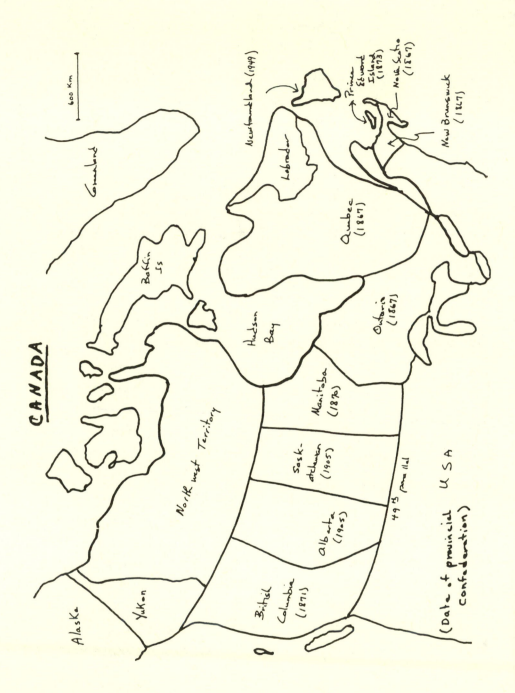

CANADA

600 Km

Greenland

Newfoundland (1949)

Labrador

→ Prince Edward Island (1873)

Nova Scotia (1867)

New Brunswick (1867)

Quebec (1867)

Baffin Is

Hudson Bay

Ontario (1867)

North west Territory

Manitoba (1870)

Saskatchewan (1905)

Alberta (1905)

49°5 para lel

U S A

Alaska

Yukon

British Columbia (1871)

(Date of provincial Confederation)

16

Selected Historical Statistics
Population (000)

Year	Maritimes[1]	Quebec	Ontario	West[2]	Total
1871	767	1,191	1,620	111	3,689
1881	871	1,359	1,926	168	4,324
1891	880	1,488	2,114	351	4,833
1901	894	1,648	2,182	647	5,371
1911	938	2,005	2,527	1,736	7,206
1921	1,000	2,361	2,933	2,494	8,788
1931	1,009	2,874	3,431	3,062	10,376
1941	1,130	3,331	3,787	3,258	11,506
1951	1,617	4,055	4,597	3,740	14,009
1961	1,897	5,259	6,236	4,873	18,265
1971	2,057	6,027	7,703	5,781	21,568
1981	2,234	6,438	8,625	7,046	24,343
1991	2,322	6,895	10,084	7,994	27,296

[1] Includes Prince Edward Island, Nova Scotia, New Brunswick and Newfoundland.

[2] Includes Manitoba, Saskatchewan, Alberta, British Columbia, Yukon and Northwest Territories.

Sources: The Canada Year Book 1921, p. 38131-7; and The Canada Year Book 1991, p. 82, and Statistics Canada.

Selected Historical Statistics
Price Indexes

Year	Index of Common Stocks[1]	Consumers Price Index[2]
1920	55.3	93.6
1930	94.0	75.2
1940	70.3	65.7
1950	146.3	102.9
1960	261.5	128.0
1970	911.0	31.9
1980	2,126.0	67.2
1990	3,421.0	119.5

[1] To 1960, 1935 - 39 = 100; after that, 1975 = 100 for Toronto Stock Exchange.

[2] To 1960, 1949 = 100; after that, 1986 = 100

Sources: M.C. Urquhart and K.A. Buckley, eds., Historical Statistics of Canada, The Macmillan company of Canada Ltd., 1956, pp. 304 and 277 up to 1960; from 1970 on, The Canadian Economic Observer, Hitorical Statistical Supplement 1990/91, Statistics Canada, 1991, pp. 92 and 49.

Selected Historical Statistics

Year	Gross National Product ($Millions)	Commercial Failures Number	Liabilities ($thousands)
1880	581		
1890	803	1,847	18,000
1900	1,057	1,355	11,613
1910	2,235	1,262	14,515
1920	5,529		
1921		2,451	73,299
1930	5,728		
1933		2,044	32,954
1939		1,392	15,089
1940	6,743		
1950	18,006		
1957		2,213	79,863
1960	36,287		
1966		3,007	247,467
1970	87,765		
1980	302,064		
1981		7,708	1,029,544
1990	647,624	11,180	2,842,848

Sources: M.C. Urquhart and K.A. Buckley, eds., Historic Statistics of Canada, The Macmillan Company of Canada Ltd., pp. 14 and 659 up to 1960; after that, The Canadian Economic Observer, Historical Statistical Supplement 1990/91, Statistics Canada, 1991, pp. 8 and 90.

Section I: Early Records

Harvey Mann
CONCORDIA UNIVERSITY, MONTREAL

ACCOUNTING FOR LES FORGES DE SAINT-MAURICE 1730-1736*

Abstract: From a capital budget, an operating budget and a partnership agreement prepared almost 250 years ago in New France, a cash Budget and balance sheets are prepared to help in an analysis of the viability of the company. This investigation into the feasibility of the project discloses a quite sophisticated use of managerial accounting. The original partnership failed, but eventually the company became a successful venture.

Accounting played a prominent role in the establishment of Les Forges de Saint-Maurice between 1730 and 1736. This is illustrated by a capital budget and an operating budget, prepared to support a request for a much-needed loan. In this paper, after an opening balance sheet is drawn up from various bits of data, the two budgets are examined and recast into more traditional forms. They are then analysed to ascertain whether decisions might have been different if present day techniques had been used. To aid in the conclusions drawn, recourse is made to an agreement between the partners. Other parts of this agreement are also examined for their accounting content. Using all the information, a new balance sheet is then prepared. It is possible to conclude that mistakes were made that may have been avoided if all the proper questions had been asked, but there is no doubt that the original concept was very sound.

Background

European explorers were first lured to North America by hopes of gold and other exotic riches, but it wasn't until 200 years after Jacques Cartier sailed up the St. Lawrence River that a more prosaic, but more useful, metal was mined and worked in New France.[1] This venture, Les Forges (ironworks) de Saint-Maurice,

---

*A great deal of original research on Les Forges de Saint-Maurice has been done by Cameron Nish, Professor of History at Concordia University, Montreal, Canada, and a leading authority on the ironworks. Although liberal use has been made of his work, it must be emphasized that the author is responsible for errors of translation and any interpretations of the data.

was started in 1730 a few miles from Three Rivers, a town half-way between Montreal and Quebec City. Although this was the first major manufacturing enterprise in New France, it was, by no means, the first in North America. This distinction is borne by a smaller venture established about 90 years earlier at Saugus, near Boston, Massachusetts,[2] approximately 400 miles southeast of Three Rivers. Several reasons can be given to explain why Saugue was started only 20 years after the first settlers arrived, while it took almost 10 times as long for a similar attempt in New France. Differences in population growth,[3] reasons behind the emigration from the old countries, the "Puritan Ethic" versus exploitation,[4] harsher weather conditions, longer trade routes, and the needs and attitudes of the mother countries[5], were all contributory factors. More important for the purpose of this paper, however, was that the American undertaking was "private enterprise", while the French enterprise required government approval at every step. This bureaucracy may have hampered industrial growth but does offer some compensations for accounting historians, since a great deal of the early information on Les Forges is available from letters of government officials and state documents that have survived in archives on both sides of the Atlantic.[6] The Saugus story, on the other hand, had to be gleaned from court records, which, actually, only tell the seamier side of the operation.

The Beginnings

The first faltering steps towards the eventual establishment of Les Forges de Saint-Maurice were taken in 1730 by a Montreal merchant, François Poulin de Francheville. He requested a 20-year monopoly from the State for the purpose of setting up an ironworks. This request was quickly granted by Gilles Hocquart, the Intendant (director), who was anxious to develop the colony and needed iron for a shipbuilding project near Quebec City. More important, de Francheville, as a true entrepreneur, did not initially ask for a subsidy or any government grant, very unusual at that time. He did, however, ask for help in recruiting experienced forgemen. This request was readily granted by the Crown, which sent two artisans from France at its own expense. By 1732, ore samples had been tested from the proposed site of the ironworks at the seignory (estate) of Saint-Maurice, with excellent results. By the end of that year, however, de Franceville realized that he had underestimated the magnitude of the project. He had spent £9,244.9s.5d[7] about one-third of his capital, and the forge was nowhere near ready for operation. To spread the risk and obtain additional capital, de Francheville decided to form a company and to involve others in the project. At the same time, he asked the French government for a loan of £10,000. The new company was set up with 20 shares, worth 1s each, de Franceville keeping 10 shares for himself. The other partners being:

> Pierre Poulin — De Francheville's brother and a Quebec City merchant François-Etienne Cugnet — a director of Domain d'Occident (western land), a member of the Superior Council of the colony, and shortly thereafter, first counsellor Bricault de Valmur — Hocquart's secretary, and Ignace Gamelin — the son of a Montreal fur trader.

The price of the seignory to the company was fixed at £6,000, but this amount did not have to be paid as long as payment of £300 per annum was made. (This is being interpreted as an open-end mortgage at 5%.) In April, 1733 the loan of £10,000 was granted by the government. From the data given in the previous paragraph it is possible to prepare the following opening balance sheet of the company.

Les Forges de Saint-Maurice
Opening Balance Sheet
April 1733

Assets		Liabilities and Capital	
Cash	£10,001	Loan payable — State	£10,000
Land	6,000	Loan — de Francheville	9,244.9s.5d.
Construction in progress	9,244.9s.5d.	Mortgage @ 5%	6,000
		Capital — partners	20s
	£25,245.9s.5d.		£25,245.9s.5d.

With the new infusion of capital, the construction of the forge progressed favourably, but unfortunately de Francheville fell sick and died in November, 1733. As can be expected, this complicated matters considerably, particularly since the government loan had been granted to de-Francheville personally. Hocquart asked Cugnet to take over the operation and early in 1734 there was finally some production. The iron, however, turned out to be of poor quality and the forgemaster, who had been brought over from France as an expert, confessed that he didn't have the required skills to run the ironworks.

By this time, £21,483 had been spent on the undertaking and there was uncertainty about the source of further funds. Although details are not available, it must be assumed that this £21,483 consisted of the £10,000 from the government, £9,244 as originally spent by de Francheville, with the balance of £2,239 coming from the five partners. In spite of this setback, Hocquart was convinced of the feasibility and desirability of the project. He asked the French government to find two new master forgemen. One, François-Pierre Oliver de Vézain was persuaded to come to the colony by a bonus of £1,200 plus an annual salary of £2,400, exorbitant payments for that time. Another master ironworker, Jacques Simonnet, was also influenced to join the operation by the promise of an equal share in the venture. Although Hocquart was prepared to abandon the Saint-Maurice site and lose the total investment, de Vézain felt, after a detailed survey, that the best available location had been chosen, even though it would be necessary to scrap most of the existing facility. By late 1735, de Vézain had prepared a detailed estimate of the capital costs necessary to set up a proper ironworks, as well as an operating budget.

The Capital Budget

The capital budget, shown in translation as Appendix A, is quite sophisticated, although in some places, the format makes it a little difficult to follow. To alleviate this difficulty, the following condensation has been prepared.

Les Forges de Saint-Maurice
Capital Budget
To prepare project for operations

Furnace
Stonework	£6,253.6s.8d.	
Housing and sheds	1,200	
Bellows, equipment & tools	2,100	
Canal, drains, etc.	1,500	
Coke shed	1,200	

Total cost for furnace		£12,253.6s.8d.
Stone crusher and washhouse		600.0 .0

Forge (Refineries, boilerhouse & workshop)
Stonework	£1,300.0. 0.
Frame & covering	2,000
Outhouses	600
4 ovens	820
Equipment & tools	5,830

Canal, drains, etc.	2,000	
Coke bunker	1,200	
Blacksmith shop	1,100	
Total cost for forge		14,850.0. 0.
Moulds, cauldrons and other cast iron		1,000.0.0.
Packhorses (16)		2,400.0.0.
Forgemaster's house		4,000.0.0.
Storehouse, stable & oven		900.0.0.
Total estimated cost of project		£36.003.6s.8d

The capital budget seems to have enough detail and preciseness to permit a reconstruction of the furnace and all the other trappings even today. A few of the amounts are calculated to the dinari but generally they appear in round figures. Later overruns proved many of the items to have been underestimated. It is obvious, from the budget, that the ironworks would be part of a "company" town. Included in the estimate was a home for the forgemaster listed at £4,000, over 10% of the whole construction cost, while facilities for the workers were already on site from the earlier construction. A later account, by a visitor to the ironworks, painted a glowing picture of the master's house, calling it the "grande maison des forges".[8] A foundry was also provided for, but the amount of £7,976.13s.4d. was not included in the budget, since it was not to be built until a definite market exisited for its products. A hint of possible future problems is discernible at the end of the report where mention was made of some extraordinary work that would be required, but without any dollar amount being given. The total estimated cost for the ironworks including the forgemaster's house, but omitting the foundry and the extraordinary work was £36,003.6s.8d.

The Operating Budget

As previously indicated, an operating budget was also prepared, see Appendix B. This was not in traditional form and profit was not computed although revenues were estimated. The expenses were grouped by work centers, under cast iron production, refineries and boilerhouses and foundry, but foundry expenses were not included in the total. The plan was to work the mill for only eight months in the year initially, since the refineries as projected could not accommodate a full year's production of cast iron from the furnace. By the same token, the market for cast iron was unknown, and the limited operation would prevent a large surplus of this material. It would seem that an eight month operating period was a prudent decision because the severe winter conditions in the area would tend to impede operations and increase costs.

The operating budget is recast below, following an income statement format:

Les Forges de Saint-Maurice
Estimated Income Statement for One Year
Based on eight months production

Sales:			
200,000 lbs. @ £200/1000 (local)		£40,000	
400,000 lbs. @ £140/1000 (France)		56,000	
100,000 lbs. iron objects @ £200/1000 (local)		20,000	£116,000
Cost of Sales:			
Raw material			
Iron ore	£ 6,000		
Coke	34,400		
Limestone	1,000		
Soil & grease	650	42,050	
Direct labor			
Furnace wages	6,800		
Refining wages	9,700		
Smelting wages	2,700	19,200	61,250
Gross profit			£ 54,750

Several shortcomings are obvious in this budget. As the budget indicated, factory expenses such as depreciation and maintenance were not covered, nor does there seem to be any provision for selling and administrative expenses. The partnership agreement does, however, shed some light. The two "working" partners, Olivier and Simonnet, were to get salaries of £3,000 and £1,500 per annum, and these amounts were included in Direct Labor in the budget. Cugnet and Gamelin were expected to manage the affairs of the company in Quebec City and Montreal, respectively, without remuneration until the business became sufficiently extensive. It is further stipulated that all other operating expenses such as administrative, selling, transport, clerical and general costs were to be met by the company and deducted before any profit sharing. No estimates were provided, however, and it is impossible to arrive at a reasonable profit estimate.

Also worthy of note was the differential pricing being recommended. This type of pricing can be justified in the circumstances. The iron shipped to France would have to compete with that produced by the local French works and with imports from Spain and Sweden. Conversely, transport costs from Europe to New France would tend to bring the actual selling price in the colony up much higher, no doubt close to the price quoted.

Cash Budget

From the information presented in the two estimates, it is possible to prepare a cash budget. There is no record of this having been done, but it is deemed important since the de Francheville's death, the financing would have to be undertaken by Cugnet and the others.

Les Forges de Saint-Maurice
Cash Requirements
To construct ironworks and for first year of operations
(Based on estimates of 1735-36)

Cash required for building of ironworks		£ 36,003
Cash required for eight months' production		61,250
Payment due to Mrs. de Francheville, etc.		9,244
Current requirements		£106,497
Payment due for seignory	£ 6,000	
Loan payable to State	10,000	16,000
Total cash requirements		£122,497

Even though this cash budget was prepared from the known information, certain assumptions had to be made. There was no indication of when the payment to Mrs. de Francheville and the former partners had to be made. The position taken was that this was a current liability, due immediately. The payment due for the seignory was definitely postponable, subject to a rental charge of £300 per annum. This payment can, therefore, be omitted from the budget, but is included for the sake of completeness. The situation is similar for the £10,000 loan from the State. As indicated in the partnership agreement, the partners had underwritten this loan. They subsequently asked the government for a deferment, which was granted. Although it is tempting to use hindsight with the amount for the construction of the ironworks, the estimate is accepted as given. This figure has to be considered as the best available information at the time. A more debatable amount is the cash requirement for the initial production. This has been shown as £61,250, the amount of the estimate for 8 months operation, with no provision for cash inflow from income. The line of reasoning taken here was that since the ironworks had not as yet gone into production:—

1. Time was required to complete the facilities.
2. There was bound to be some undetermined start-up cost.
3. Initial production would tend to be slow as the labor force became familiar with work rules.
4. Production would also tend to be slowed by the debugging and malfunction of the new, unfamiliar equipment.
5. No provision was made for working capital. There would, of necessity, a time lag between:-
   i   Production
   ii Building up of inventory
   iii Sales
   iv Transport of merchandise to customers
   v   Collection of receivables

For all these reasons, it has been decided to show the first year operating cost as a cash requirement without any offsetting sales revenue.

It is obvious that the principals had made a similar, but possibly more optimistic projection, because they asked the State for an additional loan of £100,000. If one considers all the factors at the time of the request, this amount sounds reasonable and more than adequate to complete the ironworks and start the operations. It can also be assumed that some of the partners, particularly Cugnet and Gamelin did have other resources. And once over the hurdle of the capital outlay and the start-up of production, on the basis of the projections, the cash flow would have been very good indeed.

The government seemed to have agreed with the plans by granting the loan in the form of a drawing account against the Treasury of the Navy. Aside from any other considerations, the time-frame for repayment of the loan was relatively short. With the original loan of £10,000 plus the new one of £100,000, and anticipated profit of £54,750, a payback period of a little over two years was possible under ideal conditions, once the mill was in operation. An added incentive to a quick repayment of the loan was the clause in the partnership contract that required reimbursement to the Crown before any distribution of profits.

The Contract[9]

The new partnership agreement was signed on October 16, 1736 by Cugnet, Gamelin, Olivier, Simonnet and Thomas Jacques Taschereau, Councillor of the Supreme Council of Quebec and Treasurer of the Navy. At contract date, drawings against the loan had already mounted to £42,970, and a note was signed by the partners in favor of the Crown for £52,970, which included the original £10,000.[10] From the contract, there is no doubt that a partnership was being formed, with unlimited liability and personal involvement, but with provisions for partners to disperse of their shares. It would seem that even though the corporate form of enterprise was well-known at this time,[11] no attempt was made to acquire this privilege.

The contract raises another matter of interest to accountants. When discussing possible separation of a partner from the business, reimbursement was to be by way of taking an inventory. No further information was given specifying how this is to be done, but this method was in keeping with the accepted accounting practice of that time.[12] Balance sheets were not drawn up on a regular basis, but when required, an inventory of all assets was taken and the net worth of the business was this total less the liabilities. Davis, discussing this method in 1888, accepts cost price, replacement cost at time of inventory and estimated value for damaged goods as permissible valuation Bases[13] — shades of current value accounting! Nevertheless, it would have seemed wise for the contract to specify the method to be used to avoid future disagreements.

Also of interest to accountants is the prescribed formula for dividing profits and losses. The following information is pertinent:

1. Profits and losses to be divided in proportion of original investments, i.e. Taschereau — 10%; others — 22½% each.
2. Olivier to receive £3,000 and Simonnet £1,500 per annum after all other expenses have been deducted, but these salaries are not to be considered administrative expenses. Each is responsible for his portion of the other's salary.

31

3. Other, non-listed, administrative expenses to be met by company and to be deducted before division of profit.
4. Reimbursement of loans from Crown before any profit shared.

As long as the net profit exceeded the salaries to Olivier and Simonnet and the administrative expenses, the division of profit would present no difficulty.

This is shown below, based on the estimated income statement.

Gross Profit (after salaries to Olivier and Simonnet)	£ 54,750
Less: Administrative expenses (estimate)	24,750
	30,000
Add: Salaries to Olivier and Simonnet	4,500
Profit to be divided	£ 34,500

Divided as follows:

Olivier (£3,000 plus 22½% of £30,000)	£9,750	
Simonnet (£1,500 plus 22½% of £30,000)	8,250	
Taschereau (10% of £30,000)	3,000	
Cugnet (22½% of £30,000)	6,750	
Gamelin (22½% of £30,000)	6,750	£ 34,500

Note: None of these profits, beyond the £4,500 in salaries, could be withdrawn until the loan from the government had been repaid.

A Balance Sheet

From the various bits of information in the contract and other data accumulated, it is possible to prepare the following opening balance sheet as at the date of the new partnership.

This balance sheet reveals that the partnership was starting out in a negative position, because of the commitments undertaken from the previous business. The partners' expectations, though, must have been very high, because they knew when they signed the contract that a good part of the original construction was useless. It can be argued that the partners' risk was minimal with the government putting up the £100,000, but there was unlimited personal liability and all the loans had to be repaid before any drawings could be made. It will be seen in the following brief summary of the subsequent history of Les Forgas that one partner, at least, had anticipated too much.

Les Forges de Saint-Maurice
Opening Balance Sheet
October 16, 1736

Assets			Liabilities		
Cash on hand	£	1	Loans payable — previous		
Land		6,000	partners	£	9,244
Construction in progress			Note payable — State (note 2)		52,970
(note 1)		42,970	Due re seignory (note 3)		6,000
					£ 68,124
			Partners' equity		
			Opening capital £ 1		
			Accumulated deficit (19,244)		(19,243)
		£48,971			£ 48,971

Note 1 There may have been value attributable to part of the construction completed by the previous partnership. Any amount so determined would increase the "construction in progress" and decrease the "accumulated deficit".

Note 2 The company was authorized to draw an additional £57,030 from the Treasury of the Navy against construction costs and operating expenses. This loan was repayable before any drawings by partners, other than salaries to Olivier and Simonnet.

Note 3 A rental of £300 per annum was payable until this liability had been paid.

Aftermath

Les Forges de Saint-Maurice did finally start producing in 1738, but costs escalated and sales did not meet projections. This resulted in a takeover of the ironworks by the government in 1741 and the personal bankruptcy of Cugnet in the following year. The other partners, however, were able to dispose of their personal property and seem to have gotten off scot-free. Eventually, however, Gamelin and Olivier settled with Cugnet's estate. The government operated Les Forges until 1759, at which time it fell under British military control for several years. The property was then leased to various tenants who met with varying degrees of success. During the years 1793-1846 the lease was held by Mathew Bell, who it seems worked the mill very profitably.[14] Les Forges was then sold to other private interests who continued to operate until 1883. During the almost 150 years that the ironworks were in existence, they experienced good times and bad, but they did supply the iron products needed in Canada. It has also been shown in a recent scientific study of some iron castings from the mill that the level of its production was of the highest quality.[15]

There may be areas for further research in the records of Les Forges de Saint-Maurice, particularly for the period under French control. It may even be possible to do some analysis on actual costs and production as compared to the estimates given herein, but this will have to await further translation and study. Unfortunately, records after the French era are very sketchy and may have been lost forever.

Concluding Remarks

This paper has illustrated a capital budget and an operating budget prepared almost 250 years ago, using methods which compare very favorably with those used today. The available documentation does not carry the analyses to the same depth as it would at the present time, but the estimates seem to have been adequate for the purpose. Using the figures available, a cash budget and a balance sheet were prepared that might have aided the partners in their decision-making, if they had been prepared originally. But it must be realized that this was a capital-intensive enterprise being built for the first time in a young colony with inexperienced management and labour. Even today cost overruns and financial failures are not unknown in spite of the sophisticated techniques and costly analyses performed, so it is difficult to be too critical. Also bear in mind that in spite of government support, according to the partnership agreement, all the partners staked their all in this venture, not being able to hide behind the corporate veil.

It is worthy of note that the concept of the ironworks was sound. Once into production, the mill was successful with profits being very high in some years. And most important, for almost 150 years, Canadian needs for high quality iron products were supplied by Les Forges de Saint-Maurice.

Translation[16]   *Appendix A*

"Projected expenses to be incurred in setting up and operating the ironworks in Canada", A.P.C., Series C11A, Canada, the St. Maurice Forges, vol. 110, tome 1, pp. 323-334.

Firstly

Set up costs.

Construction of the furnace.

For the furnace structure, 26 feet square by 28 feet high including the foundations, with a capacity of 87⅓ cubic fathoms(1), at £50 per cubic fathom, the sum of 4366.13.4

For the large hanging each 20 ft in breadth by 2 ft. thick and 11 ft. high, on four walls, making 24⅗ square fathoms at £16 per square fathom 391. 2.3

For the small hangings each 10 ft. in breadth by 1½ ft. thick and 11 ft. high on four walls, making 12⅗ square fathoms at £16 per square fathom 195.11.1

10,000 bricks for the walls at £40 per thousand 400

For the fire bricks for the inside walls of the furnace 600

The pipes to keep the wall of the furnace dry 300

Total for the stonework   6253. 6.8

The housing for the furnace over the crucible opening, to shelter the bellows and hoists; this being 35 ft. long and 20 ft. high, covered and roofed with layers of planks and wooden tiles, this 600

The furnace shed, covering the moulds 30 ft. wide, 30 ft. long and 20 ft. high, with walls and roof of layer upon layer of planks and wooden tiles, this 600

The furnace bellows 800

The blast-pipe, grease and flues 300

The furnace equipment comprising wheels, pulleys and lanterns 600

For the pokers and other tools 400

For the canal, drains, flagstones and waterways 1500

Shelter for the coke used in the furnace, 60 ft. long, 40 ft. wide, with a frame 10 ft. high supported by stakes and covered over with planks and wooden tiles 1200

12253. 6.8.   12253. 6.8.

For a stone crusher and washhouse for the
iron ore, with wheel and machinery   600

Forge comprising two refineries, a boilerhouse, a metal workshop with all its tools, as well as weights for the hammers and mechanical presses.

The shelter for the forge, 90 ft. long by 40 ft. wide and 15 ft. high, whose frame is covered with layer upon layer of planks and wooden tiles.

For the stonework, 10 ft. high including
the foundations, and 3 ft. thick making 108⅓
sq. fathoms at £12 per fathom   1300
    For the frame and covering   2000

For the outhouses on either side of the
shelter, where the mill wheels are kept, 90
ft. long by 10 ft. wide and 10 ft. high, supported by stakes covered over with planks
and wooden tiles   600

Four ovens: two for the refinery, one for the boilerhouse and one for the metal workshop, each with stonework at the base 8 ft. square and 1½ ft. thick, including the foot thick foundations, with their chimneys 30 ft. tall and 1 ft. thick at the base, becoming narrower from the base to the opening at the top, only 1½ ft. square.

For the stonework of each oven, each 10⅔
fathoms, making in all 42⅔ square fathoms
at £12 per fathom   512

    For the chimneys, each 6⅔ square fathoms
making in all 25⅔ square fathoms at
£12 per fathom   308   820

    For the four pairs of bellows
and trimmings   1000
    For the tuyeres, grease and flues   400
    For the cast iron wedges used in operations 100
    For the pokers, tongs and other tools   600
    For equipment for the four ovens, consisting
of axles and wheels   1200
    For the hammer weights   1000
    For the cast iron hammer   500
    For the cast iron anvil   100
    For the cords and pivots of the axle of the
mechanical hammer   200
    For the weights of the mechanical press   500
    For the wrought iron hammer   200
    For the cast iron anvil   30

For the canal, with its drains, flagstones
and waterways   2000

The coke bunker 60 ft. long by 40 ft. wide
beneath the frame supported by pickets and
covered over with planks and wooden tiles   1200

A blacksmith's shop, 15 ft. square by 8 ft.
high, covered with layer upon layer of planks
and wooden tiles   300

    For the bellows   200

    For the anvil   400   1100   14850

    For the forge and chimney   100

    For the tools   100

                                                   14850

For the molds, cauldrons and other
cast iron objects   1000

Foundry for fashioning all kinds of
iron objects (2)

The shelter, 36 ft. wide and 15 ft. tall,
covered over with layer upon layer of planks
and wooden tiles   2400

Two outhouses to shelter the wheels, 20 ft.
long by 10 ft. wide and 15 ft. high supported
by pickets covered over with planks and
wooden tiles   150

For the 32⅔ square fathoms of stonework
under the wheels at £12 per fathom   386.13.4

For the wheels, pulleys and lanterns,
wheel axles, chains and pivots   900

For the pulley components and the outhouses
with all the necessary tools and iron ware   500

For the canal, drains, flagstones and
waterway   1000

An oven designed to heat the iron to be
molten with reflected heat: 15 ft. long, 12 ft.
wide, 12 ft. tall including the foundations and 1¼
ft. thick, with its roof of 20 square fathoms at
£12 per fathom   240

For the wire netting and cast iron   340
covers   100

A blacksmith's shop similar to the
one at the forge, this   1100

    For a beam   100   1300

    For files and other tools   100

For the house for the founder and his
four workers   1000
                                                 7976.13.4

Sixteen packhorses for construction work
and carts, at £150 each   2400
    A house for the forgemaster, 40 ft. square
by 20 ft. high, with two storeys, lattices,
plastered inside and outside and walled with
planks and wooden tiles   4000
    A storehouse to keep the irons, 30 ft.
square by 8 ft. high, walled with layers of
planks and wooden tiles   550
    A stable   250
    An oven   100
                                                 36003. 6.8.

This preliminary outline does not include the house where the smiths and workers will be lodged, because the house already standing at St. Maurice will be used. The other buildings cannot remain in place, as they are standing on the ground needed for the buildings which are part of this project. The materials may be used. Its value is not entered in the present statement, as this will come under extraordinary expenses which were not foreseen when composing this preliminary outline, such as excavation of roads and other work.

Unsigned
(Olivier de Vézain?)

(1) The word translated here is Toise — fathom, which is 6 feet.
(2) The item included here is not entered, as the foundry will be set up only when there is a guaranteed market for the iron in the form of iron thongs and other various kinds of foundry products. (This note appears in the left margin of the manuscript.)

Translation   *Appendix B*

"Annual operating expenses", A.P.C., Series C11A, Canada, the Saint Maurice Forges, vol. 110, tome 1, pp. 335-339.

The furnace could be worked all year round, producing 1600 thousandweights of cast iron, of which only 900,000 lbs. could be used in the two refineries, to produce 600,000 lbs. of pig iron. Thus, 700,000 lbs. of cast iron would remain. As the extent of the market is not yet known, the project should be reduced to eight months of work, producing 1,000,000 lbs. of cast iron, 900,000 lbs. of which would be used in the refineries, leaving 100,000 lbs. over to be used in making cast iron objects for use here in the Colony.

For 1,000,000 lbs. of cast iron, the requirements are:

2000 barrels(1) of iron ore at £3 per barrel brought to the furnace, this	6000
20,000 barrels of coke to be brought to the furnace at 20s the barrel	20000
1000 barrels of limestone at 20s per barrel	1000
600 barrels of sandy soil at 20s	600
100 of candle grease at 10s	50
	£27650

Wages

A forge master	3000	
A clerk	700	
A founder	1500	
A junior founder	400	
Four labourers at £300 each	1200	£ 6800
		£34450

The 1,000,000 lbs of cast iron will come to the same amount at a rate of £34.9s per thousand. This expense is not entered here because it will be carried below as an expense of the refineries and the smelting operation.

Expenses of the refineries and boilerhouses

900,000 lbs. of cast iron at 34.9s per thousand	31005
14400 barrels of coke at 20s per barrel	14400
	£45405

Wages

A hammersmith (2)	1200		
Three boilermen at £600 each	1800		
A boilerhouse helper	300		
A refiner	1200		55105
Seven refinery employees		9700	
at £600 each	4200		
A carpenter	500		
A blacksmith	500		
		£55105	

The pig iron will come to £91.16s10d per thousand.

Smelting expenses.
1000 thousandweights of cast iron at £34.9s
    per thousand

	Wages		3445	
A moulder	1500	2700	6145
Two labourers at £600 each	1200		
		£6145	
			£61250

Foundry expenses (3)

	Wages	
A founder		1500
Four workmen at £300 each		1200
		2700

Output of the above forges.
Output of the refineries and boilerhouses.
600,000 lbs. of pig iron of which the following to be consumed by the colony:

200,000 lbs at £200 per thousand	40000	
400,000 lbs. will be sent to France at		96000
600,000 lbs. £140 per thousand	56000	

Output from smelting.
100,000 lbs. in the form of pans, slabs, cauldrons and other cast iron objects which will be used in the Colony at £200 per thousand   20000

£116000

Unsigned
(Olivier de Vézain?)

(1)   The word translated here is Pipe — a variable measure of capacity, used especially in measuring liquids. Here: barrel

(2)   These workmen will work in the metal workshop when necessary. (This passage appears in the left hand margin of the manuscript).

(3)   This expense is not entered, as the foundry will be set up only when there is a certain market for foundry irons of various kinds. (Note appears in the left margin of the manuscript).

FOOTNOTES

[1]New France, during the early 18th century, covered a vast territory entending to the Gulf of Mexico. Most of this area, however, was very sparsely populated

so that New France, as used in this paper, is only that narrow band of land along the St. Lawrence River, now part of the Province of Québec.

[2]For the story of this operation, see Hartley, *passim.*

[3]See Historical Statistics, series Z1 — 19, and Seventh Census, pp. 134-8.

[4]See Hartley, chap. 4, and Eccles, chap. 5.

[5]Hartley, p. 22.

[6]This material has been collected and published by Nash, primarily in French. Although considerable reference has been made to his research, the interpretations and analysis of the material, in this paper, are of a different nature and are examined from the perspective of an accountant rather than an historian.

[7]The monetary units used are libri (£), solidi (s) and dinari (d). 12=1s, 20=1£ (Note the British usage of £.s.d. for pounds, shillings and pence.) It is difficult to convert this amount into current dollars; some indication of its value can be perceived from the wages shown in the operating budget, which range from £300—600 per annum.

[8]Wurtele, p. 81. The literal translation of this phrase is "big house of the ironworks" but the connotation is that of "mansion".

[9]To conserve space, the translation of this document is not included in this paper. It is available to anyone interested in the details.

[10]Nish, *Cugnet,* p. 62.

[11]See the classic work by Davis, *Corporations.*

[12]Gordon, p. 59.

[13]Davis, J. D., p. 5.

[14]Wurtele, p. 87.

[15]Miller, pp. 48-9.

[16]The two translations, from the Old French, were made by Ms. Sheila A. Cushing, following Nish in *L'Actualité Economique.*

BIBLIOGRAPHY

Davis, J. D. *Manual of Standard Bookkeeping,* Montreal: John Lovell and Son, 1888.

Davis, John P. *Corporations,* New York: Capricorn Books, 1961.

Eccles, W. J. *The Canadian Frontier 1534-1760,* New York: Holt, Rinehart and Winston, 1969.

Gordon, William, *The Universal Accountant and Complete Merchant,* London: Alexander Donaldson, 1777.

Hartley, E. N. *Ironworks on the Saugus,* Norman: University of Oklahoma Press, 1957.

Historical Statistics of the United States, Washington: U.S. Department of Commerce, 1960.

Miller, Harry, *Canada's Historic First Iron Castings,* Ottawa: Queen's Printer, 1968.

Nish, Cameron, *François-Etienne Cugnet 1719-1751: Entrepreneur et Entreprises en Nouvelle-France,* Montreal: La Corporation des Editions Fides, 1975.

_____, "La Banqueroute de François-Etienne Cugnet, 1742: III. Cugnet et les Forges de Saint-Maurice (1)"*L'Actualité Economique* vol. 41, no. 4, janvier-mars 1966, pp. 762-810.

Seventh Census of Canada, 1931 vol. 1 Summary, Ottawa; J. O. Patenaude, I.S.O., 1936.

Wurtele, F. C., "Historical Record of the St. Maurice Forges, the Oldest Active Blast Furnace on the Continent of America" *Proceedings and Transactions of the Royal Society of Canada,* vol. iv, sect. 2, 1886, pp. 77-89.

Accounting for a brewery at Louisbourg*

SANDRA FELTON *Brock University*

HARVEY MANN *Brock University*

Abstract. This paper examines three accounting documents that have been preserved from records kept for a brewery built at Louisbourg, Canada, in 1759. As one of the earliest examples of English accounting in Canada, these documents provide insight into 18th century business practices in the North American colonies. Considering accounting texts of the period and documents preserved from businesses in the thirteen colonies, the study concludes that the statements prepared for the brewery were sophisticated in comparison to the accounting practices of this era.

Résumé. Les auteurs examinent trois documents comptables tirés des registres d'une brasserie établie à Louisbourg, au Canada, en 1759. Ces documents, parmi les plus anciens spécimens de comptabilité anglaise au Canada, nous renseignent sur les méthodes comptables des colonies nord-américaines du XVIIIe siècle. Compte tenu des ouvrages comptables du temps et des documents produits par les entreprises des treize colonies et qui ont été conservés, les auteurs concluent que les états dressés pour la brasserie sont d'une complexité qui tranche sur les méthodes comptables de l'époque.

Canadian historians have not generally used the term historical manuscript to include the records of business concerns and the private papers of businessmen. Historians in Canada, especially those who wrote in the nineteenth century, were preoccupied with political history. This has been Canada's loss, for business records are part of the history of this country, and the failure to appreciate this truth led inevitably to the neglect of the resource. . . . No one, however, can adequately describe the role of business in Canada's history without access to business records. (Archer, 1972, pp. 288, 290)

Although several researchers have studied colonial accounting practices in the thirteen colonies before 1779, there has been virtually no published documentation of English accounting records in the other North American colonies prior to the 19th century. This paper represents a first attempt to shed some light on this relatively unexplored area of Canadian history by examining three recovered 18th century accounting documents regarding the operations of a brewery built at Louisbourg, Nova Scotia, Canada, shortly after the capture of the fort

---

* The authors acknowledge the helpful comments of Bill Scott, the editor and the anonymous reviewers of previous versions of this paper. Persons desiring typed copies of Tables 1, 2, and 3 may obtain them from the authors.

Contemporary Accounting Research Vol. 7 No. 1 pp. 261–277

by the British in 1759. Although the documents that have been preserved may represent only a small fragment of the original accounting records, they provide insight into 18th century business enterprise and supply evidence about the sophistication of accounting practices in the North American colonies during this period.

The paper begins by outlining the historical background of this particular business venture and then proceeds with an examination of the records themselves. The analysis attempts to place the documents in their historical context, both (1) in light of accounting textbooks of the period and (2) in comparison with documents preserved from other 18th century businesses, particularly those from the thirteen colonies. The study concludes that the records that have been retrieved are sophisticated compared to the accounting practices of other colonial enterprises of this era.

The background

First settled in 1713, Louisbourg, the "great" fortress on Cape Breton Island, Nova Scotia, was built to replace the French outposts in Newfoundland and the Bay of Fundy that had been surrendered under the terms of the Treaty of Utrecht. Often called the Gibraltar of the West, Louisbourg commanded the entrance to the Gulf of St. Lawrence and dominated the northern sea route from New England to Europe (Easterbrook and Aitken, p. 92). Thus the fortress was strategically important as a seaport, fishing port, and military base.

Living conditions at Louisbourg were far from ideal. William Wood (1915) paints a very bleak picture of subsistence at the fort. Throughout this book, words such as "small," "dull," "out-of-the-way garrison town," "isolated," "crowded," and "no social life" appear to describe a quite miserable lifestyle. Donovan (1982) is less negative but still emphasizes the isolation and miserable weather of the area. From all accounts, since it was seaport as well as a military base, Louisbourg was a "drinking town." As evidence of this, Donovan (1980) cites Gilles Proulx to the effect that there were 75 official cabaret and auberges in the town plus other businesses that sold liquor without a permit. When it is further appreciated that the population was only approximately 2,000 plus transients (Moore, 1981), it would seem that Louisbourg was a promising location in which to erect a brewery.

The timing of this business venture is, of course, most significant, for the history of brewing in New France would hardly have encouraged an entrepreneur. Although beer had been brewed in Quebec as early as 1623, the French preferred wine and brandy imported from France. A royal brewery constructed under Jean Talon in Quebec in 1671 had stopped operations by 1674. Although other efforts at brewing were made in New France after that date, such attempts appear to have ceased by 1725 (Denison, 1955). Although the local habitants had engaged in home brewing since the early 17th century (Brewers Association of Canada, 1965), their output was primarily spruce beer, not the barley beer that the British preferred. Even as late as 1749, it appears that barley beer had not yet been introduced into New France (Denison, 1955).

The arrival of the British soldiers changed the situation drastically:

> Small beer was by law part of the British soldier's daily rations. . . . Winter orders for the British Army in North America, 1759–60, instructed that each post should keep on hand enough molasses "to make two quarts of beer for each man everyday. . . ." The constant demand for beer, however, guaranteed local brewers a regular market. (Bowering, 1988)

Just how auspicious a time this was for the creation of a brewing industry in Quebec is evidenced by the success of John Molson just two decades later, when he founded his brewery in the city of Montreal in 1782 (Denison, 1955).

It is, therefore, not surprising that three individuals, William Buttar, Alexander Mackenzie, and Samuel Jacobs, undertook to build a brewery in Louisbourg shortly after the capture of the fort by the British in 1759.

Of the three partners, only Jacobs is included in the *Dictionary of Canadian Biography* (vol. IV:1771 to 1800, 1979). Because of him the documents examined in this paper have survived. According to Finding Aid 195 (Public Archives of Canada, 1976):

> The records of the Samuel Jacobs estate were preserved by Edward William Gray and Michel Cornud, executors of the estate and guardians of the minor children of Samuel Jacobs, and by their successors, Frederick William Ermatinger, Charles Oakes Ermatinger, and Samuel Gale. Various records of other estates were added to the collection in the course of time. The records include personal and business correspondence, all manner of business records and books, legal papers concerning the administration of the estates, and records of the Montreal Sheriff's Office (E.W. Gray and F.W. Ermatinger were the first two sheriffs of Montreal).

Jacobs first appears as a Jewish merchant in Halifax in 1751. Although his origins are unknown, his handwritten papers indicate that neither English nor French was his native language. His handwriting reflects a trace of a German dialect, possibly from the Alsace-Lorraine area. Jacobs arrived in Quebec late in 1759 and became a prominent merchant there and at St. Denis until his death in 1786 (Mann, 1984).

Alexander Mackenzie appears to have been the accountant and active partner in the brewery venture. During this period merchants usually did their own accounting because there were few, if any, practising accountants in the British colonies (Johnson, 1976). Mackenzie's name appears at the bottom of two of the documents that have been recovered (Exhibits 2 and 3), indicating that he was the preparer of the accounting records. The similarity to the handwriting in the document in Exhibit 1 would suggest that this was also his work, although this document is unsigned.

Although no reference to Alexander Mackenzie has been found, his name suggests that he was of Scottish origin. David S. MacMillan (1972) has documented the important influence of Scottish entrepreneurs in the development of business enterprises in the North American colonies in the period from 1760 to

EXHIBIT 1

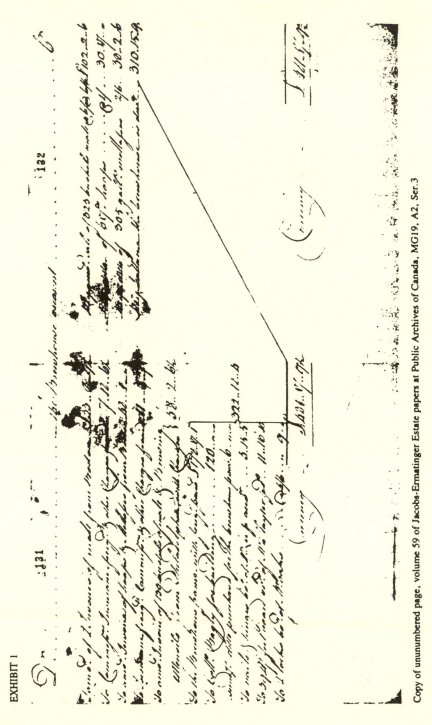

Copy of unnumbered page, volume 59 of Jacobs-Ermatinger Estate papers at Public Archives of Canada, MG19, A2, Ser.3

1825, an influence that had established roots in the Halifax area in the 1750s. These Scots were characterized by their belief in free trade and their "belief in the efficacy of education as an improver of mankind" (MacMillan, p. 46). The 18th century was the age of the Scottish Enlightenment, a time when Scotland's educational system was superior to that of England and a period in which the leading accounting textbooks written in English were authored by Scottish writers (Mepham, 1988).

William Buttar was apparently a British staff officer, as his name appears on "A List of Staff Officers belonging to ye Garrison" as "Secretary himself & Effective Servant" (London Public Records). That a British officer should enter into a business venture with a Halifax merchant and Scottish entrepreneur would not be surprising because British military and naval officers in Halifax often

participated in all types of mercantile enterprise, in co-operation with the merchants. . . . It is difficult to avoid the conclusion that the close relations between the merchants and the naval officer and officials must have often proved most profitable to all concerned (MacMillan, 1972).

The three partners started building the brewery early in 1759, no doubt with high expectations. However, in a little over one year later, the enterprise had failed, with considerable losses to the investors. The reason for this financial disaster is quite understandable and could not be blamed on lack of business acumen by the partners. In February 1760, King George II and William Pitt signed the death warrant of the brewery when they ordered Louisbourg destroyed.

Archival source of the data
The documents studied in this paper can be found in the volumes of the Ermatinger Estate held at the Public Archives of Canada, Manuscripts Division, Ottawa, Canada (MG 19, A 2, Series 3). More particularly, Exhibit 1 comes from Volume 59 and Exhibits 2 and 3 from Volume 61 of this series. Both Exhibit 1 and 2 take the form of T-accounts with a listing of debit entries on the left-hand side of the account and credit entries on the right. Exhibit 3 is a voucher for payment of "Sundry Charges" of £2.13. listed in Exhibit 2.

Analysis
The T-account format of Exhibits 1 and 2 is typical of the ledger account of the period as illustrated in 18th century accounting texts. As was customary for the period, the debit entries are prefaced by the word *to*, which indicates why the account was charged, and the credit entries by the word *by*, indicating how the account was settled (Gambino and Palmer, 1976).

Exhibit 4, included for comparative purposes, is an example of a cash account take from Alexander Malcolm's *A Treatise of Book-keeping, or Merchants Accounts; in the Italian Method of Debtor and Creditor* (1731). Whereas the entries in Exhibits 2 and 4 are listed in chronological order, those in Exhibit 1 are not dated. A noticeable difference between Exhibit 4 and Exhibits 1 and 2 is that

EXHIBIT 2

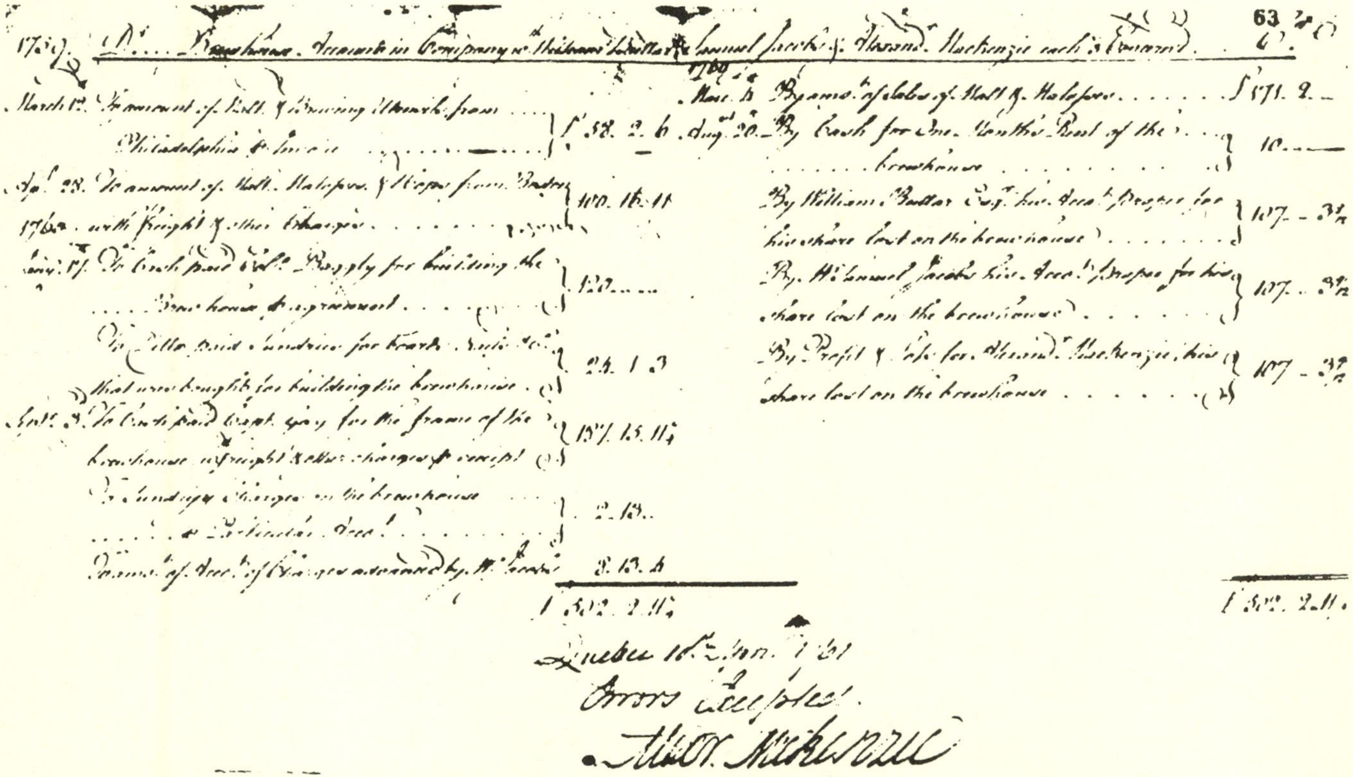

Copy of page 63, volume 61 of Jacobs-Ermatinger Estate papers at Public Archives of Canada, MG19, A2 Ser.3

EXHIBIT 3

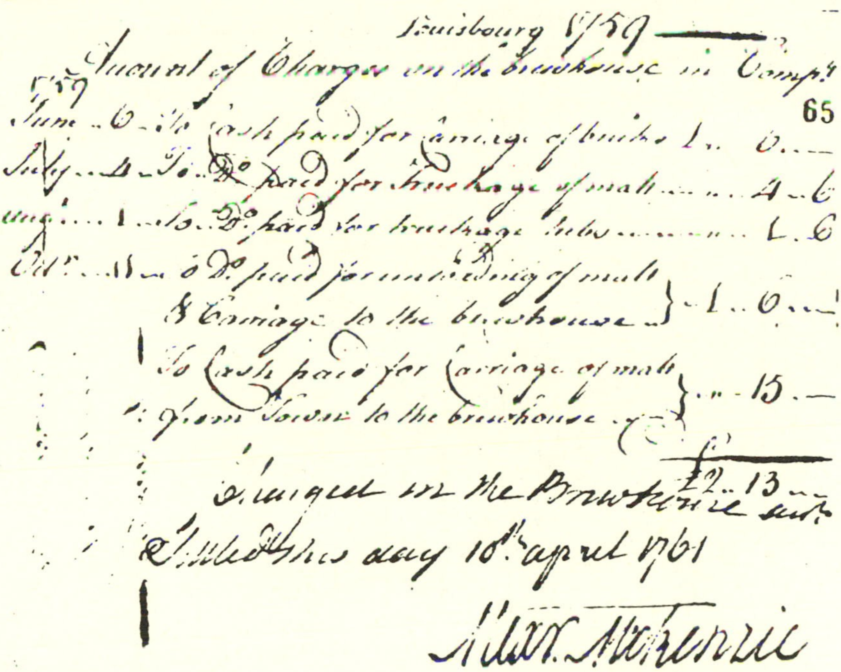

Louisbourg 1759

Account of Charges on the brewhouse in Compy 65

1759 June .. 6 .. To Cash paid for carriage of bricks 1 .. 0 .. —

July .. 4 .. To Do paid for truckage of malt ...... 4 .. 6

Augt ... 1 .. 15 .. Do paid for truckage tubs .... 1 .. 6

Octr .. 11 .. 6 Do paid for unloading of malt & Carriage to the brewhouse } 1 .. 0 .. —

To Cash paid for Carriage of malt from Town to the brewhouse } .. 15 .. —

Charged in the Brewhouse acct 2 .. 13 .. —

Settled this day 10th April 1761

Alexr. Mackenzie

Copy of page 65, volume 61 of Jacobs-Ermatinger Estate papers at Public Archives of Canada, MG19, A2 Ser.3

the former includes references to other page numbers beside almost every entry, whereas the latter contain no references to books of original entry. In addition, Exhibit 2 is signed by Mackenzie, indicating both a date and location for its preparation, something that would not normally be found in a ledger account. This notation, along with the absence of folio references, suggests that Exhibit 2—and possibly Exhibit 1—is likely not simply a ledger account, but rather a form of statement that was prepared for some users, probably for the other partners of the firm. As will be discussed later, the ledger account format was an approach advocated by some 18th century accounting textbooks for producing financial statements separate from the accounts themselves (Littleton, 1933).

It is most probable that Exhibits 1 and 2 were transcribed from the books of business of Alexander Mackenzie rather than from the records of the brewhouse itself. The credit side of Exhibit 2 shows the allocation of the losses on the brewery among the three partners. Although the losses are charged to the personal accounts of Buttar and Jacobs, they are charged "By Profit and Loss for Alexander Mackenzie." This would support the conclusion that the transcriptions were taken not from the books of the brewhouse but from Mackenzie's own business records.

Exhibit 1, the Brewhouse Account, appears to contain a listing of cash re-

EXHIBIT 4
An 18th century "Cash" ledger account

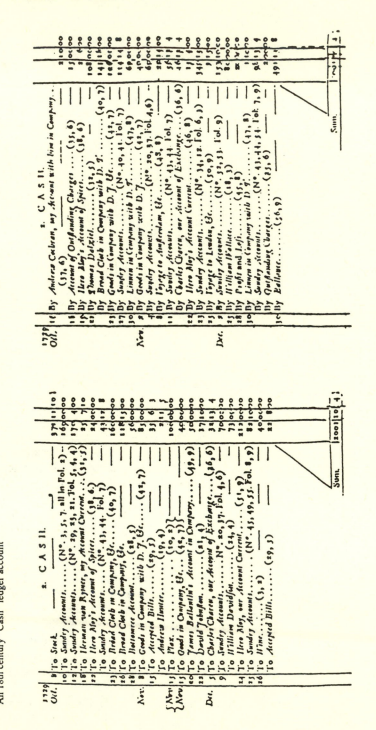

Reproduced from Alexander Malcolm, *A Treatise of Book-Keeping, or Merchants Accounts; in the Italian Method of Debtor and Creditor*, 1731

ceipts and expenditures for the enterprise. However, this is obviously not the cash account of the brewery since the debits are for expenditures and the credits are for receipts. The books of business of Alexander Mackenzie probably contained an account called *the Brewhouse Account*, which would have represented a type of asset account awaiting disposition. Into this account Mackenzie likely dumped all transactions regarding this particular business enterprise: fixed assets, expenses, and revenues. As the record-keeping agent for the partnership, Mackenzie could have used this record to prepare financial statements that would provide some orderly communication to the other partners.

The debit entries in Exhibit 1 indicate payments for raw materials (malt, hops, and molasses), brewing utensils, and the construction of the brewhouse (framing, building, sundry charges, nails, hinges, boards, and locks). It should be noted that the items are listed in this specific order with a subtotal aggregating the capital costs on the building (£322.18.4). This indicates that Mackenzie was making some attempt to organize his financial statements in a meaningful manner. The credit entries indicate amounts from sales and the amount due to balance the credits with the debits (the expenditures being in excess of the receipts by £310.15.9 1/2).

It should also be noted that the malt, hops, and molasses were imported from Boston and Philadelphia and that the charges for commission, insurance, and freight were over 20 percent of the cost of the raw materials themselves. This confirms an observation by MacMillan (1972) that, during the period from 1759 to 1762, many vessels "found profitable employment in the shipment of stores and war materials from Boston and Philadelphia to the Saint Lawrence, for high freight-rates were paid for this service" (pp. 54–55).

Exhibit 2, *Brewhouse Accounts in Company with William Buttar, Samuel Jacobs & Alexandr. Mackenzie each 3 Concerned*, contains a more complete accounting of the operations of the enterprise than does Exhibit 1. Exhibit 2 may have been prepared from Exhibit 1, or alternatively, the two exhibits may have been prepared from the same ledger account at two different times, possibly for different purposes.

All of the items from Exhibit 1 are included on Exhibit 2, although the entries are now in chronological order and the aggregation of the items has been altered. Although undated, Exhibit 1 is clearly the earlier document and provides an interim picture of the detail of particular receipts and expenditures. Exhibit 2 is a winding-up statement. It is more legalistic, shows dates, and groups similar expenditures. This is the statement that most likely would have gone to the other partners.

All of the expenditures for raw materials from Boston (the first four items in Exhibit 1) are shown in the second item in Exhibit 2 as one total amount of £100.16.11. The expenditures on the building are no longer subtotaled as they were in Exhibit 1. The cost reported for the framing of the brewhouse has increased by £8.18.10 1/4 from £178.17.1 to £187.15.11 1/4, and there are two new charges shown in Exhibit 2 that were not listed on the Brewhouse Account:

To Sundry Charges on the brewhouse
...... for Particular Accot......   £2.13.
To amot. of Acct. of Charges advanced by Mr. Jacobs   £8.13.4

The increases in costs reported in Exhibit 2 appear to be accruals that were
not included in Exhibit 1, whose totals showed only those amounts paid or
received in "Currency." Exhibit 3, which is a voucher for payment of the "Sundry
Charges" of £2.13, indicates that these charges were incurred in 1759 but not
settled in cash until April 19, 1761. These expenses are accrued in Exhibit 2,
which was prepared on March 10, 1761. However, the amount does not appear
in the Brewhouse Account even though this account was obviously prepared
after the charges were incurred in 1759. Since it includes items that are dated
1760 according to Exhibit 2 (such as the "Cash paid Colo. Baggly") it seems
reasonable to assume that the "amot. of Acct. of Charges advanced by Mr.
Jacobs" is also an accrual and that the increase in the cost of framing the
building reported on Exhibit 2 is due to "other charges for receipt" owed to
Capt. Gay for the framing but not yet paid.

On the credit side, Exhibit 2 includes a receipt for rent of the brewhouse that
was not reported in Exhibit 1, possibly because this latter document may have
been prepared before the cash was received. Also shown is the allocation of the
losses on the brewery among the three partners.

Although the analysis of Exhibit 2 indicates that Mackenzie included accruals
in the statement that he prepared for his partners, one cannot conclude that
the accruals necessarily appeared in the books of account themselves. Indeed,
there is no evidence of accruals in Exhibit 1, the Brewhouse Account, and
it would have been unusual to find accruals in the accounting records of the
period (Gambino and Palmer, 1976). In drawing up a financial statement from
his books, Mackenzie may simply have realized that a few more expenditures
needed to be made and therefore included them on the statement prepared for
his partners.

The evaluation
Although Voke (1926) suggests that 18th century colonial accounting was similar to the double entry bookkeeping of the 20th century, most later researchers
appear to disagree with this conclusion. After studying the books of several colonial enterprises, Baxter (1956) reports that, although 18th century businessmen
had some inkling of double-entry accounting:

Crude single entry was overwhelmingly the rule. I have not come across any colonial
ledger that is certainly complete. In the great bulk of the cases a trial balance is patently
impossible, as most of the impersonal accounts are lacking, the personal accounts are
not ruled off, and the work abounds in arithematical slips and other blemishes. (p. 279)

Baxter concludes that bookkeeping was employed primarily to help the colonial
merchant keep track of his transactions rather than to measure the success or
failure of his business.

Colonial merchants' accounts often consisted only of personal accounts of debtors and creditors, and many kept track only of accounts receivable, not of accounts payable, so that liabilities could be determined only from a creditor's books. Records detailing revenues, expenses, inventories, and fixed assets were seldom kept, and usually no attempt was made to balance records on a periodic basis (Kreiser, 1976).

Not only was periodic income seldom calculated, but also the preparation of a statement separate from the accounts was rarely seen in this period. The reason that so little attention was given to the preparation of financial reports was that many merchants were sole proprietors and did not need statements because they managed their own enterprises and did not need to calculate or report income for tax purposes (Baxter, 1956).

Since the first accounting textbook written in the United States was not published until 1796, colonial merchants must have depended primarily on British texts for their knowledge of accounting (Gambino and Palmer, 1976). However, many of these texts did not even discuss the preparation of financial statements. For example, this topic was not included in John Mair's (1736) *Book-keeping Methodiz'd*, which "was easily the most popular accounting text in the major American cities during the latter half of the eighteenth century" (Sheldahl, 1985). Nor is the subject included in Malcolm (1731), another text that has been described as "popular and well received" in its day (Murphy, 1987). According to Chatfield (1974) "the first modern accounting text ... (which) saw financial statements rather than ledger balances as the final step in the bookkeeping cycle" was *Principles and Practices of Bookkeeping* (1841) by Thomas Jones.

In light of these observations, the documents that have been preserved relating to the Louisbourg brewery may have been quite advanced for their day. The accounts were obviously based on double-entry bookkeeping, the preparer made an attempt to aggregate revenues and expenditures in some meaningful way on the financial statements, the enterprise's losses were calculated and allocated among the partners, and accruals were reported for unpaid expenses. But perhaps most interesting of all is the discovery of a *statement* prepared independent of the accounts themselves to report on the operations of the enterprises and the partners' losses.

In the case of the dissolution of the brewery at Louisbourg, there would have been more incentive than usual for preparing a financial report. As Littleton (1933) notes:

Another strong motive for the separation of financial statements was the settlement of partnership affairs. The closing of the books would not always suffice, for then only the one having the books would preserve a record of the situation at the moment. (p. 137)

One type of financial statement that was sometimes prepared during this period was the charge-and-discharge account. Exhibit 5, reproduced from Baxter (1956), is an illustration of a charge-and-discharge statement produced by a Boston firm in 1764. This particular example is somewhat unusual since it was prepared using Roman numerals rather than Arabic numbers. However, apart from this oddity, it is apparent that the charge-and-discharge account is not as "modern" a statement as those prepared for the Louisbourg brewery.

As Littleton (1933) notes, the charge-and-discharge statement probably originated in medieval times as a method by which stewards reported on their activities to their feudal lords. It

. . . is plainly the report of an agent, not a statement of indebtedness or of ownership . . . neither is it a receipt and disbursement statement nor a calculation of loss and gain. It is simply a well organized report upon an agent's responsibilities. (p. 126)

Whereas the statements for the brewery are based on double-entry accounting, the charge-and-discharge statement was most likely derived from documents and memoranda other than an organized ledger of double-entry accounts (Littleton (1933)).

Littleton (1933) traces the evolution of separate financial statements based on double-entry accounting to two different approaches. One approach was to produce a columnar arrangement of the data, working from the trial balance. The second method was to copy key accounts as they appeared in the general ledger. Seventeenth and eighteenth century textbook illustrations of both of these approaches, reproduced from Littleton, are shown in Exhibits 6 and 7, respectively.

It is obvious that the statements for the brewery follow the second approach rather than the first. But whereas Exhibit 7 separates the "profit and loss" account from the "balances" account, Exhibit 2 seems to combine balance sheet and income items into one statement.

That the statement for the brewery is not identical to a textbook illustration is hardly unexpected. In fact, it is surprising to discover 18th century colonial records that have been prepared so closely in accordance with the textbook accounting of the day as those for the brewery. A study of accounting in the thirteen colonies by Gambino and Palmer (1976) concludes that "in general, the level of accounting taught by the textbooks was above that practised in the (colonial) counting houses" (p. 14). Indeed, even in Britain, Jones (1985) reports that illustration of 18th century business records "in the Italian style" are "not too common," "industrial accounting records are rare," and "progress in the development of the double-entry technique and its application in Britain appears to have been slow despite the many expositions on the subject" (p. 115).

Conclusion

The study of early accounting textbooks may enlighten us about past business practices, and the examination of the archival records kept by colonial merchants provides evidence about the development of practices related to our commercial history. The brewhouse documents analysed in this paper constitute one of the earliest English Canadian accounting records that have been preserved for a business enterprise in the North American colonies. They also provide one of

EXHIBIT 5
Woodford's Charge-and-Discharge Statement

December 25, 1760 to December 23, 1764.[1]

Charge.

		s	d
Balance remaining in the hands of the accountant	"Quitt."		
Provisions left at Placentia since 1745	CC.LVIII . XVI .		I
Provisions remaining at Annapolis, at the end of last account, allowed then, but to be surcharged now	$\overset{xx}{\text{M.CC.IIII.III}}$ .XVIII .		VI
Provisions remaining at Annapolis at 25 Dec. 1760 [Long list of "sound and fit to be issued," broken, and bad — in all]	MM.CCC.XXIX . XV .		VIII
Money per warrants [Long list] $\overset{M}{\text{XVII.CC.LXXII}}$. VIII .			V
	$\overset{M}{\text{XXI.C.XLIIII}}$ .XVIII .		VIII

Discharge.

The Accountant is allowed, for food issued at Annapolis, Chignecto, etc., 26 Dec. 1760 to 23 Dec. 1764, one man for 722,904 days at 5½d.	$\overset{M\ C}{\text{XVI.V.I.XVI}}$.	XI
This agrees with lists signed by Colonel, etc.		
Expenses [chiefly to Thomas Hancock, for surveying and removing old provisions; a commission for issuing old provisions; and wastage — in all]	MM.XXVI . XIX .	ob [= ½d]
Audit fee, etc.	C.XIII .	II
Sum of discharge	$\overset{M\ C}{\text{XVIII.VII.VI}}$. XII .	ob
Provisions at Placentia not accounted for	CC.LVIII . XVI .	I
Due to government	MM.C.LXXIX . X .	VIob

[1] PRO, Audit Office, I, p. 188.

Reproduced from William T. Baxter, *The House of Hancock: Business in Boston 1724–1775* (1965), pp. 160–161.

55

EXHIBIT 6
Form of columnar statement from Dafforne, *Merchants Mirror*, 1635

[left folio]

Survey of the general-balance, or Estate-reckoning / Debitor	Thus ought your accounts to stand at the first view of the Bookes, when everything is transported out of the waste-booke into the Leager.	Thus ought your second, or Tryall Ballance to stand with the Losses.	Thus ought your True-balance to stand, which you transport into your new-bookes.
dito to Buncke..........	13688.17.8	5555. 2.-	5555. 2.-
dito to Howse King David..........	6213.15.-		
dito to Susanna Peeters Orphans..........	5571.16.8	713.14.8	713.14.8
dito to Jack Pudding my account currant	11318. 6.8	2648. 6.8	2648. 6.8
dito to Wines, 15 Butts unsold..........	1260.-.-	1260.-.-	1260.-.-
dito to French Aquae-vitae..........	3568.-.-		
dito to Rye, 18 Last, 7 Mudde..........	1877.15.8	1533.15.8	1533.15.8
dito to Concaseille..........	10080.-.-	36.-.-	36.-.-
dito to Brasill..........	10888. 3.-	70.11.8	
dito to Interest-reckoning..........	44.14.-		
dito to Profit and Loss..........	310. 2.8		
dito to Voyage to London, consigned to Jack Pudding..........	7810.-.-	1600.-.-	1600.-.-
dito to Voyage to Hamburg..........	2353. 3.-		
dito to Voyage to Danicke..........	1967. 1.-		
dito to Insurance reckoning..........	3463. 2.8		
dito to Cash..........	19561.11.-	27553. 8.-	27553. 8.-
dito to Cambrix, 11 peeces unsold..........	8000.-.-	440.-.-	440.-.-
dito to Ship the Rainbow..........	1043.12.8		
dito to Hans van Essen at Hambrogh my account currant..........	3780.-.-	60.-.-	
dito to Peeter Braseur at Danicke, my account currant..........	3805.14.8	53.12.8	
dito to Jack Pudding at London his account currant..........	917.-.-		
Samme	130544.15.-	47114.10.-	41904. 6.8

[right folio]

Survey of the general-balance, or Estate-reckoning / Creditor	Thus ought your accounts to stand at the first view of the Bookes, when everything is transported out of the waste-booke into the Leager.	Thus ought your second, or Tryall Ballance to stand with the Gains.	Thus ought your True-balance to stand, which you transport into your new-bookes.
dito By Buncke..........	8133.15.8	1325.-.-	
dito By Howse King David..........	7338.15.-		
dito By Susanna Peeters Orphans..........	4860. 2.-		
dito By Jack Pudding, my account current..........	9145.-.-	465.-.-	
dito By French Aquae-vitae..........	6960.-.-	1392.-.-	
dito By Rye..........	1788.11.8	444.11.8	
dito By Concaseille..........	13950.-.-	3906.-.-	
dito By Brasill..........	10817.12.-		
dito By Interest-reckoning..........	102.16.8	58. 2.8	
dito By Profit and Loss..........	394. 7.8	74. 5.-	
dito By Voyage to London..........	8350.-.-	3140.-.-	
dito By Voyage to Hambrough..........	3816. 6.-	1263. 3.-	
dito By Voyage to Danicke..........	1805.14.8	1838.13.8	
dito By Insurance-reckoning..........	3576. 6.-	113. 3.8	
dito By Cash..........	2408. 3.-		
dito By Cambrix-cloth..........	8105.12.-	545.12.-	
dito By Ship the Rainbow..........	1432.11.8	389.-.-	
dito By Hans van Essen, my account..........	3720.-.-		
dito By Peeter Braseur, my account..........	3751. 2.-		
dito By Jack Pudding, at London, his account current..........	3394.18.-	2377.18.-	2377.18.-
dito By Stocks, for my Just Estate..........	14592.-.-	14592.-.-	39316. 8.8
Samme	130544.15.-	41124.10.-	41904. 6.8

Reproduced from A.C. Littleton, *Accounting Evolution to 1900* (1933), pp. 138–139

EXHIBIT 7

Ledger account form of statement from Thomas King, *An Exact Guide to Bookkeeping by Way of Debtor and Creditor Done after the Italian Method*, 1717

[left folio]

Profit and Loss		Debtor
1715		£
Oct. 27	to C. S. Esq. for interest of £1000 due the 27 of April next	27 10 –
Nov. 15	to Mr. B. D.	6 17 8
23	to B. A. by Composition	15 — –
Feb. 27	to Voyage to Gibralter consigned to P. Q.	137 12 6
1716		
Mar. 26	to P. Q. my accompt current for defect in Goods	2 10 –
Apr. 27	to C. S. Esq. for interest on £1000 due the 27 of Oct. next	27 10 –
Oct. 25	to Insurance Account, lost thereby	330 — –
	to Charges on Merchandize	9 — 6
	to Household expenses	22 5 –
	to Stock gained by one year's trade	899 5 6¼
	to My Father's Will left me	5000 — –
		6477 11 2¼

[right folio]

Per Contra		Creditor
1715		£
Oct. 27	By T. C. for Interest of £500 due 27th April next	15 — –
28	By my Father's Will	5000 — –
Nov. 8	By Composition with Mr. B.	9 14 8¼
1716		
Mar. 14	By Mr. G.	27 10 –
Apr. 27	By T. O. for Interest of £500 due 27th Oct. next	15 — –
Oct. 25	By C. S. Esq. for Interest £150 due 27th inst.	5 10 3½
	By Yorkshire Cloth, gained thereby	86 6 –
	By Spanish Cloth, gained thereby	100 — –
	By Voyage to Gibralter, gained thereby	324 14 7½
	By Norwich wares, gained thereby	23 18 –
	By Exeter wares, gained thereby	14 10 –
	By Grocery wares, gained thereby	28 11 1
	By Druggets, gained thereby	10 16 –
	By Hops, gained thereby	283 10 –
	By the Flying Eagle, gained thereby	155 — –
	By Voyage to Salicia, gained thereby	377 10 6
		6477 11 2¼

[left folio]

Ballances		Debtor
1716		£
Oct. 25	to Cash resteth this day	6658 11 10
	to Yorkshire Cloth unsold	1590 — —
	to Spanish Cloth unsold	1087 10 —
	to Voyage to Gibralter for wares unsold	77 10 —
	to Mr. G. C. due to me	20 — —
	to Exeter wares unsold	215 — —
	to P. Q. at Gibralter due to me	499 12 6
	to T. O. for Principal and Interest	515 — —
	to Grocery wares unsold	404 — —
	to Sagathee unsold	120 — —
	to Fine Holland unsold	577 10 —
	to Mr. D. due to me	125 — —
	to Hops unsold	76 4 9¼
	to Voyage to Galicia for wares unsold	18 10 —
	to T. K. at Galicia due to me	385 — —
		12429 9 1¼

[right folio]

Per Contra		Creditor
1716		£
Oct. 25	By Stock	10337 5 ¼
	By C. S. Esq. due to him	871 19 8½
	By N. S. due to him	105 3 4
	By Mr. E. due to him	315 — –
	By Mr. G. due to him	300 — –
	By Mr. K. due to him	500 — –
		12429 9 1¼

Reproduced from A.C. Littleton, *Accounting Evolution to 1900* (1933), pp. 141–142 the few illustrations of a separate financial statement based on double-entry bookkeeping prepared for an 18th century business.

The analysis suggests that Alexander Mackenzie, the record keeper for the brewery, employed accounting practices that were quite sophisticated for the period. If Mackenzie was Scottish, as we have speculated, he may have been better trained than many colonial merchants, for 18th century Scotland had the best educational system in all of western Europe and was a leader in the development of accounting and economic thought.

Future research is needed to uncover other archival evidence that might establish whether or not Mackenzie's accounting practices were the exception, or whether they were typical of other 18th century enterprises in the North American colonies. Another possible direction for future research would be to examine the Scottish influence on the development of Canadian accounting practices. It is worth noting that the first society of accountants in North America met in Montreal in 1879, preceding by at least 10 years the formation of the first accounting society in the United States. Interestingly, the names of almost all of the founders of that first Canadian accounting society can be traced to Scottish origin (Mann, 1972).

References

Archer, John H., "Business Records: The Canadian Scene," in David S. MacMillan (ed.), *Canadian Business History Selected Studies, 1497–1971* (Toronto: McClelland and Stewart, 1972) pp. 208–302.

Baxter, William T., "Accounting in Colonial America," in A.C. Littleton and B.S. Yamey (eds.), *Studies in the History of Accounting* (London: Sweet and Maxwell, 1956) pp. 272–287.

———, *The House of Hancock: Business in Boston, 1724–1775* (New York: Russell & Russell, 1965).

Bowering, Ian, *The Art and Mystery of Brewing in Ontario* (Burnstown, Ontario: Federal Store Publishing House, 1988).

Brewers Association of Canada, *Brewing in Canada* (Montreal, BAC, 1965).

Chatfield, Michael, *A History of Accounting Thought* (Hinsdale, IL: Dryden Press, 1974).

Denison, Merrill, *The Barley and the Stream: The Molson Story* (Toronto: McClelland and Stewart, 1955).

Dictionary of Canadian Biography, Vol. IV: 1771–1800 (Toronto: University of Toronto Press, 1979).

Donovan, Kenneth, "Paying One's Way: Dining and Drinking in Louisbourg's Cabarets and Auberges," *Research Bulletin* No. 135 (Ottawa: Parks Canada, Minister of the Environment, 1980).

———, "Communities and Families: Family Life and Living Conditions in Eighteenth Century Louisbourg," *Material History Bulletin* (Ottawa: National Museum of Man, No. 15, 1982) pp. 33–47.

Easterbrook, W.T. and Hugh G.J. Aitken, *Canadian Economic History* (Toronto: Macmillan Company of Canada, 1975).

Gambino, Anthony J. and John R. Palmer, *Management Accounting in Colonial America* (New York: National Association of Accountants, 1976).

Jacobs-Ermatinger Estate Papers, Public Archives of Canada, MG19 A2, Series 3.

Johnson, Hans V., "Merchant-Accountants" *Management Accounting* (October 1976) pp. 57–61.

Jones, Haydn, *Accounting, Costing and Cost Estimation: Welsh Industry: 1700–1830* (Cardiff: University of Wales 1985).

Kreiser, Larry, "Early American Accounting," *The Journal of Accountancy* (July 1976) pp. 77–80.

Littleton, A.C., *Accounting Evolution to 1900* (New York: American Institute Publishing, 1933).

London Public Records Office T1–398 (London, England) p. 36.

MacMillan, David S., "The 'New Men' in Action: Scottish Mercantile and Shipping Operations in the North Atlantic Colonies, 1760–1825," in David S. MacMillan (ed.), *Canadian Business History Selected Studies, 1497–1971* (Toronto: McClelland and Stewart, 1972) pp. 44–103.

Mair, John, *Book-keeping Methodiz'd* (Edinburgh: T. and W. Ruddimans, 1736, 1st edition), facsimile reprint as vol. 12 of *Historic Accounting Literature* (London: Scholar Press, 1979).

Malcolm, Alexander, *A Treatise of Book-keeping, or Merchants Accounts; in the Italian Method of Debtor and Creditor* (London: J. Osborn and T. Longman, 1731, 1st Edition), facsimile reprint (New York: Garland Publishing, 1986).

Mann, Harvey, *The Evolution of Accounting in Canada* (Montreal: Touche Ross & Co., 1972).

———, "The Jew of St. Denis: An Introduction," *Canadian Jewish Historical Society Journal* (Fall 1984) pp. 85–89.

Mepham, Michael J., "The Scottish Enlightenment and the Development of Accounting," *The Accounting Historians Journal* (Fall 1988) pp. 151–171.

Moore, Christopher, *Fortress of Louisbourg Guide* (Louisbourg, Nova Scotia: Fortress of Louisbourg Volunteers Association, 1981).

Murphy, George, "Review Essay: Some Eighteenth Century Accounting Treatises," *The Accounting Historians Journal* (Fall 1987) pp. 1155–1123.

Public Archives of Canada, Manuscript Division, Ermatinger Estate, MG19 A2, Finding Aid 195.

Sheldahl, T.K., "American's Earliest Recorded Text in Accounting: Sarjeant's 1789 Book," *The Accounting Historians Journal* (Fall 1985) pp. 1–42.

Voke, Albert F., "Accounting Methods of Colonial Merchants in Virginia," *The Journal of Accountancy* (July 1926) pp. 1–11.

Wood, William, *The Great Fortress: A Chronicle of Louisbourg; 1720–1760* (Toronto: Glasgow, Brook & Company, 1915).

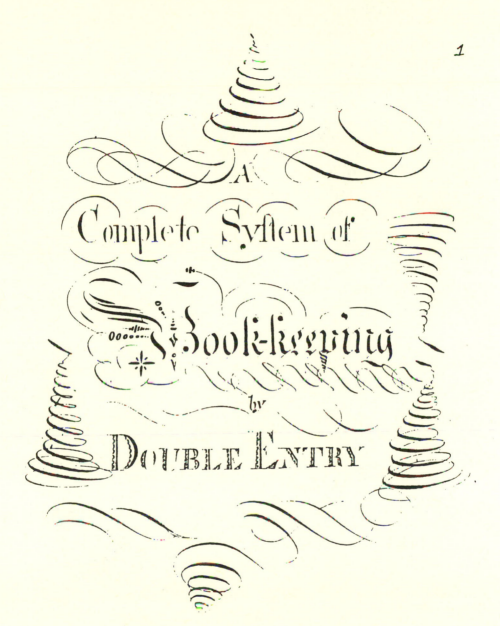

A

Complete System of

Book-keeping

by

Double Entry

Book-keeping is the Art of keeping a regular and true State of the Transactions of a Person's Affairs so that the Book-keeper may readily see at any Time what Changes are made in the State of his Affairs, various are the Methods which have been used for this Purpose. But that which is the most general & in greatest Repute, is the Method of Double Entry commonly known by the Name of Italian Book-keeping; from the first Attempt of this Nature being made in Italy, & Merchants accounts, it being in almost general Use amongst Merchants as it is very Difficult to keep a true State of their Affairs without such Methods. - - - - - - - -

2 nd The Books that are Necessary to be kept are the Waste Book, Journal, and Ledger; the Waste Book

is called from its Use; being that in which every Transaction is entered immediately after it occurs, that nothing slip the Memory. This Book begins with an Inventory of the Real and Personal Estate of the Owner; it being absolutely Necessary that he should have a true State of his Affairs at beginning of Trade. This Book is only intended as a Preparation for the Journal.

3rd The Journal is a Book in which the Waste-Book Enteries are written in a more regular Manner pointing out the Dr and Cr that the Ledger may be found with less Difficulty,

4th The Ledger Book is that in which each Subject hath a distinct and seperate Space allowed containing an equal Number of right and left Pages with its

Name written at the Head thereof being first marked
D.ʳ and C.ʳ the left Hand Pages for the D.ʳ & right Hand Pages
for the C.ʳ Entries. ————————————

General Rules

1.ˢᵗ That the Stock Account is D.ʳ for all I owe by the
Inventory, & C.ʳ for all I have in my Hands or is owing
to me mentioned in the Inventory.

2.ⁿᵈ Cash is D.ʳ for whatever is received & C.ʳ for what
Money is paid or given away.

3.ʳᵈ Profit & Loss is D.ʳ for all Losses & C.ʳ for all Gains.

4.ᵗʰ A Person's Account is D.ʳ for what I pay him or he
owes & C.ʳ for what he pays me or I owe him.

5.th An Account of Goods is D.^r for the Value of all rec.^d with the cost of Charges thereto belonging & C.^r for what any ways go out.

And in buying or selling this Rule is general. What I receive, or a Person receiving, is D.^r what I deliver or the Person delivering, is Creditor.

From what has been observed the following Rules naturally follow.

Rule. 1.st In the Ledger every Subject must be entered Double, that, for every D.^r entered I must enter its Correspondent C.^r &c. Contra.

2.nd When a set of Books are to be opened, let the Account of Stock be made D.^r for all Sums owing me & Cr for the Cash, Goods, & Debts belonging to me.

3.ʳ Let Persons to whom I owe Money have Credit in for their Accounts for the Sum due to them.

4.ᵗʰ Let the Accounts of such Persons as owe Money to me be made Dr for the Sum due to me.

5.ᵗʰ Let the Accounts of such Persons as I owe Money to, be made Cr for the Sum due to them.

6.ᵗʰ Let the Accounts of Cash, "Goods be made Dr for their Value.

Hence for every Article by which the Account of Stock is made Dr some other Account will be Cr or Contra agreable to Rule 1.ˢᵗ

7. When I receive Money.

In Payment of a Debt ⎤ cash ⎤ To the Payer,

Borrowed ——— ⎥ is ⎥ To the Lender

As a Gift ——— ⎦ Dr ⎦ To Profit & Loss

8. When I pay Money

For a Debt ——————————⎤ The Receiver ⎤ is

To the Persons who borr'd it ——⎥ the Borrower ⎥ Debtor to

As a Gift ——————————⎦ Profit & Loss ⎦ Cash.

9. When I buy Goods

For Cash ——⎤ Goods ⎤ To cash,

On Trust —— ⎥ ⎥ To the Seller,

For Goods —— ⎥ bought ⎥ To the Goods sold,

Part Trust —— ⎥ is ⎥ To the Seller in Part

Part Money —— ⎥ Dr ⎥ To Cash in Part

Part Goods ⎦ ⎦ To Goods in Part

10th When I sell Goods

For Money ————	Cash	
On Trust ———————	The Buyer	is
For Goods —————	Goods received	
Part Money ————	Cash in Part	Debtor
Part Trust ————	Buyer in Part	to
Part in Goods ———	Goods in Part	Goods sold

11th Of Discounts & Abatements

When I pay ————— ⎫ .... To Cash for
Money before due & have ⎬ She received Money Paid &
Discount allowed ——— ⎭ To Profit & Loss
~~Allowed~~ for Discount.

Money received by me ⎫ Cash Dr. To the Payer ——— ⎫
before due & I ⎬ Profit & Loss For Money received ⎬
allow Discount Profit & Loss To the Payer ⎫
thereon, Goods for Discount ⎬
damaged To Goods damaged.

Of
Balancing or Closing
the
Ledger.

1st. Begin with the First Accoumpt opened in the Ledger and Proceed regularly thro' them all, omitting only Stock & Profit & Loss which must be left open to Close.

2nd. Personal Accompts are closed to or by Balance for their Difference of their Sides where there is neither Loss nor Gain whenever either of these appears as in Case of Composition, Exchange &c. they will likewise requiere to be closed to or by Profit & Loss

III. Accompt of Goods are closed by Balance for that remainder & to or by Profit & Loss for the Gain Loss on the Staies.

IV. The Balances of Factorage commence with the Accompt of Goods which is closed with the Accompt Current for what the Factor is in advance or hath in his Hands after Deduction of Charges & Comission, and with the Accompt on Time for outstanding Debts, both which Accompts are Closed with Balance. V. The Balances in Company Books are the same as proper Trade, excepting at closing the Books, that the Share of Gain or Loss belonging to each Partner is carried to the Accompt in Company. 6. When all the Accompts are balanced: Profit & Loss is closed with Stock for the Difference, & Stock with Balance

which last if the Books are properly kept
will close itself.

To correct
Errors
in the
Ledger

There are four kinds.

I.ˢᵗ If a Debtor or Cᵣ is omitted supply that Defect
by entering it in its proper Accompt.

II.ⁿᵈ If the Dᵣ or Cᵣ is charged too much make the
opposite Dᵣ or Cᵣ by Error or the Excess.

III.ᵈ If the Dr or Cr is charged with too little Charge it again Dr or Cr by its Correspondent Accompt.

IV.ᵗʰ If the Dr and Cr be both entered on the same Side adjust it by making the opposite Side Dr or Cr by Error for the Sum of the Article misplaced & then enter the Article in its proper Place by which means the Mistake will be balanced & the Accompt properly Placed.

Foreign Trade

and

Company Accompts.

Having laid down the Fundamental Rules of Book-keeping so far as at last relates to Domestic Accompts Inow intend to Attempt the Ivestigation of Rules for Foreign & Com.ᵗ Accounts, as I propose

very soon to put such Rules in Practice.

When I receive a Bill of Exchange.

For Goods immediately sold | Bills | To Goods sold,

In Payment of a Debt | remitted | – the remitter,

As a Gift | | me Dr. to Profit & Loss

When I give out a Bill of Exchange which was

before remitted me.

For Goods bout immediately | Goods bo.ᵗ is | Debtor to

In Payment of a Debt | The receiver is | Bills,

As a Gift | Profit & Loss is | remitted me.

When a Bill of Exchange is drawn on & excepted

Payable by myself

When I pay the Bill

Bills drawn on me is Dr. to Cash for Money paid

of

Voyages

for my

Correspondent.

| When I send Goods for my Accompt of my Correspondent. - - - - - | Correspondent Dr. — | To Goods sent &c to Cash for Charges p.ᵈ by.ᵐ |
| When I receive Returns in Goods, in Bills | goods received Bills remainder | on shipping them & Dᵗ to Correspondᵗ |

of

Voyages.

When I ship	after they are enter.	Merchandize	To the
Goods	d in my Books	consigned	Goods
consigned	When bo.t on trust	my	To the
on my	& not ent.d in	Factor	Seller
own	my Books		
Accompt	But if for Cash	Dr	To Cash.

Of

INSURANCES

When I pay Money to be insured p — —	Merchandize insured p —	Debtor to Cash.
When I receive Money for a Loss — — —		lost
		To Merchandize lost
When I receive a Premium to insure	Cash Dr	To Insurance Accompt.
When I pay Money for Loss as an Insurer	Insurance Accompt Dr.	To Cash p.

Of Factorage
Accompts

When I receive Goods to be sold for Acct. of my Correspondent
A.B.

When I pay Charges on their Acct.		To Cash
If I am to pay Charge on them	The	To ye Persons to whom due
When the Goods are all sold make	Goods	To Profit & Loss for
To Balance Account of his Goods	Dr.	my Commission
Make for the mean Proceeds —		To A. B his Account

When I deliver Goods into Company

If they were my own   The Good in { To the Goods
                       Company, or {

If just bo.t for ready Money   The Voyage { To Cash

If bougt on Trust shipped make Dr To the Seller &c

When I am, an Accountant & Manager.

If I buy the Goods for the   To Cash

Company & paid for them   Voyage dr   {

If on Trust   dr   to the Seller.

If each Partner has not   Partner To Cash for my Part &

Paid his Part   dr   To each Partner for his

But if each Partner has   Voyage To Cash for my Part &

Paid his Part   dr   To each Partner for his

But if I put goods of my own   Voyage To the Accompt of

instead of Money   Dr   Goods I put into comp.y

> We can remember minutely and precisely only
> the things which never really happened to us.

Eric Hoffer [1]

CHAPTER II

THE COMPANIES REVIEWED

Introduction

Although business in Canada has existed since the founding of the country, and some records are extant since 1670, particularly those of Les Forges de St. Maurice, this study is concerned primarily with the last one hundred years. The first limited liability company in the manufacturing field in Canada was a cotton mill erected in Sherbrooke, Quebec in 1844 with a capital of 12,000 pounds,[2] but it was some time before this kind of business organization became popular. There were other limitations to the companies that could be chosen for this study. They had to be Canadian companies which were in existence over a fairly long period, preferably starting in the nineteenth century. Furthermore, these companies had to have a continuous history, and most important the financial statements had to be available, which meant, of necessity, that they were public companies. Based on a scrutiny of old stock exchange records, very few, if any, commercial enterprises were publically owned before the latter part of the nineteenth century. Canada, of course, is not unique in this respect as the American experience is similar. The major exceptions are some public utilities and railroads which are now extinct, but utilities and railroads are well represented in this study by the Bell Telephone Company of Canada and the Canadian Pacific Railroad. By the same token, the accounting profession has come into its own only within the last one hundred years, so that an examination of the financial statements of the major public companies since approximately 1870 will encompass the major portion of the growth of accounting in Canada.

This chapter will therefore serve as an introduction to the companies whose financial statements will be studied. A resume will be made of their organization, establishment, sphere of operations and their growth, as well as a brief look at the men responsible for the success of the companies. This is necessary since the financial statements of a company represent only one viewpoint of its operations and some background will make these statements more meaningful. Some of the earlier statements formed part of the ornate, hand-written minute books of director and shareholder meetings, and together they very often form the only history available of the company. As a very condensed version of the activities of an enterprise, these records do not tell of the manifold struggles, the involved people, or the millions of events that occurred over the years. Analysis, therefore, is being made from the minimal information available.

7

According to the British North America Act 1867, both Dominion and Provincial governments have the power to create companies. Railways, banks, insurance companies, and loan and trust companies are governed by special federal legislation; all other companies are under the jurisdiction of either the Federal government or one of the Provincial governments. Companies may be incorporated by 1) special act, 2) letters patent, 3) memorandum of association.[3] In addition, a few companies have been incorporated by Royal Charter. Although the type of incorporation is immaterial, this study does encompass the three different kinds; the Bank of Montreal was organized originally under a memorandum of association, was later incorporated, and then came under special legislation; The Bell Telephone Company of Canada was incorporated under special act, as was the Canadian Pacific Railroad, but both are also controlled by special legislation; the Montreal Cotton Company, Steel Company of Canada and Dominion Textile Company Limited were incorporated under the more general letters patent. The only company, whose statements have been seen, that was granted a Royal Charter to operate in Canada was the Hudson's Bay Company, but since this company for all intents and purposes was a British company and followed British accounting procedures, it does not form part of this study.

The Bell Telephone Company of Canada

The Bell Telephone Company of Canada was incorporated on April 29, 1880 by an Act of Parliament[4] at the request of Alexander Melville Bell (father of Alexander Graham Bell) and nine other gentlemen. This act was fairly modest, containing only 27 paragraphs. It gave the company the power to manufacture, purchase, build, and lease all apparatus connected with the telephone and telegraph business and to sell or let this equipment. The authorized capital stock was 5,000 shares of $100 par value, and the directors were granted the power to increase this by an additional $500,000 with the consent of a majority, in value, of the shareholders present in person or represented by proxy at a general meeting.[5] No provision was made in the act for the appointment of an auditor, nor is there any stipulation as to the kinds of records or books to be kept.

This act has been amended 11 times, up to and including March 7, 1968, usually authorizing the company to issue ever greater amounts of capital stock and augmenting its borrowing powers. By 1968 the authorized capital stock of the company was $1,750,000,000., but in 1949 there was a four-for-one stock split which reduced the par value of the common shares to $25. The allowable telephone rates to be charged by the company are first mentioned in 1892 where it is stated that the existing rates shall not be increased without the consent of the Governor in Council,[6] while other powers are controlled by the Board of Transport Commissioners and by various other Acts of Parliament. Again, no mention is made in any of the amendments to the original act of the need for an auditor, for books of account, or for financial statement content; however the amendment of 1968[7] does contain two instances which specifically exempt the company from certain sections of the Canada Corporations Act.[8] This seems to indicate that the company does have to comply with the overall law unless exempted, and hence would have to follow the procedures regarding audit,

8

statements and books of account. There is no implication that the company has not, at the very least, complied with normal practice, as will be pointed out later when both the Canada Corporations Act and the company's financial statements are discussed in greater detail.

The telephone was first patented in Canada in 1877, and originally Alexander Melville Bell leased the telephone instrument to anyone interested, with the leasee providing his own wire line. The details of handling this business became too onerous so an attempt was made to sell the Canadian patent rights in Canada. The required $100,000 could not be raised in Canada so the rights were sold to the National Bell Telephone Company of Boston. The American company sent Charles Fleetford Sise to Montreal to organize the Bell Telephone Company of

TABLE I

The following table gives some indication of the relative sums of money employed in the financing of these companies. This is shown for the reader's information and is not critical for an understanding of the paper.

Total Assets of Canadian Chartered Banks

Year End	(millions of dollars)
1867	84
1870	111
1875	183
1880	193
1885	228
1890	260
1895	322
1900	502
1905	816
1910	1,230
1915	1,738
1920	3,057
1925	2,896
1930	3,144
1935	3,079
1940	3,731
1945	7,311
1950	9,443
1955	12,702
1960	16,917

Source: M.C. Urquhart (ed.), K.A.H. Buckley (asst. ed.), Historical Statistics of Canada (Macmillan Company of Canada Ltd., Toronto, 1965), condensed from Series H 55 – 225.

9

Canada, a task already started by Alexander Melville Bell. All efforts were to be made that the company was wholly owned and operated by Canadians, but the American Bell Telephone Company agreed to invest approximately one-third of the required funds. This has dwindled to only 2 per cent at this time.[9]

The Canadian Telephone Company was incorporated at the same time for the purpose of owning the patents and rights, and of leasing the telephone apparatus to the Bell Telephone Company. This followed the method used in the United States but was dropped two years later because the Bell Telephone Company was the only large operating company in Canada as opposed to a much larger number in the United States. Between 1880 and 1881 the Bell Telephone Company had acquired the telephone operations in nine different areas stretching between the Maritimes and Winnipeg, Manitoba.

The Bell Telephone Company was forced to start its own manufacturing operation in 1882 because of the difficulty of obtaining telephones in Canada and because telephones could not be imported without invalidating the Canadian patents. This manufacturing division was spun-off in 1895 to form the Northern Electric and Manufacturing Company, which still supplies the Bell Telephone Companies and their competitors in Canada and elsewhere.[10] In actual fact, the original Bell patents were invalidated in Canada in 1885 and 1889 by the Commissioner of Patents, but by this time quite a few other patents were held by the company and in theory no telephone could be made without danger of infringement.[11]

Other companies were bought up over the years but because of large distances, difficult terrain, and sparse population, the maritime and prairie operations were sold, so that by 1909 the Bell Telephone Company was operating primarily in Ontario and Quebec. Later, however the Bell Telephone Company made substantial investments in the Maritime companies and now has a majority interest in all cases. At the present time, there are approximately 1,900 different telephone companies in Canada, all integrated under the Trans-Canada Telephone System to provide a unified national telephone system. [12]

The company has grown substantially since its inception in 1880. Although originally it was exclusively offering telephone service, it is now in "the business of moving information" as its advertising is wont to say. Constant improvement in its facilities has allowed the company to introduce new services ranging from direct distance dialing to data communications and audio-visual teaching aids. From a small beginning, the company now has more than a quarter of a million shareholders, 98% Canadian residents owning roughly 95% of the outstanding shares. It employs about 38,000 people, and has a continuing impact on the Canadian economy because of its massive investment in new construction and in research and development.[13]

The Canadian Pacific Railway Company[14]

The Canadian Pacific Railway Company first applied for and received its charter from the Canadian government in 1872, at which time the company was promised $30,000,000 and a land grant of 50,000,000 acres.[15] The group applying for this charter included an American representation headed by Jay Cooke, as well as some prominent Canadians. The government, however, insisted that there be

10

no American participation, which so riled the Americans that they made public some letters written by Sir Hugh Allen, the president of the Canadian Pacific Railway, which resulted in the fall of the government and the subsequent dropping of the charter.

Although it had to pass through territory that was mainly unpopulated and unsurveyed, and although very little was known about the agricultural possibilities of the prairies, a transcontinental railway was required if Canada were to grow. Furthermore, when British Columbia entered confederation in 1871, one of the conditions was that a railway to the Pacific would be constructed within ten years. One main constraint was that the line be built entirely in Canada and as far from the border as possible because of the fear of American domination.[16]

The government did make some desultory attempts to construct the line but by 1880 when the agreement with British Columbia was due to expire only 264 miles of rail had been laid. Private enterprise was called upon and in 1881 an Act incorporating the Canadian Pacific Railway with a capitalization of $25,000,000 was passed.[17] The government granted a further $25,000,000 and 25,000,000 acres of land and empowered the company to issue $25,000,000 bonds with the land as security, these bonds to be sold on behalf of the company by the government. The company was also ceded the track already laid.

The first Board of Directors consisted of George Stephen, president, Duncan McIntyre, vice-president, and Richard R. Angus, all of Montreal, James J. Hill of St. Paul, John S. Kennedy of New York, Henry Stafford Northcote, Pasco du P. Grenfell, and Charles D. Rose, of London, and Baron J. de Reinack of Paris.[18] The General Manager of the company during the stupendous job of construction was William Cornelius Van Horne, an American by birth and training, and subsequently a president of the Canadian Pacific Railway. The purchasing agent, who also later became a president of the company, was another American, Thomas George Shaughnessy, whose skill kept the cost of construction to a minimum. George Stephen was born in Scotland and emigrated to Canada in 1850 at the age of 21. He was president of the Bank of Montreal between 1876 and 1881, and first became acquainted with the railway business in 1877 when he, in company with Angus, a general manager of the Bank of Montreal, Donald A. Smith of Hudson's Bay Company fame, and James Hill and Norman Kitson, two Canadians living in St. Paul, bought control of the bankrupt St. Paul and Manitoba Railway.[19]

Probably one of the most difficult tasks for the management was the financing of an undertaking of this magnitude. $65,000,000 worth of common stock was sold in Canada, New York and Europe, but at a discount of over 50%. (The recording and disposition of this discount is discussed in greater detail on pages 62 and 89.) Further monies were realized from sale of first mortgage bonds ($14,600,000), a government loan of $29,000,000 plus the subsidy of $25,000,000, $3,612,500 from land grant bonds, and approximately $9,000,000 as net proceeds from sales of portions of the land grant. In spite of considerable opposition from both Canadian and American interests, and a poor money market, the line was completed in 1885, having reached the Pacific coast five years before the contract stipulated. The company proved so successful that by the following year, all obligations to the government had been settled.

11

The act incorporating the Canadian Pacific Railway contains nothing regarding auditors, reports, or books of account, but certain requirements were stipulated by the various Railway Acts under which the C.P.R. and all other railroads were and are controlled. The following paragraph, in almost identical wording, appears in every act.

> 62. The directors shall cause to be kept and, annually on the thirtieth day of June, (1) to be made up and balanced, a true, exact and particular account of the monies collected and received by the company or by the directors or (managers) (2) thereof, or otherwise, for the use of the company, and of the charges and expenses attending the erecting, making, supporting, maintaining and carrying on of the undertaking, and of all other receipts and expenditures of the company or the directors.[20]

The above requirement, as can be seen, is, in modern accounting parlance, a statement of cash-flow. Over the years, the Railway Acts have become longer and ever more demanding with more and more reporting being required by the Board of Transport. The format of these reports will be discussed more fully in conjunction with the study of the Canadian Pacific Railway's financial statements. A point of interest, though, is that there is no mention made in the act of the need for an independent auditor.

During the intervening years the company has grown continuously, expanded its operations, and diversified into many other fields. Over and beyond the initial business of the railroad, the company immediately constructed a telegraph system and built hotels, both considered as necessary adjuncts to the railroad. At the present time the C.P.R. controls a steamship line, a truck transport company, and through subsidiaries, an airline (C.P.A.) and an investment company, Canadian Pacific Investments Limited. This last named company, in turn, owns the complete voting stock of an oil and gas company, a realty company, as well as a controlling interest in other major companies such as Central-Del Rio Oils Limited and Cominco Limited. From a relatively small beginning the company has progressed to become one of the giants of Canadian industry; all this has been accomplished under private enterprise with a minimum of government aid, and often in competition with the government.

The Bank of Montreal[21]

The Bank of Montreal opened its doors for business late in 1817 as an association or limited copartnership before even applying for a charter of incorporation from the government. The name, at this time, was the Montreal Bank, and the articles of association[22] reveal several incongruities. The articles provide for a capital stock of 5,000 shares of 50 pounds each with any one person limited to 20 shares initially. If after three months the shares were not fully subscribed, a subscriber could buy a further 20 shares, and one month later, ten more shares. The shareholders were empowered to elect 13 directors but no person

12

could have more than 20 votes for which he would have to own 100 shares, based on the following voting scheme.

One and two shares –	one vote
Each two shares thereafter to ten shares –	one vote
Each four shares from ten to thirty –	one vote
Each six shares from thirty to sixty –	one vote
Each eight shares from sixty to one hundred –	one vote

The directorate was restricted to shareholders owning at least ten shares, but they also had to be natural born or naturalized subjects of His Majesty, a subject because of conquest, a person who had resided in the province for seven years, or one who had resided in the City of Montreal for three years with at least the last year immediately preceding the election. These last stipulations were no doubt inserted to ensure that no one person would gain control of the bank, and that all directors would be local people.

The articles further state that all shareholders would have limited liability, but it is difficult to see how, under present law, this could have any bearing on third parties. The business of the bank was to deal in Bills of Exchange, gold and silver bullion, and sale of pledged goods and stock, but it was prohibited from lending money on land or buildings, or for that matter from owning any land or buildings not used explicitly for the business. It seems to have been accepted as a matter of course that the bank would be issuing paper money because no specific mention is made of the power.

The nine signers of the articles are of interest because of the insight they provide as to the balance of power in the community, and the banking methods they introduced. John Richardson, considered the father of Canadian banking, was born in Scotland in 1755. However, his business training before coming to Canada was in New York with an important English mercantile house. As such he was well-versed in the banking principles of both England and the United States. However, the articles of the Bank of Montreal followed closely the charter of the First Bank of the U.S. established in 1792.[23] George Garden and George Moffatt were Montreal merchants, but one was allied with the North West Company and the other with the Hudson's Bay Company, bitter rivals at this time. Austin Cuvillier, the only French-Canadian in the group, was a member of the Legislative Assembly and an importer with French-Canadian connections. James Leslie and Robert Armour were a retired army officer and publisher, respectively. Thomas Turner and John Bush seem to have represented American commercial or financial interests, while Horatio Gates, a New Englander active in the Vermont trade, was born in Massachusetts. Gates later became president of the bank, and was instrumental in the partial financing of the bank by American interests.

A breakdown of the origins of the original subscribers is indicative of the aversion of many Canadians to a new venture. Of the 287 subscribers, 12 lived in Lower Canada outside of Montreal, 11 came from Upper Canada, three from Glasgow and five from London; 135 Montreal residents purchased 2,158 shares, while 121 Americans bought 2,360 shares! Another important American incursion (?) was the first teller of the new bank and its first professional banker,

13

Henry Stone, who was lent to the bank by a Bostonian friend. This same Stone was later to become famous in the United States as a founder of the first clearing-house system, the Suffolk Bank system, of which he was president.

After considerable difficulty, a royal charter was finally granted in 1822, thereby allowing the bank to become a public company. In spite of depression and recession, competition and political action, the bank prospered. The continued right to issue paper money was an important facet of the bank's functions until 1935 when the Bank of Canada was formed, at which time all banks lost their note-issuing privileges; however the last Bank of Montreal banknote was not withdrawn from circulation until 1949 and then "Notes in Circulation" disappeared from its balance sheet. Also, after 1935 the bank no longer acted as the government banker. The bank opened many new branches, while closing the less profitable ones. Throughout its existence foreign exchange operations have played a very important part in the profitability of the bank.

The original articles of association did touch upon accounting matters in that it was assumed that books were to be kept, and the twentieth article states in part that,

> "...the Directors shall every year, at the General Meeting, for election thereof, lay before the Stockholders, for their information, an exact and particular Statement of the amount of the Debts due to, and by the Company, specifying the amount of the Bank Notes then in circulation, and the amount of such Debts as in their opinion are bad, or doubtful; as also stating the surplus or Profit, if any remaining, after deduction of losses and provisions for dividends, ..."[24]

The various laws introduced by the government to regulate and control the banks and the banking system, however, clearly exerted a greater influence upon accounting and reporting matters. The first official document on banks was passed in 1841. Since then many acts have gone through the legislative mill, with the last revision of the Bank Act appearing in 1967. This last act had a tremendous influence on accounting practice since it required the banks for the first time to make full disclosure of their inner or hidden reserves, a figure that had always been jealously guarded. This will be explored in greater detail when the annual reports of the Bank of Montreal are discussed.

As indicated previously, the bank grew over the years; capital increased to a high of over $67 million by 1969 plus a rest account of $223 million; more than 1,000 branches were in operation, and through subsidiaries or representatives business was transacted in Europe, Japan, South America, and the United States. The Bank Act of 1944 restricted the interest rate chargeable to 6% and regulated the amount of the inner reserve, but the act of 1954 permitted the banks to lend on mortgages for the first time, and that of 1967 allowed them to compete with other financial institutions even to the extent of consumer financing. As can be seen the banks, and the Bank of Montreal particularly, have changed considerably since their inception, always an important cog in the Canadian economy, and inevitably a profitable investment to their shareholders.

14

The Montreal Cotton Company and Dominion Textile Company Limited

The Montreal Cotton Company. The Montreal Cotton Company was incorporated under letters patent in the Province of Quebec on the thirteenth day of January, 1874, with an authorized capital stock of $500,000., divided into 5,000 shares and $100 each. The incorporators of this company were the Hon. Thomas Ryan, a member of the Senate of Canada, and Charles Brydges, Thomas Cramp, William F. Kay, Alexander Cross, Edward Greene, Henry MacKay, F. Wolferstan Thomas, Henry J. Tiffin, Dugald J. Bannatyne, James S. Millar, James Coristine, William Angus, Alexander W. Ogilvy, Maurice Cuvillier, William Hobbs, Dr. George W. Campbell, all of the City of Montreal, Robert Johnstone of Cohoes, New York, and James Waltie of Valleyfield, Quebec. The purpose of the company was to acquire real estate and water power to be used for and in connection with the manufacturing of wool, cotton and other fabrics, as well as the buying and selling of all materials necessary for this purpose.[25] By 1901 the capital stock had been increased to a total of $4,000,000, and further supplementary letters patent in 1907 allowed the company to fall under the provisions of the new Quebec Companies Act 1907 in all respects.

A great deal of the original capital for the company was subscribed in England, and Cross was elected as first president of the company. He was replaced one year later by Sir Hugh Allen,[26] the same gentleman who has been mentioned previously in connection with the Canadian Pacific Railway.

The company grew originally because of the disturbance in the cotton industry in the United States due to the Civil War, and then the adoption of the National Policy in Canada in 1879 provided the spur for even more rapid development.[27] This National Policy increased the tariff on cotton importations, thereby allowing the domestic companies to prosper. However, a recession developed and the company paid no dividends for the years 1884-85-86, but business picked up again with the establishment of a print works, and the completion of the Canadian Pacific Railway. The new railway permitted the shipment of cotton goods to China, a trade which continued until the Boxer Rebellion (1900). The loss of this trade was offset by the increased demand in Canada, bolstered by ever-higher tariffs to protect Canadian industry.

Attempts were made to amalgamate the various cotton manufacturing firms into potential monopolistic combinations in order to maintain prices. Mr. A.F. Gault, president of the Montreal Cotton Company, until his death in 1903, was at one time also president of the Hochelaga Cotton Company, the Montmorency Company, the Dominion Cotton Mills, and the Canadian Coloured Cottons.[28] In 1905, a takeover bid from the organizers of the Dominion Textile Company Limited to the Montreal Cotton Company was effectively squashed by a letter from the then president, Mr. Ewing. But "progress" could not be denied, and by 1935 the Dominion Textile Company Limited was the sales agent for the Montreal Cottons. By 1948 all the capital stock of the Montreal Cotton Company was called for redemption with the company becoming a wholly-owned subsidiary of the Dominion Textiles, hence a private company, non-existent for our purposes.

15

In 1911 another company was formed under the name of the Montreal Cottons Limited which operated the Montreal Cotton Company, but there seems to be considerable confusion in the minds of all concerned because statements are available for several years around this time with what seems to be misleading titles and wrong information. Another sidelight of interest on the statements is the operation of a farm account, which according to Mr. Gurnham, in the speech previously mentioned (see footnote 26), was in operation at least until 1951.

Dominion Textile Company Limited. The Dominion Textile Company Limited was formed on January 5, 1905 by letters patent[29] to take over the properties of the Dominion Cotton Mills Company, the Montmorency Cotton Mills Company, the Merchants Cotton Company,

Figure 1				
Dominion Textile Incorporators*	Directors of Constituent Companies Before Incorporation**			
	Colonial	Merchants	Dominion	Montmorency
Black John P.				x
Forget Louis J.			x	x
Gordon Sir Charles B.				x
Grier George A.				
Holt Herbert S.	x			x
Henshaw Frederic C.				
Laing James N.				
MacKay Robert		x		x
Meredith Henry V.			✓	
Morrice David Jr.				
Williamson David				x
Yuile David				x

* The Canada Gazette
Pp. 1374-5, January 5, 1905

** This information was gleaned from various unsubstantiated sources and hence is subject to correction

16

and the Colonial Bleaching and Printing Company.[30] The original incorporators and their known affiliations in the constituent companies are listed on the preceding schedule. This differs from the Turgeon report which indicates that amongst the 16 members of the syndicate forming this company, two were directors of Montmorency, and three others were directors (one on each board) of Colonial, Dominion Cottons and Merchants.[31] The total investment of the group was $1,000,000., for which they received $500,000 in preferred stock and $5,000,000 in common shares. This included goodwill and seems to have been consummated on a "pooling" rather than a "purchase" basis. The shareholders of the original companies received senior securities, both preferred stock and bonds, for their common stock holdings.[32] Since Dominion Cotton Mills had been an amalgamation of 12 mills in 1890 and 1891, this latest merger gave Dominion Textile control over 8,300 looms and 370,000 spindles or practically 50% of the equipment in the industry in Canada.[33]

No additional financing was undertaken until 1922, when 25,000 common shares were sold at a par of $100 bringing the issued capital to $7,500,000 which was immediately increased to $15,000,000 by the formation of a new company under the same name, and justified by an appraisal of the fixed assets.[34] By 1970 the issued capital stock (common) stood at $20,278,688 , so that there has been very little change since 1922, and growth has been accomplished internally by the ploughing back of earnings. Over the years Dominion Textile has maintained its leadership in the textile industry with 15 plants, of which 14 are in the Province of Quebec, 12 subsidiary companies, and 4 affiliated companies.

There is no need to comment at this time on the accounting practices outlined above but the following quote from the Turgeon report is revealing as an example of the thinking as far back as 1935 of the responsibility of industry to the community, even ahead of the shareholders, particularly in the case of tarriff-supported companies.

The whole question of company accounting, and of the necessity of providing against possible manipulation in such accounting, demands attention as a result of the evidence to which I have referred. The textile industry is one which is engaged in the production of tariff-protected goods. It is, as has already been said, an industry for the establishment and the development of which the community has consented to tax itself. Speaking at least of such an industry, I must say that I cannot at all agree with the suggestions of secrecy which have been put forward. In my opinion, Parliament which provides the tariff has the right, I may venture, I think, to say the duty, to see to it that true facts are made known as often as necessary and practicable, concerning, among other things, the profits made by those who operate under the protection of the tariff. It should be made sure that governments, when approached for tariff changes, will always have reliable figures presented to them, that consumers, (who pay all the manufacturers' taxes in any case because they are all passed on to them in the price of the manufactured goods), should know what is going on, and that shareholders should be furnished with annual statements sufficiently clear and detailed to enable them to form a fair opinion of the value of their shares. Even under the amendments made to the Companies Act in 1934, presumably with this end in view, some of the balance sheets shown me are still quite deficient. There are reduced to the smallest possible compass, and their references to inventories and reserves are of practically no value. Reserves in themselves are not necessarily illegitimate; they may be of use and value, but they should not be kept secret from those entitled to know of them, for instance, shareholders and taxing officials. [35]

17

The Steel Company of Canada[36] (Stelco)

The Steel Company of Canada was formed in 1910 by a merger of the Montreal Rolling Mills Company, Dominion Wire Manufacturing Company, Hamilton Steel and Iron Company, Canada Screw Company, Limited and the Canada Nut and Bolt Company. These constituent companies were themselves mergers and descendants of much older companies so that this new amalgamation put under one management about sixteen different plants, and an operation integrated from pig iron and basic steel to finished products of all types.

The merger was one of several in a wave that occurred during the first decade of the twentieth century in Canada, made feasible by the growth of the Canadian economy, bolstered by the building of railways and the opening of the West, and supported by the National Policy of tariff protection. An important plus factor was the emergence of a capital market in Canada, originated by the salesmanship of E.R. Wood and his company, Dominion Securities. The architect of this merger was Max Aitken, more commonly known to the present generation as Lord Beaverbrook, who had been instrumental in organizing the Canadian Car and Foundry Company from three leading railway car manufacturers, and the Canada Cement Company Limited, made up of almost all the cement companies in Canada.[37]

Aitken was very nationalistically inclined and wanted to keep the company within the British Empire so the major portion of the financing was done in England. He purchased the Montreal Rolling Mills from the retiring owner, then negotiated with the other principals to form Stelco which then had about one-half of the finishing capacity and one-tenth of the steel ingot production in Canada. Aitken had no interest in the operation of the company, and had made many powerful enemies with his financial dealings so that after the completion of this venture he left Canada, a very wealthy man, to start a new career in Great Britain, at the ripe old age of 31.

The company was formed under the Companies Act[38] with an authorized capital of $10,000,000, 7% cumulative preferred shares, $15,000,000 in common shares, and $10,000,000 in bonds. As was common in almost all mergers during this time, the new company was capitalized at a much higher value than the companies forming the merger. In this case, $6,850,000 , in bonds, $6,500,000 in preferred stock and $11,500,000 in common stock was issued for $10,000,000 in the original companies. Mr. C.S. Wilcox, in a letter to the Royal Securities Corporation, Limited (Aitken's company) states that the purpose behind the merger is reductions in the cost of administration, selling, distribution and transportation, economies on purchases of supplies and materials, and increased efficiency through specialization.[39] There is no doubt that there is justification in these reasons, but mention could also be made of the attempt to reduce competition, and the potential for very substantial profits for the promoters of the company.

It was indicated above that very little in finances were obtained from the United States for this venture, but the Americans were and are conspicuous in other areas. Professor Kilbourn points this out very aptly where he says, "It was this kind of ready access to American technical knowledge that helped make the Canadian industrial economy in the first place".[40] Another import was collective bargaining introduced in all Stelco works in 1945 with the United Steel Workers of

18

America as the employees bargaining agent.

Stelco continued to grow throughout the years, managing to survive recession and depression, and aided by two world wars. Some indication of this growth can be seen between the production in 1910 of approximately 80,000 tons to about 3,670,000 tons in 1969, as well as the increase in capitalization from the original to over half a billion dollars in common shares and retained earnings plus long-term debt of 50 million dollars. As well the company is now a totally integrated operation from coal and iron ore properties to many plants and world wide subsidiaries manufacturing all kinds of steel products ranging from plates and sheets to pipes, fencing, etc., etc.

Figure 2						
Directors of more than one company of firms in this study in 1910.						
	Bank of Montreal 7 Directors	Bell Telephone Co. 9 Directors	Canadian Pacific Rail. 15 Directors	Dominion Textile Ltd. 10 Directors	Montreal Cottons 10 Directors	Steel Co. of Canada 11 Directors
J. P. Black				x	x	
L. J. Forget			x	x	x	
G. B. Gordon				x	x	
H. S. Holt				x	x	x
C. P. Hosmer		x	x	x		
R. MacKay	x	x	x	x		
W. D. Matthews			x			x
V. Meredith	x			x		
T. G. Shaughnessy	x		x			
Source: Annual Reports — 1910 — all except Montreal Cottons Company — direct contact.						

19

Summary

In the story of the various companies, two or three points stand out as most significant. These are the interrelationship of the directorates of these companies, the reliance of Canadian industry on the United States of America, and the impact of government policies on the growth of the companies.

The first can be seen by reference to the chart on p.19 which lists the men with more than one directorship in 1910 in the six companies being studied. Insofar as United States involvement is concerned, we see the Canadian banking system based on the tenets of Alexander Hamilton; technical know-how being provided for the Bell Telephone, The Canadian Pacific Railway and Stelco; financing done for the Bank of Montreal, the Bell Telephone, and the Canadian Pacific; and the people, Henry Stone, the first teller of the bank, Van Horne and Shaughnessy for the Canadian Pacific, and Charles Sise for the Bell Telephone. In every one of the companies concerned there is a strong bond with the United States. Nationalism, like motherhood, is a universal virtue, but it must not disintegrate into jingoism — honor where honor is due.

It would seem that without government intervention, in one form or the other, all the companies would have had difficulty in surviving and almost no hope of showing the substantial profits that they did. The Steel Company and Dominion Textile, as indicated previously, were aided greatly by the National Policy; the Canadian Pacific could not have been built without financing from the government; the Bank of Montreal benefited by handling the government accounts; while the Bell was and is a virtual monopoly, albeit under the aegis of government regulation. It can be argued that in order for Canada to survive, the government must intervene, now as much as in the past, since it is faced with an overwhelming juggernaut from the south with a population, production ability, and adventureness in business affairs, that could swallow all of Canada with very little indigestion.

CHAPTER II – FOOTNOTES

1   Thoughts of Eric Hoffer – by Eric Hoffer, The New York Times Magazine April 25, 1971, pp. 55–56.

2   Hon. Mr. Justice W.F.A. Turgeon, Report of the Royal Commission on the Textile Industry (J.O. Patenaude, I.S.O., Printer to the King's Most Excellent Majesty, Ottawa, 1938), p. 32.

3   "Special Act" refers to a specific Act of Parliament drafted especially to incorporate a company. "Letters Patent", the most common method of incorporation in Canada, is the result of an application to the government requesting a charter to form a limited company, under the Canada Corporations Act. At the present time, this power is vested in the Minister of Consumer and Corporate Affairs. "Memorandum of Association" is similar to the application for incorporation, but instead of the granting of letters patent, once this memorandum is filed and approved by the Registrar of Joint Stock Companies, it becomes the charter of the company. For further details see Canadian Corporate Secretary; the Canadian Division of the Chartered Institute of Secretaries (Sir Isaac Pitman (Canada) Limited, Toronto, 1968), passim.

20

4   S.C. 43 Victoria, 1880, Chapter 67.

5   See Table – page 9 (note $ value).

6   S.C. 55–56 Victoria, 1892, Chapter 67, paragraph 3.

7   S.C. 16–17 Elizabeth II, 1968, Chapter 48.

8   R.S.C., 1952, c. 53 as amended by S.C. 11–14 Elizabeth II, 1964–65, c. 52. Paragraph 3 (4) of the Bell Telephone Company amendment exempts the company from section 162 of the Canada Corporations Act which is concerned with preferred share voting, while paragraph 11 allows the company to make loans to shareholders in contravention of sections 190 and 193.

9   This is Bell Canada, a booklet published by Bell Canada bearing number P1 70–2, pg. 5.

10   "The Beginning of the Telephone Business in Canada", The Bell Telephone Company of Canada, Telephone Historical Collection, December, 1967.

11   Alexander Graham Bell, a booklet published by Bell Canada bearing number P1 68–76, pg. 11.

12   This is Bell Canada, loc. cit., p. 18.

13   Ibid., p. 2 and 16.

14   A good basic history of the railways in Canada is W.T. Easterbrook and Hugh G.J. Aitken, Canadian Economic History (Macmillan Company of Canada Limited, Toronto, 1956), Chapter XVIII, "The Transcontinental Railways".

15   S.C. 35 Victoria, 1872, Chapter 71.

16   James Charles Bonar, Canadian Pacific Railway Company (Manuscript, Sir George Williams University, Montreal, 1950), Vol. 1, pp. 12–16.

17   S.C. 44, Victoria, 1881, Chapter 1, An Act respecting the Canadian Pacific Railway.

18   Bonar, op. cit., p. 21.

19   Canadian Pacific Facts and Figures, compiled and edited by the General Publicity Department, Canadian Pacific Foundation Library (Gazette Printing Company Limited, 1937), pp. 22–23.

20   Dominion Railway Act, 51 Victoria, Chapter 29, in Harry Abbott, A Treatise on the Railway Law of Canada (C. Theoret, Montreal, 1896), appendix p. xxvii.

21   The major portion of the information for this section was derived from an informative and comprehensive work in two volumes detailing the history of the bank. See Merrill Denison, Canada's First Bank – A History of the Bank of Montreal (McClelland and Stewart Limited, Toronto, 1966).

22   Ibid., Appendix A, Volume 1, pp. 404–413.

23   A.B. Jamieson Chartered Banking in Canada (Ryerson Press, Toronto, 1953), p. 4.

21

24   Ibid., p. 412.

25   Quebec Official Gazette, VI, January 24, 1874.

26   Speech by Mr. C. Gurnham at the Rotary Club, Montreal, Sept. 1, 1953.

27   Turgeon, op. cit., p. 33.

28   Turgeon, op. cit., p. 36.

29   Canada Gazette, pp. 1374–1375, January 5, 1905.

30   Pamphlet, Dominion Textile Company Limited.

31   Turgeon, op. cit. pp. 119–120.

32   Financial History of Dominion Textile Company Limited, p. 7.

33   Turgeon, op. cit., p. 38.

34   Financial History, op. cit., pp. 14–15.

35   Turgeon, op. cit., p. 127.

36   Most of the information on this company came from a beautifully written book by William Kilbourn, The Elements Combined (Clarke, Irwin and Company Limited, Toronto, 1960).

37   Ibid., p. 67–68.

38   R.S.C. 1906, C. 79.

39   Ibid., p. 284.

40   Ibid., p. 116.

22

CHAPTER V

THE FINANCIAL STATEMENTS: FORM AND FORMAT

Introduction

The financial statements represent the culmination of an accountant's work. Very few people, other than fellow accountants, can visualize the endless details, the painstaking work, and the constant soul-searching that must be gone through before these statements are ready for publication. By the same token, the genius (for want of a better word) of the financial statements has seldom been adequately recognized. A countless number of financial transactions over a complete year are compressed onto one page to show how a business has done over the period, while another page purports to give the financial position of the enterprise at a certain moment in time. It is small wonder that there are some arguments as to the effectiveness and propriety of these statements; two sheets of paper must suffice to explain the ambitions and failures of the members of an organization, and their interactions with the community, the economy, and the world at large — either a magnificent obsession or a fool's paradise.

Nevertheless, accountants are still required to prepare and present financial statements. The aim of this chapter, then, is to trace the evolution of financial statements, with particular emphasis on the companies being studied, and to ascertain the changes that were made. At the same time, the attempt is made to discover how these changes came about. Format deals with the general make-up of the statements, while form is concerned with the arrangement of the accounts within the statements.

The Early Years

Financial statements, as they are seen today, are a fairly recent innovation in the history of accounting. But, even Paciolo, writing in 1494, describes the workings of the Profit and Loss Account in Chapter 27, and the Preparation of the Trial Balance in Chapter 34.[2] A later book by Gordon[3], which is available in the original, also says nothing about financial statements per se, but details are given for "balancing the ledger" in section 6 and following. Gordon, following directly in the footsteps of Paciolo, counsels the accountant in balancing or closing the ledger on an annual basis, because the space in the old ledger would be used up, and also to show the merchant the true state of his affairs. The recommended procedure is to open two new pages in the ledger called "Balance" and "Profit and Loss", and then to close all the accounts into one or the other, as appropriate; the Balance accounts are then transferred to the new ledger. This last step does have some significance in a later discussion on the "British System". It would therefore seem that a form of financial statement was available to the owner of the business if he followed these procedures, but that these statements were strictly for internal purposes.

53

Yamey[4] also traces the balancing of the books during the seventeenth and eighteenth centuries, and surmises that although the techniques were known, they were not scrupulously followed because of the close connection between the owners and their enterprises. Following through on this thought, it seems reasonable to assume that if merchants were close enough to their business not to have to close their books, they certainly would not require financial statements to ascertain the true state of affairs. And if these statements were not required, they would not have been prepared. Financial statements in more sophisticated form, therefore, had to wait until the separation of management and ownership, or at least, until the growth of business to the extent that enough people were involved in its ownership so that all could not be intimately familiar with its operations.

In spite of all this, there is proof that financial statements very much akin to those of today were being prepared even before Paciolo. De Roover offers a condensed balance sheet dated in 1399 of Francesco di Marco Datini and Company of which two original copies in much greater detail are in the Datini archives. He also shows an income statement based on data supplied by the ledger, but the form seems to be his own and not that of the company.[5] In general, though, it is felt that financial statements, for informational purposes, were first perceived and originated by some astute accountant who was merely taking a trial balance to prove the accuracy of his work.

Bank of Montreal

The exact date of the first financial statement is unknown, but the earliest one available from the companies in this study is that of the Bank of Montreal on November 6, 1828. A facsimile of this statement appears on the following pages. At first glance, this statement seems to follow the "British System" (see page 63), which the Bank did follow until 1945, but there are certain anomalies which cause some confusion. The heading of the statement shows "Debts and Credits", but the appreviations for the accounts show "Dr" and "Cr". If "Debts" is merely a misspelling of debits, then it can be assumed that, in fact, the aforementioned British System is being used, but if "Debts" is correctly spelled, then the possibility exists that the bank keeps its records opposite to the accepted norm. Debts of the Bank would appear, as shown, on the left-hand side and, of necessity, the assets would then be listed as credits. This thought can not be further developed since no reference has been found to either substantiate it or indicate a precedent.

Of further interest on this statement are the indications of conservatism, where assets are written down to expected collectible values. However, there may have been over-conservatism in the past as shown by the "Protested Note a/c" where amounts previously considered bad are brought back onto the statement. An apparent forerunner to depreciation accounting is the real estate shown at half-cost, while accrual accounting is evident when probable expense reduces the profit account. The estimated profit on operations is not great enough to offset what is called "Apparent Deficiency"; it can, therefore, be assumed that while this year did show a profit, the accumulated losses of previous years still had not been overcome. This in spite of the fact that dividends had been paid. In summary, this

54

statement appears to be a trial balance after the income and expense accounts have been closed with the "Apparent Deficiency" as a balancing amount.

Statement of the
Debts and Credits of the Montreal Bank
the 6th November 1828

	Dr.	
Stock –	187,500.00.00	
Received on account of 8th Instalment,	21,290.00.00	
		208,790,00.00
Bills payable outstanding		53.17.00
Bank Notes in Circulation		142,365.00.00
Unclaimed Dividends		112.10.00
Thomas Wilson & Co. London		12,057,15.10
Deposit accounts	59,968.15.01	
Canada Company	237.11.06	
		60,206.06.07
		423,585.09.05

Figure 5a

55

		Cr.	
Cash in the Vault, including Notes of other Banks, etc.			44,534.00.02
Quebec Branch Less Bank Notes on Hand there	20,268.00.00	114,714.16.09	
Protested Notes supposed Bad	4,214.17.09	24,482.17.09	90,231.19
Kingston Office Less Bank Notes		23,778.03.00 12,695.00.00	11,083.03.00
Notes discounted Less Wood & Co's Notes 4175. estimated at 10/-s		169,631.02.00 2,087.10.00	167,543.12.00
Protested Note a/c this sum has hitherto been considered bad - 244 2/2 however is good, and it is probable about 1377 may be obtained from Hamilton, and Caldwell, and Davidson,		15,968.02.11	1,621.07.02
Bonds and obligations will all be recovered -			22,649.12.11
Bills Receivable Wood & Co's bills 3924 9/11 which are estimated at only 10/-s included in this account, and a certificate of the Kingston WC, Bank 315		24,487.09.11 2,278.09.11	22,209.00.00
McGillivray's Debt Estimated at 5/-s and the Bank Stock at 95 per cent	22,117.17.00		11,336.03.04
Maitland's account of settlement	8,583.18.03		
William Williams	500.00.00		
I. Farrington's Debt 114 16/3 @ s6/8	381.12.01		9,465.10.04

Figure 5b

56

(Continued)

Nicol's House Debt estimated at		700.00.00
Real Estate do, - at half cost		5,645.18.02
Contingent Account and Suspense Account as last June,		8,210.18.10
The present amount of		
Discount Account	5,698.19.10	
Exchange inland account	1,235.11.10	
Interest	1,390.13.04	
Profit and Loss	639.09.06	
Rent Account	224.12.06	
Supposed profits from Quebec Account	1,800.00.00	
Supposed profits from Kingston Account	100.00.00	
At the credit of Bills of Exchange	1,071.15.06	
	12,160.02.06	

Less probable amount of Expense account	250.00.00		
And to cover the purchase of Exchange to liquidate Wilson & Co's debt, this sum besides what may be made before the balance	1,200.00.00	2,450.00.00	9,710.02.06
			13,067.17.02
			418,009.04.07
Apparent deficiency			5,576.04.10
			423,585.09.05

I hereby certify that the foregoing statement of the affairs of the Bank of Montreal is a true copy of an account made out on the 6th November last, for the information and government of the Board of Directors.

(Signed) John Molson
President

Montreal 31st January, 1829

The foregoing Certificate sworn to by John Molson Esquire, President of the Bank of Montreal this 2nd day of February 1829
Before me

(Signed) H. Griffin, J.P.

Figure 5c

By 1850 the financial statements of the Bank had taken on a more professional tone. The General Statement complied strictly with the Bank Act, and was supplemented by the following statement which appeared as part of the President's report.[6]

The amount of Income, from all sources,
Expenses of Management deducted, has
been 72,751
There have been deducted Two Half-Yearly
Dividends of 3 per cent, making 45,000
Amount of Tax on Circulation 3,975
Amount applied to reduction of the value of
Real Estate 996
Amount reserved to cover positive and probable
Losses 11,796   61,767

Making amount added to Contingent Fund..... 10,984
Raising it to the Sum of 30,048
The average amount of Discounts has been..... 1,201,699
The average amount of Deposits 302,423
The average amount of Circulation 397,548
The average amount of Specie on hand 144,106

Except for minor differences, there was very little change in the financial reports of the Bank until well after the turn of the century.Of historical significance is the introduction of Canadian dollars in 1858 alongside the pounds sterling; this continued until 1871, at which time, the sterling column was dropped. There is an improvement in the reporting of the accumulated profits in 1859 when the statement as illustrated above was changed so that it starts with the accumulated profit of the previous year, adds profits after dividends and write-offs for the current year, to arrive at the accumulated profit at the end of the year - in effect a statement of retained earnings. Unfortunately, in this first year, the so-called retained earnings do not appear on the balance sheet, although it balances, leaving the assumption that this figure is amongst the other liabilities. This, however, does not happen in future years. Finally, in 1864, the terms, Assets and Liabilities, are introduced, as well as sub-totals to set off the current portions on both sides of the General Statement. Although the British system is still in use the break has been made with what seems to be a trial balance approach.

Throughout the period from 1828 to 1913, the Bank's reporting is minimal, albeit with strict adherence to the requirements of the Bank Act. The President feels that he knows what is best for the shareholder as shown by the following excerpt from the president's speech at the annual meeting in 1883.[7]

...we have adopted the English system, and our Reports are limited to the baldest statement of facts, and it would be folly for us to put everything in the Rest[8], only perhaps to take it away again the next year. However, I will not say much about the Rest, which I hope will soon be set at rest forever, except this one remark, that nothing will so certainly contribute to uniform dividends (and uniformity is what the average investor wants); nothing, I say, will so certainly contribute to uniform dividends as a large Rest, and it will also do more than anything else to maintain the market value of

58

the stock, though that is a matter with which we, as Directors, have really nothing to do. It is our duty to manage the Bank to the best of our ability and leave the stock to take care of itself. At the same time, it is of great importance that it should not fluctuate largely,....

Montreal Cottons Company

A further progression, with more details given on operations, can be seen in the financial statements of the Montreal Cottons Company. The statements for the year ended December 31, 1877 are shown on the following pages; although these were printed, presumably to mark the first year of operations, those of the following years are elaborately handwritten. The General Statement, in this example, is on the American System, with Assets to the left and Liabilities to the right. This system will be discussed further in conjunction with the British System previously mentioned. In this case, again, the assets are ordered from the most solid, i.e. real estate, to the most liquid, while the first item on the liability side is also capital stock.

The operations portion of the statements are in the form of "T" accounts, which could conceivably be direct exerpts from the general ledger. This thought is reinforced by the names of these statements — Manufacturing Account, Farm Account, and Profit and Loss Account. Of particular interest on the Profit and Loss Account is the deduction as separate expenses of 'sample pieces delivered without charge' and 'waste stolen'. It is wondered if these items are double counted since it is assumed that they are also removed from inventory, but it is possible that they are shown in sales. At any rate, the amounts are quite insignificant and would not affect the figures materially. The Farm Account is unusual for a manufacturing company in that it is totally unrelated, but it does give some indication of the priorities of the day. This account does not appear on future reports but profits from this source are shown until 1918. It does, however, indicate an understanding of a segregation of different sources of income.

All these statements are quite sophisticated and offer considerable information to the reader. There is no difficulty in following figures from one statement to another and explanations are more than adequate on all accounts. The handling and final disposition of several of the accounts on the General Statement, such as 'charges from formation of company', 'construction interest', and 'stock arrears' have been lost to posterity, but they do indicate that many of the problems argued today in accounting circles have been in evidence for quite some time.

Canadian Pacific Railway

The early statements, 1886 — 1910, of the C.P.R. (see Appendix D for the 1899 set) are quite a contrast to the bland presentation of the Bank. Here the mass of information is almost overwhelming. The Balance Sheet, following the American System, is supported by many detailed schedules, incomes and expenses are itemized, comparative figures are given, and a statement of cash receipts and expenditures is presented. This cash-flow statement, in common with all the other schedules, is a requirement of all the Railways Acts until 1909, as scheduled. Again, it is forcibly demonstrated that accounting follows

59

THE
MONTREAL COTTON COMPANY.

31st DECEMBER, 1877.

Dr. MANUFACTURING ACCOUNT—*8 Months say 1st May to 31st December, 1877.* *Cr.*

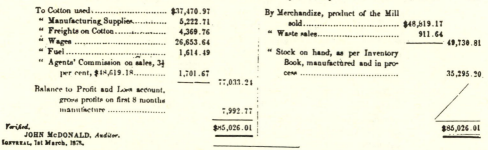

To Cotton used	$37,470.97		By Merchandize, product of the Mill		
" Manufacturing Supplies	5,222.71		sold	$48,819.17	
" Freights on Cotton	4,369.76		" Waste sales	911.64	
" Wages	26,653.64				49,730.81
" Fuel	1,614.49		" Stock on hand, as per Inventory		
" Agents' Commission on sales, 3½			Book, manufactured and in pro-		
per cent, $48,619.18	1,701.67		cess		35,295.20
		77,033.24			
Balance to Profit and Loss account,					
gross profits on first 8 months					
manufacture		7,992.77			
Verified,		$85,026.01			$85,026.01

JOHN McDONALD, Auditor.
MONTREAL, 1st March, 1878.

FARM ACCOUNT—*11 Months 31st January to 31st December, 1877.*

To Labour clearing land, seeding, stock-			By sales of Produce, Firewood, Hay,&c.,	
ing, &c.	$1,185.02		Rents of Houses, Pasturage, &c.	$1,064.04
Balance to Profit and Loss account	651.97		On hand, Live Stock and Produce	772.95
Verified,		$1,836.99		$1,836.99

JOHN McDONALD, Auditor.
MONTREAL, 1st March, 1878.

PROFIT AND LOSS ACCOUNT.

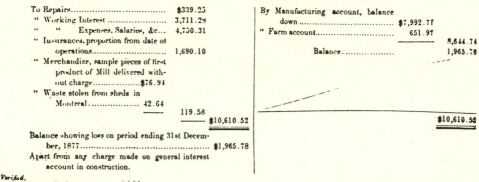

To Repairs	$339.25		By Manufacturing account, balance		
" Working Interest	3,711.29		down	$7,992.77	
" " Expenses, Salaries, &c.	4,750.31		" Farm account	651.97	
" Insurances, proportion from date of					8,644.74
operations	1,690.10		Balance		1,965.78
" Merchandize, sample pieces of first					
product of Mill delivered with-					
out charge	$76.94				
" Waste stolen from sheds in					
Montreal	42.64				
		119.58			
		$10,610.52			$10,610.52

Balance showing loss on period ending 31st December, 1877 ... $1,965.78

Apart from any charge made on general interest account in construction.

Verified,

JOHN McDONALD, Auditor.
MONTREAL, 1st March, 1878.

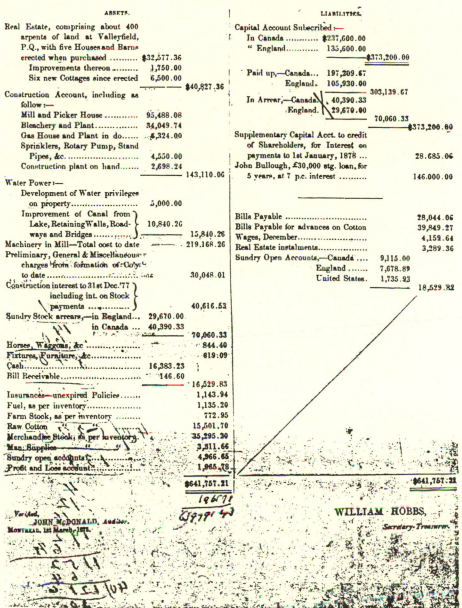

GENERAL STATEMENT.

ASSETS.				LIABILITIES.			

Real Estate, comprising about 400 arpents of land at Valleyfield, P.Q., with five Houses and Barns erected when purchased $32,577.36
Improvements thereon 1,750.00
Six new Cottages since erected 6,500.00
— $40,827.36

Construction Account, including as follow:—
Mill and Picker House 95,488.08
Bleachery and Plant............... 34,049.74
Gas House and Plant in do...... 5,324.00
Sprinklers, Rotary Pump, Stand Pipes, &c. 4,550.00
Construction plant on hand...... 2,698.24
— 143,110.06

Water Power:—
Development of Water privileges on property...................... 5,000.00
Improvement of Canal from Lake, Retaining Walls, Roadways and Bridges 10,840.26
— 15,840.26
Machinery in Mill—Total cost to date 219,168.26

Preliminary, General & Miscellaneous charges from formation of Co'y to date 30,048.01

Construction interest to 31st Dec.'77 including int. on Stock payments 40,616.53

Sundry Stock arrears,—in England... 29,670.00
in Canada ... 40,390.33
— 70,060.33

Horses, Waggons, &c 844.40
Fixtures, Furniture, &c................... 619.09
Cash........................... 16,383.23
Bill Receivable................ 146.60
— 16,529.83

Insurances—unexpired Policies 1,143.94
Fuel, as per inventory.................. 1,135.20
Farm Stock, as per inventory 772.95
Raw Cotton 15,501.70
Merchandise Stock, as per inventory. 35,295.20
Man. Supplies " " 3,311.66
Sundry open accounts 4,966.65
Profit and Loss account........... 1,965.78

$641,757.21

Verified,
JOHN McDONALD, Auditor.
MONTREAL, 1st March, 1878.

Capital Account Subscribed:—
In Canada $237,600.00
" England............ 135,600.00
— $373,200.00

Paid up,—Canada... 197,209.67
England. 105,930.00
— 303,139.67
In Arrear,—Canada. 40,390.33
England. 29,670.00
— 70,060.33
— $373,200.00

Supplementary Capital Acct. to credit of Shareholders, for Interest on payments to 1st January, 1878 ... 28,685.06
John Bullough, £30,000 stg. loan, for 5 years, at 7 p.c. interest 146,000.00

Bills Payable 28,044.06
Bills Payable for advances on Cotton 39,849.27
Wages, December....................... 4,152.64
Real Estate instalments................. 3,289.36
Sundry Open Accounts,—Canada 9,115.00
England 7,678.89
United States. 1,735.93
— 18,529.82

$641,757.21

WILLIAM HOBBS,
Secretary-Treasurer.

Figure 6b.

61

the dictates of the law, since this is the only company preparing this statement for publication.

Three reasons can be advanced for the rather strict requirements for railroads at a time when laissez-faire was more the rule of the day.

1. The machinations of railroad promoters, as outlined by Pollins[9], were well known by this time.

2. The government had a huge stake in the enterprise both financially and politically – financially from loans, advances and land grants, and politically to tie the country together from coast to coast.

3. Precedent had already been established for these requirements by the Regulation of Railways Act passed in Great Britain in 1868.

However, in spite of the seeming all-inclusiveness of these reports,. it is virtually impossible to trace some of the figures through the statements, particularly in the early years. For 1886 – 1888 the Cost of Road includes "dividends paid less net earnings to date"; until 1893 hotel construction costs are deducted from donated town sites, etc; but the most glaring offense is the non-disclosure of the issue of common stock at a considerable discount.[10] This discount of over $30 million was added to the Cost of Road, and was not adjusted until 1942 as shown on page 89 as eventually were all the other peccadillos.

The government has instituted the controls but did not follow through with adequate audit either by itself or through independent auditors; or conversely the railway had to go through at all costs, and it may be argued that the ends justified the means, but from a strict accounting viewpoint, much was left to be desired.

Bell Telephone Company

This company issued an income statement from its inception in 1880. A breakdown of receipts and expenditures in fair detail was presented, and after the first year, this statement included the surplus carry-over from the previous year. The title of the statement was consistent until 1911 as Revenue Account, December 31, 18–, when it was changed to Earnings Statement for Year 1912. There is, however, less uniformity in the Balance Sheet, which passes through several mutations in the early years. These changes are listed below:–

> 1880 Financial Statement on British System, listing the accounts as:
> Stock Account, Net Revenue, Sundry Creditors, and total, followed by Preliminary Expenses, Paid for License, fixed assets and through current assets down to Cash in Bank and on hand, and total. The fixed assets includes details of the purchase and disposal of plants and equipment.
> 1881 Financial Statement as above, plus, Statement of Assets and Liabilities on American System with subheadings for Assets, starting with Plant and License (total figure), Stores on Hand, Debtors and Cash, and total, and Liabilities, Capital Stock and Sundry Creditors, and total which is subtracted from the previous total to show Surplus, which in turn is

62

itemized as Dividend, Carried to Contingent Fund, and Balance carried forward.

- 1886 as above except that a large additional subheading is given on the Assets and Liabilities for Appropriation of Surplus.
- 1890 The title Financial Statement is changed to Balance Sheet.
- 1896 Balance Sheet as above is only one presented, on British System, and indicating additions and subtractions on the various fixed asset accounts. No change until 1910.

No definitive reason can be offered for the dual balance sheets, although it can be surmised that since this company was also under the jurisdiction of the Transport Act, the Financial Statement was its equivalent for the statement of Cash receipts and expenditures. Another possibility is that the Financial Statement was meant for British shareholders, while the Assets and Liabilities was provided for the Americans. Nevertheless, the statements are clear and straightforward and there is no difficulty in tracing accounts from one year to the next, although greater disclosure on stocks and bonds authorized and issued would have been advantageous.

Special Statement

An example of the degree of sophistication and expertise of the earlier years is shown on the following statement prepared for the Montreal Cottons Company in 1883. This summary statement first shows the net equity in fixed assets from which is deducted the deficiency in working capital to arrive at net worth, which is then itemized. A memo then indicates the contingent liabilities. This statement is worthy of the finest offered today and would be hailed by those who advocate the approach of "making it easy" for the layman to understand financial statements.

The British and American Systems

As the progression from trial balance to balance sheet is followed, it seems only natural that since debits are on the left hand side of the trial balance, the assets would also fall on the left hand side of the balance sheet. This is possibly what happened in the United States (and most European countries) to give what has been called in this paper the American System. Yet, since the balance sheet is a separate statement prepared to provide information, it should be set up in a manner to best provide this information. This theory is supported by Littleton and Zimmerman in their discussion of the British system[11]. These authors suggest that the initial responsibility of the directors was the authorization to create shares and mortgage liabilities and therefore these items should appear first on the balance sheet. By the same token, the directors were performing as stewards and this presentation was used so as to best report the status and accomplishments of their stewardship.

The British system was legalized in the Companies Act of 1862 of Great Britain[12] and illustrates the effect of legislation on accounting practice. The law forces uniformity which may be praiseworthy to provide comparability, but it also causes rigidity; the practice is

63

CHAPTER V – FOOTNOTES

1   George Santayana, Life of Reason, Vol. 1, "Reason in Common Sense".

2   R. Gene Brown and Kenneth S. Johnston, Paciolo on Accounting (McGraw-Hill Book Company, Inc., New York, 1963), pp. 83–84, 95–98.

3   William Gordon, The Universal Accountant, and Complete Merchant, (Alexander Donaldson, London, 1777).

4   B.S. Yamey, H.C. Edey and Hugh W. Thomson, Accounting in England and Scotland: 1543–1800 (Sweet & Maxwell, London, 1963), pp. 186–193.

5   Raymond de Roover, "The Development of Accounting Prior to Luca Pacioli According to the Account-books of Medieval Merchants", in Studies in the History of Accounting, A.C. Littleton and B.S. Yamey (Eds.), (Sweet & Maxwell Limited, London, 1956), pp. 142–144.

6   Bank of Montreal, Proceedings at a General Meeting of the Stockholders of the Bank of Montreal, Held at the Banking House, This Day (Monday) June 3, 1850.

7   From the speech of C.F. Smithers at the Annual General Meeting of the Bank of Montreal held June 4, 1883 (From the Gazette, of June 5, 1883).

8   The Rest is a part of the Surplus account. It consists of appropriations from undivided profits and capital surplus derived from premiums on capital stock subscriptions. This account, with the same name, appears to this day on the financial statements of the bank.

9   Harold Pollins, "Aspects of Railway Accounting Before 1868", in Studies in the History of Accounting, A.C. Littleton and B.S. Yamey (Eds.), (Sweet & Maxwell Limited, London, 1956), pp. 332–355.

10 This information is available in the Annual Statement respecting the Canadian Pacific Railway by Sir Charles Tupper, Minister of Railways, to the House of Commons on February 5, 1884 (Printed by Maclean, Roger & Co., Ottawa, 1884). On page 20 of this speech net receipts from $55 million of the shares was $25,356,828 while a further amount of $4,950,000 was received as a loan on the balance of $10 million of stock.

77

106

Section II: The Profession

Edited by GEOFFREY H. WARD, C.A.

Ward, Welch, Hall & McNair, Toronto

Practitioners Forum

It is fitting that this anniversary number should include contributions from two senior members of the profession who have been associated with their respective Institutes for more than 50 years and who are both over 80 years young. Throughout this long period they have given much useful service to the accounting profession and played an active part in the growth and development of accounting.

John Parton, F.C.A. of Winnipeg is the senior living past president of the Canadian Institute of Chartered Accountants and held office in 1918. He became a member of the Institute of Chartered Accountants of Manitoba in 1909 when he was on the staff of Webb, Read & Hegan. In 1919 the firm amalgamated with George A. Touche & Co., and as a partner he remained in public practice until his retirement in 1950. He was active on Institute committees and served on the Council of the Manitoba Institute for 37 years. In 1932 he was made a Fellow. He has written numerous articles for The Canadian Chartered Accountant and has the unusual distinction of having his work appear both in the first and now in the 50th anniversary issue.

Colonel H. D. Lockhart Gordon, F.C.A. of Toronto is a partner in Clarkson, Gordon & Co. and, at the age of 88, still takes a keen interest in the affairs of the firm which he founded nearly 50 years ago. He took his early training in England and qualified as an incorporated accountant in 1898. The same year, on his return to Canada where he was born and educated, he was admitted to the Institute of Chartered Accountants of Ontario. In 1915 he was elected a Fellow and in 1933 became president of the Ontario Institute. Fifteen years later the Institute recognized his contribution to accounting by conferring on him a life membership.

FIFTY YEARS AGO

John Parton, F.C.A.

"Those damned auditors again!" An instant grapevine would alert the office as we entered, and on all sides we would be greeted with a barrage of black looks, of forced sickly smiles — even of glances of trepidation. And when, on occasion, we would have to ask for explanations, the very air would shimmer with resentment as they were given. Had we borne the black plague we could hardly have been less welcome. Thus was the auditor received by many of his clients in the West 50 years ago.

I became a member of the Manitoba Institute in 1909, after two years with a firm in Winnipeg, with which firm and its successors I remained until my retirement ten years ago; and as my firm had offices in Saskatchewan, Alberta and British Columbia, I had ample opportunity to follow the trends of the profession throughout Western Canada.

In 1911 the profession was very much in its infancy in the West. The Institutes of Chartered Accountants of Quebec and Ontario were incorporated in the early 1880's, and had become well established and recognized for some years. British Columbia was not incorporated until 1905, Saskatchewan in 1908, and Alberta in 1910; and while the Manitoba Institute obtained its incorporation in 1886, it stood inactive until 1903 because of a general slump in business.

In saying the profession in the West was in its infancy, I am referring to its establishment as a profession, and not by any means to its individual members. I can say with certainty that the 32 members of the Manitoba Institute were thoroughly capable accountants and were doing good work. But the business public was not "sold" on the idea of audits; and with the exception of businesses which were either owned or controlled by British or Eastern Canadian houses, there was a repugnance, quite openly expressed at times, at the idea of "outside" auditors. Of course, British and Eastern houses had long learned the value of an independent audit; but most other businesses in the West had an attitude of aloofness, and regarded it as an unnecessary expense. There seemed to be an idea that the whole purpose of an audit was to prevent or discover shortages of cash, and for some years we found resentment on the part of bookkeepers, sometimes amounting to rudeness.

Working conditions, taken on the whole, were fair. In some businesses there would be a board room, and by avoiding the date of a board meeting we could work there in privacy. Usually we would work in the general office, and on some occasions a table was set up in a warehouse. As to the type of work we did, there was considerably more detail than is necessary nowadays. Today, practically all businesses have accounting machines, various methods of internal check, loose-leaf books, self-balancing ledgers and so on, and take off monthly trial balances. In many businesses, 50 years ago, none of these was in existence, and it was largely through the auditors' suggestions that they eventually were adopted. By so doing, and making recommendations for some internal checks, the auditor was able to cut down on the "check and tick" detail, of which there was plenty in and prior to 1911.

It was some time in 1912 (as I recollect) that the banks began a general practice of requiring an independent audit of all businesses which asked for loans or bank accommodations. This caused resentment from the heads of such businesses, who complained about the cost; but the banks persisted in their idea, and it is gratifying to look back after all these years and remember how heads of businesses very soon changed their minds and realized the value of audits, not only so far as the banks were concerned, but also for themselves. They began to understand that an audit was not just to catch petty embezzlements, but was concerned with the whole business and all its personnel.

I remember the case of a large financial house whose president kept documents appertaining to securities under his personal care, and when asked to produce them for the auditor's inspection, he said that he had them in his custody and would give his own certificate that they were in order. On the auditor pressing for production, at first he refused; but when the auditor said it would be necessary for him to report this refusal and to qualify his report accordingly, Mr. President acceded and produced them. Actually the securities were found to be in order, which made the resentment more difficult to understand. Those who had been distinctly unfriendly began to realize the value of the audit; suggestions were more readily received and discussed, and generally put into effect.

With the outbreak of World War I new responsibilities fell on the auditors' shoulders. The introduction of what was then a new form of taxation in Canada brought special responsibilities. This was started in 1916 with the federal business profits war tax, followed by income tax in 1917; and this form of taxation has continued to the present time with almost annual modifications and changes, adding to the necessity for study and consideration in the audits of businesses.

To sum up briefly, the principal differences in auditing practice 50 years ago and now are as follows:

1. The changed attitude of clients and staffs, resulting in a more friendly feeling toward the auditors and more ready compliance with their wishes and requirements.

2. Improvements in bookkeeping and internal controls (many of which were suggested by the auditor) which reduced the necessity of much of the detailed "checking and ticking", and enabled an efficient audit to be made by the use of "spot checks" on much of the detailed recording.

3. Office machines (adding, calculating and other bookkeeping contrivances), which were but little known — some not even invented 50 years ago — have played a great part in increasing efficiency and internal control.

To conclude with another difference from 50 years ago. While chartered accountants in Canada now number many times what they did in those days when most of them were in public practice, today approximately half the members hold positions in business, industry or in government service.

FIFTY YEARS AGO

Col. H. D. Lockhart Gordon, F.C.A.

At the time of the first issue of *The Canadian Chartered Accountant*, I was practising in partnership with R. J. Dilworth under the name of Gordon & Dilworth with our offices in the Lumsden Building in Toronto. We had a staff of about 10 chartered accountants and students. I do not remember whether we paid the students for their work. I do recall that a few years earlier as a qualified chartered accountant I was receiving only $50 a month.

An important part of our business was acting as liquidators although we were steadily increasing the number of our audit clients most of whom are still in business in Toronto today.

It was in 1913 that R. J. Dilworth and I joined E. R. C. Clarkson and G. T. Clarkson and formed the firm of Clarkson, Gordon & Dilworth. Members of the Clarkson family had been in practice in Toronto as liquidators and later as chartered accountants since 1864. I had received my early experience with the firm, then known as Clarkson & Cross. When the new firm was formed, we leased the top floor of the Merchant Bank Building at 15 Wellington Street West in Toronto. The second floor was occupied by the Bishop of Toronto while the ground floor was occupied by the bank. We soon required more space and, much to the annoyance of the Bishop, took over his floor. In 1920 we acquired the whole building which has remained our Toronto office ever since.

The work we performed as accountants in those days was very different from what we do today. Lawrence R. Dicksee, F.C.A., who was an outstanding accountant in England and the United States, published a number of articles and books in which he said that the duties of a chartered accountant were "to detect fraud and correct errors". For many years this was the public's conception of how members of the profession spent their time. I have in my files a number of statements on which we reported shortly after our firm was formed. Our report was commendably brief either in the form "audited and found correct" or "examined and found correct", and in one case we added the letters E. and O.E.

The emphasis in our work was of course the verification of the position as shown by the books, and very little attention was paid to the profit and loss account. Such procedures as the direct confirmation of accounts receivable or the attendance at physical inventories were unheard of.

A few examples will indicate the sort of assignments we were asked to carry out:

The owner of a large merchandise company in Montreal was asked by his bankers to obtain an outside opinion on his accounts receivable. He asked me to undertake the job as he did not want anyone in Montreal to know that the work was being done. When, after a considerable period, we reported that his accounts were in very bad shape and a large reserve was required, he was very annoyed and indicated we did not know what we were doing. In order to try to convince him, we gave him our notes and went over the accounts again and arrived at practically the same answer. Two years later he wrote to us in triumph saying he was now sure that we did not know our business. One account for $16,000 which we wrote off had been paid in full. This account was with a woman who operated a store. The store was burnt to the ground, and the insurance money was used to pay off the account.

On one occasion I can recall our client being most annoyed because we had failed to report that two chickens had been stolen out of the back of his delivery wagon.

The changes which have occurred in the business conditions in Toronto since those days are almost unbelievable. I used to walk to most of my clients' offices although I kept a horse and dog cart (a two-wheeled vehicle) to use when it was too far to walk or go by street car. Traffic down town was nearly all horse-drawn although motor cars were beginning to be seen on the streets.

Our office hours were 9:00 to 5:30 from Monday to Friday with three-quarters of an hour for lunch. On Saturdays we worked from 9:00 to 1:30. In those days a good hot meal would cost only 10c or 15c.

Like everything else there have been tremendous changes in office furniture and equipment. Furniture in those days consisted of wooden tables and chairs with one or two roll-top desks. The clients' books were all bound ledgers and were heavy and awkward to handle. Many clients had private ledgers with heavy brass locks containing confidential information. These could only be opened by a senior official who would permit the auditor to examine them in the private office. Because of the weight and awkward size of the books, they would be placed on high desks and we would stand and work at them all day. High stools were provided if we wished to sit down. Of course, no smoking was permitted during office hours. We used pens and coloured ink to indicate the figures we had check-

ed, and a very convenient way of storing and cleaning our pens was to stick them into a large potato on the top of the desk. A book which is never seen today was the letter book. Copies of letters were imprinted on the tissue pages of the letter book by using a letter press.

World War I marked the end of one phase of the life of the accounting profession and started it on its present road. The increased industrialization of the country and the introduction of income tax provided the chartered accountant with new opportunities to serve his clients.

The developments in the profession over the last 50 years far exceeded the expectations of those in practice in 1911. If we read the sign of the times aright, there would seem to be no limit to what lies ahead for the profession during the next 50 years. We are moving into an age of even greater complexity in business. For the chartered accountant this means even greater opportunities to be of service to his clients and contribute to the financial and economic well-being of the country.

Patriarchs of the Profession

Congratulations and best wishes are extended to the following members who have completed 50 years membership in their respective Provincial Institutes:

H. C. ANDERSON (Ont), R. J. BAKER (Ont), G. D. CAMPBELL (Ont), R. C. CAMPBELL (Que), C. D. CORBOULD (Man), DAVID COOPER (Man), H. E. CROWELL (NS), P. H. B. DAWSON (Ont), J. W. EDDIS (Ont), H. W. FIELDEN (Ont), C. V. GLADWELL (Sask), H. D. L. GORDON (Ont), B. F. GRIGGS (Man), R. W. JOHNSON (Ont), B. R. MASECAR (Sask), D. M. McCLELLAND (Ont), G. C. McDONALD (Que), R. S. McPHERSON (Ont), JOHN PARTON (Man), JOHN PATERSON (Que), W. H. PETTIT (Ont), W. W. RATHIE (Que), G. E. F. SMITH (Ont), H. F. VIGEON (Ont), SIR N. E. WATERHOUSE (Ont), F. J. WILSON (Sask), G. E. WINTERS (BC).

from
The Canadian Chartered Accountant,
Feb. 1940, pp. 76–93

THREE SCORE YEARS

Historical Highlights in the Growth and Development
of the Institute of Chartered Accountants of Ontario

By H. Percy Edwards, F.C.A., Toronto

IN reviewing the events of history as they relate to the Institute of Chartered Accountants of Ontario, one is impressed with the difficulty of presenting a readable story of the growth and development of the profession in Ontario.

Two methods are used by writers in the presentation of historical happenings. The one builds a story of individual heroism around certain facts, which are purely incidental, producing in the reader an immediate interest without lingering impressions. The other method deals with facts and enlists the co-operation of the reader in the building up of scenic effects. In this recital of incidents, the latter method will be followed. There are dates and figures to satisfy the average statistician and heroes aplenty for those who care to enter into the spirit of the times when the following events took place.

While the Institute did not receive its charter until the year 1883, the work of organization dates back to a meeting held on 11th November 1879 at the office of Robins, Myles & Co. "in response to invitations issued in the names of Messrs. William Anderson, James B. Boustead, Wm. Badenach, Thos. Bailey, E. R. C. Clarkson, A. B. Campbell, Wm. Fahey, R. H. Gray, W. F. Munroe, A. W. Murdock, Benjamin Morton and Wm. Robins, dated 6th November 1879 and sent to all the public accountants, accountants in banks, monetary institutions and insurance companies, representative bookkeepers and others in Toronto."

Eighteen persons were in attendance and upon hearing explained the purpose in calling the meeting it was resolved "That it is desirable to form an Association of Accountants for the Dominion of Canada." At this meeting Wm. Robins, Wm. Fahey, M. Robins, H. W. Eddis and Wm. Anderson were elected to be the original members of the Institute and to ballot for applicants and prepare a constitution and by-laws, and it was resolved "That it be an instruction to the original members now elected to frame the rules, as far as possible on the model of the Institute of Accountants of Great Britain, and also to provide that the original mem-

76

bers shall themselves be submitted to any examination imposed upon members who may hereafter be elected."

Several meetings of the original members were held at which thirty-two applicants were balloted upon and elected to membership. A constitution and by-laws were prepared and consideration given to the matter of incorporation.

The first general meeting was held on 10th December 1879, with an attendance of twenty-four original and elected members. The original members, in conformity with the understanding at the time of their election, retired and submitted their applications for membership. Upon a ballot being taken they were elected to membership. The constitution and by-laws of the "Institute of Accountants and Adjusters of Canada" were adopted.

The meeting proceeded to elect the Council by balloting for the nine Fellows who shall, with the President and Vice-President, constitute the same. The result of the ballot was the election of Messrs. Wm. Anderson, Hugh Scott, Wm. Badenach, E. R. C. Clarkson, James E. Day, Wm. Robins, Charles Robertson, James Watson and D. O'Reilly. The meeting was adjourned and upon being reconvened on 23rd December, Charles Robertson was elected President and Wm. Anderson Vice-President of the Institute. The meeting was adjourned to 30th December at which time the members ballotted to elect two members to Council to fill vacancies resulting from the election of the President and Vice-President. On the first ballot F. J. Minet was elected but the second, third and fourth ballots failed to elect a second member. The meeting was then adjourned to 6th January 1880 at which time H. W. Eddis was elected to Council on the first ballot.

Between adjournments of the general meeting, Council met and appointed Wm. Robins to be Secretary-Treasurer and instructed him to procure the necessary books and stationery. James E. Day undertook to see the President of the Board of Trade as to getting the use of their rooms. The Secretary reported to Council on 22nd January that $80.00 in fees had been received and an account opened with the Imperial Bank; also that he had purchased a table for $20.00 which was approved.

That the accountants of those times experienced a pressure of work during the early months of the year seems

77

115

to be borne out by the fact that general meetings called for 30th January and 19th February failed for lack of a quorum and the Council meeting of 10th March suffered a similar fate.

At its meeting on 15th March 1880, Council ordered that the offer of the Board of Trade for the use of a room at $80.00 per annum, without taxes, be accepted. Little time was lost in completing the arrangements and moving the table, and such other furnishings as may have been acquired, into the new offices, for the records indicate that a general meeting of the members was held on 15th April in the rooms of the Institute at the Board of Trade.

Meanwhile Council considered the question of examination subjects and diplomas and the extension of its field of influence. Committees were appointed to confer with accountants in Hamilton and London. Success attended this effort to the extent that eight persons from London and one each from Brantford and Belleville submitted applications and were received into membership. Among these persons was J. W. Johnston of Belleville who later served on Council and as President of the Institute. From Hamilton were received eight applications including those of J. J. Mason and W. F. Findlay who are numbered among the earlier elected Presidents who so ably directed the Institute's affairs.

In May 1880 a Committee was appointed to purchase a book case and lamps for the room. Up to this time there is no indication that books had been purchased or donated for the purposes of equipping a library, but doubtless some unrecorded acquisitions had taken place, as the first recorded purchase was in January of the following year when "It was recorded that Dun, Wiman & Co.'s book on Mercantile Law be purchased for the use of the Institute."

On 31st December 1880, the Institute closed its accounts and presented its first annual report which showed a total membership of fifty-nine, of whom forty-three were residents of Toronto, eight of Hamilton, six of London and one each of Belleville and Brantford. Total receipts as shown by the audited financial statement amounted to $526.00, derived from entrance fees and annual subscriptions at the rate of $10.00 each from Toronto members and $6.00 each from members outside of Toronto. The sums

78

116

so collected from each member were apportioned equally between entrance fees and annual subscriptions.

Disbursements during the year included, in addition to the usual items of rent, printing and stationery, postage, etc., the cost of table and cartage $21.00; bookcase $28.00; ballot box, lamps, etc. $12.00, allowance to the Secretary of $40.00, and a balance of cash on deposit amounting to $68.33 was carried forward to the new year.

Under the Presidencey of Wm. Anderson the work of organization and education continued. "The Secretary was empowered to open a correspondence with the Institutes of Accountants of Great Britain, having in view an affiliation with them for the mutual benefit of members of each Institution on both sides of the Atlantic." This effort was not successful and in his report to Council on 23rd September 1881, the President stated that upon the occasion of his late visit to England he had been informed "The Charter of the English Company however prevented such affiliation," a condition which still exists.

A series of addresses was given by members of the Institute upon subjects of interest to the membership and to the business public. The first of these was given by the President on 22nd March 1881 at Shaftsbury Hall upon the subject "The value and scope of accountants' work." Press reports the following day in *The Globe, The Telegram* and *The Mail* indicated a well attended meeting and an instructive address.

Other papers were read during the year. On 21st April E. R. C. Clarkson addressed a meeting upon the subject of "Insolvency" and one month later H. W. Eddis spoke on the subject "Balance sheets." In September, October and November, three papers were given, the first by W. A. Douglas "The Accounts of building and loan societies," the second by J. T. Moore on "Life insurance contracts" and the last on the subject of "Joint stock company's bookkeeping" by J. W. Johnson of Belleville.

Application for Incorporation—An unsuccessful attempt was made to secure incorporation by Special Act of the Legislature. In his address to the annual meeting the President reported that the government had not acceded to the request, but stated, "We earnestly recommend our successors in office to renew the application next session, with, we trust, a more favourable result."

During that year the membership was increased by fifteen new members in Toronto and thirty from other places including Kingston and Cobourg not previously represented. Revenues from entrance fees and annual subscriptions reached a total of $464.00, an excess over expenditure of $59.81, for the year, so that with the balance brought forward from the previous year of $68.33 the Institute closed its accounts with a favourable bank balance of $128.14 "which it was expected would be increased by some subscriptions which may still be collected."

By special permission of His Worship the Mayor and the City Council, President S. B. Harman presented his inaugural address in the Council Chamber at the City Hall on 18th May 1882. Before a large attendance of prominent citizens and members Mr. Harman reviewed the progress of growth and development of the Institute and similar societies in other parts of the world, particularly in Great Britain.

The aims and objects of the Institute were dealt with at great length and reference made to the fact that schools and colleges "to foster and encourage science and art, have been founded to give the stamp of efficiency to those they send forth as their recognized alumni; but the profession of an Accountant seems to have been hardly yet recognized as one deserving like evidence, or that free-masonry of association which has done so much to elevate other callings."

Another quotation from his address is particularly interesting in the light of the present day organization of our profession throughout Canada. He said "and another point I take pleasure in suggesting hopefully, if not prophetically, namely, that the Institute of Ontario may so advance in public favour, that the other Provinces may follow the movement, and the day be not far distant, when, by a happy union, Canada at large may become the field of labour and usefulness of a Dominion Institute."

In closing Mr. Harman impressed upon his audience that "the arduous profession of an accountant is one which, rightly undertaken, elevates the labour employed, and raises the treatment of figures to the nature of a science, thus justifying the motto adopted for the seal of the Institute of Accountants of Ontario 'Scientia et Labore.'"

80

The reader may have noticed that the name of the Institute has been varied from that originally decided upon. From time to time the minutes of meeting indicate that the constitution had been subjected to amendment but, unfortunately, in no case has the specific amendment been recorded.

Events of importance marked the year of 1882. The City of Toronto invited the Institute to be represented upon a committee charged with arranging for the semicentennial celebration, to be held in 1884 of the incorporation of Toronto in 1834. An invitation was extended by the Institute of Accountants and Bookkeepers of New York to be represented at its first annual meeting to be held on 15th March 1883.

Addresses by W. A. Douglas upon the subject "Financial fallacies" in October and by R. H. Tomlinson on "Commercial crises" in November of that year would seem to indicate that business and financial conditions were suffering from some sort of disturbance. Nevertheless the Institute renewed its application to the legislature for a Special Act of Incorporation.

In presenting its petition for incorporation great care was taken to acquaint the members of the legislature with all phases of the Institute's objects and activities. When presented the petition was accompanied by a list of 211 names of accountants from 22 cities and towns in Ontario and elsewhere.

On 9th March 1883, the President addressed the Institute and at some length reviewed the events respecting the Charter "which," he said, "it was a matter of satisfaction had been successfully carried in the Legislature and was now the law of the land as 46 Victoria (1882-3) Chapter 62."

And so, cradled in a voluntary association, was born the "Institute of Chartered Accountants of Ontario."

No time was lost in amending the by-laws to conform to the Act of Incorporation, and those members not specifically named in the petition were asked to renew their application for membership. One hundred and sixteen immediately responded and were duly elected members.

The financial statement for the year showed revenues from all sources to be $755.00 which included $30.00 proceeds

81

119

from the sale of a table, presumably that piece of furniture purchased for $20.00 as already noted. Expenditures totalled $638.55 and an accumulated balance of cash on hand and on deposit of $244.59, was carried forward to the succeeding year.

Due to the heavy demands upon the time of the President and Council in obtaining the charter of incorporation and the work of organization which immediately followed, a formal presentation of the accounts was not made, but instead two years' accounts were presented to the annual meeting held on 7th March 1884. The report of the President stated the position of the membership to be: charter members, 17; members re-elected, 115; new members elected after charter, 29; members awaiting re-election, 2; members awaiting election, 12—a total of 175 of whom 78 were resident in Toronto and 97 elsewhere. The balance of cash on hand and in bank was $411.40, with $264.00 annual dues in arrears but considered good.

At this meeting were recorded resolutions of condolence to the families of Charles Robertson and William Anderson, whose deaths were recorded as of the first and second Presidents of the Institute.

Mr. Harman retired from the Presidency and was succeeded by J. J. Mason, Mayor of the City of Hamilton. In passing, it is worthy of note that Mr. Harman served the City of Toronto as its Chief Magistrate during the years 1869 and 1870.

In his inaugural address, delivered to the meeting of the Institute, President Mason referred to the Institute's incorporation and particularly to the services rendered by the retiring President in this regard. He dwelt at some length upon the lack of educational facilities in the schools and colleges as they related to the subjects of bookkeeping and political economy, and the position the Institute must take to promote the skill and competency of its members as a duty imposed by its charter.

Reference was made to "the advance of progress in the Dominion of Canada in its development of manufacture and commerce and the extension of banking and railway enterprises and their demand for extreme care and precaution in the method of keeping accounts."

Qualifying Examinations—In the period which followed,

82

120

Council completed the framing of rules for the examination of candidates for the Diploma of Fellowship and the Certificate of Competency. The requirements of examination for the diploma called for "such high qualifications and recognized efficiency, as shall warrant the Council in endorsing the candidate for the practice of a public accountant."

The certificate required of the candidate a familarity with the principles which govern all accounts and the exhibition of good methods in his own department. He was not expected to exhibit a knowledge of "modes of recording and distributing which prevail in lines of business foreign to his own experience." A wider range of knowledge than that required was taken into account and a certificate was graded according to the marks obtained in excess of the number required to pass. Holders of the certificate were privileged to enter for higher grade for one-half the original fee.

In his report to the annual meeting held on 17th April 1885, the President referred to the rules regarding examinations and the granting of diplomas and certificates to its members. He "earnestly hoped that as the important question of Diplomas and Certificates has now been decided, the prosecution of the work of the Institute will be vigorously conducted and that the members generally during the coming year will avail themselves of the opportunity of obtaining Diplomas and Certificates as authorized by the Act of Incorporation."

The quotation just given appears to deserve more than passing mention. There is, in the minds of many, an impression that the early members secured the privilege of designating themselves chartered accountants without passing through the examination experience. The writer has always understood that examination has been the only gateway to the qualifying as a chartered accountant. This appears to be borne out by the records, for we find the name of E. R. C. Clarkson among the petitioners for the Charter of Incorporation and later as having presented himself for examination for the diploma entitling him to use the designation "Chartered Accountant."

Further confirmation is given to this position in the absence of any mass effort toward the granting or obtaining this title. In fact at each holding of examinations, the number of persons presenting themselves for examination is small and then, as now, there were those who failed to satisfy the requirements placed upon intending candidates.

The affairs of the Institute progressed in an orderly manner without incident calling for special mention here. That all members had not availed themselves of the invitation to sit for examination is evidenced by a minute of Council in October 1887, whereby the Secretary was instructed to notify those not in full membership to desist in using the term "Chartered Accountant."

The following month Council published a declaration that the designation "Chartered Public Accountant" shall belong exclusively to Fellows of the Institute practising as public accountants while continuing in membership.

The first recorded granting of the diploma to members of other accounting societies was upon the application of Michael Crawley, who, upon production of his certificate of Fellowship in the Society of Accountants and Auditors of London, England, was awarded the diploma of this Institute.

From this time until 1894 there is no item of particular interest to record. Meetings of Council and committees were frequent. By-laws were from time to time amended and improved to meet the needs of the Institute. Examination procedure was improved upon and the publication of examination papers, previously used, produced some revenue by their sale to intending candidates who in those days were handicapped by the absence of texts and other means of preparation for examination.

Admission of Women—In 1894 Council met to consider the case of a lady who was an unsuccessful candidate for the diploma at the recent examinations. A general discussion took place and it was decided if an offer of an Associate Certificate would be acceptable to her, it would be issued as provided by the by-laws. The lady in question notified Council that the offer of the Associate Certificate was acceptable to her, and so was postponed for a short time the problem of admitting women to practise in the profession.

The postponement was brief, for in the following year three more applications of like nature were received and

84

considered by Council. In the discussion which followed many and varied were the reasons given by the individual members for admitting or barring of women as members. Some expressed the opinion that the nature of the accountant's duties in factory and arbitration work was unsuitable for ladies; some considered that "the employment of women clerks was detrimental to the value of male labour;" one feared that in the case of all other conditions, as to skill and academic standing, being equal, employment would be given to women because of the lower fee which would be asked. Others expressed themselves as considering that proficiency shown in passing the examinations should be the test as to their admissibility. Upon a vote being taken it was unanimously decided against the admission of women to membership and in reaching this decision Council was in a large measure guided by the precedent of other intellectual societies. Upon this decision the Council of 1912 refused the applications of two ladies desiring to sit for examination.

While upon this subject it may be permissible to bridge the gap of years and deal finally with this question. With each application discussions followed and eventually ladies were permitted to qualify and sit for examination. The changed attitude of other professions and the general entry of women into the business life of the time were the determining factors. In February of 1930 among those admitted to membership was Mrs. Helen Burpee (née Sutcliffe), the first lady to qualify and become a chartered accountant in Ontario.

Lest an impression may have been given to the reader that the period from 1887 to 1894 was without activity, it should be stated here that the Presidents and Councils of those years vigorously pursued a policy of improving the organization and standing of the Institute in its sphere of influence.

Early Educational Efforts—Regular meetings were held and papers read by leading members upon subjects of particular interest to members and students. Text books were recommended to students to assist them in preparing for examinations. Arrangements were made with Upper Canada College, which school had established a department devoted to the study of accounts, and also with the Northern

85

Business College, Owen Sound, and the Ontario Business College, Belleville, to become affiliated with the Institute.

The masters of these affiliated schools being members of the Institute, it was arranged that they should conduct the primary examinations of the Institute, under rules to be prepared by the Examination Committee. Other business colleges became affiliated from time to time, to enjoy the same privilege.

Students' Association—This manner of conducting the primary examinations through the facilities of affiliated schools was established under rules framed by the examination committee in 1893. The committee drew up forms for the use of applicants for examination and membership. There were five of these forms of which one is to be noted, viz., "Student-Associate." The adoption of this registration and application was the beginning of the Students' Association which was to become an important factor in the education and preparation of students for membership in the Institute.

Reference has been made to the membership which in 1884 stood at a total of 175 members all told. During the ten years following, the numerical strength of the Institute was greatly reduced. Many of the earlier members did not avail themselves of the invitations to qualify for the designation of chartered accountant, mainly for the reason that they were not engaged in public practice and therefore saw no advantage in doing so. Many names were struck from the roll because of non-payment of their annual dues. The roll in 1894 showed a total registration of 78 members. This roll further shows that total charges to members for annual subcriptions, entrance and examination fees in that year amounted to $623.00, not including arrears from the previous year amounting to the sum of $183.50, and as collections for that year amounted to only $506.00, the amount of $300.50 in arrears was carried forward to the following year.

While sustaining loss in numbers the Institute gained in quality of men who took the affairs of their profession very seriously. Up to this time there had been three complaints lodged with Council having to do with the conduct of members in their professional practice. This is evidence of the desire then, as now, to keep the standard of practice on such a plane as would demand the confidence of the business public in its members.

A subject which received more than passing attention was that of municipal accounting and in this regard representations were made to the government of the day for legislation which would improve the conditions then existing.

It will be remembered there was a favourable cash balance amounting to $128.14 at the close of the year 1881, but despite the reduced membership revenue, and the expenditures made to promote and further its objects, the financial statement for the year 1894 showed a balance of funds on deposit of $360.44 to the credit of the Institute.

Dominion-wide Organization—We move forward again over a period of progress to the year 1902 when on 15th February a special general meeting was called to discuss a public notice to the effect that an application would be made to Parliament to incorporate an Institute of Accountancy which would provide that its members would be permitted to style themselves "Chartered Accountants."

The opinion of this meeting was that the application constituted a grave menace to the Institute and that the co-operation of like bodies should be sought to oppose the application. Assurances of co-operation were received from the societies in Montreal and Winnipeg and a decision was reached that opposition should be in the form of an application to parliament for a bill which would include the desirable features, but at the same time safeguard the interests of existing bodies.

Efforts were made to reach an agreement with the promoters of the bill whereby objectionable clauses granting educational powers would be removed and the corporate name and titles changed so as not to conflict with those made commercially valuable by this Institute. In the result the original bill was amended and Section 3 provided,—

"The Association shall be composed of all members in good standing of existing provincial incorporated institutes and associations, who shall apply for membership within one year after the passing of this Act, and of any other persons of whose qualifications and fitness the Council approves."

On 15th May 1902, the Act to Incorporate the Dominion

Association of Chartered Accountants received assent. In his report to the annual meeting of the Institute in July 1902 the President, Wilton C. Eddis, referred to this Act and stated "what influence it will have on us chartered accountants, or this Institute, it is premature and would be unwise to form an opinion." He indicated that the members of the Institute would have the position of charter members of the Association and probably would shortly be invited to attend its first meeting.

Nothing more was heard about this matter until about November when the Institute took appropriate steps to qualify its members to become members of the Dominion Association under the terms of section three of the Dominion Act. It was then learned that the plan of organization of the Dominion Association was such as to include the majority of the Ontario Institute members on terms less favourable than had been anticipated.

For six years the Dominion Association carried on as an independent organization of professional accountants while the Ontario Institute continued to function as formerly. With two bodies, each qualifying chartered accountants in accordance with its own standards, the public mind was becoming confused in the acceptance of the degree.

In an effort to clear up this situation the Institute, in 1908, sought from the Ontario Legislature powers to regulate and control the practice of the profession in that Province. An act was passed, which by its terms reserved the right to use the designation "Chartered Accountant" to the members of the Ontario Institute.

Upon the passing of this Act legal representatives of the Institute in England and Wales conferred with those of the Ontario Institute and an agreement was reached so as to avoid any possible difficulties which might arise. The Dominion Association, however, asked and obtained an Order of Disallowance.

Then followed an extensive campaign of articles in one of the leading financial journals which were intended to inform the business public upon the facts relating to the organization of the profession in Ontario and elsewhere in Canada. The effect and result was to bring the Dominion Association and the various Provincial Societies together, and a settlement of all problems was reached when the

88

Dominion Association passed under the control of all the Provincial Societies of whom it was henceforth to be composed. Re-enactment of the disallowed legislation was asked and obtained. Matters of organization were completed which established the profession in Canada upon a basis the equal of any other country.

The difficult experiences through which the Institute had passed were not reflected in its statistical record. In 1908 the report of President J. W. Johnston, delivered to the annual meeting held that year in Belleville, stated that the membership at that time consisted of 105 associates and 22 fellows. During that year 87 applications were received for permission to write the Primary examination, for the Intermediate 111, and for the Final 33 applications.

Financial conditions had improved. During that year $306.77 of net revenue was carried to surplus account, and the accumulated surplus amounted to $1,715.36, of which over $1,000 was on deposit and over $300 invested in furniture account.

The Students' Association, as may be gathered from the number of applicants for examination, was an active body and conducted series of lectures to aid its members in preparation for the examination ordeal. In the early days the examinations were indeed difficult. By comparison with those of today they may not so appear but on the other side of the ledger is to be noted that there were no prescribed study courses to guide the student or indicate the matter upon which the examiner might delight to test his skill and competency. In a later chapter we shall follow the efforts of the Institute to equip its students and members for the tasks which lay ahead.

The library had grown to a total of 117 units including text books, journals and financial reports although carried conservatively at $9.43 in the balance sheet.

We have reached at this point the twenty-fifth anniversary of incorporation. Those who met in Belleville in that year included some who had been active throughout the development of the Institute, and to them the pride of achievement during the quarter century became an incentive to lead the way to greater progress.

The hope of the first President, S. B. Harman, that other provinces might follow the movement of Ontario was being

89

realized. A society in Montreal had already been incorporated in 1880, Manitoba followed with an incorporation in 1886, Nova Scotia was next in 1900. Following the incorporation of the Dominion Association, the profession in British Columbia obtained its charter in 1905. In 1908, the year of the Dominion-Provincial differences, Saskatchewan granted incorporation, to be followed in 1910 by Alberta; New Brunswick was a "war baby" born in 1916, and in 1921 the Prince Edward Island Institute was incorporated, thus completing the organization of chartered accountants throughout Canada.

By 1913 the affairs of the Institute had grown to such proportions that it became necessary to appoint a full time Registrar to fulfil the requirements of that office. To that position was appointed W. J. Valleau who rendered faithful and valuable service over a long period of years. Upon his retirement in 1935 he was unanimously elected an Honorary Life member of the Institute.

In 1911 the first issue of THE CANADIAN CHARTERED AC-COUNTANT was published by The Dominion Association of Chartered Accountants. Shortly after his appointment as Registrar of the Ontario Institute, Mr. Valleau assumed the duties of Editor of the magazine until succeeded by Austin H. Carr in 1930 upon his appointment as Secretary-Treasurer of the Dominion Association. The development of the Magazine under the direction of Mr. Carr is a matter of Dominion Association history and has no place in this narrative. It is a matter of satisfaction to the Institute that through the temporary use of its facilities it has accelerated the more recent development of the Dominion Association affairs.

Profession and the Great War—The profession in Ontario, as elsewhere, looks back upon the years of the Great War with a sense of pride that the Institute and its members played their part with distinction in that drama. The annual report upon the affairs of the year ending 30th June 1918 showed that the Institute had expended the sum of one thousand dollars in the purchase of a Lewis machine gun and seven hundred dollars had been subscribed to the British and Canadian Red Cross Societies. This contribution amounted to thirty-seven per centum of the Institute's surplus, accumulated over a period of thirty-eight years.

90

The total enrolment of members and students stood at two hundred and fifty-two, of whom sixty had enlisted for overseas service prior to the introduction of compulsory service. To this number, approximately twenty-five per centum, there were many others who also served in like manner and in other capacities for which their training and skill admirably fitted them.

The financial burdens imposed by the war produced a system of taxation which immediately broadened the scope of the accountants' work and established a higher requisite standard of skill and knowledge in the profession.

Accordingly educational facilities were geared up to keep pace with the greater demands upon the professional accountant. The library facilities had been improved and the number of volumes stood at 445, a sizable increase over the number previously reported.

Courses of Instruction—With the stepping up of examination standards the greater was the necessity of providing a study programme for the student body. A board of instruction, consisting of George Edwards, Chairman; T. Watson Sime, Rutherford Williamson and R. Easton Burns, was appointed to negotiate with existing schools for such a course of instruction. Arrangements were completed with Queen's University to conduct the courses on behalf of the Institute.

The Board of Instruction was appointed on 10th January 1921, and under its direction a Select Committee of members of the Institute in collaboration with the Faculty of the University produced a course of lessons which were put into operation on 1st January of the following year. These courses called first, second and third year were designed respectively for primary, intermediate and final examinations and it was made compulsory that students complete the respective courses before sitting for examination.

The effort was a creditable one both from the standpoint of speed in preparation and thoroughness of the material supplied. Its reception by the students indicated that it was filling a long felt need.

The Institute might have capitalized upon these courses by making them available to any who wished to subscribe, but decided to restrict their use to its registered students.

The courses were, however, made available to the students of other provincial bodies with whom Ontario had affiliation through the Dominion Association.

The study courses have been constantly under revision and have been expanded so as now to provide instruction over a five-year period. So well has this course been received that one might say it is "standard equipment" for students of six out of the nine Provincial Institutes. The widespread use of the Ontario study course has done much to bring about a uniformity of standards among the various Institutes; in the year 1939 the nine Provincial Institutes agreed upon a standardized examination for their candidates qualifying for membership.

In 1933 another milestone was passed when in a manner befitting the occasion the Institute celebrated its Golden Anniversary. The celebration took the form of a dinner at which over four hundred members and students were in attendance. Guests honouring the gathering included the Premier of the Province, the Mayor of Toronto, representatives of the Law Society and other professional bodies together with representatives from the Dominion Association, the Provincial Societies and the American Institute of Accountants. This occasion being of recent date is well within the recollection of the majority of our members, and was well reported in THE CANADIAN CHARTERED ACCOUNTANT in the March issue of that year.

A mark of the success achieved during the half-century is the membership of 591 persons, many of whom have taken residence in countries throughout the world. At this writing the Institute boasts of a total membership of 844 with 437 registered students progressing towards their degree of Chartered Accountant.

Financially the Institute has now reached the position that it has accumulated a surplus sufficient for any contingency which might arise. Accordingly it has revised downward, the annual fees of its members so that revenues about equal expenditures and services are rendered at cost. This position has been attained since 1924, for it was in that year that the surplus of $8,553.01 was almost wiped out by the failure of the Home Bank. The loss provided for out of surplus amounted to $8,318.07 upon which no recoveries have been realized. It was the irony of fate that this de-

92

pository was the only one of the chartered banks which did not engage a chartered accountant to audit its accounts.

In its recovery the Institute has not profited financially from its study courses. Any surplus from their operation is used in revising and keeping up to date the subject matter of the lesson material.

The position of the Institute of Chartered Accountants today is the result of much time and thought given unstintingly by members too numerous to have allowed of individual mention here. Upon the walls of the Council Chamber arranged in the order of their tenure in office are the portraits of all the Institute's Past Presidents keeping watch over the deliberations of their successors in the direction of the Institute's affairs.

Toronto, 28th December 1939.

GEORGE EDWARDS
The Great Organizer[*]

The man who set the tone for the Institute of Chartered Accountants of Ontario was George Edwards. True, others began the Institute. And, now that Edwards has been safely dead for thirty years, other chartered accountants run it. But in many ways, the Institute still behaves the way George Edwards taught it to. It still exhibits that wonderful combination of innocence, arrogance, enthusiasm, idealism and egocentricity which has been its hallmark since Edwards made it his masterpiece.

Edwards was born in Toronto in March 1861. His father William had emigrated from England and was appointed secretary (deputy minister) of the provincial Department of Public Works in 1868, a position he held for over thirty years. Edwards received his academic training at Toronto Collegiate Institute and with private tutors, and in 1880 went to work as a clerk in Toronto. Small and dapper, he was, apparently, an impressive young man. In 1885 when Edwards was twenty-four, George Jewell of London met him while in Toronto to collect his FCA. Later Jewell's son recalled that his father had, on returning home, predicted that Edwards would one day occupy a prominent position among the accountants in Ontario.

Edwards became a chartered accountant in 1889 and a fellow the following year. His first employment as a chartered accountant was with E.R.C. Clarkson. Recognizing Edwards's talents, Clarkson paid him $2.50 a day when the going rate was $2. Edwards practised by himself for a while in 1889, and then joined Alexander Hart-Smith to form the Edwards and Hart-Smith firm. In 1903 Hart-Smith died and

---

[*] Transcribed from Creighton, P., A Sum Of Yesterdays, Being A History Of The First One Hundred Years Of The Institute Of Chartered Accountants Of Ontario, 1984, The Institute of Chartered Accountants of Ontario, pp. 130-135.

in 1904, William Pomeroy Morgan, a stepson of Hart-Smith, joined the firm. Edwards Morgan was born and became the first firm in Canada to develop a branch office network; prior to World War I it had offices in Toronto, Montreal, Winnipeg, Calgary and Vancouver. The firm changed its name in 1957 and in 1962 it merged into Deloitte, Plender, Haskins and Sells.

Edwards was elected to the council of the Institute of Chartered Accountants of Ontario in 1890 and gained prominence rapidly. He was president for the three years 1895, 1896 and 1897 and again in 1903. From then until 1926, Edwards was either a member of the council or chairman of some important Institute committee, principally the board of instruction. It is a reasonable bet that for over thirty years, nothing much happened in the Institute of which Edwards did not approve.

Building on the base which his father's senior position in the Ontario civil service gave him, Edwards was tireless in trying to influence the provincial government in favour of the Institute. His first triumph came in 1897, when among other amendments to the Municipal Act, he got the following provision included:

> That a proper person to conduct municipal audits should
> be a fellow of the Institute of Chartered Accountants of
> Ontario or some other expert accountant.

Edwards continued his efforts in 1907 with a lot of careful work related to the Ontario Companies Act revisions. The 1907 act consolidated a myriad of predecessor acts; it also picked up the latest revisions to the English Companies Act. The end result was a statute which was undoubtedly the leading Companies Act in Canada. It also, in some viewers' eyes, was one of the most forward acts in the English-speaking world at the time; it was, indeed, used as the model for the revision of the federal act in 1917.

In the 1907 revisions, Edwards did not try to acquire a monopoly position in Ontario for the chartered accountants but rather tried to secure the auditor's position, whoever the auditor might be. In fact, when the Trust and Loan Companies Act was amended some ten years later, he actively opposed the attempt by the provincial government to limit the position of auditors in trust companies to members of the Institute. His opposition was based on his clearsighted perception that the price would be the admission to membership of all the non-chartered accountants already active in the field. This he opposed vigorously on the grounds that there was not enough professional work available in such audits to justify the lowering of the Institute's membership standards.

His greatest success with the Ontario Legislature was, undoubtedly, the series of amendments to the Chartered Accountants act passed in the period 1909-11, which would have limited the right to use of the designation "chartered accountant", in Ontario, to a member of the Institute of Chartered Accountants of Ontario. These amendments were disallowed, consistently, by the Dominion government, on the encouragement of the rival Dominion Association of Chartered Accountants.

Edwards always spoke his mind, too. Writing in 1909 to the editor of the *Monetary Times*, after the disallowance of one of the Ontario chartered accountancy acts by the Dominion government, he said:

> It is the most recent incident in a seven years fight
> for a principle, and is not a quarrel between
> individuals excepting to the extent that certain gross
> breaches of faith on the part of individuals have
> embroiled Canadian Accountancy interests in a dispute
> for which there is small hope of settlement, so long as
> the Dominion Association fails to live up to the

> obligations imposed upon it by its own act of incorporation.

The impasse between provincial and national bodies was resolved in 1911 when the new form of the Dominion Association of Chartered Accountants (now the Canadian Institute of Chartered Accountants) was adopted. The Dominion Association ended its attempts to rival the Ontario Institute. Under the new arrangement the Dominion Association became, really, the national arm of the various provincial institutes.

During the 1914-18 World War, Edwards worked in Ottawa on the Imperial Munitions Board and the Edwards Morgan firm represented the Imperial government in Canada. For his war work Edwards was created a Commander of the Order of the British Empire (CBE) and might, in a kinder political climate, have had a title. He also acquired a lot of influential friends and acquaintances. A number of ministers of finance both asked for, and listened to, his advice. Edwards was active, for example, in representations to the federal government in the early 1920s when the Bank Act was revised, following the crash of the Home Bank. And his firm audited the general accounts of the Dominion of Canada for three years during the 1920s.

Edwards's other professional accomplishments were legion. He was president of the Dominion Association of Chartered Accountants in 1913. He was the managing editor of the *Canadian Chartered Accountant* magazine when it began publication. He was one of the founders, and the first president, of the Canadian Society of Cost Accountants in 1919. He was, also, the instigator of the Institute-run correspondence course of instruction, which was better known, for half a century, as the Queen's course. To honour Edwards for his contribution to chartered accounting education, and perhaps more mundanely for his ability as a fundraiser in the Queen's University capital-raising drive of the early 1920s, the university gave

Edwards an honorary doctorate. Edwards is also the person who sold the idea of reciprocity in membership - the concept of a common membership standard -to the various provincial institutes of chartered accountants in Canada.

He had all the great man's willingness to decide other people's fates for them. Most of Edwards's sons were taken into the family firm. One of his major weaknesses as a manager was his conviction that everybody called Edwards, obviously, must be a partner in his firm. The office was simply stiff with people called Edwards. There were three sons, and innumerable cousins, nephews, and assorted relatives. This made it difficult, however, to retain the non-family staff in the firm.

The family was also recruited to help with the Institute. One son, H. Percy Edwards, sat on innumerable committees and eventually became president. On the other hand, Oswald, another son, was less of a success in his father's eyes. Oswald did not like Institute work; in the Edwards family, however, this was really not negotiable. Oswald relates how he was forced back, eventually, onto the subterfuge of doing his job so well that he never was asked back. His first task was to set a cost accounting examination: he made it so hard that no one passed!

Edwards made a lot of money from his public accounting practice and his investments and lived well. He had a big house in Parkdale on the lakefront in the western suburbs of Toronto. He liked power boats and owned big ones. He bought the site of a burnt-out hotel in Bala, Ontario and build himself a lovely summer home, complete with a room for the Anglican Bishop of Toronto and an Anglican church out behind.

In the 1920s and 1930s George Edwards had if not the best, then, assuredly, the second best accounting practice in Toronto. His client list made contemporaries wildly envious. His office was smaller than Clarkson, Gordon, the largest in the city, but not markedly so. His success was a tribute to his character and ability, but he lacked any notion of building up his firm. He was not as adept, for example, as Colonel H.D.L. Gordon in attracting and retaining the services of outstanding younger accountants. His predilection for his family did not help. Both in his family and firm he found it too easy to override the objections and the points of view of others.

It was only in the Ontario Institute that Edwards found other people of like ability, who were willing to stand against him. This seemed to be the challenge he enjoyed and it is the Ontario Institute which is Edwards' real monument. Through that Institute he had a profound effect on the development of professional accounting in Canada today. This is not to detract from the great work of the Montreal accountants, or of those other giants of the Institute in Toronto, but simply to state the obvious, that in any short list of the great Canadian accountants Edwards has to come near the top.

On November 15, 1926, the Institute recognized its obligation to George Edwards and gave him a banquet. Over two hundred accountants attended. A fancy program was printed, speeches were made, songs sung, toasts given, an illuminating address presented and an invitation extended for him to sit for a portrait. The portrait was completed and it hung for years in a prominent position in the Institute's offices at 10 Adelaide Street East in Toronto. It may be significant of the waning of Edwards's influence that when the Institute's new building was opened in 1954, at 69 Bloor Street East in Toronto, none of the organizing committees made the slightest objection to shunting Edwards's portrait quietly into the dimmer recesses of the library. Perhaps, as Edwards had died in 1947, they were not averse to supplanting the king.

RESEARCH CONTRIBUTIONS TO CANADIAN STANDARDS:

A RETROSPECTIVE

Ross M. Skinner

I have always believed that one's environment has a very strong influence on one's beliefs and actions. As I near retirement from active participation in professional pursuits, I feel an urge to reflect on the way my own career was shaped by its environment. This somewhat extended account, in essence, stems from that urge. Its focus is on professional research since research constituted a significant part of my career.

I. INITIAL DEVELOPMENT

I joined Clarkson Gordon (then called Clarkson, Gordon, Dilworth and Nash) in October 1945, just after the conclusion of World War II. Unlike most of the other larger firms (small by today's standards) that operated on the "pool" system, Clarkson's followed the "staff" system whereby

Research in Accounting Regulation, Vol. 3, pages 197–217.
Copyright © 1989 by JAI Press Inc.
All rights of reproduction in any form reserved.
ISBN: 0-89232-998-X

professional staff were assigned to individual staff reporting to an individual partner, and having a defined group of clients to look after. I was fortunate enough to be assigned to one of the staffs reporting to J. R. M. (Jack) Wilson, a young partner, aged about 36, who was even then developing recognition as the most competent technical partner in the firm.

At that time the Firm had 3 offices and some 20 partners in all, 12 of them in Toronto. It was not a highly structured organization. With its staff system of operation it was not unlike a set of small firms within a firm, and this was considered highly desirable in order to maintain the sense of personal and professional responsibility for the clients' interests. However, the strong leadership of Colonel Gordon, the founder of one of the principal components of the firm, made up for whatever it lacked in formal organization. In 1945 the Colonel was beginning to reduce his active participation and the mantle of leadership was passing to his older son, Walter Gordon, together with his close friend and associate, J. Grant Glassco.

The core activity of a public accounting firm in 1945 was auditing. Virtually all partners were generalists who were expected to look after all the needs of audit clients and to train staff reporting to them. It was an innovation in the profession when Grant Glassco undertook to acquire special expertise in taxation and built up a reputation preparing and presenting claims, for clients and nonclients alike, for special consideration under the wartime Excess Profits Act. (Under that Act, companies paid a tax on deemed excess profits which reached 100 percent, with 20 percent refundable after the war. Excess profits were defined as all profits in excess of a base consisting of average profits for the period 1936-1939. A company could, however, go before a board and argue that its base should be adjusted because its profits in that period were unduly depressed or for other reasons.)

The education of a CA in 1945 was the joint responsibility of the Institute, the employing firm, and, of course, the student himself. In Ontario, a registered student was required to take a 5 year correspondence course from a high school degree, which was reduced to 4 years for those holding a BA, and 3 for those holding a B.Comm. The course was administered by Queen's University. Much of the course material was drafted by Queen's faculty members, but it was carefully reviewed for accuracy by a committee of the Institute. (I served a term on that committee in the 1950s, and well remember Professor Leonard's surprise when I told him that, contrary to his draft lesson on financial institutions, Canadian chartered banks still had secret reserves.)

There were also 3 sets of examinations, with an exemption for B.Comm.'s from the primary set. The basic texts to be used with the course of study were Smail's *Auditing* and a book by Smails and Walker (I think) on accounting principles. These were supplemented by shorter publications on more specialized topics, and, in the more advanced years, by Montgomery's *Auditing*. The latter text by then was in its seventh edition, and was a most useful all-purpose text, in that it covered accounting principles as well as auditing techniques. In its choice of texts, the course neatly summarized the transition from British influence to American influence on the profession. Smail's works were in the British tradition, especially in their extensive reproduction of leading case law; Montgomery's text was wholly American. To a large extent the texts were descriptive and "how-to-do-it" in nature, without much emphasis on theory or policy. I well remember my sense of exhilaration in my final year upon reading George O. May's book *Financial Accounting: A Distillation of Experience*. Until that time I had not appreciated the historical development of accounting, or realized the importance of concepts to its application.

The accounting firms were responsible for giving their students exposure to an adequate variety of work experience and teaching how audit procedures were applied in practice. To this end, each firm of any size would have its own code of audit ticks and instructions for using audit stamps, its devices for formalizing audit procedures, such as "audit charts" and various forms of questionnaires, and its design of working papers, especially for the record of balance sheet work.

II.   THE 1945 AUDIT ENVIRONMENT

The typical audit in Canada in the 1930s consisted of two main segments. The "current audit" consisted of detailed examination of the mainly documentary evidence for all transactions recorded in the books of account during the year. The "balance sheet" audit consisted of verification, using both internal and external evidence, of the balances of assets and liabilities that it was proposed to include in the financial statements and satisfying oneself that they were properly grouped and described so as to give a "true and correct view" in the words of the law. The current audit was directly intended to monitor the "stewardship" of management and, in particular, to uncover any traces of employee fraud. The balance sheet audit was directed more to the auditor's statutory duty to report on the financial statements of corporations. This Canadian approach to auditing was derived from British precedent and contrasted with common practice in the United States which tended to be much more concentrated on verification of the balance sheet supplemented by analyses of individual profit and loss accounts, somewhat along the lines of what would be called "analytical review" today.

In the 1930s, or even before, it was apparent in Canada that the complete detailed audit was becoming impractical because of the volume of transactions. The answer, in large corporations at least, was to conduct a "test audit," rather than a detailed audit. Typically, the examination of a year's transactions was reduced to a test by reducing the number of months examined to four or fewer. The month(s) selected were theoretically to be chosen at random. My impression was that the justification for the reduction in audit effort was more a rationalization of expediency than a conclusion from any well-thought-out theory. True, there was a rudimentary idea of sampling embodied in the concept of the test audit. Also, the theory that larger companies would automatically be less subject to fraud and error, because the division of functions among employees could be designed to provide "internal check," carried some conviction. But neither of these ideas was well enough developed to indicate *to what extent* it was safe to reduce audit procedures.

III.   THE SENSE OF PROFESSIONAL OBLIGATION

Colonel Gordon, as a matter of policy, felt that the Firm should play a leadership role in the affairs of the profession. That included the responsibility to be active in the development and propagation of good auditing standards. (Accounting, prior to World War II, was still regarded very much as a matter for professional judgment rather than standards.) No doubt there was an element of self-interest in the concern of the profession's leaders for good auditing standards. Public recognition of the profession's right to practice depended on its standards. Also, court cases had established that the question whether a professional was negligent would be judged, by and large, by the standards of his peers. It was therefore wise for any individual firm to make sure that its particular view of appropriate procedures should be widely adopted within the profession. Nevertheless, I am sure that the sense of obligation to the profession was an ethical imperative as well as practical.

World War II created a strain on accounting firms as it did on virtually every form of enterprise. The great majority of professional staff were of an age to join the services. Thus, from 1940 on, a pattern developed whereby staff would be hired and, perhaps after only a few months, would resign to join up. The gap was filled in part by hiring of "audit clerks," a large number of them women, who did not register as students-in-accounts, but merely took the job as they would any other. (Some women, but not a large number relatively, did enroll and qualify as CAs.) Thus the staff mix of all C A firms was heavily weighted by students with little experience and by audit clerks who were hired to do a job but had little intention of making it their career.

Clarkson's answer to this problem was twofold. The Firm ran a series of Saturday morning lectures to train the junior staff. And it developed its first audit manual for staff in 1942—in effect, an audit text (although perhaps lacking in explanation of the "why" for procedures) especially written to incorporate firm policies and routines. The very specific aim of the manual was to give every staff member a guide they could take with them on the job, so that if a senior were temporarily unavailable and they were uncertain where to start or what to do next, they could turn to their manual and get on with it. In this way, the manual substituted, in part, for the training and lessons that junior students had not yet had and that audit clerks would never get. In line with the Firm's sense of professional responsibility, it had its lecture series edited and gave it to the Institute for publication. The title was something along the lines of "Duties of a Junior Accountant," but because of its yellow cover it was popularly known as "the Yellow Peril." Likewise, the Firm's audit manual formed the basis, somewhat later, of a small text under the authorship of H. C. Dell and J. R. M. Wilson that ran through several editions and was included in the Institute's educational program for many years.

IV. PERSONAL DEVELOPMENT

Just like any registered student, my principal aim beginning in October 1945 was to learn to perform an audit, to complete the course of study, and to pass the examinations. The work, initially, was somewhat boring except for its novelty to me. However, with each passing year it became more challenging and interesting as the scope for judgment increased and the variety of business situations encountered steadily broadened. Also, one was continually learning. It seemed to many of us that when we mastered some skill we rarely had much opportunity to apply it, but immediately moved on to some unfamiliar task. The common complaint of clients that they were regularly sent junior staff who "learned on them" was very largely true. However, there was not much that CA firms could do about it. The CA training gave staff members highly saleable skills in a short period of time, so that many left for jobs in industry within a few years of qualification. Thus the firms were forced into a routine of continuously hiring new students right out of school and training them, only to see them take their skills elsewhere.

In my initial hiring interview, Jack Wilson told me that one of the principal sources of satisfaction in a CA career (as well as providing the icing on the cake in terms of income) was "special work." To some extent special work meant what we would call management advisory services today, but the fit is not exact. In 1945 there were far fewer information specialities than there are today. CAs were seen as experts in the interpretation of numbers. In the absence of established expertise on a narrow subject area, CAs were likely to be called upon to study and advise in the establishment of financial policy, the implementation of a law or regulation, or other such matters. The development of the profession's expertise in income tax was the natural outcome of this. In effect, CAs became the specialists in this field. In other subject areas more narrowly focused specialists emerged and took over.

Special work was rewarding materially and intellectually, but it could be demanding. Since it could not be planned for in advance, the usual custom was to ask the apparently best qualified audit partner to take on each new special assignment as it came in and make ad hoc (and usually inadequate) arrangements for other partners to take on part of his normal audit load. Since it was important that partners build strong personal relationships with their clients, there were distinct limits to such load sharing. Nevertheless, successful completion of special assignments added to a partner's stature in the firm, so that, for the most part, the extra work was taken on gladly.

Almost by definition, special work required highly talented and widely experienced individuals. There was much less scope for the use of junior staff than on the normal audit engagement. Nevertheless, some research and number crunching could often be delegated. Owing to the recognized importance of special work, the partner responsible could legitimately ask for the assistance of the most able staff members no matter what partner that member reported to. Thus it was clear to all staff below the level of partner (as well as to partners themselves) that selection to work on a special assignment was an indication of the Firm's regard for one's talents.

I was probably lucky in receiving some special assignments early in my career. One of the first major audit clients I worked on was Union Gas, with headquarters in Chatham, Ontario. In 1947 the company, after many years of shrinking production from its own natural gas wells, signed a contract with an American pipeline company for the import of significant volumes of gas from Texas. Under these changed circumstances, it was appropriate to seek a new structure of rates for the company. George Richardson, a senior partner with a particularly powerful and enquiring mind, was asked to prepare testimony to be presented to the regulatory board in support of the company's application, on the subject of the fair rate of return to be allowed the company. At least partly because I had some familiarity with the company, and probably because it was thought my B.Comm. degree had taught me much more about economics and finance than it actually had, I was detailed to assist Mr. Richardson.

At that time public utility regulation was not highly developed in Canada, and there was no established pattern for setting rates. What form of testimony would be useful was, therefore, rather unclear. Mr. Richardson and I went to New York to see what American precedents there were. I did some digging in the library of the American Institute, while Mr. Richardson was interviewing Standard Statistics (now Standard and Poor's) to commission a special survey designed to show cost of capital. I was lucky enough to be able to turn up some worthwhile literature on the subject of rate setting. Mr. Richardson was highly delighted because it helped him shape his whole approach to the testimony.

That was the first of many assignments having to do with public utility regulation in which I participated over the next 25 years, first as an assistant and ultimately as the Firm's leading expert in public utility accounting and rates. These and a number of other financial and economic studies over the years brought me a reputation within the Firm as a researcher with skills going beyond accounting and auditing, and brought me into contact with all the senior partners, including Walter Gordon and Grant Glassco, with both of whom I worked on special assignments.

V. FORMALIZATION OF A RESEARCH RESPONSIBILITY

I was admitted to the partnership on April 1, 1954, at age 30. A typical audit partner oversaw 2 or occasionally 3 audit staffs, each having 7 or 8 staff members on average (although a staff responsible for the work of a very large client could be quite a bit larger). Although a new partner might start out with only one staff for a year or so, I was able to start out with 2 since I had experience in a more junior capacity with many of the clients assigned to me.

At that time it was an understood policy of the Firm that every client partner had a personal responsibility to maintain his professional competence in accounting, auditing, and tax. At the same time, it was becoming increasingly evident that people needed help in keeping up with the accelerated pace of development of these areas. This had been recognized formally for more than ten years in the tax area through the assignment of some partners to specialize full-time on tax matters. These specialists were available to educate client partners on new developments and to assist in or even handle particularly complex tax problems of clients.

Things were different in the core areas of accounting and auditing. These were so central to the profession's mission that the idea of an accounting and auditing specialist seemed unnatural. Nevertheless, as the Firm grew, the need for policies in addressing contentious issues to ensure a consistent Firm response became apparent. There was also a need to help busy partners become aware of new developments. Finally, there was a need to make sure that the Firm's audit procedures remained appropriate and up-to-date as conditions changed. These needs were recognized informally at first rather than through any formal change in the Firm's organizational structure. However, a vehicle for disseminating Firm policies and creating awareness of new developments was provided in the form of accounting, auditing, and tax "notebooks," distributed to partners and managers, and containing memoranda on important policies and current matters of interest. Jack Wilson was responsible for keeping the accounting and auditing sections of the notebooks up-to-date.

By 1954 Jack was taking on more responsibilities, along with some other of the younger partners, for the operating direction of the Firm, as both Walter Gordon and Grant Glassco were becoming more involved in interests outside the Firm. He therefore coopted me as soon as I was admitted to the partnership to help him keep the notebooks in shape. More important than that, he instructed me to consider whether the Firm's organization of audit engagements and its procedures were satisfactory in all respects.

As I recall, the first formal announcement to the partners at large that I was to take on this responsibility was made at the 1956 annual partners' meeting. (There was no specific title that went with the job—it was a few years later that a more formal organizational structure for the Firm provided the title of "National Director of Accounting and Auditing Standards" as one member of the newly formed National Office.) I was asked to report to the partners at the 1956 meeting my ideas on the direction of Firm research in auditing. The program I sketched at that time was the basis for such research effort as I was able to make for the next several years, and to some extent shaped the work done by Rod Anderson and Don Leslie after me.

VI. INITIAL IDEAS

My initial concern was with the planning and organization of the audit. By the 1950s, most of the work done in both the "current" and the "balance sheet" segments of the audit was on a test basis. Auditing literature had formalized two ideas—namely, that a test was justified on the general principle of a sample being representative of the whole, and also that the extent of test should relate to the strength of the client's internal controls. My concern was with the practical implementation of these propositions. Specifically, I could not see that our work demonstrated a logical link between internal controls and extent of testing. There were two problems—we did not review internal controls well, and, even if we did, it was difficult to demonstrate a direct connection between the findings of that review and our decisions on extent of testing.

When I joined the firm in 1945, the review of internal control was supposed to be conducted early in the current audit segment of the audit. As a junior auditor, I had only the vaguest idea of how to set about a review. I cannot recall ever receiving any worthwhile instruction on the subject, and my Institute lessons, although explaining the concepts of internal check and internal control, were not very helpful in explaining how one actually made a review in practice. Naturally, too, this was an area in which one could not expect much help from client's staff. Not infrequently, the reaction of client staff to any questioning on the subject of internal controls was anger that their integrity was being questioned. Early on in my training the Firm introduced internal control questionnaires, patterned, I think, after those in Montgomery's Auditing. But these also seemed unsatisfactory in practice. How could one evaluate five "Yes" answers and two "No" answers?

My observation, therefore, throughout my first ten years of practice, was that the review of internal control was a mere warm-up exercise, after which we got down to the real audit-that is, following the standard procedures laid down in the audit manual, usually to the same extent as in the previous year. As far as I could tell from contacts with staff or other firms, this situation was general. This false position the profession was in bothered me.

The problem was how to improve it in a practical way. My reasoning was that internal controls had to be built in to a client's systems and routines for carrying on its activities and recording their results. We needed an accurate understanding of the systems to evaluate the controls. Therefore, our emphasis should shift from review of controls directly to review of the systems, from which we could deduce the apparent controls. Such an approach might also be more workable in practice, since clients' staff were less likely to become uncooperative if asked questions about the functioning of the systems than if asked directly about controls, implicitly questioning their honesty.

Following this line of thinking, I told the partners in 1956 that I hoped to work along the lines set out below:

1. Devise a scheme for describing a client's systems in a standard format that could be readily understood by someone other than the describer.
2. Devise a procedure for linking that description with an evaluation of internal control.
3. Build in to the program automatic drafting of letters to management with respect to weaknesses in controls.
4. Consider whether some more formal way could be found to relate weaknesses uncovered in internal controls to the extent of audit procedures. In this connection, explore the possible application of scientific sampling techniques to guide the extent of audit tests.
5. Finally, consider whether a direct spin-off benefit to the client could be obtained by adapting our record of review of the client's system so that it could also provide valuable suggestions to the client from the standpoint of efficiency, or, at least, pinpoint areas where a more detailed study might be beneficial.

VII.   EARLY RESEARCH EFFORTS

This statement of objectives was well received by the partners. Implementing the program was another matter. Even though I had been assigned responsibility for professional research within the Firm, I still had responsibility for two audit staffs, a workload at least equal to that of other young partners, especially if fairly frequent special assignments were counted in. The theory (not without merit) was that the person responsible for research should also be responsible for making sure its results could be applied in practice. Unfortunately, it is also true that, in life, tasks of long-range importance tend to be pushed aside by the merely urgent. Especially in a service profession, no one can control the timing of client's needs for service, or ignore them when they arise. These sorts of demands made it very difficult to perform any concentrated thinking and research. I did have an assistant assigned to me to work in this area, but his time was fully taken up by the task of keeping our accounting and auditing policy notebook memos up-to-date, and generally keeping up with and creating awareness within the Firm of current professional developments.

Accordingly, the sum total of progress on my program in the period 1956-1960 was very small. I started out with three ideas. The first was that the systems description should be in narrative form, so that it could be read and understood. The second was that the description should be structured in some logical flow so that staff members would find it easy to proceed step by step, and any gaps in the description would be more readily apparent. To this end, I directed that the narrative should be organized in natural cycles, corresponding to the business activity and recordkeeping of the client, with each cycle to be described "from cradle to grave," beginning with the initial activity in the cycle and carrying on to the final record in the accounts. Thus, in an ordinary manufacturing company the cycles were:

- Purchasing—covering order initiation and authorization; receipt and approval of quality of goods and services; receipt and checking of invoices; recording of amounts payable and issuance of payment; and any collateral checks and recording.
- Selling—covering order receipt and approval; requisition of goods and shipping; preparation of invoices; recording of sales and receivables; recording of payments; and any collateral checks and recording.
- Payrolls—covering hiring and termination procedures; production of records on which pay is based; preparation and distribution of pay; and collateral records of deductions and earnings.
- Costing—covering inventory costing and generally any use of accounting data for management purposes.

- Books of Account—covering entries in the general ledger and interim financial statements.

My third idea was that the system description should be set down on the left side of a wide sheet of paper, and in columns beside it should be placed comments on internal control strengths and weaknesses and suggested modifications of our standard audit procedures or specifications of extent of tests to adapt the audit to the particular situation of the client.

I had my staffs experiment with this approach in a number of small to medium sized client engagements in the late 1950s, leaving the more challenging question of larger audit engagements till we had some experience in simpler situations. The experiment was only partially successful. It did seem to produce results in terms of a better understanding of the internal controls and how the audit should be adapted to them. But it also had some significant problems. The approach depended upon the ability of the staff member performing the review to express himself clearly in writing, and not all were up to this task. Moreover, it is far too easy to leave lacunae in a systems description when it is in a narrative form. Also, the task of systems description was quite time-consuming, and it was evident that the difficulty would multiply in larger and more complex engagements.

VIII. DEVELOPMENT OF ANALYTICAL AUDITING

About 1960 our program accelerated. There were several contributing factors. We realized that we would have to devote more effort if we were to make real progress with our R. and D. To facilitate this, my two existing staffs were transferred to a new partner (although I retained what we called "A" partner responsibility for the larger clients), and to replace them a new "experimental" staff was formed and given responsibility for a collection of clients with whom I had had no previous acquaintance. It was hoped that, with the reduction in the amount of my overall direct responsibility for clients, more time would be available for audit development work, as well as the increasing responsibilities of the now officially recognized position of National Director of Accounting and Auditing Standards.

The members assigned to my new experimental staff were deliberately selected to be typical of the calibre of our staff members generally. The intent was to make our experiments honest—but we cheated in one important particular. Rod Anderson, who at that time had been with the Firm for two or three years and had already made his mark as one of our most brilliant students in a generation, was assigned to the staff. (I should also concede that subsequently, as individual staff members were promoted or rotated to other positions, new students assigned to the staff tended to be selected from our most promising recruits.)

About this time, also, we committed ourselves to write a textbook on auditing. Our client, Copp Clark Publishing, had recently been acquired by the English publisher Pitman's, who specialized in the publication of business-oriented books. Pitman's were of the opinion that a Canadian auditing text would strengthen their presence in Canada and might well be adaptable to the U.S. and English markets as well. Jack Wilson, for his part, felt that authorship of such a text would be good for the Firm and would also provide a forum by which we could expose to the profession at large the fruits of our audit experiments. I was rather reluctant to take on this new task, particularly since I had just become a member of the CICA Accounting and Auditing Research Committee which would add to the demands on my time. However, I eventually agreed to make the effort, provided Rod would be free to work with me on it.

Rod's addition to our development efforts paid off in short order. It was he who conceived the idea of recording our systems descriptions in flow charts, using a set of symbols specially adapted to accounting processes. And it was he (with the assistance of other staff members, notably Steve Lowden) who worked out details whereby we made a record of our compliance tests in a compact form at the foot of the flow charts. With this addition, we had what we thought was a practical way to implement my basic ideas—the basic features of the approach being the cycle flow basis of describing the client's systems and the flow charting techniques.

Having developed and tested our ideas within our experimental staff in 1960-1961 we were ready to phase in implementation. We first introduced the ideas to a sample of other staffs in Toronto and some other offices in order to gain broader experience. Then, either in the Spring of 1962 or 1963 (my memory is not perfectly certain), we put on training sessions for all staff in all offices, so that our new techniques would be adopted in all but smaller audit engagements as soon as it was practical to phase them in. (It was recognized that creation of flow charts initially would be more time-consuming than keeping them up-to-date.) This marked the end of the major development work on this project although, of course, refinements continued to be made as we gained experience.

Our commitment to write an auditing text now began to weigh upon us.

As Rod attained increased seniority, the demands on his time naturally multiplied. Now there were two of us for whom the immediate crisis was continually crowding out matters of long-term importance. In essence, we accomplished nothing worthwhile, and even the most indulgent of publishers might be excused for feeling impatient. About this time, as I will recount shortly, I committed myself to what was for me a far more interesting task. We arrived, therefore, at a compromise solution. We offered Pitman's an immediate book on our flow-charting system, with the promise that Rod would in due course produce the full-scale auditing text that was originally intended. The result was *Analytical Auditing*, published in 1966, the bulk of which was written by Rod over a very short period of time. As co-author, I had the rare experience of having little difficulty accepting the drafting of my colleague, and most of the credit for the book belongs to Rod. The book was reasonably successful without ever receiving much promotion from Pitman's. It was translated into four foreign languages, usually as a result of some foreign accountant approaching us so that the book could receive wider distribution in his country, (Oddly, there are two versions in Spanish, since the Argentine accounting community was not happy with the original translation done in Mexico.)

This, in effect, marked the end of my involvement in auditing research. Rod was admitted to the partnership some time before the book was published, and shortly thereafter my job was split, with Rod becoming National Director of Auditing Standards and I retaining responsibility in the accounting area. In his new position Rod had no shortage of work to do. There was, in particular, the continuing challenge of keeping up with the auditing implications of computers. Rod was the prime mover in developing a videotaped course in computer concepts to improve the computer literacy of partners and staff. This course was given to the Institute for wider distribution in the profession, and licensed by it for use by the AICPA and, I believe, one or more of the British institutes. Rod also spent an enormous amount of time in researching and trying to work out the application of statistical sampling techniques to auditing. As a result he continued to find it difficult to devote time to writing a full-scale auditing text. It was not until 1977 that *The External Audit* was finally published. Two years later, his studies on statistical sampling, in conjunction with partner Don Leslie and Albert Teitlebaum of McGill University, bore fruit in the form of *Dollar-Unit Sampling: A Practical Guide for Auditors*. This work, was awarded the Wildman Gold Medal by the American Accounting Association.

One footnote to this history may be of interest. At the CICA annual conference in Winnipeg in the Fall of 1963, two partners of McDonald Currie made a presentation on their newly developed method for evaluation of internal control. I was pleased to find that, working entirely independently, they had come up with ideas very similar to our own. In particular, there was a striking similarity in the way they and we broke down our systems analysis into cycles, although their manner of recording and evaluating internal controls was far different from our flow charts. Evidently, the breaking down of systems description into naturally connected segments has intuitive appeal. Similar ideas played a prominent part in an Arthur Andersen (U.S.) publication on evaluation of internal control published in 1978, some fifteen years later.

IX.   MY TRANSITION TO ACCOUNTING RESEARCH

The shift to accounting principles and standards as my major interest began with my appointment as a member of the CICA Accounting and Auditing Research Committee in September, 1959. The Committee was then putting the final touches on Bulletin 17, dealing with the wording of the auditor's standard report. The principal change recommended in the Bulletin was the addition of the words "in conformity with generally accepted accounting principles applied on a basis consistent with the preceding year" to the auditor's opinion. The Bulletin stated that this change in wording did not represent a change of substance from previous practice. It was merely intended to emphasize the auditor's obligation to respect accepted opinion when forming his own professional opinion.

At the end of the meeting at which final approval was given to the Bulletin (my first meeting, I think) one of the members said to me in jest: "One of these days we'll have to get around to saying what generally accepted accounting principles actually are." Even though the remark was intended as a joke, it stuck in my mind as having serious merit. Experience had led me to believe that the idea of "general acceptance" was not very helpful in resolving differences of opinion. In the first place, it seemed to me there were a lot of issues on which we did not have general agreement and were unlikely to get it if we waited for opinion to coalesce. Second, I did not believe that simple acceptance necessarily should be the last word. I thought there ought to be some theory, or conceptual framework if you will, from which the best solutions to particular accounting issues ought to be deducible. Only if such a framework existed were we likely to obtain internal consistency in financial reporting. Of course, it did seem possible to me, perhaps even probable, that some implicit framework reflecting collective experience underlay most accepted accounting principles. But, if so, wouldn't it be better to try to state that framework explicitly, rather than to try to solve each issue that arose on its own, by deciding what was "accepted" by what could only logically be a nose-counting process?

This underlying point of view influenced all my actions as a Committee member. It was during my term of membership that the CICA commenced its policy of commissioning research studies, at least partly with the idea that such studies would form a point of departure for future Committee recommendations. I don't remember now who first suggested this new policy—it may even have been myself. Certainly, I was strongly in favor. Another project which I know I initiated was one to produce a book on accounting by nonprofit organizations. I was bothered at the time by the observable absence of generally accepted principles common to different types of nonprofit organizations and the marked diversity of practice even within a single type. My proposal was to put together a book in which each chapter would describe the accounting practices found within a particular type of nonprofit organization, using a standard format for each chapter. Individual authors familiar with the particular type of organization covered would be recruited to draft each chapter. By this means, I hoped we would provide evidence of the lack of uniformity in practice. Also, I hoped that by asking ourselves why the accounting differed from one type to another we would be helped to make rational recommendations of general application that could fit the different circumstances found in the real world. This proposal for a book was approved by the Committee, and I undertook to line up authors for individual chapters on churches, hospitals, universities, school boards, charitable and welfare societies, social clubs and so on. This I did, taking on the responsibility for the chapter on university accounting myself.

In due course, I became chairman of the Committee. My next object of attack was business accounting principles. Just about this time, the first research studies were appearing in the new series sponsored by the AICPA in conjunction with the inception of the APB. Research studies Nos. 1 and 3 on the basic postulates and broad principles of accounting received a strongly unfavorable reaction. In my judgment this was partly because they dared to be different in some of the ideas they expressed, and partly because their high level of abstraction made it difficult for people accustomed to thinking in terms of narrow individual problems to see what the studies would do for them. In other words, whatever the merit of the ideas in the studies, they were not a tactical success. I thought we could do better. I thought a more hopeful approach would be to produce a description of current practice, try to identify the implicit principles on which it was based, point out any internal conflicts so that they could be attacked individually, and finally, stand back from the structure and examine its basic premises to see whether some fundamental rethinking was called for. I persuaded the Committee we should try to do a research study along these lines, and drafted terms of reference embodying the thinking just described.

The approval for this project predated by at least a year the AICPA's approval of a research study by Paul Grady to produce an ''inventory'' of GAAP. Our project, although similar in some respects, was much broader in conception. It was not only to list GAAP, it was also to codify the principles in a rational, articulated manner, and it was to evaluate them critically. However, the other side of the coin was that Grady completed his study within a year or two. It took us far longer.

My first task was to find someone to write the study. I approached a number of academics and thoughtful practitioners to undertake it. Being sensible men, they all realized the terms of reference were very demanding and begged to be excused. After a number of such rejections, I concluded that if it was to be done, I would have to do it myself. By this time I was positive the job needed to be done, and frankly, I wanted to be the one to do it. Accordingly, I got the Firm to agree that this dedication of my time was worthwhile and, as already mentioned, managed to shift the prime responsibility for our auditing text to Rod Anderson. To reduce the time commitment, which I originally estimated at 1200 hours, I resigned from the chairmanship of the CICA Research Committee after completion of only one year out of the standard two-year term.

My first obligation, however, was to finish my chapter for the book on non-profit accounting. This I did over the course of a busy year. Unfortunately, in spite of our best efforts, only one other volunteer fulfilled his commitment. Finally, it was decided that the project would have to be abandoned. I was asked to revise the chapter I had drafted on university accounting so that it could be published on a stand-alone basis as one of the Institute's research study series. This I did, and the result was the study *Canadian University Accounting*, completed in late 1964 and published in 1965.

I then set out in earnest to write my study on accounting principles. By mid-1965 I had what I reckoned to be half the study in draft form. Then the special work impediment struck again. Our Regina partners obtained an assignment to make a special study of the accounting and financial reporting procedures of Saskatchewan Power Corporation and insisted that I was essential to head it up. This study took upwards of three months. I came back to a considerable backlog of client and other work in Toronto, and was shortly involved in another special study—fortunately considerably shorter—for the Saskatchewan Government Insurance Office. It was near Christmas before there was any opportunity to get back to my study. By this time my momentum was lost. My vision of where I was to go from where I had left off in the study had become fuzzy. In the course of clarifying it in my mind, I changed direction sufficiently that much of the first part of the study had to be rewritten.

This was pretty much the pattern of the next several years. Almost every time I cleared the decks for an extended period of concentrated work on the study, I would find my flow of thinking and effort interrupted in short order by some new assignment that demanded attention. The difficulty was intensified when one of our ablest partners suffered an untimely death from a heart attack. I had to step in and take the lead responsibility for perhaps our most important client. In addition to generating a steady stream of accounting issues in its far flung operations, that client often asked for assistance on special projects, such as investigations connected with possible mergers and acquisitions, which always had to be completed at high speed and on short notice. It was the sort of client relationship that any professional auditor would find stimulating and challenging—but it did make sustained progress on my study almost impossible.

Ultimately, after many interruptions and much rewriting, the study was completed in the Fall of 1971, some 7 years and 1800+ man-hours of work after it was begun. I had asked a number of people to review my drafts, but only two or three provided comments and criticisms in any depth. However, before publication the study was apportioned out among members of the CICA Research Committee of the time for review. As a result of this review, the study almost had more influence before publication than after. It was observable for some time that my ideas played a considerable part in the Committee's deliberations. That does not mean, of course, that the study's ideas were always accepted—but at least they were considered. Conversely, it must be acknowledged that the comments of the Committee members before publication helped improve the study.

Because it was so lengthy, the study was published by the CICA as a hard cover book rather than in the standard research study format, under the title *Accounting Principles: A Canadian Viewpoint*. It is fair to say the book was well received, and it continued to be read and consulted for far longer than usual in these fast-moving days.

After publication of the book in 1972, my energies were fully occupied for some time by the ever increasing demands of the National Accounting Standards Department (which by now had grown to a complement of several partners and managers), continuing client responsibilities, and continuing special work. By the mid-1970s, certain health problems were making it difficult to sustain the stress of all these activities, and a change in career emphasis seemed indicated. I resigned from the partnership in 1976, since I did not think it right to continue as partner if I was not prepared to devote my energies to the Firm to the fullest possible extent. The Firm's Executive, however, made a very generous arrangement with me, in effect giving me carte blanche to work on whatever I wanted, but continuing in an advisory and consulting relationship with the Firm. Some years later it was decided that my continuing close relationship with the Firm would be more publicly evident if I rejoined as a partner, but no change in our working relationship was intended. So it continued until I reached the normal retirement age for partners, and even after, since I retained my office and secretarial support until completion of my latest book in 1987.

In the period from 1976 to 1987 my concentration was on accounting research issues and consulting.

- J. J. Macdonnell, the Auditor-General of Canada invited me to chair an advisory committee on government accounting and auditing in 1975. This position gave me an insight I had previously lacked into issues of governmental financial reporting. It subsequently led to my participation in the CICA research study on that subject and more recently to an advisory role in the Federal Government Reporting Study sponsored jointly by the offices of the Comptroller-General of the United States and the Auditor-General of Canada.
- In the mid-1970s, of course, much attention was paid to the issues of Current Value Accounting. I directed the production of a videotaped presentation for clients and other interested parties outlining the basic concepts and issues. In 1977, I wrote one of the supplementary papers for the Ontario government-sponsored Committee on Inflation Accounting. The paper was entitled *The Significance of*

*Debt Financing to an Enterpriseduring an Inflationary Period and
the Implications thereof to a System of "Inflation Accounting."*

- One practical accounting problem that has interested me very much
  is that of accounting for a firm's obligations under its pension plans.
  In my 1972 book I made the observation that the accounting standards put in place around 1965, although an improvement on previous practice, did not provide fully satisfactory answers. It became
  increasingly evident to auditors in the inflationary 1970s that the
  standards gave incomplete guidance, were capable of abuse, and
  often were abused. To help in the rethinking that clearly was going
  to be necessary, I produced a monograph, published by the Firm in
  1980, under the title *Pension Accounting, the Problem of Equating
  Payments Tomorrow with Expenses Today.* Subsequently, I served
  on the FASB task force on the subject. As a member of the task
  force, I was dismayed to observe the very wide range of opinion
  and the inbuilt prejudices on the subject. Unfortunately, I fear the
  standards issued by the FASB and CICA in 1985/86 fall far short of
  a solution to the problems in this area, undoubtedly because of the
  wide divisions of opinion. It may be that government-mandated
  changes in pension plans will by themselves narrow the range of
  accounting possibilities. If not, I predict the problems will fester
  and require reconsideration in the 1990s.
- As the FASB Conceptual Framework studies emerged and it became evident that the Board was struggling in its efforts to make
  some sense out of the concepts of recognition and measurement, the
  thinking that led me to undertake the study on accounting principles
  in the 1960s re-emerged. My 1972 book was becoming quite dated
  by 1983 owing to changes in standards since 1972, and perhaps
  even more because of entirely new issues that had arisen since the
  book was written. I felt it would be useful to bring the book up to
  date. I wanted to do more than that, however. I wanted to promote
  understanding by placing present accounting standards firmly within their historical setting and within a solid framework of theory. I
  wanted, also, to reflect further upon that theory in view of developments since 1972. Hence I set about writing a new book. At the
  beginning, I thought of a two volume work—one being a critical
  survey of accounting theory, and one a critical survey of accounting
  standards. I concluded, however, that accounting theory today (in
  particular, what the academic world is interested in) is so fragmented, and contains so many conflicts, that to survey and make

sense of both theory and standards would be a task beyond my energy and competence. Even as it is, the book I eventually produced in 1987, under the title *Accounting Standards in Evolution*, was a substantial compression of my original drafting.

This concludes the story of my research interests. I know that many others can claim equal or greater achievement. This personal memoir may be justified, however, as a reminder of the satisfaction attainable from a balance between service to clients and broader service to one's profession.

The Accounting Historians Journal
Vol. 11, No. 2
Fall 1984

George J. Murphy
UNIVERSITY OF SASKATCHEWAN

EARLY CANADIAN FINANCIAL STATEMENT DISCLOSURE LEGISLATION

Abstract: The Ontario Companies Act of 1907 was one of the earliest legislative enactments to require presentation at company annual meetings, and specify the content of, the financial statements of commercial and manufacturing companies. The study describes the background to this important event and points to the two main influencing forces—the office of the Provincial Secretary and the equally active and informed Institute of Chartered Accountants of Ontario. The concern for disclosure suggests that Ontario was in the forefront of accounting development in the latter part of the nineteenth and the first decade of the twentieth centuries.

The turn-of-the-century financial statement requirements of the Canadian Province of Ontario constitute one of the earliest pieces of legislation in English-speaking countries to mandate shareholder disclosure of income statement and minimum balance sheet information for general commercial and manufacturing corporations. The background to this legislation exposes the complex and intermingled influences underlying this important event. Such influences as existing disclosure in regulated industries, an active and progressive-minded office of the Provincial Secretary in charge of Companies Act legislation, a political and economic environment that developed a tradition for government intervention and for federal-provincial jurisdictional disputes in commercial and industrial activities, an awareness and concern for recommended accounting changes in other countries, and a remarkably active and well-informed provincial association of accountants, the Institute of Chartered Accountants of Ontario (ICAO), all figured prominently in establishing the legislation.

The author appreciates the helpful comments of his colleagues, Professors V. B. Irvine, W. D. Lindsay, and T. Musser; the use of the libraries of the Ontario Archives, the Institute of Chartered Accountants of Ontario, and the Ontario Legislature; and the financial assistance of a Leave Fellowship Award from the Social Science and Humanities Research Council of Canada.

This study attempts to describe and assess influences which brought about this financial statement legislation. The evidence derives mainly from bills and statutes of provincial and federal jurisdictions, minutes of the ICAO, files of the office of the Provincial Secretary and corporate financial statements of the first decade of the twentieth century. The sequence of discussion relates to the legislation in question, the political and economic environment in Ontario that supported such legislation, the prominence of the ICAO, the activities of the office of the Provincial Secretary, the influence of the legislation including its impact on corporate financial statement reporting practices and lastly, some concluding comments.

Early Ontario Companies Acts Legislation

The Ontario Companies Act of 1907 is likely the most pathbreaking piece of corporate disclosure legislation in Canadian history.[1] According to its chief architect, Assistant Provincial Secretary Thomas Mulvey, the Act attempted to prevent stock promotional abuse, to consolidate the legislation relating to numerous commercial enterprises which had previously commanded individual legislation, and to incorporate some of the regulatory features of the optional First Schedule requirements of the English Companies Act of 1862.[2] Of particular importance were the compulsory requirements to file a prospectus, to engage an auditor, and to provide an income and expenditure statement and a detailed balance sheet to shareholders at the annual meeting.[3] The sections of the 1907 Act containing financial statement requirements for annual meetings are reproduced in Figure 1.

The requirement to present an income and expenditure statement at the annual general meeting was carried forward from the legislation of 1897.[4]

The Political and Economic Environment in Ontario

Though Canada, and particularly Ontario, inherited many of the traditions of Britain, the size, proximity, and power of the United States presented examples to be followed. In Canada, size, regionality, and ethnic differences (Quebec) pointed towards the adoption of a federal system of government as opposed to the unitary system of Britain. The provinces had powers relating to local concerns such as property, civil rights, civil law, education, provincial company charters, municipal government and direct taxation. The

Figure 1

Financial Statement Disclosure Requirements of the Ontario Companies Act, 1907. Selections from Section 36.

36 (2) At such meeting the directors shall lay before the company,

    (a) A balance sheet made up to a date not more than three months before such annual meeting;

    (b) A statement of income and expenditure for the financial period ending upon the date of such balance sheet;

    (c) The report of the auditor or auditors;

    (d) Such further information respecting the company's financial position as the Letters Patent or the by-laws of the company may require;

and, on resolution affirmed by shareholders holding at least five per centum of the capital of the company, shall furnish a copy thereof to every shareholder personally present at such meeting and demanding the same.

36 (3) The balance sheet shall be drawn up so as to distinguish at least the following classes of assets and liabilities, namely:

    (a) Cash;

    (b) Debts owing to the company from its customers;

    (c) Debts owing to the company from its directors, officers and shareholders;

    (d) Stock in trade;

    (e) Expenditures made on account of future business;

    (f) Land, buildings and plant;

    (g) Goodwill, franchises, patents and copyrights, trademarks, leases, contracts and licenses;

    (h) Debts owing by the company secured by mortgage or other lien upon the property of the company;

    (i) Debts owing by the company but not secured;

    *(k) Amount received on common shares;

    (l) Amount received on preferred shares;

    (m) Indirect and contingent liabilities.

    *No entry for (j) is given in the Act.

federal government retained control over foreign affairs, trade and commerce, currency, criminal law, indirect taxation, postal services, federal company charters, banking, railways, and navigation, as well as residual authority in matters not specifically allocated to the provinces. Mulvey acknowledged, in explanation of the background to the 1907 Act, that though "the courts were always under the influence of the English decisions . . . , Legislatures obtained their inspiration from the United States"—especially with regard to the chartering of companies by letters patent as opposed to the English method of registration and memoranda of association.[5]

The assignment of authority was such as to give rise to federal-provincial jurisdictional disputes, particularly, for our purposes, in matters relating to the chartering of companies and professional societies. The jurisdiction in which companies incorporated was of great concern to politicians and legislators, who were mindful lest they drive away corporate control from their domains.[6] Ontario's progressive interest in corporate regulation was constantly tempered by the considerable lag in time of comparable federal legislation.[7] Though incorporation fees for the Ontario and federal jurisdictions were kept competitively comparable,[8] government-required filing of Annual Returns (available to the public) relating to shareholders and directors, and their past and present addresses, callings and shareholdings, were initially much more onerous in Ontario.[9] By 1900 the Extra Provincial Corporation Act of Ontario required federally incorporated companies to comply with the Annual Return filing of the Ontario Companies Act.[10] Similarly, in the 1907 Act, Ontario attempted to make its mandatory prospectus provisions apply to all companies doing business in Ontario, whether incorporated there or not.[11] Some companies with purely local interests engaged in the "charter ploy" which meant that they would try to incorporate federally and avoid the harassment of uncooperative provincial legislatures.[12] Federal-provincial disputes over incorporation remained matters of continuing conflict in the first two decades of the century.[13]

Incorporation disputes spilled over into the accounting profession. Provincial incorporation of the ICAO in 1883 had granted what was felt to be exclusive right to the designation "Chartered Accountant."[14] However, members of the Dominion Association of Chartered Accountants (DACA), which had been federally incorporated in 1902,[15] began to use the same name. The cause of the ICAO was taken up by the Ontario legislature, ever willing to support provincial claims; but intended provincial legislation was "disallowed" by the federal powers.[16] It was not until 1909, after much legislative and professional jurisdictional wrangling, that membership in the DACA was restricted to, and became automatic for, members of provincial institutes of chartered accountants. An additional irritant to the Province of Ontario and the ICAO, during this period was the claim by English chartered accountants that colonial legislation (in regard to designation) could not apply to their members practising in Canada.[17]

The political and economic environment in Ontario prior to and at the turn of the century was both supportive of business and mindful of the social obligations that business must accept. The Ontario government has been characterized as one in which "the language of business, the methods of business, the concerns of business for economy and expertise were reflected in [its] policies. . . ."[18] This spirit coexisted with a host of mandatory public financial statement disclosure requirements for such regulated enterprises of public interest as utilities, municipalities, railroads, savings and loan associations and insurance companies.[19] In the latter part of this period, the Conservative government under the leadership of J. P. Whitney, and in the American "progressive" tradition, "reflected a recognition of the rise in the province of an urban industrial society"—a society in which government intervention and direction were to be expected.[20] The Companies Act of 1907 was accompanied by equally path-breaking legislation relating to mining, workmen's compensation, health and education, and most notably the formation of the controversial government-owned Hydro Electric Power Commission of Ontario. Business was scarcely in a position effectively to object to such intervention since as Bliss comments

> . . . for generations the Canadian Manufacturers' Association existed primarily to lobby for continued or increased tariff protection. No organization in Canada was so deeply opposed to free enterprize in business than the CMA. Because of its effectiveness in championing state intervention and in demonstrating to other groups how to follow its lead, the CMA did more than any other organization to encourage the development of collectivism in Canada. It was socialism's best friend in Canadian business.[21]

The amount of public disclosure of financial statements in the late nineteenth and early twentieth centuries was certainly considerable. That disclosure pertained not only to those companies that were by statute required to publish, but also to those companies of a commercial or manufacturing nature that were not. Despite concerns over revelations of reporting ambiguities issuing from the Royal Commission on Insurance,[22] the *Financial Post* in 1907 was able to pronounce that "nearly all the most important companies have adopted a straight-forward policy of publicity of earnings and condition."[23]

Following, in many instances, counterpart legislation in England, the interventionist hand of government had mandated certain public disclosure of the financial affairs of those companies deemed to be of general public or fiduciary interest. In Ontario by 1877, the operating returns of companies incorporated under the General Road Companies Act were required to be forwarded to the Municipal County Council.[24] Similar provisions required timber hauling companies to forward returns to the Commissioner of Public Works.[25] Gas- and waterwork companies were required to publish operating information and to have a statement of debts and liabilities available for inspection by shareholders and creditors.[26] Municipal institutions were required to appoint auditors, to have an abstract of receipts, expenses, assets, and liabilities open for inspection and published, and to file "a true account of all debts and liabilities to the Treasurer of Ontario" if there were outstanding loans.[27] Building societies were required to provide a "full and clear" statement of assets and liabilities to the Provincial Treasurer —abstracts of which were to be published by the latter.[28] Railways were required to forward "a true, exact and particular account of the money collected and received" to the Provincial Secretary[29] and insurance companies were required to provide a balance sheet and income statement in prescribed detail to the Provincial Treasurer.[30] Earlier, in 1873, mutual fire insurance companies were required to forward, under prescribed categories, detailed balance sheets and income statements to the Provincial Secretary and Registrar, a synopsis of which was to be published in the Ontario Gazette.[31] In 1892, insurance companies were required to have auditors[32] and by 1896 street railway[33] and electric railway[34] companies were obliged to forward detailed financial statements to the Provincial Secretary. Comparable counterpart legislation existed at the federal level for banks,[35] insurance[36] and railway companies.[37]

General practice among such regulated companies well before the turn of the century, was to publish or to have represented, their financial statements in such publications as *The Monetary Times* and *The Globe.* By the turn of the century, prospectuses were commonly published in such media[38] and easy access to the affairs of many of the nonregulated commercial and manufacturing enterprizes representing the bulk of such listings on the Toronto Stock Exchange was obtainable through annual anthologies of financial statements.[39] The publication of these anthologies was undertaken very likely with the support and sponsorship of the Toronto Stock Exchange, though early Exchange listing regulations of 1905 and 1912 required that "a full statement of the affairs of the company" be provided *only* at the time of the listing application.[40] Quite clearly a strong tradition for financial statement disclosure was in existence at the time of the 1907 Ontario Act

The Institute of Chartered Accountants of Ontario (ICAO)

The fact that the financial statement requirements of the 1907 Act were virtually written by the ICAO[41] is not surprising in light of that organization's tradition of spirited and informed membership. First organized in 1879,[42] the Institute's subsequent incorporating legislation of 1883 granted it a charter "as an intellectual and educational movement to raise the standard of accountancy" and required "the promotion . . . of knowledge, skill and proficiency of members of the Institute . . . and to these ends the establishment of classes, lectures and examinations and the prescription of such tests of competency, fitness and moral character. . . ."[43] It is likely that the Institute's remarkable vigor, prominence and authority were engendered by the organizational activity necessary to fulfill that educational mandate. Within ten to fifteen years of inception,[44] the Institute had established a tradition for regular meetings during the year, to which the public was invited and at which papers relating to accounting matters were delivered. In commenting on this tradition, the President of the ICAO acknowledged the importance of keeping the Institute before the eyes of the public and raising the standards of the profession.[45] Regulations were devised categorizing the various divisions of competency that were recognized, and periodic examinations were set to determine that competency. The highest level, "Fellowship," required a thesis to be prepared—the presentation of which became a tradition at one of the regular meetings.[46] By 1893, virtually all founding members had submitted to qualification of competency by examination.[47] The notice for the sitting of exams, questions and answers to exams, the proceedings of the annual meetings and the accounting papers delivered at regular meetings were commonly reported on, often at great length, in the financial press.[48] As early as 1893, the Institute sought out and accredited various colleges and schools that were able to provide sufficient accounting education to students to qualify for the introductory level of competency.[49] Yearbook publication began in 1896. Papers delivered at meetings were being published in professional journals;[50] reprints of the papers were frequently distributed among Ontario businessmen; and several attempts to begin a regular journal were discussed.[51] Efforts to establish a formal Institute library were finally successful in 1903.[52] Prior to that time, Institute committees regularly urged the Toronto Public Library to carry a wide range of accounting related books. The influence and concerns of the ICAO extended throughout Canada as it sought to initiate uniform examinations and standards for emerging Chartered Accountants Institutes in Manitoba and Nova Scotia.[53] A student society formed by the Institute[54] intensified the concern for lectures and the publication[55] of textbooks and examinations. An impressive list of texts authored by Institute members developed including

Canadian Accountant by S. G. Beatty and J. W. Johnson, 9th ed., 1892.

Canadian Standard Bookkeeping by J. W. Westervelt, 3rd ed., 1904.

Joint Stock Company Accounts by D. Hoskins, 3rd ed., 1907.

Joint Stock Company Bookkeeping by J. W. Johnson, 7th ed., 1884.

Municipal Accounting by F. H. Macpherson (exact dating not established).

Factory Cost Accounts by W. C. Eddis and W. B. Tindall, 3rd ed., 1904.

Manual for Accountants by W. C. Eddis, 1899.

Primary Accounting Manual by D. Hoskins (exact dating not established).

Expert Bookkeeping by C. A. Fleming, 1892.

Bookkeeping for Joint Stock Companies by D. Hoskins, 1901.

The Eddis and Tindall text has been singled out by Garner as being influential on American practice by dismissing "as being entirely inadequate the nonintegrated cost systems which had been advocated so strenuously by the English."[56] It is noteworthy that all of these authors except Fleming either attended, or sent letters to, the meeting at which the Institute presented its financial statement recommendations for the Ontario legislation. Quite clearly, Institute membership was sufficiently interested and independently well-informed to be able to advise provincial legislators on matters of financial statement disclosure. No reference exists in the minutes indicating knowledge or influence of the optional model financial statements of the 1862 English Companies Act.

The Institute's relations with the government were highly visible from the beginning. President Harmon, under whom incorporation was sought in 1883, was a former mayor and treasurer of the city of Toronto. Vice president Mason held similar offices in Hamilton and was related by marriage to J. M. Gibson, a subsequent Provincial Secretary and Lieutenant Governor of Ontario. The large public meeting of the Institute which preceded the petition for incorporation was held in the offices of the city of Toronto. The interaction with government was not only of a self-serving nature in which the Institute, usually unsuccessfully, sought a monopoly for its services in particular areas of legislative concern, but also of a broader professional nature. Recommendations were forwarded to the Provincial Secretary[57] relating to municipal accounting in 1888, to the federal Finance Minister[58] relating to the duties, certificate, and qualifications of bank auditors in 1890, and to the Secretary of State[59] relating to the Dominion Companies Act of 1902. A Legislative committee of the Institute Council was formed in 1895. Deputations to the Provincial Cabinet with regard to qualifications of auditors doing municipal work successfully obtained mention in the legislation of institute members' qualifications.[60] Meetings at the federal level with the Minister of Finance in 1897 were concerned with the formation of an inter-provincial Dominion accounting association and with uniformity in the handling of bankruptcies.[61] Institute standards (through their qualifying examinations) were recommended for all public accountants by the financial press.[62] In the face of the federal government's incorporation of the Dominion Association of Chartered Accountants, the provincial government's jurisdictional concerns were also served as it responded positively to the Institute's lobby to restrict the C.A. (chartered accountant) designation to members of the ICAO.[63] The appointment of an American auditor to perform some investigatory work for the Provincial government invited an enormous amount of Institute-organized resistance and embarrassing publicity for the Government in the press.[64]

The first draft bill leading to the 1907 legislation included the ICAO recommendations which had been made almost a year previous at the specific request of the Provincial Secretary.[65] The latter, together with his Assistant, attended a special Institute meeting to hear members' comments on the legislation.[66] The Provincial Secretary, his Assistant and the former Provincial Secretary were all awarded honorary Fellowships in the Institute, as was the editor of Canada's leading financial newspaper *The Monetary Times.*

The chief source of strength in the ICAO at the turn of the century was certainly Canadian in its origin. The guiding spirit in the Institute at this time was George Edwards, whose father was an Ontario government civil servant. The Institute was always mindful of the somewhat more lengthy traditions of public accounting in England and of the English legislation relating to matters of accounting and auditing, but the Institute minutes betray little "mother-country" influence beyond that. English Chartered Accountants could become members of the ICAO upon application (a privilege that was reciprocated!) but they came to Canada as individuals, not as members of English accounting firms who would set up international branches. The split between native and English influence that Merino indicates existed in America up to 1905,[67] seemed to have no counterpart in the ICAO's history.

In America, the Report of the Industrial Commission had held back from recommending mandatory company audits because of a concern for the ability of the public accounting profession to respond.[68] No such reservations were entertained in the considerations leading up to the mandatory audit provisions of the 1907 Ontario Act. Nor were Institute members unassuming in their feelings of prominence. In 1902, the President proclaimed the ICAO as being "the leading and recognized head of the accounting profession on the continent."[69] In 1907, after returning from meetings of the American Association of Public Accountants, the President with similar modesty stated at the annual general meeting that he was "pleased to report in point of excellence of work and results the Ontario Institute is certainly far in advance of any of the State Associations."[70] Edwards proclaimed, in *The Monetary Times,* that the Ontario Institute's standards . . . were higher than those of any other in Canada or the United States."[71] It may be observed that from 1894 to 1910, Institute membership grew from 78 to 130.

Background to the 1907 Act and the Efforts of the Office of the Provincial Secretary

Prior to the 1907 legislation in Ontario, the public's legal right to information about the financial affairs of commercial and manufacturing companies was limited to access to the company Annual Returns that were required to be filed with the Provincial Secretary and which contained summary information about the capital stock and detailed information concerning the names, addresses, occupation, and shareholdings of each shareholder and director. The books of the company filing such information were also open for the inspection of creditors and shareholders. Court-approved inspections and optional audit requirements accompanied these provisions, together with the requirement for directors to present an income and expenditure statement at the annual general meeting. The foregoing procedures were embodied in the 1897 Ontario Companies Act. By 1907 however, the legislative emphasis had shifted markedly from providing information about the capital stock, directors, and shareholders, to furnishing investors with a prospectus, and shareholders with audited, detailed information about the results of the directors' handling of the company's operations. An investor point of view inspired much of the legislation. The creation of "private companies" was the device which legislators used to allow small, closely-held corporations to avoid filing a prospectus.

The office of the Provincial Secretary was an active source of proposals for legislative control over corporations. The 1897 Ontario Companies Act was preceded by an intensive investigation of the corporate legislation of other countries and of several American States.[72] The office was therefore aware of the extremely progressive draft legislation of the state of Victoria in Australia and of the English Davey Committee Report.[73] The first reading of the Bill[74] preliminary to the 1897 legislation contained the mandatory provisions for audit and detailed financial statements to shareholders in the optional form prescribed by Table A of the First Schedule of the 1862 English Companies Act (Figure 2 shows the form of Balance Sheet); however concern lest such provisions prove too onerous for small companies prompted withdrawal of these provisions.[75] Only the requirement to supply an income and expenditure statement to the annual meeting remained in the Act.

An employee of the office of the Provincial Secretary, J. D. Warde, was the author through at least seven editions (1884-1907) of *The Shareholders' and Directors' Manual*. This text,[76] dedicated to the Provincial Secretary and acknowledging the helpful reviews of the Assistant Provincial Secretary, Thomas Mulvey, and one of the most prominent ICAO members, George Edwards, recommended full disclosure in matters of financial statement presentation and put forward as a model of disclosure the balance sheet prescribed by Table A. Legislators' comments at the federal level in support of an unsuccessful 1894 Companies Bill incorporating broad disclosure provisions argued for the public right to greater

Figure 2

Balance Sheet Optional Requirements of Table A of the First Schedule of the English Companies Act of 1862.

C.89.   25° & 26° VICTORIÆ.   A.D.1862.

Companies, &c.   (First Schedule.)

Balance sheet table from the First Schedule of the English Companies Act of 1862, Dr. (Capital and Liabilities) and Cr. (Property and Assets) sides.

Dr. — BALANCE SHEET of the ... CAPITAL AND LIABILITIES.

I. CAPITAL.
Showing:
1. The Number of Shares
2. The Amount paid per Share
3. If any Arrears of Calls, the Nature of the Arrear, and the Names of the Defaulters.
4. The Particulars of any forfeited Shares

II. DEBTS AND LIABILITIES of the Company.
Showing:
5. The Amount of Loans on Mortgage or Debenture Bonds.
6. The Amount of Debts owing by the Company, distinguishing—
(a.) Debts for which Acceptances have been given.
(b.) Debts to Tradesmen for Supplies of Stock in Trade or other Articles.
(c.) Debts for Law Expenses.
(d.) Debts for Interest on Debentures or other Loans.
(e.) Unclaimed Dividends.
(f.) Debts not enumerated above.

VI. RESERVE FUND.
Showing:
The Amount set aside from Profits to meet Contingencies.

VII. PROFIT AND LOSS.
Showing:
The disposable Balance for Payment of Dividend, &c.

CONTINGENT LIABILITIES.
Claims against the Company not acknowledged as Debts. Monies for which the Company is contingently liable.

Cr. — Co. made up to ... 18 ... PROPERTY AND ASSETS.

III. PROPERTY held by the Company.
Showing:
7. Immovable Property, distinguishing—
(a.) Freehold Land -
(b.) " Buildings -
(c.) Leasehold "
8. Movable Property, distinguishing—
(d.) Stock in Trade -
(e.) Plant
The Cost to be stated with Deductions for Deterioration in Value as charged to the Reserve Fund or Profit and Loss.

IV. DEBTS owing to the Company.
Showing:
9. Debts considered good for which the Company hold Bills or other Securities.
10. Debts considered good for which the Company hold no Security.
11. Debts considered doubtful and bad. Any Debt due from a Director or other Officer of the Company to be separately stated.

V. CASH AND INVESTMENTS.
Showing:
12. The Nature of Investment and Rate of Interest.
13. The Amount of Cash, where lodged, and if bearing Interest.

172

knowledge of the financial affairs of large commercial and manufacturing endeavors.[77]

The appointment of T. Mulvey as Assistant Provincial Secretary in 1904 was followed by the election of J. P. Whitney's Conservative government and appointment of W. J. Hanna as Provincial Secretary. Hanna, a prominent businessman, and particularly Mulvey, the scholarly and progressive minded civil servant, were the moving forces behind the 1907 Act. Under their directions, draft legislation was circulated to many interested parties in 1906 and 1907, and many hearings and much correspondence with the office of the Provincial Secretary preceded enactment in 1907. Possibly because of the carefully orchestrated, widespread discussion of the legislation, the bulk of the evidence in the files of the Provincial Secretary in the Ontario Archives is generally supportive.

The moving spirit behind the legislation was largely Mulvey, whose concern for greater information for the investing public oftentimes ran counter to the prevailing business sentiments for corporate secrecy at a time when the promotion of stock without prospectus information was not uncommon. Mulvey was particularly concerned with stock promotion abuses and his main attention and enthusiasm in the legislation centered on the mandatory prospectus requirements and on the stock allotment provisions that would inhibit the prevalent practice of stock watering. The bulk of the correspondence in the Provincial Secretary's files was similarly directed. The financial statement disclosure requirements, while fitting in with Mulvey's general theme for the provision of increased information, were not the thrust of the legislation and it may well be that these annual reporting requirements (because of their complementary nature) rode along on the coattails of the provisions directed at stock promotion abuse.[78]

With regard to mandatory prospectuses, Mulvey stated "we have no desire to drive people away from incorporating under our Act, but it is far better to let scalliwags go elsewhere than to allow them to do as they please under the Ontario laws."[79] Though a marginal note on an internal copy of draft legislation in the files of the Provincial Secretary[80] indicated that some American States had equivalent financial statement disclosure requirements, no specific references to such legislation were otherwise available nor could any other reference to American influence be found in the files of the Provincial Secretary, in the voluminous public writings of Mulvey or in the financial press. (Horack,[81] Kuhn,[82] and Sterrett[83] all emphasize the ineffectiveness of whatever little American annual reporting requirements were then extant.) The legislative mould was the Companies Acts of England, but Mulvey improved on them most notably by ensuring that companies could not avoid the prospectus provisions and by requiring an income and expenditure statement and a detailed balance sheet. For the financial statement disclosure requirements, he accepted without change the recommendations of the ICAO. The Act itself was consistent with the legislative pattern of the progressive-minded Whitney government.

The Impact of the Legislation

Some tentative comments are possible with regard to the effect on corporate reporting practices of this legislation in 1907. The *Annual Financial Review—Canadian* requested corporations to forward information on their financial affairs for publication in its annual anthology. The vast majority of those commercial and manufacturing companies whose stocks were listed on the Toronto Stock Exchange forwarded their financial statements and/or information from the Annual Returns required by the Provincial Secretary or the federal Secretary of State.[84] Of companies in the anthology incorporated in Ontario, only one of five in 1905 did not provide financial statements and by 1910 all twenty-one were doing so. Of federal or other-province companies, where mandatory provision of financial statements to shareholders did not exist, nine of seventeen did not provide financial statements in 1905 and by 1910, only seven of thirty-four were not doing so. A subjective review by the author of the amount of information disclosed in the commercial and manufacturing financial statements indicated only a marginal improvement in 1910 statements over those of 1905. In both years these statements, while in some instances aggregating accounts that were required to be distinguished, usually contained more information than the 1907 legislation required.

The legislation—though little concern is apparent in the files of the Provincial Secretary!—also covered mining companies. Evidence with regard to the impact on disclosure of these financial statements is more forceful in demonstrating the impact of the legislation. In 1906 immediately prior to the 1907 legislation, seventeen of twenty-eight companies listed in the *Annual Financial Review—Canadian* did not disclose their financial statements; in 1908 all but four of thirty-five disclosed. Related provincial mining company legislation is somewhat perplexing. The Supplementary Revenue Act[85] of 1907 required that mining companies pay a 3% tax on income in excess of $10,000. However neither this statute nor the later consolidation statute of 1914, though they painstakingly set forth the expenses which were to be regarded as valid deductions in arriving at taxable income, made any reference to the required minimum and audited format of the 1907 companies act legislation—format which it would seem would have been complementary to the purposes of the revenue act.

The number of firms voluntarily disclosing at the provincial level prior to 1907 and at the federal level prior to 1910 was considerable. The example of mandatory disclosure of regulated corporations (England had much the same required disclosure for regulated firms), the concern for financing from the investing public, the likely encouragement of the Toronto Stock Exchange and the moral suasion certainly of the office of the Provincial Secretary and possibly of some of the members of the ICAO may in varying degrees have been influential.[86] No provisions existed at the federal or provincial level for the imposition of income taxes prior to 1907. The infrequent requirement to pay income taxes at the municipal level prior to 1907 likely did not occasion the filing of financial statements which would have been available to the public.[87]

The response in the financial press to the financial statement provisions of the 1907 legislation was not unexpectedly silent, since the legislation had been openly discussed for the previous one and one-half years. The legislation was not attributed to any grand corporate scandals proceeding from financial statement inadequacies; and the tradition for legislated mandatory disclosure in the many regulated areas of enterprise together with voluntary disclosure by nonregulated companies, may have made the absence of such legislation for commercial and manufacturing firms appear anachronistic.

The Ontario legislation served as a model for other provinces. The federal government itself in 1917 enacted identical disclosure legislation and acknowledged its debt to Ontario in this regard.[88] In 1909 Mulvey became the Under Secretary of State of the federal government and once again (possibly with support from George Edwards, who had been brought to Ottawa by the federal government during World War I) was the initiating spirit in the office of the Secretary of State for this legislation at that level.[89] In the first two decades of the century, governments and bureaucracies were sufficiently small or nonlabyrinthine that the strong leadership of an individual could make a difference.

Concluding Comments

The 1907 Ontario legislation is significant in the evolution of corporate disclosure because it is one of the earliest statutes in the English-speaking world to make detailed financial statements mandatory for commercial and manufacturing companies, and also because it is one of the earliest occasions on which an accounting organization has demonstrated its influence on disclosure legislation. The varied and complementary circumstances under which these financial statement provisions took place are instructive.

Prior to the legislation, voluntary disclosure of such information for these companies had been regarded as uniformly good. Similarly, there existed a long-standing legislative tradition for required disclosure among those regulated enterprises having a public or fiduciary interest. The general demand for change was therefore directed towards the various needs which a mandatory prospectus would satisfy. Required financial statement disclosure rode along on the coattails of the rationalizing of numerous incorporating statutes, of the concern for stock promotional abuse and of the general movement to greater societal control of corporate operations. It was the concern for the investing public that particularly informed the mind of the chief government proponent of the legislation, Thomas Mulvey. The Act, in total, was consistent with the reforming spirit of the Whitney government.

Though Mulvey copied much of the prospectus legislation from England, for financial statement disclosure purposes he bypassed the recommendations of the Davey Committee and the provisions of the English Companies Act of 1900 and sought out the aid of the well regarded and highly visible ICAO. The Institute, with its lengthy record of competence engendered by a mandated, onerous, and well publicized involvement in education, was sufficiently confident in its own abilities to propose disclosure unique to legislation at that time. The record of achievement of the ICAO for the period from 1880 to the legislation of 1907 invites comparison with other accounting institutes for those years.

FOOTNOTES

[1] Ontario, Statutes, (1907).

[2] Mulvey, (1907), pp. 81-82; and Ontario Archives, correspondence of T. Mulvey with G. Staunton, February 20, 1907.

[3] Ontario, Statutes, (1907), Secs. 97, 123 and 36 respectively. The mandatory audit provisions followed the English Act of 1900, but the Ontario requirements for an income statement and a detailed balance sheet predated English concern by a full three and two decades respectively.

[4] Ontario, Statutes, (1897), Sec. 75.

[5] Mulvey, (1918), p. 129.

[6] Ontario Archives, correspondence of T. Mulvey with G. Staunton, February 20, 1907.

[7]Federal legislation equivalent to the Ontario Act of 1907 followed only a full decade later in 1917.

[8]Canada, Canada Gazette, (June 21, 1902); and Ontario Sessional Paper No. 33.

[9]MacInnes, (1900), p. 4.

[10]Ontario, Statutes, (1900), Sec. 12.

[11]Ontario, Statutes, (1907), Sec. 95(2).

[12]Armstrong and Nelles, (1973), p. 164.

[13]Mulvey, (1918), pp. 124-39.

[14]Ontario, Statutes, (1883), Sec. 2.

[15]Canada, Statutes, (1902).

[16]ICAO, Minutes, (February 15, 1902, July 19, 1907, Dec. 27, 1907, and Minutes of Annual General Meeting July 18, 1908).

[17]Edwards, (1910), p. 283.

[18]Brown and Cook, (1974), p. 86.

[19]See references to statutes following.

[20]Humphries, (1966), pp. 500. A certain government hostility to corporate abuses and power was also evident: see Humphries, (1966), p. 272 and Bliss, (1982), p. 5.

[21]Bliss, (1980), p. 130.

[22]Canada, Royal Commission on Life Insurance, (1907).

[23]*The Financial Post*, (February 16, 1907), p. 1.

[24]Ontario, Statutes, (1877), ch. 152, sec. 146.

[25]Ontario, Statutes, (1877), ch. 153, sec. 27.

[26]Ontario, Statutes, (1877), ch. 157, secs. 22, 32 and 33.

[27]Ontario, Statutes, (1877), ch. 174, secs. 254-257 and 363.

[28]Ontario, Statutes, (1877), ch. 164, secs. 67-68.

[29]Ontario, Statutes, (1877), ch. 155, secs. 26, 36.

[30]Ontario, Statutes, (1877), ch. 160, secs. 26-27 and Schedule B.

[31]Ontario, Statutes, (1873), ch. 44, sec. 72.

[32]Ontario, Statutes, (1892), ch. 39, sec. 29.

[33]Ontario, Statutes, (1896), ch. 50, sec. 16.

[34]Ontario, Statutes, (1895), ch. 38, Schedule C.

[35]Canada, Statutes, (1886), ch. 120, secs. 24, 66 and Schedule B.

[36]Canada, Statutes, (1886), ch. 45, sec. 19 and Form A.

[37]Canada, Statutes, (1888), ch. 29, sec. 299 and Schedule One.

[38]See for example *The Monetary Times* (January 11, 1901), pp. 898-900 and (February 22, 1901), p. 1108.

[39]See various issues of *The Annual Financial Review—Canadian* from 1901 to 1941..

[40]Toronto Stock Exchange Bylaws, Rule 26 of 1905 and 1912. A long time employee of the Exchange, L. Lowe confirmed in conversation with the author the close and complementary relationship between the Exchange and the publisher W. R. Houston and supported the implication that the Exchange had no specific regulation with regard to the disclosure of annual financial statements at the turn of the century. Houston maintained his offices with one of the member firms of the Exchange and subsequently in the Exchange building itself; for much of the 1920s and 1930s, he was the Assistant Secretary of the Exchange.

[41]ICAO, Minutes, Figure 1 is almost identical with the recommendations of February 8, 1906.

[42]ICAO, Minutes, (November 11, 1879).

[43]Statutes, Ontario, (1883), Preamble and Sec. 2.

[44]ICAO, Minutes (1885-1900). See also Edwards (1909), pp. 1984 and 2038.

[45]ICAO, Minutes, (July 19, 1901).

[46]ICAO, Minutes, April 1894. (Exact date not given.)

[47]Edwards, (1915), p. 336.

[48]For example ICAO, Minutes (March 22, 1881; November 4, 1885; November 25, 1886; April 19, 1888).

[49]ICAO, Minutes, March 20, 1893 and February 28, 1895. By 1895 affiliation was established with Northern Business College, Upper Canada College and The Ontario Business College.

[50]See four articles by ICAO members A. C. Neff, W. T. Kernahan, and W. C. Eddis in January, February and March issues, 1899, of *Accountics.*

[51]ICAO, Minutes (October 6, 1885, March 21, 1889, June 20, 1893, November 23, 1906, July 19, 1907). Concern expressed for publishing "Questions and Answers" to Institute exams (March 26, 1891).

[52]ICAO, Minutes (October 22, 1885, February 21, 1893, July 17, 1903).

[53]ICAO, Minutes (July 15, 1904).

[54]ICAO, Minutes (January 4, 1900).

[55]ICAO, Minutes (October 4, 1893).

[56]Garner (1954), pp. 266-267.

[57]ICAO, Minutes (April 19, 1888).

[58]ICAO, Minutes (March 21, 1890).

[59]Ontario, Archives RG8 1-1-D, File 3240.

[60]ICAO, Minutes (April 9, 1897).

[61]ICAO, Minutes (March 19, 1897).

[62]*The Monetary Times* (Sept. 14, 1900), p. 841.

[63]Ontario, Statutes (1908), Sec. 13. This Act was disallowed at the federal level.

[64]ICAO, Minutes (April 14, 1905).

[65]ICAO, Minutes (February 8, 1906), and Ontario, Bill 101, Sec. 35.

[66]ICAO, Minutes (January 18, 1907).

[67]Merino (1975), pp. 145-154.

[68]Merino (1975), p. 285.

[69]ICAO, Minutes (July 18, 1902).

[70]ICAO, Minutes (July 19, 1907).

[71]*The Monetary Times* (May 15, 1909), p. 2038.

[72]Ontario, Archives, RG8 1-1-D, Files 1822, 3640-49.

[73]The Victoria legislation was revised in 1910 to bring it into conformity with English law, Gibson (1979), p. 33. Corporate legislation of the province of British Columbia in 1904 mandated a detailed income and expenditure statement and the balance sheet detail of Table A of the First Schedule of the English Companies Act of 1862, but rescinded these requirements in 1910 to conform to the disclosure requirements of the English Companies Act of 1900.

[74]Ontario, Bill 74, Secs. 60-61.

[75]Ontario, Archives, RG8 1-1-D. An internal memo of January 30, 1902 from G. E. Lumsden, the Assistant Provincial Secretary to J. R. Stratton, the Provincial Secretary, indicated that these provisions would "work a hardship" on small or close corporations.

[76]Warde (1900), pp. iii-vi, 262, 339.

[77]Canada, Senate Debates (June 13, 1894), pp. 523-524.

[78]Note that the first draft bill to amend the Companies Act in 1905 pertained only to the prospectus provisions. This Bill was deferred and later incorporated in the 1907 legislation. Ontario, Bill 100 (1905).

[79]Ontario, Archives, RG 8 1-1-D. Letter of Mulvey to G. L. Staunton, February 20, 1907.

[80]Ontario, Archives, RG8 1-1-B-1, Box 3.

[81]Horack (1903), pp. 83-86.

[82]Kuhn (1912), pp. 144-146.

[83]Sterrett (1910), pp. 242-243.

[84]Checked for the years 1900 (11 of 13) and 1905 (17 of 19) to the Exchange listings in *The Monetary Times* and for 1911 (75 of 77) to *The Globe.*

[85]Ontario, Statutes (1907), Sec. 6.

[86]Recent interest in voluntary disclosure provides interesting hypotheses. See Mumford (1982), Watts and Zimmerman (1979), Morris (1979) and Ma and Morris (1981).

[87]An enquiry of the City of Toronto Archives provided correspondence (July 12, 1982) which indicates that in 1905 and 1906 the only taxes exacted by the municipality of Toronto were personal.

[88]Canada, Statutes (1917), Sec. 105, and Mulvey (1920), p. 54.

[89]Mulvey as the then federal Under Secretary of State, spoke to legislation at the hearings of the Senate Standing Committee on Banking and Finance, July-August, 1917.

BIBLIOGRAPHY

Accountics. New York: The Accountics Association.

Armstrong, C. and Nelles, H. W. "Private Property in Peril: Ontario Businessmen and the Federal System, 1898-1911." *Business History Review,* Vol. 47 (Summer 1973), pp. 158-176.

Bliss, M. "Singing the Subsidy Blues." *Canadian Business* (September, 1980), pp. 128-132.

——————————————. "Canada in 1907." *The Financial Post* (January 16, 1982), pp. 5-6.

Brown, R. C. and Cook, R. *Canada 1896-1921: A Nation Transformed.* Toronto: McLelland & Stewart, 1974.

Canada, *Canada Gazette.* Dominion of Canada.

Canada, *Royal Commission on Life Insurance,* 1907. Ottawa: King's Printer, 1907.

Canada, *Senate Debates.*

Canada, Statutes. Revised 1886. *The Bank Act.* 49 Vict., ch. 120.

Canada, Statutes. Revised 1886. *The Insurance Act.* 49 Vict., ch. 45.

Canada, Statutes. *The Railway Act,* 1888. 51 Vict., ch. 29.

Canada, Statutes. *An Act to Incorporate the Dominion Association of Chartered Accountants,* 1902. 2 Edward VII, ch. 58.

Canada, Statutes. *The Companies Act Amendment Act,* 1917. 8 Geo. V, ch. 25.

Edwards, G. "Chartered Accountants in Canada." *The Monetary Times,* 1909.

Edwards, G. "Organization—Its Objects and their Attainment." *Journal of Accountancy,* Vol. 10 (August 1910), pp. 275-285.

Edwards, G. "Accountancy in Canada." *Journal of Accountancy,* Vol. 20 (November 1915), pp. 334-347.

Garner, S. Paul. *Evolution of Cost Accounting to 1925.* University, Alabama: University of Alabama Press, 1954.

Gibson, R. W. "Development of Corporate Accounting in Australia." *The Accounting Historians Journal,* Vol. 6 (Fall 1979), pp. 23-38.

Horack, F. E. *The Organization and Control of Industrial Corporations.* Philadelphia: C. F. Taylor, 1903.

Humphries, C. W. "The Political Career of Sir James P. Whitney." Unpublished doctoral thesis, University of Toronto, 1966.

ICAO (Institute of Chartered Accountants of Ontario). Minutes. 1879–1910.

Kuhn, A. K. *A Comparative Study of the Law of Corporations.* New York: Columbia University, 1912.

Ma, Ronald and Morris, Richard, "Disclosure and Bonding Practices of British and Australian Banks in the Nineteenth Century," Paper, University of New South Wales, 1981.

MacInnes, C. "A Dominion or Ontario Charter?" *Canada Law Journal,* Vol. 36 (January 1900), pp. 3–6.

Merino, B. D. "The Professionalization of Public Accounting in America: A Comparative Analysis of the Contributions of Selected Practitioners 1900-1905." Unpublished doctoral thesis, University of Alabama, 1975.

Morris, Richard, "Corporate Disclosure in a Substantially Unregulated Environment: New South Wales During the Nineteenth Century," Working Paper, School of Accountancy University of N.S.W., June 1979.

Mulvey, T. "Company Law in Ontario." *Canada Law Journal,* (February, 1907), pp. 81–85.

_____. "The Companies Act." *The Canadian Chartered Accountant,* Vol. 8 (October 1918), pp. 124–141.

_____. *Dominion Company Law.* Toronto: The Ontario Publishing Co., 1920.

Mumford, M. J. *Towards a Theory of Corporate Disclosure.* Lancaster Accounting and Finance Working Paper Series No. 17, 1982.

Ontario Archives. Files of the Provincial Secretary.

Ontario. Bill 74. *An Act Respecting the Incorporation and Regulation of Joint Stock Companies.* First Reading (February 19, 1897).

Ontario. Bill 100. *An Act to Amend the Ontario Companies Act.* First Reading, March 30, 1905.

Ontario. Bill 101. *An Act Respecting Joint Stock and Other Companies.* First Reading January 28, 1907.

Ontario. *Sessional Papers.* Report of the Secretary and Registrar of the Province for the Year 1899.

Ontario. Statutes. *Mutual Fire Insurance Company Act,* 1873. 36 Vict., ch. 44.

Ontario. Statutes. Revised 1877. *The General Road Companies Act.* 40 Vict., ch. 152.

Ontario. Statutes. Revised 1877. *Joint Stock Companies for Transmission of Timber Act.* 40 Vict., ch. 153.

Ontario. Statutes. Revised 1877. *An Act Respecting Joint Stock Companies Supplying Cities, Towns and Villages with Gas and Water.* 40 Vict., ch. 157.

Ontario. Statutes. Revised 1877. *An Act Respecting Insurance Companies.* 40 Vict., ch. 160.

Ontario. Statutes. Revised 1877. *An Act Respecting Building Societies.* 40 Vict., ch. 164.

Ontario. Statutes. Revised 1877. *The Railway Act of Ontario.* 40 Vict., ch. 165.

Ontario. Statutes. Revised 1877. *An Act Respecting Municipal Institutions.* 40 Vict., ch. 174.

Ontario. Statutes. *An Act to Incorporate the Institute of Accountants of Ontario,* 1883. 46 Vict., ch. 64.

Ontario. Statutes. *The Insurance Companies Act,* 1892. 55 Vict., ch. 39.

Ontario. Statutes. *The Electric Railway Act,* 1896. 59 Vict., ch. 38.

Ontario. Statutes. *The Street Railway Act,* 1896. 59 Vict., ch. 50.

Ontario. Statutes. *The Ontario Companies Act,* 1897. 60 Vict., ch. 28.

Ontario. Statutes. *An Act Respecting the Licensing of Extra-Provincial Corporations*, 1900. 63 Vict., ch. 24.

Ontario. Statutes. *The Supplementary Revenue Act*, 1907. 7 Edw., ch. 9.

Ontario. Statutes. *The Ontario Companies Act*, 1907. 7 Edward VII, ch. 34.

Ontario. Statutes. *An Act to Incorporate the Institute of Chartered Accountants of Ontario*, 1908. 8 Edw. VII, ch. 42.

Sterrett, J. E. "Legislation for the Control of Corporations." *Journal of Accountancy*, Vol. 9 (February 1910), pp. 241-247.

The Annual Financial Review—Canadian. Toronto: Houston's Standard Publications, 1901-1941..

The Financial Post. Toronto.

The Globe. Toronto.

The Monetary Times. Toronto.

Toronto Stock Exchange. *Minutes and Bylaws*. Toronto.

Warde, J. D. *The Shareholders' and Directors' Manual*, 6th ed., 1900. Toronto: The Canadian Railway News Co. Limited.

Watts, R. L. and Zimmerman, J. L. "The Demand for and Supply of Accounting Theories: The Market for Excuses." *The Accounting Review*, Vol. 54 (April 1979), pp. 273-305.

The impact of competition among occupational segments on the professionalization of the occupation is examined with data on the evolution of accountancy in Canada. It is shown that intraprofessional competition is an important factor directing and pacing the professionalizaton of accountancy defined in terms of educational standards, the symbolic attributes of professionalism, and achievement of occupational licensing. An analytic typology of professional segmentation is developed to locate the present study with respect to studies of segmentation in medicine, law, and engineering.

Professionalization and Intraprofessional Competition in the Canadian Accounting Profession

ALAN J. RICHARDSON
Queen's University

This article explores the intersection of two developments in the sociology of the professions. The first development is the empirical observation, following Bucher and Strauss (1961), that the professionals are segmented occupations, each segment holding different values and attempting to enact a distinct professional identity. This perspective emphasizes the process of interaction among segments of the profession as each segment attempts to maintain its identity and establish its domain (Barber, 1965; Gilb, 1966; Freidson, 1976; Armstrong, 1979).

The second development is the conceptualization of "profession" as a culturally and historically specific form of occupational control (Johnson, 1972; Friedson, 1983). It is thus claimed that the parameters of

Author's Note: *The author gratefully acknowledges the support of the School of Business and the School of Graduate Studies and Research, Queen's University, and the Department of Accounting and Center for the Advancement of Professional Accounting Education, University of Alberta, and a SSHRC Doctoral Fellowship.*

WORK AND OCCUPATIONS, Vol. 14 No. 4, November 1987 591-615
© 1987 Sage Publications, Inc.

591

professionalism, that is, the attributes of an occupation necessary to sustain and legitimate a claim to professional status, can be understood only by examining the dialectic relationship between the professionalization of an occupation and the social structures and processes in which that occupation is embedded (Johnson, 1977; Huer, 1980; Larson, 1977). The attainment of professional status within this perspective involves the skilled production of social imagery and ongoing negotiation of occupational privilege (Portwood and Fielding, 1981).

At the intersection of these extensions to traditional perspectives on professionalization is the proposition that the interaction of occupational segments is an important aspect of the "internal dynamic" (Klegon, 1978) that motivates the professionalization of an occupation and simultaneously defines the nature of professionalism in that occupation. That proposition is explored in this article with data—drawn from professional journals, commissioned histories, internal documents, and interviews—on the evolution of the Canadian accounting profession.[1]

This article begins by developing a typology of professional segmentation in order to locate the present study with respect to other studies of the phenomenon. This allows the generality of observations on accountancy to be bounded subject to further empirical work. The article will then document the extent and focus of competition within accountancy and, finally, examine the effect of this competition on the professionalization of accountancy in terms of the development of educational standards and symbolic attributes, and the achievement of occupational licensing.

THE NATURE OF
PROFESSIONAL SEGMENTATION

Professional segmentation is not a unitary phenomenon. For example, in accountancy, segments have been identified by common material interests (Siegel, 1977; Montagna, 1974: 159-160), values (Rosenberg et al., 1982; Hastings and Hinings, 1970), or tasks (Johnson, 1977; Montagna, 1974: 175-179), and by the existence of district professional associations (Johnson and Caygill, 1971; Carr-Saunders and Wilson, 1933). Similarly, in medicine, segments have been defined by the location and focus of practice (Armstrong, 1979), the existence of shared goals for reform (Perrucci, 1973), and modes of treatment (Starr, 1982; Bucher and Strauss, 1961).

These empirical definitions of segmentation reflect two dimensions of the phenomenon: the range of bases over which segmentation may occur, and the relationships among segments. These dimensions may be combined, as in Figure 1, to identify categories of professional segments. It is argued below that the consequences of segmentation for practitioners and the professions vary over these categories.

The bases of segmentation that are most often identified are status and task. Child and Fulk (1982: 180), for example, following Sorokin (1947), identify these as the bases of "vertical" and "horizontal" segmentation, respectively, within the five professions they examined (see Freidson, 1986: 211). The relationships among segments may be dichotomized as those segments within an association (subsidiary segments) and those that exist as independent associations (independent segments). This dimension of segmentation reflects a continuing concern within sociology over the organization of the professions (Turner and Hodge, 1970: 31-33) and is consistent with the importance attributed to the "consolidation" of a profession (Gilb, 1966; Larson, 1977; Powell, 1979).

Typically, more than one type of segmentation will be found within a profession. For example, in the British legal profession, both independent segments (e.g., the Law Society and British Legal Association) and subsidiary segments (e.g., the salaried solicitors' and local government groups within the Law Society) exist (Podmore, 1980). Empirically, however, the relative importance of each category has varied depending on the stage in the profession's history and the strategies adopted by different segments to advance their interests.

The early history of the English medical profession, for example, was dominated by the interaction of independent task segments, represented by the physicians', surgeons', and apothecaries' guilds. As each guild developed expertise and aspirations in the same areas of practice, these tasks distinctions broke down and status considerations predominated. The formation of the British Medical Association in 1856 and the General Medical Council in 1858 internalized this status hierarchy within a single professional body. The recent history of the profession indicates the growing importance of subsidiary task segments (Stevens, 1971; Portwood and Fielding, 1981; Armstrong, 1979).

The type of segmentation that predominates will shape the issues

| | | Relationship Among Segments | |
		Subsidiary	Independent
Bases of Segmentation	Status	e.g. Medicine/Law (historically)	e.g. Accounting
	Task	e.g. Medicine (recently)	e.g. Engineering

Figure 1: An Analytic Typology of Professional Segmentation

facing a profession and, arguably, the course of professionalization. The existing literature suggests some general effects of segmentation, but no attempt has been made to detail these effects or to link them to particular types of segmentation. The case study reported in this article examines one type of segmentation, but tentative descriptions of behavior in each quadrant of the typology will be presented. Differences among types of segments may be seen in the degree of career mobility available to practitioners; the degree of dependency among segments and, consequently, the extent to which practitioners can be expected to conform to dominant values; and the likely form and focus of interactions among segments.

The most-often-identified segments are status segments within existing associations (subsidiary-status segments). In these cases, the structure of a profession—its ethics, mission, technologies, and public image—is defined by the elite segments (Smith, 1958; Larson, 1977). Lower-status segments are presumed to accept this situation because membership in the association aids in competition with other occupations and a potential career path exists through the institutions that support the status hierarchy (Larson, 1977; Podmore, 1980; Paterson, 1983). They may also be subject to censure or expulsion should they oppose the objectives of dominant segments and, in any case, are socialized to accept those standards as legitimate (Larson, 1977). Rothman (1979) summarizes these effects by suggesting that conformity is attained through the dependence of lower-status segments on colleagues for access or advancement.

A corollary of this point is that the degree of conformity will depend on the concentration of resources under elite control. Heinz and

Laumann (1982), examining the Chicago Bar, suggest that segmentation within the bar is based on status but find no evidence of elite domination. They attribute this to the inability of the elite to control worksites and the fine division of labor among law firms. The bar association has also relinquished control over licensing and discipline to the courts and, therefore, this source of control is unavailable to elite segments.

Heinz and Laumann's study is complicated by the presence of multiple bases of segmentation (status, task, ethnoreligious) that combine to separate practitioners concerned with corporate or personal affairs. Although the authors identify status as the dominate basis of segmentation, some characteristics of the profession, such as the low mobility among segments, are more characteristic of subsidiary task segments (described below). Their findings clearly reflect the complex segmentation of the bar in that city.[2]

Subsidiary task segments also face pressures for conformity. Larson (1977: 230-231) suggests that specialists, due to their narrower cognitive base and greater codification of knowledge, face the risk of losing control over the application of their knowledge (see Child and Fulk, 1982: 181-182). In order to safeguard their status, specialists must remain within the umbrella organization of generalists for whom the balance of technique and judgment (i.e., the technicality/indeterminacy ratio; Jamous and Peliolle, 1970) supports their claim to professional status. This situation may be reinforced by a referral system that ensures that clients are directed to specialists through general practitioners.

De Santis (1980: 179-236) suggests a different basis for the integration of subsidiary task segments. She finds that the "professional dominance" (Freidson, 1970) of medicine emerges from competition among segments over the distribution of tasks. This competition not only establishes an internal division of labor, it also ensures that tasks are allocated to those practitioners with the greatest competence. This in turn strengthens medicine's claim to these tasks with respect to competing occupations. Individual task segments, therefore, depend on interaction with other segments to maintain the dominance of the profession as a whole.

There is a marked tendency for interaction among subsidiary segments to be structured as individual rather than group actions. For example, competition or conflict among subsidiary segments is typically dealt with on an individual basis as a matter of ethics (e.g., Berlant, 1975; Auerbach, 1976), and the advancement of segment interests occurs primarily through individual competition for institutional positions (teaching positions, executive offices in professional associations). Only under rare circumstances are segment interests pursued on a group basis and then typically only to alter the structure within which individual negotiations occur, for example, exerting pressure to alter ethical standards (Podmore, 1980: 5-7; Child and Fulk, 1982: 181; De Santis, 1980: 229).

In spite of pressures for conformity, subsidiary segments are seen as the focal point of change in a profession (Bucher and Strauss, 1961; Rosenberg et al., 1981; Child and Fulk, 1982). And, at the very least, they may be an impediment to the dominant segment's attempt to gain legislative recognition of the profession's status (Kronus, 1976; Begun and Feldman, 1981). A key empirical and theoretical question, therefore, is to specify under what conditions subsidiary segments arise and gain influence. The work on radical groups within the professions (e.g., Perrucci, 1973; Powell, 1979) and on the division of labor undertaken from a negotiated order perspective (e.g., Pettigrew, 1973: chap. 5-6; Freidson, 1976; Rothman, 1979) is relevant to this task.

When independent status segments exist within a profession, a different range of phenomena is observed. While elite segments continue to shape the profession, the consequences for lower-status segments do not encourage conformity. First, since it is possible to publicly differentiate segments, the development of the profession by elite segments reinforces and expands the status differential. Unlike the situation described for subsidiary segments, lower-status groups gain little benefit from the advancement of elite segments. Lower-status groups, therefore, are motivated to decrease the status differential in order to increase their own status and to undermine attempts by the elite segments to gain exclusive recognition.

Second, lower-status groups are not subject to discipline by the dominant group and do not perceive opportunities for career paths that span work settings in which different associations are dominant. Mobility among segments is restricted due to varying entrance requirements and, typically, an unwillingness to recognize credentials granted by other associations. In this case, segment conflicts remain group conflicts and focus on the marketplace and the courts. The action of competing groups are typically framed as "encroachment or charlatanism" (Godde, 1960), and the relative strength of credentials becomes the key point of debate.

Where independent task segments exist within a profession, it is difficult to maintain the public image of a single profession, and boundary disputes among associations and with related occupations are frequent (Smith, 1958; Rothstein, 1968). The specialization of practitioners generally precludes mobility among segments, and the distinct concerns of each segment prevents the development of common programs (Gerstl and Hutton, 1966). These observations lead Perrucci and Gerstl (1969) to describe engineering, the archetype of a profession dominated by independent task segments, as a "profession without community." They could not find a core set of values and institutions on which engineering could claim to be a single, coherent profession.

As this brief discussion shows, the nature of segmentation in a profession affects the issues facing practitioners and the strategies that groups may use to secure professional status. The remainder of this article presents a historical case study of interaction among segments in the accounting profession. In their pioneering survey, Carr-Saunders and Wilson (1933) described independent segments in accounting as an anomaly among professions. Independent segments have continued to dominate the profession, primarily based on status (Johnson and Caygill, 1971; Stacey, 1954), but, since World War I, also based on task, particularly the separation of public and management accounting. This article, therefore, contributes to an understanding of professional segmentation primarily within one quadrant—independent/status—of the typology presented above (this characterization of the accounting profession will be dealt with more fully below). It is complementary to work on subsidiary segments in medicine (Stevens, 1971; Berlant, 1975; Starr, 1982) and law (Auerbach, 1976; Halliday and Cappell, 1979), and to studies of independent task segments in engineering (Rothstein, 1968; Perrucci and Gerstl, 1969).

THE CURRENT STATUS OF THE
ACCOUNTING PROFESSION IN CANADA[3]

Accounting is a "reserved title" occupation in Canada. Associations may certify the competence of their members and authorize them to use a distinctive title and designation, but they do not have exclusive practice rights. There are currently five such associations in Canada: Chartered Accountants (CA), Certified General Accountants (CGA), Certified Management Accountants (CMA), Accredited Public Accountants (APA), and the Guild of Industrial, Commercial and Institutional Accounts (ICIA).

The right to practice as an accountant is generally unregulated. The exception to this rule is public accounting (typically defined as adding credibility to financial information by conducting an audit and presenting a signed public opinion on the adequacy of the information). This is the highest status accounting role, garnering prestige and income well above accountants in industry or bookkeepers (Tremain, 1977). Public accounting is regulated in 6 of 10 provinces. CAs have exclusive public practice rights in two provinces, represent the majority on licensing boards and in practice in three other provinces, and are codominant (with CGAs and CMAs) on the licensing board of one province. It should be noted that this regulation is permissive; accountants who gain a license to practice as public accountants do not necessarily give up other forms of practice.

The technology of the profession, accounting and auditing standards, is largely controlled by the CAs, who maintain a handbook of standards. These standards are accepted as authoritative by the Canada Corporations Act, which governs reporting federally incorporated companies, and by the securities exchange commissions,which govern reporting by publicly traded companies. The handbook is also widely accepted on a voluntary basis by companies not subject to these sources of regulation. An independent standard-setting body, sponsored by the CGAs, exists but has no noticeable impact on the profession. The CAs, numerically and in terms of legal rights, are clearly the dominant professional body. The CGAs and CMAs, which are close to each other in size and status, occupy a secondary position, while the remaining bodies represent few accountants and do not significantly affect the development of the profession as a whole.

THE COMPETITION
FOR PROFESSIONAL STATUS

The current organization of the profession reflects over a hundred years of interaction among associations and the state. The first accounting associations were formed in Quebec and Ontario in 1879. It has been suggested that the coincident formation of these groups reflected concern by local practitioners that English associations were expanding their domains to include the "colonies" (Allan, 1982: 2; Johnson and Caygill, 1971; Johnson, 1982). Both groups adopted the

CA, Chartered Accountant, designation that had gained prestige in Great Britain.

Additional groups quickly formed in other provinces—Manitoba in 1886 and Nova Scotia in 1901—also using the CA designation. Each association operated primarily within their own province. In 1902, however, an independent group was incorporated federally, in spite of opposition from the provinces, as the Dominion Association of Chartered Accountants, DACA, and began offering their CA designation across Canada. For the next eight years, the provincial and federal associations engaged in a running battle in the courts, legislature, and press over the right to use the CA designation. In 1909 and 1910, these conflicts were resolved by merging all CA associations in Canada, with the DACA acting as a federal coordinating body (Hoole, 1963: 12; Mann, 1976; Creighton, 1984: 63-64).

About the same time, other associations were emerging and entered into competition with the CAs. These associations segmented the profession on various bases. The CGAs (formed in 1908) and CMAs (formed in 1920) were initially concerned with accountants in industry. Both associations, but particularly the CGAs, gradually developed an interest in public accounting. The Institute of Accountants and Auditors of the Province of Quebec (formed in 1912) represented francophone accountants in opposition to the anglophone-dominated CA association. The Certified Public Accountants (CAPs; formed in 1918) and APAs (formed in 1938) represented accountants opposed to the education requirements of the CA association. The number of associations peaked in the mid-1940s, with at least 10 distinct accounting associations operating in Canada (Richardson, 1985).

Although a variety of bases of segmentation have been noted, the common interest of these associations was the high prestige public accounting role; the essence of segmentation in the profession has been access to and the status of audit clients. In order to secure this role, and the higher status that it provided, associations attempted to establish their claims *in comparison with other associations*. This competition occurred within a widely held, but poorly specified, belief that accountancy was, or should be, a profession (see Larson, 1977: 228). The competition for status had two consequences: (1) It created procedures and symbols that served to legitimate and constitute professional status in this field, and (2) it encouraged the escalating commitment of associations to these procedures and symbols as each attempted to maintain its comparative advantage. These effects will be demonstrated in the development of educational standards and the symbolic attributes of the profession, and achievement of occupational licensing.

EDUCATION

The adoption of educational programs by occupations, particularly university affiliations, as part of a program of professionalization can be seen as filling two roles. First, these programs serve to legitimate claims for special privilege (Larson, 1977; Portwood and Fielding, 1981). In accounting, the existence of education programs was prima facia evidence of the technical content of the field and allowed practitioners successfully completing these programs to signal their competence. The development of such programs, therefore, legitimated claims to privilege based on expertise. In addition, and equally important, was the use of these programs to control access to the profession, which served to assure the public that existing practitioners were not attempting to create a monopoly.[4]

Second, educational programs may serve to focus the training of practitioners on a particular body of knowledge and values. This creates a degree of "cognitive exclusiveness" (Larson, 1977) on which professions could lay claims to occupational license. This role presumes and requires that particular educational processes should possess some comparative advantage in conveying a codified body of knowledge. The comparative advantage of universities in training accountants is moot (Ferris, 1982) and education for a career in accounting continues to involve university-based and profession-based programs. Even when licensing exists, experience may be accepted as a substitute for formal education.

Up to this point in the history of accounting, educational programs aimed at legitimating professional status appears to dominate their role in standardizing the productive knowledge of practitioners. For example, Englebert (1962: 148-49), commenting on a proposal to require that all Chartered Accountants have a university degree, stated:

The reasoning behind this recommendation is based on the fact that university education has long been recognized by other established professions as a prerequisite for admission and the public, generally, has come to think of the professions as synonymous with university graduation. There is little comfort in accountants telling themselves they

192

have all the basic attributes of a profession if they cease to be accepted as such and not sought to supply professional service.

The degree required could be in any field. It was a purely institutional requirement and not a technological imperative (Richardson, forthcoming).

The educational requirements of CA associations thus emerged as part of a program to secure social recognition as a profession. These requirements were the minimum necessary to meet commonsense expectations of professionalism. Over the first 20 years of the profession's history, however, the rhetoric of educational aims developed more than the educational programs themselves. This situation changed as competing associations developed and began to use education standards as a resource to establish their status. The effect of competition will be demonstrated in the adoption of mandatory examination, apprenticeship requirements, university-based courses, and the requirement of university graduation.

MANDATORY EXAMINATIONS

The major development in accounting education prior to 1900 was the Institute of Chartered Accountants of Ontario's (ICAO) adoption of a three-stage examination program in 1895. Each stage had different age and experience requirements, but no supervised preparation was offered. In addition, whether or not a candidate would be examined was at the discretion of the council. The first mandatory examinations appeared under the charter of the Institute of Chartered Accountants of British Columbia (ICABC) in 1905. The ICABC had attempted to gain a charter that exempted founding members from examination in return for bearing the costs of incorporation (a common practice). The bill was opposed by other associations until it was amended to include a mandatory examination requirement. The examinations were given by CAs from Ontario and England. At the time of application for incorporation, the ICABC had 86 members, after the examinations only 4 members remained.

Although the intent of other associations may have been to block the ICABC, or to restrict its membership, the result was to establish a higher level of qualification and standard of entry, which was now part of the definition of professionalism in accounting. Mandatory examinations for membership in associations became the norm after this point; for example, this requirement was included in the charters of the CGA association (1908), and CA associations in Alberta (1910) and New Brunswick (1916).

APPRENTICESHIP REQUIREMENTS

In order to qualify as a CA, candidates were required to undertake independent studies followed by an apprenticeship in public practice. The latter requirement created a bottleneck, as the number of applicants far outnumbered the available positions for apprentices. The CPAs and CGAs both formed to provide an alternative route to professional status. They granted credit toward their designation for *any* accounting experience, regardless of the particular context in which it was gained, but otherwise duplicated the education requirements adopted by the CAs (Mann, 1976: 175).

The CPAs attempted to discredit the CAs' apprentice requirements:

> In non-industrial areas of Canada employment by a practicing accountant may provide very restricted experience. Students may, indeed, have no training in the practice of accounting and auditing as applicable to limited liability companies, and it is quite unlikely that their experience will include the audit of a corporation of substantial magnitude. Students serving their period of training in such areas and subsequently moving into a highly industrialized district will probably soon discover the lack of adequate training. Such restricted experience is not generally comparable to that obtained by an employee of a large industrial, manufacturing, or commercial company.

> Employment by a public practitioner is not necessarily an invulnerable argument that one who seeks to become public accountant is adequately trained. Conversely it is not an invulnerable argument that other employment does not afford appropriate experience.

The CAs reacted to this type of criticism by requiring that students apprentice in the offices of CA members and began an inspection program to ensure that students received diverse experience in public accounting. These changes were intended to guarantee the quality of experiential training received by candidates and highlighted an essential difference between the CAs and other associations. The standard also ensured that CA students would apprentice in CA firms rather than in

194

emerging CPA public practices. Since students were used by these firms to perform routine accounting functions, the standard served both the economic interests of firms as well as maintaining control over the CAs student body.

UNIVERSITY-BASED COURSES

The formal education of accountants was initially handled by proprietary schools such as the Nicholson Institute of Cost Accounting and the Shaw Correspondence School. Although each association held its own examinations and sponsored speakers, the education that candidates received was basically the same. This changed in 1921, when the ICAO contracted with Queen's University to provide courses and administer the association's examinations. This model rapidly spread among CA associations, each provincial association becoming affiliated with a local university or requiring Queen's University's correspondence course (Mann, 1976: 31). This affiliation also allowed an exchange of legitimacy symbols between the newly established business programs and the CAs (see Light, 1983). A notable example is the granting of honorary degrees to accountants by both McGill and Queen's University in 1922 (*CCA*, 1922: 158).[5]

The CAs adoption of university-based training coincided with a move by the CGAs to expand their domain into public practice. This was marked by an advertising campaign beginning in 1916, and the formation of a separate association of CGAs in public practice in Quebec in 1920. This put the CGAs in direct competition with the CAs. The move to university education clearly differentiated the CAs from the CGAs and other rival associations. It has since become the explicit policy of the CAs to maintain their educational standards at the forefront of the profession (e.g., *CCA*, 1932: 100). The issue resurfaced during the early 1950s when the CGAs incorporated in British Columbia and began offering a training program through the University of British Columbia. Coulter (1975) reported the following:

> For two years the CGA course was superior to the CA course. This got
> their fire up and the CAs have never been overtaken since. This was an
> excellent accomplishment for the accounting profession and the public.

The APAs and CGAs used private correspondence schools until the 1950s; the ICIA continues to represent graduates of correspondence courses (Swinburne, 1982; Ross and Brown, 1978). The CPAs kept pace with the CAs by arranging a program of instruction through the University of Toronto.

A UNIVERSITY DEGREE REQUIREMENT

The final step to a university degree requirement was taken by the CAs in 1970-1971. This was first proposed in 1959 based on observations that other professions had adopted a university degree requirement (in accounting, New York CPAs and English CAs had adopted a degree requirement in 1945 for accountants entering public practice) and that the public expected professionals to possess university qualifications (Englebert, 1962: 148-149). It also reflected the growing complexity of accounting technique, the hiring trends of accounting firms, and the tendency of good students to continue through to university. The concern remained, however, that this step was necessary to remain at the forefront of the profession:

> These are changes which can and must be accepted, and at as rapid a rate as possible if the [CA] profession is to survive and remain in the forefront. To delay such changes will undermine the present enviable position of the profession [*ICABC,* March 12, 1966: 5].

The university degree requirement has, to date, been adopted only by the CAs. The CGAs (Sinotte, 1981: 12) and the ICIA (Ross and Brown, 1978) have explicitly rejected the idea of requiring a university degree. These groups formed in opposition to the perceived elitism of CA associations and are ideologically opposed to entrance criteria or systems of training that narrow access to the profession. The CMAs are also opposed to requiring a university degree. In Alberta, for example, after the CAs adopted this policy, the CMAs withdrew a by-law that prohibited their members from using their designation to claim competence in public accounting. It was felt, prior to 1970, that any member with aspirations in public accounting could qualify for the CA designation. The degree requirement, however, effectively precluded this option for many members.

SYMBOLIC ATTRIBUTES

Certain attributes of occupations become key symbols for public recognition as professions. The possession of a designation, or a code of ethics, may provide an occupation with access to status and rewards previously out of reach. This occurs either because the symbol has been established as an indicator of quality, or is generalized from a context in which such a link has been established. The CA associations in Ontario and Quebec adopted the symbols of professionalism established by British accounting associations or, more generally, on the lead provided by the medical profession (Richardson, forthcoming). These were the sources of the institutional "myths" (Meyer and Rowan, 1977; Hall, 1979) on which the profession drew to establish its legitimacy (see Boland, 1982).

Although the influence of competition on the adoption of professional symbols by associations can be seen in many areas (such as the adoption of university affiliations, as noted above), it is perhaps most marked in the adoption of professional designations. In this regard, two designations have particular salience: the CA designation established in Great Britain, and, following the development of close economic ties between Canada and America after World War I, the CPA designation. Two concerns are evident in the use of designations: first, that associations gain control over a designation that is recognized as a mark of quality; second, that no other association gains control of any similar designation that the public might accept as equivalent. Both conditions are necessary to ensure the comparative advantage of possessing a designation.

The CA designation, by the late 1800s, was accepted as a symbol of excellence and integrity in accounting, due to its development and use in Great Britain. Control over the use of that designation thus became very important in the careers of accountants. It has been mentioned, for example, that the initial formation of accountants associations in Ontario and Quebec has been attributed to a movement by accounting associations in Britain to gain exclusive rights to use the CA designation throughout the commonwealth.[6] Similarly, the struggle between the ICAO and the DACA was primarily over the right to use this designation and resulted in the restructuring of the DACA as a federation of provincial CA associations.

The "CA" was so jealously guarded that the CAs opposed the charter of the Canadian Accountants Association (*CA*A), until they changed their name to the General Accountants Association (*GA*A) (Bentley, 1938: 9). A similar conflict arose when the society of Industrial and Cost Accountants of Ontario applied for charter with the right to offer the CIA, Certified Industrial Accountant, designation. This was resolved by changing the designation to RIA, Registered Industrial Accountant (Allan, 1982: 31).

With the "Americanization" of Canadian business after World War I, the CPA designation, which was well established in the United States, also gained value in Canada. The Canadian CAs developed a close relationship with the CPAs in the United States explicitly to "improve [their] professional standing" (*CCA*, 1920: 81). This relationship had more instrumental consequences in subsequent years when the American CPAs gave support to the CAs opposition to the creation of a CPA designation in Canada (*CCA*, 1922: 161). The CPA designation was blocked from use in Canada until 1936, when the Association of Accountants and Auditors of Ontario, on the strength of informal ties to the government of the day, gained the right to use the designation. The CPAs and CAs merged in 1962, in part due to pressure from American CPA firms, who were affiliated with CA firms in Canada, to remove the confusion experienced by their clients who used CPAs in the United States but not in Canada. The CAs maintain the rights to the CPA designation to ensure that it does not reappear in Canada.

OCCUPATIONAL LICENSE

Occupational licensing represents one way in which the comparative status of occupations or occupational segments may be institutionalized (Freidson, 1986: chap. 4, p. 19-37). Licensing enlists the power of the state in securing task domains and providing customers with a degree of protection where ex post remedies are insufficient. Attempts by accounting associations to use licensing to reinforce status differences have faced two difficulties. First, there is no consensus on which tasks should be limited to licensed practitioners. And second, since associations are segmented by status rather than task, practitioners dealing with regulated tasks may be in any association. The development of occupational licensing in accounting has, therefore, required complex negotiations aimed at defining areas of practice in which regulation was necessary and coupling the status hierarchy with a division of labor among associations.

The rise of accounting associations coincided with the institutionalization of accounting roles in legislation, for example, the "Insolvent Acts" in Quebec (1984, 1869, 1875) and similar acts in other provinces (Mann, 1976: 43-52). These acts created roles that accountants could fill but did not give particular occupational groups that mandate. As competing associations were created, there were incentives to have these acts amended in order to gain exclusive practice rights and to formalize status distinctions among groups. The CAs in British Columbia, for example, focused on the existence of competing associations in their first, unsuccessful, attempt to close the profession:

> These men (members of other associations) have no standing at all, they are simply small bookkeepers. They amply demonstrate the evil we are trying to cure. Various small societies of men such as these spring up and hand themselves certificates at little family gatherings. We, through the incorporation of our Institute, just want to prevent such unqualified men from holding themselves up as qualified. We want to prevent this province from being overwhelmed with unqualified men [Sloan, *Vancouver Times,* Nov. 15, 1921: 10].

It quickly became clear that the CAs could not prevent competing associations from forming. Their strategy, therefore, was to concentrate their efforts on the high prestige public accounting role. This strategy was adopted in spite of the fact that their membership has always been equally divided between accountants in public practice and those working in other contexts. In Ontario, this was marked by an amendment to the Chartered Accountants Act in 1910 that required that two-thirds of the ICAO council be public accountants.

In 1980, the CGAs formed to provide a mechanism to advance the field of management accounting now partially abandoned by the CAs. The CAs saw this as a positive development (*CCA,* 1922: 254):

> It will be clear that there was at the outset a perfectly good understanding as to the spheres of activity that the CAs and [CGAs] should occupy, and one, which, if faith were kept, would lead to a harmonious working arrangement between the two organizations.

They were not concerned that the CGA charter was based on theirs, preferring to attribute this to expediency rather than any desire to enter the field of public accounting (*CCA,* 1922: 255). It became increasingly clear, however, from the CGAs' creation of a public accounting association in Quebec and their attempts to organize in other provinces, that the CGAs would attempt to expand their domain wherever possible.

In 1920, the CAs, mirroring developments in the United States and England (*CCA,* 1920: 31), created a management accounting branch called the Canadian Society of Cost Accountants. In engineering this split, the CAs created a charter that limited the new society to management accounting and a quasiprofessional status, that is, they would not have a designation nor attempt to create a monopoly in their field (*CCA,* 1920: 45). This new body was designed to challenge the CGAs on their own territory while being specifically denied access to the preferred domain of the CAs.

The creation of the society was an attempt to undermine challenges to the CAs' status by creating an independent task segment and linking the existing status hierarchy to task domains. This ultimately failed, in part because the society *was* independent and could not be forced to remain in the domain to which it was assigned, and because competing associations did not accept the division of labor that the CAs had attempted to enact. Thus, in spite of these informal attempts to achieve a division of labor, competition for public accounting roles remained intense.

In 1945, the first general legislation limiting the right to conduct audits was created in Quebec. The state of the profession at the time has been characterized as "chaos," with six associations representing accountants in public practice and repeated attempts by associations to "close" the profession in their favor (Collard, 1980: 28-33). Finally, the Quebec government, faced with competing proposals for licensing legislation from each of the major associations, "closed" the profession, merging existing organizations into one group, to be known as CAs, and limiting future entry to the profession to those who could pass an examination process jointly administered by CAs and academics from major Quebec universities. The act gave the CAs exclusive rights to public accounting (broadly defined) for most companies.

The closure of the profession in Quebec led other associations to reconsider their own positions. In Ontario, the ICAO moved to negotiate legislation with other associations before the government could impose closure. The act that was finally drafted proposed the creation of a board, composed of members of each accounting group in proportion to its size, which would set standards of entry and practice. Based on estimates, the board was made up of eight CAs, five CPAs, and two "others" to represent independent accountants and smaller associations. The standard for entry to the field reflected the lowest common denominator of the training requirements of the two dominant groups (CAs and CAPs) on the board. This level of qualification was then used to define *public accounting,* that is, to put boundaries on the scope of regulated practice. The act defined public accounting as those activities associated with the preparation and/or auditing of financial statements. This is a broad definition including routine accounting work as well as more judgmental aspects.

Once all public accountants had registered, it became evident that the numbers used to apportion representation on the board had been seriously in error. In fact, independent accountants dominated public practice at that time. Within a short period of time, however, due to the entrance criteria that had been established, the merger of CPAs and several smaller groups, and finally the merger of the CPAs and CAs, the independent group declined and the CAs emerged with a clear majority in public accounting and control of the Public Accountants Council.

Following the merger of the CAs and CPAs in 1962, the Public Accountancy Act was amended. The amendment raised the entry requirements to the final examination of the ICAO, that is, membership in the ICAO, and revised the definition of public accountancy to the provision of an opinion on the validity of financial statements rather than the preparation of such information. It was argued that this narrower definition better reflected the areas of accountancy where public protection was necessary and justified the higher educational standards that limited access to this market to members of the ICAO.

The ambiguity of task boundaries and the competition for status continue to be driving forces in the development of the profession. In 1974, the CGAs petitioned for changes to the act that would broaden the definition of public accounting and allow their members access to this field (Leal et al., 1980, chap. 6). The petition was turned over to a government ministry and subsequently to a committee for study. The committee agreed that the current definition of public accountancy is too narrow and recommended rescinding the mandate given to the ICAO. These recommendations have not yet been acted on by the government.

DISCUSSION

The accounting profession in Canada, as in other countries (e.g., England: Stacey, 1954; Willmott, forthcoming; and America: Previt and Merino, 1979), is a network of independent associations competing for prestigious accounting roles. This article has attempted to document the effect of interaction among these segments of the professionalization of accountancy in Canada. It is suggested that the phenomena observed may be generalized to a class of professions characterized by the existence of independent associations segmented according to the status of members and their work. Within this context, it was shown that the ability of associations to publicly differentiate themselves, and the lack of mechanisms by which the elite segments could enforce their preferences, encouraged competition for professional status and access to professional roles among associations. This competition occurred within a poorly specified but widely shared ideological conviction that accounting was a profession. Competition among associations, therefore, had two effects. First, associations continually escalated their commitment to professional standards and symbolism in order to establish their superiority to other associations on a range of professional criteria. It was shown, for example, that the need to establish the symbolic attributes of the profession, or to gain an explicit social mandate, arose only in the face of competition for the professional role in the field of public accounting. The continual escalation of education requirements may have been required by the nature of the task, but also served as a means of closing the profession and securing domains. Even the division of labor between public and managerial accounting associations can be traced to competition among occupational segments for the key professional roles.

Second, the competition for professional status resulted in the definition of professionalism in this particular sphere of activity. Although there was consensus among associations that accounting was a profession, the operational meaning of professionalism in accounting was unclear. The competition among associations, therefore, was not simply pushing associations along a scale of predetermined steps toward professionalism. Each response to competitive pressures was defining what professionalism would mean to this field. In some cases, this would involve the explicit use of the model provided by other professions (e.g., the adoption of a university degree requirement). In other cases, the standards emerged as an unexpected consequence of interactions (e.g., the mandatory examination requirement). Each innovation in association structure, procedure, and symbolism, of course, was subject to a pragmatic social test of whether or not it assisted the association in gaining recognition and increased privilege. The social context of interactions was, therefore, also a key factor in shaping the definition of professionalism in accounting.

The competition among associations documented in this article has not resulted in a stable network of associations arrayed along a status continuum. The associations have developed in parallel and each has a claim to professional status. Attempts to couple the status hierarchy to task segmentation, such that the elite segment would have exclusive access to public accounting, have failed as members within each association continue to occupy a diverse range of professional niches and negotiations with the state have produced mixed results. The current movement in the profession is to encourage the development of subsidiary segments, explicitly recognizing the specialization of members within each association. These developments are analogous to those noted in the development of other professions, but their analysis requires a theory of segment evolution that has yet to emerge. The typology developed in this article may serve as a base from which to develop such a theory and to gain a better understanding of the phenomena of professional segmentation.

NOTES

1. The Canadian accounting profession is organized provincially, with significant variations in law and professional structure among provinces. This sketch of the profession, therefore, necessarily omits those details that are not of theoretical relevance. The profession was first organized in Ontario and Quebec, and these provinces account for the majority of practitioners. The article, therefore, concentrates on these two provinces.

2. These results, as well as the work of Child and Fulk (1982) and Freidson (1986: 19-37), suggest that the institutional context of practice may be a significant basis of segmentation. In essence, these studies suggest that variables identified as the basis of segmentation in other studies are clustered according to context. If this is so, it may be possible to identify archetypes as an alternate framework for the exploration of professional segmentation.

3. Detailed sources for the incidents described are available in Richardson (1986). All associations are referred to by their most recent designations. It must be noted that in most cases the designation and associations' names have changed during the history of the profession.

4. The CAs in Ontario, for example, were initially rejected when they applied for a charter as a "voluntary organization." They reapplied as "an educational and intellectual movement" and were successful. Brown (1905/ 1986) attributes this to the concern of the Liberal government of the day that accountants were seeking "class legislation." The rhetoric of educational aims served to assure the government that the association would operate according to universalistic criteria.

5. The *Canadian Chartered Accountant*, CCA, is the official journal of the Canadian Institute of Chartered Accountants. These references are to editorial comments in this journal.

6. The British accounting associations continued to pressure the Canadian associations. In 1911, in order to secure legislation providing the ICAO with exclusive rights to use the CA designation in Ontario, the ICAO developed a "registered society list." Any member of associations on this list could, on application and without examination, be admitted as a member of the ICAO. This placated the British associations, who , of course, were included on this list, and incidentally set in motion pressures for the uniformity of entry and training requirements for CA Institutes across Canada in order that they could grant reciprocal memberships.

REFERENCES

ALLAN, J. N. (1982) History of the Society of Management Accountants of Canada. Hamilton: SMAC.

ARMSTRONG, D. (1979) "The emancipation of biographical medicine." Social Sci. and Medicine 13a: 1-8.

AUERBACH, J. S. (1976) Unequal Justice. New York: Oxford Univ. Press.

BARBER, B. (1965) "Some problems in the sociology of the professions," in K. S. Lynn (ed.) The Professions in America. Boston: Houghton Mifflin.

BEGUN, J. W. and R. D. FELDMAN (1981) A Social and Economic Analysis of Professional Regulation in Optometry. Washington, DC: Department of Health and Human Services.

BENTLEY, W. (1938) History of the General Accountants Association, 1980 to 1938. Canadian General Accountants Association. (mimeo)

BERLANT, J. L. (1975) Profession and Monopoly. Berkeley: Univ. of California Press.

BOLAND, R. J. (1982) "Myth and technology in the American accounting profession." J. of Management Studies 19, 1: 109-127.

BROWN, R. (1905/1958) A History of Accounting and Accountants. New York: Kelley.

BUCHER, R. and A. STRAUSS (1961) "Professions in process." Amer. J. of Sociology 66: 325-334.

CARR-SAUNDERS, A. M. and P. A. WILSON (1933) The Professions. Oxford: Clarendon.

CHILD, J. and J. FULK (1982) "Maintenance of occupational control." Work and Occupations 9, 2: 155-192.

COLLARD, E. A. (1980) First in North America, One Hundred Years in the Life of the Ordes Des Comptables Agrees Du Quebec. Montreal: OCAQ.

COULTER, J. (December 1975) "Letter to the editor." CGA Magazine: 6.

CREIGHTON, P. (December 1975) "Letter to the editor." CGA Magazine: 6.

CREIGHTON, P. (1984) A Sum of Yesterdays. Toronto: Institute of Chartered Accountants of Ontario.

De SANTIS, G. (1980) "Realms of expertise: a view from the medical profession," in J. A. Roth (ed.) Research in the Sociology of Health Care (Vol. 1). Greenwich, CT: JAI.

ENGLEBERT, R. (1962) "A diamond jubilee progress of the professions in Canada." Canadian Chartered Accountant 81, 2: 147-152.

FERRIS, K. R. (1982) "Educational predictors of professional pay and performance." Accounting Organizations and Society 7, 3: 225-230.

FREIDSON, E. (1970) Professional Dominance. New York: Atherton.

FREIDSON, E. (1976) "The division of labour as social interaction." Social Problems 23, 6: 304-313.

FREIDSON, E. (1983) "The theory of professions: state of the art," in R. Dingwall and P. Lewis (ed.) The Sociology of the Professions. London: Macmillan.

FREIDSON, E. (1986) Professional Powers. Chicago: Univ. of Chicago Press.

GERSTL, J. E. and S. P. HUTTON (1966) Engineers: The Anatomy of a Profession. London: Tavistock.

GIBB, C. L. (1966) Hidden Hierarchies: Government and the Professions. New York: Harper & Row.

GOODE, W. J. (1960) "Encroachment, charlatanism and the emerging profession: psychology, sociology and medicine." Amer. Soc. Rev. 25: 902-914.

HALL, R. (1979) "The social construction of the professions." Sociology of Work and Occupations 6, 1: 124-126.

HALLIDAY, T. C. and C. L. CAPPELL (1979) "Indicators of democracy in professional associations: elite recruitment, turnover and decision-making in a metropolitan bar association." Amer. Bar Foundation Research J., 4: 699-767.

HASTINGS, A. and C. R. HININGS (1970) "Role relations and value adaptations: a study of the professional accountant in industry." Sociology 4: 353-366.

HEINZ, J. P. and E. O. LAUMANN (1982) Chicago Lawyers: The Social Structure of the Bar. New York: Russell Sage Foundation/American Bar Foundation.

HOOLE, A. H. (1963) A Brief History of the Institute of Chartered Accountants of Manitoba: 1886-1961. Winnipeg: ACAM.

HUER, J. (1980) "Professional callings and called professions: ideology, rhetoric and legitimation." Humanity and Society 4, 4: 297-320.

JAMOUS, H. and B. PELIOLLE (1970) "Changes in the French University Hospital System," in J. A. Jackson (ed.) Professions and Professionalization. Cambridge: Cambridge Univ. Press.

JOHNSON, T. (1972) Professions and Power. London: Macmillan.

JOHNSON, T. (1977) "The professions in the class structure," in R. Scase (ed.) Industrial Society: Class, Cleavage and Control. New York: St. Martin's.

JOHNSON, T. (1982) "The state and the professions," in A. Giddens and G. MacKenzie (eds.) Social Class and the Division of Labour. Cambridge: Cambridge Univ. Press.

JOHNSON, T. and M. CAYGILL (1971) "The development of accountancy links in the commonwealth." Accounting and Business Research (Spring): 135-173.

KLEGON, D. (1978) "The sociology of professions." Sociology of Work and Occupations 5, 3: 259-283.

KRONUS, C. L. (1976) "The evolution of occupational power: an historical study of task boundaries between physicians and pharmacists." Sociology of Work and Occupations 3: 3-37.

LARSON, M. S. (1977) The Rise of Professionalism. Berkeley: Univ. of California Press.

LEAL, H. A., J. A. CORRY, and J. S. DUPRE (1980) The Report of the Professional Organizations Committee Ministry of the Attorney General of Ontario. Toronto: Queen's Park Printer.

LIGHT, D. W. (1983) "The development of professional schools in America," in K. H. Jarausch (ed.) The Transformation of Higher Learning, 1860-1930. Chicago: Univ. of Chicago Press.

MANN, H. (1976) The Evolution of Accounting in Canada. Montreal: Rouche Ross.

MAYER, J. W. and B. ROWAN (1977) "Institutional organizations: formal structure as myth and ceremony." Amer. J. of Sociology 82, 2: 340-363.

MONTAGNA, P. D. (1974) Certified Public Accounting: A Sociological View of a Profession in Change. Houston: Scholars Book Co.

PATERSON, A. (1983) "Becoming a judge," in R. Dingwall and P. Lewis (eds.) The Sociology of the Professions. New York: St. Martin's.

PERRUCCI, R. (1973) "In the service of man: radical movements in the professions." Soc. Rev. Monograph 20.

PERRUCCI, R. and J. GERSTL (1969) Profession Without Community: Engineers in America Society. New York: Random House.

PETTIGREW, A. M. (1973) The Politics of Organizational Decision-Making. London: Tavistock.

PODMORE, D. (1980) "Bucher and Strauss revisited—the case of the solicitors' profession." British J. of Law and Society 7: 1-21.

PORTWOOD, D. and A. FIELDING (1981) "Privilege and the professions." Soc. Rev. 29, 4: 749-773.

POWELL, M. (1979) "Anatomy of a counter-bar association: the Chicago Council of Lawyers." Amer. Bar Foundation Research J., 3: 501-542.

PREVIT, G. J. and B. D. MERINO (1979) A History of Accounting in America: An Historical interpretation of the Cultural Significance of Accounting. New York: Ronald.

RICHARDSON, A. J. (1985) "The professionalization of accountancy in Canada." Proceedings of the Canadian Academic Accounting Association, Montreal, May.

RICHARSON, A. J. (1986) A Reference Chronology of the Evolution of the Accounting Profession in Canada. Univ. of Alberta, Canada. (mimeo)

RICHARDSON, A. J. (forthcoming) "The production of institutional behaviour." Canadian J. of Administrative Sciences 3, 2.

ROSENBERG, D., C. TONKINS, and P. DAY (1982) "A work role perspective on accountants in local government departments." Accounting, Organizations and Society 7, 2: 123-137.

ROSS, H. and G. BROWN (1978) History of the Guild of Industrial Commercial and Institutional Accountants. Toronto: GICIA. (mimeo)

ROTHMAN, R. A. (1979) "Occupational roles: power and negotiation in the division of labour." Soc. Q. 20: 495-515.

ROTHSTEIN, W. G. (1968) "Engineers and the functionalist model of the professions," in R. Perrucci and J. Gerstle (eds.) The Engineers and the Social System. New York: John Wiel.

SIEGEL, G. H. (1977) "Segmentation in the accounting profession." Ph.D. dissertation, University of Illinois at Urbana-Champaign.

SINOTTE, G. (December/January 1981) "President's report." CGA Magazine.

SMITH, H. L. (1958) "Contingencies of professional differentiation." Amer. J. of Sociology 63: 410-414.

SOROKIN, P. (1947) Society, Culture and Personality: Their Structure and Dynamics. New York: Harper.

STACEY, N.A.H. (1954) English Accountancy, 1800-1954. London: Gee.

STARR, P. (1982) The Social Transformation of American Medicine. New York: Basic Books.

STEVENS, R. (1971) American Medicine and the Public Interest. New Haven: Yale Univ. Press.

SWINBURNE, F. (1982) "History of accounting bodies in Canada," Industrial, Commercial and Institutional Accountants J. 1: 34-36.

TREMAIN, D. J. (1977) Occupational Prestige in Comparative Perspective. New York: Academic Press.

TURNER, C. and M. N. HODGE (1970) "Occupations and professions," in J. A. Jackson (ed.) Professions and Professionalization. Cambridge: Cambridge Univ. Press.

WILLMOTT, H. (forthcoming) "Organizing the profession." Accounting Organizations and Society.

Who Audits ? The Emergence of Hegemony
in the Ontario Accountancy Profession.

Alan J. Richardson

Queen's University

Presented to the

Queen's University Conference on Behavioural and

Social Accounting, Kingston, Ontario July, 1986

Portions of this paper have been published in

"Corporation and Intraprofessional Hegemony:

A Study of Regulation and Internal Social Order"

Accounting Organizations and Society

V14 N 5/6 (1989): 415-431. We are grateful to

Anthony Hopwood, Editor-in-Chief, for his

permission to reprint this material.

The author would like to acknowledge the assistance of M.Wright in performing
reliability checks on the coding procedures used in this paper.

Who Audits ? The Emergence of Hegemony in
The Ontario Accounting Profession

The emergence of a distinct auditing profession in Ontario, Canada is examined from Gramsci's hegemonic perspective. The history of the profession is analysed in terms of the use of strategies of "transformism", the co-optation of leaders of subordinate groups into the elite group, and "expansive hegemony", the adoption of values of the subordinate groups by the dominant group, by one segment of the profession. The success of these strategies is assessed through an analysis of the ideologies of various groups within the profession. The theoretical and practical limitations of elite hegemony are discussed.

In the majority of countries, the right to perform audits is limited to a select group of accountants (AICPA, 1975). This group is the elite of the profession typically garnering prestige and economic rewards well above the average for all occupations (Tremain, 1977). In traditional sociological theory, the position of these groups is regarded as a consequence of their ethical and cognitive superiority over other practitioners (e.g. Parsons, 1954). This approach has been criticised, however, because the practices used to identify and justify the current position of these groups have not always been present, are often found in lower status groups, and do not guarantee the qualities which they purport to signal (Larson, 1977; Freidson, 1970; Berlant, 1975). An alternate approach, adopted here, is to regard the emergence of such groups as a political process and to inquire into the strategies used by occupational groups to gain and maintain privilege (Larson, 1977; Portwood and Fielding, 1980).

This paper examines the question of "who audits" in historical perspective, tracing the emergence of an auditing profession from among a relatively undifferentiated group of accountants over one hundred years in one jurisdiction. The approach taken is to regard accountancy as a "segmented" occupation (Bucher and Strauss, 1961), i.e., an occupation composed of distinct subgroups, operationalized as separate professional associations, each holding different values and attempting to enact a distinct professional identity. The paper traces the emergence of one such group into a position of "hegemonic dominance", or "intellectual and moral leadership" (Gramsci, 1971: 57), within the profession, reflected in that group's control of the audit function.

The paper is composed of five sections. The first section provides an introduction to Gramsci's work on the role of political hegemony in the maintenance of relations of dominance. Section two describes the structure of the

1

accounting profession in Ontario and documents the dominance of the Chartered Accountants (CAs) over other accountants. Section three and four then examine the history of the profession in terms of the use of two major strategies, identified in Gramsci's work, to achieve hegemony. The fifth section changes perspective from historical to contemporary in order to document the ideology which underlies the current organization of the profession and, hence, the dominance of the CAs. The paper concludes with a discussion of the limitations of elite hegemony in accountancy.

The Hegemonic Perspective

Gramsci's writings on political hegemony are used as a theoretical basis for exploring the emergence of the structure of the profession. This presumes that accounting, unlike professions such as engineering, has been segmented on the basis of status rather than, or in addition to, task (Johnson and Caygill, 1971; Richardson, 1987). The emergence and maintenance of the structure of the profession is, thus, a political process rather than one dictated by instrumental rationality.

Gramsci was concerned with mechanisms by which class structures were maintained. He differentiated between mechanisms operating in "civil" society and those operating in "political" society. Civil society refers to interactions among groups in the absence of authority relations. Class structures may arise in civil society on the basis of the spontaneous consent given by subordinated individuals to the dominant group. Gramsci referred to this relation between groups as hegemonic domination.

Political society refers to interactions between groups on the basis of structures of authority. Class structures arise in political society through the creation of laws and the distribution of rights and privileges on an authoritative

2

basis. Political society is maintained, in the final analysis, by direct domination such as the use of coercion by the police, military and courts. Gramsci argued that the class structure of society is primarily created through civil society and only when voluntary consent is withdrawn, i.e. hegemony fails, will direct domination be used to maintain class structures.

Hegemony refers to consent based on beliefs that relations of dominance are natural and legitimate. There must exist, therefore, an ideology, or system of beliefs, which so infuses a culture that competing positions are contained within an "ideological space" which supports the status quo (Hall, 1977). The realistically perceived alternatives must be simple variations on existing conditions rather than radical disjunctures.

Hegemony may be achieved by "transformism" and/or "expansive hegemony" (Mouffe, 1979). Transformism refers to the absorption of key members of subordinate groups into the dominant group. This process of co-optation is regarded as achieving a "passive consensus" which cannot provide true hegemonic dominance as subordinate groups will continually spawn new leaders. Expansive hegemony refers to the adoption of key values of subordinate groups and the creation of an ideology which supports the class structure and is genuinely accepted as a "national will" (or general will in Rousseau's sense).

It must be stressed that although hegemony operates at an ideological level, its motivation is economic and is used to maintain the dominant group's position at the center of economic activity. This fact places a limit on the extent to which an elite group can use expansive hegemony to maintain its position. At some point the contradiction between the values which it claims to hold, and must reflect significantly in its actions and rhetoric, and its position in the economic structure of society will become too great. The elite segment must then either

3

relinquish its hold, or more precisely, will be forced to relinquish its hold, or turn to mechanisms in political society to maintain its position.

The key medium through which hegemony is achieved is thus the ideology through which people view economic activity and their place in the economic order. For Gramsci, ideology was the terrain on which groups struggled for dominance and the clash of hegemonic principles on this terrain was the essence of class struggle.

<u>Professional Dominance in the Ontario Accounting Profession</u>[1]

Accounting is a "reserved title" occupation in Ontario. This means that associations may certify the competence of their members and provide a distinctive title but they do not have exclusive practice rights. As of 1983 there were five such associations in Ontario: Chartered Accountants (CA), Certified General Accountants (CGA), Certified Management Accountants (CMA), Accredited Public Accountants (APA), and the Guild of Industrial, Commercial and Institutional Accountants (GICIA). In addition, three other groups have played an important role in the history of the profession: the Independent Public Accountants Association (several distinct groups using this name sequentially) (IPAA); the Certified Public Accountants (CPA) who merged with the CAs in 1962; and, the International Accountants and Executives Corporation (IAEC) which merged with the APAs in 1958 (Mann, 1976; Ross and Brown, 1978; Swinburne, 1982).[2]

The right to practice as an accountant is unregulated in Ontario -- with the exception of public accounting (defined as adding credibility to financial information, primarily through conducting an audit, and presenting a signed public opinion on the adequacy of the information). Public accounting has been regulated since 1950 through the creation of a Public Accounting Board which

4

216

licences accountants meeting certain criteria. In 1983, 98.6% of licenced accountants in Ontario were CAs. This represents a marked increase over 1951, the first year of operation of the Board, when 35.6% of licenced accountants were CAs (see Table 1).

Table 1: Licenced Accountants in Ontario

Year	Existing Licences*				New Licences**			
	CA	CPA	OTHER	%CA's	CA	CGA	OTHER	DENIED
1983	7451	-	106	98.6	418	0	0	5
1982	7172	-	120	98.4	508	0	0	9
1981	6850	-	277	96.1+	509	0	1	19
1980	6476	-	424	93.9	514	0	0	11
1979	6074	-	438	93.3	588	0	0	11
1978	5929	-	460	92.8	439	0	0	8
1977	5317	-	488	91.6	547	1	2	9
1976	5011	-	525	90.5	618	1	1	16
1975	4586	-	540	89.5	462	2	1	13
1974	4217	-	565	88.2	410	1	0	21
1973	3956	—	583	87.2	281	2	0	14
1972	3749	-	605	86.1	321	2	2	17
1971	3526	-	629	84.9	314	1	4	14
1970	3355	-	660	83.6	288	5	1	17
1969	3215	-	688	82.4	241	0	2	20
1968	3116	-	703	81.6	223	10	1	11
1967	2920	-	722	80.2	264	6	2	16
1966	2723	-	740	78.6	215	11	1	15
1965	2610	-	764	77.4	128	7	0	17
1964	2535	-	795	76.1				
1963	2533	-	802	76.0++				
1962	1767	659	830	54.3				
1961	1647	600	797	54.1				
1960	1468	518	799	52.7			***	
1959	1421	463	829	52.4				
1958	1304	427	832	50.9				
1957	1211	378	856	49.5				
1956	1123	323	867	48.6				
1955	1005	323	869	45.7				
1954	842	305	889	41.4				
1953	740	302	881	38.5				
1952	658	291	858	37.3				
1951	613	295	815	35.6				

5

+   the ICAO granted CAs to 270 others and 60 CGAs;
++   the ICAO granted CAs to 1112 CPAs and 25 CGAs.

Sources:

*   abstracted from the 'Summary of licencees', Annual Report of the Public Accountants Councils for Ontario, 1965-1983;

**   abstracted from the 'Report of the Applications Committee',Annual Report of the Public Accountants Council for Ontario, 1965-83;

***   data unavailable, from 1951-64 the activities of the council were reported to licencees by letter, these letters are no longer on file.

The CAs' numerical dominance is reinforced by their control of the technology of public accounting -- accounting and auditing standards. The Canadian Institute of Chartered Accountants (CICA) prepares and maintains a handbook of standards which has been accepted as authoritative by the Canada Corporations Act which governs reporting by federally incorporated companies, and by the provincial securities exchange commissions which govern publically traded companies. The Handbook is also widely used on a voluntary basis by companies not subject to these sources of regulation.

The standard-setting process is administered by the CICA through the Accounting Research Committee (now the Accounting Standards Board and Auditing Standards Committee) which includes representatives of the CGA, CMA, and Financial Executives Institute of Canada (FEIC). It may be noted, however, that over 90% of FEIC members are CAs and nominees of the FEIC and CMA have often been CAs. The CGAs withdrew their support from the committee in 1981 claiming that they were unable to exert any influence. They subsequently sponsored an independent standard-setting body but this body has had no noticeable impact on the profession.

The CAs, both numerically and in terms of legal rights, are the dominant professional group. The CGAs and CMAs, which are close to each other in size

6

and status, occupy a secondary position while the remaining associations represent few accountants and do not significantly affect the development of the profession. The rise of the CAs to this position of dominance will be charted in terms of the use of transformism and expansive hegemony. It must be noted that this is not a complete analysis of the social position of the CAs. The ties between the CAs and the state, and the CAs relationship with clients are also relevant.

Transformism

The use of transformism to establish the hegemony of the CAs may be divided into two eras. During the first era, 1879 to 1902, the Institute of Chartered Accountants (ICAO) was the only accounting association in the Province. The focus of transformism in this era was the leaders of groups in society whose support, passive or active, was necessary to secure the social position of the Institute. This included members of the governing party, elite independent practitioners and heads of proprietary commercial schools. The second era, 1902 to 1983, saw the rise of competing associations and a shift in emphasis of transformism to establishing the hegemony of the Institute within the profession. The target of transformism in this era became those accountants in public accounting roles. This is the highest status role in the profession, garnering social recognition and rewards well above accountants in industry. Control of this segment of accounting, therefore, was necessary to achieve dominance in the profession.

The need for such tactics is evident in the Institute's attempt to gain a provincial charter in 1882. The legislature was dominated by rural representatives (Liberals) who saw the Institute as an attempt to create a monopoly and, consequently, rejected the application (Brown, 1905). The next year the Institute recruited more politically acceptable members to fill its executive positions and

7

reapplied. The President and Vice - President on the second application were both municipal politicians and prominent members of the Anglican Church and Masonic Order which were strongly represented in Government. A meeting in City Hall attended by many Toronto businessmen was then staged which passed resolutions urging government to grant the Institute a charter (Creighton, 1984: 13). On February 1, 1883, the ICAO finally gained its charter.

The Institute repeatedly sought out leaders of groups in areas in which it intended to operate. Following the first meetings in 1879, the Institute organized 'safaris' (Creighton, 1984: 7) to recruit prominent accountants in outlying regions. These campaigns were successful and by the time of incorporation 210 accountants were listed as members. The Institute also awarded memberships to the headmasters of commercial schools in the Province which were likely sources of new members. One notable example was the election of Mrs. M.L. Rattray, Principal of Shaw Correspondence Schools, to membership in 1885 becoming the Institute's first woman member. In 1896, however, women were banned from membership to strengthen social support for those holding the CA designation. This policy was not reversed until 1930.

In 1902 the Dominion Association of Chartered Accountants (DACA) was established and began granting their own CA designation. The ICAO unsuccessfully opposed the incorporation of the DACA and, thereafter, sought legislation to give the ICAO exclusive rights to the CA designation in Ontario. This action was inconclusive. The ICAO succeeded in gaining provincial legislation guaranteeing their rights but the DACA succeeded in having the Act declared ultra vires in the courts. In light of this stalemate, the leaders of the ICAO and DACA met in 1908 at the meetings of the American Association of Public Accountants and agreed to reorganize the DACA as a federation of the

8

existing provincial Institutes. Members of the DACA were given membership in the ICAO as part of this reorganization.

The ICAO's attempt to gain control of the CA designation in Ontario drew the attention of the British Colonial Office. The Colonial Office was concerned that if the ICAO was successful, British CAs would lose the right to use their designation in Ontario. The ICAOs solution was to create a "Registered Societies" list. Members of any society on this list, which included all British associations, could gain membership in the ICAO without examination and retain the right to use the CA designation.

The existence of senior accountants who were not CAs continued to concern the Institute. In 1917, two senior accountants were admitted to membership after writing "secret" examinations (Creighton, 1984: 75). Both men were partners of prominent accounting firms. It was important to the CAs that accountants admitted to membership in this manner be recognized leaders in the field. That year, for example, the Ontario government proposed amendments to the Loan and Trust Companies Act which would require auditors to be CAs. The Institute rejected this honour on the grounds that it would pressure them to accept as members "unqualified" accountants currently performing that work. Similarly, in 1916, the ICAO rejected an application for membership under special terms from an accountant with a small local practice by the name of Chester Walters. At that time Walters did not have the stature to seriously jeopardize the Institute's position. He was, however, to form the CPA Association.

As new associations arose in Ontario -- e.g. the Canadian Accountants Association in 1908 (incorporated in 1913 as the General Accountants Association using the CGA designation), the Society of Independent Accountants and Auditors in 1918 (incorporated as the United Accountants and Auditors in Canada in

9

1920), and the Association of Accountants and Auditors in 1921 (incorporated in 1926, eventually known as the Certified Public Accountants Association of Ontario [CPAAO] using the CPA designation) -- the objective of transformism shifted from attempting to secure the social position of the profession to attempts to establish the position of associations with respect to others within the profession.

For example, in 1933 the ICAO attempted to arrange special exams for a group of prominent CPAs, the major rival to the ICAO. In this case, the membership of the ICAO rejected the move, calling a meeting which passed a resolution banning the practice. The Council defended its proposal claiming that admission of these men would strengthen the Institute, pre-empting government intervention and countering criticism that the Institute was creating a monopoly (Creighton, 1984: 145)

The strategy adopted by several associations was to establish a numerical presence in the profession through mergers (see Table 2). This became common after the imposition of closure on the profession in Quebec in 1946. This political solution to the problem of rival groups in Quebec prompted efforts to obtain a civil solution in Ontario. At the same time, the ICAO recognized the opportunity to gain a political solution. In 1947, the ICAO drafted regulatory legislation which would secure legal protection of the dominant status they sought. The ICAO suggested the creation of a Public Accountants Council to regulate the profession. The council would include representatives of each association in proportion to the number of member actively involved in public accounting. According to estimates prepared by the ICAO, this would give the ICAO 75% of the seats on council, the remaining 25% would be split equally between the CPAAO and "other" groups. The government, however, encouraged the groups

10

to negotiate (discussed in the next section).

Table 2: Mergers and Attempted Mergers Within
the Ontario Accounting Profession

Year	Success	Accounting Association**						
		IPAA	IAEC	CA	CPA	CGA	CMA	APA
1922	NO				+	+		
1946	NO			+	+			
"	PARTIAL				+	+		
"	YES	+			+			
1952	NO		+		+			+
1957	YES	+						+
1958	YES		+					+
1960	NO			+	+			
"	YES			+	+			
"	NO					+	+	
1969	NO	+		+				+
1972	NO					+	+	
"	PARTIAL	+		+				
1980	YES					+		+
1981	YES	+		+				
Participation Rate* (%)		37	13	40	47	33	13	33

+ indicates that the association participated in the merger negotiations
* participation rate = (# of participations/total # of mergers) x 100
** column headings use the most recent designation of accounting associations and includes negotiations involving all predecessor associations.

After a number of meetings, the CPAs withdrew and attempted to strengthen their position by absorbing public accountants in other groups. They succeeded in absorbing the Independent Accountants Association of Ontario (about 100 people) and about 100 CGAs. The Toronto branch of the CGAs refused to join and continued in operation although their Directors had surrendered the association's charter. The CPAs also negotiated with the APAs and the IAEC. Although the executives of these associations approved the merger,

11

the CPA membership voted against implementation.

This wave of mergers shifted the numerical strength of associations. As a result, when the composition of Council was settled in 1950 the ICAO was given 8 members, the CPAAO 5 members, and 'other' accountants 2 members. As Table 1 demonstrates, in spite of efforts to organize the profession, independent accountants predominated in public accounting.

The legislation named the ICAO and CPAAO as "qualifying bodies" requiring all future accountants to complete their training programs and intermediate examinations to qualify as public accountants. This requirement allowed the CPAS and CAs to gain numerical dominance in the field. The ICAO reinforced this by merging with the CPAAO in 1962 and granting membership to 60 CGAs in public practice. The Public Accountants Act was then amended to name the ICAO as the sole qualifying body and to raise the entrance standard to their final examination. The dominance of the ICAO was further solidified by absorbing the majority of "other" public accountants in 1981.

The growth in the number of CAs in public practice from 1951 to 1981 can be decomposed as follows. First, 16% of the growth is due to the absorption of members of other associations and independent accountants by the ICAO. Second, 84% of the growth is due to CA students qualifying for practice. Although the proportion of growth due to transformism is significant, the effectiveness of this tactic, both prior to and after the enactment of legislation, is due to its selectivity. The ICAO targeted and successfully co-opted only those accountants in public practice.

Expansive Hegemony

The routine absorption of accountants from other associations into the ICAO could not in itself establish the dominance of the Institute. Each incident

12

224

resulted in a period of relative peace, a passive consensus on the place of each association, but the interests which the ICAO had co-opted soon redeveloped in other associations. These groups have repeatedly challenged the ICAO and attempted to establish themselves as equals in the field of public accounting. These challenges have failed in part because of the financial and political strengths of each association, but also because the ideology of the ICAO, reflected in its structure and defense against challenges, is largely accepted by other associations.

The ideology under which the CAs operate is a form of professionalism which has evolved to serve the interests of accountants within the Province. The initial adoption of this occupational form came about as a response to the demands of the state. The 1881 Bill petitioned for "corporate powers" by claiming, simply, that the ICAO was a "voluntary association". The Institute sought the right to "charge and take such fees from scholars, students or candidates as may be thought fit and promote the welfare of members". The use of the FCA designation (Fellow of the Chartered Accountants) was granted to any member "so long as they remain subscribing members of the Institute". The revised version submitted in 1883 referred to existing Institutes in England, and to the role of the ICAO as "an intellectual and educational movement". It also reduced the emphasis on payment of fees, completely removing references to the payments by students. As Creighton (1984:12) notes, the details of this petition were constructed to support the Institute's claim for recognition: the list of members was padded with the names of prominent accountants who were not members or who had initially been members but who had since resigned; and, the listing of past presidents was manipulated to create a more impressive heritage.

These changes served to associate the Institute with symbols which had a

13

strong basis in social legitimacy (Dowling and Pfeffer, 1975). On one hand, the new members and executives of the Institute established a tie to the social groups which constituted the governing party. These practitioners possessed attributes which Bourdieu and Passeron (1977) refer to as "cultural capital", i.e. general indicators of social status and power. On the other hand, the revised purposes of the Institute were shaped to reflect the priorities and social philosophies of the day.

The formal recognition of the ICAO as a professional body did not, however, secure its social position. The Institute was subject to charges that their entrance requirements created a "close corporation" [sic] (Bentley, 1938) and allowed "favouritism" in the selection of members (Edwards, 1921). Their education programs were criticized as narrow and inadequate (CPAAO Annual Report, 1949) and as creating a financial hardship which inhibited high quality training (Smails, 1926).

The Institute responded by refining and developing their examination and education process. The examination process was formalized with double blind grading to ensure objectivity. A program of course work was developed to prepare students for examinations and this grew into a university-based curriculum. The apprenticeship programs were overhauled. Offices which had articling students were inspected to ensure that students received broadly based and high quality experience. And the practice of indenturing students to a firm was replaced with registration with the Institute to allow students greater choice of workplace.

Through these actions the Institute was able to conform with the image of professionalism held by the public and developing within accountancy. Each of the major associations were developing similar procedures and structures

14

(Richardson, 1986). This aspect of expansive hegemony, while crucial to establishing the status of accountancy as a profession, did not, therefore, serve to differentiate the accounting associations which were competing for professional roles.

In order to achieve a division of labour among associations, a series of explicit negotiations centered on attempts to regulate public accounting and to establish its boundaries were undertaken. These negotiations centered on attempts to regulate public accounting and to establish its boundaries, particularly the distinction between public and cost or management accounting. The latter issue is typically referred to as "rationalizing" the profession.

Table 3: Negotiations Within the Ontario Accounting Profession

Year	Reason	Success	ACCOUNTING ASSOCIATION*						
			IPAA	IAEC	CA	CPA	CGA	CMA	APA
1913	Rationalization	Yes			+		+		
1920	Rationalization	Yes			+			+	
1948	Regulation	No	+		+	+			
1949	Regulation	No	+		+	+	+	+	
"	Rationalization	Yes			+			+	
1959	Rationalization	No			+		-	+	
1961	Rationalization	Yes			+	+		+	
1962	Rationalization	Partial			+	+	+	+	
1981	Rationalization	Yes			+		+		
Participation Rate (%)			20	0	100	40	40	60	0

+ participant in negotiations;
- invited to participate but declined

* column headings use the the the most recent designations of accounting associations and includes negotiations involving all predecessor associations.

The attempt to negotiate a division of labour began as soon as rival

15

associations emerged. The first organized competition came from the CGAs. The CGAs consisted of accountants in industry, notably employees of the Canadian Pacific Railway, and in negotiations with the CAs at the time of incorporation, agreed to limit their activities to advancing the status of accountants in industry. The CAs felt that this agreement would allow a "harmonious working relationship between the two organizations" (Canadian Chartered Accountant [CCA], 1922:254).

In the decade following incorporation, however, the CGA membership grew to include both public and management accountants, and the association began forming provincial chapters and advertising the CGA designation which, they claimed, was proof of competence as a public accountant. In 1920, following the United States and Great Britain, the CAs formed the Canadian Society of Cost Accountants. The Society was intended to provide a forum for accountants in industry to satisfy their needs for affiliation, social identification and advancement of their technical skills. It was explicitly "not intended to be a professional body" (CCA, V10:45). The Society was created to fill the role to which the CGAs had initially agreed but had subsequently exceeded.

The president of each provincial Institute sat on the Society's first Council, and the Institutes continued to appoint half of the Council for the next five years. This link served to provide the Society with sufficient resources and expertise to ensure its success, and to guide its actions into its "legitimate" domain (CCA V10:34). A break from this format occurred in 1938 when the Society voted to establish a training program and offer a designation. The issue divided the Society. A number of members who believed that the Society should serve those who interpret financial information rather than training those who must prepare it left to form the Controllers Institute. When the Society put this plan into effect

16

228

in 1941, however, it assured the ICAO that this did not represent a change in the domain occupied by the Society and that they "would not grant the use of the degree designation as a standard of qualification for practice in public accountancy" (Allan, 1982:32).

The next challenge to the ICAO came from an association which eventually became the "Certified Public Accountants". It was also known as the Society of Independent and Public Accountants, United Accountants and Auditors (UAA), and Accountants and Auditors of Ontario. In 1922 the UAA attempted to take over the CGA association to gain their designation granting authority. It was the intention of the UAA to use the CGA designation as a rival signal to the CA designation. The incumbent CGA executive rebuffed the UAA attempt, reaffirming their emphasis on cost accounting and their intent to meet the challenge provided by the Society of Cost Accountants (Creighton, 1984:124).

The UAA incorporated in 1926 as the Accountants and Auditors of Ontario using the LA, Licentiate in Accounting, designation. In 1933 the group began granting the IPA, Incorporated Public Accountant, designation and in 1936 changed to the CPA designation. Between 1936 and 1950 the association concentrated its activities in the public accounting field.

In the late 1940's the CAs drafted regulatory legislation and suggested that they and the CPA's form a regulatory council in proportion to the number of members each had in public practice. The CAs decision to include the CPAs recognized the fact that the CPAs included many highly placed civil servants with close ties to government. It was thought that these ties would allow them to block legislation which excluded their members. Initial estimates of the numbers of public accountants in each association indicated that the CAs were in the majority. The CPAs began negotiating mergers with other groups to establish a coalition

17

to represent the interests of non-CA accountants (discussed in the last section). Once the CPAAO strengthened its position, negotiations resumed.

One outcome of these negotiations was the Public Accountants Act of 1950 which established a Council to control entry to the practice of public accounting. The Act established the following definitions:

'public accountancy means the investigation or audit of accounting records or the preparation of or reporting on balance sheets, profit and loss accounts or other financial statements, but does not include bookkeeping, or cost accounting, or the installation of bookkeeping, business and cost systems;

public accountant means a person, alone or in partnership with others, carries on the practice of accountancy and in connection with that practice offers his services for reward to members of the public ...'

In order to qualify as a public accountant, it was necessary to pass the intermediate exam of either the CPAAO or the ICAO. This state continued for ten years, during which time the public accountancy membership of the CPA and CA grew rapidly compared with other accounting groups.

The CGAs, after a partial merger with the CPAs in 1950, began to rebuild and, in 1957, regained their charter. Many of the CGAs who had joined the CPA in 1950 were now involved in the CGA rebirth, giving the association a significant proportion of public accountants. This development lead the CPAAO to ban joint membership in accounting associations. This forced members caught between the two associations to choose. Since all CPA members had the right to licences as public accountants by virtue of their membership, the CGAs who did leave that organization were, understandably, mainly those in public accounting. The CGAs, once again, had become an association of industrial accountants.

In 1959 the CAs and CPAs began merger negotiations. The treatment of CPA students in industry became a major issue. While the formal education of

18

CPAs was similar to the CAs, the CPAs accepted practical experience gained in any context. The CAs were willing to accept CPA students in public practice but would not extend that offer to students whose experience, in the opinion of the CAs, was inadequate to prepare them for public practice. The situation was resolved through negotiations between the CAs, CPAs and CMAs. The CMAs took over the CPA training program, extending the CMA program from four to five years and strengthening their university affiliations, and accepted CPA students in industry into membership on completion of their training.

The merger was consummated in 1962 after the CA had overcome internal resistance to the marriage. The Public Accountants Act was subsequently amended to read:

'public accountant means a person who either alone or in partnership engages for reward in public practice involving,

(i) the performance of services which include causing to be prepared, signed, delivered and issued and financial, accounting or related statement, or

(ii) the issue of any written opinion, report or certificate concerning any such statement, where by reason of the circumstances or of the signature stationary or wording employed, it is indicated that such person or partnership acts or purports to act in relation to such statement, opinion, report or certificate as an independent accountant or auditor or as a person or partnership purporting to have expert knowledge in accounting or auditing matters, but does not include a person who engages only in bookkeeping or cost accounting ...'

The change in the two definitions is largely one of scope. The 1962 definition more narrowly defines the role of a public accountant and it is this narrow role which justifies the high standards demanded of auditors. This, in turn, was based on the separation of accounting practitioners into two streams represented by separate associations.

The attempted merger of the CPAs and CGAs had brought most of the

19

CGAs in public practice into membership in the CPA. The subsequent merger of the CAs and CPAs had further concentrated public accountants within the ICAO and this was reinforced by bringing 25 CGAs in public practice into the CA as part of the amendments to the Public Accountants Act in 1960. There was thus achieved a separation of public and cost accounting.

The CGA's and CMA's represented cost accountants and provided similar training programs. It was suggested, by the Ontario government among others, that these bodies merge to form an association to represent the interests of cost accountants. Negotiations were initiated but soon foundered as the CGAs reaffirmed their committment to both public and management accounting. This commitment reflected a contradiction between the economic organization of the profession and the division of labour which had been achieved giving the CAs exclusive public practice rights.

CA firms require "technicians" to perform routine duties. The firms use CA students, members of other associations to fill these roles and non-accounting personnel. Millie (1967) reported that 23% of the staff of CA firms fell into the latter two categories. With the switch to a university degree standard for CAs approved in 1970 and implemented in 1972, however, many firms could not afford to hire CA students as technicians and the number of members of other associations working in CA firms increased. The training provided by the CGA or CMA associations combined with experience gained in public accounting firms recreated constituencies of "public accountants" in management accounting associations most notably among CGAs.

This issue had concerned the CAs for a number of years. In 1967 a report recommended the creation of a technician category within the Institute arguing that such a group would "reduce substantially any need for the practicing firms

20

to employ students of other accounting bodies" (Millie, 1967). This recommendation was not followed up and in 1979 D.C. Scott (past president of the CA's) chided his peers for continuing to hire these students: "it seems dumb to hire CGAs. To sponsor those whose public intention is to bury us, does not seem very smart" (Creighton, 1984:319).

The conflict between the CGAs and CAs became public in 1974 when the Professional Organizations Committee (POC) of the Attorney General's Office was created to look into problems in several professions including accountancy. These events are considered in depth in the next section and are summarized here. The POC considered the definition of public accounting and its implications for the licencing regime which would be supported by the state. The division of labour in accounting was not challenged by the POC, and the Staff Report (Trebilcock et al., 1979) recommended that the definition of Public Accounting be narrowed to include only those financial reports required by statute. Presumably the existence of statutory requirements would indicate the cases in which protection of public interests was deemed most crucial and where the standards of competence must be highest. The final report of the committee (Leal et al., 1980) rejected the staff study, citing claims by the CMA and CGA that such a definition implied that their members were qualified to perform audits on some firms but not others, even though there is no difference in the complexity of the assignments. In addition, many non-audit reviews of financial information have the same intent, i.e. adding credibility, as statutory audits. The committee thus recommended a broad definition of public accounting and hence supported the claims of other accounting bodies, with lower entrance requirements, for access to this field.

It is clear that the organization of accountancy in Ontario is still in a state

21

of flux. The final section of this paper examines the hegemonic basis of the dominance of the CAs. This analysis suggests some likely directions of future interactions in the profession.

The Ideology of Accountancy

The success of CAs in establishing hegemony over the audit function through the strategies of transformism and expansive hegemony may be assessed by the extent to which groups within the profession share a common ideology. Ideologies, understood as systems of values and beliefs, are usually implicit in the actions of individuals and are taken - for - granted by those involved. The exception is during "critical situations" which Giddens (1979: 124) describes as "a set of circumstances which... radically disrupts accustomed routines of daily life". This disruption causes the assumptions which underlie routine activity to be explicitly raised as the key problematic of interaction. In this section, the most recent attempt by the CGAs to challenge the dominance of the CAs is used to identify and compare the ideologies of groups in the profession and to assess the extent to which the CAs have established their hegemony.

The CGA organization has repeatedly put forward claims for access to the public accounting field. In 1957 and 1961 the CGAs petitioned to be named a qualifying body under the Public Accountancy Act. These petitions were withdrawn when CGA's then in public practice were given CAs as part of the 1962 CA/CPA merger and subsequent amendments to the Act. In 1974 the CGA suggested broad changes in the composition of the Public Accountants Council which would give each association representation on the Council and, therefore, access to public practice.

The 1974 petition coincided with similar problems in other professions and the Attorney General's office created the Professional Organizations Committee

22

(POC) to consider these situations. Specifically, the POC was given a mandate to consider:

> '(1) the appropriateness of the existing division of functions and jurisdictions of these professional groups;... (2) the possible creation of new professional groups and sub-groups or the amalgamation of groups within these professions;... (3) the need for recognition and definition of roles of paraprofessionals;... (4) the amount of control these professional groups should have over the training and certification of their members;...' (Leal et al., 1980:1)

The POC provided a forum in which the CGA could air its views and, hence, forced the ICAO to legitimate its position in the profession.

The ICAO assured members that it would oppose the CGA petition. In its 1977 annual report, however, the Institute recognized that professions, in general, were facing pressure to allow greater competition. The amendment of the Federal Combines Investigation Act (concerning the creation of monopolies contrary to the public interest) in 1976 to include service industries and the recommendation of the McRuer Commission on Civil Rights (1967) that no professional body be allowed to maintain dominance over groups in the same field are examples of these pressures. In spite of these indicators of the times, the ICAO remained confident that it would fare well under the POC study. It was even suggested that the current state of affairs in the profession reflected these values.

In 1978, the ICAO noted that the composition of the POC favoured their view and the President of the ICAO assured members that the status quo would be maintained. By 1979, however, the ICAO found that the POC staff study was considering alternatives contrary to their prior expectations. The study adopted an economic perspective to determine the appropriate organization of accounting. This perspective implicitly rejects the CAs claim to be a profession and subjects it to economic tests of market efficiency rather than sociological tests of

23

professionalism.

Four "principles" were used to assess the current situation and possible alternatives: (1) the protection of vulnerable interests; (2) fairness of regulation; (3) feasibility of implementation; and, (4) public accountability. In the words of the staff report (Trebilcock et al., 1979:40):

'... one cannot simply proceed on the basis of which interests one wishes to favour over others. Rather, one requires generally accepted principles to apply such that the ultimate judgements about the balancing of competing claims will command widespread support.'

It is clear, however, that the value-standards, understood as situation specific values used to evaluate and legitimate action, adopted by the POC were not those widely held within the profession but were consistent with the CGA petition. The following year the committee's recommendations were put before the legislature and the ICAO expressed their opposition.

The debate over the legitimacy of the dominance of the CAs centered around the value-standards which should be used as normative bases for organizing the profession. The value-standards used by each party during this challenge were examined through a content analysis of documents presented to the POC. This analysis is summarized in Table 4.

The two main parties in the dispute were the CAs and the CGAs. The Public Accountants Council (PAC) also submitted a brief, however, this only received the approval of the CA members of the council and a minority brief was also submitted by the elected members of the Council (all APA's). The views of four groups -- CAs, CGAs, APAs and the PAC -- are thus represented in this analysis.

24

	Body Citing Standards			
	CA	CGA	APA	PAC
Equity				
(1) of treatment under existing norms	0	9.1	38.5	0
(2) of existing norms	0	3.0	7.7	0
(3) of representation	0	6.1	7.7	0
(4) of opportunity to practice (based on a realistic assessment of skill needs	4.1	18.2	7.7	6.3
	4.1	36.4	61.6	6.3
Unity				
(1) of standards	16.3	0	11.5	18.8
(2) of public accounting	4.1	0	3.9	12.5
(3) of accounting overall	0	6.1	0	0
	20.4	6.1	15.4	31.3
Public Interest				
(1) responsive to community/government	8.2	21.2	3.9	6.3
(2) choice among practitioners	0	6.1	3.9	0
(3) high standards of practice	28.6	9.1	3.9	37.5
(4) continuing education/discipline	10.2	12.1	0	12.5
(5) unspecified	0	3.0	0	0
	47.0	51.5	11.7	56.3
Consistency				
(1) with laws	4.1	0	0	0
(2) with past agreements	10.2	0	0	0
	14.3	0	0	0
Opportunity				
(1) for social mobility (multiple paths)	0	6.1	11.5	0
(2) for social mobility (single path)	14.3	0	0	0
	14.3	6.1	11.5	0
Efficiency of Regulation	0	0	0	0
Number of Times Value-Standards Cited	49	33	26	16
Number of Paragraphs Reviewed	115	71	38	23

*The reliability of the coding procedures used in this analysis was tested in two ways: test-retest reliability of the main coder was 0.88 (over twenty pages of text with three months between codings), and interrater reliability was 0.67 (Holsti, 1969: 0.47 when corrected for base rates according to the Scott index of reliabilty). Details of the procedure are provided in Richardson, 1985a: Appendix B.

25

The CAs argued that the organization of the profession should be based on a single, high standard of competence administered by a single body within the public accounting field. These values are also reflected in the brief prepared by the PAC who felt that "the training and examination standards set by the ICAO are sufficiently high to ensure a fair degree of protection to the public and that this standard should not be lowered."

The Council, although dominated by appointees of the ICAO, responded to the CGA petition as an independent body, noting that "since the Petition deals with matters that are the responsibility of this Council it is considered appropriate that Council should express its views."

The three APA members of Council submitted a minority brief on the CGA petition. As shown in Table 4, while reaffirming the principles of unity and high standards, the APA's suggested a different institutional framework for their enactment. They suggested that the Public Accountants' Council, reconstituted to eliminate the dominance of the ICAO, be given "the power to determine the qualifications necessary for licencing and responsibility for establishing and maintaining standards of excellence required of licencees." The APA's brief argues that the present Council has not exercised its perogatives in an equitable manner. They describe the Council's actions as an "abuse of power".

The value-standards cited by the CGA contrast markedly with those cited by the ICAO. In the seventen categories used in the analysis, there are only four categories which are cited by both the CGA and the ICAO. Seven categories are cited only by the CGA, while the remaining six were cited by the ICAO but not by the CGA. The CGA called for representation of all accountants, regardless of specialty, on any controlling body and access to professional status through a diversity of career paths based on a functional specification of the necessary level

26

of competence. They also support the existence of multiple accounting bodies, arguing that the combination of marketplace competition and collegial control is more effective than collegial control alone in safeguarding the public interest. Along with this view is the contention, contrary to the CAs, that the public is able to differentiate between accounting designations (see Perry, H. (Executive Director, CGAAO) CGA Magazine V10:27-28).

In areas where the CGA and CAs agree in principle, there are differences in emphasis. For example, while both clearly recognize that the profession must safeguard the "public interest", the CAs see this as being accomplished through high standards of initial competence and practice (set and maintained by the profession), while the CGA sees this as being accomplished through competition among practitioners and responsiveness to environmental forces (particularly government policy).

Interestingly, the CGA call for representation of all associations on any board set up to control entry to public accounting was rejected by the CMA, who were not included in the discussions and indicated (through the ICAO) that they did not desire such a role. The CMA annual reports of the period, however, indicate a less clear cut response to the proposal. They express a willingness to "accept the responsibility of licencing ... members" and provide "all necessary support facilities."

The Report of the POC released in April, 1980 describes the situation in the profession as "a history of recurring outbursts of organizational rivalry and recurring attempts to snatch harmony from the jaws of discord." The Report recommended that:

> (1) the CGA should be incorporated by statute (rather than letters patent) and should be given the CGA as a reserved title;
> (2) each of the CMA, ICAO and CGA should be empowered to grant

27

licences;

(3) all current public accountants, not members of either the CMA or ICAO, should become members of the CGAAO;

(4) the definition of public accounting should be expanded to include any action designed to add credibility to financial information;

(5) each association adopt and enforce the CICA handbook as the standard of auditing practice;

(6) public accountants should be licenced by passing a common examination set by a Public Accounting Licencing Admissions Board (PALAB) composed of representatives of each association, colleges and universities, and the Ontario Securities Commission; and,

(7) the ICAO transfer its uniform final examination role to the PALAB to serve as the common examination for public accountants.

These recommendations, while "recognizing the pre-eminence of the ICAO in the profession", would remove the dominance enjoyed by the ICAO.

In the year following the release of the report, the unaffiliated public accountants, who had not been contacted by the POC during its deliberations, approached the ICAO seeking membership. The ICAO regarded this as evidence of the preferences of this group on the organization of the profession. "They wished to become CAs and they wanted the Institute to remain the only qualifying body for public accounting licences." The ICAO saw granting this group membership as being "in the public interest and ... totally consistent with our commitment to a single standard". A motion accepting them into membership without examination was passed by an overwhelming majority (5070 to 930).

The CGA, however, saw the same event as "an apparent attempt to undermine the POC recommendations." Specifically, the move contradicted the recommendation that all unaffiliated public accountants become CGAs. The APAs merged with the CGAAO in 1981.

In 1982, the CGA, following the POC report, applied for incorporation by statute. Their bill was opposed by the ICAO, CMA and PAC who succeeded

28

in having auditing deleted from the association's list of educational responsibilities, and in having a clause added which denied CGAs the right to practice as public accountants. The ICAO recognized that this Act would allow the CGA to "obtain the enhanced credibility that a statutory umbrella would provide." In recent advertisements the CGA continues to list auditing as one of the possible careers for its graduates.

Discussion

The basic pattern explored in this paper has been identified in other professions (eg Freidson, 1970; Johnson, 1977, 1982; Armstrong, 1979) but attention to political processes within the accounting profession is only recently gaining attention (eg Armstrong, 1985; Willmott, 1986; Loft, 1986). This approach to studying the profession is consistent with attempts to consider the role of accounting in its social and organizational context (Burchell et al., 1980; Tinker, 1980). It supports this effort by demonstrating that who practices accounting, and how professional roles are organized, can have a significant impact on accounting practice (Parker, 1977). The accounting profession is not simply a passive medium through which social forces are transcribed into accounting theory and practice. It is a social system which contributes independently to the shape of accounting practice.

This paper has focused on the strategies used by one segment of the profession to gain and maintain a dominant position within the profession. The CAs have used tactics in both civil and political society. In civil society, they have attempted to gain consensus on the division of labour in the profession and their entitlement to the public accounting role. This has involved the co-optation, or in the vocabulary of the profession "grandfathering", of individuals whose interests coincide with those of the Institute. This strategy has been limited by the

29

concern of existing members that public respect for the designation would be "watered down" by bringing individuals into membership without the usual training and examinations. There is also concern about the increasing competition among CAs that this strategy creates. The strategy has also been limited due to the recognition by other accounting groups that this strategy is being used. The CGAs, for example, made this statement to the POC: "And if we can leave you with no other impression, it would really be that ... we are not anxious to join the ICAO. They are entitled to their regiment, and we are entitled to our regiment" (Leal et al., 1980). In editorials at this time, the CGA called on their members to remain loyal.

The second strategy in civil society has been to be responsive to critics and to adopt the values used to assess associations' right to special privilege. This has resulted in competition among associations to remain the "most" professional. Each association has adopted education and examination processes of increasing rigor and have made significant innovations in procedures to ensure continuing competence. Unfortunately, the simultaneous development of these procedures in several associations precludes their use in attempts to differentiate associations. There have also been explicit negotiations among associations to establish a division of labour. These have been reasonably successful, particularly when combined with the use of transformism to bring about congruence between the tasks assigned to different associations and the work roles of members. The difficulty is that the economic organization of the profession contradicts its institutional structure. In the ICAO, which clearly dominates public accounting, members are increasingly finding employment in management accounting roles. And in public practice, licenced accountants continue to use members of management accounting associations to perform routine audit work. The result is

30

that the Institute comes under criticism from its own members for not providing services to those in management accounting roles while being challenged from without by accountants who believe they have sufficient training and experience in public accountancy to qualify for a licence to practice.

When the beliefs of accountants are examined, it is clear that the CAs have failed to establish hegemony in accountancy. Although numerically the CAs ideology is supported by a majority of accountants, a significant minority holds views which do not legitimate the CAs dominance of public accounting. Increasingly, therefore, it has been necessary for the ICAO to turn to mechanisms in political society to maintain their position. This has included the development of regulation for public accounting, the use of their position on the Public Accountants Board to restrict access to licences to practice as a public accountant, and opposition to attempts by other groups to improve their status in the courts, legislature and before public inquiries. The use of political mechanisms, of course, has been in addition to a continuing attempt to achieve a civil solution.

The overall picture which emerges from this study is one of a profession in "process" (Bucher and Strauss, 1961). The definition of public accountancy and the identification of those practitioners who will be deemed qualified to undertake this work is still emerging from the interaction of various segments within the profession. The institutional structure of public accounting which exists at any point in time is clearly a transient equilibrium of forces acting on and within the profession.

31

Footnotes

1. Details of the incidents described and sources may be found in "An Interpretative Chronology of the Development of Accounting Associations in Canada" published in this volume.

2. Throughout this paper accountants and associations will be referred to by their most recent designation. Although this may not be historically correct in all instances, it is necessary to ensure the readability of the paper.

32

Index of Abbreviations

APA	Accredited Public Accountant
CA	Chartered Accountant
CCA	Canadian Chartered Accountant (Magazine)
CGA	Certified General Accountant
CICA	Canadian Institute of Chartered Accountants
CMA	Certified Management Accountant
CPA	Certified Public Accountant
CPAAO	Certified Public Accountants Association of Ontario
DACA	Dominion Association of Chartered Accountants
FCA	Felow of the Chartered Accountants
FEIC	Financial Executives Institute of Canada
GICIA	Guild of Industrial, Commercial and Institutional Accountants
IAEC	International Accountants and Executives Corporation
ICAO	Institute of Chartered Accountants of Ontario
IPA	Incorporated Public Accountant
IPAA	Independent Public Accountants Association
LA	Licentiate in Accounting
POC	Professional Organizations Committee
UAA	United Accountants and Auditors
PAC	Public Accountants Council

33

Bibliography

AICPA Professional Accounting in 30 Countries (New York: American Institute of Certified Public Accountants 1975)

Allan, J.N. History of the Society of Management Accountants of Canada, (Hamilton: SMAC 1982)

Armstrong, D. 'The Emancipation of Biographical Medicine', Social Science and Medicine, (1979) V13a:1-8.

Armstrong, P. 'Changing Management Control Strategies: the role of competition between accountancy and other organizational professions' Accounting Organizations and Society (1985) V10 N2: 129-148

Bentley, W. History of the General Accountants Association 1908 to 1938 mimeo, (1938) Canadian General Accountants Association

Berlant, J.L. Profession and Monopoly (Berkeley: University of California Press 1975)

Bourdieu, P. and Passeron, J.C. Reproduction in Education, Society and Culture (London: Sage 1977)

Brown, R. A History of Accounting and Accountants (New York: Kelley 1905[1968])

Bucher, R. and Strauss, A. 'Professions in Process', American Journal of Sociology, (1961) V66:325-334.

Burchell, S., Clubb, C., Hopwood, A. and Naphapiet, J. 'The Roles of Accounting in Organizations and Society' Accounting, Organizations and Society (1980) V5 : 5 - 27

Carr-Saunders, A.M. and Wilson, P.A. The Professions (Oxford: Clarendon Press 1933)

Crieghton, P. A Sum of Yesterdays (Toronto: Institute of CharteredAccountants

34

of Ontario 1984)

Edwards, G. 'The Educational Responsibilities of the Chartered Accountants Societies' Canadian Chartered Accountant (1921) V11: 147-152

Dowling, J.B. and Pfeffer, J. 'Organizational Legitimation' Pacific Sociological Review (1975) V18 N1: 122-136

Freidson, E. Professional Dominance (New York: Atherton 1970)

Giddens, A. Central Problems in Social Theory (Berkeley: University of California Press, 1979)

Gramsci, A. Selections from the Prison Notebooks of Antonio Gramsci (Hoare, Q. and Smith, G.N. trans.) (New York: International Publishers, 1971)

Johnson, T. and Caygill, M. 'The Development of Accountancy Links in the Commonwealth' Accounting and Business Research (1971) Spring: 135-173

Johnson, T. 'The Professions in the Class Structure', in Scase, R. (Ed.), Industrial Society: Class, Cleavage and Control, (New York: St. Martin 1977)

Johnson, T. 'The State and the Professions' in Giddens, A. and MacKenzie, G. (Eds.) Social Class and the Division of Labour Cambridge: Cambridge University Press 1982)

Larson, M.S. The Rise of Professionalism, (Berkeley: University of California Press 1977)

Leal, H.A., Corry, J.A. and Dupre, J.S. The Report of the Professional Organizations Committee (Ministry of the Attorney General of Ontario, Toronto: Queen's Park Printer 1980)

Loft, A. 'Towards a critical understanding of accounting: the case of cost accounting in the U.K., 1914-1925' Accounting Organizations and Society

35

(1986) V11 N2: 137-170

Mann, H. The Evolution of Accounting in Canada, (Montreal: Touche Ross and Company 1976)

Millie, I.E. 'Report to the Council on the use of Technicians' mimeo, Institute of Chartered Accountants of Ontario (April, 1967)

Mouffe, C. 'Hegemony and Ideology in Gramsci' in Bennett, T.; Martin, G.; Mercer, C. and Woollacott, J. (Eds.), Culture, Ideology and Social Process, (London: Open University Press 1981)

Parker, R.H. 'Research needs in accounting today' Accounting Historians Journal (1977) V4 N2

Parsons, T. Essays in Sociological Theory (Glencoe: Free Press 1954)

Portwood, D. and Fielding, A. 'Privilege and the Professions' Sociological Review (1981) V29 N4: 749-773

Richardson, A.J.' Legitimation, Professionalization and Intraprofessional Competition' unpublished Doctoral Dissertation, Queen's University, Canada (1985a).

----'The Professionalization of Accountancy in Canada' Proceedings of the Canadian Academic Accounting Association, (Montreal, May 1985b)

----'Professionalization and Intraprofessional Competition in the Canadian Accounting Profession' Work and Occupations V14 N4 (1987) 591-615

----'The Production of Institutional Behaviour' Canadian Journal of Administrative Sciences, V3 N2 (1986): 304-316

Ross, H. and Brown, G.History of the Guild of Industrial Commercial and Institutional Accountants mimeo, (Toronto: GICIA 1978)

Smails, R.G.H. 'Letter to the Editor' The Accountant (March 6, 1926)

Swinburne, F. 'History of Accounting Bodies in Canada', Industrial, Commercial

36

and Institutional Accountants Journal, (1982) V1:34-36.

Tinker, A.; Merino, B.D. and Neimark, M.D. 'The Normative Origins of Positive Theories: Ideology and Accounting Thought' Accounting Organizations and Society (1982) V7 N2: 167-200

Trebilcock, M.J.; Tuohy, C.J. and Wolfson, A.D. Research Directorate Staff Study (Toronto: Ministry of the Attorney General 1979)

Tremain, D.J. Occupational Prestige in Comparative Perspective (New York: Academic Press 1977)

Willmott, H. 'Organizing the Profession' Accounting Organizations and Society, (1986)

37

The Accounting Historians Journal
Vol. 16, No. 1
June 1989

Alan J. Richardson
QUEEN'S UNIVERSITY

CANADA'S ACCOUNTING ELITE: 1880-1930

Abstract: This paper provides an analysis of "elite" accounting practitioners during the formative years of the Canadian accounting profession (1880-1930). The social characteristics of this group in comparison with the Canadian population and the links between the accounting elite and other elite groups in society are used to evaluate the extent to which the profession achieved democratic ideals of access and social mobility for all members of society. The operation of the accounting profession as a democratic institution is argued to be an important aspect of the profession's claim to serve the public interest.

The professions have earned a place of privilege in western societies. They have gained legislative recognition, and often protection, of their occupational domains from the state. They also have been given rights of self-government within a narrowly defined sphere in recognition of the difficulties experienced by laymen in evaluating the quality of professional practice. The powers exercised by the professions have lead observers such as Gilb [1966, 1981] to characterize them as "private interest governments." In the same way that public governments act to translate a society's values (or sub-set of those values) into law and an authoritative allocation of resources, the professions act to create and enforce laws (eg. licensing and ethics), to impose taxes (eg. professional dues) and to provide access to market opportunities (eg. areas of restricted practice) and positions of political power (eg. executive positions in professional associations). The privileges granted to the professions by society carry a responsibility, meeting this responsibility justifies the continuation of those privileges.

The professions' place in society is justified by claims that they serve the public interest. Within liberal democracies the

This work has been supported by grants from the D.I. McLeod Fund, the Advisory Research Committee and Principal's Development Fund, Queen's University. The research assistance of Kathy Klaas and Lynn MacDonald on this project is gratefully acknowledged. The paper has benefited from the constructive criticism of Tony Dimnik, Norm Macintosh, Dean Neu and the *Journal's* reviewers.

concept of the public interest has two implications for the professions. First, it implies that practitioners will meet the needs of *individual* clients within the norms of professional practice. This aspect of the public interest underlies confidentiality rules and the concern that all members of society should have access to professional services (eg. the Hippocratic Oath). It is also presumed that practitioners will limit themselves to areas in which they are technically competent and will ensure that the highest professional standards are followed. The public interest is thus served through the competent performance of socially valued skills equally available to all members of society.

Second, the public interest concept implies that the professions should be open to all members of society with the ability and desire to gain the necessary skills. The professions are seen as an important medium for social mobility [eg. Giddens, 1973; Parkin, 1979], they provide the career paths which allow individuals to achieve their potential in society. It is recognized, however, that in any society characterized by a complex division of labor and bureaucratic organizations all individuals will not be equal in wealth, status or power. Michel's [1958 [1911]] "Iron Law of Oligarchy" assures that the overall direction and policy will be set by an elite who occupy the "command posts" [Mills, 1956] of the profession. Most democratic theorists accept the existence of elites as a functional necessity [eg. Lipset and Bendix, 1959; but see Bachrach, 1967] but, to paraphrase Thomas Jefferson, require that elites should represent an aristocracy of achievement based on a democracy of opportunity. The public interest is thus also served through the provision of opportunities for individuals to advance their status in society through membership in a profession.

This paper focuses on the latter issue and presents an analysis of elite practitioners during the formative years of the accounting profession in Canada (1880-1930). Drawing on the theory of democratic elitism [cf. Bachrach, 1967; Prewitt and Stone, 1973], accountancy may be said to be a democratic institution, and, therefore, fulfill its responsibility to the public interest in the second sense described above, if three conditions are met. First, all members of society must have the opportunity to become an elite member of the profession. This implies that there should be no systematic biases in recruitment to the profession. The study of elites provides indirect evidence on this requirement by demonstrating the existence of ascriptive criteria affecting individual achievement in the profession. If these criteria are public knowledge, self-selection to the profession will bias recruitment patterns.

The study of elites, however, provides direct evidence on a second requirement that all social interests be represented within the elite. As Porter [1957] has noted, the study of elites "is an attempt to discover the principles on which a social system allocates certain types of individuals to . . . positions of power and, thereby, denies power to others." Under ideal conditions one would expect that individual attributes unrelated to the instrumental performance of a task would be unrelated to success in that field of endeavor. It has been argued that this should be particularly true in the early years of the development of industrial economies when entrepreneurial activity is most prevalent and highly rewarded [Kaelble, 1981]. It is clear, however, that certain criteria such as gender, religion or ethnicity have and do affect the career success of individuals. By examining the social characteristics of elite accountants, the non-instrumental bases for stratification and occupational closure [cf. MacDonald, 1985] of the profession can be identified.

Finally, a third criteria for evaluating the profession's service to the public interest is to determine the extent to which the elite of the accounting profession is independent of elites in other sectors of the economy, and thus able to exercise "checks and balances" on each other. While the concept of independence of auditors is well established in the accounting literature, this criterion extends the profession's responsibility to that of remaining independent of larger social interests which might influence the profession's institutional structure or practices.

The paper is organized as follows. The first section describes the sample selection procedures and method of analysis to be followed. This is followed by a three-way comparative analysis between (1) the Canadian accounting elite, (2) the Canadian (non-accounting) social elite and (3) the general population (where applicable). This analysis covers education and careers, ethnic and religious affiliation, and political preferences and offices, and social and service club memberships. The paper concludes with a discussion of the results.

METHOD

While the *concept* of an elite is established in the sociological literature, the *operationalization* of the concept has been problematic [cf. Giddens, 1974; Moyser and Wagstaffe, 1987]. In essence, the problem of operationalization concerns (1) establishing the boundaries of the functional or institutional sphere for which an elite is to be identified and (2) identifying specific individuals within this sphere who qualify as members of the elite. For example, in Porter's [1957] classic study of the Canadian economic elite, the economic sphere was defined as 170 "dominant" corporations identified by their control of assets and market share in their respective industries; the Canadian economic elite was then identified as those directors of the dominant corporations resident in Canada. Both of these aspects of Porter's definitions have been challenged. Ashley [1957] suggests that the dependence of economic activity on the banking industry and the dense network of interlocking directors between the banks and other sectors of the economy is such that the directors of banks alone define the economic elite. Pahl and Winkler [1974] have also suggested that the key decision-makers in corporations are the members of the executive committees and only these members should be considered part of the elite [cf. Heap, 1974, for other definitional problems in Porter's work].

The operationalization of an "accounting elite" is no less beset with difficulty. One possibility is to use an inventory of institutional positions in order to define the elite analogously to Olsen's [1980] study of *The State Elite in Canada*. It would be possible to identify directors of professional associations, senior partners in accounting firms and accounting educators as part of the elite. This approach, however, would omit accountants in industry and the public sector, and would ignore accountants in public practice who were not members of accounting associations. The latter oversight would be particularly serious in the early years of the profession prior to its consolidation.

It is also difficult to use work roles to establish basic boundaries on the sphere of influence as may be possible in professions such as medicine or law. Accounting has developed licensing and certification processes relatively recently and over the last hundred years the occupation of accountancy has referred to a shifting task domain. For example, much of the early accounting work focused on bankruptcies but has grown to include and be refocused on auditing, taxation and management advisory services [cf. Jones, 1980]. The term "accountant" thus is a linguistic category with a shifting task referent; in part any study of the evolution of accounting is a study of the semantics of occupational labels. It would bias any study of the profession to impose *a priori* constraints on the task domain into which this term was mapped at any point in history [see Stewart *et al.*, 1980, for an extended discussion of this issue].

The resolution of these issues adopted in this study is to use the methodology of Mills [1945] and Lipset and Bendix [1962] to identify the elite. Their approach is to recognize that elite status is a complex mixture of social prestige, wealth and power. The elite is not, therefore, restricted to any set of institutional positions; rather, it is recognized that allocative and authoritative dominance may also be exercised informally. They rely on the complex social judgments of the editors of biographical dictionaries as the basis for the identification of the elite. These judgments may then be validated by analysis of the elites' standing on objective but partial measures of power and privilege (eg. institutional and market positions). Subclassifications of the elite into functional areas can be accomplished based on the biographical data relying on the historical contingent terms in which individuals position themselves within society. Lipset and Bendix [1962] provide a comparison of this method with other approaches to elite identification which indicates its validity.

The subjects of this study are those individuals listed in *Canadian Who's Who* [1910 and/or 1936 editions] and/or *Who's Who in Canada* [1910 - 1930 editions]. *Canadian Who's Who* was first published in 1910 by the Times Publishing Company of London, England. In 1932, the copyright to this title was purchased by Alfred Leonard Tunnel and, in 1936, in association with Sir Charles George Douglas Roberts, produced a second edition. The 1936 edition incorporated *Canadian Men and Women of the Time* (Edited by Henry James Morgan) which had been published in 1898 and 1912. *Who's Who in Canada* was published by International Press Ltd. These data bases are widely used as a means of gathering data on the elite of Canadian society [eg. Porter, 1967; Clements, 1975; Olsen, 1980].

Both listings include the major political, industrial, academic, artistic, and religious figures of the time in addition to numerous individuals who had been nominated to them (in the case of *Canadian Who's Who*) or whose name had appeared in major newspapers or magazines (in the case of *Who's Who in Canada*). The listings are not identical, but together provide a representative cross-section of Canada's social elite. It must be noted that both sources had a policy of having individuals verify the information included under their name. While this adds to the reliability of the data, it allows for a self-selection bias; individuals failing to confirm or provide information were not included. This feature may explain the absence from this list of such prominent accountants as George Edwards (although other

members of his firm were included) and John Hyde and E.R.C.
Clarkson (although their sons are included and their entries note
that their fathers were prominent Chartered Accountants).
Other prominent names (such as Samuel Harman, president of
the ICAO at the time of incorporation) are missing because they
were deceased at the time of compliation of the first volume in
1898. The list produced thus provides a representative sample
and not a comprehensive listing of elite accountants over the
first fifty years of the profession's existence.

Two samples from these data bases are used in the analysis.
The first sample uses all individuals listing accounting or
auditing as part of their biography (this may be as an occupation or as part of their training). This selection criteria produced
seventy-nine (79) names which are listed in Appendix A. The
second sample consists of a random selection of non-accounting
listings. For convenience, this sample consisted of the first
non-accounting listing appearing on the same page as an accounting listing (the non-accounting sample is thus matched for
year of listing). This selection criteria also produced seventy-
nine (79) names. Where appropriate, comparison data on the
general population has been drawn from the 1891 or 1931
Census of Canada.

THE ACCOUNTING ELITE'S POSITION
IN THE PROFESSION

The method of identifying the accounting elite in this study
is essentially reputational. It is a necessary starting point to
validate this definition of the elite by analysis of this group's
position within institutions and the market place (a further
validation would require evidence of the decision-making roles
taken by this group, but such information is as yet unavailable).
If this method is valid, this group should include, for example,
the executives of accounting associations and senior partners of
the larger accounting firms.

The group identified as the accounting elite in this paper
were significantly involved in organized professional activities.
Among the 79 accountants, 66 were CAs (23 were FCAs), 1 was a
member of the Society of Accountants and Auditors, and 1 was a
member of the Corporation of Public Accountants of the Province of Quebec (CPAPQ); 11 indicated no memberships in
professional bodies. Among the CAs, 3 listed additional memberships in the Canadian Society of Cost Accountants (CSCA), 3
in the Society of Accountants and Auditors, 4 in the National
Association of Cost Accountants (USA), and 1 in the CPAPQ. The

list includes 25 Presidents of various CA Institutes, 1 President of the CPAPQ and 1 President of the CSCA. A further 17 had served on the executive board of professional associations.

Among the accounting group, 18% were employed in industry, 3% in education, 4% in the civil service, 75% in public accounting (2 in other pursuits). By comparison, among the non-accounting groups, 21% were in industry, 15% in education, 17% in civil service and 47% in other pursuits (primarily professions). Among the public accounting group, 45% were partners in the large public accounting firms while the remainder were in small partnerships. Particularly prominent among the large firms are P.S. Ross and Company of Montreal with six partners listed and the Clarkson partnerships (names varies over this period) also with six partners listed. All of the (then) major public accounting firms are represented in the elite.

The accounting sample, based on these data, appears to include those individuals in key positions within both professional associations and accounting firms. It appears reasonable to use this group as a sample of the elite in the profession. The remainder of this paper will examine the social characteristics of this sample and their position in society compared with the general population and the elite in other sectors of Canadian society. In all cases, the implicit hypothesis is that the elite will be representative of Canadian society if recruitment to these positions reflects democratic ideals.

Birthplace and Religious Affiliation

The birthplaces of the two elite groups and the Canadian population as a whole are listed in Table 1. For comparison, census data for 1931 and 1881 are included. The 1931 census data reflect the population for the time period in which the elite were identified. The 1881 census data reflect the population at the likely period of birth of the 1931 elite (this follows the assumption of Clement, [1975], but note that this comparison assumes either low rates of immigration or the slow integration of immigrants into society). Neither the accounting nor the non-accounting groups are representative of the population as a whole regardless of the census year used for comparison. The proportion of native born among the non-accounting elite (75.9%) is roughly equal to the proportion of native born in the population (77.6%). The accounting elite has a lower proportion of native born (57.5%) and has an unusually high proportion of individuals born in Great Britain (England, Scotland or Ireland) compared with either the population as a whole or the non-accounting elite. Ontario born individuals are overrepresented in both elite groups, while Quebec born individuals are under-represented. This finding is consistent with Porter's [1957] study of the economic elite of Canada in the mid 1950s which found that in spite of the rough equality of numbers between those with English and French backgrounds (the two dominant cultures in Canada at the time of Confederation), those of Anglo-Saxon origin dominated the elite.

Cook and Brown [1974] note that the industrialization of Quebec did not advance the social status of francophones in the same way as anglophones. The background of French immigrants led them to develop small scale manufacturing based on craft skills. The social values of this group, reflecting Catholic teachings, did not favor rapid capital accumulation and thus the investment funds in the province tended to remain under anglophone control. Observers of the growing anglophone economic dominance of this province lamented the lack of economic leaders among the francophone population but inspite of these concerns, few francophones achieved positions of economic power [Cook and Brown, 1974: 131-135].

Table 1
Percentage of Distribution of Birthplace

Place of Birth	Elite Accounting	Non-Accounting	1931 Census of Canada	1881 Census of Canada
British Columbia	0	1.20	2.39	0.8
Prairie Provinces	0	4.82	12.55	1.8
Ontario	36.25	34.94	26.93	34.0
Quebec	18.75	15.66	25.98	30.8
Maritime Provinces	2.50	19.28	9.73	18.8
Sub-total for Canada	57.50	75.90	77.58	86.20
England	23.75	9.64	7.19	3.9
Ireland	7.50	2.41	1.04	4.3
Scotland	10.00	4.82	2.70	2.7
Sub-total for Great Britain	41.25	16.87	10.93	10.90
Other	1.25	7.23	11.31	3.0

Chi-Square =   28.1 df = 8 $p<0.05$ accounting elite vs non-accounting elite
Chi-Square = 107.3 df = 8 $p<0.05$ accounting elite vs 1931 census
Chi-Square =   23.2 df = 8 $p<0.05$ non-accounting elite vs 1931 census
Chi-Square = 115.2 df = 8 $p<0.05$ accounting elite vs 1881 census
Chi-Square =   23.4 df = 8 $p<0.05$ non-accounting elite vs 1881 census

The skewed ethnic origins of the accounting elite becomes particularly noticeable when compared with other levels of the occupational status hierarchy within accountancy. The 1931 Census provides data on th country of origin of two groups within accountancy: the lower level bookkeepers (and cashiers) and the higher status group of accountants and auditors. The degree of detail of origins reported in Table 1 is not available on these groups in the Census data. Table 2 provides a comparison of the ethnic origins across bookkeepers, accountants and the accounting elite. As this Table shows, at increasing levels of this status hierarchy, there is an increasing proportion of the group born in Great Britain and a decreasing proportion born in Canada. Although this trend is marked, "nativism" does not appear to have been a major issue in Canada unlike Miranti's (1988) observations of New York State.

Table 2
The County of Origin of Accountants, Bookkeepers and the Elite

Country of Origin	Percentage of		
	Accounting Elite	Accountants	Bookkeepers
Canada	57.5	59.7	73.3
Great Britain	41.3	35.1	21.1
Other	1.2	5.2	5.6

The data on birthplace and religious affiliation are not independent as different regions tend to be dominated by particular religions. The relationship between elite membership and religious affiliation does, however, provide additional information on the ascriptive criteria affecting membership in the elite. Both the accounting and non-accounting elites show significant differences in religious affiliation compared with the population as a whole, particularly the high proportion of Anglicans. The two elite groups are only marginally different with the accounting elite being more homogeneous than the non-accounting elite.

In comparing Table 1 and 3 it may be noted that there is a disparity between recruitment from Quebec (which is predominately French-Canadian, francophone and Roman Catholic) and the proportion of Roman Catholics in the accounting sample. It may be inferred from this discrepancy that accountants were selectively recruited from the anglo-saxon minority in that province.

Table 3
Percentage Distribution of Religious Affiliations

Religion	Elite Accounting	Elite Non-Accounting	1931 Census of Canada
Anglican	41.67	34.29	15.76
Baptist	4.17	10.00	4.27
Presbyterian	15.28	20.00	8.39
Protestant	8.33	4.29	0.23
United	16.67	15.71	19.44
Sub-total for Protestant Sects	86.12	84.29	48.09
Catholic	6.94	14.29	41.30
Jewish	0	1.43	1.50
Other	6.94	0	9.11

Chi-Square =   13.8 df = 7 p<0.06 accounting elite vs non-accounting elite
Chi-Square = 295.3 df = 7 p<0.05 accounting elite vs census
Chi-Square = 124.5 df = 7 p<0.05 non-accounting elite vs census

Political Affiliations and Political Office

The political affiliations of those members of the elite stating a preference is shown in Table 4. Although both elite groups are similar in the large proportion claiming to be independent, they differ markedly in their affiliation to the two main parties (a rough cross-cultural comparison with the USA would equate the Conservatives and Republicans and the Liberals and Democrats). The accounting elite has strong Conservative allegiances while the non-accounting elite overall favors the Liberal party. As Porter [1967] notes, the political spectrum covered by these parties in Canada is narrow and skewed to the right. Both parties are linked to the business community and political affiliations of this nature are unrelated to such things as memberships on Boards of Directors. It may be noted that

Table 4
Percentage Distribution of Political Affiliations

Affiliation	Elite Accounting	Elite Non-Accounting	1930 Federal Election Results by Ridings Held
Conservative	48.60	25.70	55.90
Liberal	20.00	51.40	35.90
Independent	31.40	20.00	1.20
Other	0	2.90	6.90

Chi-Square = 612   df = 3 p<0.05 accounting elite vs election results
Chi-Square = 20.5 df = 3 p<0.05 accounting elite vs non-accounting elite
Chi-Square = 252   df = 3 p<0.05 non-accounting elite vs election results

none of the accountants claimed affiliation with the "other" political parties which were represented in the legislature. These parties represented agricultural interests (eg. the United Farmers Party) which were not represented among the elite accountants.

Table 5 displays the political offices held by each group. There is no statistically significant difference between the two groups but there is evidence that the accounting group tends to be active at a lower level, i.e. focused on more narrow constituencies, than the non-accounting group. The high proportion of accountants on Boards of Trade suggests an indirect influence on, at least, municipal politics. Weaver [1975], for example, notes the strong influence of Boards of Trade on civic reform during this period.

Table 5
Political Office

	Percentage of Elite	
	Accounting	Non-Accounting
Board of Trade (or Commerce)	25.3	8.9
Political Party Office	3.8	3.8
Alderman	2.5	0
Reeve/Mayor	8.9	5.1
Member of the Provincial Legislature	5.1	6.3
Member of Parliament	0	1.3
Member of Senate	0	2.5

Chi-Square = 9.4 df = 6 NS

Directorships

Acheson [1973:189] argues that between 1880 and 1910, Canada shifted from an economy of small family concerns or partnerships to one in which joint stock companies were the dominant organizational form. One measure of accountants' roles in controlling these enterprises is the extent to which they had gained seats on the Boards of Directors. On average, members of the accounting elite held 1.562 directorships while the non-accounting elite on average held 1.651 directorships (NS). The types of organizations in which each group held directorships is summarized in Table 6. There is no significant difference in the rates of participation in the types of organizations for which each group served as directors. It may be noted that 42.9% of directorships held by the accounting elite and 54.4% of directorships held by the non-accounting elite were concerned with non-profit organizations. These groups were clearly involved in leading roles in all the major institutions of society.

Table 6
Directorships

Type of Organization	Percentage of Directorships Reported	
	Accounting Elite	Non-Accounting Elite
Charity/Religious	15.3	13.8
Finance/Banking	12.2	14.7
Manufacturing	30.6	23.3
Utility/Transportation	10.2	6.9
Natural Resource	4.1	0.9
Professional	5.1	12.1
Other*	22.5	28.5

* Primarily hospitals
Chi-Square = 8 df = 6 NS

Social and Service Clubs

Both elite groups were members of numerous social and service clubs. These clubs appear to have serve two functions [Clements, 1975]. First, they were a meeting place where deals could be struck and information exchanged. Second, and perhaps more importantly, membership in these clubs served as signals about the social characteristics and position of individuals. The accounting group, on average, belonged to 0.654 service clubs and 3.086 social clubs while the non-accounting elite, on average, belonged to 0.535 service clubs and 2.488 social clubs. In neither of these cases is there a statistically significant difference between the two groups. The three most common social and service clubs joined by each of the elite groups are listed in Table 7. Based on the complete list of memberships, there are no significant differences for membership by the elite groups in either social clubs (chi-square = 14.8 df = 13 NS) or service clubs (chi-square = 10.4 df = 8 NS).

Education

The data sources used in this study provide a listing of the educational institutions attended by each individual. These institutions were categorized in hierarchal order as public schools (1), high school and private commercial schools (2), and universities and colleges (3). The average educational attainment of the accounting elite on this scale was 1.872 while the

Table 7
Social and Service Club Memberships

Service Clubs	Percentage of Elite Reporting Membership*	
	Accounting	Non-Accounting
Mason	35.4 (1)	31.6 (1)
Rotary	13.9 (2)	5.1 (3)
Kiwanis	5.1 (3)	1.3
IOOF (Odd Fellows)	1.3	7.6 (2)
Social Clubs		
Canadian	20.3 (1)	11.4 (1.5)
Montreal	16.5 (2)	6.3 (4.5)
St. James	11.4 (3)	7.6 (3)
University	3.8	11.4 (1.5)
Manitoba	3.8	6.3 (4.5)

see text for a statistical comparison
* the bracketed numbers give the rank of each club in terms of the percentage of the elite reporting membership.

educational attainment of the non-accounting elite was 2.566 (F = 28.3, p < 0.01). The educational level of the accounting group to 1910 was not significantly different than the group listed in the 1930's (1.875 vs 1.871 NS). The non-accounting group, however, showed some increase in the average education over this period (2.25 vs 2.642, F = 3.6, p = 0.06). Acheson [1973:200] provides similarly classified data for the industrial elite of 1885 and 1910 which yield values of 1.42 and 1.9 respectively. These data suggest that accountants' education may have initially exceeded that of clients but that they soon found themselves at a disadvantage.

Accouting education was available in universities in Canada as early as 1913 and the Chartered Accountants began a program of correspondence courses in conjunction with Queen's University in 1920. The senior members of the profession, however, were more likely to have gained their training from commercial schools and apprentice programs. The state granted accounting associations the right to certify the competence of their members but has never been involved in setting minimum qualifications. These forms of education allow selection of candidates to be based on the particular values of accounting firms or associations. Access to designations such as the state administered CPA in the United States was not an option in Canada.

Gender

Both elite groups in the sample were predominately male. The accounting elite, however, had no female members while 7% of the non-accounting elite were women (F = 6 p < 0.05). The 1931 Census provides evidence that the gender bias evident at this level of the occupational status hierarchy was not as extreme at other levels. Among the accountants and auditors category in the 1931 Census 3.5% were women, while among the bookkeepers and cashiers category 42% were women. The importance of gender to success may be indirect. The service and social clubs to which the elite belonged tended to be exclusively for men (eg. the National, York, Toronto, Montreal, etc. among social clubs and the Masons etc. among service clubs). This reflected a general bias in society at this time and created obstacles to the integration of women into the elite.

DISCUSSION

The results presented above may be summarized by distinguishing between the attributes of the elite groups (gender, education, birthplace, religion and political preferences) and their achievements (political offices, directorships, service and social club memberships). The attributes are regarded as relatively enduring qualities of individuals upon which social selection mechanisms may be based. The achievements represent the institutional positions to which individuals aspire and are selected. Grouped in this manner, the results comparing the accounting and non-accounting elites show a striking pattern; on all attributes these groups differ, but in terms of achievements they are the same (see Table 8).

Table 8
Summary of Comparisons Between the Accounting and Non-Accounting Elites

Variable	Comparison of Accounting and Non-Accounting Elite
Gender	exclusively male
Education	less educated
Birthplace	more foreign born, particularly from U.K.
Religion	more homogeneous, more Anglican
Politics	more likely to support the Conservative party
Political Office	No significant difference in number or type of offices
Directorships	No significant difference in number or type of directorships
Service Clubs	No significant difference in number or type of clubs
Social Clubs	No significant difference in number or type of clubs

This pattern suggests that accountants have successfully integrated into Canada's social elite. They participate in the social networks which allow the exchange of information and the development of trust between groups in different functional areas. They have also taken their place in the political and economic offices which allow them to influence economic development and policy. At the same time, however, it is clear that the accounting group was evolving according to social criteria statistically different from that of the social elite in general. It is to these criteria that the discussion now turns.

The differences between the accounting elite and other groups noted in the analysis above reflect the social context in which accountants sought to improve the status of their occupation. In the late 1800s, accountancy was disorganized, subject to frequent scandals and generally held in low repute. The early accounting associations sought to improve their position in the profession by differentiating themselves from the mass of practitioners. The exclusiveness of the early associations was in part based on competence but the effectiveness of this program of status enhancement also was due to the social characteristics of members.

The period examined in this article was one of great instability in Canada; a period which Cook and Brown [1974] characterize as "The Great Transformation." The formal creation of the nation in 1867 was, at the beginning of the period, still a part of living memory and could not be taken for granted. It also was not clear what form the Canadian identity would take as the nation developed. The traditional ties to England were strained by the influx of immigrants from Europe and by the growing economic influence of the United States. The relationship between French and English speaking groups was tense particularly at times when Canada was called upon to support wars (the Boer and First World Wars) which francophones regarded as British concerns. Canada was becoming an urban nation during this period. In the cities, social inequalities were magnified and the control of traditional institutions over society were weakened [cf. Bothwell *et al.*, 1987]. All of these factors created circumstances in which social characteristics were valued as signals of individuals' values and beliefs, and as indicators of how they might behave in the face of changing social conditions.

In many cases, social characteristics also signalled technical competence. Porter [1985] has noted that the Canadian educational system has been notoriously slow in adapting to changing occupational demands. As a consequence, in many technical areas (eg., architects, physical scientists, physicians and surgeons) recent immigrants form a high proportion of qualified practitioners. In accounting, given the type of qualifications required, Great Britain was the natural recruiting ground. This was supported during this period by the dominance of British foreign investment [McDougall, 1958], creating a natural flow of personnel along with assets. As well, British investors may have preferred auditors and accountants of known quality. It may be noted that when Queen's University became the focal point of Canadian accounting education in 1920, it went to England to recruit the required faculty members.

The United States usurped England's place of privilege as the main source of funds in the early 1920s. There is some evidence that this changed the focus of the profession from the UK to the USA. For example, when the CSCA adopted examination and training requirements in 1927, it followed the USA example rather than the UK in the content of its curriculum [Allend, 1982]. It would be worthwhile testing the hypothesis that the recruitment of non-native born accountants after 1930 focused increasingly on the United States.

In spite of the importation of technical experts from Great Britain, the accounting elite lagged behind the educational levels achieved by other members of Canada's elite. The evidence presented above suggests that this gap was widening over the study period. The education of accountants was clearly an issue in the profession during this period. In 1880, bookkeeping was taught at the public school level with more advanced education available privately or by experience. By 1913, largely through the efforts of the Chartered Accountants, it was possible to earn a Bachelor of Accountancy degree through the University of Saskatchewan [Editorial, *Canadian Chartered Accountant*, V.3, 1913/1914:50] and by 1920, the education program for all Chartered Accountants was administered through Queen's University [Creighton, 1984:106-108]. The rapid advancement of educational requirements in accountancy appears to be related in large part to attempts to differentiate groups of practitioners [Richardson, 1987], but may have also been related to the elite's perceived "under education" compared with their social peers. The relative lack of educational criteria on which accountants could differentiate themselves resulted in a greater emphasis on social characteristics.

Canada is an ethnically plural society in which many

cultures are represented. The social elite, however, are primarily English speaking of British descent. This is particularly true of those in positions of economic power [Porter, 1957]. The dominance of immigrants from Great Britain and native-born from outside Quebec reflects this bias among the accounting elite. One piece of evidence that this bias affected more than just the elite of the profession is the formation of the Institute of Accountants and Auditors of the Province of Quebec (IAAPQ) in 1912, to represent the interests of French-speaking accountants in Quebec. This group successfully argued for incorporation on the basis of the lack of francophone accountants in existing associations [Editorial, *Canadian Chartered Accountant*, V.3, 1913/1914:119].

The differential representation of birthplaces and cultures also is reflected in the religious affiliations of the accounting elite. The dominance of Anglicans reflects in part the recruitment of men from Great Britain, but also captures the differential emphasis of protestant education systems on commercial education when compared with catholic school systems (the institutional reflection of Weber's *Protestantism and the Spirit of Capitalism*). The low percentage of Jews in the accounting elite appears to generalize to the organized profession. Creighton [1984:301-302] notes that Jewish accountants practiced exclusively with Jewish clients and experienced difficulty integrating into the organizational hierarchy of the ICAO. It was not until the mid-1960s that Jewish accounting firms began to play a significant role in the market place.

It is noteworthy that on the social characteristics where there are differences between the accounting and non-accounting elite, the accounting elite shows an exaggeration of the characteristics which differentiate the non-accounting elite from the Canadian population as a whole. Although they differ statistically, the two elite samples share the ascriptive criteria used to achieve social closure. The data presented does not indicate whether or not these criteria assured simply that the traits of the accountants would be homogeneous or also ensured the intergenerational stability of accountancy. There is evidence that the latter may also be true, for example, the larger firms [eg. Ross and Clarkson] were, by 1930, controlled by second generation accountants (sons taking over the practices of their fathers) and the requirement of apprenticeships with low or no salary restricted entry to those families with financial resources to support their sons through their period of training. These data suggest that a study of intergenerational mobility in accounting would also be worthwhile.

To return to the three issues in the introduction:

1. accountancy in its formative years in Canada does not appear to have been open to all members of society, factors such as gender [cf. Richardson and McKeen, 1988], religion and ethnicity affected the ability to enter the professional associations, gain an accounting education and achieve success (elite status) in the profession;

2. the elite of the profession does not represent the full array of social interests, the elite are homogeneous with respect to social backgrounds and contemporary experiences and, therefore, are unlikely to advance the general interests of society or potential accounting practitioners;

3. the elite of the profession is significantly linked with other sectoral elites, both functionally (eg. through directorships) and socially (eg. through clubs), members of the accounting elite are not independent in this sense.

CONCLUSION

Recent sociology of the professions and accountancy, in particular, has argued for the need to examine the emergence of professional institutions and the development of professional technologies in historical context [Larson, 1977]. This follows from the observation that ahistorical research tends to reify current social arrangements and to portray them as functional necessities. Historical research corrects this tendency by exploring the problematic development of the professions and identifying the alternatives foregone in arriving at current structural arrangements. This paper focuses on the formative years of the accounting profession in Canada (1880-1930). It attempts to enrich our understanding of the forces shaping accountancy in Canada by examining the social characteristics of key decision-makers in the profession during this period. These characteristics provide evidence about the interests shaping the structure of the profession.

The data presented in this paper demonstrate the integration of the accounting profession into Canada's social elite by the 1930s. The characteristics of this group of elite accountants suggests that success in the profession during this period was based on ascriptive criteria which ensured the homogeneity of the elite. Specific incidents in the history of the profession were cited to argue that these criteria affected the rank-and-file of the profession and not just a select group. The data thus suggested that the integration of accountancy into the overall pattern of social control by sectoral elites had significant implications for who would be allowed to practice and, by implication, the way in which accountancy was practiced.

REFERENCES

Acheson, T.W., "Changing Social Origins of the Canadian Industrial Elite, 1880-1910," *Business History Review*, V47, N2 (1973):189-217.

Allen, J.N., *History of the Society of Management Accountants of Canada*, Hamilton: SMAC (1982).

Ashley, C.A., "Concentration of Economic Power," *Canadian Journal of Economics and Political Science*, V23, N1 (1957).

Bachrach, P., *The Theory of Democratic Elitism*, Boston: Little Brown (1967).

Bothwell, R., Drummond, I., English, J., *Canada 1900-1945*, Toronto: University of Toronto Press (1987).

Boyd, M., Goyder, J., Jones, F. E., McRoberts, H. A., Pineo, P. C. and Porter, J., *Ascription and Achievement: Studies in Mobility and Status Attainment in Canada*, Ottawa: Carleton University Press (1985).

Clements, W., *The Canadian Corporate Elite: Economic Power in Canada*, Toronto: McClelland and Stewart (1975).

Cook, R. and Brown, R. C., *Canada, 1896-1921: A Nation Transformed*, Toronto: McClelland and Stewart (1974).

Creighton, P., *A Sum of Yesterdays*, Toronto: Institute of Chartered Accountants of Ontario.

Giddens, A., "Elites in the British Class Structure" in Stanworth, P. and Giddens, A. *Elites and Power in British Society*, Cambridge: Cambridge University Press (1974).

Giddens, A., *The Class Structure of Advanced Societies*, New York: Harper & Row (1984).

Gilb, C. L., *Hidden Hierarchies*, New York: Harper and Row (1966).

Gilb, C. L., "Public or Private Governments?" in Nystron, P. C. and Starbuck, W. H. (ed.) *Handbook of Organizational Design*, Oxford: Oxford University Press (1981).

Heap, J., *Everybody's Canada*, Toronto: Lorimer (1974).

Jones, E., *Accountancy and the British Economy 1840-1980*, London: Batsford (1981).

Kaelble, H., *Historical Research on Social Mobility*, London: Croom Helm (1981).

Larson, M. S., *The Rise of Professionalism*, Berkeley: University of California Press (1977).

Lipset, S. M. and Bendix, R., *Social Mobility in Industrial Society*, Berkeley: University of California Press (1962).

MacDonald, K. M., "Social Closure and Occupational Registration," *Sociology*, V19, N4 1984:541-556.

McDougall, D. M., "The Economic Growth of Canada and the United States, 1870-1955," unpublished Ph.D. dissertation, Johns Hopkins University (1958).

Michels, R., *Political Parties*, New York: Free Press (1968).

Mills, C. W., "The American Business Elite: A Collective Portrait," *The Tasks of Economic History* (supplementary issue of the *Journal of Economic History*, December (1945):20-44).

Mills, C. W., *The Power Elite*, New York: MacMillan (1956).

Moyser, G. and Wagstaffe, M., *Research Methods for Elite Studies*, London: Allen and Unwin (1987).

Miranti, P. J., "Nativism and Professionalism: The Competition for Public Accountancy Legislation in New York During the 1890's," *Social Science Quarterly*, V69 (June 1988):361-380.

Olsen, D., *The State Elite*, Toronto: McClelland and Stewart (1980).

Pahl, R. E. and Winkler, J. T., "The Economic Elite: Theory and Practice" in Stanworth, P. and Gidden, A. *Elites and Power in British Society*, Cambridge: Cambridge University Press (1974).

Parkin, F., *Marxism and Class Theory*, New York: Columbia University Press (1979).

Porter, J., *The Vertical Mosaic*, Toronto: University of Toronto Press (1967).

Porter, J., "The Economic Elite and the Social Structure in Canada," *The Canadian Journal of Economics and Political Science*, V23 (1957).

Porter, J., "Canada: The Societal Context of Occupational Allocation" in Boyd *et al.* op.cit.

Prewitt, K. and Stone, A., *The Ruling Elites: Elite Theory, Power and American Democracy*, New York: Harper and Row (1973).

Richardson, A. J., "Professionalization and Intraprofessional Competition in the Canadian Accounting Profession," *Work and Occupation*, V14, N4 (1987):591-615.

Richardson, A. J. and McKeen, C. A., "Women Pioneers in Accounting in Canada Before 1930," Working Paper, School of Business, Queen's University, Kingston, Canada (1988).

Stewart, A., Prandy, K. and Blackburn, R. M., *Social Stratification and Occupations*, New York: Holmes & Meier (1980).

Weaver, J. C., "Elitism and the Corporate Ideal: Businessmen and Boosters in Canadian Civic Reform, 1890-1920" in McCormack, A.R. and Macpherson, I. (eds.) *Cities in the West*, National Muesuem of Man Mercury Series, History Division, Paper No. 10 (Ottawa, 1975):48-73.

APPENDIX A
THE ACCOUNTING ELITE 1880-1930*

1	Adams, Arthur William	41	Laporte, J.R.
2	Adams, Ernest Hall	42	McCannel, Donald H.
3	Adamson, William James Thompson	43	Maclachan, W.M.
4	Allen, Loftus Annesley	44	Mapp, K.A.
5	Anderson, John	45	Martin, Norman L.
6	Anscomb, Herbert	46	McCannel, Donald A.
7	Apedaile, Joseph Leonard	47	McClelland, D.M.
8	Barber, George	48	McDonald, George Cross
9	Belanger, Aurelien	49	McLennan, F.D.
10	Bender, Joseph M.	50	Mitchell, Alister F.
11	Bennett, E. James	51	Molson, H deM
12	Blatch, George L.	52	Mulholland, G.M.
13	Bronskill, Frederick George	53	Nash, Major A.E.
14	Brown, Samuel G.	54	Neff, Arthur C.
15	Carmichael, W.R.	55	Peckham, S.B.
16	Chambers, Norman G.	56	Pettit, W.H.
17	Clarkson, Geoffrey T.	57	Roberts, C.P.
18	Coulter, Thomas J.	58	Ronald, W.S.
19	Crawford, J.E.	59	Rooke, George C.
20	Crehan, Maj. M.J.	60	Ross, Brig. Gen. J.G.
21	Crowell, Harvey E.	61	Ross, J.W.
22	Dalglish, K.W.	62	Russell, G.A.
23	Dowie, Col. L.A.	63	Scott, G.W.
24	Durnford, George	64	Scott, Charles S.
25	Dykes, R.F.	65	Shanon, C.A.
26	Fisk, Arthur K.	66	Shepard, A.B.
27	Fleming, C.A.	67	Stiff, F.J.
28	Gonthier, George	68	Sutherland, James B.
29	Gordon, Ltd. Col. H.D.L.	69	Thomas, D.S.
30	Guilfoyle, H.E.	70	Thompson, W.H.A.
31	Henderson, W.A.	71	Thompson, J.C.
32	Higgins, Fred P.	72	Thompson, W.G.
33	Hindsley, N.	73	Tindale, Arthur S.
34	Howson, Ernest J.	74	Turville, Frank P.
35	Hudson, J.D.	75	Wade, Osler
36	Jamieson, Henry Tomkinson	76	Webb, Lt. Col. H.J.
37	Jephcott, W.G.H.	77	Whyte, Andrew
38	Johnson, J.W.	78	Wilson, J.
39	Kennedy, Robert H.	79	Winter, George E.
40	Kerr, G.R.		

* All accountants listed in *Canadian Who's Who* (1st and 2nd Edition), *Who's Who in Canada* (1910 - 1930), and/or *Canadian Men and Women of the Times* (1889 and 1910).

Section III: Standard Setting

Financial Statement Disclosure Requirements of the Ontario Companies Act, 1907. Selections from Section 36.

36 (2) At such meeting the directors shall lay before the company,

   (a) A balance sheet made up to a date not more than three months before such annual meeting;
   (b) A statement of income and expenditure for the financial period ending upon the date of such balance sheet;
   (c) The report of the auditor or auditors;
   (d) Such further information respecting the company's financial position as the Letters Patent or the by-laws of the company may require;

and, on resolution affirmed by shareholders holding at least five per centum of the capital of the company, shall furnish a copy thereof to every shareholder personally present at such meeting and demanding the same.

36 (3) The balance sheet shall be drawn up so as to distinguish at least the following classes of assets and liabilities, namely:

   (a) Cash;
   (b) Debts owing to the company from its customers;
   (c) Debts owing to the company from its directors, officers and shareholders;
   (d) Stock in trade;
   (e) Expenditures made on account of future business;
   (f) Land, buildings and plant;
   (g) Goodwill, franchises, patents and copyrights, trademarks, leases, contracts and licenses;
   (h) Debts owing by the company secured by mortgage or other lien upon the property of the company;
   (i) Debts owing by the company but not secured;
   *(k) Amount received on common shares;
   (l) Amount received on preferred shares;
   (m) Indirect and contingent liabilities.

   *No entry for (j) is given in the Act.

STANDARDIZATION OF SHAREHOLDERS' ACCOUNTS AND AUDITORS' REPORTS AND CERTIFICATES.

By J. C. Gray, C.A. (Scot. and Can.,) Toronto.

ACCOUNTANTS will notice with satisfaction from the October number of the "Journal of Accountancy" that the American Institute of Accountants are to appoint a committee to consider the standardization of accounting procedure. Whether or not the objects of this proposed committee will include the question of the standardization of auditors' accounts and reports is not clear, but no doubt their work is bound to touch on this more or less, particularly as there would appear to be a considerable field for betterment in this respect which could be handled to advantage at the same time.

·When the labors of this committee are completed and its report and recommendations are available for the use of other societies it would be an opportune moment for the Canadian societies to take these up and adapt them, where suitable and desirable, to conditions in this country. It is with the object of anticipating this event and of making a few observations of my own that this article on "Standardization of Shareholders' Accounts and Auditors' Reports and Certificates" is written.

The following should always be borne in mind when drawing up and submitting accounts of a company for its shareholders' use and information :—

1. The provisions of the Companies' Acts regarding the information to be given on a balance sheet should be observed. As these are given in Section 12 of The Companies' Act Amendment Act, 1917, it is unnecessary to refer to them in detail.

2. The accounts should be set up and prepared in such a manner that one year or period may be readily compared with another. The wording used should be simple and clear, and technical terms should be avoided where possible. When one takes into consideration the fact that the majority of the shareholders of most public companies do not understand very much about accounting the desirability for the above is apparent.

3. Where a company is a public one, sufficient information should be given in its annual accounts to enable a prospective investor in its stock, through the medium of the stock exchange, to size up its financial position quickly, and, without seeking further information from outside sources than is necessary, to decide whether or not he will invest. Moreover, the stock exchange will always regard with more favor those stocks which are backed up with financial statements that are clearly and simply drawn up than those that are not. This also applies to bankers, who, as

193

a rule, are not very well informed in the art of understanding and determining financial positions of companies and the values of investments, and, consequently, will be inclined to listen more eagerly to petitions for credit which are supported by accounts that they can understand.

It can, therefore, be understood that the manner in which a company's accounts are prepared, and by this I do not mean the neat, and sometimes the rather flashy way in which they are bound, although, if this is not overdone, it counts in their favor, may take quite an important place in an investor's or banker's estimation.

In Accounts Nos. 1, 2 and 4, which I submit herewith, are embodied what I understand to be the most recent accounting practice in the United States, to which I have added a few ideas and suggestions of my own.

Balance Sheet—Account No. 1.

Referring to the balance sheet first of all as being the most important of the accounts which are submitted to the shareholders of a company, and which is, indeed, the only financial statement that they are legally entitled to, I would draw attention to the

Arrangement and Order of Assets and Liabilities.

The arrangement that I have adopted is that of starting off with the assets that can be most quickly and readily realized at the least sacrifice and finishing with those that have no value at all, except under unusual circumstances. For example, the cash in bank appears before the inventories, which occasionally have to be liquidated at a loss or in completing unprofitable orders. Cash, too, can be realized at very short notice, whereas inventories, as a rule, cannot. With regard to the arrangement of the liabilities, I have started off with those that are most immediately and urgently due for settlement, followed by those that are deferred, such as the bonds, and have finally shown the capital and surplus, for which, as a rule, no definite dates have been arranged for repayment. It is the practice of many accountants to start off the balance sheet with the capital assets, followed by the current assets, and complete the debit side with the deferred charges to operations, and on the credit side to start with the capital, followed by the bonds, current liabilities, reserves, and finish up with the surplus. The most notable advantage to be gained by using the method that I have adopted in these accounts is that, with the majority of people who are studying balance sheets, be they investors, bankers, stock brokers or the general public, the most important feature in their eyes is the liquid position of the company. Hence, the first things that they look to are the amount of cash on hand, what the accounts re-

194

ceivable amount to, how large the inventories are as compared with the turnover, and how far the total of these is able to take care of the current liabilities.

With prospective investors in the company's bonds, of course, the security in the form of capital assets is the most important thing to be considered, but these gentlemen are few in number as compared with those interested in stock and shares.

In concluding this paragraph, let me refer to the ease with which one, on taking up the balance sheet, is able to ascertain that the current assets exceed the current liabilities by $2,435,-135.62, and that the bonds are secured four times over by the capital assets. Can this information be as readily and quickly obtained from Account No 3, which, I regret to say, is a form of balance sheet only too commonly used?

Investments.

The inclusion of investments among current assets is noticeable, since the treatment of such assets on balance sheets is very frequently to show them as distinct from either capital or current assets, and in a section of their own. Where the investments are in such readily liquidated securities as government bonds, I do not see any good reason for distinguishing them from other current assets, for, although there is a tendency for their market value to vary from time to time, and, although moneys in bank earn a lower rate of interest, there is practically no difference between the two, so far as facilities to liquidate both are concerned. Both are repayable at par, the bonds at some date in the future, and the cash at once—except so far as the bank may elect to make use of a prerogative that it seldom cares to exercise.

Investments by a company in the stock of a competitor whose stock it may propose to acquire the control of, should, however, but only so long as it does not own the controlling interest, be shown on the balance sheet under the head of "Investments" and distinct from the current or capital assets. The reasons for this are that these investments cannot, as a rule, be readily and quickly realized, and that they are not made for the purpose of investing the company's surplus cash to the best advantage, pending its utilization in the business to meet future requirements, but for the future development and extension of the business. To this extent these investments partake more of the nature of capital than of current assets.

Where the controlling interest of another company is owned the rules regarding holding company balance sheets should be observed.

Prepaid Expenses.

The inclusion of prepaid taxes and insurance, etc., among current assets is worthy of comment. It is the custom among

195

accountants at present to show these under "Deferred Charges to Operations," and the explanation that I would offer for the suggested change in treatment is that, since taxes and insurance are almost entirely eventually absorbed in overhead expense (that is, where the company is a manufacturing one), they automatically become part of work-in-progress through the distribution of the overhead expense, and should, therefore, not be treated differently from work-in-progress in the balance sheet. The same applies to factory supplies. With reference to stationery, advertising material, and that proportion of the taxes and insurance which, having regard to the floor space, value of equipment and furniture, etc., allocated to and used by the selling and administrative departments of the business, is chargeable to the latter as part of their expense, I consider that the values of these, as inventoried and computed, respectively, should be set up in the balance sheet under the head of "Deferred Charges to Operations." No doubt there is a small cash value attachable to these inventories, and possibly something could be obtained for the unexpired taxes from the purchaser of the company's business in the event of its sale or liquidation, but, as a balance sheet is always supposed to represent the position of the company as a going concern, I do not consider it correct to include these under "Current Assets," except, of course, that part of taxes and insurance which, as I have already mentioned, will eventually become part of work-in-progress.

Capital Assets.

With regard to the capital assets of a company, it is sometimes desirable, and cannot under any circumstances be harmful, to show the increases or decreases in these since the last statement. This information can, of course, be gleaned by comparing the two statements, so that it is doubtful whether it is any advantage at all to show the comparison as suggested above. Should it be done, it would be necessary to start off the balance sheet with the capital assets instead of with the current assets, since the inclusion of the headings necessary to give this information in the middle of the statement would give the latter a rather clumsy and overbalanced appearance.

Bond Interest Accrued.

So far as I have been able to discover, there is no accepted rule providing whether this should be shown on the balance sheet as a current liability or as part of the bonded indebtedness. I have included it as part of the latter on account of its not being due for immediate payment. In other words, I have treated this item as a deferred liability. In the event of the company going out of business or defaulting on its bond interest, the outstanding

196

and accrued interest on the bonds would, together with the principal thereof, be redeemed out of the proceeds of the sale of the company's capital assets on which they are secured. Until these contingencies materialize, however, bond interest due for payment and accrued bond interest have no preferable charge on the assets of the company. In view of these remarks, I am of the opinion that the correct way to show bond interest due for payment is under "Current Liabilities" and accrued bond interest as part of the bonded indebtedness.

Unclaimed Dividends.

On most balance sheets of public companies that I have inspected I notice liabilities brought on for unclaimed dividends, the cash in bank set apart to meet these being shown as part of the cash in bank and on hand.

It would appear to me that this practice is incorrect, inasmuch as immediately the money is set aside by the company to meet these dividends it loses its claim thereon, and, consequently, cannot treat this as part of its assets or the liability therefor as part of its liabilities.

Balance Sheet Generally.

The segregation of the reserve for depreciation under "Reserves," instead of as a deduction from capital assets, as it is frequently shown, and the fact that unissued capital stock is not treated as treasury stock, which is an altogether different thing, are the only other points worthy of particular notice.

It may be argued that the balance sheet as submitted by me goes into too great detail, but this can be adjusted as circumstances demand. For example, it is by no means necessary or required by law to subdivide the inventories as between manufactured goods, goods in process of manufacture, and raw materials and supplies, nor is it always desirable to give as full particulars as I have done of how the capital assets are made up, except to state how much of these consists of goodwill.

Profit and Loss Account—Account No. 2.

Account No. 2 is straightforward, and calls for little or no explanation. The information given by me in this statement might be more condensed, as, for example, the dividends need not be given in detail, and if this were sufficiently done it would be possible to incorporate the whole profit and loss account in the balance sheet under the head of "Profit and Loss Account" instead of giving it in the form of a separate statement. The former is quite a common practice in the balance sheets of many large companies.

The profit and loss account, as I have presented it, indicates that the profits for the year were $854,500.00, and that,

197

after providing $35,000.00 for necessary reserves and $210,000.00 for dividends, here remained a surplus for the year of $609,500.00, or 15.2375 per cent. on the common shares. In certain profit and loss accounts that have come before my notice it has only been possible after rearrangement thereof to determine whether or not there was a surplus on the year's operations. The following profit and loss account of one of our leading Canadian industrial companies—Account No. 5—gives an example of what I mean. This shows that the surplus at the commencement of the year dwindled from $403,300.05 to $242,801.70 at the end of the year. It *does not show* that the net profits fell short of preference dividend requirements by $160,498.35.

Clearness in accounts is, in my opinion, most essential, and auditors should never rest content that they have done their duty by the shareholders of the companies whose books they are auditing until they have furnished for their information and use such a statement of the company's affairs as they (the shareholders) can readily understand and without an undue amount of analysis, comparison, etc.

Operating Account—Account No. 4.

It is seldom either necessary or advisable to furnish the shareholders of a company with such detailed information of operations as I have given in Account No. 4, but as an example of what, in my opinion, their directors are entitled to expect from its executives, I give it for what it is worth. The chief recommendations, to my mind, are the clearness with which the total net sales, the manufacturing cost of sales, the selling expense, the administration and general expense, etc., and the resulting net profit on operating are set forth. The percentages of cost of sales and of expenses on sales are also given, as is also the percentage of manufacturing expense on productive labor. All this information is immediately available for ready comparison with other years, and what is true of years can also be said for shorter periods, since the system of accounts from which this information is derived should permit of similar information being available for the latter.

Auditors' Reports and Certificates.

The Companies' Act Amendment Act, 1917, in Section No. 11 provides that the auditors of a company shall make a report in which they shall state: (a) whether or not they have obtained all the information and explanations they have required; and (b) whether, in their opinion, the balance sheet referred to in their report is properly drawn up so as to exhibit a true and correct view of the state of the company's affairs, according to the best

198

of their information and the explanations given to them, and as shown by the books of the company.

In spite of this requirement, it is still the practice of many accountants to issue their accounts with the notations of "audited and found correct," "certified correct," "audited," etc., attached. Sometimes one only finds their names, as, for example, "John Jones, Auditor." Needless to say, these offenders are seldom chartered accountants.

A form of certificate which complies with legal requirements and is to the point, and does not say more or less than is necessary, is, to my mind, found in the following :—

Toronto, 1st December, 1918

To the Shareholders,

The Toronto Manufacturing Company, Limited,
1400 Queen Street South,
Toronto.

I report to the Shareholders of the Toronto Manufacturing Company, Limited, that I have examined the books and accounts of the company for the year ending 31st December, 1917, and that all my requirements as auditor have been complied with.

(Then state qualifications, if any.)

A provision of only $100,000.00 has been made for depreciation, but all repairs and renewals to buildings, plant and equipment have been charged to operating account.

Subject to the above remark, I hereby certify that the attached balance sheet at 31st December, 1917, Account No. 1, is, in my opinion, properly drawn up so as to exhibit a true and correct view of the company's affairs at that date, according to the best of my information and the explanations given me and as shown by the books of the company at that date.

J. C. Gray,
Chartered Accountant, Auditor.

Conclusion.

In an article on such a subject as the foregoing one is naturally limited by the space available, and, in any event, it is extremely difficult to explain as clearly as one would wish the many points and questions involved without reference to more actual accounts and statements than it is possible for the same reason to give. The accounts used by me are those of a manufacturing company, and, consequently, certain of the remarks which I have made are only applicable to such and cannot appropriately be applied to the accounts, say, of a bank or a real estate or mining company. The principles of arrangement and classification are, however, interchangeable to quite an appreciable extent.

199

The Toronto Manufacturing Company, Limited.

Balance Sheet as at 31st December, 1917.

ASSETS.

Current Assets :—

Cash in Bank and on Hand......... $		500,000.00	
Investments :—			
$500,000.00 in Dominion of Canada 5½% (First Victory) Loan Bonds, repayable 1st December, 1922, at Cost, plus Accrued Interest to Date (Market Value, $494,835.62)		502,335.62	
Prepaid Expenses :—Insurance and Taxes Unexpired, etc.		9,000.00	
Accounts Receivable :—			
Trade Accounts and Bills Receivable. $	480,000.00		
Less :—			
Reserve for Doubtful Accounts	10,000.00		
	$470,000.00		
Advances to Officers	5,000.00		
Owing by Directors	1,300.00		
		476,300.00	
Inventories as certified to :—			
Manufactured Goods. $	500,000.00		
Goods in Process of Manufacture ...	150,000.00		
Raw Materials and Supplies	2,350,000.00		
		3,000,000.00	
Total Current Assets			$ 4,487,635.62

Sinking Fund Assets :—

Cash in Hands of Trustee			364.38

Capital Assets :—

Land . ... $	460,000.00		
Buildings	540,000.00		
Plant and Machinery ...	7,550,000.00		
Small Tools and Equipment	250,000.00		
Office Furniture and Fixtures	25,000.00		
	$8,825,000.00		
Goodwill, Patents, Trade Marks, etc..	2,175,000.00		
Total Capital Assets			11,000,000.00

Deferred Charges to Operations :—

Sundry Prepaid Expenses .... $	1,000.00		
Discount on Bond Issue—unabsorbed Balance	75,000.00		
Total Deferred Charges to Operations.......		76,000.00	
			$15,564,000.00

Approved on behalf of the Board.

.... Directors.

200

The Toronto Manufacturing Company, Limited.
Balance Sheet as at 31st December, 1917.
CAPITAL AND LIABILITIES.

Current Liabilities :—

Trade Accounts Payable, and Accrued Salaries and Wages, Charges, etc. (including Provision for War Tax)	$1,275,000.00	
Loans from Banks, secured under Section 88 of the Bank Act..........	725,000.00	
Dividend No. 8 on Preference Shares for three months to date, declared, payable 1st February, 1918......	52,500.00	
Total Current Liabilities....		$ 2,052,500.00

Bonded Indebtedness :—

First Mortgage 6% 20-year Gold Bonds, due 1st March, 1929 :—			
Authorized $3,000,000.00			
Issued $2,500,000.00			
Less :—			
Redeemed to date. 250,000.00			
		$2,250,000.00	
Add :—			
Interest Accrued to Date......	45,000.00		
			2,295,000.00

Reserves :—

Reserve for Contingencies .... $ 100,000.00		
Do. for Depreciation 750,000.00		
Do. for Extraordinary Repairs and Renewals 150,000.00		
		1,000,000.00

Capital Stock :—

Authorized :—		
Preference—35,000 shares, 7% Cumulative of $100.00 each.. $3,500,000.00		
Common—40,000 shares of $100.00 each 4,500,000.00		
	$8,000,000.00	
Issued :—		
Preference—30,000 shares, 7% Cumulative of $100.00 each, fully paid $3,000,000.00		
Common—40,000 shares of $100.00 each, fully paid 4,000,000.00		
		7,000,000.00

Profit and Loss Account :—

Balance at credit thereof, per Account No. 2.....	3,216,500.00	
		$15,564,000.00

NOTE.—There is a Contingent Liability for Bills Receivable under Discount amounting to $150,000.00.

201

The Toronto Manufacturing Company, Limited.

Profit and Loss Account for Year ending 31st December, 1917.

Profit from Operations for Year ending 31st December,
1917, after deducting $100,000.00 for Depreciation
and providing for War Tax $1,002,914.38
Add: Interest from Investments 7,835.62

$1,010,750.00

Deduct: Bond Interest .... $ 150,000.00
Proportion of Discount on
Bond Issue 6,250.00   156,250.00

Net Profits from Operations for Year..... $ 854,500.00

Less:
Transferred to Reserve for Contingencies .... $ 15,000.00
Transferred to Reserve for Extraordi-
nary Repairs and Renewals 20,000.00   35,000.00

$ 819,500.00

Less:
Dividends on Preference Shares :—
No. 5 for three Months ending 31st
March, 1917 .... $ 52,500.00
No. 6 for three Months ending 30th
June, 1917 .... 52,500.00
No 7 for three Months ending 30th
September, 1917 .... 52,500.00
No. 8 for three Months ending 31st
December, 1917 .... 52,500.00   210,000.00

Surplus for Year = 15.2375% on Common Shares $ 609,500.00

Add:
Balance at credit of Profit and Loss at
31st December, 1916 .... $2,679,000.00
Deduct: Adjustments thereon. 72,000.00   2,607,000.00

Balance at Credit of Profit and Loss at 31st December,
1917, per Account No. 1 .... $3,216,500.00

The Toronto Manufacturing Company, Limited.

Balance Sheet as at 31st December, 1917.

ASSETS.

Land and Buildings—less Depreciation .... $	750,000.00
Plant and Equipment—less Depreciation	7,075,000.00
Sundry Equipment—less Depreciation	250,000.00
Goodwill, etc.	2,175,000.00
Investments (detailed)	502,700.00
Cash in Bank and on Hand.........................	500,000.00
Accounts Receivable, less Reserve for Doubtful Accounts	476,300.00
Inventories	3,000,000.00
Prepaid Expenses	10,000.00
Discount on Bond Issue	75,000.00
	$14,814,000.00

Approved on behalf of the Board.

Directors.

CAPITAL AND LIABILITIES.

Capital :—

Preference—Authorized $3,500,000.00		
Common—Authorized 4,500,000.00		
	$8,000,000.00	
Less: In Treasury 1,000,000.00		$ 7,000,000.00
Bonds $2,500,000.00		
Less: In Treasury 250,000.00		
		2,250,000.00

Liabilities :—

Trade Accounts and Accrued Charges............	1,275,000.00
Loans from Banks	725,000.00
Preference Dividend No. 8.....................	52,500.00
Accrued Bond Interest	45,000.00
Reserve for Contingencies	100,000.00
Reserve for Extraordinary Repairs and Renewals......	150,000.00
Profit and Loss Account	3,216,500.00
	$14,814,000.00

NOTE.—There is a Contingent Liability for Bills Receivable under Discount amounting to $150,000.00.

203

ACCOUNT No. 4.

The Toronto Manufacturing Company, Limited.

Operating Account for Year ending 31st December, 1917.

Sales .			$10,100,000.00	
Less: Returns and Allowances			100,000.00	
Net Sales				$10,000,000.00
Deduct: **Manufacturing Cost of Sales** (70% of Net Sales.)				
Inventory of Manufactured Goods at 31st December, 1916		$ 600,000.00		
Add :—				
Cost of Production :—				
Materials used :—				
Inventories of Raw Materials and Work-in-Progress at 31st December, 1916	$2,600,000.00			
Add :—				
Purchases of Raw Materials during year (including duty, freight and cartage)	4,040,000.00			
	$6,640,000.00			
Deduct :—				
Inventories of Raw Materials and Work-in-Progress at 31st December, 1917	2,500,000.00			
	$4,140,000.00			
Productive Labor	1,725,000.00			
Manufacturing Expenses (60% of Productive Labor).				
Non-prod. Labor. $ 525,000.00				
Maint. and Repair 250,000.00				
Depreciation .. 100,000.00				
Superintendence . 25,000.00				
Insce. and Taxes 125,000.00				
Light, Heat and Power . 80,000.00				
Miscellaneous . . 50,000.00				
Forward . $1,155,000.00	$5,865,000.00	$ 600,000.00	$10,000,000.00	

204

The Toronto Manufacturing Company, Limited.

Operating Account for Year ending 31st December, 1917.—Continued.

Forward	$1,155,000.00	$5,865,000.00	$ 600,000.00	$10,000,000.00

Less :—

Proportion chargeable to Selling and General Expense	120,000.00	1,035,000.00	6,900,000.00

$ 7,500,000.00

Deduct:

Inventory of Manufatured Goods at 31st December, 1917 ....   500,000.00

Total Manufacturing Cost of Sales...... $ 7,000,000.00

Deduct: **Selling Expense** (10% of Net Sales).

Salesmen's Salaries	$250,000.00
Branch Expense	340,000.00
Commission	75,000.00
Travelling and Hotel Expenses.....	65,000.00
Shipping Expense	55,000.00
Freight and Cartage outward	70,000.00
Proportion of Manufacturing Expense (as above)	70,000.00
Miscellaneous	75.000.00

Total Selling Expense 1,000,000.00

Deduct: **Administration and General Expense (5% of Net Sales).**

Office Salaries	$275,000.00
Executive Salaries	75,000.00
Printing, Stationery and Office Supplies	15,000.00
Telephones, Telegrams and Cables.	7,000.00
Provision for Bad and Doubtful Debts	25,000.00
Proportion of Manufacturing Expense (as above)	50,000.00
Miscellaneous	53,000.00

Total Administration and General Expense   500.000.00

Deduct: **Interest and Discount paid, less received (.25% of Net Sales)** 25,000.00

Deduct: **Provision for War Taxes (4.72% of Net Sales)** 472,085.62   8.997,085.62

Balance: **Profit on Operating for Year ending 31st December, 1917 (10.03% of Net Sales)** .... $ 1,002,914.38

205

ACCOUNT No. 5.

The Montreal Manufacturing Company, Limited.

Profit and Loss Account for Year ending 31st December, 1917.

Profit from Operations for Year ending 31st December,

1917 . ... $230,027.30

Add : Interest from Investments 4,586.59

$234,613.89

Deduct : Net loss on Investments realized. $ 112.24

Interest on First Mortgage Bonds 90,000.00

90,112.24

$144,501.65

Add : Balance at credit at 31st December, 1916,

brought forward 403,300.05

$547,801.70

Deduct : Dividends on Preference Shares for year :—

No. 5 ... . $26,250.00

No. 6 .... 26,250.00

No. 7 .... 26,250.00

No. 8 .... 26,250.00

105,000.00

$442.801.70

Deduct : Transferred to Reserve for Depreciation.... 200,000.00

Balance at credit at 31st December, 1917, per Balance Sheet $242,801.70

206

IV

CANADA

In Canada, the principal national organization of accountants is The Canadian Institute of Chartered Accountants, having a membership in excess of 19,000. With headquarters in Toronto, the Canadian Institute (or CICA) is a federation of the chartered accountants' institutes of the ten Canadian provinces. Prior to a reorganization in 1971, it was governed by a 30-member Council and an eleven-member Executive Committee. Effective in 1971, the Canadian Institute is headed by a 22-member Board of Governors and a seven-member Executive Committee. Eighteen of the Board members are appointed by the provincial institutes in accordance with the following assignments (which reflect relative membership sizes): four from Ontario; three from Quebéc; two each from Alberta, British Columbia, and Manitoba; and one each from New Brunswick, Newfoundland, Nova Scotia, Prince Edward Island, and Saskatchewan. Two of these 18 members are selected by the Board to serve on the Executive Committee. The four remaining members of the Board, the President, Vice President, Secretary, and Treasurer, are ex-officio members of the Executive Committee. The President and Vice President are chosen for one-year terms by the Board of Governors on recommendation of the outgoing Executive Committee. The Secretary and Treasurer are nominated for office by The Institute of Chartered Accountants of Quebéc (Quebéc Institute) and The Institute of Chartered Accountants of Ontario (Ontario Institute), respectively, and must be confirmed by the Board. All members of the Board, save the President and Vice President, serve for three-year terms. A full-time Executive Director is the seventh member of the Executive Committee. The incumbent is R. D. Thomas, a chartered accountant.

THE CANADIAN ACCOUNTING PROFESSION
IN HISTORICAL RELIEF

To a strong degree, the structure of the Canadian public accounting profession mirrors the relationship between the

269

Canadian Government and the ten provincial governments, a unique federalism that has long been the subject of controversy in Canada. The British North America Act of 1867, by which the U.K. Parliament created the confederation known as the Dominion of Canada, parcelled governmental authority among the Canadian Parliament and the several provincial legislatures. The former was given authority

> to legislate upon matters deemed to be for the general advantage of Canada, customs, defense, railways, navigation, post offices, bankruptcy, banking, patents and so forth. The provincial legislatures were given the exclusive right to legislate upon matters of local concern, municipal, judicial, licence, property, education and civil rights and numerous other matters.[1]

When the Canadian Institute was founded in 1902 (under the name, The Dominion Association of Chartered Accountants, which was changed in 1950-51), it entered into competition with the existing provincial institutes in Quebéc, Ontario, Manitoba, and Nova Scotia. Until then, the provincial institutes had been establishing and enforcing their own minimum standards for conferring the professional designation, chartered accountant. The national body thus sought to assume authority for a function that had been regarded as purely provincial. After some seven years of legislative jousting over the claims of national and provincial bodies to regulate the accountancy profession, an accord was reached in 1909, and effectuated the following year, by which the memberships of each of the provincial bodies and the national group were "mutually absorbed." Thereafter, the provincial institutes were charged with training and examining candidates for membership and maintaining a surveillance over the professional performance of members — consistent with the duties delegated to the provinces of licensing, educating, and conferring civil status. The national body was to "concern itself solely with the welfare of the constituent societies, and to promote a friendly understanding among them."[2]

---

[1] Geo. Edwards, "Accountancy in Canada," *The Journal of Accountancy*, November, 1915, p. 339.

[2] Edwards, *ibid.*, p. 341. Also see *The Story of the Firm, 1864-1964: Clarkson, Gordon & Co.* (privately printed, 1964), pp. 51-54; R.R. Thompson, "The Development of the Profession of Accounting in Canada," *The Canadian Chartered Accountant*, March, 1939, esp. pp. 177-79 (which draws heavily on the Edwards article); J.E. Smyth, "Notes on the Development of the Accountancy Profession (Part II)," *The Canadian Chartered Accountant*, December, 1953, pp. 291-92; and the *CICA Handbook*, pp. 3-4.

This was a uniquely Canadian solution, respecting the historical distinctions between the federal and provincial spheres of authority. The provincial institutes admit members, design and enforce a code of ethics, collect dues and allocate a portion thereof to the federal body, and select the federal officers. Thus, while all members of the provincial institutes automatically become members of the Canadian Institute, no federal elections are held. The officers of the provincial institutes choose, directly or indirectly, the officers of the Canadian Institute.

A year after putting into effect the agreement between the provincial institutes and the national organization, the latter commenced to issue a quarterly, now monthly, journal, the *Canadian Chartered Accountant.* Its current circulation is 30,000.

Much of the early history of the Canadian public accounting profession, save for what has already been discussed, resembles the experience in Great Britain. Furthermore, as the considerable Scottish immigration has affected the development of the country (the first two Prime Ministers were Scots), the Canadian accounting profession was bound to be strongly shaped by accountants immigrating from the country whose accounting profession was the first to organize itself. Wrote Thompson:

> Among these settlers have been Scottish accountants, so that to a large extent the foundation of the profession in Canada can be traced to the influence, initiative, and activity of these men.[3]

In the last decades of the nineteenth century, accountants were increasingly called upon to act as "official assignees" of insolvent estates on behalf of the creditors. But the continuity in accountant-client relationship had to await the emergence of industrial corporations and the consequent companies legislation which, in Canada, has been enacted at both the federal and provincial levels.

In 1917, a Dominion companies act required the appointment of an auditor to report to the shareholders, following the Ontario Act of 1907 (in which the Ontario Institute had a role), which in turn reflected the British Companies Act, 1900. By 1939, two of the then nine provinces still had not placed similar requirements in their laws. Differences among the provincial acts and between them and the federal act continue to persist, although most large industrial companies today are incorporated under the federal

[3] Thompson, *op. cit.*, p. 172.

legislation.[4] Amendments passed in 1934 to the Dominion act set forth a series of minimum disclosure requirements for balance sheets and profit and loss statements, again largely paralleling prior companies legislation in Great Britain. Yet "the most significant changes in the Canadian Act," writes Murphy, "went far beyond the requirements of the English Act."[5] The 1934 act gave legal status to consolidated statements, following practice in the United States, for consolidated statements were not formally recognized in British companies legislation until 1947. In 1935, minor changes were made in the 1934 act. Later amendments are discussed below.

Federal income tax legislation was first passed as a wartime measure in 1917, and while the tax law has not required that taxpayers have independent audits, those who elect to have audits ordinarily file their audited financial statements and the auditors' unabridged report with their return.

Although the early development of the Canadian public accounting profession (and companies legislation) bore a striking resemblance to that in Great Britain, a Canadian chartered accountant was able to say in 1951:

> While the profession in Canada owes much of its form to British professional attitudes, the approach to specific problems in Canada is now much more influenced by American thinking than by British thinking.[6]

This shift in orientation came about mainly for two reasons. First, and far less important of the two, American textbooks, which began to issue from the presses in the 1910s and 1920s, gradually superseded the standard British texts in Canada. Thus Dicksee, Pixley, Leake, and Lisle gave way to Hatfield, Kester, Finney, Montgomery, and Himmelblau. A Canadian literature began abuilding in the 1920s and 1930s by Smails and others, but it was on a small scale in comparison with the American output.

---

[4] Of the 100 largest manufacturing, resource, and utility companies in Canada, according to the July 11, 1970 issue of *The Financial Post* (page 11), 60 are federally incorporated. Ontario is second, with 17. Of the first 40 companies in the same list, 32 are federally incorporated. A 1967 study by The Toronto Stock Exchange found that 232 of 449 listed, domestic industrials were federally incorporated. Ontario again was second, with 149. In the case of mining companies, however, 210 of 307 were incorporated in Ontario. Twenty-three of the domestic oil companies, according to the study, were incorporated in Alberta; 16 were federally incorporated.

[5] George J. Murphy, letter to the *Canadian Chartered Accountant*, September, 1971, p. 183.

[6] Smyth, *op. cit.*, p. 292.

A more important development that focused Canadian eyes on the United States was the growing volume of American investment in the Canadian economy. Prior to World War I, the London capital market satisfied the bulk of Canada's needs for expansion of wheat production, lumbering, and railway building. In the 1920s, however, the inflow of capital from the United States began to gather momentum, much of it being in the form of direct investment as opposed to portfolio holdings. The pace of U.S. direct investment accelerated greatly following World War II, so that of the $15-billion non-resident investment in Canada in 1957, over $11-½ billion was held in the United States and some $2-½ billion in the United Kingdom (all in Canadian dollars). Approximately two-thirds of the U.S. capital was in the form of direct investment, implying not only ownership and control but also policy direction. The nature and size of this capital movement provoked an "intangible sense of disquiet" in Canada, as suggested by the following 1958 assessment:

> Manufacturing, mining and petroleum are the areas of investment where non-resident controlled companies represent more than half of the total capital invested. In manufacturing alone, excluding petroleum refining, the non-resident controlled portion is nearly 50%, in petroleum 70%, and in other mining approximately 55%. Most of these concerns are controlled in the United States.[7]

Of the total foreign direct investment in Canada at the end of 1964, at least 80 percent represented ownership and control by U.S. companies.[8] At the end of 1970, the book value of U.S. direct investment in Canada was estimated at US $22.8 billion.[9]

Since the financial statements of the Canadian subsidiaries of U.S. parents eventually have to be consolidated in accordance with "generally accepted accounting principles" in the United States, an important segment of the Canadian profession, i.e., the technical partners of firms that were auditing the Canadian subsidiaries, have had to become acquainted with U.S. practice. Furthermore, Canadian companies seeking capital in U.S. securities markets, while using accepted Canadian practices in their financial statements, are required by the U.S. Securities and

[7] The investment data and the quotation are drawn from Henry G. Norman, "Foreign Investment in Canada," *The Canadian Chartered Accountant*, August, 1958, pp. 132-35.

[8] Melville H. Watkins, "Impact of Foreign Investments: The Canadian-U.S. Case," *Columbia Journal of World Business*, March-April, 1969, p. 23.

[9] R. David Belli and Julius N. Freidlin, "U.S. Direct Investment Abroad in 1970," *Survey of Current Business*, October, 1971, p. 28.

Exchange Commission to disclose in their reports the magnitude of any significant effect on net income of the difference between the two countries' practices.[10]

Coupled with earlier British investment in Canada, the heavy capital movements across the U.S.-Canadian border led to the establishment in Canada of offices of British and U.S. public accounting firms, notably the latter. As these offices grew, in some instances they were brought under the aegis of a newly formed Canadian firm which itself became a partner of the founding foreign firm. Certain American firms, however, preferred to coordinate their Canadian offices from headquarters in the United States. Choosing a different strategy, several indigenous Canadian firms forged links with large U.S. firms, each representing the other in their respective countries. To the extent, therefore, that these internationally minded firms influenced professional thinking in Canada — and it seems fair to say that their influence has been strong — an importation of American concepts and practices was inevitable.

Thus, the Canadian accounting profession, which has always shown an active interest in, and knowledge of, accounting and auditing practices in Great Britain and the United States, was driven by economic circumstances to regard U.S. practices with a greater sense of immediacy. Whether the Canadian profession, which would probably trace its intellectual heritage to Scotland more than to anywhere else, would have done otherwise in the absence of the invasion of large amounts of U.S. capital, is open to speculation. A combination of the Scottish respect for the practical benefits of higher education[11] and the much faster development in the U.S. than in Great Britain of university study as a normal avenue into the accounting profession might have led in a small way to a gradual importation, via the few Canadian universities then offering coursework in accounting, of the American philosophy and attitudes. This transference, if it has been occurring at all, may be about to accelerate, as nine of the ten provincial institutes have decided to require a university

---

[10] See *Accounting and Other Requirements for the Sales of Foreign Securities in the U.S. Capital Market* (New York: American Institute of Certified Public Accountants, 1962), p. 18.

[11] Galbraith recalls that the strongest case for higher education among the Scotch townspeople in his Southwestern Ontario hometown was that it had "independent utility for improving a man's position in the community or preparing him for a profession. . . ." John Kenneth Galbraith, *The Scotch* (Baltimore: Penguin Books, 1966), p. 87.

degree, and a growing fraction of Canadian accounting professors have taken at least one degree, increasingly the doctorate, in the United States.

This historical review, albeit brief and inadequate, portrays the Canadian profession as (1) having been organized in a unique federative style, (2) having been affected initially by Scottish values within a framework of laws based upon precedents in Great Britain, and (3) having later acquired a closer identification with U.S. ways and attitudes. Notwithstanding these latter two tendencies, the Canadian profession has retained a strong sense of independence and self-determination, and is not inclined to copy other systems or solutions.

Canadians are fond of saying that they often choose a position somewhere between the British and the Americans. Perhaps more so than the accounting profession of any other country, Canadians are familiar with accounting developments abroad. The reports on developments in other countries, which appear in the "Research" (formerly "Accounting Research") and "Accounting Abroad" departments of the *Canadian Chartered Accountant,* and frequent international comparisons in the biennial *Financial Reporting in Canada* attest to a wide-ranging and critical faculty.

EMERGENCE OF THE ACCOUNTING AND AUDITING RESEARCH COMMITTEE

Having thus portrayed the Canadian profession in broad outline, it is not difficult to understand why the Canadian Institute formed an Accounting and Auditing Research Committee which began to issue a series of technical bulletins for the guidance of members following World War II.

Leaders of the Canadian profession have regularly studied developments in the profession in other countries. In February, 1937, the editor of *The Canadian Chartered Accountant* drew attention to the founding of The Accounting Research Association (ARA) in Great Britain.[12] The ARA, he observed, was intended to create close cooperation between the universities and the profession in encouraging the conduct and publication of research studies.

---

[11] "Accounting Research in England," Editorial Comment, *The Canadian Chartered Accountant,* February, 1937, pp. 91-92.

> To what extent [wrote the editor] can the profession in Canada support this laudable effort? . . . Because of their close contact and co-operation with the universities in several provinces, our Institutes have an unusual opportunity for suggesting to the faculties of commerce in the universities some lines of investigation. The topics for research in the programme of the Association in England indicate many studies which may also be pursued in Canada.[13]

The editor's endorsement of the British initiative was strong and enthusiastic.

Since 1934, the Canadian Institute had had a Committee on Terminology, but little had yet been achieved. In July, 1937, however, the Chairman of the committee began a monthly "Terminology Department" in *The Canadian Chartered Accountant*. Shortly thereafter, the beginnings of a dictionary of terminology were issued in looseleaf form under the title, "Accounting Terminology for Canadian Practice."

Doubtless the Canadian profession was also aware of events then transpiring in the United States. In 1932-34, committees of the American Institute of Accountants (as the American Institute of Certified Public Accountants was then known) and the New York Stock Exchange proposed the adoption of a new form of the auditor's report and of five "accounting principles." Beginning in 1934, the new Securities and Exchange Commission (SEC) took a strong interest in accounting and auditing, especially in the form of financial statements and complementary disclosures. In 1936, the newly reorganized American Accounting Association issued "A Tentative Statement of Accounting Principles Underlying Corporate Financial Statements," and two years later the American Institute published a monograph entitled *A Statement of Accounting Principles*, written by Professors Thomas H. Sanders, Henry Rand Hatfield, and Underhill Moore.

Alert to these developments, the membership of the Canadian Institute decided at the 1938 annual meeting to "co-operate with Queen's University in a programme of research into accounting procedure and principles..."[14], as a result of which the Executive Committee in the following year appointed a Research Committee (retitled Accounting Research Committee in 1941). The negotiations between Queen's and the Canadian Institute's

---

[13] *Ibid.*, p. 92.
[14] "General Notes," *The Canadian Chartered Accountant,* April, 1939, p. 288.

new committee, owing to the onset of World War II, never matured into a transaction.[15]

In the immediately ensuing years, the Accounting Research Committee was relatively inactive. In 1943, it promulgated a recommendation to members on the accounting treatment of the refundable portion of Dominion Excess Profits Taxes [16] — the first instance in Canada of formal advice or guidance on a technical matter being given by a professional accounting body to its members.

It soon became evident that a series of pronouncements on technical subjects would be needed. The issuance in 1940 of SEC Regulation S-X, a comprehensive document calling for disclosures considerably more extensive than those required by the Dominion Companies Act, 1934-35, coupled with a fear that one or more bodies outside the profession might begin to prescribe the form and content of financial statements if the profession did not assert itself, seemed to motivate most of this activity. [17] To be sure, Canadians began to sense the lack of *Canadian* authoritative support for best practice.

A Committee on Co-operation with Stock Exchanges was formed, consisting of the chairmen of like provincial committees in Ontario, Quebéc, Alberta, British Columbia, and Manitoba. Liaison was quickly established with the New York Stock Exchange, the Toronto and Montreal stock exchanges, the Montreal Curb Market, the Investment Dealers Association, and various other interested bodies.[18]

As for the Accounting Research Committee, it felt the need for research staff in order to move ahead. [19] In August, 1945, the Council authorized the Executive Committee to engage the services of a research director. C. L. King, a 30-year-old chartered accountant, became the Canadian Institute's Secretary and Research Director on September 1, 1946. Also in 1946, the

---

[15] C. L. King, "Accounting and Auditing Research in Canada," *The Canadian Chartered Accountant*, January, 1950, p. 22.

[16] "Refundable Portion of Excess Profits Tax," *The Canadian Chartered Accountant*, February, 1943, p. 140. Also see the *1943-1944 Year Book* of The Dominion Association of Chartered Accountants, pp. 8-9.

[17] See H. G. Norman, "Dominion President's Address," *The Canadian Chartered Accountant*, October, 1944, p. 206, and J.R.M. Wilson, "Standards of Disclosure," unpublished speech delivered before The Institute of Chartered Accountants of Ontario, November, 1946, pp. 3-4.

[18] "Committee on Co-operation with Stock Exchanges," *1944-1945 Year Book* of The Dominion Association of Chartered Accountants, p. 8.

[19] *Ibid.*

Executive Committee authorized the Accounting Research Committee to prepare and publish reports on its own responsibility and enlarged its size to 14 members. [20] In this respect, the Canadian Institute preferred American over English practice. In 1942, The Institute of Chartered Accountants in England and Wales (English Institute) had begun a series of Recommendations on Accounting Principles, which were issued on the authority of the Council. The Accounting Research Bulletins which had been published since 1939 by the American Institute, however, were issued on the authority of a senior technical committee, not the Council. The Canadian committee also adopted the policy, begun by its American counterpart, of requiring a two-thirds majority for approval and of publishing members' dissents. The English Institute, by contrast, never disclosed the votes of the Council, the required minimum for approval being a "substantial majority."

While in the U.S. the accounting and auditing areas were apportioned to separate committees, in Canada they were combined in one, apparently in the belief that the two subjects contained a high degree of interdependency. Accordingly, in 1946 the name of the Accounting Research Committee was changed to "Accounting and Auditing Research Committee."

While the American Institute's two series of bulletins on accounting and auditing seldom dealt with questions of disclosure and the form and content and financial statements, the Canadian Institute's committee gave these subjects a high priority. In the U.S., the SEC had largely pre-empted the field on such matters, but in Canada it was evidently hoped that the provincial legislatures and the Canadian Parliament would be guided by the profession's initiatives.

That one motive behind the reactivation of the committee was a concern over possible governmental interest in financial reporting seems to have been borne out by the experience of the committee's first two Bulletins. Bulletin No. 1, issued in October, 1946, proposed disclosure standards for annual financial statements of manufacturing and mercantile companies. It had originally been drafted by a committee of the Ontario Institute, some of whose members also belonged to the Accounting and Auditing Research Committee. [21] Bulletin No. 2, issued six

---

[20] "Accounting Research Committee," *1946-1947 Year Book* of The Dominion Association of Chartered Accountants, p. 7.

[21] *Ibid.*

months later, dealt with the auditor's role and financial disclosures in regard to prospectuses; in part, the second Bulletin incorporated disclosure standards set forth in Bulletin No. 1. The formal issuance of both Bulletins was preceded by the publication in the *Canadian Chartered Accountant* of "tentative statements" and an exposure period of five to six months.[22] Even before Bulletin No. 2 could be issued in final form, the Ontario Securities Commission eagerly adopted the contents of both Bulletins in a policy statement entitled "Notes re Financial Statements Under Section 49 of The Securities Act, 1945."

A vigorous program of liaison followed the issuance of the first two Bulletins. Discussions were held with representatives of the Toronto, Montreal, and Vancouver stock exchanges, the Investment Dealers Association, and security analysts and financial journalists in the principal financial centers. As a result of these meetings, the Toronto and Vancouver stock exchanges and the Investment Dealers Association endorsed Bulletin No. 1, and the two exchanges sent copies of the Bulletin, together with a letter recommending the adoption of the standards in reports to shareholders, to their listed companies. The meetings with the financial journalists were intended to be informational to the Committee and educational to the writers.

In the area of terminology, the Committee continued the work of the old Committee on Terminology. In 1957, after some ten years of experimentation, it sponsored "without the official sanction of the Institute or of any of its committees" the publication of a 77-page book, *Accounting Terminology*. Three

---

[22] Following these two Bulletins, the committee unanimously decided not to publish future exposure drafts in the *Canadian Chartered Accountant;* instead, copies marked "Tentative and Confidential" were to be sent to all members of the Canadian Institute. "The Committee thought that this method would avoid anyone acting on the draft of the statement, and finding later that the final statement had been altered in some particulars." *1947-48 Year Book* of The Dominion Association of Chartered Accountants, p. 9. Before another exposure draft could be issued, however, the Committee reconsidered its earlier decision and concluded that the publication of exposure drafts in any form would be misleading to readers who were uninformed about the Committee's procedures. *1948-1949 Year Book,* pp. 9-10. The next exposure draft to be published, as noted below, was in the June, 1967 issue of the *Canadian Chartered Accountant,* on income tax allocation. Since then, exposure drafts have also been published in the Canadian Institute's journal, and reprints widely distributed, for the pronouncements on prior period adjustments, extraordinary items, and capital transactions. Exposure drafts on earnings per share, diversified operations, unaudited financial statements and accounting summaries, and interim financial reporting to shareholders, were announced and discussed (but not reproduced) in the *Canadian Chartered Accountant,* the drafts themselves being sent directly to members of the Canadian Institute and other interested parties.

years later, a version in French was published. In 1962, the 517 terms defined in the earlier book were expanded to 854 in *Terminology for Accountants,* which was translated into French the following year.

The Committee was exceedingly reluctant, however, to pursue questions of auditing procedure. It observed that the English Institute had "carefully avoided" any guidance statements on the subject of auditing,[23] and the Committee may have believed that the activity in this field by the American Institute had been imposed on the profession by the SEC, initially as a result of the celebrated McKesson & Robbins case of 1938-39. The Committee's reasons for not issuing Bulletins on auditing were said to be the following:

> Some members of the committee feel that if any such bulletins were issued the members of the profession would be exposing themselves unnecessarily to liability. Others feel that publication of such bulletins has a tendency to detract from the professional nature of the practice of public accounting and they point to the fact that no other profession lays down rules as to the manner in which work is normally to be performed by its members.[24]

In 1951, however, the Committee issued two Bulletins in the area of auditing procedures, one which gave formal recognition to the auditing procedures already in use for inventories, and another which recommended a standard form of the auditor's report. Yet, as late as 1958, in a Bulletin on the confirmation of receivables, the Committee made known its hesitancy to express itself on auditing:

> The Committee on Accounting and Auditing Research has generally limited its bulletins on auditing to questions of professional standards and the forms of auditors' reports, in which a measure of uniformity is desirable. In the opinion of the committee, a bulletin setting out standards of auditing procedure should be issued only when the exceptional nature of a problem calls for formal recognition of an acceptable practice.[25]

In 1959-60, the Committee seemed to relax somewhat this policy, as it issued three more Bulletins on auditing, two of which superseded the Bulletins issued in 1951.

---

[23] Report of the Accounting and Auditing Research Committee, *1950 Annual Report* of the D.A.C.A., *loc. cit.*

[24] *Ibid.*

[25] "Confirmation of Receivables," Bulletin No. 15, Accounting and Auditing Practice Statements issued by The Committee on Accounting and Auditing Research of The Canadian Institute of Chartered Accountants (April, 1958), p. 1.

A provision contained in the Government's proposed Income War Tax Act in late 1947 gave impetus to the Committee's work in accounting principles. Section 4 of the bill was as follows:

> Subject to the other provisions of this Part, income for a taxation year from a business or property shall be determined in accordance with generally accepted accounting principles.[26]

When lawyers began to ask representatives of the accounting profession for an explication of "generally accepted accounting principles," they were informed that the term had not been codified in Canada and that the profession would prefer that it be removed from the bill, which it was. At that, the Committee resolved to begin the process of issuing Bulletins on particular facets of "generally accepted accounting principles," hoping eventually to codify the term. It chose accounts receivable as its first subject, believing it to be noncontroversial. It was anything but noncontroversial, because many companies had created bad-debt allowances in the 1930s which, in the light of conditions in the 1940s, were excessive. The companies, however, were "locked in" to their excessive allowances, as they had been set up when tax rates were much lower than the excess-profits rates of the 1940s. Bulletin No. 4, on "Accounting for Bad Debt Losses," which recognized the dilemma, was issued in January, 1950.

The Committee then turned to inventories, dividing the subject into "cost" and "market" considerations. Once again, a topic was more difficult than the Committee had imagined. Bulletin No. 5, "The Meaning of the Term 'Cost' as Used in Inventory Valuation," issued in November, 1950, reflected the permissiveness found in Recommendation 10 of the English Institute and Accounting Research Bulletin No. 29 of the American Institute on which the Canadian pronouncement seemed to be patterned. A Bulletin on market did not follow. The Committee apparently realized that the codification of accounting principles was a much more challenging task than had been imagined.

In 1952-53, the Committee directed attention to the impact of inflation on financial statements. A special meeting was called in May, 1952 to which a number of persons engaged in industry, commerce, and finance were invited, in order to discuss:

> (a) Replacement accounting, having regard to the recommendations of the Business Income Study Group in the United States [which

---

[26] *Report of Proceedings*, Conference on the Income Tax Bill, December 8th and 9th, 1947, Ottawa (Canadian Tax Foundation), p. 5.

were published in *Changing Concepts of Business Income*] , and
other related literature.

(b)   The form, content, and terminology of financial statements.[27]

It was reported that "considerable animated discussion took
place."[28] Although the members of the Committee appeared to
believe that any provision for the replacement of assets at higher
costs should be made from accumulated profits and that
accounting should adhere to the cost concept, "it was immediately
evident that this view was not shared by some of the senior
accountants in industry and it was strongly urged that the problem
should be explored further."[29] A committee entitled "The
Committee to Enquire into the Effect of the Changing Value of
the Dollar on Financial Statements" was thereupon appointed, its
members consisting of five senior financial executives from
industry, three from financial institutions of whom two were
economists, one appointee from the Government's Department of
Finance, four chartered accountants in practice, and the CICA
Research Director. A little more than a year later it was reported
that the effort had been abandoned because of "the absence of
any permanent organization or any indication that material
progress was being made by accounting bodies in other countries. . . ."[30]

During the first two decades of the Committee's reinvigorated
program, Bulletins were issued on the average of one per year.
While it is not always easy to classify the Bulletins into the three
broad areas which they were intended to comprehend, i.e.,
accounting principles, auditing procedures, and disclosure standards, the Bulletins most directly concerned with matters of
accounting principle would be the following:

3   The Accounting Treatment of Income Taxes
      in Some Special Circumstances   June, 1948

4   Accounting for Bad Debt Losses   January, 1950

5   The Meaning of the Term "Cost" as
      Used in Inventory Valuation   November, 1950

---

[27] Report of the Accounting and Auditing Research Committee, *1952 Annual Report*
of The Canadian Institute of Chartered Accountants, p. 14.

[28] *Ibid.*

[29] *Ibid.*

[30] Report of the Accounting and Auditing Research Committee, *1953 Annual Report*
of The Canadian Institute of Chartered Accountants, p. 12.

9 The Use of the Term "Reserve" and
Accounting for Reserves   January, 1953

10 Depreciation, Capital Cost Allowances
and Income Taxes   September, 1954

11 Surplus   August, 1955

12 Loss Carry-Over Tax Credits
(Superseding No. 3)   August, 1956

19 Financial Statements of
Unincorporated Businesses   July, 1961

21 Accounting for the Costs of
Pension Plans   August, 1965

24 Accounting for Government Grants
for Fixed Assets   September, 1967

26 Accounting for Corporate Income
Taxes (Superseding Nos. 10 and 12)   September, 1967

A direct comparison of the Committee's output with that of the American Institute's Committee on Accounting Procedure is not feasible for several reasons. One, a single Canadian committee has been issuing Bulletins in areas that have occupied two or more committees of the American Institute. Two, it is possible that the American committees' initiatives in certain areas were accepted in Canada without the need for a Canadian pronouncement. Three, the Canadian committee had on only few occasions (e.g., diversified operations, land development companies) been prodded into action by Federal or provincial authorities, in contrast to the continuing dialogue in the United States between the SEC and technical committees of the American Institute.

In the Canadian committee's first 26 Bulletins, only five dissenting votes were reported. This record suggests that innovation, at least in controversial areas, was not intended. The following passage from the Committee's 1950 report lends credence to this view:

> It is inevitable, and on reflection it is obviously desirable, that bulletins in this series will contain little that is new to the members of the profession. It would, in fact, be deplorable if the bulletins did contain such surprises, for what the committee is attempting in this series is to set out what it believes to be those principles or procedures which are generally accepted by the profession. . . . The value of the bulletins, if

they are generally accepted by members of the profession, lies in the fact that the profession itself and not someone else is saying what may be considered to be good accounting practice in Canada.[31]

Yet in Bulletin No. 10, a hope emerged that the Committee might break new ground. The subject was the always-contentious allocation of income taxes, and in the end the Committee compromised by accepting both the "flow-through" and allocation approaches, while expressing a preference for the latter. In spite of its permissiveness, Bulletin No. 10 evoked the first dissent. That was in 1954.

It was not until Bulletin No. 24, issued thirteen years later, that the second and third dissents were registered. Accounting for government grants was the subject.

Two more dissents were filed the same year, 1967, when Bulletin No. 26 strongly endorsed the practice of income tax allocation. To be sure, the division within the committee that was so evident in Bulletin No. 10 had haunted many of its later meetings. Yet the importance of Bulletin No. 26 transcends the subject with which it deals, for it made evident a new policy of going beyond accepted practice in the Committee's pronouncements on accounting principles. It was issued following four years of difficult debate within the Committee. So controversial and sensitive was the subject that the Committee revived its long-discarded policy of publishing exposure drafts in the *Canadian Chartered Accountant.* The penultimate draft appeared in the issue of June, 1967 and was preceded by a "pre-exposure draft" in August, 1965.[32]

---

[31] Report of the Accounting and Auditing Research Committee, *1950 Annual Report* of The Dominion Association of Chartered Accountants, p. 10. At the close of the quotation, one detects a veiled reference to influence from outside the country, likely the United States.

[32] A "qualified assent" by three Committee members in Bulletin No. 26 vividly shows how a U.S. pronouncement on accounting practices applicable to an industry having strong interests in Canada can have an impact on Canadian accounting. In 1967, when the Bulletin was issued, the U.S. oil and gas industry did not allocate income taxes in regard to the intangible drilling costs on successful wells. (See *Report on Certain Petroleum Industry Accounting Practices, 1967* (New York: American Petroleum Institute, 1967), p. 28, Table V.) In their qualified assent, the three Committee members cited this accounting policy of U.S. oil and gas companies and concluded that it would be impracticable to try to gain acceptance of the Bulletin among the U.S.-dominated oil and gas companies operating in Canada. Relying in part on a chapter in the Canadian Institute's research study on oil and gas accounting, the Committee nonetheless rejected an exemption of the industry from the Bulletin's recommendation that income tax allocation be followed.

Shortly after the issuance of Bulletin No. 26, the American Institute's Accounting Principles Board approved Opinion No. 11 in support of "comprehensive" income tax allocation. But Opinion No. 11 exempted the oil and gas industry pending completion of

What factors contributed to the Committee's change in posture? First, there had been a growing dissatisfaction in the profession with the Committee's lack of leadership. A special Study Group was appointed in late 1966 to inquire into the Committee's organization and terms of reference. Its report, dated July, 1967, was adopted the following September by the Canadian Institute's Executive Committee and Council. Among its recommendations were that the Committee should promote *"higher* and *more nearly uniform* standards for the accounting profession in Canada" and should publish "recommendations on *sound* accounting and auditing practices."[33] (Emphasis added.)

Second, increasingly during the 1960s, younger men were being appointed to the Committee. They were probably more inclined to innovate than their predecessors. Third, the large firms themselves were becoming more research-minded in their internal operations.

A factor that cannot be entirely dismissed, and which may have contributed in part to the concern about the Committee's role as a leader, was the developments in the United States. In late 1966, the Accounting Principles Board (APB) had unanimously approved two Opinions in controversial areas (pensions and extraordinary items/earnings per share), raising hopes that real progress was finally being made. Furthermore, in late 1966 and 1967, it was known that the Board was drafting an Opinion that endorsed "comprehensive" income tax allocation – a development that probably was noted by the Canadian committee as it completed work on Bulletin No. 26.

THE NEW RESEARCH PROGRAM: PHASE ONE

Yet Bulletin No. 26 was not the first sign that the Committee believed it should depart from its traditional role of synthesizing

---

the American Institute's accounting research study on extractive industries. In view of the industry exemption in Opinion No. 11 and the intransigence of the oil and gas industry on the question, a *de facto* industry exemption in Canada was deemed unavoidable. Consequently, Canadian public accounting firms have not insisted on qualifying their opinions in those instances where intangible drilling costs are not tax-allocated and full disclosure of this departure from Bulletin No. 26 is shown in the footnotes to the financial statements.

[33] "Reorganization of the Institute's Research Activities" Accounting Research, *Canadian Chartered Accountant,* March, 1968, p. 196.

accepted practice. In 1961, it decided to inaugurate a series of research studies. Two years later, when the first study was published, the Chairman of the Committee commented on this "new departure":

> It will be appreciated that, initially, bulletins represent only the views and recommendations of the Committee, and. . . their usefulness and authoritative status depend almost entirely on the degree of acceptance which they receive. Bulletins, therefore, usually have dealt with topics on which there is believed to be a large degree of unanimity of opinion.
>
> Whether or not for this reason, the fact remains that all bulletins issued since 1957 have dealt with auditing techniques and methods of reporting, rather than the basic accounting problems. . . .
>
> The nature of many of these accounting problems is such that little or no possibility exists of finding a ready solution which will receive sufficient general acceptance to justify a bulletin. The first requirement is for detailed research into each alternative method or procedure and, if possible, of finding a logical basis on which to recommend the adoption of one alternative in preference to others. . . . In this way it is hoped to crystallize public opinion, and reduce the areas of controversy to the degree that the Research Committee will be justified in issuing a bulletin on the topic.[34]

The objective of the Canadian Institute's new research program, therefore, differed in one key respect from that of the American Institute's program, which was launched in 1959. While the latter placed primary emphasis on discovering the underlying postulates and principles which might point the way toward eventual agreement on particulars, the former sought a "logical" means of selecting the best alternative accounting method or procedure.

Another clue to the philosophy of the new series of research studies was given by the Director of Research a year later, in the form of two objectives:

> 1. To provide a series of carefully reasoned studies of areas of interest to the accounting profession; and
> 2. To provide a means of exposing important subjects for review by members of the Institute, and other interested persons, in the hope of getting a cross-section of opinions on areas in which the Committee was considering the issuance of a bulletin.[35]

---

[34] John R. Church, "Research Studies – A New Departure," Editorial, *The Canadian Chartered Accountant*, January, 1963, pp. 25-26.

[35] Foreword by R.D. Thomas, in T.A.M. Hutchison, *Reliance on Other Auditors*, A Research Study (Toronto: The Canadian Institute of Chartered Accountants, 1964), n.p.

It was evidently believed that through careful reasoning, wide exposure, and the solicitation of opinions from many sources, difficult questions of accounting principle would become more tractable. Since the Committee's Bulletins carried no force beyond their persuasiveness, it was perhaps felt that the prior publication of research studies might, among other things, create a climate in which subsequent Bulletins based on the studies would be more susceptible to general acceptance. It might also have been hoped that the issuance of the studies themselves would lead to the improvement of accounting practice.

Through 1971, ten research studies on accounting subjects were published, as follows:

> *Use and Meaning of "Market" in Inventory Valuation* (1963), by Gertrude Mulcahy
>
> *Accounting Problems in the Oil and Gas Industry* (1963), by W. B. Coutts
>
> *Accounting for Costs of Pension Plans* (1963), by W. B. Coutts and R. B. Dale-Harris
>
> *Accounting for Costs of Financing* (1964), by H. S. Moffet
>
> *Overhead as an Element of Inventory Costs* (1965), by J. K. Walker and G. Mulcahy
>
> *Financial Reporting for Non-producing Mining Companies* (1967), prepared by a study group
>
> *Finance Companies – their Accounting, Financial Statement Presentation, and Auditing* (1967), by St. Elmo V. Smith
>
> *Canadian University Accounting* (1969), by R. M. Skinner
>
> *Accounting for Real Estate Development Operations* (1971), prepared by a study group
>
> *Accounting for Trust and Loan Companies in Canada* (1971), prepared by a study group.[36]

The study on non-producing mining companies was undertaken at the request of The Toronto Stock Exchange.

---

[36] Two research studies on auditing subjects have been published:
> Reliance on Other Auditors
> The Hospital Audit

The first of these two studies led directly to Bulletin No. 22 and has apparently had an important impact on practice. In addition to the research studies, the Committee has commissioned several "audit technique studies," of which the examples published to date are the following:
> Materiality in Auditing
> Internal Control in the Small Business
> Internal Control and Procedural Audit Tests
> Confirmation of Accounts Receivable
> Good Audit Working Papers
> Confirmation of Trade Accounts Payable

Of the ten research studies, only one — the study on pensions — has been followed by a Bulletin on the same subject, although parts of a few other studies may be found in two or three Bulletins. Six studies have dealt with the accounting practices in particular industries.

In a departure from standard procedure, a draft of the study on the accounting practices of real estate development companies was circulated in late 1970 to several hundred persons associated with the industry as well as to all interested parties. [37] The study group was anxious that the study reflect the variations in conditions found in different parts of the country. The response to the request for comments was regarded as quite good: Some provincial institutes went so far as to organize discussion groups. The completed study was published the following year.

Although it is difficult to generalize about the differences between the Canadian Institute and American Institute's research studies, one distinguishing characteristic does boldly stand out: length. While the Canadian studies ordinarily do not exceed 50 pages, those of the American Institute seldom run *fewer* than 100. "Academic" is probably a term that practitioners would use to describe the American studies, yet some of the longest of these have been written by practitioners.

The experience with the nine Canadian studies seems not to suggest a preoccupation with putting out Bulletins on the same subjects shortly thereafter. By contrast, all of the first eleven American studies, with the exception of No. 11, have led either to an Opinion or a Statement of the Accounting Principles Board.

The Canadian studies are done either by one or more authors aided by an advisory panel or by a study group consisting of experienced individuals in the subject area under investigation. This second approach tends to be used in the more controversial and sensitive areas in order to bring into the study a full consideration of competing viewpoints. All American studies, by contrast, are done by the first approach.

So far, the authors and members of the study groups have all been chartered accountants. All but two of the authors, in fact, have been past or present members of the Accounting and Auditing Research Committee. The two other authors were a member of the Institute's research staff, and a onetime editor of

---

[37] See the announcement of the draft study, Accounting Research, *Canadian Chartered Accountant,* December, 1970, pp. 414-15.

the "Accounting Research" department of the *Canadian Chartered Accountant.* In this respect, the authors have been thickly involved in the Institute's ongoing technical operations. The same can be said for somewhat more than a majority of the authors of American studies.

As will be seen, this comparison anticipates the second phase of the Canadian Institute's research program, which has endeavored to pursue more basic research and to bring more academicians into the effort.

THE NEW RESEARCH PROGRAM: PHASE TWO

In 1964, the Canadian program of research studies seemed to lose some of its "applied" flavor. In that year, the Committee authorized a study on "generally accepted accounting principles" — in the same year that the Accounting Principles Board commissioned Paul Grady to undertake an "inventory" on the same subject. Grady's study was published in 1965, but by the end of 1971, the Canadian study had not yet appeared. It is scheduled for publication in 1972.

A second injection of the philosophy of basic research was provided in 1967 by the special Study Group referred to above. Among its recommendations was the following:

> In our view it is essential that the Research Committee, to a much greater extent than it has in the past, should engage in initiating and overseeing basic research at the frontiers of our profession rather than gathering together to record the best current practice.[38]

In discussing the Study Group's proposal, the Canadian Institute's Associate Director (now Director) of Research acknowledged the traditionally "practice-oriented" approach of the Committee and said:

> To be realistic it must be admitted that the Institute's research programme has not produced any major new knowledge that is vital to the continuation of the profession and its leadership in the field of accounting. . . . [U]nless positive steps are taken to initiate and maintain the development of new knowledge, the whole accounting function will soon become useless.[39]

[38] "Reorganization of the Institute's Research Activities," *op. cit.*, p. 197.
[39] Gertrude Mulcahy, "Pure Research — An Essential Ingredient of the Institute's Programme," Accounting Research, *Canadian Chartered Accountant*, September, 1968,

The Associate Director of Research interpreted the new research direction as calling for "pure" research,[40] which would involve, of necessity, active participation by the growing number of chartered accountants engaged in full-time university teaching. The first product of the move in this direction was an empirical study of Canadian experience with pooling of interests and purchase accounting, done by three academic researchers in collaboration with the Canadian Institute and The University of Western Ontario.[41]

In 1969, while the University of Western Ontario study was still in progress, the research director made it known to academicians that the Committee invited proposals for research studies from the universities. To this end, six guidelines were tentatively established by the Committee:

(i)   The subject must be of current significance.

(ii)   There must be a commitment on the part of the University or School of Business and not just individual academicians personally.

(iii) The University or School of Business must satisfy the Committee that they have, in fact, the staff and personnel to undertake the project.

(iv)   The projects should, preferably, be capable of completion within a 6 - 8 month period.

(v)   Those Universities or Schools of Business who are interested in participating in projects on a joint basis should present the Research Committee with a definite proposal.

(vi)   The actual selection of projects each year will be on the basis of the best proposal that is presented to the Committee but rotation among the various Universities would be desirable.[42]

p. 185. In January, 1969, Gertrude Mulcahy became the first person to dedicate full time to the position of Director of Research, although she had been a full-time Associate Director for a number of years. Her predecessors either divided the Directorship with the heavy duties of Secretary or Executive Director (C.L. King and R.D. Thomas) or were university faculty working part-time at the Canadian Institute (L.G. Macpherson).

[40] *Ibid.*, pp. 185-86. A dissent from this view is found in Howard Ross, *Financial Statements: A Crusade for Current Values* (New York: Pitman Publishing Corporation, 1969), pp. 82-87. Ross has been President of the Quebéc and Canadian Institutes, Chairman of the Accounting and Auditing Research Committee, and a partner in a large firm of chartered accountants. He is now Dean of the Faculty of Management, McGill University.

[41] Samuel A. Martin, Stanley N. Laiken, and Donald F. Haslam, *Business Combinations in the '60's: A Canadian Profile* (Toronto and London, Ont.: The Canadian Institute of Chartered Accountants and The School of Business Administration, The University of Western Ontario, [1970]).

[42] Gertrude Mulcahy, "The Research Programme of the Canadian Institute of Chartered Accountants," *Proceedings*, Third Annual Conference, Canadian Regional Group, American Accounting Association, York University, June, 1969, p. 32.

It was added that the Committee had in mind not only joint sponsorship but also joint financing. A maximum annual Institute contribution of $10,000 was mentioned, but straitened financial conditions since 1969 might oblige the Institute to commit a lower sum. Recently, the research director contacted eight universities about a research project similar to the University of Western Ontario undertaking, but dealing with the accounting implications of the Government's White Paper on income tax reform. At most schools, there was insufficient interest or unavailable staff. If the Canadian Institute continues in this direction, it will be going opposite to the trend at the American Institute, which began with academic authors and has in recent years been assigning studies mainly to practitioners.

In future research studies, it is planned that a close working relationship between the author or authors and the advisory panel will be maintained, as was done in the University of Western Ontario study. The Committee believes that the scope and framework of the studies must be monitored throughout the research and writing process if they are to respond to the research needs of the Committee.

Research studies on accounting subjects currently in process deal with changing financial values, the translation of foreign currency, the financial reporting of life insurance companies, depreciation accounting, and (as noted above) generally accepted accounting principles. Because of current discussions concerning the possible establishment of a research foundation (see below), the Committee has decelerated the authorization of new studies until a decision on future financing is made.

In the middle and latter 1960s, the larger Canadian firms began to expand their technical and research staffs. Several firms have designated a partner having few or no client responsibilities to direct the research/technical staff. Since "research" means different things in different firms, generalizations do not come easily. In the last few years, the Canadian Institute's research director has met with the research/technical partners of several of the large firms in order to become better informed about the nature and direction of their research activities.

THE NEW APPROACH TO ISSUING PRONOUNCEMENTS

Since the effective creation of the Committee in 1946, the members resident in the Eastern financial centers of Toronto and

Montreal dominated the Committee's deliberations, partly because of geography and partly as a result of their more extensive experience with the technical problems under discussion. In fact, the Toronto and Montreal members were organized as a subcommittee to meet several times a year and formulate proposals for the entire Committee to consider. But at the one meeting each year of the full Committee, the members from the other provinces regarded their vote as comparable to the Royal Assent.

The Toronto/Montreal subcommittee also tended to be too large for effective draft-writing, so in 1961 it was divided into Toronto and Montreal sub-subcommittees. Eventually, the work load became heavy even for these two smaller bodies.

An aim of the aforementioned special Study Group, therefore, was to achieve a greater degree of participation by all parties. Its recommendations were as basic to the Bulletin-issuing process as to the research program. The Study Group's proposals, as implemented in 1967, increased the Committee membership to twenty and divided it into three geographical sections; created a steering committee consisting of the section chairmen, the general chairman, the Director of Research, and the Associate Director of Research; and organized its work to assure a more deliberate approach and a greater degree of participation by all Committee members. Under the new plan, a member may be Chairman of the full Committee for one year, usually after having been a section chairman for one or two years.[43]

According to the new plan, the steering committee recommends topics for consideration. Once the full Committee approves a topic, the research staff prepares a resource paper, pulling together opinions and information on extant practice not only in Canada but abroad as well. Utilizing the resource paper, the geographical section to which the topic has been assigned, known as the "initiating section," draws up a "statement of principles." Submission of the "statement of principles" to the full Committee is the key stage, for the Committee's decision at this point will shape, in general terms, the position eventually to be reflected in a pronouncement. If the Committee approves the "statement of principles," the initiating section prepares a draft of the pronouncement, which, after examination by the Committee and

---

[43] An exception was made in 1971, when the 1970-71 Committtee Chairman was reappointed for a second year.

exposure to the profession and other interested parties, would be promulgated.

Each regional section — Eastern, Central, and Western — consists of public practitioners from both large and small firms, an industry representative, an academician, and (in one section) a government representative. All members must be chartered accountants. Industry representatives were first appointed to the Committee in 1963. The American Institute added industry representatives under its new research program in 1959. The Canadian committee has included full-time academicians since 1946 (save for 1961-63), the American committee since 1939.

A final reform resulting from the report of the Study Group replaced the series of numbered Bulletins by a subject-indexed, cross-referenced Handbook in looseleaf form. The final version of a committee pronouncement, therefore, would be a "Handbook release," consisting of new page inserts revised to reflect the Committee's recommendations. A separate Bulletin would not be issued. Dissents and the names of dissenters would not be recorded,[44] although it was hoped that the sense of the dissenters' comments would be reflected in the discussion of alternative methods. The Handbook approach goes a step further than the American Institute which, in 1968, while continuing to publish separate APB Opinions, began collaborating with a commercial publisher in the preparation of subject-indexed, looseleaf compilation of all pronouncements in effect. Both Institutes believe that a subject-oriented, cross-referenced handbook will make the pronouncements easier to understand and use.

Since inaugurating the Handbook approach, the Committee has issued releases ("research recommendations") on extraordinary items/prior period adjustments, earnings per share, financial

---

[44] The Study Group's reason for dropping dissents was reported as follows:

We find that the Bulletins, as now designed, tend to become frozen in form and content, and are amended only by a complete rewording. This is partly because the format makes it impossible to amend a Bulletin without a complete reprinting, but largely because each Bulletin is identified with the names of the Committee members who approve it.

This identification with individuals and the publishing of dissenting opinions had resulted in a tendency for Bulletins to contain built-in compromise in order to minimize the number of dissents. If a dissenting opinion does appear, it gives undue importance to the views of one or two members of the Committee compared with the views of the majority. We believe this may result in a disservice to the profession. "Reorganization of the Institute's Research Activities," *op. cit.*, p. 198.

The members of the Study Group were drawn from the membership of the Accounting and Auditing Research Committee.

reporting of diversified operations, and interim financial reporting to shareholders, as well as on a number of auditing matters. While the research recommendation on extraordinary items/prior period adjustments was closely patterned after a previous U.S. pronouncement, the recommendation on earnings per share departed in a material respect from its U.S. counterpart. When the Canadian pronouncement on interim financial reporting to shareholders was issued, the Accounting Principles Board had not yet exposed its draft on the subject. Exposure drafts of proposed Canadian pronouncements, which are ordinarily open for comments for a 60-day period, have been issued on long-term intercorporate investments and business combination disclosure. As in other countries, the subject of accounting for business combinations has been particularly difficult for the Committee to resolve. Although its research study was completed in 1969, the Committee has so far been able to agree only on the terms of disclosure. Guidance is in earlier stages on funds statements, consolidated statements, and certain aspects of corporate income taxes.

In 1969, it was decided not to continue publishing exposure drafts in the *Canadian Chartered Accountant,* for it seemed that this medium had educed few letters of comment. Instead, some 22,000 copies of exposure drafts are distributed to a mailing list which includes all Institute members, the provincial institutes, the principal stock exchanges, major investment firms, and the Investment Dealers Association, among others. Individual letters are sent together with exposure drafts to about 400 companies. Most of the comments are submitted by corporate officials. The Director of Research writes personal letters to all authors of comments, explaining why their suggestions were or were not adopted by the Committee. In addition, when a research recommendation is announced, an article appears in the *Canadian Chartered Accountant* summarizing and analyzing the suggestions received, including reasons why the Committee made changes in the original draft.[45]

In 1969, without prior issuance of an exposure draft, the Committee added to the Handbook a "departure disclosure" requirement essentially identical to that contained in the

---

[45] See, e.g., "Financial Reporting of Diversified Operations: Comments Received on Exposure Draft," Accounting Research, *Canadian Chartered Accountant,* May, 1971, pp. 359-61.

American Institute's Special Bulletin of 1964.[46] The key provisions are as follows:

> Where the accounting treatment or statement presentation does not follow the recommendations in this Handbook, the practice used should be explained in notes to the financial statements with an indication of the reason why the recommendation concerned was not followed. (Handbook Sec. 1500.05)

> Where financial statements reported on by the auditors depart from a recommended accounting treatment or statement presentation, and the departure is not disclosed in notes to the financial statements, the auditors should make such disclosure in their report. (Handbook Sec. 2500.20, reflecting a minor amendment of original Sec. 2500.18)

These provisions cannot be enforced, however, until the several provincial institutes amend their codes of ethics to require compliance. The initial reactions of the provincial institutes have been cool, and such amendments are not expected soon. The "departure disclosure" raises afresh the federal-provincial controversy.

OTHER CICA RESEARCH ACTIVITIES

Two other activities of the Canadian Institute's research staff deserve mention.

Since 1955, the Canadian Institute has published the biennial *Financial Reporting in Canada,* which presently analyzes the reporting practices of 325 Canadian companies. While its format is similar to that of the American Institute's annual *Accounting Trends and Techniques,* the Canadian publication tends to give less attention to accounting and disclosure areas where substantial uniformity exists, concentrating instead on divergenices. *Financial Reporting* also makes frequent references to U.S. and British pronouncements and to comparable figures in *Accounting Trends and Techniques,* while the American publication rarely looks beyond the domestic scene for comparisons.

In 1964, the Accounting and Auditing Research Committee, with the approval of the Canadian Institute's Executive Committee and Council, authorized the Director of Research to write

---

[46] That the Committee was able to achieve agreement so rapidly (although not without opposition from provincial representatives in Council) of the "departure disclosure," while the American Institute required a year-and-a-half of difficult debate to do the same, suggests how Canada can take advantage of precedent in another country.

the auditors of companies whose financial statements contained departures from the Committee's recommendations. A wide array of responses was received, ranging from indignant rejections to expressions of gratitude for help in persuading a client to accept the Committee's recommendations. Because of an increase in other demands on the research staff, the program was suspended a few years ago. It has been suggested that the Canadian Institute replace the earlier, more expensive program with one by which the Committee or research staff would investigate complaints of substandard reporting.

COST OF THE RESEARCH AND HANDBOOK PROGRAM

As might be surmised from this description of the Canadian Institute's accounting research and Handbook program, the scale of activity has enlarged significantly in the last few years. The Canadian Institute now has a full-time research staff of five. Although it economizes to some extent by trying to avoid unnecessary duplication with the larger program of the American Institute,[47] a present membership base of approximately 19,000 may not be large enough, especially in view of the share of provincial dues that is remitted to the federal body, to support the ambitious program of research and pronouncements — unless an alternative funding source is found.

Exhibit I depicts the comparative growth, in terms of aggregate costs, of the combined research and pronouncement programs in both accounting and auditing of the Canadian and American Institutes.[48] In 1969-70, the cost of the Canadian program was more than three times that of the program in 1964-65. By the end of the same five-year period, the cost of the American program had grown to four times the figure for 1964-65.

In 1969-70, the Canadian Institute's cost of $161,300 represented a per-capita cost of almost $9.00. Though the American Institute's per-capita cost of 1968-69 for a much larger program was only slightly higher ($9.32, in Canadian dollars), the

---

[47] For example, a representative of the Canadian Institute has ordinarily attended the symposia and (now) public hearings held by the Accounting Principles Board on problems being considered by the Board.

[48] Since the Canadian Institute's figures for 1970-71 were compiled and classified on a basis that makes comparability with prior years difficult, figures for the most recent year are not presented.

EXHIBIT I

COMPARATIVE COSTS OF CICA AND AICPA RESEARCH AND PRONOUNCEMENT PROGRAMS IN ACCOUNTING AND AUDITING

(In Canadian dollars unless otherwise indicated)

The Canadian Institute of Chartered Accountants (CICA)

Fiscal Year	(1) Cost of Accounting and Auditing Research Committee	(2) Total fees (dues)	(3) Membership	(4) Dues per Capita (2)/(3)	(5) Cost as Percent of Dues Base (1)/(2)	(6) Cost per Capita (1)/(3)
1959-1960	$ 18,063	$ 88,610	9,107	$ 9.73	20.4%	$1.98
1960-1961	28,784	94,295	9,722	9.70	30.5	2.96
1961-1962	32,971	103,340	10,335	10.00	31.9	3.19
1962-1963	27,087	118,133	12,132	9.74	22.9	2.23
1963-1964	39,600	127,400	12,834	9.93	31.1	3.09
1964-1965	46,800	162,200	13,555	11.97	28.9	3.45
1965-1966	48,500	212,700	14,363	14.81	22.8	3.38
1966-1967	76,500	323,600	15,443	20.95	23.6	4.95
1967-1968	117,800	421,600	16,302	25.86	27.9	7.23
1968-1969	133,800	436,400	17,155	25.44	30.7	7.80
1969-1970	161,300	542,500	18,100	29.97	30.7	8.91

SOURCES: Col. (1) from the financial statements published in the CICA Annual Reports and the bi-monthly *Dialogue* (figures for 1968-1969 and 1969-1970 are modified to include the cost of mailing Handbook releases to CICA members without charge); Cols. (2) and (3) from CICA Annual Reports, *Dialogue*, and the office of the CICA Executive Director.

EXHIBIT I
(Cont'd.)
COMPARATIVE COSTS OF CICA AND AICPA
RESEARCH AND PRONOUNCEMENT PROGRAMS IN
ACCOUNTING AND AUDITING

American Institute of Certified Public Accountants (AICPA)

Fiscal Year	(1) Cost of Accounting and Auditing Programs*	(2) Total Dues (000)	(3) Member-ship	(4) Dues per Capita (2)/(3)	(5) Cost as Percent of Dues Base (1)/(2)	(6) Cost per Capita (1)/(3)
1962-1963	US$225,000	US$1,529 (US$1,673)**	47,000	US$32.53 ($35.17)***	14.7% (13.4%)	US$ 4.79 ($ 5.18)***
1963-1964	216,000	1,626 (1,757)	50,000	32.52 (35.16)	13.3 (12.3)	4.32 (4.67)
1964-1965	200,000	1,723 (1,859)	53,000	32.51 (35.15)	11.6 (10.8)	3.77 (4.08)
1965-1966	296,000	1,830 (2,045)	57,000	32.11 (34.71)	16.2 (14.5)	5.19 (5.61)
1966-1967	400,000	1,937 (2,214)	60,000	32.28 (34.90)	20.7 (18.1)	6.67 (7.21)
1967-1968	505,000	2,062 (2,416)	64,000	32.22 (34.83)	24.5 (20.9)	7.89 (8.53)
1968-1969	595,000	2,816 (3,241)	69,000	40.81 (44.12)	21.1 (18.4)	8.62 (9.32)
1969-1970	800,000	2,967 (3,590)	75,000	39.56 (47.86)	27.0 (22.3)	10.67 (11.23)

(*)   Includes Accounting Principles Board, Committee on Auditing Procedure, and the accounting and auditing research programs. Overhead has been applied.

(**) Figures in parentheses include the annual transfer to the General Fund from the AICPA Foundation Fund (through 1967-1968) and from the Accounting Research Association Fund (since 1967-1968).

(***) Figures in parentheses in Cols. (4) and (6) are expressed in Canadian dollars converted at the rate of .925 for all years but 1969-1970, for which an estimate of .95 was used. These translations reflect the exchange rates then in force and are concededly a poor substitute for price-level data on the comparative costs of the services purchased by the two Institutes in their respective economies. If, for example, the number of the Canadian monetary unit for services purchased by the CICA Accounting and Auditing Research Committee were approximately 80 percent of the number of the U.S. monetary unit expended for like services by the American Institute, the exchange rate for purposes of Col. (6) would be better expressed as .8 to 1.

SOURCES: Cols. (1) and (3) from the office of the AICPA Executive Vice President; Col. (2) from the financial statements published in the October or November issues of *The CPA*.

share of the American Institute's dues dollar devoted to the program was 9.6 percentage points lower (i.e., 21.1% v. 30.7%) than the comparable Canadian figure, suggesting a smaller dues base per capita than for its American counterpart. As one runs down the annual per-capita figures (Col. (6)) for both Institutes since 1962-63, those for the American Institute are always higher. Yet in every year, the Canadian Institute outspends the American Institute as a percent of the dues dollar (Col. (5)). The explanation lay in the consistently lower dues per member in Canada than in the United States, as reflected in a comparison of the figures in Col. (4) for the two countries.

Furthermore, between 1962-63 and 1967-68, the American Institute was able to supplement dues support with a transfer from the AICPA Foundation Fund of an amount approximating the direct costs of the accounting research and pronouncements program. In 1967, the American Institute replaced the AICPA Foundation for this purpose by the Accounting Research Association in order to broaden the base of contributions. In 1969-70, the Association received contributions ("dues") from member firms and individuals of US $509,321. The balance in the Association Fund as of August 31, 1970 was US $9,139.

To help cover the rising costs of the research program, the Executive Committee of the Canadian Institute has been considering the establishment of a foundation, perhaps similar to the American Institute's Accounting Research Association.[49]

The foregoing figures are, in fact, only a fraction of the *total* cost of the research and pronouncements programs. Omitted are the substantial costs incurred by accounting firms, companies, universities, and Government agencies in freeing the time of their representatives on the Accounting and Auditing Research Committee and in providing them with staff assistance. Similar costs, when not reimbursed, are applicable to the authors and the members of study groups for research studies. It would seem fair to estimate the portion of the total cost which is not reflected in the Institute's accounts at more than $1,750,000 a year.

---

[49] Task Force 2000, in a report submitted in 1970, proposed a "Research and Development Foundation" which would adopt an inter-disciplinary approach to basic and applied research in accounting theory and techniques. *Canadian Chartered Accountant*, November, 1970, pp. 334-35.

ROLE OF GOVERNMENT IN ACCOUNTING MATTERS

At present, there is no law or agency in Canada which regularly enforces compliance with the Committee's Handbook releases on accounting principles.[50] The accounting and auditing provisions of Canada's Federal and provincial companies legislation, in the spirit of the British companies acts and all but a few Accounting Series Releases of the U.S. Securities and Exchange Commission, are limited to matters of disclosure, terminology, and the independent auditor's representations.

Amendments to the Canadian and provincial companies acts have tended to follow the SEC's changing disclosure requirements (frequently given their first expression in Canada through Bulletins of the Canadian Institute's Accounting and Auditing Research Committee) and reports of the periodic British company law committees together with the resulting amendments to the British Companies Act.

Ontario company law has consistently been the most progressive in Canada, especially in regard to public financial disclosures. When the Canada Corporations Act, 1965, overhauled the Federal companies law for the first time since 1934-1935, many of the most important changes were foreshadowed in the 1953 revision of the Ontario act. British Columbia and Manitoba extensively revised their companies acts in 1964-1965, and Ontario again amended its corporations act in 1966 and 1970, further extending its disclosure requirements.

When it is known that companies legislation is under revision, the Canadian Institute and most of the provincial institutes prepare submissions for their respective legislatures. Parts of a 1964 Bulletin on disclosure standards and an earlier Bulletin on the auditor's report were reflected in the Canada Corporation Act, 1965. The recommendations of the Ontario Institute have been influential in successive amendments to the provincial act.

A section contained in a recent bill to amend the Canada Corporations Act illustrates the influence of British companies legislation. Patterned after Section 17 of the British Companies Act, 1967, it would have required companies formed under the

---

[50] Since at least 1968, the Department of Consumer and Corporate Affairs has been contemplating the introduction of a bill in the Canadian Parliament to create a national securities commission (CANSEC). The Canadian Institute's Federal Legislation Committee has publicly supported the idea. Predictably, the provincial governments have resisted it. As of this writing, a bill has not yet been introduced.

Canadian act to disclose sales and profits by major classes of business activity. When the bill was introduced in the Canadian House of Commons in May, 1969, the Minister of Consumer and Corporate Affairs

> emphasized that the proclamation of this section of the act would be delayed, partly because businessmen, accountants in particular, are still considering criteria for determining what constitutes a "class" of business.[51]

In one important respect, the section of the Canadian bill differed from Section 17 of the 1967 British Companies Act. In the latter, the additional disclosures appear in the directors' report, while the Canadian disclosure would have appeared in the notes to the audited financial statements. Perhaps because of this difference, the portion of the Canadian requirement pertaining to profits was deleted from the bill in 1970, shortly before it was enacted into law.

Probably the most influential provincial securities commission is that of Ontario. While the Ontario Securities Commission (OSC) is primarily concerned with questions of disclosure, in mid-1969 it took the unprecedented step of issuing a policy statement on a matter of accounting principle. The incident arose over the accounting practices of Revenue Properties Co., Ltd., a Canadian company which had its shares listed on both the American Stock Exchange (in New York) and the Toronto Stock Exchange. In early 1969, the SEC's accounting staff questioned the company's practice of recognizing profits on all land sales in the year of sale. In some situations, the SEC allows foreign registrants to use accounting practices accepted in their home countries but not "generally accepted" in the United States, so long as full disclosure of such departures is provided and, where the difference between the foreign and U.S. treatments has a significant effect on the company's reported net income, that the amount of such effect is disclosed in a prominent and clear manner.[52] At that time, neither the OSC nor the CICA's Accounting and Auditing Research Committee had spoken on the subject of land development accounting, and it was evident to the OSC that a

---

[51] "Proposed Changes in Federal Company Law," News Release dated May 22, 1969 from the Department of Consumer and Corporate Affairs, p. 3. Although the CICA Accounting and Auditing Research Committee had previously added diversified operations to its list of subjects deserving study, the introduction of this bill in May, 1969 made it a matter of high priority.

[52] See *supra*, ftn. 10.

Canadian pronouncement was needed on short notice. To fill the void in Canadian accounting authority, the OSC issued a policy statement which adopted as its core the bulk of SEC Accounting Series Release No. 95.

The OSC's action on Revenue Properties took the Canadian accounting profession by surprise. To minimize the likelihood of future such occurrences, the Accounting and Auditing Research Committee created a subcommittee on liaison with securities commissions and stock exchanges. This new committee, which has members or representatives in all provinces, is expected to provide the parent committee with "early warning" on matters coming before those bodies.

INTEREST IN ACCOUNTING PRINCIPLES
BY OTHER GROUPS

Stock Exchanges.

The Toronto Stock Exchange, Canada's principal exchange, has so far shown little interest in accounting principles. In the area of financial disclosures, the Exchange began to require quarterly financial statements of its listed companies only as recently as January 1, 1969.[53]

Financial Executives.

As a group, the Financial Executives Institute (Canada) has not until very recently been active on accounting principles. Depending on the subjects of proposed Bulletins, individual companies or industry groups have taken an interest. FEI (Canada) does not have a full-time staff, and the main thrust of its activities has been to make representations before the Canadian Government on various matters.

Financial Analysts.

Both the Montreal Society of Financial Analysts and The Toronto Society of Financial Analysts have been eager commentators on CICA exposure drafts. The Canadian Institute's

---

[53] *Annual Review, 1968,* The Toronto Stock Exchange, p. 6.

research staff has been attempting to improve its liaison with financial analysts as well as other interested groups. Thus far, neither the investment dealers nor the bankers have evinced much interest in accounting principles.

Financial Press.

The Toronto *Globe and Mail,* together with Canada's two major financial weeklies — *The Financial Post* and the *Financial Times of Canada* — report the "accounting beat" with regularity and acuity. The Canadian Institute sponsored "press seminars" in January and April, 1969 to acquaint reporters with the work of the Accounting and Auditing Research Committee.

The Financial Post has since 1951 sponsored an annual contest for the most informative corporate annual reports. Unlike the annual-report competition in the *Financial World* (U.S.), which seems to be concerned almost exclusively with format, design, and typography, *The Financial Post's* contest includes a professional evaluation of the accounting content of financial statements. For this purpose, the *Post* applies criteria formulated by the Canadian Institute and uses judges who are chartered accountants. The judges' specific evaluations of the financial statements are published in the *Post.*

Other Groups.

Liaison with the real estate industry, especially in the wake of the Revenue Properties episode, has not been entirely smooth. At first, an organization known as Urban Development Institute (Ontario), began a program of issuing Statements on Accounting Practices. In 1970, UDI (Ontario)'s Accounting Practices Committee, whose membership was composed almost entirely of chartered accountants, issued three Bulletins. While UDI (Ontario) has said that its accounting program is being carried out in collaboration with the Canadian Institute, the latter denies this.

In 1970, a Toronto-based association, the Canadian Institute of Public Real Estate Companies (CIPREC), was formed. It represents itself as an organization having national scope, in contrast to UDI (Ontario), whose membership is confined to one province. In 1970-71, UDI (Ontario) and CIPREC began to work together on accounting, and both submitted comments on the draft of the CICA research study on accounting for real estatement development operations.

In early 1968, The Society of Industrial Accountants of Canada, an examining body with a membership in excess of 5,500, seriously considered issuing a "Statement of Opinion" directly opposed to Bulletin No. 26 of the Canadian Institute. Although the Society had created a Committee on Accounting Principles and Practices in 1966 with a three-part charge, the first of which was

> To prepare as a guide to members, opinions on applications of accounting principles and practices in reporting to and on behalf of management,

no such opinions had been published. Strong beliefs held by some members of the Society's National Board evidently led to the preparation of a draft of "Opinion No. 1," dated March, 1968 and bearing the title, "Depreciation of Fixed Assets and Deferred Income Tax Accounting." After a vigorous debate, the National Board decided that it would be more helpful to the profession to issue a research study than to compete with the Canadian Institute. The study, which would be the Society's first of its kind in the accounting principles area, is scheduled to appear in 1972. The Society now feels, somewhat like the National Association of Accountants in the U.S., that it should be active in the area of accounting principles.[54]

CONCLUDING REMARKS

In developing its own research program and completely redesigning the structure and operation of its Accounting and Auditing Research Committee, the Canadian profession has made evident a policy of relying less on an adaptation of U.S. and British practices in favor of enhancing its capacity to identify and resolve distinctively Canadian problems.

In 1961, when the research program was inaugurated, the Canadian Institute's Executive Committee stated the challenge as follows:

> [I] f the Canadian profession does not develop its own body of research material, our members, and the Canadian business community generally, will be compelled to accept many, if not most, of the

---

[54] For a discussion of the Society's research program, see J. W. Ross, "Research by the Society of Industrial Accountants," Accounting Research, *Canadian Chartered Accountant,* November, 1970, pp. 342-44.

standards recommended from outside of Canada. Since Canadian laws, customs and economic conditions are sufficiently different from those of other countries, it is essential that we develop our own body of material even though this may involve some duplication of the research activities of accounting bodies in other countries.[55]

---

[55] Quoted in "Reorganization of the Institute's Research Activities," *op. cit.*, p. 196.

A Descriptive Analysis of
Selected Aspects of the Canadian Accounting
Standard-Setting Process
John H. Waterhouse

Discussants' Comments
David G. Ward
A. Wayne Hopkins

Reply to Discussants' Comments

Synopsis of Discussion

Abstract

This paper describes and analyses several aspects of the process whereby accounting standards are established in Canada. The research is intended to provide information that will be useful to those charged with the responsibility for structuring the standard-setting process. This includes, in the first instance, the Canadian Institute of Chartered Accountants (CICA) which, within the existing legal and regulatory framework, has the authority to establish accounting standards. How accounting standards should be selected is also a public policy issue with a number of general economic and social implications.

Canadian accounting standards are accorded legal status under the Canada Business Corporations Act and are mandatory for most businesses whose securities are traded in organized markets. Accounting standards have the potential to affect the distribution of wealth among various members of society. The essence of the standard-setting problem is to balance competing private standard preferences with each other and with public interest considerations in such a manner that standards are perceived to be legitimate by those who are required to follow them and by governments from whom the quasi-legal authority to establish them has been received. Two processes are felt to underlie the standard-setting process, a political process, which is concerned with accommodating conflicting preferences, and a legitimation process, which is concerned with establishing credibility for specific standards and for the standard-setting process in general.

The Accounting Research Committee (ARC), the body responsible for selecting accounting standards, is structured and follows procedures consistent with its political role. However, Committee members do not perceive their activities as having a dominant political or legislative dimension. They state that experience with practice and reasoning from practice rather than conceptual considerations or the economic consequences of alternative standards dominate in their decisions. While the ARC solicits feedback on its proposals from a large number of its constituents through the exposure draft process, a relatively small number of large businesses and accounting firms dominate in the responses. Most proposals seem to enjoy broadly based support, especially proposals that are consistent with American accounting standards. On balance, exposure draft responses appear to have a relatively minor impact on ARC decisions.

Canadian accounting standards do not appear to be supported or justified on the grounds that they are consistent with a conceptual framework, are derived from accounting theories, or are consistent with

John Waterhouse PhD is Associate Professor of Accounting, Faculty of Business Administration and Commerce, University of Alberta. He is a past president of The Canadian Academic Accounting Association.

other research findings. Standards seem more likely to be justified on the grounds that they reflect economic reality, are consistent with the accounting standards of other countries, or have resulted from experience and professional judgment.

Two policy implications are stated. First, as the economic environment within which accounting standards are established becomes more complex and changeable, it may become more necessary – although at the same time more difficult – to anticipate and assess the economic and social consequences of accounting standards before they are established. This may require that more resources be devoted to accounting research. Second, it is suggested that the standard-setting process be less secret and more open to public scrutiny.

Introduction

The purpose of this paper is to describe and analyse some aspects of the process whereby accounting standards are established in Canada. The legal right to set Canadian accounting standards rests largely with the Canadian Institute of Chartered Accountants (CICA). The *CICA Handbook* is accorded considerable legal authority under federal and provincial corporations and securities legislation. Under this legislation, the accounting standards adopted by the CICA virtually assume the status of law. Delegation of this quasi-legislative authority by the state to a professional organization such as the CICA is presumably justifiable on the grounds that the prerequisite technical knowledge base rests with members of the CICA and that such knowledge will be exercised in the public interest.

The means whereby the CICA's quasi-legal authority is exercised is of both professional and public concern. From the accounting profession's perspective, the right to establish standards is a source of prestige, status, and, potentially, economic gain. Thus, it is in the profession's interests to demonstrate that the process is working effectively in issuing socially desirable standards. The public's interest in accounting standard setting arises from the potential of accounting standards to affect wealth distribution. The social desirability of such wealth distribution or redistribution, is, presumably, of interest to legislators and other public interest groups. Accounting researchers are interested in the standard-setting process to the extent that they may desire to present relevant evidence for standard setters and to the extent that such information may contribute toward the development of a descriptive theory of how accounting standards are determined. In describing some aspects of the standard-setting process, this paper provides some initial and tentative evidence on how these responsibilities are being discharged by the CICA.

The paper is organized as follows. Section I reviews briefly the reasons why accounting standards are a public interest issue. This review also suggests some issues that may be relevant in evaluating the standard-setting process. Section II provides a general overview of the structure of the CICA's standard-setting mechanism, focusing on the role of the Accounting Research Committee (ARC). Section III reports the results of a survey conducted to determine the evidence, information, and criteria that members of the ARC state that they use in selecting standards. In Section IV, the results of analysing responses to four recent ARC exposure drafts are reported. This analysis provides some indication of the degree to which the ARC appears to be responsive to concerns expressed by some interested

I wish to thank several individuals and organizations for their assistance with this research. The CICA and especially R.D. Thomas and G. Mulcahy were very helpful in developing the data base. Several partners in Clarkson Gordon provided valuable insights into the subject matter of this paper. My special thanks are owed to Alex Milburn for his able assistance throughout the project and to Al Rosen for his advice in its inceptive phase.

constituents. Finally, Section V provides a summary and states the study's conclusions.

Section I

Before one can reasonably understand and evaluate the existing standard-setting process in Canada, it seems desirable to gain some understanding of the reasons for the existence of a standard-setting mechanism and the role it serves. This, in turn, implies a need to understand the role that accounting information plays in the economy. Armed with a conceptual framework we can begin to define some relevant variables and issues in the Canadian standard-setting process on which descriptive information is lacking.[1]

Financial statements serve a number of purposes. One role for accounting information is to reduce uncertainty about a firm's earning power and future cash flows. In this role an important objective for accounting is to provide information that may be useful for making decisions by individuals who do not have direct access to a firm's internal financial records. Another function of accounting information is to provide a means for reaching and enforcing contracts between the firm and its managers, owners, creditors, and suppliers. For example, accounting information may provide a basis for managerial incentive contracts or a basis for lending agreements such as debt covenants or dividend restrictions. A third role for accounting is to provide information on which regulatory, taxation and other public policy decisions may be based.

In discharging each of these informational roles, accounting data may significantly affect the economic well-being of the entity that is being accounted for and of the information recipient. Since the self-interests of the various parties affected by accounting information may diverge, the potential for conflict over which specific accounting method should be used in a particular setting clearly exists. Such conflicts could presumably be settled on a case-by-case basis. For example, when negotiating a debt covenant agreement, the parties to the contract could negotiate the set of measurement and disclosure rules under which the contract terms would be discharged. Alternatively, if some prior set of rules existed that each party could agree to follow, some of the costs of negotiating could be avoided. Thus the desire to avoid costly contract negotiation provides some inducement to develop a "generally accepted" set of accounting rules that could be applied in a variety of settings or for a variety of purposes.

In this setting, there are incentives to agree upon some set of rules, but there may be disagreement over the specific form of a given rule. This suggests that one role of a standard-setting agency is to reconcile the competing preferences for particular measurement or disclosure rules in such a manner that the final decision is viewed as legitimate or reasonable by potentially affected parties. The legal status given to CICA standards by Canadian corporations and securities laws is one means whereby accounting standards gain legitimacy. But accounting information is also consumed in a competitive environment where alternative sources of information exist. Thus, both historically and currently, general acceptance by management and others arises voluntarily. The tradition in accounting is one of searching for acceptable and accepted standards, where legitimacy arises from the perception that the standards adopted are fair, reasonable, and equitable.

Focusing only on the private incentives that may exist for individuals to reach agreement on accounting standards provides an incomplete picture of the role of a standard-setting body. For, if the social costs and benefits of accounting information differ from its private costs and benefits, the quantity or quality of the accounting information produced in an unregulated market may differ from the social optimum. This may occur if accounting information is a public good, that is, where the quantity consumed by one individual does not diminish the quantity available to others. This may lead to the underproduction of information. For example, insufficient incentives may exist for public disclosure of extraordinarily profitable firms or industries. Thus, accounting standard setters should be concerned with the social as well as the private costs and benefits of alternative measurement and disclosure policies.

The possibility that accounting information has a social value that differs from its private value suggests that accounting standard setters should be concerned with the social as well as the private consequences of accounting information. Indeed, the notions that individual preferences for accounting information may diverge, and that accounting information has a social or public value, imply that accounting policy makers face social choice questions similar in many ways to those faced by makers of public policy in other fields of government and regulation. In such settings it has been shown by Arrow [1951] that it is impossible to construct a social choice rule that is sensitive to individual preferences and that meets a minimal set of rational choice conditions. Furthermore, Demski [1973] has demonstrated that no set of criteria such as objectivity, consistency, or relevance exists that will optimally rank accounting standards in relation to individual preferences. Thus, accounting standard setters face difficult social choice questions where no objective, theoretically defensible criteria or choice procedures can be relied upon to rank competing standards in relation to individual preferences.

The impossibility of a theoretically defensible social choice rule or a set of technical criteria for ranking individuals' preferences for accounting standards highlights the difficulty faced by the CICA and other standard-setting bodies. The essence of the problem is to balance competing private preferences for accounting standards with each other and with general public interest considerations in such a manner that the standards selected are perceived to be legitimate by those who voluntarily or otherwise adopt and use accounting methods and by governments, from whom quasi-legal authority over their establishment has been received. The choice is complicated further because there is substantial uncertainty about the economic and political consequences of proposed standards.

This characterization of the standard-setting process draws attention to two separate but related underlying processes. One part of the standard setter's role is legislative-political, in that it involves reconciling competing social and private interests in which accounting standards are mandated. A second and related part of the process attempts to maintain legitimacy for the political role. Here, the concern is to justify locating control over a political process in the private sector and to gain general acceptance for accounting standards.

Failure by standard setters to deal effectively with either the political or legitimation role may cause a disruption of the process. For example, Zeff [1978] has argued that the failure of the Accounting Principles Board (APB) to deal with the political and economic consequences of accounting standards led to its demise. A number of examples from the US and Canada of situations in which standards have been promulgated and later have been withdrawn, overruled by a government agency, or significantly modified could be offered. Such situations result from a failure of specific standards to gain legitimacy and cumulative failures of this kind may challenge the legitimacy of the process in general.

Legitimation may occur in several ways. If the standard choice problem is defined as an essentially technical question, and if the prerequisite technical expertise from which standards are derived mainly rests with a professional organization, then that organization's control over standard setting may be legitimated. From a US perspective, the search for basic principles or postulates of accounting, for a conceptual framework, or for basic objectives may be an attempt to legitimate accounting standards by defining the problem as an essentially technical issue [Dopuch and Sunder, 1980]. For example, the Financial Accounting Standards Board (FASB) has argued that a conceptual framework would, among other things, provide a frame of reference for resolving accounting questions and a guide to the body responsible for establishing accounting standards [FASB, 1976a, pp. 5-6]. Accounting research may also be used to legitimate accounting standards choices. Watts and Zimmerman [1979] have argued that accounting theories are useful justifications in political lobbying over accounting standards.

Casual observation suggests that Canadian standard setters have been much less concerned with basic principles, with a conceptual framework, or with the development of accounting theories than have their US counterparts. Yet Canadian standards have a higher legal status than do US standards. This raises the general question of the grounds on which the

Canadian standard-setting process is legitimated. The main objective of the research reported below is to explore the grounds on which accounting standards are established and legitimated in Canada, concentrating on the interplay between political and legitimation processes.

It is in this context that several specific research questions concerning the ARC of the CICA are framed. These questions fall into three general categories. First, what is the structural composition of the ARC and under what procedures does it operate? The ARC is the social choice mechanism employed by the CICA for the past eight years and its structure, composition and procedures have a potentially important bearing on which accounting issues are raised and on how issues are settled. Second, what information, objectives, and criteria do members of the ARC think are important for making policy choices? This question is intended to shed light on the internal workings of the ARC and on how or whether its members perceive the private and social choice issues described above. The third category focuses on the exposure draft stage of the standard-setting process and asks: Who submits responses to exposure draft material and what impact on the Committee's final position do these comments appear to have? These questions are important because the exposure draft procedure is presumably employed to solicit the opinions and preferences of a broad cross-section of individuals and corporations for proposed standards. The manner in which these opinions and preferences are sought and accommodated is seen as an important part of the legitimation process for accounting standards.

It should be emphasized at this point that the research described below is strictly descriptive in nature. No hypotheses are presented or tested. No opportunity is provided to test and reject hypotheses related to a theory of accounting standard setting. Nor can the research lead to any normative conclusions with regard to how accounting standards should be set. Rather, the intent is to provide descriptive information on how some aspects of the process are believed to have behaved over a particular time period. This evidence, combined with other information, may assist others in evaluating and improving the process, and may point to ways in which other accounting research may be made more relevant to standard setters.

Section II

This section provides a condensed[2] overview of the CICA standard-setting structure. Readers who are already familiar with the structure and proceedings of the ARC should proceed directly to Section III. Adopted in 1973, the present structure was reviewed recently by the CICA Special Committee on Standard Setting. Several proposals for restructuring the procedures employed to decide on accounting standards came out of this review, and as a result certain changes to the standard-setting structure are expected. While it is perhaps unfortunate that the present study was conducted just prior to a period of change, it nevertheless seems important to provide an overview description because of the possible importance of this structure to several decisions made during the 1970s. The structure may be an important influence on how issues are raised, the kinds of evidence made available to the decision makers, and who had access to the process.

The ARC has been delegated the authority by the CICA Board of Governors to establish accounting standards on its own responsibility. The ARC is a twenty-two person, volunteer committee comprised of one representative from each of the Canadian Council of Financial Analysts (CCFA), the Financial Executives Institute of Canada (FEIC), the Canadian Certified General Accountants Association (CCGAA), and the Society of Management Accountants (SMA); two accounting academics; and sixteen chartered accountants from public practice. ARC members are directed to vote based on their own experience and judgment and not according to the views of their firms, companies, or associations. Each Committee member may have up to ten associates from whom confidential advice on proposed standards may be sought. The ARC is divided into three geographic sections, each assisted by a research manager. Proposed changes to the existing set of standards are advanced by the sections for approval by the whole Committee.

Topics reach the agenda of the ARC and its sections through the Accounting Research Steering Committee. This Committee includes the ARC chairperson, the chairpersons of each ARC section, the CICA Director of Accounting Research and the General Director of Research for the CICA. Proposals to study and make recommendations on a topic are acted upon by the entire ARC. Proposed topics reach the Steering Committee and hence the ARC from a number of possible sources. One source is the Accounting Research Advisory Board, a twenty-member committee comprised mainly of non-accountants. The Advisory Board is intended to alert the ARC to new subjects and to provide informed criticism on what has been done. Another source of agenda topics is the ARC members themselves. Also, any person, group, or organization can submit a proposal for studying a particular issue. Developments in other countries may also result in a topic being considered for inclusion on the Committee's agenda. It should be emphasized however that the ARC itself is responsible for both initiating and completing a project.

Once approved, projects are developed in several stages. A section's research manager prepares material outlining problem areas, alternative solutions, and an outline of authoritative writing on the subject. The section to which a project has been assigned prepares a statement of principles, which is an outline of perceived basic issues, an indication of some alternatives considered, and a statement of reasoning for certain choices. The statement of principles is sent to associates for comment and feedback. When the entire Committee has agreed on the statement of principles, a draft recommendation is prepared for discussion and eventual agreement by the section and full Committee before an exposure draft is prepared. When agreement on the draft recommendation has been reached by the ARC an exposure draft is published and circulated to approximately 40,000 accountants, business organizations, and other potentially interested parties for comment. Exposure draft comments are reviewed by the initiating section and by the ARC. These comments may result in changes to the proposed standard. If two-thirds of the full ARC supports the revised proposal it is approved as a revision to the *CICA Handbook*.

ARC members have potential access to information on emerging problems, alternative solutions, and the preferences of interest groups at several stages in the above process. Information on the perceived feasibility and consequences of proposed standards might be obtained from associates and from exposure draft respondents. Input on which issues should be tackled is provided for at several stages, although the Steering Committee and the ARC itself clearly bear the responsibility for setting their own priorities. Staff support is provided with the intent of making research findings and other authoritative writing available to Committee members. However, this research function seems to consist largely of a selective review of some accounting literature and the organization of material into an outline of problems and solutions rather than original research on, for example, the expected economic impact of proposed standards.

From the perspective of the framework on accounting and standard setting presented in Section I above, the ARC's existing structure and procedures seem to have certain merits. The present structure permits input from many potentially interested parties. The composition of the ARC, the availability of input from associates, and the exposure draft process all enable interested constituent groups to express their preferences or opposition with regard to specific issues and proposed standards. However, certain user groups such as shareholders or prospective shareholders, who may rely on accounting information to assess a firm's earning power and future cash flows, do not seem to be directly represented in the process.[3] Whether this results from a lack of interest or a lack of opportunity is unknown.

In comparison with other public policy agencies or social choice mechanisms, including the FASB, the ARC appears to work in substantial secrecy. Its meetings are not open to the public, no public hearings are held, and it publishes little information on the reasons for its choices. As a result, the ARC's decisions and procedures have been less open to public scrutiny than have those of, for example, the FASB. Whether the ARC's secrecy reflects Canadian institutional and political realities in general or whether it is the result of a more purposeful strategy by the CICA to maintain its autonomy is open to speculation at this point. Nevertheless, such secrecy may inhibit public accountability. And, to the extent that public accountability is necessary to maintain legitimacy, there is a potential deficency in the process.

This overview of the standard-setting structure has provided some indication of how accounting policy choices are made in Canada. In some respects the process seems well suited to balancing competing standard preferences and to maintaining the legitimacy, credibility, and integrity of financial statements. Some possible deficiencies were also noted. However, these observations must remain extremely tentative in the absence of any information on how ARC members use the data that is made available to them, on what objectives ARC members hold, and on the criteria they employ in making standard choices. It is these issues to which we now turn our attention.

Section III

Clearly, the ARC plays a pivotal role in deciding which accounting standards are adopted. Ideally, to gain an understanding of how such policy decisions are made, one would like to know the information, criteria, and objectives that Committee members actually use in making accounting policy decisions. Determining how decisions are actually made could prove to be prohibitively costly in that it would likely involve extensive observation of Committee meetings and in-depth interviews of Committee members. As a methodological compromise, a questionnaire survey of Committee members was conducted, supplemented by interviews with some of them. The object of this exercise was to provide some insight into how Committee members believe they go about the task of setting accounting standards. It should be noted that the perceptions and beliefs of individual Committee members may differ in significant ways from the underlying reality of how the Committee as a whole actually makes decisions.

Methodology

A two-part questionnaire was designed by the author (see Appendix).[4] The questions in the first part attempted to determine Committee members' perceptions of their role and function, their perceptions of the environment within which accounting standards are established and their perceptions of the objectives of accounting and of standard setting. This part did not focus on any specific standard. The second part of the questionnaire attempted to track a specific standard, Translation of Foreign Currency Transactions and Foreign Currency Financial Statements, from the reasons why the issue was raised to the reasoning behind the final decisions. The foreign currency issue was chosen for study because of its controversial history. It was felt that the issues, problems and reasoning behind this standard would be clearly defined.

The questionnaire was revised several times. The most significant revision resulted from discussions with one person who was a member of the ARC when the foreign currency issue was addressed. A large number of changes were made as a result of this pre-test in an attempt to address issues in a manner that the respondents would find meaningful.

A list of individuals who were members of the ARC when several recent *Handbook* revisions were released was obtained from the CICA. Twenty-one individuals were identified as being members of the ARC when the foreign currency issue was addressed. Questionnaires were mailed to each of these persons. Also six questionnaires were mailed to ARC members who were not directly involved in the foreign currency issue. Fifteen completed questionnaires[5] were received from the twenty-one foreign currency respondents. These respondents completed Parts I and II of the questionnaire. Two individuals who were not directly involved in the foreign currency issue responded to Part I, which dealt with issues that were not specific to the foreign currency revision. Thus, the results reported below are based on fifteen responses to Part II and seventeen responses to Part I.

Post-response interviews were held with four of the foreign currency respondents. The purpose of these interviews was to solicit an elaboration of the responses and to determine how the questions were being interpreted. The findings of these interviews are not directly reported below, but they are indirectly incorporated in the results section. Proceeding from the general to the specific, the results of Part I are reported first.

Results – Part I

Part I of the questionnaire focused the respondent's attention on ARC activities in general. This part of the questionnaire attempted to determine: (1) how ARC members perceive their role; (2) how they perceive the environment within which accounting standards are set; and (3) what objectives they perceive for accounting and for the standard-setting process. The questionnaire responses are discussed below according to these a priori categories. Because of the small sample size, no attempt was made to determine if any statistical association existed among the responses to the questions in each category.

Perceptions of the ARC's role

The purpose of a number of questions was to determine whether ARC members perceive their role to be a political one as opposed to a purely technical one. Section I of this paper noted that accounting policy decisions sometimes involve trading off the preferences of some interest groups or individuals against the preferences of others. It was also noted that standard setters have incentives to maintain the legitimacy of the

Table 1: Response Frequencies on ARC's Role

Question	Strongly Agree	Agree	Neutral	Disagree	Strongly Disagree	Average
(3) Legislative activity	1	5	0	8	3	2.59
(4) Economic consequences	0	8	2	7	0	
(5) Balance preferences	0	1	1	11	4	1.94
(7) Cost benefit trade-off	0	3	4	5	5	2.29
(17) Managerial motives	0	4	1	10	2	3.00
(19) Analysts' motives	4	9	0	3	0	3.87
(20) Conflicting motives	1	2	4	6	4	2.41
(1) Basic concepts	0	3	4	5	5	2.29
(6) Conceptual framework	0	4	7	3	3	2.71
(11) Economic reality	2	10	0	3	1	3.59
(14) Decision making	3	9	1	4	0	3.65
(10) Leadership role	0	11	2	4	1	3.24
(26) Detailed standards	0	2	1	10	3	2.12

process. Based on this consideration, private control over standard setting may be justified on the grounds that superior technical knowledge rests with the private sector. In this case, standard setting may be seen (by the standard setters) as an insular activity based on specialized technical and professional considerations. Responses to the thirteen questionnaire items that were intended to examine these issues are summarized in Table 1.

Four questions, 3, 4, 5, and 7 were directly concerned with determining whether ARC members perceive their activities as political. On balance, Committee members did not seem to see their role as primarily a political one. A majority disagreed with the statement that standard setting involves trading off the interests of various affected parties, as reflected in the responses to Questions 3, 5, and 7. The respondents were evenly divided on whether accounting standards have significant economic consequences for business firms (4) and they did not see standard setting as a process of trading off possible costs and benefits (7). In a related vein, the respondents did not see the interests and motives of managers, shareholders or financial analysts as necessarily conflicting. These views are reflected in the responses to Questions 17, 19, and 20.

These observations seem to lead to the conclusion that standard setting in Canada is not perceived by the standard setters as a political activity. The potential economic consequences of standards do not appear to weigh heavily on the Canadian standard setters' minds, and most do not see standard setting as a quasi-legislative like activity. This view by standard setters stands in marked contrast to the legislative-political role of standard setting defined by the framework presented above.

On the other hand, one is somewhat pressed to present a clear description of how standard setters do perceive their role. The following observations may be drawn from the responses:

1. The responses to Questions 1 and 6 suggest that, at best, Committee members are ambivalent about the value of "basic concepts" or a conceptual framework.
2. Committee members see their activities as involving a search for standards that reflect economic reality (Question 11), and that provide useful information (Question 14).
3. A clear majority feel that accounting standards tend to follow rather than lead good accounting practice, as witnessed by the responses to Question 10, and most believe that standards should not be detailed and specific in their requirements (Question 26).

Taken together, these responses seem to suggest that judgment and experience are the primary elements of the standard-setting process. This conclusion is based on the observation that the respondents do not seem to perceive a dominant political or legislative dimension to their activities, they do not perceive great value in a conceptual framework, and they do not uniformly perceive that accounting standards have important economic consequences. A substantial majority believe that standards can be chosen on the basis of a decision about which accounting methods best reflect economic reality, and that standards tend to follow rather than lead good accounting practice. Economic reality is a matter of subjective judgment. Also, if standards follow rather than lead good practice, experience would seem to be an important input to the decision process. But, there was little willingness on the part of the respondents to recognize that perceptions of economic reality may differ among individuals or that the experience of Committee members may vary substantially.

Perceptions of the environment of standard setting

Another set of questions was concerned with how Committee members see the context within which accounting standards are established in Canada. Of particular concern here are the assumptions that Committee members make regarding financial statement users and securities markets, and the relationship they perceive between Canadian and US financial accounting standards. Responses to these questions are presented in Table 2.

Questions 8, 9, and 18 were designed to see if Committee members believe that financial statement users are relatively naive or relatively sophisticated, as would be consistent with the notion of efficient capital markets. A majority of the respondents disagreed with the statement that disclosure issues are more important than measurement issues (Question 8) and that financial statement users can separate useful from irrelevant data (Question 9),[6] and the majority agreed that most financial statement users are not capable of understanding complex accounting issues (Question 18). While these responses may suggest a naive user orientation, a majority of the respondents did not feel that the primary role of the accounting profession is to look after the interests of less influential financial statement users (Question 21).

Table 2: Response Frequencies on Environment

Question	Strongly Agree	Agree	Neutral	Disagree	Strongly Disagree	Average
(8) Disclosure vs. measurement	0	3	1	10	3	2.94
(9) Naïve users	3	4	2	7	1	3.06
(18) User understanding	3	6	3	5	0	3.41
(20) Conflicting motives	1	2	4	6	4	2.41
(21) User primacy	1	3	4	6	2	2.88
(22) User influence	3	7	1	6	0	3.41
(23) Consistency with US standards	0	16	1	0	0	3.90
(25) Canadian firms — US GAAP	0	0	0	11	6	1.65

The respondents did not see the interests of corporate managers and shareholders as conflicting (Question 20). A substantial majority of the respondents disagreed with the statement that left to their own devices most corporate managers would disclose very little financial information (Question 17). When combined with the view that some financial statement users are influential enough to get the information they want irrespective of which accounting standards are established (Question 22), these views may suggest the perception that alternative sources of information exist and that accounting information exists in an "information market." This is consistent with the view volunteered by some respondents in the post-questionnaire interviews that there is no "conspiracy" by corporate managers and others to mislead investors or to obscure the results of operations.

The perceived relationship between US and Canadian accounting standards is a separate environmental issue. The respondents unanimously agreed with the statement that Canadian accounting standards should be consistent with those promulgated in the US because the business environment in the two countries is essentially the same (Question 23). At the same time, the respondents were adamant in their belief that US standards should not prevail in Canada even for Canadian companies registered with the Securities and Exchange Commission (SEC) in the US, or for Canadian subsidiaries of US corporations (Question 25).

Accounting and standard-setting objectives

The intent of this set of questions was to assess more closely the perceived objectives or purposes of accounting. This concern stemmed from the possibility that accounting information may serve several different purposes but that the desired properties of accounting data demanded for each purpose may be incompatible. For example, if one assumes that the major purpose of accounting is to provide *ex ante*, decision-relevant information, then a criterion such as predictability would seem appropriate for making

Table 3: Response Frequencies on Perceived Objectives

Question	Strongly Agree	Agree	Neutral	Disagree	Strongly Disagree	Average Response
(14) Accounting should be decision relevant	3	9	1	4	0	3.65
(16) Custodianship is the main objective	1	7	3	6	0	3.18
(12) Standards should limit choice	2	6	0	7	2	2.94
(13) Managers economic interests are tied to standards	0	11	3	2	0	3.56
(15) Accounting measures should be standardized	0	4	3	8	0	2.73

policy choices. In contrast, if one assumes an accountability objective, where *ex post* information would be relevant, criteria such as objectivity and verifiability may be appropriate. As noted by Ijiri [1975], employing one of these sets of criteria rather than the other may lead to quite different sets of accounting standards. The results of the questions which attempted to examine these issues appear in Table 3.

Questions 14 and 16 posed the decision-relevance and accountability-custodianship issues respectively. The respondents did not perceive a conflict between these objectives, as most of those who agreed that the main purpose of financial accounting is to provide useful information also agreed that the main purpose is to report on the custodianship of resources.

Questions 12, 13, and 15 attempted to expand on this issue somewhat. Following Ijiri's arguments, accountability is important because the entities' and managers' economic interests are tied to the content of financial statements and thus the purpose of standards is to increase the measure's "hardness" by increasing standardization and verifiability, and to limit the choice of accounting methods that managers would otherwise have. The responses to Questions 12, 13, and 15 were not consistent with these views. While a strong majority of the respondents believed that managers' economic interests are tied to financial statements (Question 13), the respondents were almost evenly divided on the question of whether the main purpose of standards is to limit managerial choice over standards (Question 12), and a majority disagreed with the statement that accounting measures should be highly standardized and verifiable (Question 15). These responses would seem to suggest that Committee members hold different and possibly conflicting views on the objectives of accounting and of standards.

Results—Part II

Part II of the questionnaire focused on a specific policy decision and sought Committee members' opinions on six aspects of the CICA foreign currency Recommendations (*CICA Handbook*, Release 26, 1978). These aspects were: (1) Committee members' knowledge of the predominant accounting methods employed prior to Release 26; (2) some reasons for why the issue was addressed when it was; (3) the Committee members' initial positions on several issues on which the Committee reached a decision; (4) whether Committee members agreed with the resolution of these issues and the reasons for their disagreement, if any; (5) what sources of information Committee members found useful in reaching their final positions; and (6) the relative importance of several reasons for the final position they reached. A summary of the fifteen responses to these issues is presented below.

Existing practice

Questions 1 and 2 asked for an opinion on which translation methods and recognition criteria predominated in practice prior to Release 26. All fifteen respondents agreed that the current, non-current rate was the predominant method of translation. There was no unanimity, however, over which method of recognizing translation gains and losses was used by most companies. This disagreement over which recognition criteria were most commonly employed perhaps reflects actual divergence in practice and Committee members' diverse experience. It may also suggest a need for systematic research to inform Committee members about existing company practices and the reasons behind companies' choices.

Reasons for a decision

Question 3 asked the respondents to rate the importance of six reasons why the foreign currency issue was raised when it was. The response frequencies and average importance ratings are displayed in Table 4. The average importance ratings were determined by weighting the five response categories by 1 through 5, with "of no importance" assigned a value of 1 and "extremely important" a value of 5. Although the differences among the average ratings were not large, reasons 3(b), that some corporations were choosing to account for foreign currency fluctuations in ways that did not adequately reflect economic reality and 3(c), that existing practice lacked uniformity, were rated as being most important. The economic reality issue was raised repeatedly in the pre-test and follow-up interviews with ARC members. In the context of the foreign currency issue this was frequently taken to mean that exchange rate fluctuations were becoming more pronounced and existing practices were not adequately reflecting the risk engendered by such fluctuations. In this context, some Committee members perceived a leadership role for the ARC in drawing the attention of accountants and managers to the

Table 4: Response Frequencies for Reasons Why the Foreign Currency Issue was Raised

Question	Of No Importance	Marginally Important	Of Some Importance	Important	Extremely Important	Average Rating
3(a) Inadequate disclosure	0	2	2	8	1	3.62
3(b) Did not reflect economic reality	0	1	1	9	2	3.92
3(c) Lack of uniformity	0	1	4	4	5	3.77
3(d) Lack of audit authority	3	2	4	1	3	2.92
3(e) Abuse of choice	0	3	5	4	2	3.36
3(f) US-Canadian inconsistencies	0	3	2	8	1	3.50

possible effects, such as increased risk, of more pronounced exchange rate fluctuations. Some of those who were interviewed expressed the opinion that the profession had the responsibility to make business aware of the exposure risk they were facing.

Nevertheless, it is difficult to conclude from this data that any one specific reason for the foreign currency issue being placed on the ARC's agenda dominated all others.

Initial and final positions

The purpose of Questions 4 and 5 was to see if different Committee members shared the same positions on several issues in Release 26 both before and after the Committee's deliberations. Table 5 summarizes the responses to Question 4 regarding pre-deliberation positions. The data displayed in Table 5 shows some initial diversity in the preferences for certain positions. For example, the respondents had heterogeneous preferences as to the timing of the recognition of unrealized translation gains and losses (4(b)). On the other hand, few respondents held a strong initial position on the temporal method of translation (4(a)). This apparently reflected the fact that many Committee members were not

Table 5: Initial Positions on Key Issues

Question	Strongly Favoured	Favour	No Initial Position	Oppose	Strongly Opposed
4(a) Temporal method	1	1	10	1	1
4(b) Recognition criteria	1	6	3	3	1
4(c) Hedging gains	0	7	7	0	0
4(d) Foreign debt coverage	2	1	1	5	5

familiar with the temporal method because it was not widely used at the time of the ARC's deliberations.

In response to Question 5 – "Did you agree with the Committee's resolution of all the above issues when *Handbook* Revision 26 was released?" – ten of thirteen respondents said no. At least one respondent reported being in disagreement with at least one of the four issues listed in Question 4. Most of the ten disagreed with the position that foreign debt used to finance specifically identifiable assets should not be considered self-liquidating. Some respondents stated that during the course of their deliberations, Committee members developed strongly held preferences and beliefs, which were not easily compromised. Apparently the conflicts of opinion over the resolution of certain issues were not completely resolved within the Committee. Some individuals reported that they went along with the final decisions in spite of personal reservations because they perceived a need to reach some solution or because of a perceived need for consistency with the comparable US standard.[7]

Sources of information

Question 6(i) attempted to determine the sources of information that Committee members felt were most important to their final positions. These responses are summarized in Table 6. Most sources of information were rated as important, with exposure draft comments, sectional meetings, and associates' comments being rated as most important. However, with the exception of item (j) (discussions with government officials), which was rated very low, no one source of information seemed to be substantially more important than any other.

Table 6: Importance of Information Sources

Source	Extremely Important	Important	Of Some Importance	Marginally Important	Of No Importance	Average Rating
(a) Research studies	3	9	3	0	0	4.00
(b) Staff research summaries	2	10	3	0	0	3.93
(c) Associates' comments	4	8	3	0	0	4.07
(d) Clients	3	5	4	1	2	3.40
(e) Exposure draft comments	4	11	0	0	0	4.27
(f) Section meetings	8	4	0	0	2	4.14
(g) Informal discussion	3	7	4	0	1	3.73
(h) ARC meetings	7	4	1	3	0	4.00
(i) Experience	7	3	2	2	1	3.87
(j) Government	0	0	0	3	12	1.20

Table 7: Importance of Decision Criteria

Factor	Extremely Important	Important	Of Some Importance	Marginally Important	Of No Importance	Average
(a) Reflect economic reality	6	7	0	1	1	4.07
(b) Affect managerial decisions	2	3	5	4	0	3.21
(c) Consistent with US	0	6	6	1	1	3.21
(d) Legal liability of auditors	0	2	0	2	11	1.53
(e) Decrease management manipulation	2	5	4	3	1	3.27
(f) Consistent with concepts	2	7	4	1	1	3.53
(g) Useful for decision making	5	8	2	0	0	4.20
(h) Costly to implement	0	0	8	5	1	2.50

Decision criteria

Question 6(ii) sought to determine the factors or criteria that Committee members believed were important in making choices on issues in the foreign currency translation standard. These responses are presented in Table 7. Of the eight factors that the respondents rated, "assisting interested parties in making decisions" and "reflecting economic reality" were rated most highly. Discussions with some of the questionnaire respondents indicated a definite association between these two variables in the thinking of some Committee members. They expressed the belief that information reflecting economic reality will be useful to decision makers. The possible subjective nature of economic reality was not always admitted by those with whom interviews were conducted.

In general, the above data would seem to suggest substantial diversity in approach to decision making within the ARC. No clear pattern is apparent in the criteria considered to be important or in the information sources ARC members find useful. To some degree the responses may support the conclusion, reached from the responses to part I of the questionnaire, that many decisions are the result of professional judgment on the part of ARC members. The respondents seem to rely on internal discussion, experience and the opinions of others including their associates and the exposure draft respondents. The usefulness for decision making of the information provided and the extent to which it reflects economic reality seems to have a predominant influence on the choice of standards. Clearly such factors are general and somewhat subjective.

Summary

It seems fair to conclude from the preceding discussion that the Committee members who responded to the questionnaire do not perceive a political or legislative dimension to standard setting. This perception may accurately reflect the reality of standard setting in Canada, it may be the result of defensive posturing by the respondents, or it may simply be that the questionnaire did not draw attention to the relevant political issues. The respondents also did not seem to perceive or to articulate the possibility that some of their criteria and objectives may lead to contradictory conclusions. Professional judgments based on subjective definitions of economic reality and on discussions with associates and other Committee members, plus feedback from exposure draft comments, seem to be the important elements in the decision-making processes of individual Committee members. One interpretation of these observations is that experience with practice and reasoning from practice, rather than quasi-legislative compromise or theoretical concepts, underly the ARC's decision making.

However one interprets these data, it is clear that the ARC actively seeks information and feedback from individuals and corporations who are not directly involved in making accounting standard decisions. The exposure process is the most extensive feedback mechanism. It is to this process that we now turn our attention.

Section IV

As noted in Section II above, opportunities exist at several stages in the CICA's standard-setting process for interested individuals to provide input to the ARC. The last such point is in response to exposure draft material. Exposure drafts are the means by which the ARC seeks reactions from a broad cross section of those affected by *Handbook* Recommendations. The exposure draft stage is potentially crucial for maintaining the legitimacy of the process. For it is through the exposure draft process that previously unreconciled and possibly competing standard preferences may be expressed. Thus, information on who responds to exposure draft material, the preferences expressed by exposure draft respondents, and the apparent impact of exposure draft comments would appear to be important for understanding the ARC's standard-setting activities.

This section provides descriptive information on the exposure draft respondents and their comments on four recent *Handbook* Releases: (1) Research and Development Costs, (2) Leases, (3) Segmented Information, and (4) Foreign Currency Translation. Four proposed standards were selected for study to provide coverage of opinions on a broad range of measurement and disclosure issues.

Exposure draft respondents
Approximately 40,000 copies of each exposure draft are distributed by the CICA. Of these about 1,000 are distributed to corporate officials, industry

Table 8: Number of Exposure Draft Responses

Respondent Group	Research and Development Costs	Leases	Segmented Information	Foreign Currency Translation
Business firms	22	35	39	52
Accounting firms	10	12	10	9
Industry, trade and professional associations	4	4	3	4
Individuals	4	12	13	27
Total	40	63	65	92

organizations, stock exchanges, and securities commissions. About 2,500 are distributed to other organizations participating in ARC activities including the Canadian Certified General Accountants Association (CCGAA), the Financial Executives Institute of Canada (FEIC), the Canadian Council of Financial Analysts (CCFA), and the Society of Management Accountants (SMA).

In excess of 36,000 are distributed to members of the CICA and to CA students through the provincial institutes [Thomas, 1979]. Table 8 shows the responses to each of the four exposure drafts analysed. Inspection of Table 8 reveals that in absolute terms, the response rate is generally very low. As a proportion of total population, however, these responses do not appear to differ dramatically from those received by the FASB [Haring, 1979]. Proportionately more business firms than other groups respond. And there is substantial variance in the number of respondents according to the issue addressed, with more than double the respondents to the foreign currency exposure draft than to the research and development exposure draft.

As revealed in Table 9, most respondents replied to only one exposure draft. A total of eighty-six different business firms responded to the four exposure drafts that were analysed. Fifty-two business firms responded to one exposure draft while six business firms responded to all four exposure drafts. Similarly, of the fifteen accounting firms that responded to any of the exposure drafts, seven responded to all four and six responded to only one. As might be expected, the most frequent responders tended to be from the so-called "big eight" accounting firms, although two of the large multinational accounting firms did not submit a response to any of the four exposure drafts. Individual respondents most frequently responded to one of the four issues. Such respondents were overwhelmingly chartered accountants in public practice or in industry. Less than one-half of the industry, trade, and professional respondent group were business associations, with the remaining responses in this group coming from professional associations and government or regulatory agencies. The proportion of single-issue

Table 9: Exposure Draft Response Frequencies

Respondent Group	1 Response	2 Responses	3 Responses	4 Responses	Total
Business firms	52	17	11	6	86
Accounting firms	6	1	1	7	15
Industry, trade, and professional associations	10	1	2	0	13
Individuals	50	3	0	0	53
Total	118	22	14	13	167

responses is highest in the case of individual respondents and industry, trade, or professional organizations.

Table 10 presents additional information on the business firms that responded to the four exposure drafts. The lower panel of Table 10 shows some ownership characteristics of these respondents. Forty of the eighty-six corporate respondents were SEC registrants[8] or subsidiaries of SEC registrants in 1977, the year chosen for this analysis.[9] The proportion of SEC registrants is clearly higher for the most frequent responders. A relatively small proportion of the business respondents were closely held companies for which financial statements were not publicly available. Slightly less than one-half the business respondents were publicly traded

Table 10: Size and Ownership Characteristics of Business Firm Respondents

Characteristic	1 Response	2 Responses	3 Responses	4 Responses	Average/Total
Size					
(a) Average assets ($000,000)	619[1]	1,363[2]	1,857	1,832	819
(b) Average sales ($000,000)	397[1]	1,473[2]	2,594	1,638	1,157
Ownership:					
(a) SEC registrant or sub. of SEC registrant	20/52	8/17	7/11	5/6	40/86
(b) Publically traded non-SEC	26/52	8/17	4/11	1/6	39/86
(c) Closely-held	6/52	1/17	0/11	0/6	7/86

[1] Based on 30/52 respondents
[2] Based on 13/17 respondents

on (primarily) Canadian or other non-US securities markets. The proportion of non-SEC filers is larger for the less frequent respondents than for the more frequent respondents.

The upper panel of Table 10 shows that the responding business firms had average asset sizes of $819 million and average annual sales of $1,157 million. Multiple-issue respondents, those responding to two or more exposure drafts, tended to be larger firms than were single-issue respondents. The size statistics displayed in Table 10 may overstate the average size of single-issue respondents because data were unavailable for twenty-two single-issue respondents and for four two-issue respondents. The missing data appear, on average, to be from smaller companies or relatively small, wholly-owned subsidiaries, thus biasing the observed averages upward. Nevertheless, size statistics strongly indicate that most of the exposure draft respondents, particularly the most active respondents, are very large corporations.

The fact that large corporations tend to respond to exposure drafts is not surprising. First, large corporations are more likely to have the resources to respond. In fact a few business firms seem to make a policy of responding to all or most exposure drafts even if they have no substantive comments or strong preferences to express. Secondly, larger corporations are more likely to be affected by many of the issues the ARC addresses. For example, large corporations are more likely to engage in research and development, meet segmentation criteria, and have foreign currency transactions or foreign operations. Finally, large corporations may have a greater stake than small businesses in financial reporting standards because they are potentially more subject to regulation, and are potentially more affected by political factors. Both regulation and political sensitivity may be partly based on the information contained in financial statements.

Exposure draft preferences

Several potentially contentious issues in each of the four exposure drafts were identified from a review of the exposure draft material, by noting the issues discussed in the research column of *CAmagazine*, and by observing which points drew the most comment from exposure draft respondents. In most cases major issues were easily identifiable either because of their importance to the accounting standard or because of the number of comments they drew. For example, in the case of research and development costs, the recommendation that development costs should be capitalized met both criteria. In other cases, such as with the leases exposure draft, no single issue apart from capitalization itself seemed to predominate either in the exposure draft comments or conceptually.

All exposure draft comments were reviewed and the respondent's position on the issues was noted. Respondents were classified as agreeing with, disagreeing with, or expressing no opinion on the issues. Also, the respondent's overall or general preference for or against the proposed standard was recorded. In most cases the respondent's position on specific issues and on the proposed standard in general were fairly clear and thus could be recorded as "favour" or "oppose" without difficulty. In those instances where the respondent's position was not clear, or where the respondent did not refer to a specific issue, a "no comment" response was recorded. Thus, in the analysis presented below, a respondent's position is recorded as "favour" when there was a clear indication of support for the ARC's exposure draft position, "oppose" when an explicit disagreement was stated, and "no comment" when the respondent's position was not clear or when no position was stated.[10]

It should be noted that the exposure draft process was designed, in part, to afford various groups and individuals the opportunity to express opposition to proposed standards. Since those who favoured a position were less likely to respond, the proportions of "favour" to "oppose" comments should not be viewed as representative of the overall proportion of support or opposition in the population.

The following analysis focuses primarily on those issues on which the ARC changed its position after the exposure draft process, and on which the ARC's final or exposure draft positions differed from those adopted by the FASB. The ARC's exposure draft position may itself have represented a compromise on the basis of previous input such as, for example, the personal experience of ARC members, and associates' comments. Thus the results that follow describe only a part of the process by which competing private standard preferences may be made known to Committee members. In those cases where the ARC's position changed after the exposure draft period, the aim was to determine whether the change was consistent with support or opposition from any identifiable group of respondents. However, without knowledge of the specific thoughts of each ARC member it was clearly not possible to determine whether exposure draft support or opposition *caused* the ARC to change its position. As this was an *ex post facto* analysis, no causal inferences could be made. In addition, the analysis focused on issues where the ARC adopted a position different from that of the FASB, in order to examine whether pressure for Canadian accounting standards to be identical with those in the US was being expressed by any identifiable respondent group.

Research and development

Table 11 presents a summary of the preferences expressed by respondents on the research and development exposure draft in general and on whether certain development costs should be capitalized and amortized against future revenue. The recommendation that development costs be capitalized differed from the treatment of development costs required by FASB Statement of Financial Accounting Standards No. 2 [FASB, 1974] in the US. No significant changes were made to this standard after the exposure period.

Table 11: Responses to Research and Development Cost Exposure Draft

Issue	Business Firms		Accounting Firms	Government Agencies, Industry, Trade, and Professional Associations	Individuals	Total
	Non-SEC	SEC				
Overall	F = 3/7 O = 2/7 NC = 2/7	F = 6/15 O = 5/15 NC = 4/15	F = 9/10 O = 0/10 NC = 1/10	F = 0/4 O = 0/4 NC = 4/4	F = 0/4 O = 0/4 NC = 4/4	F = 18/40 O = 7/40 NC = 15/40
Development costs should be capitalized	F = 0/7 O = 4/7 NC = 3/7	F = 0/15 O = 12/15 NC = 3/15	F = 4/10 O = 4/10 NC = 2/10	F = 2/4 O = 0/4 NC = 2/4	F = 2/4 O = 0/4 NC = 2/4	F = 8/40 O = 20/40 NC = 12/40

F = favour; O = oppose; NC = no comment (position not stated or unclear).

Eighteen of the forty responses were classified as being in general agreement and seven of forty as disagreeing with the ARC's overall position on accounting for research and development costs. Proportionately, the greatest support for the ARC's position came from CA firms, with nine of the ten responding firms supporting the ARC's overall position. Support from other classes of respondents was mixed, with nine of twenty-two business firms supporting the ARC's position and seven of twenty-two opposing it. The proposal that development costs be capitalized and amortized against future revenues received no explicit support from business firm respondents, and sixteen of twenty-two explicitly expressed disagreement with it. All other respondent groups were fairly evenly divided in their support for the ARC's position on capitalizing development costs. Overall, twenty respondents explicitly expressed disagreement with the development cost proposal and eight explicitly supported it.

Segmented information
The positions of the respondents to the segmented information exposure draft are displayed in Table 12. While a fairly large number of different issues were raised by the exposure draft respondents, most had a clearly identifiable position with regard to whether or not segmented information should be required in financial statements. Few specific issues drew a significant number of responses. The ARC did change its position on two issues after the exposure period: the requirement that segmented information be included in interim reports was dropped, as was the proposal requiring disclosure of the amount of sales to significant customers. FASB Statement of Financial Accounting Standards No. 14 (SFAS No. 14) [FASB, 1976b], the comparable US standard, requires that revenue

Table 12: Responses to Segmented Information Exposure Draft

Issue	Business Firms SEC	Non-SEC	Accounting Firms	Industry, Trade and Professional Associations	Individuals	Total
Overall	F = 16/22 O = 6/22 NC = 0/22	F = 8/19 O = 10/19 NC = 1/19	F = 7/9 O = 2/9 NC = 0/9	F = 1/3 O = 0/3 NC = 2/3	F = 6/13 O = 3/13 NC = 4/13	F = 38/66 O = 21/66 NC = 7/66
Should segmented information be in interim reports?	F = 0/22 O = 1/22 NC = 21/22	F = 0/19 O = 0/19 NC = 19/19	F = 0/9 O = 0/9 NC = 9/9	F = 0/3 O = 0/3 NC = 3/3	F = 0/13 O = 0/13 NC = 13/13	F = 0/66 O = 1/66 NC = 65/66
Should major customer information be disclosed?	F = 0/22 O = 3/22 NC = 19/22	F = 0/19 O = 6/19 NC = 13/19	F = 1/9 O = 1/9 NC = 7/9	F = 0/3 O = 1/3 NC = 2/3	F = 0/13 O = 2/13 NC = 11/13	F = 1/66 O = 13/66 NC = 52/66

F = favour; O = oppose; NC = no comment (position not stated or unclear).

from major customers be disclosed. In other respects the CICA reporting requirements for segmented information are similar to those required under SFAS No. 14. A firm meeting the requirements of SFAS No. 14 would be in compliance with CICA requirements but the converse is not necessarily true.

Table 12 shows that the exposure draft's overall position enjoyed substantial support, with those explicitly favouring the overall position outnumbering those explicitly opposed by almost two to one. Some differences among the classes of respondents should be noted. Within the group of business respondents, those business firms that were required to file financial statements with the SEC were almost twice as likely to support the ARC's position as were non-SEC respondents. Interestingly, however, six of the twenty-two SEC respondents opposed the ARC's position even though these firms would be required to report such information to the SEC. A variety of reasons were cited by these opposing companies. They included: the disclosure of segmented information would create labour negotiation problems; all companies, including those not publicly traded, should be required to report segmented information because otherwise those required to report would be placed at a competitive disadvantage; additional exemptions should be provided; and companies should have non-disclosure rights. About one-half of the non-SEC companies opposed the ARC's overall position. As compared with business firms, proportionately fewer accounting firms or individuals opposed the overall requirement that segmented information be required.

Somewhat surprisingly, only one of the sixty-six respondents, and that one a SEC registrant, explicitly opposed the inclusion of segmented information in interim financial statements. This observation is surprising because the ARC changed its position from the exposure draft position, which required segmented information in all financial statements, to the *Handbook* Recommendation, which requires information only in annual financial statements. It would appear that the ARC's change did not occur as a result of broadly based opposition from exposure draft respondents. In addition, the one business firm that did explicitly object to the interim reporting provision, as noted above, was an SEC registrant. As such, the company would be required to report segmented information on an interim basis in the US if it described its financial statements as conforming with generally accepted accounting principles. Thus the firm's position, that the interim reporting provision would impose burdensome accounting costs, is somewhat suspect. This would seem to reinforce the point that the ARC's change of position was not motivated by comments on the exposure draft.

The ARC also changed its position on whether to require that the amount of sales to significant customers be disclosed. As may be seen from Table 12, some opposition to this proposal came from all respondent groups, although only about one-fifth of all respondents explicitly objected to it. This issue is another example of a change by the ARC from a position consistent with the FASB requirement to one that is inconsistent with it. The opposition by SEC registrants is therefore difficult to explain, since this information would be a part of their SEC filing. Opposition from other respondent groups was based on a variety of considerations, including the belief by some respondents that such a disclosure would harm their competitive position. However, no consistent set of reasons underlying the respondents' objections was apparent. Nor did they present any evidence on the potential impact of the standard. Whether or not the ARC's position on this issue changed as a result of the objections raised by the exposure draft respondents is, of course, a matter of speculation. However, with regard to this specific issue, a change in the ARC's position was associated with objections raised by a variety of sources.

Leases
Responses to specific issues in the exposure draft on leases were difficult to analyse. The leases exposure draft was a complex one, covering many sub-issues. No specific sub-issue seemed to draw comment from a significant number of respondents. However, most respondents clearly expressed support or opposition to the overall requirement that certain leases be accounted for in a manner similar to accounting for the purchase or sale, and associated financing, of long-term assets. A classification of the responses to the statement in general is presented in Table 13.

The only significant opposition to this exposure draft came from the

Table 13: Responses to the Leases Exposure Draft

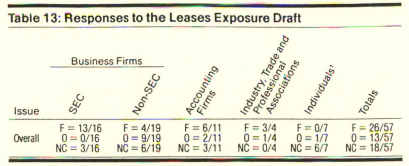

Issue	Business Firms		Accounting Firms	Industry, Trade and Professional Associations	Individuals[1]	Totals
	SEC	Non-SEC				
Overall	F = 13/16 0 = 0/16 NC = 3/16	F = 4/19 0 = 9/19 NC = 6/19	F = 6/11 0 = 2/11 NC = 3/11	F = 3/4 0 = 1/4 NC = 0/4	F = 0/7 0 = 1/7 NC = 6/7	F = 26/57 0 = 13/57 NC = 18/57

F = favour; 0 = oppose; NC = no comment (position not stated or unclear).
[1] Some comments from individuals were not classified.

non-SEC business respondents, with almost one-half of those responding expressing opposition to the proposed requirements. Among the various reasons stated by this group for opposing the leases recommendation were: (1) the requirements may force a breach of debt covenant agreements; (2) the tax implications of lease agreements were not properly recognized; and (3) capitalizing leases would result in "misleading" financial statements, as in the case where retail chains would be required to capitalize the value of leased property. These arguments appear to be a mixture of economic reality and economic consequences issues. No SEC registrant explicitly objected to the exposure draft, and a clear majority expressed support for it. Most accounting firm, individual, and association respondents supported the thrust of the ARC's recommendations on leases.

Foreign currency
Table 14 classifies the foreign currency exposure draft responses. The foreign currency issue drew relatively heavy and mixed comments, with about one-third of the respondents opposing its overall thrust. About seventy-five per-cent of the non-SEC business respondents opposed the ARC's overall position as compared to about twenty per-cent opposition by SEC respondents, twenty-five per-cent opposition by CA firm respondents, and about twenty per-cent opposition by individuals and associations. Conversely, the bulk of the support for the foreign currency exposure draft position came from SEC business firms, CA firm respondents and selected individuals.

The respondents' positions on three specific issues in the foreign currency translation exposure draft were analysed. These issues were: (1) whether the temporal method of translation should be employed; (2) whether unrealized exchange gains and losses on long-term monetary assets and liabilities should be amortized over the total life of the related item; and (3) whether gains or losses resulting from translation of foreign financed and held assets should be recognized in income. The ARC's

Table 14: Responses to the Foreign Currency Exposure Draft

Issue	Business Firms SEC	Non-SEC	Accounting Firms	Industry, Trade and Professional Associations	Individuals	Totals
Overall	F = 19/26 0 = 5/26 NC = 2/26	F = 4/22 0 = 16/22 NC = 2/22	F = 6/8 0 = 2/8 NC = 0/8	F = 3/5 0 = 0/5 NC = 2/5	F = 8/27 0 = 7/27 NC = 12/27	F = 40/88 0 = 30/88 NC = 18/88
Should the temporal method be used?	F = 5/26 0 = 5/26 NC = 16/26	F = 1/22 0 = 13/22 NC = 8/22	F = 3/8 0 = 0/8 NC = 5/8	F = 1/5 0 = 1/5 NC = 3/5	F = 3/27 0 = 13/27 NC = 11/27	F = 13/88 0 = 32/88 NC = 43/88
Unrealized exchange gains or losses — total life	F = 3/26 0 = 21/26 NC = 2/26	F = 3/22 0 = 14/22 NC = 5/22	F = 3/8 0 = 4/8 NC = 1/8	F = 0/5 0 = 5/5 NC = 0/5	F = 2/27 0 = 16/27 NC = 9/27	F = 11/88 0 = 60/88 NC = 17/88
Self-sustaining foreign operations	F = 0/26 0 = 4/26 NC = 22/26	F = 0/22 0 = 7/22 NC = 15/22	F = 0/8 0 = 1/8 NC = 7/8	F = 0/5 0 = 1/5 NC = 4/5	F = 0/27 0 = 2/27 NC = 25/27	F = 0/88 0 = 15/88 NC = 73/88

F = favour; O = oppose; NC = no comment (position not stated or unclear).

exposure draft position on when unrealized exchange gains or losses should be recognized differed from the FASB's position, which was that all such gains or losses should be taken to income in the current period. The ARC modified its position on this issue slightly after the exposure period. Instead of requiring gains or losses to be amortized over the asset or liability's total life, gains or losses were to be amortized over the remaining life of the related items. The ARC's position on the use of the temporal method and on self-sustaining foreign operations was identical to that of the FASB both before and after the exposure period.

Some differences in the patterns of responses on these issues emerged from the analysis of the exposure draft comments. First, whether business firm respondents favoured or opposed an issue appears to have depended in part on whether or not the respondents were SEC registrants and on whether the ARC's position was consistent with that of the FASB. For example, five of twenty-six SEC registrants opposed the proposed temporal method of translation, whereas thirteen of twenty-two non-SEC registrants opposed the same issue. However, both SEC and non-SEC respondents opposed the ARC's proposal for recognizing exchange gains and losses, an issue on which the ARC differed from the FASB. It should be noted however, that this pattern did not follow for the issue of whether self-sustaining foreign operations should be considered differently from non-covered assets. Here, both SEC and non-SEC registrants opposed the

ARC's position, although the ratio of non-SEC opposers to respondents was double the ratio of the SEC opposers to respondents. Nevertheless, on balance, these data seem to suggest that the preferences of business firms for or against the specific issues are partly dependent on whether the firm is an SEC registrant and whether the ARC's position is consistent with that of the FASB.

Of the responses from other groups, those of CA firms seemed to be more closely aligned with those from the SEC business firms while the individual respondents' positions were closer to those from non-SEC business firms. This trend was particularly noticeable on the issue of whether the temporal method of translation should be employed. The reasons for this similarity are not clear.

Summary

Several points that emerged from the analysis of exposure draft comments deserve to be emphasized at this point. First, the ARC gets feedback through the exposure draft process from a relatively small group of self-selected respondents. Large industrial and commercial organizations constitute the bulk of the business firm respondents, an observation consistent with related studies conducted on US standard setting. (For example, see Watts and Zimmerman [1978] and Hagerman and Zmijewski [1979].) Responses from large national and multinational accounting firms predominate in the accounting firm responses. There appears to be little or no direct input from user groups at the exposure draft stage, nor is there any appreciable input from other accounting groups such as accounting academics, or members of the SMA or CCGAA. In short, the process mostly involves a small number of large business and accounting firms with periodic input from a few members of the profession and some trade and industrial associations.

The responses to exposure draft comments indicate that it would be a mistake to assume that business firms are consistently opposed to the ARC's proposed accounting standards or that accounting firms consistently favour the proposed standards, as has been suggested by Stamp [1979]. On the assumption that a respondent who was classified as "favouring, overall" agreed with both the thrust of the proposed standard and with the fact that a standard on the given topic was being issued, most of the standards examined enjoyed broadly based support by both business and accounting firms. A possible exception to this generalization is provided by non-SEC corporate respondents, a larger proportion of whom opposed proposed standards than did any other identified group.

Broadly based opposition to any specific issue was most marked on those issues where the ARC's position differed from that of the FASB. Two examples were the proposal that development costs be capitalized and the proposal that unrealized foreign currency exchange gains or losses be amortized over the total life of an asset or liability. Such opposition was broadly based but was most pronounced among SEC registrants. A number of exposure draft comments explicitly noted a preference that Canadian standards be identical with their US counterparts. These comments came especially from SEC business firm respondents and from some accounting firms.

The above analysis suggests that the number and sources of exposure draft comments have a relatively minor impact on the ARC's decisions. The number of opposing comments received by the ARC on the three issues on which a change of position occurred did not differ markedly from the number of opposing comments on those issues where no change of position occurred. No changes occurred in the position on the capitalization of development costs ($0=20/40$), or on the use of the temporal method ($0=32/88$), or on the recognition of foreign currency gains or losses from self-sustaining foreign operations ($0=15/88$). Changes did occur on the requirements that segmented information be included in interim reports ($0=1/66$), that major customer information be disclosed ($0=13/66$), and that unrealized exchange gains be amortized over the total life of the asset or liability ($0=60/88$). These observations, plus the fact that few changes in the ARC's position occur after the exposure period, suggest that such changes should not be viewed as resulting from intense political activity or concerted lobbying efforts by exposure draft respondents.[11] On the contrary, the number of exposure draft comments expressing support for or opposition to the ARC's exposure draft position does not appear to be the only, or perhaps even the main, determinant of the ARC's final position. This, in spite of the fact that twelve of fourteen questionnaire respondents stated that exposure draft responses were important or extremely important sources of information in reaching their final decisions.

Section V

This paper has reviewed several aspects of the Canadian accounting standard-setting process. Section I reviewed some of the reasons why a standard-setting mechanism exists. We concluded that standard setters face conflicting demands. On the one hand mandatory accounting standards have the potential to occasion wealth transfers among individuals. This effect of accounting standards, combined with the possibility that standards have a public value different from their private value suggests the existence of conflicting preferences as to which accounting standards should be adopted. To the extent that the standard-setting process must reconcile competing preferences, it is political. On the other hand, standard setters must be concerned with legitimating the standard-setting process in general as well as the specific standards they adopt. CICA control over standard setting may be justified on the grounds that the specialized knowledge base on which standards rest is unavailable to the state and that such expertise will be exercised in the public's interest. The manner in which these conflicting demands are reconciled was the subject of enquiry of this paper.

The structure of the ARC, the way in which its members say they make decisions, and its use of exposure draft comments appear to reflect these conflicting demands. The ARC's structure and procedures are such that, nominally at least, input from a variety of user and preparer interests can be made at several points. Problems may be brought to the attention of the ARC through a number of channels and from multiple sources. Input from associates and the exposure draft process would seem to provide opportunities for many affected parties to express their preferences concerning standards. However, the Committee itself consists mostly of practising accountants, little direct input from user groups appears to be forthcoming, and the Committee's activities are largely secret.

Individual ARC members also appear to reflect the conflicting demands placed upon them. They state that they rely heavily on information from exposure draft comments and from associates in making decisions. On the other hand, Committee members apparently do not perceive a legislative or political dimension to their activities. One way of characterizing the manner in which ARC members say they make decisions is that they apply professional judgment based on their experience and on subjective economic reality criteria. Such findings are consistent with the idea that standard setting requires specialized technical expertise, which is unavailable except to senior practitioners in the field. Whether the professional values that may accompany this expertise act as a surrogate for the public interest is, of course, still open to question.

Some of the same conflicts appear to underlie the ARC's response to exposure draft comments. The process itself and the CICA's substantial efforts to encourage responses appear to be attempts to involve affected constituents in the decision-making process. When asked to rate the importance of various sources of information, Committee members state that exposure draft comments are very important. Yet the actual impact of such comments was difficult to evaluate. The study's data are most consistent with the view that the ARC does not treat comments as votes and that the ARC reserves for itself the right to respond to comments in the manner that it sees fit. Exposure draft comments do not seem to be the most important part of the process whereby a consensus on which accounting standards should be adopted is sought.

The Canadian standard-setting process does not appear to be supported by an extensive research base. If standard setting were seen by the participants as a political activity, there would be a demand for research findings supporting the positions of various advocates. No direct evidence was uncovered that such is the case in Canada. The CICA research activity appears to concentrate on extant authoritative writings (i.e., the conclusions reached by standard-setting bodies in other countries) and to a much more limited extent on summarizing normative positions presented in accounting literature. No exposure draft comment reviewed cited or presented research findings to support the view being expressed. Nor did Committee members express any felt need for research findings that would assist them in predicting the consequences of proposed standards. Whether this results from a dearth of accounting research conducted in Canada or whether little Canadian research is conducted because standard setters and other interested parties have not been receptive to it, is open to question.

In summarizing certain aspects of the standard-setting process in Canada, the following generalizations seem justified. Standard setters do not see their role as political or legislative. Nor did the data suggest that the same legitimation processes underlie Canadian accounting standards as apparently underlie US standards. The respondents did not seem to place much confidence in being able to reason from a conceptual framework, or much emphasis on accounting research or on accounting theories. They expressed little concern with the economic consequences of accounting standards. It seems that experience with practice and reasoning from practice lie at the base of the ARC's decisions and it is these factors rather than theories, concepts, or research that provide the grounds for legitimating standards and the standard-setting process.

Whether individual Committee member's experience with practice will continue to be sufficient grounds for establishing and legitimating accounting standards is an important and open issue. As the economic environment becomes more complex and changeable, the impact and consequences of accounting standards may become more difficult to assess and anticipate. When problems arise which those in practice have not had much experience with, such as inflation accounting, the grounds for choice may become shaky. As managerial and other user groups become better educated, users may require more complete explanations of the reasoning behind certain choices. The growing importance of accounting information for regulation and taxation decisions combined with its increasing cost may create a demand for more thorough reasoning of the economic and social impact of accounting standards. While no direct conclusion on how accounting standards should be established can be drawn from this descriptive research, its findings suggest some issues that should be considered by those in a positon to decide how accounting standards should be established.

Notes

1. Some of the source literature for this review includes Demski [1973], May and Sundem [1976] and Watts and Zimmerman [1978].
2. More extensive reviews are available in Mulcahy [1977] and Thomas [1978]. The present review is condensed from these sources.

3. The ARC's composition does include a financial analyst; the information preferences of financial analysts, may, however, diverge from those of shareholders.

4. A third part of the questionnaire, the responses to which are unreported here, solicited demographic information from the respondents.

5. Six eligible ARC members did not respond to Part II of the questionnaire. Of these six individuals, one objected to the questions and wrote a detailed explanation of the reasons for his objections. One person responded stating that his recollection of the issues discussed was not good. Three individuals did not state reasons for their lack of response and one individual could not be located.

6. Question 9 is a compound question and is therefore open to different interpretations.

7. Clearly the ARC experienced great difficulty in resolving these issues, as is witnessed by the fact that it took the unusual step of meeting with several exposure draft respondents.

8. Companies were automatically classified as SEC registrants if evidence that their securities were listed in US capital markets could be found. Where no such evidence was found, a letter was written to the company asking them to verify that they were not a SEC registrant.

9. Exposure draft release dates were: for Research and Development Costs, February 1977; for Segmented Information, May 1978; for Leases, January 1978, and for Foreign Currency Translation, June 1977. Data on the corporate respondents were gathered for one year, 1977, to simplify the analysis and presentation.

10. The results of this tabulation were compared with the relevant summary of comments published in the research column of *CAmagazine*. In those instances where tabulations were reported in *CAmagazine* the two tabulations were virtually identical.

11. Political activity could of course take place before proposed standards reach the exposure draft stage. There was, however, no indication of this, either formally or informally.

References

Arrow, K.J., *Social Choice and Individual Values*, 1st. edition (John Wiley and Sons, 1951).

Demski, J.S., "The General Impossibility of Normative Accounting Standards," *The Accounting Review* (October 1973), pp. 718-723.

Dopuch, N. and Shyam Sunder, "FASB's Statements on Objectives and Elements of Financial Accounting: A Review," *The Accounting Review* (January 1980), pp. 1-22.

Financial Accounting Standards Board (FASB), *Accounting for Research and Development Costs*, Statement of Financial Accounting Standards No. 2 (Stamford, Conn.: FASB, October 1974).

_____ , *Tentative Conclusions on Objectives of Financial Statements of Business Enterprises* (Stamford, Conn.: FASB, 1976a).

_____ , *Financial Reporting for Segments of a Business Enterprise*, Statement of Financial Accounting Standards No. 14 (Stamford, Conn.: FASB, December 1976b).

Hagerman, R.L. and M.E. Zmijewski, "Some Economic Determinants of Accounting

Policy Choice," *Journal of Accounting and Economics* (August 1979) pp. 141-161.

Haring, John R., "Accounting Rules and 'The Accounting Establishment,'" *Journal of Business* (Vol. 52, No. 4, 1979), pp. 505-519.

Ijiri, Y., *Theory of Accounting Measurement* (AAA, 1975).

May, Robert G. and Gary L. Sundem, "Research for Accounting Policy: An Overview," *The Accounting Review* (October 1976), pp. 747-763.

Mulcahy, G., "CICA Accounting Recommendations – The Process and Procedures of Their Development," Paper presented at The Clarkson Gordon Foundation Accounting Workshop, York University, May 1977.

Stamp, E., "The Watts Report: An Uncertain Trumpet," *The Accountant's Magazine* (January 1979), pp. 10-12.

Thomas, R.D., "Setting Accounting and Auditing Standards," *CAmagazine* (September 1978), pp. 60-63.

———, "Have We Heard From You Lately?" *CAmagazine* (October 1979), pp. 77-80.

Watts, R.L. and J.L. Zimmerman, "Towards a Positive Theory of Determination of Accounting Standards," *The Accounting Review* (January 1978), pp. 112-34.

———, "The Demand for and Supply of Accounting Theories: The Market for Excuses," *The Accounting Review* (April 1979), pp. 273-305.

Zeff, S.A., "The Rise of 'Economic Consequences,'" *Journal of Accountancy* (December 1978), pp. 56-63.

Appendix

Questionnaire Survey of Selected ARC Members

Part I

Please indicate the strength of your agreement or disagreement with the following statements as they apply to ARC activities in general.

[Each question was followed by the scale: Strongly Agree; Agree; Neutral; Disagree; Strongly Disagree.]

1. Most accounting issues can be solved by reasoning from a few basic accounting concepts, such as the entity concept or the going concern concept.

2. The essential difficulty in establishing accounting standards is to convince those who use or are affected by financial statements that the proposed standard is the right one.

3. Standard setting in accounting is like a governmental or legislative activity in that preferences of various interested parties such as management, shareholders, and other interested parties should be acknowledged and accommodated.

4. Most accounting standards have economic consequences of a significant magnitude for the business firms required to adopt them.

5. In choosing between (among) accounting alternatives, the most important consideration is to balance the preference of various interested parties.

6. Many accounting issues will be resolved when a comprehensive conceptual framework for accounting is developed.

7. Establishing accounting standards is essentially a matter of trading off the costs

and benefits associated with proposed standards among different groups and individuals.

8. Generally speaking, disclosure issues are much more important than measurement issues in accounting.

9. On the whole, financial statement users are able to separate useful information from false, misleading or irrelevant data in financial statements and other corporate reports.

10. Accounting standards tend to follow rather than lead good accounting practice.

11. Choosing between (among) accounting alternatives is really a matter of deciding which standard will best describe economic reality for most companies.

12. The main purpose of financial accounting standards is to limit the choice that managers would otherwise have in reporting to shareholders and other financial statement users.

13. Managers' economic interests are closely tied to the content of the financial information they disclose.

14. The *main* purpose of financial accounting is to provide information useful for making investment and disinvestment decisions.

15. Accounting measures should be highly standardized and verifiable.

16. The main purpose of financial accounting is to report on the custodianship of resources under the command of individuals or organizations.

17. Left to their own devices, most corporate managers would disclose very little financial information.

18. Most financial statement users are not capable of understanding complex accounting issues.

19. On balance, financial analysts are in favour of substantially expanded financial disclosure by corporations.

20. The financial reporting interests of corporate managers and shareholders are most often in conflict.

21. The accounting profession should establish standards that look after the interests of less influential financial statement users such as shareholders with small holdings.

22. Some financial statement users such as bankers or financial analysts are influential enough to get whatever financial information they want from corporate managers irrespective of which accounting standards are established.

23. Canadian accounting standards should generally be consistent with those promulgated in the US because the business environment in the two countries is essentially the same.

24. Accounting standards tend to follow rather than lead good accounting practice.

25. Canadian firms that file with the SEC and Canadian subsidiaries of US multinational corporations should be allowed to follow US GAAP when reporting in Canada.

26. Accounting standards should be detailed and specific in their requirements.

Part II

Prior to the release of *Handbook* Revision 26, Translation of Foreign Currency

Transactions and Foreign Currency Financial Statements, Section 1500.13 required that the basis for translation of amounts from foreign currencies to the currency in which the financial statements are expressed be disclosed, and that the amount of net current assets in countries with exchange restrictions be disclosed. Also, paragraph 3210.05 required disclosure where the carrying value of a long-term liability differed from the liability translated at the rate of exchange prevailing at the date of the balance sheet.

Handbook Revision 26 would have required companies to adopt the temporal method for translating assets and liabilities recorded in a foreign currency. Unrealized gains and losses related to the translation of monetary assets and liabilities with lives extending beyond the end of the subsequent fiscal year would have been amortized over the remaining life of the asset or liability. Foreign debts used to finance specifically identifiable foreign assets were not to be considered as self-liquidating and therefore translation gains and losses on such debt were to be included in net income.

1. Prior to *Handbook* Revision 26, which was the *predominant* method for translating foreign currency transactions and for translating the financial statements of subsidiary, investee, or other foreign operations?

_____ Current rate
_____ Current, non-current rates
_____ Monetary, non-monetary
_____ Temporal
_____ Other (please specify)

2. Prior to *Handbook* Revision 26, how did most companies recognize unrealized gains and losses translations?

_____ Charging all such gains and losses to income of the current period
_____ Charging only certain gains and losses to income
_____ Charging all or certain types of gains and losses to equity
_____ Deferring and amortizing some or all gains and losses
_____ Other (please specify)

3. What do you believe were the major shortcomings of Canadian practice before *Handbook* Revision 26 which necessitated action by the ARC? Please rate the importance of the following reasons.
[Parts a – f were followed by the scale: Extremely Important; Important; Of Some Importance; Marginally Important; Of No Importance.]
(a) Some corporations were not adequately disclosing the effects of foreign currency fluctuations.
(b) Some corporations were choosing to account for foreign currency fluctuations in ways that did not adequately reflect economic reality.
(c) Existing practice lacked uniformity.
(d) Audit firms lacked the authority to require that the most informative accounting methods be adopted.
(e) Some corporations were abusing their freedom of choice by choosing to account for foreign currency fluctuations in self-serving ways.
(f) Too many inconsistencies between Canadian and US practice were developing.
(g) Other reasons (please specify).

4. Please indicate below whether you *initially*, that is before discussing or debating the issue within the Committee, favoured or opposed the position

which was finally adopted by the Committee on the following issues:

[Parts a – d were followed by the scale: Strongly Favoured; Favour; No Initial Position; Oppose; Strongly Opposed.]

(a) The temporal method for translating foreign currency transactions and foreign operations should be used.

(b) Only certain unrealized gains and losses on translation should be recognized in the current period's income.

(c) Gains and losses arising from the translation of unperformed forward exchange contracts should be amortized over the life of the contract if the contract extends beyond the following fixed period.

(d) Foreign debt used to finance specifically identifiable foreign assets should not be considered self-liquidating.

5. (a) Did you agree with the Committee's resolution of all the above issues when *Handbook* Revision 26 was released?

    _____   Yes   _____   No

(b) On which of the above issues were you in disagreement with the Committee's decision?

6. The following two questions are concerned with describing how your position on the above issues developed and evolved while the issues implied in *Handbook* Revision 26 were under consideration by the ARC.

[All items in parts (i) and (ii) of this question were followed by the scale: Extremely Important; Important; Of Some Importance; Marginally Important; Of No Importance.]

(i) Please rate, in the space provided, the importance of the following *sources* of information to your final position:

    (a) Background or self-directed technical reading such as research studies published in journals or technical reports.

    (b) Research summaries presented by the CICA staff.

    (c) Associates' comments.

    (d) Discussion with clients.

    (e) Exposure draft comments.

    (f) Discussions and argumentation in Sectional Committee meetings

    (g) Informal discussions with business colleagues or others.

    (h) Discussions and argumentation in full ARC meetings.

    (i) Past experience in dealing with issues.

    (j) Discussions with government officials.

(ii) This question attempts to determine the reasoning behind your final decision on the issues in *Handbook* Revision 26. A list of factors that may have influenced your decisions on the issues in this *Handbook* revision appears below. In the spaces provided, please rate the importance of each factor to your own decisions on the issues above:

    (a) Application of the standard would have resulted in information capable of reflecting economic reality in most circumstances.

    (b) The standard would have significantly affected managerial decisions regarding foreign currency transactions.

    (c) The standard would have resulted in practice consistent with that in the US.

    (d) The legal liability of audit firms would have been significantly affected if the proposed standard had been adopted.

(e) Application of the proposed standard would have foreclosed opportunities for managers to manipulate reported financial results.

(f) The proposed standard would have been consistent with accounting concepts such as the matching concept.

(g) The resultant information would have assisted interested parties in making decisions about the reporting entity.

(h) The resultant standard would have been costly to implement.

Discussant's Comments
David G. Ward

I would like to thank the organizers of the Symposium for inviting me to attend these discussions. At the risk of giving a "preview" of my comments, I must say that this is the first time in four years of standard-setting activity that I have attended – or, perhaps more importantly, been invited to attend – what might be described as an academic gathering. In addition, to set my comments in the context of my professional experience, I should let you know that I have not spent any time in the research activity carried on by my firm, Coopers & Lybrand.

To further qualify my credentials to discuss an academic's paper, I propose to start by telling you a joke. Last summer I attended the Stanford Executive Program in Palo Alto for eight weeks. Our yearbook contains an inventory of jokes, many told by Chuck Horngren. The one I will quote is from Bill Davis, a marketing professor who was in a friendly competition with Horngren, the accountant, for the best joke award: "Horngren and I went to South America. As we flew over the Andes I asked him how old the mountains were. 'Oh, about two billion and seven years.' 'How do you know that?' 'Well, I was down here seven years ago and they told me then they were two billion years old.'" Then Horngren told the one about the Financial Accounting Standards Board, which I will translate to "Canadian": "The Accounting Research Committee, unloved, feels like a lone tree in the midst of a thousand dogs."

In a more serious vein, I would now like to discuss the subject of John's paper and, more broadly, the theme of this Symposium, under three main headings: (1) comments on author's observations; (2) the future of standard setting as standards become more controversial; and (3) the role of academic research in the formulation of standards.

Comments on author's observations

First of all, I must say that the research technique employed, that of a multiple choice questionnaire followed by selected telephone interviews, has made it difficult for the author to resolve fully what would appear to be conflicting responses. The issues raised in the questions are complex and interactive, and I am not surprised that John had difficulty in drawing conclusions – some of the issues could tie up the Accounting Research Committee in discussion for several hours.

In addition, the paper does not deal with the important role in standard setting played by the CICA Research Studies activity, headed by John

David Ward CA was at the time of the Symposium a Partner of Coopers & Lybrand, Toronto and Chairman of the CICA Accounting Research Committee. He is currently with Barrick Investments, Toronto.

Denman. A research study preceded the foreign currency standard, and we have two valuable research contributions on the subject of pensions, one by Ross Skinner and the other by Ross Archibald, to form a knowledge base for the standard "Accounting for Employer Pension Costs" now being developed. These are current examples of the contribution of research to our deliberations – we have also had this in the past.

That said, I would like to discuss three issues that have been raised: (1) secrecy, in the context of what the author terms "legitimating" our process; (2) whether or not there is a legislative or political dimension to the Accounting Research Committee's activities; and (3) the uses and abuses of exposure draft comments.

Secrecy

John has identified an important issue, and an area where I believe that greater efforts must be made by the Accounting Research Committee to break down the barriers. The perception of secrecy arises in the first place because we have tended to be secretive, but also because, quite frankly, not too many people are interested in our deliberations (that is, until they are affected, after which they become very interested!). Our actual secrecy has evolved from a concern that if our deliberations are public, the uneven course that we often must follow to reach a conclusion will confuse our constituents and discredit the process. It should also be said that it is easier to be secretive than to be open!

My personal belief is that we have to open up our process, perhaps in the following ways:
1. By using discussion papers on important issues to set out the alternatives available and to provide a preliminary indication of the Committee's position and the reasons supporting that position.
2. By creating an overview group consisting of members drawn from a broad cross-section of users, as envisaged by my partner, Morley Carscallen, as Chairman of the Special CICA Committee which recently reported on standard setting.[1]
3. By holding public hearings or, to use a gentler word, discussions after the exposure draft has been issued but before final *Handbook* release. We did this with selected exposure draft respondents on foreign currency translation, and the day spent was very helpful to the Accounting Research Committee members and, I believe, to the respondents as well.
4. With broader use of advisory groups, as is now being done with foreign currency translation.

The cost of these steps is time, but many are of the view that this time would be well spent. We would produce a standard that might have better acceptance as more people would have participated in its development. People participating in this process would also come to understand better the conflicting issues that often underlie a particular standard.

Legislative or political dimension

John states in his conclusions that Committee members do not attribute an economic or political role to the process of setting standards. I disagree and am surprised at this statement, perhaps because we are partway through discussions on the Petroleum and Gas Revenue Tax (PGRT) and Petroleum Incentives Program (PIP) where the CICA has been explicitly threatened with legislation of accounting standards by senior federal civil servants and the choice of one accounting standard over another has clear economic implications.

Current cost accounting is another standard we have been working on for some time – and that is probably an understatement – that has clear implications for the allocation of capital. Tables of figures are now being published by *Business Week* and by stockbrokers, not to mention accounting firms, that set out important economic comparisons. Investment in food retailing is probably a better hedge against changing prices than being in the steel manufacturing business!

All in all, I find John's assertion surprising, but I do not have any basis other than a faith in my fellow Committee members' intelligence to disagree with it.

Uses and abuses of exposure draft comments

First and foremost, the Accounting Research Committee does not view or use comments as ballots on particular standards but rather to gain information on matters affecting the standard that may not have been considered by the Committee. We also receive useful arguments against positions we have taken, and we are sometimes persuaded that our position is wrong or that it could be better explained.

One of the most difficult "political" situations that we have to deal with is the view that we do not take into account comments received. We do, but it should be remembered that we have discussed the subject over a period of several months and have already addressed many of the issues raised in exposure draft comments. Also, we have a voting rule that requires a two-thirds majority vote to initiate or to change a principle. This tends to freeze exposure draft positions, which are approved by a two-thirds majority, as it takes a two-thirds vote to change that position; I have tussled with this rule several times. I think that it is right, but would welcome any suggestions.

I would now like to turn to the future of accounting standards in Canada and the part that can be played by academics in standard setting.

The future of standard setting as standards become more controversial

I am sure that every Accounting Research Committee chairman, halfway through his term, feels that standard setting is at the crossroads. Recent standards are more of a nature that "bite" – segmented reporting, related party transactions, and current cost accounting, and a draft guideline on forecasts all tend to be controversial.

Current support for standards and the *CICA Handbook* is, by my assessment, good but under pressure. Accountants who have personal or business disagreement with the standards are, in some cases, choosing to ignore them and are pressuring auditors to accept their position. Positions being taken by auditors differ for varying reasons. Some of these positions are valid, but many – in my view – are the result of an unwillingness to "stand up and be counted." I have tried not to bias my conclusion by the fact that setting accounting standards is a thankless activity in Canada today, albeit a rewarding professional experience because of the learning and the contact with fellow professionals it involves.

I see important changes occurring in the standard-setting process, many of which are set out in the Report of the CICA Special Committee on Standard Setting.[1] The move will be towards a more open process using more resources, probably at a greater cost to members.

The important change from the perspective of academic input is the recommended move to task forces. These groups, specially selected for each major project, will provide a vehicle for greater specialist input than has been the case to date – but don't let me excite you with these possibilities without first talking to you about some of the roadblocks.

The role of academic research in the formulation of standards
I should start by saying that appropriate research will continue to be important as part of the process, and that this importance will grow. But I must also say that I am not sure that academics have been fulfilling their role. My experience with the academic community, from contacts on the Accounting Research Committee, has been positive. But my impression is that not many important pieces of original research have been done by the academic community on subjects related to current standard setting – what might be termed practical research – other than those where the CICA acted as the catalyst.

Harsh words, perhaps, but I have tested these views with a few of my peers and found them confirmed.

What is to be done? There should be more communication between the academic community and standard setters although this is a two-way street. The academic community's participation in the process, which has been good in the past, needs to be increased. This does not necessarily mean time-consuming Accounting Research Committee membership but, rather, for example responding to exposure drafts and raising problems with existing standards. Finally, academics should contribute more original and practical research on subjects of current and future interest to standard setters.

I trust that my comments will be viewed in their proper perspective. I am not saying that the relationship between standard setters and academics is poor but merely that I see significant room for improvement. This is especially important given John's view that research will become an important supplement to practical experience – a view that I share.

Notes

1. Special Committee on Standard Setting, *Report to CICA Board of Governors* (Toronto: CICA, December 19, 1980).

Discussant's Comments
A. Wayne Hopkins

I would like to begin by complimenting John on a thoughtful, well-written, readable paper.

This paper, like many of the others, is lengthy. I was not consoled by Alex Milburn's appeal to authority in his statement to Symposium participants that readers should be "willing to study the information with reasonable diligence." But, perhaps part of the price of dealing with important issues such as those this Symposium addresses is a considerable commitment on the part of interested parties. I am pleased to be here today, Mr. Chairman, and would like to thank The Clarkson Gordon Foundation for the invitation and opportunity to share in the work that will take place today and tomorrow.

Three categories of research questions were formulated and posed in the paper:

1. The structural composition of the Accounting Research Committee (ARC) and its operating procedures were reviewed to assess which accounting issues are raised and how issues are settled.
2. To shed light on the internal workings of the ARC, an attempt was made to determine the information, objectives, and criteria used by members in making policy decisions.
3. Responses to exposure drafts were summarized by category and an attempt was made to determine the impact of the responses on the pronouncements.

Research of this nature is difficult. Asking people how they make decisions, or for the criteria used in decision making, for example, is a weak method of capturing policy decisions, as the author acknowledges in the introduction to Section III. For some reason, many of us do not have a good understanding of how we ourselves operate, although we may very well be able to describe in detail how our associates come to decisions and the influences that are brought to bear in their decision-making processes. In addition, the group dynamics were not captured in the questionnaire instrument used by the author.

This research was in progress at the same time that a high-profile Special Committee, commissioned by the CICA Board of Governors, was meeting and addressing the same problem, and the papers were produced at about the same time.[1] I have some empathy for this type of situation because ten years ago I was preparing to submit a proposal on the Structure for Establishing Accounting Principles and Enforcing Compliance in the United States at the same time that the Wheat Committee was meeting.[2]

Wayne Hopkins PhD CA is Associate Professor of Accounting, Faculty of Administration, University of Regina. He previously taught at the Universities of Manitoba and Colorado.

From a study of submissions to the Wheat Committee, I concluded that the problems were well understood; it was solutions that were elusive.

Rather than addressing the research questions posed or the findings of the study, I will restrict my comments to three elements of the paper that I view as important. They are: (1) the difference between the author's perception of the role of the standard setter and that of ARC members, (2) the element of secrecy, and (3) the importance of research in the present standard-setting process.

Role of the standard setter

One of the findings of the study is that ARC members do not see their role as political or legislative. They view themselves as providing judgment and experience in establishing accounting standards that reflect economic reality and that provide useful information.

This role contrasts markedly with the framework presented by the author in Section I of the paper. A line of reasoning that appears to have been heavily influenced by articles in US journals led to the observation that one part of the standard setter's role is legislative-political in that it involves reconciling competing social and private interests. A related aspect attempts to find justification for the control over a political process residing in the private sector.

It is not surprising that a finding based on Canadian experience is at variance with a framework formulated on the basis of US influences. Standard setting in the US evolved to a legislative-political function in the seventies because of the perceived notion that otherwise the public sector would exercise its legal right to establish accounting standards.

The climate in Canada is not similar. The political, legal, and social environments in the two countries are quite different. The Americans tend to be much more adversary than Canadians, are readier to involve the courts to resolve problems or find scapegoats, and are prepared to lobby politicians in pressing for acceptance of their viewpoint. US Congressmen in turn have been willing to exert pressure on the Securities and Exchange Commission (SEC) in response to the lobbyists and the SEC has mounted increasing pressure on standard setters. This situation is partially attributable to the separation of legal authority to establish accounting principles from actual responsibility for completion of the task. The legal authority rests in the public sphere with the SEC while the responsibility lies in the private sector with the Financial Accounting Standards Board (FASB), and formerly with the Accounting Principles Board (APB). In addition, the accounting profession in the US was bombarded with an unfavourable press in the sixties, which conveyed a message of increasing dissatisfaction with accounting and accountants.

In Canada, the institutional arrangements for establishing accounting standards are now and were ten years ago different from those in the US. The legal authority for establishing accounting principles and disclosure rules is different, and politicians in Canada are much more reluctant to become involved in the accounting standard-setting process. We do not have as litigious an environment nor have we had as many significant lawsuits relating to the adequacy and application of accounting standards. Publicity in the financial press has been quite different and the willingness of third parties to intervene in the standard-setting process is not parallel in the two jurisdictions.

Let us be careful not to advocate a ten-year-old American solution for standard setting to a current Canadian problem when the environments are not the same.

Secrecy

Both Professor Waterhouse and the CICA Special Committee on Standard Setting (SCOSS)[3] expressed concern about secrecy in the standard-setting process. Waterhouse referred to three issues: (1) ARC meetings are not open to the public, (2) public hearings are not held, and (3) little information is published on the reasons for choices by the ARC.

SCOSS expressed concern that it was difficult for outsiders to influence the process. The first communication from the ARC most often comes at the exposure draft stage, and a perception exists that the Committee may be unwilling to move from its considered position in arriving at a final conclusion to be published as a *Handbook* pronouncement. SCOSS was also concerned that exposure draft responses were not available to the public.

Both Waterhouse and SCOSS indicated that increased openness will lead to increased credibility, but the issues raised by the two reports and their implications were quite different. The Special Committee advocated a greater opportunity for outside parties to participate at all stages of development and recommended that exposure draft responses be made available to the public upon request unless submitted in confidence. Although Professor Waterhouse did not state a preference for a "sunshine law," he did refer to open meetings and public hearings.

Interestingly, and in contrast to SCOSS, Waterhouse suggested that one of the merits of the existing process is that it permits input from many interested parties – a broadly based ARC, associates of ARC members, and respondents to exposure drafts. Further, he stated that the ARC actively seeks information and feedback from individuals and corporations who are not directly involved in making accounting standards decisions. Nevertheless, feedback, in the form of exposure draft responses, is limited and from a relatively small group of self-selected respondents.

Whether the limited response is attributable to the standard-setting process or to the inaction of non-respondents is an important question. SCOSS suggested it is the process. The view was expressed that outsiders are unwilling to respond to what is perceived to be a considered position with limited chance of altering that position.

Preference as to a considered position or an earlier exposure is a matter of personal style. I prefer a considered position. There is nothing inherently wrong with the ARC taking a position from which it must be persuaded to change if, in fact, the Committee is occasionally persuaded to change the view expressed in the exposure draft. And the ARC has changed its position. There are examples of re-exposure drafts and *Handbook* releases which differ from the exposure draft. As an associate of one of the Committee members, I have witnessed instances in which the recommendations have been changed at the exposure draft stage from the statement of principles formulated at the pre-exposure draft stage. I suggest this indicates a Committee responsive to the views of others although I must admit that I do not know the reasons for the changes.

It is unlikely that as many changes would be allowed if the process were completely in the public eye. There would be a reluctance to risk the credibility of the profession by making public several changes in position in the development of a standard. Perhaps we are simply talking about a difference in timing. Whether we call the first external communication from the ARC an exposure draft, a tentative statement of principles, a discussion paper, or something else, the first release must come, in my view, only after due deliberation.

One of the criticisms of the FASB procedure of due process is that a tentative position is *not* taken at the discussion memorandum stage. This criticism may result from groups working at cross purposes. The FASB wishes to expose the issues in a discussion memorandum in the hope of soliciting the views of interested parties whereas some individuals wish to know the direction the FASB is taking in order to obtain an early indication of whether or not the standard setters are on the "right road."

In my view, more open discussion of tentative positions will increase the political nature of the standard-setting process in Canada. The present confidential system with extensive use of associates provides an opportunity for diverse views from a large cross-section of individuals. It facilitates freedom of discussion and reduces the political aspects of the process. It allows ARC members to act as individuals and not as representatives of their firms' or clients' positions. An open process would almost certainly negate this benefit.

If there is dissatisfaction with the present process, it may be because:
1. The process is not working well in the sense that the associates do not make a significant contribution. I am not in a position to judge the contributions of the associates.
2. The selection process of associates is *ad hoc*. Some may believe it should be more deliberate. If left on an *ad hoc* basis, the ultimate representation is left to chance. On the other hand, if some group is responsible for selecting the associates, the process is more restrictive and the final group of associates may be less diverse.
3. The contribution or participation of a large number of individuals is not

at present well understood. This is a communication problem that can be resolved through education rather than through a drastic change to complete openness which might be accompanied by an increased level of politicization.

In summary, I agree that there should be accessibility to a public record and that reasons for choices should be disclosed. I have reservations about the cost/benefit relationship associated with open meetings and public hearings. I believe there is sufficient opportunity to influence the results at present, and I doubt there would be an increase in the number of interested parties who contribute if the process were extended to achieve the appearance of greater public accountability. If there is dissatisfaction with the results, a change in the composition of the ARC, with less control by the CICA, is likely to have greater potential for different outcomes than is a move to greater accountability.

Finally, there is a large overriding constraint under which the ARC operates that already assures a certain amount of openness, albeit in another jurisdiction. That constraint is a very real desire for standards to be consistent with US standards whenever possible. Perhaps that goes a long way towards explaining why most of the standards examined by John Waterhouse enjoyed broadly based support by both preparers and attestors with one possible exception – non-SEC respondents. To put it in a slightly different context, maybe much of the discussion of proposed standards has already taken place during the due process procedures of the FASB.

Research

Four of the findings in the Waterhouse report related to research or the absence of it in the present standard-setting process. They are:

1. Practice and reasoning from practice lie at the base of ARC decisions.
2. Little emphasis is placed on accounting research and accounting theory.
3. The ARC is not overly concerned with the economic consequences of accounting standards.
4. Little confidence is placed on reasoning from a conceptual framework.

Although decision making always benefits from judgment and experience, we live in an increasingly complex world, and "economic reality" is personal to each member of the standard-setting body. The increasing complexity makes it imperative that research be undertaken to facilitate the decision-making process, since decision making can benefit from research as well as from judgment and experience.

It seems appropriate to end on the research note and to move to a simple subject like pension costs this afternoon – an area in which we can bring our considerable experience and judgment to bear and where little or no research is necessary for ARC members to pool their collective wisdom.

Notes

1. Special Committee on Standard Setting (SCOSS), *Report to CICA Board of Governors* (Toronto: CICA, December 19, 1980).
2. The report of the Study Group on the Establishment of Accounting Principles (which was chaired by Francis M. Wheat) was entitled: *Establishing Financial Accounting Standards: Report of the Study on Establishment of Accounting Principles* (New York: AICPA, 1972).
3. See note 1.

Reply to Discussants' Comments

I will address three related issues raised by Wayne Hopkins and David Ward in their discussion of my paper. The first is whether or in what sense the process of establishing Canadian accounting standards is in fact and in the perception of standard setters a political-legislative process. Two related issues are: (1) the extent to which secrecy should surround the standard-setting process, and (2) the role that academic research should or can play in assisting standard setters.

The central point raised by both discussants goes to the very core of the standard-setting issue: is the process of establishing accounting standards really a political or legislative process and is it perceived by Canadian standard setters to be so? Professor Hopkins argued in his comments that because the social, legal, and regulatory environments of Canada differ from those of the United States, one cannot state that Canadian standard setters face the same legislative-political problems as do their American counterparts. David Ward implicitly disagreed with this view; he expressed surprise at my observation that Accounting Research Committee (ARC) members did not state that they perceive a legislative or political role for standard setting in Canada. The role standard setters play and their perception of it are both crucial to an analysis of the standard-setting process and to the judgments one may wish to make regarding reform of the process.

To some degree accounting standard setting is a political-legislative activity irrespective of the specific political, legal, and social environments within which standards are established. The essential elements of the argument as to why, or in what sense, standard setting is political were as follows. First, in both Canada and the United States the minimum quantity and the specific type of accounting information produced is regulated. That is, accounting standards have a legal or quasi-legal status and are, for the most part, mandatory for a sizeable number of business firms. Secondly, at least some compulsory accounting standards have the potential to occasion wealth transfers among some economic agents. Accounting standards may occasion wealth transfers from corporate shareholders to auditors by increasing audit fees, from the shareholders of one corporation to those of another by providing information which may attract competitors to profitable industries, from shareholders to debtholders as may result upon the mandatory capitalization of lease obligations, etc. As a consequence of these economic effects, various economic interests will hold different preferences for accounting standards, or for whether a particular mandatory standard should exist at all. Thirdly, given a set of diverse and potentially conflicting preferences, is there any objective (i.e., non-political) way that the "best" accounting standard can be selected? If we make the ethical judgment that individuals' preferences should count, thereby precluding a dictatorial system, the answer is no. Moreover, no general principle such as objectivity, relevance, or "meets with economic reality" can be employed to select socially optimum accounting standards. The absence of an objective way for aggregating diverse accounting standard preferences places standard setters in the position of having to trade off the preferences of some individuals against those of others. It is in this sense that standard setting is political: standard setters must subjectively compromise the preferences of some individuals or groups for those of other individuals or groups. The essential elements of the argument, which are conditional on the general political, social, or legal environment, are (1) that accounting standards are mandatory, (2) that the economic interests of individuals are affected by accounting standards, and (3) that individual preferences should be taken into account in selecting standards. In these respects, the environments of Canada and the United States are similar and therefore the framework presented in Section I of my paper argued, based on American literature, that Canadian accounting standard setting has a legislative-political dimension to it.

Whether or not standard setters perceive that they have a political or legislative role to perform, they in fact do as long as standards are mandatory, have some economic impact, and are, at least in principle, sensitive to individual preferences. Unlike David Ward, I did not find it especially surprising that some of the standard setters whom I surveyed either did not perceive this aspect of their role or, if they did, were reluctant to admit it. Legislative actions which have an impact on the economic welfare of individual members of society are most often taken within the jurisdiction or under the authority of an elected body. Where such authority has been delegated to a professional organization such as the CICA, it can be reclaimed if the process is seen to be blatantly political or if constituents become sufficiently dissatisfied with the results. Thus, admitting to the political-legislative role of a standard setter may call into question the legitimacy of a standard-setting mechanism located in the private sector. For this reason, the background section of my paper postulated a dual process underlying standard setting. One part of the process deals with the political aspect of the role. A second part is concerned with legitimation. Specific standards require legitimation and the process itself, including its location at the CICA, needs to be legitimated if the profession is to retain control over standard setting. Defining the process of choosing standards as a political or legislative process may decrease its legitimacy, hence the reluctance to perceive or admit to its political nature. Instead, standard setters may attempt to define the problem of which standards should be adopted in technical, conceptual, or professional terms.

Both discussants addressed the question of secrecy in Canadian standard setting, as did my paper. My concern with secrecy stemmed from the ethical position that individual preferences should count when mandating standards which have economic consequences. Interestingly, Wayne Hopkins, who appears to believe that standard setting is not a political process, is not as concerned with secrecy as David Ward, who seems to perceive a legislative-political dimension to standard setting. My own value judgment is that standards should be sensitive to individual preferences and that individuals will be more likely to make their preferences known to the standard-setting body if they believe that their opinions are at least considered. The best way to demonstrate that the process is sensitive to the preferences of constituents is to open it up. The counter-argument, that the process must be kept secret because it necessarily follows an uneven course, is most meaningful if one sees standard setting as a search for truth. A political process follows, virtually by definition, an uneven course. Surely it is in the best interest of the profession and society in the long run to acknowledge the process for what it is – a search for compromise – and to design a choice mechanism accordingly. To my mind this means opening it to public scrutiny.

A final issue relates to the role that academic accounting research can and should play in the standard-setting process. Whether or not a particular research project is seen to be of practical benefit depends in part on how standard setters and researchers see the essential nature of the standard-setting problem. The type of research information that those who define the problem in essentially technical terms will find useful or relevant is likely to be quite different from the type of research that those who see the problem as a social choice issue will perceive as being helpful. In the first case, research that searches for consistency between a proposed alternative and a conceptual framework or that purports to show that a particular accounting method more accurately reflects economic reality than do the alternatives is likely to be seen as important, practical, or original. On the other hand, if the problem is seen as a political or legislative one, information on the likely economic consequences of a proposed standard may be valued for the same reasons.

This is not to argue that there is an abundance of relevant research available in Canada at this time, or that any research project would be capable of resolving the question of which accounting standard should be selected. Rather, the perception that there is insufficient research to support the standard-setting function adequately stems from (1) differences of opinion on the nature of the standard-setting problem, (2) the inability of any research project to resolve accounting issues, and (3) a dearth of qualified researchers in Canada with the time and financial support to conduct relevant research. I fully support David Ward's call for greater liaison between standard setters and academics, but I caution both researchers and standard setters against forming unrealistic expectations for the practical impact of such efforts. To my mind, accounting research might play a role in formulating accounting standards analogous to the role played by economic research in formulating economic policy. Economic research may assist economic policy makers in forecasting the effects of economic policies, but the ultimate question of who should bear which costs and who should receive which benefits for a policy alternative is a political one. Similarly, accounting research may help us understand the consequences of alternative standards, but the ultimate choice will remain a political one.

Synopsis of Discussion

The discussion opened with the suggestion that a possible reason for Waterhouse's findings that Canadian standard setters gave a low ranking to the political element of their role was that, until recently, choices between accounting policy alternatives have not been perceived to have great economic effects. One participant observed that no one will go to the trouble of demanding a particular accounting disclosure or refuse to provide it unless the perceived economic incentive is large enough to warrant the effort. He noted, though, that the scene in Canada is changing, as more decisions are being made by the CICA Accounting Research Committee that have an obvious economic impact. He cited segmented disclosure, current cost accounting, and accounting for the Petroleum and Gas Revenue Tax and the Petroleum Incentives Program. (Another participant expressed the view that the latter two issues bring Canada to the point the US was at in the early 1960s with the investment tax credit.) The suspended *Handbook* Recommendations on foreign currency was also cited as an example of this changing scene. It was suggested that significant economic consequences were not foreseen, so that little research was done and considerations relating to economic consequences were incorrectly assumed to be unimportant.

In sum, this discussion suggested that as Canadian standard setters become involved in more issues such as the above that have, or are perceived to have, economic effects, it is likely that greater political pressure will be felt by standard setters. It was felt that this is likely to lead to demand for research on the economic effects of proposed standards.

Much of the subsequent discussion centered on the need for research on the economic effects of proposed standards, the difficulty of doing such research, and the possible impact of its findings on the decisions of standard setters. While there seemed to be agreement that it is important for standard setters to know about the possible economic effects of any proposed standard, it was observed that such research is very difficult to do. Current research methodology does not allow us to predict how people will react to a standard once it is in place. The FASB standard on foreign currency was cited by a US participant. He observed that the public record of comments on the Exposure Draft preceding this standard shows that, for the most part, there was agreement with the proposal. Yet after the standard was finalized, many found it unacceptable. He suggested that we do not have the research technology to predict with any degree of accuracy how people will react. Another participant replied that this lack of technology does not relieve the profession of the responsibility for at least doing some "soft" research to understand as best we can the possible consequences of proposed standards. For example, financial statement figures can be calculated giving effect to proposed changes under various possible circumstances – in order to grasp the possible effects better. A participant from industry noted that a few large Canadian companies are paying more attention to the economic effects of proposed standards and are doing research of this sort. Some others thought that this is the exception rather than the rule, however.

One participant suggested that if the standard-setting process was opened up (through, for example, making exposure draft comments available to the public, having public meetings, etc.), comments on exposure drafts would likely be less self-serving than they otherwise might be. Another participant viewed self-serving representations as very useful to the Accounting Research Committee – it is better to have them at the exposure draft stage than later, he said. It was also suggested that there would be more scope for academics to be usefully involved in the research process if exposure draft comments were on the public file – as has been recommended by the CICA Special Committee on Standard Setting.

With respect to Waterhouse's questionnaire results, it was suggested that the low ranking for economic effects as a factor in standard-setting decisions may be because the Accounting Research Committee respondents themselves did not recognize that possible economic effects played a part in their decisions. There was a comment that perhaps the thinking of many Committee members is not as broad as it should be, and that their approach is too much oriented to dealing with accounting issues by following rules and to pursuing the belief that there is one right answer, so that economic effects are viewed as largely irrelevant.

On the other hand, one academic participant wondered whether the responses to the questionnaire may have been affected by "honest posturing" on the part of Committee members – which may have obscured what is really happening. Professor Waterhouse agreed that this is a problem with surveys and that, in his view, the only way his research could have been designed to be sure as to what is really going on, and to capture the political element, would be to follow a project through from beginning to end, attending all meetings and reviewing all information sources used.

There was some discussion of how items are chosen for the Accounting Research Committee's agenda. It was thought that topics get on the agenda after becoming issues in practice – a result of (1) basic economic changes (such as the growth of pension funds), (2) US pronouncements on the topic, or (3) government legislation (e.g., government grants).

ACCOUNTING STANDARD SETTING..A NEW BEGINNING

EVOLUTION, NOT REVOLUTION[1]

By Edward Stamp, FCA

On behalf of the Study Group on Corporate Reporting, I recently completed writing Corporate Reporting: Its Future Evolution, a research study that will be published this month by the CICA. Although the objectives of corporate reporting have been -- and still are being -- studied in the United States, the United Kingdom and Australia, the CICA study is the first to take a practical approach. Because the study establishes a framework for the setting of accounting standards, it is certain to be of interest to all members of the profession and the general business community, both here in North America, and abroad.

This article will outline some of the main features of the study, but first it is essential to explain why it was undertaken. The best way to do this is by looking at some of the problems that accounting standard setters have to face.

ACCOUNTING STANDARD SETTING BECOMING MORE DIFFICULT

The setting and enforcing of accounting standards throughout the world are becoming increasingly difficult tasks. The problems have become particularly acute in the United States where the responsibility for accounting standard setting was taken out of the hands of the American Institute of Certified Public Accountants in 1973 and handed over to the newly-established Financial Accounting Standards Board. Yet the situation in the U.S. does not appear to have improved to any great extent. The level of criticism voiced in the early 1970s has not diminished and, in fact, in the last few years the U.S. Congress and the Securities and Exchange Commission

---

[1]Transcribed from original script of CA Magazine, Sept. 1980, pp.38-43.

have joined the chorus. The FASB has, however, committed substantial resources of time, manpower and money to the development of a conceptual framework, which it hopes will specify the fundamental concepts upon which accounting standards should be based and from which they should be developed. The FASB expects that when this framework is complete, it will set the course for financial accounting and reporting for many years to come.

Across the Atlantic, the British Accounting Standards Committee (which, through the participation of the Irish Institute, also sets standards for Eire) was established early in 1970. Until then there had been no mandatory accounting standards in the United Kingdom, but, now that they are being produced, they are attracting increasing amounts of criticism. Although the expressions of opposition to British standards have not been as fierce as in the United States, they have nevertheless caused the British Accounting Standards Committee to undertake a comprehensive review of the whole process of standard setting. The British have displayed some interest in the notion of establishing a conceptual framework, but they have yet to make any material commitment of resources to such a project.

On the broader international scene, both the United Nations and the Organization for Economic Cooperation and Development are actively considering whether to intervene in the process of establishing international standards. This task, at the moment, is the responsibility of a private sector organization, the International Accounting Standards Committee, which is concerned that their job will become more complicated by the intervention of international governmental agencies. A further complication exists in Europe because of the fact that, under the Treaty of Rome, the European Commission has the right to issue directives on accounting standards that the member states of the European Community must incorporate into legislation.

The pressures for reform, and the criticisms of accounting standard setting, have also been evident in Canada. The Canadian criticism has been less vocal, and its effects have been less damaging than that in the United States, partly perhaps because of differences in national character and partly because the legal and constitutional environment in this country is different in a number of important respects from that in the United States. Nevertheless, criticism of accounting standards in Canada has been increasing, and some of its most recent manifestations have been concerned with standards designed to deal with accounting for foreign exchange translation, deferred taxation, pensions, leaseholds and inflation accounting.

OBJECTIVES OF CORPORATE FINANCIAL REPORTING

It does not take much reflection to realize that if improvements are to be made in the processes of accounting standardization, and hence in the quality of the standards themselves, it is necessary not only to look at the institutional aspects of the matter (now being considered by a committee under the chairmanship of Morley P. Carscallen, FCA) but also to examine the objectives and the conceptual underpinnings of the standards themselves.

In examining the objectives and the conceptual foundations of accounting it has to be recognized that accounting is not an end in itself. On the contrary, accounting, accounting standards and financial reporting are utilitarian in that they provide the means by which people's needs for information to make economic and other decisions can be met. Thus, if we were to attempt to summarize the objectives of corporate financial reporting, albeit in the abbreviated form of a single sentence, it might read:

"To provide adequate information about the real economic position and performance of an enterprise to all potential users who need such information to make decisions."

This, of course, provides only a brief summary of the objectives of corporate financial reporting, and they are examined in much greater detail in the research study to be published later this month. It is clear, however, that even a simplified expression of objectives leads naturally to a consideration of several further important questions, such as: Who are the users of published financial reports? What are the information needs of such users? What criteria can be used not only in deciding whether these needs are being satisfied but also in establishing accounting standards to ensure that the needs can be satisfied?

It is not possible to provide the answers to all of these questions in an article; that is why the research study was written. The abbreviated definition of corporate financial reporting given above, however, also focuses attention on some important conceptual aspects of the problem of accounting standard setting that are worth examining in this article.

WHAT IS "ECONOMIC REALITY"?

To begin with, it is clear that accounting is concerned with representation of economic reality. There must be only a few people who really suppose that it is the intention or the purpose of accountants to deal with fictions or illusions. "Economic Reality" seems clear enough. It lies all around us in the form of real estate, buildings, plant and equipment, vehicles, ships, aircraft, inventories of raw materials, work in process, and finished goods of all kinds. We also recognize it in its less tangible forms, such as debts receivable and payable, stock and bond certificates, bank deposits, business goodwill, and so on. To many people it is most evident in the form of cash -- either in their pockets, or in the form of pay cheques, dividend or interest cheques, or other negotiable paper that is readily convertible into cash.

Yet, when we think carefully about the measurement of the value of this economic reality -- the task that is entrusted to accountants -- it becomes clear that this is not something that can be done in an unambiguous fashion. Even cash loses its value in times of inflation, and the measures of the value of all other assets depend on whether we are interested in how much the asset cost when it was bought originally, how much it would cost today, or how much it could be sold for today. Indeed, it has to be recognized that all values reside ultimately in the future, since it is our estimate of the benefits that we shall derive from an asset in the future (ultimately, in economic terms, in the form of cash flows) that determines its value to its owner today.

Clearly, measures of economic reality cannot be unambiguous. all manner of judgments are necessary in making measurements of value. Similar judgments are required in measuring income, which, in its broadest sense, is represented by changes in value. It will also be observed that since income (which is generally thought of as measuring what has happened in the past) depends on measures of value, it becomes impossible to divorce the past from both the present and the future when an accountant attempts to measure past performance.

WHAT IS THE NATURE OF ACCOUNTING?

Thus, many of the uncertainties of accounting measurement result from ambiguities in the aspect of value we are trying to measure. Others result from uncertainties that are inherent in our inability to predict the future. Still others depend on more subtle problems, such as the question of whether or not it is, in principle, possible to make unambiguous accounting allocations, such as are required in measuring depreciation, cost of sales, etc.

Because of all of this, many people have concluded that accounting is an "art", an attitude that bewilders people who are impressed -- however wrongly - by the apparent precision and certainty of a public company's balance sheet.

Others who have thought about the nature of accounting regard it as a social science, similar in many ways to law, and see the authority of accounting standards depending on a consensus.

Still others see accounting as a subject whose problems could be solved if they were tackled in the same fashion as in the natural sciences, where hypotheses are propounded in an attempt to explain observed facts. The hypotheses are then either supported or rejected by using them to make predictions that are tested against further empirical evidence.

And still others argue that accounting standard setters should adopt the approach used in certain branches of mathematics, such as geometry, where axioms are established -- through intuition or through observation -- and from which an internally consistent set of standards (theorems) is developed through a process of logical analysis.

Perhaps the most obvious way of looking at accounting is to regard it as a language, a vehicle whereby information is conveyed from the preparer to the user of financial statements. Yet, although this view presents a vivid description of the nature of accounting, it is not very fruitful, since it provides little guidance as to how to go about developing the language in such a way as to maximize its utility and its acceptability to its users.

Corporate Reporting considers all these issues in detail, and draws conclusions as to the best way in which standard setting and, consequently, corporate financial reporting, should evolve in the future in Canada. It really is not possible to set a course for the future development of accounting standard setting unless one is clear not only as to the objectives of financial reporting, but also as to the nature of accounting itself.

CONCEPTS

In examining the nature of accounting, we also need to ask what are the underlying concepts on which financial reporting and accounting standards rest. If such fundamental concepts do in fact exist, are they permanent and universally applicable? Or do they change over time and from place to place (depending on the environment); and, if they do, then how can they be regarded as fundamental?

It is not hard to appreciate that variations are possible. For example, income -- and the related concept of value -- can be defined in several different ways and, although some of these measures may be less objective (in the sense that less precise or reliable measures are possible), they may be more useful. Considerations of this kind have weighed heavily in the minds of accountants in recent years as they have grappled with the problem of inflation accounting. If different concepts of income and of value are possible -- and they clearly are -- and if they are of varying degrees of objectivity and usefulness -- and they clearly are -- then accountants and others are faced with the problem of deciding which concepts should be used.

MEETING THE NEEDS OF USERS

This immediately raises the questions of who are the users of financial reports and what are their needs. It is clear that accounting standards cannot be developed with much confidence until there is agreement between the preparers of financial reports and the standard setters as to which of all of the various possible user groups a public company is accountable, and in what manner it is accountable to each group. This is not necessarily a purely legal question. On the contrary, it is one in which the whole community has an interest, and it seems highly desirable that the accounting profession should provide a lead.

Although considerations of this kind are clearly important in the process of accounting standard setting, they are not sufficient in themselves either in judging the quality of the accounting standards that are produced or in assessing the extent to which a company has been successful in accounting to outside users. It is, therefore, essential that both accounting standard setters and the preparers of company financial reports and the users of such reports should have available a set of criteria they can use to (1) judge the quality of accounting standards; (2) choose between possible alternative standards on any given subject; and (3) assess the usefulness of published company reports to those who use the information in them. A substantial section of the research study is devoted to a detailed consideration of these important questions.

THE RESOLUTION OF POTENTIAL CONFLICTS OF INTEREST

It must always be borne in mind that none of the processes referred to earlier, namely setting standards, producing (and auditing) company financial reports, or using the information provided in such reports, is without cost. On the other hand, presumably none of these activities would be undertaken in the first place if they did not generate benefits. Financial information is not a free good (even though it may appear to be so to some of the people who use it), and it is clearly essential to weigh the costs against the benefits when deciding what action to take in the area of standard setting.

This is, of course, much easier said than done. Although, in many cases, it is only the marginal costs and benefits that need to be considered, the sum total of each is almost always impossible to estimate. The problem is further complicated by the fact that in many cases the costs and the benefits are divided unevenly among the various parties involved.

Further complications arise from the fact that there will often be conflicts or potential conflicts of interest between the preparers of financial statements and the users in deciding what information should appear in published financial statements. Auditors, and ultimately the accounting standard-setting body, are the professional arbiters in this process.

It is not only between the preparers and users that such conflicts or potential conflicts may arise. It is also possible that conflicts of interest will arise between different categories of user groups as to what information is appropriate and how it should be supplied in published financial reports. There will, of course, be many instances where such conflicts or potential conflicts are non-existent, but it is naive to suppose that this disposes of the problem. If the danger of conflicts were not important enough to cause any concern, then there would be no need to have any accounting standards at all, and it would be unnecessary for the community to invest so heavily in the provision of auditing services by professional accountants.

Another issue the research study deals with is the extent to which the evidence accumulated in research on the efficient market hypothesis is relevant to the problems of accounting standard setting, and whether the need for standards in areas such as depreciation accounting and leaseholds (to name just two) has been diminished -- if not eliminated -- by efficient market evidence. The conclusion of the research study is that standards are indeed still required in these areas, and the impact of efficient market research on accounting standard setting is likely to be much less than was once supposed.

THE DANGERS OF OSSIFICATION

A question of broad interest and concern, dealt with in the study in some detail, is related to the overriding purpose of accounting standards. The process of accounting standardization is generally regarded as necessary to narrow the areas of difference in financial reporting. The intention is to improve the comparability of the financial reports prepared by different entities by ensuring that like situations are treated in the same manner, in accounting terms, by different companies. The aim is, therefore, to achieve greater uniformity of accounting treatment throughout the country. This immediately raises two important questions that are dealt with in some detail in the research study. First, is such an increase in uniformity possible? (And if not, why not?) Second, if it is, how can we ensure that the processes of legitimate innovation in accounting measurement and disclosure are not stifled?

Without innovation financial reporting will ossify, and flexibility is therefore essential if accounting standards are to evolve to keep pace with the changes that are constantly occurring in technology, financial techniques, user decision needs, social, political and economic conditions, etc.

A related problem is the fear that, in our attempts to achieve improved comparability of accounting through increased uniformity, we are not only diminishing the flexibility that leads to innovation, but are also accelerating the trend towards "books of rules". There is much concern that the scope for professional judgment will thereby be sharply decreased. Such concern is justified and, indeed, the very existence of accounting as a true profession could be jeopardized.

Yet the alternative, which is to rely more heavily on professional judgment and less on detailed standards, raises the difficult question a to how judgment of this kind can be defined, how society can ensure that the best qualities of judgment are applied and how the users of financial reports can be satisfied that consistent standards of judgment are being exercised across the whole of the financial reporting spectrum.

All of these problems are likely to be rendered more acute by the possibility, or the probability, that current value figures may in future supplement (and perhaps eventually supplant) the conventional historic cost figures in published financial statements. Such a step entails a recognition that more than one basis of valuation may be used in financial statements in the future. If this should happen, it will be because the Accounting Research Committee and the preparers of financial statements jointly recognize that the needs of the users of published financial statements can be met only by the provision of such further information.

This raises the further question -- one that needs to be given the most serious consideration -- as to whether the needs of all of the various user groups can be satisfied by one set of "general purpose" financial statements. If not, we have to ask ourselves whether the additional information should be published in the form of supplementary statements, or by adding further columns to the present style of financial reports.

WILL A U.S. "CONCEPTUAL FRAMEWORK" MEET CANADIAN NEEDS?

Corporate Reporting deals with these and other questions in much greater detail than it is possible to do here. One of the most important questions the study addresses -- not so far mentioned in this article -- is the problem of whether the approach towards a conceptual framework that the FASB is now adopting is suitable for Canada. If it is, then it might well be argued that the best strategy for the CICA to adopt would be to wait until the FASB has reached its final conclusions and then adopt those conclusions holus bolus in Canada.

The research study presents a strong argument, however, that, although the FASB approach may be appropriate for the needs of the United States, it is not suitable for Canada. The American approach depends too much on normative, axiomatic and even authoritarian prescriptions, and it is also too narrow in its scope since it is confined largely to the needs of investors. In fact, the FASB's stated primary concern is with the needs of investors, whereas in Canada, for reasons outlined briefly in the following paragraphs, it would seem appropriate to acknowledge the interest of a much wider group of users.

It is not unnatural that there should be differences of approach between the United States and Canada. Appendix II of The Adams Report[2] sets out some of the major differences between the U.S. and Canadian environments. As The Adams Report was mainly concerned with auditing, it naturally stressed the differences between the legal environments in the two countries, since it is such differences that have been largely responsible for the much greater incidence of litigation against public accountants in the U.S. than in Canada. But the differences defined by The Adams Report are relevant to accounting standard setting as well. In addition, there are some broader differences that need to be considered, because they go a long way towards explaining why a solution to the problem of accounting standard setting that might be suitable in the United States is not necessarily appropriate in Canada.

---

[2]The Report of the Special Committee to Examine the Role of the Auditor (The Adams Report), CAmagazine (April 1978).

The history of the two countries is quite different. The United States broke away from Britain as a result of the Revolutionary War with that country. Canada, by contrast, has evolved as an independent, bilingual, federal nation within the Commonwealth, and its parliamentary and legal systems (which are quite different from those in the United States) are based on the British model. Within the United States, the West was won with the gun. More orderly means were used in Canada, and Canadians still tend to take a less adversary approach towards the solution of their problems than is the custom in the United States. Similarly, there is a greater emphasis on social justice and social welfare in Canada. All the Canadian provinces have had medicare systems in existence for a number of years. These systems are operated by governments of all shades of political opinion, and a wider spectrum of political opinion, and a wider spectrum of political belief is tolerated in Canada than in the United States. The climate of public opinion in Canada is receptive to the notion of wider corporate responsibility, and welcomes it, and there is more public participation in the economy (through publicly owned corporations) in Canada than in the U.S.

When it comes to specific accounting matters, the standards issued in Canada by the CICA have the support and legal backing, not only of the federal government, but also of the provincial securities commissions. This is quite different from the position in the United States. Moreover, as the surveys referred to in The Adams Report have determined, roughly 95% of the chief financial officers of large Canadian enterprises who are members of the Financial Executives Institute are chartered accountants, whereas in the United States only about 35% of the members of the FEI are CPAs.

All of these differences are important to accountants. They are among the many reasons why Canada is so clearly a unique nation, quite different in its background, character and outlook from the United States. As a Canadian citizen now living in England, who makes frequent trips to Canada and the United States, I have always been puzzled by Canadian concern about "national identity". To me, Canada is so obviously different from the United States that I would find it quite impossible to mistake one country for the other. None of this of course means that accounting standards developed in Canada must necessarily be different from those issued in the United States. It seems quite obvious that the fewer such differences the better, if only because of the close trading and financial relationships between the two countries, as well as their contiguity. But differences in environment mean that a different approach is required in Canada, and Corporate Reporting sets out the approach that is considered to be best for this country -- and quite possibly for other countries that share our fundamental legal, constitutional, political and social traditions -- such as the United Kingdom, Australia and New Zealand.

A FRAMEWORK OF OUR OWN

What is clearly important is that whenever it is decided, because of conditions peculiar to Canada, that accounting standards promulgated in this country are to be different from those in the U.S. (or in the U.K., or by the IASC), there should be a full and complete explanation of the practical and conceptual reasons supporting the Canadian position.

The research study to be published later this month specifies in considerable detail the conceptual and practical analysis that is required for developing accounting standards. As explained earlier, Corporate Reporting examines in detail the objectives of financial reporting, outlines the needs of all the various user groups, and argues in favour of a wider accountability to the users of published financial statements. It also answers many of the questions raised in this article. Yet, the research study is not a kind of philosopher's stone that can magically provide golden solutions to the problems that now beset accounting standard setters throughout the world.

What it can and does do is establish a clear and integrated set of criteria that should be used by standard setters, as well as by the preparers and users of financial information, in the processes of:

- Developing new standards.
- Evaluating and modifying existing standards (or, occasionally, withdrawing them).
- Choosing between alternative courses of action, both in developing standards and in applying them.
- Assessing proposals for changes in standards. (Those who make such proposals should justify them in terms of the same criteria used by standard setters and preparers.)
- Deciding whether there is justification for differences between Canadian standards and those of other jurisdictions.
- Assessing the quality of the accountability of companies subject to Canadian standards.

All these processes require the exercise of judgment. If this is to be done consistently, and if the quality of the judgment is to be properly assessed, then clearly defined criteria are essential.

The research study specifies 20 criteria that should be used in making judgments about accounting standards. Among the most important are objectivity, relevance to user needs, verifiability, substance over form, materiality and cost-benefit effectiveness. In varying degrees, however, all 20 of the criteria must be weighed in the balance in making accounting judgments. "Balance" is a key issue because, as the research study emphasizes in its lengthy discussions of the criteria, improvements in respect of one of them can generally be obtained only at the expense of a reduction in compliance with one or more of the others. Thus, improved relevance (for example, in introducing current value accounting) generally has to be obtained at the cost of lower objectivity and verifiability of the data to be reported.

Of the 20 criteria proposed in the study, eight conflict with each other in this way, five more are generally compatible with the rest, and the remaining seven are constraints (an example is data availability) that may affect any of the other 13.

The use of these criteria will enhance the judgment of standard setters and others, and will help greatly in making the exercise of judgment more consistent and credible than it has been in the past.

The study's proposals constitute a conceptual framework for the development of accounting standards in Canada, a framework that can be used to ensure that the future evolution of financial reporting in this country will be directed -- and be clearly seen to be directed -- to meeting users' needs.

The changes proposed are not radical; they are evolutionary. They will, however, require careful thought and consideration by all members of the CICA -- not only before implementation but in the years to follow.

Edward Stamp, FCA, is director of the International Centre for Research in Accounting and Endowed Research Professor at the University of Lancaster, England. He was a partner in Clarkson Gordon in the early 1960s. He has also held professorial chairs at Edinburgh University and the University of Wellington in New Zealand. He was the American Accounting Association Distinguished International Visiting Lecturer in 1977, and has lectured widely in North America, Europe, Africa, Australasia, Asia and Japan.

DO WE NEED A CANADIAN CONCEPTUAL FRAMEWORK?[*]

By Joel H. Amernic and W. Morley Lemon

It has been four years since the CICA published *Corporate Reporting: Its Future Evolution*, a research study that, according to its preface, hoped to "provide a blueprint for the evolution of a rational and generally acceptable system of accounting standards in Canada." Was this a vain hope? Not much has been heard since on the subject, which may lead one to believe that either we do not need a Canadian conceptual framework, or we do but the research study apparently did not fill the bill.

We will first consider what the potential advantages and disadvantages are for the profession, reporting companies, shareholders, creditors and other financial statement users of having a coherent, written Canadian conceptual framework for financial reporting. We believe that a case can be made for designing and implementing one. Second, we will evaluate the CICA research study to see if it, or parts of it, would be suitable, or whether it is in need of extensive reworking if it is to form the basis for such a framework.

What is a Conceptual Framework?

Before assessing whether or not it makes sense to have our own Canadian conceptual framework, it seems reasonable to settle on an understanding of what we are talking about. The US Financial Accounting Standards Board (FASB), in an early document entitled *Scope and Implications of the Conceptual Framework Project* (December 2, 1976), likened a conceptual framework to a constitution, an apt description since a constitution, according to one dictionary definition, is defined as "the system of fundamental laws and

---

[*]Transcribed from original script of *CA Magazine*, July 1984, pp. 22-27.

principles that prescribes the nature, functions, and limits of a government or other institution."

More specifically, the FASB, in its 1976 document, defined a conceptual framework for financial reporting as:

> "a constitution describing it as a coherent system of interrelated objectives and fundamentals that can lead to consistent standards and that prescribes the nature, function, and limits of financial accounting and financial statements. The objectives identify the goals and purposes of accounting. The fundamentals are the underlying concepts of accounting, concepts that guide the selection of events, and the means of summarizing and communicating them to interested parties. Concepts of that type are fundamental in the sense that other concepts flow from them and repeated reference to them will be necessary in establishing, interpreting, and applying accounting and reporting standards."

There can, conceivably, be a variety of accounting constitutions or conceptual frameworks. For example, one type might define reporting objectives quite narrowly, while another might favour broad objectives. Similarly, one type might define the elements of financial reporting specifically, while another might not. Further, differences concerning substantive matters, such as who is being reported to, might distinguish one type from another.

Our interest here, however, is in whether we need a formal, written conceptual framework at all. Most practitioners and academics would probably agree that we now have a fragmented, inconsistent and largely unwritten framework – which is not a constitution in any meaningful sense of the word.

The Case for Developing a Written Framework

The case for a Canadian conceptual framework is obviously not clear-cut, but we believe the need is there. And the need is not just academic. Gordon Fowler, for example, recently asserted that:

> [From] the point of view of a public practitioner who must constantly exercise professional accounting judgment, the need for a conceptual framework of accounting is achingly clear. ... In my opinion, judgments based on an objective, internally consistent, and generally accepted conceptual framework would provide more useful information to financial statement users than judgments based on subjective factors, which are more difficult to interpret and apply. Without some form of conceptual framework, professional accounting judgments are based on little more than personal experiences and biases.[1]

A conceptual framework can be used to help guide the standard setters. As Walter P. Scheutze[2] explains, there are basically two opposing methods of setting standards. The first is "a situation-by-situation approach," resulting in "inconsistent accounting recognition for similar events." The second, a conceptual approach, "attempts to develop accounting standards based on a structure of coordinated concepts," thus setting the reasoning environment within

---

[1]Gordon C. Fowler, "A Public Practitioner's View of Corporate Reporting: Its Future Evolution," in Sanjoy Basu and J. Alex Milburn (editors), *Research to Support Standard-Setting in Financial Accounting: A Canadian Perspective* (Proceedings of the 1981 Clarkson Gordon Foundation Research Symposium).

[2]Walter P. Scheutze, "The Significance and Development of the Conceptual Framework," *Journal of Accounting, Auditing and Finance* (Spring 1983).

which a body such as the CICA's Accounting Standards Committee deliberates, and ensuring that a consistent approach is taken.

Without such a framework, "politics" might become a dominant factor in standard setting.[3] One has to wonder, for example, whether accounting for Petroleum Incentive Program (PIP) grants would have been an issue at all if the profession could have pointed to deferral and amortization as being consistent with an accepted, published conceptual framework.

The possibility of the profession being seen to accommodate a particular interest group would be far less likely were its standards to have the force of a conceptual framework behind them. Such a framework, therefore, would strengthen the profession's position in its dealings with various lobby groups, including clients and government. In fact, in a socio-political environment like Canada's, in which both the power and the responsibility to set financial accounting standards have been given by government to the profession via legislation, the development of such a framework would appear to be crucial.

As K.V. Peasnell pointed out in a recent article, the "Canadian Institute would appear to have a great need of a [conceptual framework]. How can it show that its efforts at developing (and enforcing) accounting standards are proceeding in a fair, logical and highly professional manner other than by setting out the framework within which it is operating?"[4]

---

[3]David Solomons makes an eloquent, if somewhat overreaching, plea for minimizing the effect of "politics" on accounting in "The Politicization of Accounting," *Journal of Accountancy* (November 1978).

[4]K.V. Peasnell, "The Function of a Conceptual Framework for Corporate Financial Reporting," *Accounting and Business Research* (Autumn 1982), p. 254.

A conceptual framework would also be of value in buttressing the independence of public accountants. The notion of independence has long been a basic tenet of the profession because the value of a practitioner's work rests to a large degree on the extent to which he or she is perceived to be independent and not subject to influence. Not all accountants think of themselves that way, though.[5] Any means of enhancing their independence, therefore, deserves serious attention. Surely, having a conceptual framework to fall back on when dealing with clients over contentious issues would be one such means."

A conceptual framework would, moreover, as the FASB pointed out in its 1976 document, provide "a frame of reference for resolving questions in the absence of a promulgated standard." Even when there are no contentious accounting issues, practitioners must often decide whether the treatment of an event not covered by specific *Handbook* Recommendations complies with GAAP. A body of literature setting out a specifically Canadian framework would be useful in such situations, as the issue could be resolved by reasoning within a coherent framework to a greater extent than is possible now. As Scheutze indicates, one important benefit of a conceptual framework is that predictability "by both users and preparers of how an accounting issue ultimately will be resolved will be enhanced."

A coherent, Canadian conceptual framework might also be of benefit to the education of students entering the profession because it would likely give them a better understanding of practice, especially as it is revised to be consistent with the framework.

---

[5]Joel H. Amernic and Nissim Aranya, "Public Accountants' Independence: Some Evidence in a Canadian Context," *The International Journal of Accounting* (Spring 1981.).

Practice would not then be viewed as "just a series of ad hoc, arbitrary rules" (Scheutze's words), to be learned by rote, but as the detailed application of a "structure of coordinated concepts." Even authoritative rules that were inconsistent with the framework would be better understood since students would now have a benchmark against which to judge the "deviant" standard.

Not only does a conceptual framework have a potentially important role to play in education, but it can also serve to provide important support for accountancy's claim to hold professional status. Sociologists and others often define a profession as having (among other attributes) a cognitive base –a generalized and systematic central knowledge base. It seems reasonable to suggest, therefore, that if a coherent, published conceptual framework existed, and if practice evolved out of applying that framework to specific issues, we would have a better claim to professional status.

The Case Against

While we obviously favour the idea of a Canadian conceptual framework, we must not ignore the "cons," the most obvious of which are technical in nature.

For one thing, it may be difficult for the different groups, both within and outside the profession, who may have different views on the nature and objectives of financial reporting, to agree on a single conceptual framework.

Witness the 10 years the FASB has been working on its conceptual framework. Indeed, throughout the period of development of a conceptual framework, some parties who hold opposing views may be just using the opportunity to provide support for different specific accounting rules, based on motivation fueled by self-interest.[6] Because of the profound and pervasive role that a conceptual framework will play, we should not expect that the process of agreeing on one will be easy or of short duration. After all, the development of any constitution is often fraught with bitterness that extends over a considerable period of time, until a workable compromise and consensus is achieved. An interesting question (that we do not address) involves the "political" question of how to develop a voting mechanism for adopting a conceptual framework – it seems that "politics" is unavoidable in accounting.

Because a Canadian conceptual framework could very well be different from, say, a US or UK framework – reflecting cultural, political and environmental differences – this would logically lead to different financial reporting standards, providing a good rationale for creating a unique Canadian conceptual framework. If, however, the conceptual frameworks of different countries were to differ for no good reason, then we might simply be creating more unjustified differences in international accounting.

Of course, we should not ignore the direct costs involved in developing a conceptual framework, nor the opportunity costs to standard setters, practitioners and others who would be called on to make representations in this regard. Proponents virtually take it as an article of faith that such costs would be small compared to the benefits to be derived, but that remains to be seen.

Consider, also, that a conceptual framework may be too flexible, too general in nature. As William W. Holder and Kimberly

---

[6]R.L. Watts and J.L. Zimmerman describe similar scenarios in "The Demand for and Supply of Accounting Theories: The Market for Excuses," *The Accounting Review* 54 (1979), pp. 273-305. Recently, their view has been criticized. See, for example, E.A. Lowe, A.G. Puxty and R.C. Laughlin, "Simple Theories for Complex Processes: Accounting Policy and the Market for Myopia," *Journal of Accounting and Public Policy* 2 (1983), pp. 19-42.

Ham Eudy point out, this would lead to "incomplete or inadequate conceptual expressions ... to resolve operational controversies in practice."[7] For a conceptual framework to do its job adequately, it should not be possible to use it to support opposing accounting treatments for the same accounting event.

The other side of the coin is that a written conceptual framework may be too inflexible and thereby constrain professional judgment. Of course, the degree to which such a framework is flexible or inflexible will presumably reflect - at least in the long run - the preferences and influences of the parties affected by it.

Now that we have discussed the pros and cons, we are ready to take a closer look at the CICA's research study, *Corporate Reporting: Its Future Evolution*, written by Professor Edward Stamp, FCA, on behalf of an institute study group. Keep in mind that what we need and what we are arguing for is a well-designed supportable written framework that will serve the profession well over an extended period of time.

An Overview of the Study

The study's first chapter outlines an interesting cross-section of problems that the study group thought accounting standard setters must address:

- Ambiguity of "economic reality."
- Nature of accounting (an art? a science?).
- What are accounting's underlying concepts? Are they permanent?

---

[7]William W. Holder and Kimberly Ham Eudy, "A Framework for Building An Accounting Constitution," *Journal of Accounting, Auditing and Finance* (Winter 1982).

- To whom are public companies accountable?
- Standard setters must have a set of criteria to help them.
- Costs and benefits of standards must be considered.
- Users and preparers may have conflicts of interest.
- Possible implications of the efficient market literature.
- Is uniformity possible or desirable?
- Should some indication of "margin of error" be reported?
- Can user needs be satisfied by one set of "general purpose" financial statements?
- How should standards be enforced?

Chapter 2 covers "some perplexing conceptual issues," such as accounting allocations, difficulties encountered in defining income, the choice of capital maintenance concept and valuation bases for assets and liabilities.

In Chapter 3, the study group sets out its reasons for believing accounting standards are needed, fundamental among them the separation of ownership and management, and the influence of large public corporations on several groups in society. Brief mention is also made of some of the objections to standardization raised by management and public accountants. These the study group dismisses, suggesting that standard setters should consider the potential costs (for example, loss of competitive position) as well as the benefits of new standards. Standards, they say, "should be framed in such a way as not to stifle innovation." The chapter concludes with the comment that the efficient market literature does not negate accountants' concerns with either information overload or the needs of other users (that is, those not acting in the stock market).

It is in Chapter 4, which deals with the objectives of corporate financial reporting, and in the following four chapters, that the study group's approach to setting accounting standards is explained. In brief, its approach is user oriented and thus similar in major respects to the FASB's conceptual framework. Chapters 5 and 6 discuss users and their information needs and Chapter 7 the criteria for assessing the quality of standards and of corporate accountability. Chapter 8 addresses the issue of differences among users' needs.

Chapter 9, focusing on the development of a conceptual framework, begins by asking, "What is the nature of accounting?" and concludes that it is most like law. Further, because the study group sees problems in portraying reality, it concludes that adopting an authoritarian approach in which accounting concepts such as revenues, expenses, assets and so on are given formal definitions is not useful.

At this point, the research study provides a short critique of the FASB's conceptual framework, arguing that proceeding from a set of definitions (for assets, liabilities and so on) is inappropriate because (1) different users may have different preferred definitions, thus any the FASB proposes must be too general, and (2) some important concepts may be omitted from the definitions. On this last point, the study says that the FASB's definition of an asset "does not specify the level of aggregation of separate items that are to be considered as an asset."

Chapter 10 dismisses the FASB's conceptual framework project as being unsuitable for Canada (because it is too normative, axiomatic and narrowly oriented toward investors), explaining that it is natural there should be differences of approach between the two countries due to environmental differences. The focus then shifts to the chapter's main topic, a proposed conceptual framework, the basis for which was set forth in Chapters 4 through 8.

The study argues for more resources for the Accounting Standards Committee (AcSC), justification by the AcSC of its positions by reference to the criteria and user needs set out in previous chapters, and that it "should be made clear to anyone (or any organization) that wishes to comment on exposure drafts or standards, or make proposals for change, that their argument should be justified in relation to the same sets of criteria that the Research Committee itself uses in justifying its pronouncements when they are issued." The study group concludes the chapter by saying that a rule-book approach (such as the FASB's) "runs counter to our notions of professionalism," and that a framework should follow a common law approach based on precedent and a means of appeal. This procedural suggestion is perhaps one of the study's major contributions.

Chapter 11 examines several "extensions" of financial disclosure, and strongly recommends "that a full explanation should be provided by the [AcSC] as to how the standard meets the objectives and criteria laid down in this Study, and how it is expected that the information resulting from the implementation of the new standard will be useful to the various user groups in meeting their needs."

Chapter 12 lists some of the study's implications for the AcSC and for auditors: "better standards (clearly based upon known criteria) should be easier to apply and interpret"). The study ends with this interesting statement that, "to the extent that the [AcSC] is unwilling to adopt any of the proposals in this study, it should be prepared to explain its reasons for taking such a position."

An Evaluation of the Study

The writing of conceptual frameworks is not a new activity in accounting. They have appeared, in various forms, more or less regularly for over 40 years.[8] What distinguishes the more recent writings from those of the past is the fact that the institutions that sponsored them and the authors who wrote them hoped they would have a fundamental impact on the structure of financial accounting and reporting. As the CICA study group wrote: "It is hoped that this study as a whole will provide a blueprint for the evolution of a rational and generally acceptable system of accounting standards in Canada." Was the study group being too optimistic?

Approach to Standard Setting

The sequence the study group suggested to setting accounting standards – moving from objectives to users to user needs (criteria) and, finally, to standards – is a "user-oriented, deductive" approach and, as such, is similar to the FASB's conceptual framework (although, as we shall see, the particular components are somewhat different). At first glance, this approach appears to represent a significant break from the way standards were set in the past (namely, by codifying existing practice – an inductive approach – and by reacting to current crises). Indeed, eminent accounting academics have for years argued for a user-oriented, deductive approach to standard setting. Such an approach is normative in the sense that it provides a means of accepting or rejecting accounting methods.[9]

---

[8]One of the earliest examples of such a conceptual framework is found in W.A. Paton and A.C. Littleton, *An Introduction to Corporate Accounting Standards*, Monograph No. 3 (American Accounting Association, 1940).

[9]Robert R. Sterling, "A Statement of Basic Accounting Theory: A Review Article," *Journal of Accounting Research* (Spring 1967), pp. 95-112, and *Theory of the Measurement of Enterprise Income* (Lawrence, Kansas: The University Press of Kansas, 1970).

The broad approach the study group has set out is certainly appealing. As our concern is with whether the study will likely result in a successful normative approach to standard setting, we will focus on what we regard as three important preconditions for success which we found lacking in the study.

Three Preconditions to Success

First, as Watts and Zimmerman point out,[10] normative approaches to accounting decision making cannot hope to succeed unless they are based on an understanding of the factors influencing the standard-setting process, especially the behaviour of various interest groups. "This understanding is necessary to determine if prescriptions from normative theories ... are feasible." In other words, positive theory must precede a normative approach to decision making. A normative approach cannot stand alone. We must have a good idea of the likelihood of affected groups supporting a proposed "ideal" standard; in so doing, the CICA might not have had to suspend its standard on foreign currency translation in February 1979, just four months after its release, for example.

The study group criticized the FASB's conceptual framework for being "normative, even authoritarian" because it proceeded to build its user-oriented scheme from basic axioms and definitions set out in Statement of Financial Accounting Concepts No. 3, "Elements of Financial Statements of Business Enterprises" (1980). Nevertheless, though its approach is not built on a so-called axiomatic base, it is virtually identical in general outline to the FASB: both follow

---

[10]Ross L. Watts and Jerold L. Zimmerman, "Towards a Positive Theory of the Determination of Accounting Standards," *The Accounting Review* (January 1978), pp. 112-34.

the deductive, user-oriented approach flowing from objectives. Simply put, both "suffer" from being normative.

To be fair to the CICA research study, however, it does couple its normative approach with a plea that standards must win general acceptance, and also suggests a "common law" approach to implementing its standard-setting system. The problem with the study is that it does not go far enough. That is, it does not explicitly identify the need for positive research in accounting as a prerequisite for its normative approach, but merely urges that standards that pass its criteria and meet its objectives be publicly justified: "To win general acceptance ... it is necessary that there be public justification of the standards and a public explanation as to how the standards are seen as meeting the criteria and the objectives of good financial reporting."

This leads to a second precondition for success – the selection of objectives. As the study aptly points out, "The main reason for defining the objectives for corporate reporting is to assist in the process of devising adequate means for achieving them." Simply put, under a user-oriented, normative approach, defining objectives is the fundamental step; a proposed standard can score high on several criteria, but if it fails to meet the objectives of corporate reporting, it is not a legitimate candidate for an accounting standard.

The point we wish to make is that no only do the Canadian study's objectives, which it sets out in Chapter 4, differ from the FASB's (in SFAC 1), but that the difference is symptomatic of a general feature of any approach to accounting decision making requiring that objectives be pre-specified; namely, that they must be defined not in relation to an individual, but to a social activity (financial accounting) and, thus, reflect the objectives of user groups. Users may not have uniform objectives for corporate reporting (as there are generally several diverse, and often competing, categories of users). The study group recognized that problem and dealt with it in Chapter 8 by suggesting that alternative measures be disclosed; deciding on the limits of such additional disclosures might be difficult, though.

A more fundamental problem is raised by the study group's use of the "dominant group" approach which, in the case of user-oriented schemes for setting accounting standards, ignores the objectives of other groups and individuals affected by corporate reporting. Dopuch and Sunder put it thus: "A user-primacy notion in the selection of objectives of financial accounting which ignores how firms' managers are likely to adjust their behaviour to the new information system (and how this adjustment in management behaviour will affect the interests of the so-called users) represents a very short-sighted view of the whole problem. As such, solutions derived from this simplified approach will not work. A similar argument could be offered regarding the exclusion of the auditors from the "primary" groups whose interests must be explicitly considered in any realistic set of objectives of financial accounting."[11]

Certainly, Dopuch and Sunder's pessimism concerning the user-oriented approach to defining accounting objectives is of great concern and has major implications for such issues as "general acceptance"; that is, should all groups involved in the accounting process accept (or at least accede to) new accounting standards? If standards are set in ways that ignore the objectives of nonuser participants (managers and auditors, for example) in the accounting process, the likelihood of general acceptance decreases. For

---

[11]Nicholas Dopuch and Shyam Sunder, "FASB's Statements on Objectives and Elements of Financial Accounting: A Review," *The Accounting Review* (January 1980), p. 15.

instance, the FASB's Statement of Financial Accounting Standards No. 8, "Accounting for the Translation of Foreign Currency Transactions and Foreign Currency Financial Statements," was apparently promulgated without consideration for the objectives of managers of multinational companies (which may have adversely affected their bonuses, say), consequently, they lobbied intensely against it.

By arguing for the withdrawal from a dominant (user) group approach to formulating objectives of corporate reporting, Dopuch and Sunder appear to support the notion that the objectives of other groups, such as auditors and managers, should be included in the corporate reporting objectives. Such a view would tie in very neatly with a positive approach to accounting. It seems reasonable to suggest, then, that the objectives of major participant groups in the accounting process (corporate management, accountants and various users) should be incorporated into these objectives, if only to improve the likelihood of these new standards being "generally accepted."

Thus, we view *Corporate Reporting: Its Future Evolution's* "user-orientation" in formulating objectives as too narrow, possibly leading to conflicts among participants in the accounting process. Paradoxically, the Canadian study's objectives are much broader than the FASB's, and may in fact be too broad to be useful. The study group itself, though it was aware of this trap in setting objectives, did not appear to have heeded its own advice since the study's objectives - being broad - are not as useful as the FASB's in performing the basic function of objectives, namely, helping to select standards.

A third precondition for success is that the users must be carefully defined. This precondition is closely related to the objectives issue just discussed. The study group used the concept of "accountability" to identify the users of corporate financial statements, and ended up with 15 different categories, each with a legitimate interest in receiving and using published financial statements and wide variety of needs. The criteria for being included as a "user" is not spelled out in sufficient detail and, consequently, the list suffers from being not persuasive.

The study also claims that the "range of user groups is much broader than that being considered by the FASB" since the latter focuses on information for investment and credit decisions. In its SFAC No. 1, however, FASB specifically assumes that information that satisfied investors and creditors should be useful to all parties interested in an enterprise. The bulk of users' needs identified in the Canadian study is indeed closely related (if not identical to) the needs of investors and creditors. Thus, the differences between it and the FASB on this score are more apparent than real. Indeed, by explicitly identifying so many diverse user groups, the study group may impede the standard-setting process by emphasizing the differences in information needs between user groups, rather than the commonalities.

The General Quality of Argument and Evidence

Even though the Canadian study and the FASB's conceptual framework are similar in many substantive areas, major differences are evident. The differences involve mainly the degree to which positions and conclusions taken in the study are supported by argument and/or empirical evidence. Even though the study calls for research (to identify users' needs, for example), it appears not to have employed substantive research. For example, the study group's choice of approach to formulating financial accounting objectives is not supported by argument or empirical evidence. The list of (overly broad) objectives set out in Chapter 4 is only weakly supported, and constraints are often intermingled with objectives.

18

Much is made of environmental differences between Canada and the United States – and the influence of these purported differences on setting standards – without providing convincing evidence as to the differences and their effects. The listing goes on.

Did the Study Fulfil its Terms of Reference?

The terms were:

- To identify the various groups who have a legitimate claim to corporate information.
- To examine the objectives of corporate reports published in the private sector and the underlying concepts on which they rest, and to recommend the form of financial reporting needed.
- To identify the entities that should report publicly.
- To identify the type of information that each reporting entity should provide to the various groups.
- To consider the implications to the auditor of its conclusions.
- To make specific proposals for implementing the conclusions arrived at.

As Sterling, quoted earlier, said of the American Accounting Association's 1966 Committee to Prepare a Statement of Basic Accounting Theory: "This is indeed a large order, so large that hardly anyone would be surprised if the committee failed." We can say the same of the CICA's study in terms of the degree to which its terms of reference went unfulfilled.

Keep in mind, however, that failure by a committee – especially one engaged in suggesting rules for institutional decision making in a field such as accounting – is not necessarily a bad thing. First, even if the document it produced failed as a whole, parts of it might still be important (as is the case with the study). Second, failure is almost guaranteed since the users of such a document have diverse goals and points of view and may be expected to react to the proposed recommendations using criteria not used by the committee (and possibly not felt to be relevant at the time). Indeed, likely the most important contribution a work such as the research study can make is to stimulate reaction by groups with different points of view. At least their biases will then be made public.

Let us now examine the degree to which each term of reference was, in our estimation, fulfilled.

The first term of reference ("to identify the various groups who have a legitimate claim to corporate information") forced the study group to adopt a user-oriented approach to formulating accounting objectives. An important contribution of the study, when evaluated in this light, is the selection of the criterion of accountability as a means of identifying user groups. The notion of accountability goes beyond statutory and contractual relationships and leads to the problem of identifying when the accountability relationship is strong enough between a corporation and a particular group to require that that group be included as a user of financial accounting information and thus have its needs considered when standards are set. This is a complex and interesting issue. Within the framework of a user-oriented approach, the study group succeeded.

The second term of reference consisted of three parts. The first called for an examination of the objectives of corporate reports published in the private sector. It is not clear whether this was to be a survey of what current objectives appeared to be, or a normative exercise in defining what objectives should be. In any event, the study group opted for the latter, and produced an overly broad, user-oriented list of weakly supported objectives: As for the second part ("examine the ... underlying concepts on which they rest"), there is no evidence of this being attempted, nor is there evidence of the third part ("recommend the form of financial reporting needed") being fulfilled, aside from some vague statements about possible extensions of financial disclosure in Chapter 11.

The third term of reference ("to identify the entities that should report publicly") is fulfilled by fiat early in the study, when the group writes that its study "is confined to the accounting standardization problems of those financial statements, subject to audit, that are published by Canadian public companies." Is this what the CICA intended when it set out that term of reference? Was it a reasonable term of reference? Without answers to those questions, we cannot come to a conclusion about the importance of the research study with respect to the third term of reference. We suspect, however, that a more substantive consideration of the issue was called for (for example, "Do large, private companies have accountability relationships to various outside groups, which would lead one to conclude that they should report publicly?"). Thus, even though the study group fulfilled this term of reference by fiat, it certainly did not succeed with respect to it third term of reference.

Nor did it succeed with the fourth, "to identify the type of information that each reporting entity should provide to the various groups." A mere list of broad user needs (as in Chapter 6) does not make such an identification. As for the fifth term of reference ("to consider the implications to the auditor of the conclusions of the study"), those implications are spelled out in chapter 12. And Chapter 10 sets out "specific proposals for implementing the conclusions arrived at in the study," as requested by the sixth term of reference, although they are somewhat vague.

On balance, it seems fair to conclude that Sterling's comments are fitting for the study group. The terms of reference and the final report do not bear enough resemblance to each other. Perhaps the terms of reference were unfair. Maybe they were unattainable.

The Canadian vs. the FASB study

The study group argues that because Canadian and US environments differ, the approach taken in applying the standard-setting process should as well. Since such a view has important implications for standard setting in both countries, it should be based on persuasive and sound reasoning.

This issue of environmental differences is first raised in Chapter 1, which states that the criticism in Canada "has been less vocal and its effects have been less damaging" than in the United States. It suggests that the reasons for these differences are "the differences in national character" and differences in the "legal and constitutional environment."

The study group's inventory of differences between the two countries set out in Chapter 10, includes the following:

- "The history of the two countries is quite different. The United States broke away from Britain as a result of a Revolutionary War ... Canada, by contrast has evolved ... and its parliamentary and legal systems ... are based upon the British model."
- "Within the United States, the West was won with the gun. More orderly means were used in Canada, and Canadians still tend to take a less adversary approach towards the resolution of their problems than is the custom in the United States."
- "There is a greater emphasis on social justice and social welfare in Canada."

- "A wider spectrum of political belief is evident in Canada than it is in the United States."
- "The climate of public opinion in Canada is receptive to the notion of wider corporate responsibility ..."

Even if those statements were true (and the research study's authors would be hardput to prove the value-judgments among them), the study does not develop a case for showing how those differences lead to a different approach in implementing the process of standard setting. The study group members have convinced themselves, however, that they have made a sound argument and, thus, can go on to suggest a "common law" approach for implementing a suitable standard-setting process for Canada.

Food for Thought

We must conclude that the research study contains significant deficiencies. Thus, it seems reasonable to suggest that more thought be given to formulating a Canadian conceptual framework. By reacting to the study, practitioners and others interested in Canadian accounting – and in international accounting in general – can, we hope, begin the process. Indeed, as we said, earlier, perhaps the most important contribution of a work such as the study is to stimulate reaction.

Joel H. Amernic, FCA, an associate professor in the Faculty of Management Studies, University of Toronto, has been chairman of its accounting division for the past two years and is the accounting coordinator of the Ontario Institute's School of Accountancy.

W. Morley Lemon, Ph.D., CPA, CA, associate chairman of the accounting group and associate professor of accounting at the University of Waterloo, is presently serving on the Advisory Group for the CICA research study Materiality in Auditing.

financial statement concepts

TABLE OF CONTENTS

	PARAGRAPH
Purpose and scope	.01-.06
Objective of financial statements	.07-.12
Benefit versus cost constraint	.13
Materiality	.14
Qualitative characteristics	.15-.21
Elements of financial statements	.22-.35
Recognition criteria	.36-.43
Measurement	.44-.47
Generally accepted accounting principles	.48-.50

PURPOSE AND SCOPE

The purpose of this Section is to describe the concepts underlying the development and use of accounting principles in the general purpose financial statements (hereafter referred to as financial statements) of profit oriented enterprises.[1] Such financial statements are designed to meet the common information needs of external users of financial information about an entity. .01

The Committee expects this Section to be used by preparers of financial statements and accounting practitioners in exercising their professional judgment as to the application of generally accepted accounting principles and in establishing accounting policies in areas in which accounting principles are developing. .02

This Section does not establish standards for particular measurement or disclosure issues. Nothing in the Section overrides any specific Recommendation in another Section of the Handbook or any other accounting principle considered to be generally accepted. Any inconsistency between this Section and another Section will be reviewed by the Committee when that other Section is re-examined. .03

Financial statements

Financial statements normally include a balance sheet, income statement, statement of retained earnings and statement of changes in financial position. Notes to financial statements and supporting schedules to which the financial statements are cross-referenced are an integral part of such statements. .04

[1] The Committee is developing financial statement concepts for non-profit organizations in a separate stage of the Financial Statement Concepts project.

1000.04

.05 The content of financial statements is usually limited to financial information about transactions and events. Financial statements are based on representations of past, rather than future, transactions and events although they often require estimates to be made in anticipation of future transactions and events and include measurements that may, by their nature, be approximations.

.06 Financial statements form part of the process of financial reporting that includes also, for example, information in annual reports outside the financial statements and in prospectuses. While many financial statement concepts also apply to such information, this Section deals specifically only with financial statements.

OBJECTIVE OF FINANCIAL STATEMENTS

.07 In the Canadian economic environment, the production of goods and the provision of services are, to a significant extent, carried out by investor-owned business entities in the private sector and to a lesser extent by government-owned business entities. Debt and equity markets and financial institutions act as exchange mechanisms for investment resources.

.08 Entity ownership is often segregated from management, creating a need for external communication of economic information about the entity to investors. For the purposes of this Section, investors include present and potential debt and equity investors and their advisers. Creditors and others who do not have internal access to entity information also need external reports to obtain the information they require. In the case of financial institutions, investors, creditors and others include depositors and policyholders.

.09 It is not practicable to expect financial statements to satisfy the many and varied information needs of all external users of information about an entity. Consequently, the objective of financial statements focuses primarily on information needs of investors and creditors. Financial statements prepared to satisfy these needs are often used by others who need external reporting of information about an entity.

.10 Investors and creditors are interested, for the purpose of making resource allocation decisions, in predicting the ability of the entity to earn income and generate cash flows in the future to meet its obligations and to generate a return on investment.

.11 Investors also require information about how the management of an entity has discharged its stewardship responsibility to those that have provided resources to the entity.

Objective

.12 The objective of financial statements is to communicate information that is useful to investors, creditors and other users in making resource allocation decisions and/or assessing management stewardship. Consequently, financial statements provide information about:

1000.05

(a) an entity's economic resources, obligations and equity;

(b) changes in an entity's economic resources, obligations and equity; and

(c) the economic performance of the entity.

BENEFIT VERSUS COST CONSTRAINT

The benefits expected to arise from providing information in financial statements should exceed the cost of doing so. This constraint applies to the development of accounting standards by the Committee. It is also a consideration in the preparation of financial statements in accordance with those standards, for example, in considering disclosure of information beyond that required by the standards. The Committee recognizes that the benefits and costs may accrue to different parties and that the evaluation of the nature and amount of benefits and costs is substantially a judgmental process.

.13

MATERIALITY

Investors, creditors and other users are interested in information that may affect their decision making. Materiality is the term used to describe the significance of financial statement information to decision makers. An item of information, or an aggregate of items, is material if it is probable that its omission or misstatement would influence or change a decision. Materiality is a matter of professional judgment in the particular circumstances.

.14

QUALITATIVE CHARACTERISTICS

Qualitative characteristics define and describe the attributes of information provided in financial statements that make that information useful to investors, creditors and other users. The four principal qualitative characteristics are understandability, relevance, reliability and comparability.

.15

Understandability

For the information provided in financial statements to be useful, it must be capable of being understood by investors, creditors and other users. Investors, creditors and other users are assumed to have a reasonable understanding of business and economic activities and accounting, together with a willingness to study the information with reasonable diligence.

.16

Relevance

For the information provided in financial statements to be useful, it must be relevant to the decisions made by investors, creditors and other users. Information is relevant by its nature when it can influence the decisions of investors, creditors and other users by helping them evaluate the financial impact of past, present or future transactions and events or confirm, or correct, previous evaluations. Relevance is achieved through information that has predictive value or feedback value and by its timeliness.

.17

(a) **Predictive value and feedback value**

Information that helps investors, creditors and other users to predict future income and cash flows has predictive value. Although information provided in financial statements will not normally be a prediction in itself, it may be useful in making predictions. The predictive value of the income statement, for example, is enhanced if abnormal items are separately disclosed. Information that confirms or corrects previous predictions has feedback value. Information often has both predictive value and feedback value.

(b) **Timeliness**

For information to be useful for decision making, it must be received by the decision maker before it loses its capacity to influence decisions. The usefulness of information for decision making declines as time elapses.

Reliability

.18 For the information provided in financial statements to be useful, it must be reliable. Information is reliable when it is in agreement with the actual underlying transactions and events, the agreement is capable of independent verification and the information is reasonably free from error and bias. Reliability is achieved through representational faithfulness, verifiability and neutrality. Neutrality is affected by the use of conservatism in making judgments under conditions of uncertainty.

(a) **Representational faithfulness**

Representational faithfulness is achieved when transactions and events affecting the entity are presented in financial statements in a manner that is in agreement with the actual underlying transactions and events. Thus, transactions and events are accounted for and presented in a manner that conveys their substance rather than necessarily their legal or other form.

The substance of transactions and events may not always be consistent with that apparent from their legal or other form. To determine the substance of a transaction or event, it may be necessary to consider a group of related transactions and events as a whole. The determination of the substance of a transaction or event will be a matter of professional judgment in the circumstances.

(b) **Verifiability**

The financial statement representation of a transaction or event is verifiable if knowledgeable and independent observers would concur that it is in agreement with the actual underlying transaction or event with a reasonable degree of precision. Verifiability focuses on the correct application of a basis of measurement rather than its appropriateness.

1000.18

(c) **Neutrality**

Information is neutral when it is free from bias that would lead investors, creditors and other users towards making decisions that are influenced by the way the information is measured or presented. Bias in measurement occurs when a measure tends to consistently overstate or understate the items being measured. In the selection of accounting principles, bias may occur when the selection is made with the interests of particular users or with particular economic or political objectives in mind.

Financial statements that do not include everything necessary for faithful representation of transactions and events affecting the entity would be incomplete and, therefore, potentially biased.

(d) **Conservatism**

Use of conservatism in making judgments under conditions of uncertainty affects the neutrality of financial statements in an acceptable manner. When uncertainty exists, estimates of a conservative nature attempt to ensure net assets or net income are not overstated. However, conservatism does not encompass the deliberate understatement of net assets or net income.

Comparability

Comparability is a characteristic of the relationship between two .19 pieces of information rather than of a particular piece of information by itself. It enables investors, creditors and other users to identify similarities in and differences between the information provided by two sets of financial statements. Comparability is important when comparing the financial statements of two different entities and when comparing the financial statements of the same entity over two periods or at two different points in time.

Comparability in the financial statements of an entity is enhanced .20 when the same accounting policies are used consistently from period to period. Consistency helps prevent misconceptions that might result from the application of different accounting policies in different periods. When a change in accounting policy is deemed to be appropriate, disclosure of the effects of the change may be necessary to maintain comparability.

Qualitative characteristics trade-off

In practice, a trade-off between qualitative characteristics is often .21 necessary, particularly between relevance and reliability. For example, there is often a trade-off between the timeliness of producing financial statements and the reliability of the information reported in the statements. Generally, the aim is to achieve an appropriate balance among the characteristics in order to meet the objective of financial statements. The relative importance of the characteristics in different cases is a matter of professional judgment.

ELEMENTS OF FINANCIAL STATEMENTS

.22 Elements of financial statements are the basic categories of items portrayed therein in order to meet the objective of financial statements. There are two types of elements: those that describe the economic resources, obligations and equity of an entity at a point in time, and those that describe changes in economic resources, obligations and equity. Notes to financial statements, which are useful for the purpose of clarification or further explanation of the items in financial statements, while an integral part of financial statements, are not considered to be an element.

.23 The elements defined herein are the most common categories of items portrayed in financial statements. The existence of other items is not precluded. In practice, a balance sheet may include, as a category of assets or liabilities, items that result from a delay in income statement recognition. Criteria for the recognition of items in financial statements are discussed in paragraph 1000.39.

.24 Net income is the residual amount after expenses and losses are deducted from revenues and gains. Net income generally includes all transactions and events increasing or decreasing the equity of the entity except those that result from equity contributions and distributions. Investors, creditors and other users frequently use net income as a measure of economic performance.

Assets

.25 Assets are economic resources controlled by an entity as a result of past transactions or events from which future economic benefits may be obtained.

.26 Assets have three essential characteristics:
   (a) they embody a future benefit that involves a capacity, singly or in combination with other assets, to contribute directly or indirectly to future net cash flows;
   (b) the entity can control access to the benefit; and
   (c) the transaction or event giving rise to the entity's right to, or control of, the benefit has already occurred.

.27 It is not essential for control of access to the benefit to be legally enforceable for a resource to be an asset, provided the entity can control its use by other means.

Liabilities

.28 Liabilities are obligations of an entity arising from past transactions or events, the settlement of which may result in the transfer or use of assets, provision of services or other yielding of economic benefits in the future.

1000.22

Liabilities have three essential characteristics: .29

(a) they embody a duty or responsibility to others that entails settlement by future transfer or use of assets, provision of services or other yielding of economic benefits, at a specified or determinable date, on occurrence of a specified event, or on demand;

(b) the duty or responsibility obligates the entity leaving it little or no discretion to avoid it; and

(c) the transaction or event obligating the entity has already occurred.

Liabilities do not have to be legally enforceable provided that they .30 otherwise meet the definition of liabilities; they can be based on equitable or constructive obligations. An equitable obligation is a duty based on ethical or moral considerations. A constructive obligation is one that can be inferred from the facts in a particular situation as opposed to a contractually based obligation.

Equity

Equity is the ownership interest in the assets of an entity after de- .31 ducting its liabilities. While equity in total is a residual, it includes specific categories of items, for example, types of share capital, contributed surplus and retained earnings.

Revenues

Revenues are increases in economic resources, either by way of .32 inflows or enhancements of assets or reductions of liabilities, resulting from the ordinary activities of an entity, normally from the sale of goods, the rendering of services or the use by others of entity resources yielding rent, interest, royalties or dividends.

Expenses

Expenses are decreases in economic resources, either by way of .33 outflows or reductions of assets or incurrences of liabilities, resulting from the ordinary revenue-earning activities of an entity.

Gains

Gains are increases in equity from peripheral or incidental transac- .34 tions and events affecting an entity and from all other transactions, events and circumstances affecting the entity except those that result from revenues or equity contributions.

Losses

Losses are decreases in equity from peripheral or incidental transac- .35 tions and events affecting an entity and from all other transactions, events and circumstances affecting the entity except those that result from expenses or distributions of equity.

RECOGNITION CRITERIA

.36 Recognition is the process of including an item in the financial statements of an entity. Recognition consists of the addition of the amount involved into statement totals together with a narrative description of the item (e.g. "inventory" or "sales") in a statement. Similar items may be grouped together in the financial statements for the purpose of presentation.

.37 Recognition means inclusion of an item within one or more individual statements and does not mean disclosure in the notes to the financial statements. Notes either provide further details about items recognized in the financial statements, or provide information about items that do not meet the criteria for recognition and thus are not recognized in the financial statements.

.38 The recognition criteria below provide general guidance on when an item is recognized in the financial statements. Whether any particular item is recognized or not will require the application of professional judgment in considering whether the specific circumstances meet the recognition criteria.

.39 The recognition criteria are as follows:

(a) the item has an appropriate basis of measurement and a reasonable estimate can be made of the amount involved; and

(b) for items involving obtaining or giving up future economic benefits, it is probable that such benefits will be obtained or given up.

.40 It is possible that an item will meet the definition of an element but still not be recognized in the financial statements because it is not probable that future economic benefits will be obtained or given up or because a reasonable estimate cannot be made of the amount involved. It may be appropriate to provide information about items that do not meet the recognition criteria in notes to the financial statements.

.41 Items recognized in financial statements are accounted for in accordance with the accrual basis of accounting. The accrual basis of accounting recognizes the effect of transactions and events in the period in which the transactions and events occur, regardless of whether there has been a receipt or payment of cash or its equivalent. Accrual accounting encompasses deferrals that occur when a cash receipt or payment occurs prior to the criteria for recognition of revenue or expense being satisfied.

.42 Revenues are generally recognized when performance is achieved and reasonable assurance regarding measurement and collectibility of the consideration exists. Gains are generally recognized when realized.

1000.36

Expenses and losses are generally recognized when an expenditure or .43
previously recognized asset does not have future economic benefit. In
some cases, a transaction or event results in the recognition of both
revenues and expenses that are linked to each other in a cause and effect relationship, in which case, the expense is matched with the revenue and included in income in the same accounting period. In other
cases, expenses are not linked with revenues but are related to a period on the basis of transactions or events occurring in that period or
by allocation. The cost of assets that benefit more than one period is
allocated over the periods benefited.

MEASUREMENT

Measurement is the process of determining the amount at which an .44
item is recognized in the financial statements. There are a number of
bases on which an amount can be measured. However, financial statements are prepared primarily using the historical cost basis of measurement whereby transactions and events are recognized in financial
statements at the amount of cash or cash equivalents paid or received
or the fair value ascribed to them when they took place.

Other bases of measurement are also used but only in limited circum- .45
stances. They include:
(a) Replacement cost – the amount that would be needed currently to
    acquire an equivalent asset. This may be used, for example, when
    inventories are valued at the lower of historical cost and replace-
    ment cost.
(b) Realizable value – the amount that would be received by selling
    an asset. This may be used, for example, to value temporary and
    portfolio investments. Market value may be used to estimate real-
    izable value when a market for an asset exists.
(c) Present value – the discounted amount of future cash flows ex-
    pected to be received from an asset or required to settle a liabili-
    ty. This is used, for example, to estimate the cost of pension bene-
    fits.

The concept of capital maintenance used in financial statements also .46
affects measurement because income in an economic sense exists only
after the capital of an entity has been maintained. Thus, income is the
increase or decrease in the amount of capital contributions and distributions. Financial statements are prepared with capital maintenance
measured in financial terms and with no adjustment being made for
the effect on capital of a change in the general purchasing power of the
currency during the period.

Financial statements are prepared on the assumption that the entity is .47
a going concern, meaning it will continue in operation for the foreseeable future and will be able to realize assets and discharge liabilities in
the normal course of operations. Different bases of measurement may
be appropriate when the entity is not expected to continue in operation for the foreseeable future.

GENERALLY ACCEPTED ACCOUNTING PRINCIPLES

.48 Generally accepted accounting principles is the term used to describe the basis on which financial statements are normally prepared. There are special circumstances where a different basis of accounting may be appropriate, for example, in financial statements prepared in accordance with regulatory legislation or contractual requirements.

.49 The term generally accepted accounting principles encompasses not only specific rules, practices and procedures relating to particular circumstances but also broad principles and conventions of general application, including the underlying concepts described in this Section. Specifically, generally accepted accounting principles comprise the Accounting Recommendations in the Handbook and, when a matter is not covered by a Recommendation, other accounting principles that either:

(a) are generally accepted by virtue of their use in similar circumstances by a significant number of entities in Canada; or

(b) are consistent with the Recommendations in the Handbook and are developed through the exercise of professional judgment, including consultation with other informed accountants where appropriate, and the application of the concepts described in this Section. In exercising professional judgment, established principles for analogous situations dealt with in the Handbook would be taken into account and reference would be made to:

(i) other relevant matters dealt with in the Handbook;

(ii) practice in similar circumstances;

(iii) Accounting Guidelines published by the Accounting Standards Steering Committee;

(iv) International Accounting Standards published by the International Accounting Standards Committee;

(v) standards published by bodies authorized to establish financial accounting standards in other jurisdictions; and

(vi) CICA research studies and other sources of accounting literature such as textbooks and journals.

The relative importance of these various sources is a matter of professional judgment in the circumstances.

.50 In those rare circumstances where following a Handbook Recommendation would result in misleading financial statements, generally accepted accounting principles encompass appropriate alternative principles. When assessing whether a departure from Handbook Recommendation is appropriate, consideration would be given to:

(a) the objective of the Handbook Recommendation and why that objective is not achieved or is not relevant in the particular circumstances;

1000.48

(b) how the entity's circumstances differ from those of other entities which follow the Handbook Recommendation; and

(c) the underlying principles of accounting alternatives by referring to other sources (see paragraph 1000.49).

The identification of these circumstances is a matter of professional judgment. However, there is a strong presumption that adherence to Handbook Recommendations results in appropriate presentation and that a departure from such Recommendations represents a departure from generally accepted accounting principles.

[THE NEXT PAGE IS PAGE 201]

Section IV: Legislation, Inquiries and Regulation

Financial Statement Disclosure and Corporate Law: The Canadian Experience

GEORGE J. MURPHY*

The changes that have taken place over time in Canada relating to the financial statement disclosure requirements of Canadian corporate law have had a variety of sources of influence. These influences have come from both England and the United States as well as from within Canada. Canadian legislation has at times been ahead of and at other times lagged behind English and American legislation. The purpose of this paper is to chronicle the changes in legislated financial statement disclosure requirements and to indicate, where possible, the source of the influences which gave rise to those changes. The evolution will be seen to reflect the English and American influences but have found a uniquely Canadian resolution—one which may have important implications for the profession in Canada.

Apart from the relevant incorporating statutes and regulations, evidence for the study was sought in legislative debates, proceedings of governmental committe hearings, briefs and submissions made by various parties to committees of enquiry, and in the considerable professional, academic, and financial literature. Since the provincial Ontario legislation has tended to lead the federal Canadian legislation, both jurisdictions were examined.

*George J. Murphy is professor of accounting at the University of Saskatchewan, Saskatoon, Canada. Some of the material for this paper is drawn from the author's Working Paper Number 20 of the Academy of Accounting Historians, "The Evolution of Corporate Reporting Practices in Canada." The author wishes to thank his colleagues, Professors G. Baxter, W. J. Brennan, V. G. Irvine, and D. Lindsay, for their helpful comments.

1877 TO 1917

On the federal Canadian level, the first disclosure provision requiring that ". . . directors of every company lay before its shareholders a full and clear printed statement of the affairs and financial position of the company at or before each general meeting . . ."[1] was enacted in 1877. The more specific requirement that such statements be presented annually was incorporated in the 1902 Act.[2] Many federally incorporated companies, prior to the mandatory presentation of the profit and loss statement in the legislation of 1917, interpreted these provisions as applying only to the balance sheet.[3]

Ontario has been the center of commercial and financial activity in Canada, and it is therefore not surprising to find its legislation well ahead of the federal jurisdiction. The Ontario legislation of 1907 and 1953 are outstanding examples of this leadership. Even the earliest provincial legislation of 1897 seemed to anticipate the modern emphasis of the income statement over the balance sheet by requiring the preparation of a statement of "income and expenditure."[4] Indeed, an audited balance sheet was to be presented at the annual meeting only if the by-laws of the company so directed. The Ontario Companies Act of 1907, in addition to requiring the statement of income and expenditure and the audited balance sheet, specified certain disclosures relating to the balance sheet.[5] These provincial requirements are detailed in exhibit 1 because with respect to the provision of the income statement and the detail to be included in the balance sheet, they are the earliest significant corporate disclosure requirements of any English, American, or Canadian jursidiction. With additional requirements relating to disclosure of values received for shares issued and of amounts amortized in respect to fixed assets and goodwill, the 1917 federal legislation[6] is a direct copy of the 1907 Ontario provisions.

An understanding of the reasons for the early prominence of Canadian legislation is not wholly complete. The inspiration of the 1907 Ontario legislation is attributed to the recommendations of the Institute of Chartered Accountants of Ontario by T. Mulvey, who had been both the federal under secretary of state and the Ontario assistant

[1]Canada, Statutes, *Canada Joint Stock Companies Act*, 1877, 40 Vict., ch. 43, sec. 87.
[2]Canada, Statutes, *The Companies Act*, 1902, 2 Edward VII, ch. 15, sec. 88.
[3]See, for example, various annual anthologies of financial statements in *The Annual Financial Review—Canadian* (Toronto: Houston's Standard Publications 1901-1916).
[4]Ontario, Statutes, *The Ontario Companies Act*, 1897, 60 Vict., ch. 28, secs. 75 and 84.
[5]Ontario, Statutes, *The Ontario Companies Act*, 1907, 7 Edward VII, ch. 34, sec. 36.
[6]Canada, Statutes, *The Companies Act Amendment Act*, 1917, 8 George V, ch. 25, sec. 105.

**Exhibit 1. Financial Statement Disclosure Requirements
of the Ontario Companies Act, 1907**

At such meeting the directors shall lay before the company

a) A balance sheet made up to a date not more than three months before such annual meeting.
b) A statement of income and expenditure for the financial period ending upon the date of such balance sheet.
c) The report of the auditor or auditors.

The balance sheet shall be drawn up so as to distinguish at least the following classes of assets and liabilities, namely:

a) Cash;
b) Debts owing to the company from its customers;
c) Debts owing to the company from its directors, officers and shareholders;
d) Stock in trade;
e) Expenditures made on account of future business;
f) Land, buildings and plant;
g) Goodwill, franchises, patents and copyrights, trademarks, leases, contracts and licenses;
h) Debts owing by the company secured by mortgage or other lien upon the property of the company;
i) Debts owing by the company but not secured;
j)*
k) Amount received on common shares;
l) Amount received on preferred shares;
m) Indirect and contingent liabilities.

---

*No entry for j) is given in the original act.

provincial secretary.[7] The Institute recommendations may well have drawn on the extensive optional disclosure requirements in the model articles, Table B, of the English Act[8] of 1856 and on the suggestions of the committee that made recommendations for changes in the English Act[9] of 1900. (Hatfield has acknowledged the significance of the model articles on American practices.)[10] Though the Engish Act of 1900 required a mandatory audit,[11] there was requirement neither for the provision of an income statement nor for any minimum details to be included in the balance sheet. The English Act of 1908 put forward only the very general requirement that a balance

[7]T. Mulvey, *Dominion Company Law* (Toronto: The Ontario Publishing Co., 1920), p. 54.
[8]Great Britain, Statutes, *Joint Stock Companies Act*, 1856, 19 and 20 Vict., ch. 47.
[9]H. C. Edey and Prot Panitpakdi, "British Company Accounting and the Law 1844-1900," in *Studies in the History of Accounting*, ed. by A. C. Littleton and B. S. Yamey (London: Sweet and Maxwell, 1956), p. 374.
[10]H. R. Hatfield, "Variations in Accounting Practice," *Journal of Accounting Research* (Autumn 1966): 172.
[11]Great Britain, Statutes, *Companies Act*, 1900, 63 and 64 Vict., ch. 48.

sheet, showing ". . . such particulars as will disclose the general nature of these liabilities and assets, and how the values of those fixed assets have been arrived at," must be forwarded to the Registrar of Companies.[12]

Sources of influence from within Canada are various. The Institute of Chartered Accountants of Ontario is likely to have had a strong self-interest in the mandatory audit provisions of the 1907 act. Revelations of the Royal Commission on Insurance[13] had alerted the financial community to abuses in corporate accounting practices. Similarly, the Ontario Conservative government of J. P. Whitney was certainly of a disposition to constrain the corporate "laissez-faire" attitudes of the day.[14]

At the federal level, several factors were influential in the promulgation of the 1917 Act: the concern for mergers and the profit in corporate promotions,[15] the rash of bankruptcies at the beginning of World War I,[16] the bank failures culminating in the bank legislation of 1913,[17] and the existence of a pattern for legislation in the Ontario Act[18] of 1907. Very likely, however, the single most immediate reason for the 1917 Act was the imposition of the Tax Acts of 1916[19] and 1917.[20] The mandatory audit provisions and the minimum disclosure requirements would provide a more consistent and comparable base upon which taxes could be levied. "Taxation equity" would also be satisfied by having a respected professional attest to the adequacy of financial statement disclosure. The complementary nature of the 1916-17 Tax Acts and the 1917 audit and disclosure provisions is implicit in several commentaries of that time.[21] No additional evidence was uncovered from any source—the financial press, legislative

---

[12]Great Britain, Statutes, *Companies (Consolidation) Act*, 1908, 8 Edward VII, ch. 69.
[13]Canada, *Royal Commission on Life Insurance* 1907 (Ottawa: King's Printer, 1907).
[14]Witness the mining legislation, the formation of the publicly owned Hydroelectric Power Corporation and the government intervention in the bankruptcy of the Consolidated Lake Superior Company. C. W. Humphries, "The Political Career of Sir James P. Whitney" (Ph.D. Dissertation, University of Toronto, 1966), pp. 301-410; and J. Schull, *Ontario Since 1867* (Toronto: McLelland and Steward, 1978), pp. 125-78.
[15]A. Raynauld, *The Canadian Economic System* (Toronto: Macmillan Company of Canada, 1967), 149-50; and O. D. Skelton, *General Economic History of the Dominion 1867-1912* (Toronto: Publishers Association of Canada, 1913), pp. 259-61.
[16]M. C. Urquhart and K. A. Buckley, eds., *Historical Statistics of Canada* (Toronto: Macmillan Company of Canada, 1965), p. 659.
[17]Canada, Statutes, *The Bank Act*, 1913, 3 and 4 George V.
[18]Mulvey, *Dominion Company Law*, p. 54.
[19]Canada, Statutes, *Business Profits War Tax Act*, 1916, 6 and 7 George V.
[20]Canada, Statutes, *The Income War Tax Act*, 1917, 7 and 8 George V.
[21]See for example, Canada, *House of Commons Debates*, vol. 6, 1917, p. 5937; and J. Parton, "Merchandise Inventories and the Auditor's Responsibility Therefor," *Canadian Chartered Accountant* (October 1917): 99.

debates, economic and legal histories, or accounting literature existing in *The Canadian Chartered Accountant*—to indicate why this
audit and disclosure legislation was passed at a time when the efforts
of the whole country were devoted to the war. At the annual meeting
in 1918, the president of the Canadian Institute drew attention to the
passage of the act but made no further comment.[22]

1917 TO 1935

The noteworthy legislation in this period occurred at the federal level
in 1934[23] and 1935.[24] Mandatory income statement disclosure related
to directors' and executive officers' fees and salaries, depreciation,
taxes, investment income, nonrecurring profits and losses, amortization of any asset, and interest on long-term debt. The transactions in
the various surplus accounts must be disclosed and their year-to-year
reconciliation demonstrated. Balance-sheet disclosure must include
the valuation basis of receivables, investments and marketable securities, inventories, land, buildings and plant, and, if the fixed-asset
valuation is based on appraisal, the date of the appraisal and the
name of the appraiser. The preparation of consolidated statements,
though long since used in practice, was now officially permitted.
Where consolidated statements were not prepared, the investment in
the shares of, and loans to, subsidiaries must be disclosed together
with the treatment of their aggregate profits and losses.

Internal influences were likely of greatest importance on the 1934-
35 Canadian legislation. Little concern for increased disclosure was
evident during the 1920s when economic events were buoyant; however, with the fall in values relating to the stock market crash of 1929
and the depression of the 1930s, the Canadian public began to clamor
for more information. The highly respected Professor R. G. H.
Smails[25] and a study group of Queen's University professors[26] called
for improved disclosure. Financial commentary, particularly *The
Financial Post*, added to the clamor.[27] The immediate stimulus[28] for

[22]J. Hyde, "The President's Address," *Canadian Chartered Accountant* (October 1918):
93-103.
[23]Canada, Statutes, *Companies Act*, 1934, 24 and 25 George V, ch. 33.
[24]Canada, Statutes, *Companies Act*, 1935, 25 and 26 George V, ch. 33.
[25]R. G. H. Smails, "Directors' Reports—A Criticism and Suggestion," *Canadian
Chartered Accountant* (September 1931): 101-3.
[26]Members of the Department of Political and Economic Science at Queen's University,
"Financial Manipulation: A Project of Reform," *Queen's Quarterly* (May 1933): 274-
77.
[27]"Audit Responsibility Urged in 1932 Statements," *Financial Post* (21 January 1933),
p. 11. Also see *Financial Post* (24 June 1933), p. 12; (16 December 1933), p. 11, and (6
May 1933), p. 11.
[28]See Canada, *Senate Debates* (1934), p. 452.

the 1934 legislation was provided by the Conference of Commissioners on Uniformity of Legislation which had prepared draft legislation. Though reporting practices clearly needed improvement, most of the incentive for the legislation came from a need to correct abuses in corporate promotion and capitalization.[29] In 1931, the Canadian Institute of Chartered Accountants made proposals for uniform legislation relating to financial statements and also made a submission to the federal government for the 1934 legislation.[30]

Though the English Companies Act[31] of 1928 made mandatory the provision of an income statement, very little minimum disclosure was required in the financial statements beyond the need to specify directors' fees, the nature of the valuation of fixed assets, the treatment of subsidiary profits and losses, and the amount transferred to reserve accounts. It was only with respect to these last four items that the 1928 English legislation was in advance of the 1907 and 1917 Canadian legislation. The latter, on the other hand, required much more detailed information in the balance sheet than that of the English legislation. The 1934-35 Canadian legislation, as previously outlined, far exceeded the 1928 English legislation. Indeed, the provisions relating to the disclosure and reconciliation of surplus accounts were incorporated into Canadian law to remedy some of the English Act's deficiencies[32]—deficiencies that may well have permitted the 1929-30 English Royal Mail Steam Packet Scandal to occur. The differences in Canadian and English requirements are discussed at length here to dispel the general misbelief that, up to this time, the Canadian financial statement disclosure legislation was a mere copy of that of the English. While many aspects of the corporate audit provisions had indeed been copied from English legislation, the Canadian disclosure requirements were well ahead of their English counterparts.

Though no evidence was uncovered to demonstrate the specific effect of American influence on the Canadian legislation, there were many signs portending America's future pervasive influence on Canadian thought and practices. American theory and practices including *Uniform Accounting* (1917) and *Verification of Financial*

---

[29]W. A. Macintosh, "Economics and Accountancy," *Canadian Chartered Accountant* (December 1932): 407. See also J. L. Ralston, "Discussions on Dominion Companies Act," *Canadian Chartered Accountant* (February 1935): 87; and Canada, *House of Commons Debates* (29 May 1934), pp. 3454-58.

[30]Neither report could be located by the writer.

[31]Great Britain, Statutes, *Companies Act*, 1928, 18 and 19 George V, ch. 45.

[32]R. G. H. Smails, "Students' Department," *Canadian Chartered Accountant* (September 1934): 283.

Statements (1929) were carefully reported on and extolled in the Canadian literature.[33] Professor Smails of Queen's University, a member of the Institute of Chartered Accountants in England and Wales, went so far as to recommend American texts as being theoretically superior to those of the English.[34] It is, however, quite likely that similar events in both America and Canada—stock promotion abuses and financial reporting inadequacies—gave rise to the virtually coincident 1934-35 Canadian and 1933-34 American legislation and that the Canadian legislation can therefore be explained without reference to the United States. In America, government intervention may have come as a sudden jolt, but in Canada, the vehicle of correction, the Companies Acts, had existed for many years and undoubtedly, by contrast, the 1934-35 legislation can be regarded as an evolution rather than a revolution.

1935 TO 1953

The Ontario Corporation Act[35] of 1953 constituted the first significant revision of that province's legislation since 1907. It is of major importance in the Canadian geneology because the disclosure provisions are so recognizably modern. They were virtually written by the Institute of Chartered Accountants of Ontario.[36] Once again, they were the direct model for the federal legislation which was to appear ten years later. The additional disclosure requirements related to the provision of much more informational detail in the income and retained earnings statements, the balance sheet, and the financial statement footnotes. Restrictions were placed, as well, on the wording and treatment of the various surplus and reserve accounts.

Apart from laying the foundations for modern disclosure requirements in Canada, this Ontario legislation is particularly interesting because of its inspiration. Though there was some concern[37] for improving the federal 1934-35 and particularly the 1907 Ontario provisions,[38] there were no important instances of business scandals

---

[33]C. A. Clapperton, "The Balance Sheet," *Cost and Management* (July 1927): 10.
[34]R. G. H. Smails, "Students' Department," *Canadian Chartered Accountant* (May 1935): 367.
[35]Ontario, Statutes, *The Corporations Act*, 1953, I Eliz. II, ch. 19.
[36]J. G. Glassco, "Accounting in a Modern World," *Canadian Chartered Accountant* (April 1955): 212. Glassco was president of the Canadian Institute in 1955.
[37]See, for example: W. G. Leonard, "A Plea for Greater Frankness in Financial Representations," *Canadian Chartered Accountant* (July 1942): 12-13; C. A. Ashley, "Uniform Accounting," *Commerce Journal* (April 1943): 1-9; W. F. A. Turgeon, *Royal Commission on the Textile Industry* (Ottawa: King's Printer, 1938), p. 127.
[38]R. G. H. Smails, "Students' Department," *Canadian Chartered Accountant* (September 1943): 197.

or corporate malfeasance to fan the flames of change as happened with the 1934-35 legislation. The author's conjecture that the legislation took place first because the provincial statutes had not been revised since 1907 and were now well behind the federal legislation, and second, because the model for revised disclosure had already been framed in the Canadian Institute of Chartered Accountants' Bulletin No. 1, is confirmed by the then secretary to the Select Committee on Company Law.[39] The secretary also indicated that the enquiry and revision were made possible at that particular time because

the number of members of the House of the government party far exceeded the total number of members in the opposition parties and the use of the Select Committee gave Mr. Frost (the Premier of Ontario) an opportunity of keeping many of his backbenchers actively employed, especially between sessions when most of the work of the Select Committee was done.

The 1953 legislation illustrates the increasing influence of the Institutes of Chartered Accountants. The disclosure provisions of that Act were a virtual copy of the recommendations of the Ontario Institute to the Select Committee.[40] These recommendations were, in turn, based wholly on the Canadian Institute's first bulletin on recommended disclosure standards in 1946.[41] The substantive authorship of this bulletin is attributed to the Committee on Accounting and Auditing of the Ontario Institute.[42]

As English influence continued to wane in importance, American influence tended to increase. The disclosure provisions of the English Act[43] of 1947 went little beyond the 1934-35 Canadian legislation. However, the accounting standards and guidelines of the Securities and Exchange Commission (SEC) following 1935 and those of the American Institute commencing in 1939 were well ahead of Canadian thought and practice[44] and were invariably repeated and commented on favorably in *The Canadian Chartered Accountant*. The close

---

[39]S. Lavine, in correspondence with the author, dated 10 June, 1970.

[40]The Special Committee of the Legislature of the Province of Ontario charged with the Revision of The Companies Act (Ontario) and Related Acts, *Proceedings*, vol. 15 (Oct. 6, 1952).

[41]*A Statement of Standards of Disclosure in Annual Financial Statements of Manufacturing and Merchandising Companies*, Bulletin #1 (Dominion Association of Chartered Accountants, 1946).

[42]J. R. M. Wilson, "Standards of Disclosure" (Address to Dominion Association of Chartered Accountants, Montreal, 11 September 1946).

[43]Great Britain, Statutes, *The Companies Act*, 1947, 10 and 11 George VI, ch. 47.

[44]See, for example, SEC Accounting Series Release No. 7, "Analysis of Deficiencies Commonly Cited by Commission in Connection with Financial Statements" (May 1938), reprinted in *Federal Securities Law Reports* (Washington: Commerce Clearing House, undated).

relationships between many American and Canadian professional accounting firms also served to highlight disclosure differences between the two countries.[45] The vehicle for this influence now became the Canadian Institutes as they carefully screened American thought and practices before making their own recommendations. Canadian commentators at times envied the incentive provided in America by the existence and activity of the SEC.[46]

1953 TO PRESENT

The most notable legislation of the 1960s was the Canada Corporations Act[47] of 1964-65 and the Ontario Securities Act[48] of 1966. The federal legislation initiated by the Senate[49] is, with a few additions, almost identical to the 1953 Ontario legislation. Though there were increasing signs of dissatisfaction with the inadequacies of corporate reporting,[50] neither the provincial nor federal legislation was the result of widespread notoriety or discontent. Senate debates acknowledged that the 1934-35 legislation was simply out of date and that the revision was copied from the existing Ontario legislation.[51] Similarly, the Kimber Committee[52] which made recommendations for the Ontario Securities Act changes was established not because of any particular grievance or scandal, but rather because of a concern that the law was in need of review.[53] Following the Kimber Report, the Ontario Securities Act was drastically revised, giving ongoing surveillance of Canada's chief exchange, the Toronto Stock Exchange, to the Ontario Securities Commission. Though this commission holds powers at the provincial-listed security level similar to those of the American SEC,[54] it has not created an elaborate financial statement review process, nor has it attempted to promulgate its own accounting guidelines.[55]

[45]Howard Ross, of Touche Ross & Co., in correspondence with the author dated 21 August 1972.
[46]Glassco, "Accounting," p. 212.
[47]Canada, Statutes, *Canada Corporations Act*, 1964-1965, 13 and 14 Eliz. II, ch. 52.
[48]Ontario, Statutes, *The Securities Act*, 1966, 14 and 15 Eliz. II, ch. 142, Part XII.
[49]Senate of Canada, *Proceedings of the Standing Committee on Banking and Commerce*, 26 Parl., 1964.
[50]In response to which the Canadian Institute issued the first of its recommended standards on disclosure, Bulletin No. 1, in 1946.
[51]Canada, *Senate Debates* (1964), pp. 515-18.
[52]Attorney General of Ontario, *Report of the Attorney General's Committee on Securities Legislation in Ontario* (Toronto: Queen's Printer, 1965).
[53]J. R. Kimber, in correspondence with the author, dated 3 July 1970.
[54]See Ontario, Statutes, *The Securities Act*, 1966, 14 and 15 Eliz. II, sec. 139, Part XIV.
[55]Some exceptions do exist. See "Recognition of Profits in Real Estate Transactions," *Ontario Securities Commission Bulletin* (Toronto: Ontario Securities Commission, July 1969).

Though the federal and provincial legislation of the mid 1960s were not initiated by widespread dissatisfaction with corporate reporting, they were preceded by a relatively quiet but fairly steady stream of concern.[56] That concern grew to very broad proportions following the mid 1960s and served to thrust the Canadian Institute into a position of great prominence. The American influence which was acknowledged in the Kimber Report's recommendations continued as Canadians closely observed the many aspects of American accounting practice that were being publicly questioned during this period.

A financial failure of significant proportions—the Atlantic Acceptance Company[57]—in 1965 is likely a turning point in the attitude of the public and the financial community with regard to corporate regulation and financial disclosure requirements. From this time onward, governments and boards of enquiry seemed increasingly willing to respond to what were felt to be corporate shortcomings. The Atlantic Acceptance failure brought into question, among other things, the appropriateness of loans to affiliated companies, income reporting practices of financial institutions, and parent auditors' responsibility with regard to the subsidiary auditor's work. This failure, together with a rash of other major financial corporate crises,[58] spurred a concern for reform at many levels.[59] The concern for improved disclosure was accompanied by an increasing demand for narrowing the range of acceptable accounting practices.[60] Principles and standards as well as increased disclosure were now being demanded.

---

[56]See the *Report of the Royal Commission on Banking and Finance* (Ottawa: Queen's Printer, 1964), pp. 350, 560-61; and the *Report of the Attorney General's Committee on Securities Legislation in Ontario* (Toronto: Queen's Printer, 1965), p. 7.

[57]Ontario Lieutenant Governor in Council, *Report of the Royal Commission Appointed to Enquire into the Failure of Atlantic Acceptance Company Limited* (Toronto: Queen's Printer, 1969), 4 volumes. Note Mr. Justice Hughes' impatience at the slowness of the accounting profession in resolving issues, pp. 1589-90.

[58]For example, British Mortgage and Trust, Alliance Credit Corporation, Prudential Finance Corporation, Windfall Oils and Mines Limited, Revenue Properties Ltd., Corporation Foncier de Montreal, and the Commonwealth group of companies experienced either failure or major financial crises.

[59]"Finance Company Bill Arousing Business' Ire," *Financial Times* (2 December 1968), p. 3.

[60]See E. C. Harris, "Access to Corporate Information," in *Studies in Canadian Company Law*, ed. J. S. Ziegel (Toronto: Butterworths, 1967), p. 491; also R. H. Jones, "Do Those Financial Statements Really Inform the Shareholder?" *Financial Post*, (18 September 1965), p. 13; and the Director of Research of the Canadian Institute G. Mulcahy, "The Auditor's Report on Consolidated Statements," *Canadian Chartered Accountant* (April 1966): 288.

Modest alterations were legislated in the Ontario Corporations Act[61] of 1970. It was, however, the Canadian Securities Administrators[62] in 1972, the Canadian Business Corporations Act[63] in 1975, and the Ontario Securities Act of 1978[64] that proposed the boldest legislative requirement in response to perceived disclosure and uniformity inadequacies. National Policy No. 27 of the Canadian Securities Commissions indicates that the Canadian Institute Handbook must be used to determine what constitutes generally accepted accounting principles. Greater ease and flexibility in making changes in financial statement requirements are provided in the Canada Business Corporations Act and the Ontario Securities Act by relegating such matters to the Regulations. These Regulations similarly require that financial statements be prepared in accordance with the Handbook. Only with respect to the reporting of diversified operations does the federal legislation go beyond Handbook requirements.[65]

The accounting profession has moved from a pleading or advocacy position to a legislative position. Henceforward, the recommendations of the Institute Handbook are the law of the land. This startling result had little, if any, debate or discussion in the professional literature, though some foreshadowing was evidenced in 1971 in *Proposals for a New Business Corporations Law for Canada* which indicated that

it should not be left to the persuasive powers of the accounting profession to see to the implementation of improved financial reporting practices, because the unscrupulous will tend to observe only the minimum legal requirements.[66]

(It was only in 1973 that the Ontario Institute's Rules of Professional Conduct required departures from the Handbook to be justified.[67])

[61]Ontario, Statutes. *The Business Corporations Act*, 1970, 19 Eliz. II, ch. 25. The Lawrence Committee had earlier indicated that "no present need had been demonstrated for amendments of major significance to the financial disclosure provisions of the Ontario Act," The Legislative Assembly of Ontario, *Interim Report of the Select Committee on Company Law—1967* (Toronto: Queen's Printer, 1967), par. 10.1.4.
[62]Canadian Securities Commissions, "National Policy No. 27, Generally Accepted Accounting Principles" (Toronto: CCH, 1972), vol. 2, 54-864.
[63]Canada, Statutes, *Canada Business Corporations Act*, 1975, 23 Eliz. II.
[64]"Publications under the Regulations Act," *Ontario Gazette*, part II (28 July 1979).
[65]*Canada Business Corporations Act Regulations* (Toronto: Richard Dee Boo, 1976), p. 189. It should be noted that a submission by the Institute succeeded in having removed those draft regulations which conflicted with or were redundant with the Handbook. See Canadian Institute of Chartered Accountants, *Draft Regulations Under the Canada Business Corporations Act* (Toronto: CICA, 1975).
[66]*Proposals for a New Business Corporations Law for Canada* (Ottawa: Queen's Printer, 1971), part 13, par. 327.
[67]See G. Mulcahy, "Ontario Institute's New Rules re Accounting Standards," *CA Magazine* (August 1973): 50.

The Public Accountancy Amendment Act of Ontario[68] in 1962 had given members of the Institute of Chartered Accountants of Ontario the exclusive right to the practice of public accounting in Ontario. It may have been only inevitable then that the Ontario Securities Commission, as a member of the Canada Securities Commission, would, when confronted with a mood for reform, look for help from the agency to whom a monopoly had been granted. The earlier-mentioned suggestion that legislation was needed to aid the persuasive powers of the professional accountants may also have been influential in the minds of legislators and securities commissioners.

POSTSCRIPT

The position of the Canadian Institute and its rule-making office would seem to be somewhat different from that of its counterpart institutes in England and America. In the former country, the minimum legal requirements for disclosure continue to be set forth in the Companies Acts.[69] Recommendations of the English Institute are not acknowledged in English legislation, although undoubtedly as in Canada prior to the most recent legislation, Institute recommendations would be regarded as an acceptable standard in the event of enquiry or litigation.

In America, the Securities and Exchange Commission controls accounting practices. Though it acknowledges the pronouncements of the Financial Accounting Standards Board (FASB) as having substantial authoritative support, its on-going close surveillance of accounting matters, through its own releases or in the countermanding of FASB pronouncements, leaves little doubt where short-run as well as long-run command resides.

From the turn of the century in Canada, the legislative authorities have relied heavily on the Institutes to provide the framework for financial statement disclosure. Since the mid-1960s, there has been an increasing public demand to narrow the range of acceptable accounting practices as well as to provide greater disclosure. The extension of these trends has resulted in the formal delegation of the determination of standards and disclosure requirements to the Institute. Institute recommendations are now law, and the various powers within

---

[68]Ontario, Statutes, *The Public Accountancy Amendment Act*, 1961-1962, 10 and 11 Eliz. II, ch. 113. This monopoly position is now being questioned in *Professional Regulation*, the study of the Professional Organization's committee appointed by the attorney general of Ontario.
[69]Most recently in Great Britain, Statutes, *Companies Act*, 1976, 24 and 25 Eliz. II, ch. 69 and previously in *Companies Act*, 1967, 15 and 16, Eliz. II, ch. 11.

securities and corporate legislation can be called upon to enforce compliance.

Though the Institute seems to have warmly welcomed its new task,[70] it is not one without extremely heavy responsibilities. When power is given to determine accounting standards, the responsibility to undertake this task in a competent and timely fashion also follows. Though recourse to prior American discussion and research on many of the problems that would confront the Institute would be an invaluable aid, the burden of standard setting is likely to grow at an increasing rate. If insufficient resources are devoted to this task or if improper standards are set, or if standards for particular events or activities have not been set at all, the Institute bears enormous responsibility. To the extent that reliance on the Handbook is complete, the blame for a serious financial scandal that could be attributed to improper or inadequate standards might well redound directly to the discredit of the Institute. In such an event, the Institute might be particularly vulnerable or exposed since, unlike the Financial Accounting Standards Board, the various committees that propose and define standards are composed largely of volunteer members holding relatively short-term appointments.[71] The Institute would be unwise to minimize in any way the significance of the responsibility which it now bears.

[70]Mulcahy, "New Rules re Accounting Standards," p. 50.
[71]See Canadian Institute of Chartered Accountants, "Rules of Membership and Principal Terms of Reference of Accounting Research Committee as approved by Board of Governors," *CICA Handbook* (September 1973).

DIRECTORS' REPORTS—A CRITICISM AND SUGGESTION

By R. G. H. Smails, B.Sc. Econ., C.A.

THE Canadian general companies acts* require directors to make a report to shareholders for discussion at the annual general meeting. The report is to comprise an audited balance sheet, a general statement of profit and loss, and "such further information respecting the company's financial position as the special act, letters patent or by-laws of the company require." This statutory report is, normally, the only process by which directors account for their stewardship to their employers and the only means by which the shareholders can judge of the efficiency of their stewards and the condition and prospects of their company. In spite of these all-important considerations the typical directors' report to shareholders is a vacuous document scarcely worth the paper on which it is printed. As Mr. Justice Wright said in the course of his summing-up in the trial of Lord Kylsant, . . "one cannot help wondering, whether those who manage big companies do not forget sometimes that the body of directors of the company are the agents of the shareholders, that they owe them full information subject to proper commercial and reasonable necessities, and that it is the shareholders' interests they have to study. They are not to regard shareholders as sheep who might look up if they were not fed." Happily, of recent years, a slight improvement is perceptible and Canada can boast of a few men who are turning some part of their talent to the construction of reports that are both

*With the regrettable exceptions of those of Manitoba, New Brunswick and Prince Edward Island.

100

informative and interesting. We salute these pioneers but leave them for the moment to consider how and why the vast majority of those documents remain either crudely or ingeniously uninformative.

What can be said of the balance sheet? The first thing to be said is that a balance sheet is subject to inherent limitations and cannot by itself tell the whole story of a company's fortunes and condition. It is essentially a technical document requiring interpretation by those who have prepared it in order to be completely intelligible to others; its valuations are inevitably matters of personal opinion; it makes no attempt at valuation of management which is frequently the biggest factor in success. As Sir Gilbert Garnsey has said: "It is extremely important that shareholders and others should realize the limitations of even the best accounts; the shorter the period covered by the accounts the greater are the limitations. It may be that too much is expected from balance sheets; in essence they are historical records and correct conclusions can hardly be drawn from a hurried survey of temporary conditions, but rather by a careful examination, with the object of distinguishing between permanent tendencies and temporary fluctuations."* Much uninformed criticism of published balance sheets proceeds from failure to realize these things and to understand that a balance sheet does not profess to exhibit, on its face, the market value of the enterprise to which it relates. At the same time it has to be admitted that in spite of its inherent limitations a balance sheet can be so drawn and worded as to enable an intelligent lay reader, who studies it in conjunction with earlier balance sheets and the president's commentaries, to form his own opinion of the condition and trend of the enterprise. A balance sheet which does not answer this test is subject to some remediable defect for which its authors are responsible. A study of the published balance sheets of one hundred Canadian industrial companies selected at random has revealed that not one of them was free from remediable defects of this type. In twelve cases terminology employed was so ambiguous or highly technical as to be wholly unintelligible or intelligible only to a trained accountant; excessive grouping of assets and liabilities marred respectively

*"Limitations of a Balance Sheet," Canadian Chartered Accountant, Vol. XIX, page 131.

101

forty-eight and sixty balance sheets; in seventy cases the basis of valuation of assets was not revealed. These results indicate that little attempt is made to use the balance sheet as a means of informing shareholders and the public, and that the report is prepared perfunctorily merely to satisfy the requirements of the statute.

The statement of profit or loss accompanying the balance sheet is rarely more than a summary of the surplus account showing the net profit from operations of all kinds, the amount of depreciation reserved, income tax incurred and interest and dividends paid on securities. Less exception can be taken to the paucity of information in this part of the report, for to disclose to shareholders details of trading income and expense would, in some cases, be to furnish rivals with valuable information—and perhaps to shake the consumer's faith in the intrinsic value of the product! But even here secretiveness seems to be practised on occasion for its own sake without regard to any useful purpose served, and information that would be of great interest to shareholders and no value to competitors is withheld at the dictate of ancient custom.

Nor does the president's message which is usually appended to the balance sheet and statement of profit and loss commonly attempt to repair the deficiencies of these accounts. Most of such messages, instead of interpreting the accounts and amplifying the information to be derived from them, are formal and platitudinous. Usually attention is drawn to the amount of operating profit as disclosed by the profit and loss statement, this figure is perhaps compared with that for the previous year and the amount available for common dividends computed, a note of confidence in the future is sounded, and the directors "again wish to express their appreciation of the faithful and efficient service rendered by the staff throughout the year." There is little more than this—year in, year out.

For the regrettable state of affairs which has been sketched above, the directors as authors of the report are, of course, responsible. In defence they constantly argue that it is not in the interests of shareholders that they should have information because competitors may glean valuable knowledge of the business. Such an argument carries little weight, for the reports stop far short of the point where to give any more information would be to

102

impart confidential knowledge of this kind. This is particularly true of the balance sheet, for the figures which are of value to commercial opponents are not balance sheet items at all but those which relate to revenue and have to do with trade turnover, margins of profit, costs of manufacture, etc. In short, the argument, to use the words of the President of the Society of Incorporated Accountants and Auditors "in ninety-nine cases out of a hundred is all humbug.* An alternative line of defence is to plead that shareholders are ignorant and apathetic, interested only in profits and that they are given all the information that they want or are capable of digesting. But who is to say which is cause and which effect, the ignorance and apathy of the shareholders or the secretiveness of the directors? Is there not anyhow amongst every body of stockholders an intelligent minority deserving of better treatment? Is not the public at large, as the source of new capital, worthy of cultivation? To the last question directors may retort that they get capital from the investment banker who in turn has his own effective methods of extracting it from the public. But to the first two questions no such cynically conclusive retorts are possible. Our own submission is that in ninety-nine cases out of a hundred the "economy of information" practised by directors has nothing whatever to do with the pleas advanced above but is due to a fear that shareholders who are allowed and encouraged to take an intelligent interest in the affairs of the company will interfere with its management and thereby bring ruin on the company and desolation on its directors. (In the hundredth case the explanation lies in fraudulent intent to conceal but this exceptional case is not the occupation of the present article). We believe this fear of intervention to be entirely unfounded for it is a root principle of the companies acts that directors shall be given powers commensurate with their responsibility. In application of this principle the acts, while reserving to the shareholders ultimate control of the company's broad policies have secured inviolably to the directors the right to administer the affairs of the company in all things.

The dawn of a new era of interesting and informative

*Mr. Morgan, quoted by Mr. H. V. Alexander in debate on the Companies (Amending) Bill, 1927. The Accountant, Vol. LXXVIII, p. 323.

103

reports will not be ushered in by legislation; so much is admitted by all who have given the matter earnest thought. The statutes already require that a balance sheet be presented, that a certain minimum of detail be given in the balance sheet and that the accounts must be audited before presentation. They cannot usefully go further than this. Attempts to impose a stereotyped form of balance sheet upon all the infinitely varied enterprises that may be incorporated under a general act are doomed to failure—and have failed historically as under the earlier British acts. Attempts to regulate the content of the president's message would only aggravate the evil they sought to cure. These things are properly and inevitably left to the discretion of directors. We are thus forced to the conclusion that the only hope for improvement lies in directors being educated —by the more enlightened members of the craft and by experience—out of the belief that a well informed shareholder is an interfering shareholder. It is for this reason that the lead now being given by the directors of a few of the largest Canadian companies deserves the widest possible publicity.

It is not within the scope of this paper to consider in detail the distinguishing features of the "new model" reports but a brief reference to some of these features is necessary. The balance sheet shows in an adjacent column the corresponding figures of the last report (in one instance in our possession these were printed in red ink); the original cost and basis of valuation of assets is clearly indicated; each significant asset and liability is distinguished; group totals for different classes of assets and liabilities are given; where necessary the items are annotated to explain in non-technical language their exact nature and significance; all proprietorship equity accounts are congregated and the total divided between the different classes of security holders. In addition to such features as these which are common to all balance sheets each individual statement affords scope for initiative in the lucid presentation of facts or conditions peculiar to the enterprise in question. It is more difficult to generalize upon the Profit and Loss Statement and impossible to generalize upon the content of the president's report. With regard to the former it may however be said that the total net profit or loss from trading operations is a figure to which shareholders are most certainly entitled

104

and disclosure of which cannot prejudice the business in competition. Details of the non-operating income including income from investments, non-recurring profits or losses, appropriations from reserves (secret or otherwise) should be distinguished at least in total and in most cases detail may reasonably be demanded. (In this connection it is of interest to note that the R.M.S.P. Co., according to the Attorney General transferred from hidden reserve to surplus account between the years 1922 and 1927 the sum of five and a half million pounds and meanwhile succeeded in conveying to shareholders the impression that the operations of the company were consistently profitable whereas in fact heavy losses were being taken). In some instances the total of sales may reasonably be given and in all cases some criterion of the trend of sales (such as volume or percentage increase or decrease) can be disclosed with impunity to the company and great interest to its shareholders. The president's message should, as has already been suggested, interpret the foregoing accounts to the shareholders and include the results of a skilled analysis of the present condition and future prospects both of the company in particular and the industry in general. A report which has recently attracted much favorable comment in financial circles—it is that of a packing company—works out certain important comparative ratios (both balance sheet and profit and loss), explains the significance of these ratios, reviews the present position of the company and by means of a study of hog prices and production over a number of years throws some light on future prospects. Mention has been made of this one specific document not because it can or should be slavishly copied but because it serves as an admirable example of what can be done by the exercise of initiative and imagination to develop an intelligent, loyal and farsighted body of stockholders. The opportunities are numberless.

In conclusion it is fitting to enquire how, if at all, the professional accountant can promote the cause of informative directors' reports. The responsibility for running the business is on the directors not the auditor, and any suggestion that the auditor should directly interfere with the report of the directors to their shareholders would be gross presumption. The duty of the auditor *qua* auditor is to express his opinion upon the accuracy of the balance sheet

105

which the directors propose to put before the company. He has no control over the form and content of that balance sheet but must tell the shareholders in what respects, if any, it is incorrect or misleading. If he does this unequivocally he has performed his whole duty. We may say then that in his statutory capacity the auditor can promote the cause under consideration only by avoiding negative qualifications and ambiguous phraseology in his own report upon the balance sheet. This in itself would be no mean advance, for truisms such as the one which cost the auditor so dear in *Re London and General Bank* ("the value of the assets is dependent upon realization") are not infrequently met in our own time. Of far greater importance, however, is the influence which the auditor can bring to bear upon the directors in his extra-legal capacity of general business consultant. This influence in many cases can be exercised over the entire contents of the directors' report but it is natural and proper that it should be brought to bear especially on the form and content of the balance sheet. Much useful work is already being done in this connection quietly and unobtrusively, but there is probably scope for more. *The Accountant* has for the past two years conducted a column entitled "Finance and Commerce" in which company reports are subjected to scrutiny and commended or denounced without fear or favor not according to the amount of profits they disclose but according to the kind and amount of information they provide. The column has provided a service entirely different from that of the financial papers but at least as valuable, and has done much to stimulate and direct professional interest in a matter bordering very closely on accounting practice. We wonder if there is not room for a similar service in Canada where, as in England "the present tendency in company practice cannot fail to be very disquieting both to professional men and to many of those who are engaged in company work."

106

accounting principles and practices

Government intervention– the PIP grant accounting controversy

by Robert H. Crandall, Queen's University

Canada's National Energy Program (NEP) was announced with fanfare in October 1980. If the NEP worked according to plan, Canada would eventually find enough new oil to be energy self-sufficient, and it would be owned by Canadians.

The NEP had a number of provisions to accomplish these goals. The first was a new tax of 8 per cent on revenue produced by existing oil and gas wells called the Petroleum and Gas Revenue Tax (PGRT). Secondly, to offset the impact of the PGRT on Canadian-owned companies that were willing to explore in the frontier areas, the federal government introduced the Petroleum Incentive Program (PIP) grant system. The grants could be as high as 80 per cent of the exploration expenditures, but to receive the top amount the company doing the exploration had to be substantially Canadian-owned, and do its exploration in "Canada Lands" in the far north or off the east coast. Naturally, this arrangement was not received favorably by foreign-owned oil producers in Canada, or by Alberta.

The Liberal government in Ottawa thus found itself with enemies on a variety of fronts because of the NEP. Foreign investors, particularly in the United States, objected to paying a heavy new tax, the PGRT, in order to finance Canadian competitors' activities in drilling for oil. The government of Alberta felt similarly discriminated against: companies producing oil in Alberta were forced to pay the PGRT as they sold Alberta's underground wealth (thus making oil exploration in that province less attractive) so that wealth could be returned through PIP grants to those who explored outside Alberta in the "Canada Lands." Newspapers regularly carried stories of drill rigs leaving Alberta for the United States, where exploration had become more attractive.

The oil industry in Calgary listened to the budget speech of Tuesday, October 29, 1980 with particular interest since they knew the NEP would affect them pro-

foundly. Depending on a company's tax position, the implication of the NEP was that a company that got the full 80 per cent grant would have to provide less than ten cents of its own money for each dollar spent on exploration; the rest would come from public grants or tax relief. Generally, the oil companies in Calgary thought the cash flow impact on Canadian-owned companies would be about neutral. In Toronto, Norcen corporate analysts had been running computer simulations of possible initiatives the company might take, and were more optimistic.

A difference of opinion

While the cash flow prospects were favorable or neutral, the potential impact on the reported net income of the oil companies was not good at all. The key issue was that the CICA's Accounting Standards Committee (AcSC) (called the Accounting Research Committee at the time) would regard the PGRT as an expense of the period in which it was payable, with the PIP grants being treated as a reduction of the exploration expenses they were tied to. Since most Canadian oil companies wrote off these exploration expenses over an extended period of time, this would mean that the impact of PIP grants on reported income would be similarly delayed.

The CICA's opinion about the appropriate accounting treatment of PIP grants was not one to be ignored, since the federal corporations act effectively required that financial statements of companies incorporated under the Act should be drawn up according to the CICA *Handbook*, and the Ontario Securities Commission had a similar requirement for all companies whose shares traded in that province.

The implications of the November 1980 budget sank in quickly, and activity proceeded in three main groups: (1) the CICA's Accounting Standards Committees; (2) the Canadian-owned part of the oil industry; and (3) the Ottawa policy makers.

56

The early signs of impending trouble became evident in Calgary in February 1981 when representatives of the oil industry met to discuss the accounting implications of PIP grants. There clearly existed a group of senior oil company executives who wanted accounting treatment in the NEP era to follow in the footsteps of the pre-NEP era. To do this, they wanted the part of the PIP grant that equalled the PGRT payment to be "offset," so that only the remainder of the PIP grant would be treated as a reduction of the cost of exploration. If this were done, they said, then their results would be comparable with prior years (and reported income would be higher in the early years of exploration).

Another group in Calgary was involved. It consisted of partners of the major firms of Chartered Accountants that dealt with clients in the oil industry. They met monthly in the Petroleum Club as an "Ad Hoc Committee" to discuss accounting issues. Most of the people in the Ad Hoc group felt, initially at least, that PIP grants fitted the description of a government grant to help in the acquisition of fixed assets, and hence the accounting treatment was already covered under Section 3800.26 of the CICA *Handbook* which said, "Government assistance towards the acquisition of fixed assets should be either: (a) deducted from the related fixed assets with any depreciation calculated on the net amount; or (b) deferred and amortized to income on the same basis as the related depreciable fixed assets are depreciated." Clearly, the AcSC had thought about this issue already, and had developed a standard well before the present controversial NEP had been launched.

At a Calgary meeting of oil industry people in February 1981 this difference of viewpoint became very evident. Ominously, the Petro-Canada representative held out strongly for the offset treatment, and was joined by representatives of some other oil companies.

Compromise proposed

A group of oil industry executives in Calgary decided they would take the initiative in working out a compromise between the CICA position in favor of the "grant" approach and the "offset" approach they wanted. Most of them knew they would have to go to the financial markets to raise the funds needed for the exploration contemplated by the NEP. They believed that the underwriters would want to price their securities at a less favorable rate if they reported a lower net income because of the CICA stand. The validity of this view is controversial, but there is no question that it was widely believed.

The plan they most favored was one in which the federal government would simply not collect the PGRT to the extent it matched their PIP grants. In effect, instead of taking it away though PGRT and giving it back through PIP, the federal government would do neither. Hence the companies would have no PGRT on their Income State-

ment, and would only receive a net PIP grant. The working group thought they had an implied understanding from the CICA that this would be acceptable, and hoped to persuade the federal government to use this approach since the cash flow would be the same. They were to be disappointed.

The Calgary oil industry executives found themselves making many trips to Ottawa following the introduction of the NEP, and this gave them an opportunity to try to convince senior policy makers at the federal capital, such as the Deputy Minister of Finance, Ian Stewart, of the merits of their approach. They pointed out that the CICA was not likely to make a major change in its position so long as the PIP grants were given in the form of grants — the *Handbook* position had been stated years before, and positions were now hardened. In addition, the CICA would not like to be seen bowing to political pressure or it would lose its credibility as an impartial setter of accounting standards. They pointed out that the CICA likely had political influence far beyond its membership. "I said it was one thing to pick on an industry that was heavily concentrated in Alberta," one industry executive recalls, "but quite another thing to pick on the CA profession when they're all across Canada behind every lilac bush."

The Ottawa spokesmen were sympathetic but firm. As much as they regretted antagonizing the chartered accountants, the NEP was an important instrument of government policy and could not be frustrated by the stand of the CICA. The proposal to amend the NEP along the lines suggested by the industry just wouldn't work. Politically, it didn't make sense to make amendments to the NEP when it was under such fire because it might be misinterpreted as a sign of retreat. Technically, it wasn't possible to integrate PIP into the PGRT because of Canada's international tax treaties. "We were caught between a rock and a hard place," was the summary of one of the oil company participants, and this effort to work out a compromise came to an end about May 1981.

The ultimate weapon

It became clear early in 1981 that the federal government thought its ultimate weapon with the CICA lay in the Canada Business Corporations Act (CBCA). They would change the CBCA to permit the use of offset accounting for PIP grants.

Meanwhile, AcSC had been busy examining its position and surveying those affected to find out how much support it had. On March 11 there was a meeting in Calgary with auditors and industry representatives. This meeting had been organized with the help of the major petroleum associations. Those present came down clearly in favor of the CICA position, although critics later said that those invited had been mainly financial, not chief executive, officers.

The key people in AcSC were aware of these criticisms and arranged another meeting, this time in Toronto, on March 23, 1981. Present were representatives of Norcen, PanCanadian, Husky Oil, Petro-Canada, the federal Department of Finance, and Energy Mines and Resources. Although the meeting did not end in agreement, those present do not remember it as unfriendly, although the possibility of government legislation to resolve the issue was mentioned.

Although the March 23 meeting was amicable, the move to change the CBCA to permit offset accounting gathered momentum in Ottawa. In early April the Deputy Minister of Finance called a senior CICA staff member, the General Director of Research (R.D. Thomas), to make sure the AcSC members realized the NEP was a high-profile issue in the federal cabinet, and that changes to the CBCA to permit offset accounting were contemplated if the CICA persisted in its stand. The response from Thomas was that the cabinet should be prepared for "holy war" if they proposed to amend the CBCA, since the CICA did not intend to back down. Reverberations of the dispute appeared in the *Financial Post* in an article entitled "PIP makes jitters in the oil patch."

In mid-April AcSC circulated drafts of the Accounting Guideline it proposed to issue when the legislation creating PIP grants became law. The draft Guideline essentially said that accounting for government grants had already been covered under Section 3800. The members of AcSC Steering Committee thought they were bending over backwards to make sure their reasoning on this issue was known ahead of time. Those favoring offset accounting felt differently; they thought the issue was still under discussion, and felt affronted at what they saw as a preemptive move by AcSC. Copies of the draft Guideline were sent to the Minister and Deputy Ministers of Finance and Energy, to the main participants in the dispute in Calgary, the provincial securities commissions, and members of Parliament who were CAs. It would be difficult to say that the Guideline had not been widely communicated to those who might be interested.

AcSC followed up on the issue of the draft Guideline with a press conference on April 22 at which the Chairman of AcSC was going to address the assembled press on the role of AcSC and the reasons for its stand on this issue. Only one outside reporter turned up for the briefing and the luncheon that followed, Chris Robinson of the *Financial Post*.

By this time the audit firms with major oil companies as clients were having an uncomfortable time because the battle lines were clearly formed, and pressure on the audit firms to support their clients' position was building. The Chairman of AcSC, David Ward, was a partner of Coopers & Lybrand, a firm with energy-related clients. To ensure that he could fill the role of Chairman of AcSC without feeling pressure from clients, his firm instructed

him not to attend any client-related committees within his firm until his term as Chairman was over. The next Chairman, Robert Rutherford of Thorne Riddell, had similar instructions from his own firm.

A reply of sorts to the publication of the Guideline was the Interim Report of Norcen for the quarter ended March 31, 1981. Norcen used offset accounting, contrary to the Guideline, and had some strong words in favor of doing so.

It was now clear to the members of the AcSC that the issue was not settled. About the same time, the group in Calgary that was working to mediate a solution in favor of offset had concluded that there was no hope. It was a standoff, and from May 1981 to the late fall of that year other issues pressed in and PIP lay unresolved; the AcSC draft Guideline was now out, and Norcen continued to ignore it in calculating its income in its Interim Reports for the end of June, and September. Everyone knew the crunch would come when the annual report was issued, and the auditors had to report. For most companies, this would be around the beginning of March 1982.

Prior to the end of 1981 some preliminary work had been done in the offices of those who favored offset to see what changes needed to be made to the Canada Business Corporations Act (CBCA) to make it possible for firms to use offset accounting if they wished. On examination it turned out to be not all that easy. While the CBCA could be amended to permit the use of offset, there was the troublesome issue of the auditors' report. Under the rules of most provincial Institutes of Chartered Accountants, the auditors were required to qualify their report if the financial statements do not conform with the accounting standards laid down in the *Handbook*. If an auditors' report is qualified over an issue of accounting reporting (which this would be), then the securities commissions, such as the Ontario and Alberta Securities Commissions, could suspend the trading privileges of the affected company until the issue was cleared up — probably after a public hearing. The CBCA had somehow to provide that the auditors would give an unqualified opinion, or the federal objectives would be frustrated.

While the federal government was determined, at the most senior levels, to amend the CBCA if necessary, it was by no means unanimous in Ottawa that this was the best course of action if it weakened the process of accounting reporting in Canada. Many important government functions, such as corporate income taxation, relied on the integrity of accounting reports and there was a reluctance to tamper for the sake of a political initiative like the National Energy Policy, however important it might be at the moment. In addition, Canada was a party to international accounting standards agreements designed to harmonize accounting reporting, and some in Ottawa saw the proposed change to the CBCA as a significant step backwards. People who held this view were not, however,

57

at senior policy levels at the Ministry of Energy Mines and Resources.

The controversy heats up

AcSC issued advance copies of its official version of the Accounting Guideline in mid-January 1982, and "that's when the hardball really started" according to the President of PanCanadian. The Guideline was distributed to all *Handbook* subscribers, and to those who got the original draft.

By January 1982 AcSC was facing the distinct possibility of legislation being passed to change the CBCA to permit offset accounting for PIP grants. The legislation essentially proposed that a federally incorporated oil company could apply to the federal government to use offset. If it received such permission, then not only could it use offset but — and this was particularly galling to the professional accountants — the auditors' report was required to say that offset accounting constituted generally accepted accounting principles.

If the auditor was going to be required by law to say that offset accounting constituted generally accepted accounting principles — when his professional body had already issued a Guideline to say it didn't — then one response was to somehow make this clear in the auditors' report itself. Accordingly, the Auditing Standards Committee of the CICA (AuSC) set to work on an Auditing Guideline that might be issued in response to a change in the CBCA. The implications such a modified report might have for companies regulated by securities commissions was something all were aware of.

By this time the situation was clearly serious, and in the latter part of February 1982 there were meetings between the President of the CICA, Dennis Culver, the members of AcSC and AuSC, and senior representatives of major firms of chartered accountants. It was clear that the members of the accounting profession felt resentment that the government would tamper with the setting of accounting standards, but there was disagreement as to how firm a stand the CICA (it was now a larger issue than simply the authority of AcSC) should take. The "hawks" felt a hard stand had to be taken, or there would be no end of government intervention in standard setting to satisfy political needs of the moment, and in the end the credibility of the reporting system would be lost. "It was a time to give in or dig in," as one of the hawks put it. The moderates questioned whether this was the time or the issue for such a stand.

Clearly, those who favored a firm stand convinced the others, because in the middle of February 1982 the Ministry of Energy, Mines and Resources got a rather extraordinary letter. It was written on plain paper, with no return address, and was brief. The signatures took the most space. It described the proposed initiative to set accounting and auditing standards by government regula-

tion as "completely inappropriate" and "a serious reflection on the integrity of the Institute and its thirty-two thousand members." It concluded by offering assistance in attempting to find a solution but if that failed, "to join with our Institute in opposing the contemplated regulation by all reasonable means at our disposal."

The letter was signed by the most senior or executive partners of Arthur Andersen & Co.; Campbell, Sharp; Clarkson Gordon; Collins, Barrow/Maheu, Noiseux; Coopers & Lybrand; Deloitte Haskins & Sells; Dunwoody and Company; Ernst & Whinney; MacGillivray & Co.; Price Waterhouse; Raymond, Chabot, Martin, Paré & Associés; Thorne Riddell; and Touche Ross & Co. Many of these firms received substantial fees from various federal departments and agencies; firms do not lightly antagonize a client, so the letter was a measure of their concern.

The Friday after this letter was mailed, a meeting was held in Ottawa between the CICA and the Minister of Energy Mines and Resources, the Honorable Marc Lalonde, and his staff. This meeting was not a pleasant one. Those sympathetic to the CICA stand recall the Minister as being pleasant but blunt: he did not intend to let the CICA interfere with the public perception of the National Energy Policy, and regrettable as overruling the CICA with legislation might be, it was an outcome that would be used if the CICA forced his hand. The CICA representatives said they could not agree to the Minister's demands since they had arrived at their stand carefully and with due consultation with the parties concerned. To change their stand simply because the Minister demanded it would be contrary to their role as an independent and politically neutral standard-setting body. One participant remembers the Minister's attitude as "treating us like a bunch of shiny-assed bookkeepers."

For those favoring the government view, the CICA's stand was infuriating. Why did the CICA have to be so rigidly inflexible now, when it appeared they had been more accommodating to others over earlier issues? Why did they posture about remaining pure about setting accounting standards when they had already lost their virginity to the oil companies? Why did they insist on an accounting policy that favored the multi-nationals and discriminated against Canadian companies, when they knew the NEP's purpose was to do the opposite? Didn't they understand the interventionist philosophy of this government, and particularly the Minister of Energy? Was this anglophone establishment telling the Minister that they would govern the country, not him?

The meeting ended with both sides angry at what transpired, so it was hardly appropriate for setting the atmosphere for another meeting the following Wednesday, this time in Toronto at the Granite Club. The President of the CICA, Dennis Culver, had been involved for some time, and he chaired the meeting. The participants sat around a table in the shape of a hollow square, with the Chairman seated at one end with senior staff of AcSC beside him. Those favoring offset mostly sat down one side of the table and those favoring the CICA position down the other.

This meeting went no better than the one with the Minister. The Minister's representative stressed that they were there to "make a deal," and expressed the hope that they could arrive at a mutually satisfactory conclusion. The CICA representatives explained again that accounting standard setting was a long process of consultation and discussion, and they were not in a position to make changes for the reasons they had already advanced. There was a confrontational atmosphere in the room, and one time the two sides went into a huddle in a separate part of the room to discuss their next move. Not surprisingly, no agreement came out of the meeting.

The Ontario Securities Commission intervenes
The Ontario Securities Commission (OSC) had been watching these developments with unease. The OSC is charged with maintaining an efficient capital market that operates with integrity, and it viewed political intervention into standard setting as undesirable.

The Commission received information that led it to believe that in early March the federal government intended to issue (shortly after the abortive meeting at the Granite Club), an Order-in-Council along the lines threatened by the Minister of Energy at the meeting with the CICA the previous week. It prepared a formal legal Notice to be published in the OSC Bulletin which would, on this issue, (1) remind companies that mandatory CICA regulations must be complied with unless specific permission to the contrary had been obtained from the OSC; and (2) require companies with reservations in their auditors' reports as to their accounting treatment to appear at a public hearing.

Since the whole point of the proposed Order-in-Council was to permit companies to use offset, get an unqualified audit report, and get easier access to capital markets, the OSC stand was obviously serious. The OSC told the legal counsel for the federal government about the proposed Notice and he persuaded the OSC to give him a week to try to work something out with the federal government that would make such a Notice unnecessary. The OSC agreed, giving him until the next printer's deadline of noon, Friday, March 12.

During that week the remaining advocates of offset considered their position. Possibly they could persuade the OSC to hold a hearing on the merits of the CICA proposal, although this was unlikely given the OSC's traditional support of the standard-making authority of the CICA. Possibly they should let the Order-in-Council go ahead and fight it out with the OSC and other securities commissions and — just possibly — with the CICA in the courts.

On Wall Street there was a rumor that the CBCA would be amended to permit the government to expropriate shares held by non-Canadians in Canadian energy corporations. That week's edition of the Financial Post came out on Thursday with an article, "PIP Grant Sparks Row in Accounting." It quoted the OSC Chairman, Henry Knowles, as saying, "If this (i.e., federal legislation to control accounting standards) goes through, it will destroy the credibility of the accounting profession as a self-regulating and policing organization." Knowles also added, "Our business is full, true and plain disclosure."

Government backs down
At 11:45 of the last day, March 12, the Chairman of the OSC received a phone call to say that the federal government would not be proceeding "at this time" with the Order-in-Council. The proposed Order was not issued. The following week Norcen, one of the main advocates of flow through, put out a news release about its net income for 1981. It used the CICA grant method.

A week after the March meeting at the Granite Club the Minister of Energy wrote a frigid letter to the President of the CICA. In it he said, "The unsatisfactory nature of these discussions led me, and those of my colleagues who have responsibilities in this area, to review the entire nature of the relationship between government and the accounting profession in the area of financial reporting for federal government purposes. You may expect to hear from me in this regard."

The anger in Ottawa at the "CICA monopoly," as it came to be called, did not die away. Work went on with the intricate drafting of the proposed legislation. Meanwhile the CICA was putting plans in place to inform its members as widely as possible about the issues, while at the same time removing any mention of the confrontational aspects of the issue. In May representatives of the CICA appeared before the Standing Committee on Energy Legislation of the House of Commons to explain their stand on the PIP accounting issue. The questions asked them appeared to indicate that most of the honorable members didn't understand the issue and didn't care to.

At some point in April or May 1982 the decision formed in Ottawa that there was not enough to be gained in pushing through the proposed legislation. Anger at the CICA had not subsided all that much, but the political decision was made that it wasn't worth it. The Minister had counted his friends and he didn't have enough. On the other hand, there was no reason for him to forget who his friends were.

This article was researched and prepared while the author was on sabbatical leave at the National Office of Deloitte Haskins & Sells, Toronto. While that firm provided assistance, the views expressed are solely those of the author. A more complete English version, suitable for teaching purposes, is available from Dr. A.K. Mason, Deloitte Haskins & Sells, P.O. Box 6, Royal Bank Plaza, Toronto M5J 2J1.

59

HOW THE REGULATORS SEE US[1]

By Stanley M. Beck and Paul G. Cherry

The performance of auditors has been the subject of intense scrutiny and mounting criticism lately, fuelled perhaps by some spectacular business failures. In Canada, the financial misfortunes of the Canadian Commercial and Northland banks received extensive media coverage. The banks' auditor were lambasted by the hardhitting, no-nonsense inquiry headed by Mr. Justice Willard Z. Estey.

It is tempting to conclude that the issue is simply the responsibility of auditors to detect, report and possibly predict business failures. Or, put more positively, to verify an enterprise's viability as a going concern. We shall leave this for others to debate. We believe the issue of audit failures goes far beyond the relatively narrow, albeit high-profile, area of business failures.

Are we experiencing more audit failures today? By that we mean the failure by auditors to discharge their professional responsibilities adequately. Audit failures, or at least reported failures, have not reached epidemic proportions in Canada. Thousands of financial statements are issued and reported on without incident each year -- an impressive performance.

Using insurance claims and litigation as indicators, the track record of Canadian auditors is significantly better than that of their American colleagues. Perhaps this simply reflects the greater resources of the Securities and Exchange Commission (SEC) in enforcement matters and the generally more litigious US environment with its contingency fees and class actions.

---

[1]Transcribed from original script of CA Magazine, Oct. 1987, pp.40-44.

Most audit failures to date have involved errors of omission and commission; normal audit procedures, properly executed, or a proper interpretation of evidence already gathered would have detected the problem. The risk of audit failures resulting from errors of this sort is probably diminishing, particularly for larger companies. Large audits involve many professionals, often with different levels of expertise and experience, and are generally subject to quality-control procedures to ensure normal audit procedures have been properly applied.

THE REAL RISK OF AUDIT FAILURES

Some might conclude that the risk of audit failure has declined. To the contrary. It's a new, rapidly changing, increasingly complex world characterized by large and growing organizations. It's also a jungle -- fiercely competitive and multinational. Information has become a commodity; opinions are sought, obtained, communicated and compared quickly and widely.

How are auditors bearing up? Although the "bad actors" may be relatively few in number, the profession as a whole must keep its members within bounds or run the risk of the few tarnishing the reputation of the many. We are also concerned that trends may be developing that, if unchecked, could undermine the audit function.

In our view, the real risk of major audit failures relates to judgment errors, inadequate understanding of the business being audited and lack of professional will. The Estey report illustrates the growing importance of judgement and business sense to the profession. The bank's auditors were evidently well aware of the accounting practices that caused Judge Estey so much concern.

Estey criticized "technicalities of accounting rules" if their result offends common sense. In his view, the auditors "enslaved themselves to management decisions" by a restrictive interpretation of their role and an expansive interpretation of the role of management and the directors. Still, Estey cannot be taken as the final determination of what is acceptable accounting and auditing practice for banks.

Some auditors will undoubtedly argue that his understanding of auditing standards and the role of auditors was seriously, even fatally, flawed. Flawed or not, it would be foolhardy of the profession to ignore the warning. After all, who can disagree with his acid test of an audit as "the overall impression of a neutral observer who 'stands back'"? And who can expect to pass this test without professional will?

THE MACDONALD COMMISSION

In 1985, the CICA established the Commission to Study the Public's Expectations of Audits, chaired by William A. Macdonald, a prominent lawyer. If the commissioners, all independent volunteers, find there is a gap between the public's wants and needs and what audits can reasonably accomplish, their report, expected sometime this year, will recommend changes.

The staff of the Ontario Securities Commission (OSC) made a submission to the Macdonald commission that dealt at length with some serious issues facing auditors today. Both accounting and auditing matters were addressed, because the two are inextricably linked. The major points raised in the submission and discussed here reflect the very real problems OSC accountants face on a daily basis.

Accounting Standards

We support the style of accounting standards presently reflected in the CICA Handbook -- broad statements of principles and a minimum of detailed rules. It is essential, however, that the general framework be complete. There are a number of important accounting issues for which standards are lacking entirely or are too general to be of practical value. The objective should be to reduce significantly the alternative accounting treatments for any given transaction.

The present approach relies heavily on professional judgment to flesh out the general standards in a manner consistent with them. Once again we see how important professional will is in our present system.

Unfortunately, it's not working the way it should. Similar transactions are being accounted for in radically different ways. Some accountants and auditors seem to take the position that, in the absence of a clear Handbook Recommendation to the contrary, anything goes. Others resort to a strict, literal interpretation of the Handbook (ignoring anything not in italics), following the letter but not the spirit of the Recommendations. They seize on any source (often US pronouncements) that supports their position, but dismiss anything that goes against their desired result on the grounds that it's not a Canadian rule and can therefore be ignored.

It is highly dangerous, and often misleading, to borrow bits and pieces from foreign sources without adopting all the other related treatments that foreign GAAP would have required. The result can be a highly biased presentation contrary to the clear intent of the standard setters.

Accountants and auditors must restore whatever credibility they may have lost. They cannot escape responsibility, even by relying on other experts or specialists. Handbook Section 5360.14, "Using the Work of a Specialist", requires that the auditor "should satisfy himself, based on his knowledge of the business and his knowledge of the specialist's methods," that the expert's work and findings are reasonable for the intended purposes.

There is no escaping it -- auditors must strongly assert their independence and exercise sound professional judgment in assessing any proposed financial presentation.

The standard-setting process must respond more quickly. The capital markets cannot afford to wait years while the standard setters deliberate on a topic. Nor should all complex accounting problems necessarily find their way into the Handbook. Still, we are pleased to note recent actions being taken by the CICA, such as the decision to expand the use of guidelines to provide timely guidance on emerging issues and on the potential impact of new US standards in Canada, and the creation of the Accounting Standards Financial Institutions Task Force. These are steps in the right direction, but they're not enough.

A forum should be created to identify and debate emerging issues, perhaps along the lines of the Emerging Issues Task Force recently established by the US Financial Accounting Standards Board. Representatives of preparers, major user groups, regulators and auditors would be invited to participate -- their objective to establish a consensus quickly on the appropriate response to issues. We expect a consensus would be reached on most issues.

These views -- what might be described as "best thinking" -- should be widely circulated. The onus would be on practitioners to justify departures from the consensus. To the extent the consensus view becomes well-established practice (that is, GAAP), no further action by the CICA might be required. In some situations, a guideline might ensue; in a few, Handbook Recommendations would ultimately be required to replace the stop-gap measures.

The Importance of Strong Self-Discipline

The OSC supports self-regulation. Rather than prosecute delinquent accountants and auditors on criminal charges under Section 118 of the Securities Act, we generally prefer to refer such matters back to the profession for action. But the profession must improve its disciplinary procedures. Its processes are slow and shrouded in secrecy, much of their impact lost due to the lengthy lag before disciplinary action is finally taken.

The disciplinary process focuses on the individuals involved. When audit reports are issued by partnerships -- some very large and well known -- the public identifies with the partnership, not the partners. When something goes wrong, the firms should be held accountable by their peers. The time has come to develop effective sanctions against partnerships and professional corporations as well as against individuals.

Enforcement matters fall within the jurisdiction of the provincial institutes. Regional, national, international and even worldwide accounting organizations audit many Canadian companies. In part, this is a response to the needs of a growing clientele of national and multinational companies. The profession cannot ignore the fact that as the business activities of their clients become more national in scope, the financial statements of those clients are being used across the country. The damage to the profession and to the public that might flow from uneven and inadequate enforcement could have national repercussions. The time has come for a national approach to disciplinary matters.

Discipline must be effective and must be perceived as such. In this way, credibility will be preserved and perhaps enhanced. Strong and effective discipline is essential in a system that places so much importance on the exercise of sound professional judgment. It must be strong self-discipline, or regulators will have to take a more active role as an enforcer.

Meaningful Financial Analysis

It is becoming clear that users do not fully understand the limitations of present-day financial reports. Nor do they fully appreciate the concepts of materiality and judgment applied in auditing them. Management is in the best position to explain and interpret their companies' results and the nature of the financial reporting process.

The CICA Handbook already requires disclosure of information by industry segments. We are concerned that extremely broad definitions of industry segments are being used. Many large entities report as a single business. Accordingly, they do not segment their revenues, expenses, operating profit or loss of identifiable assets in any meaningful way in their financial statements. Yet the very annual reports, prospectuses, information circulars and similar documents of which those financial statements form a part often contain reports on the various different operating divisions and product lines.

In the United States, SEC registrants are required to publish a management discussion and analysis of financial condition and results of operations -- an MD&A. More specifically, an MD&A discusses a company's liquidity, capital resources and results of operations, all of which are necessary to gain an understanding of it financial condition, changes in that condition and results of operations. An explanation of changes, known material trends and unusual events are also disclosed. The MD&A does not form part of the financial statements.

Both the CICA and the securities commissions have an important role to play in improving the quantity and quality of financial analysis. The time has come for some form of MD&A disclosures in Canada. The OSC and the Commission des valeurs mobilières du Québec have a joint project under way and hope to publish draft proposals for comment shortly. At the same time, the CICA should bolster its segmented disclosure requirements, which are presently being interpreted in a way that makes it possible to avoid meaningful segmentation in many instances.

MD&A and segmented information should support and reinforce each other. The regulators and standard setters should develop criteria for industry segmentation that would serve as the framework for both sets of requirements.

It is encouraging to note that seven of the "Big Eight" US accounting firms have called for auditors' involvement in reviewing and reporting on MD&A. We understand the Auditing Standards Board of the American Institute of Certified Public Accountants has agreed to publish such a standard. Said its chairman Jerry Sullivan: "This is a clear indication to our critics that we're willing to involve ourselves in this area of so-called soft information." When we and the Commission des valeurs mobilières du Québec have issued our joint proposals, we will be urging the CICA to take similar action.

OUR OBJECTIVES: CLARITY, RELEVANCE AND INTEGRITY

Paul Guy, chairman of the Quebec Securities Commission, explained to Judge Estey that the rationale for the regulation of financial reporting is "most notably to enable investors to make an enlightened judgment as to the real financial situation of companies that solicit investment from the public and the value to be accorded to securities issued by those companies". In his words, the regulator seeks "financial statements that readily and unambiguously convey a clear image of a company's financial situation."

The group of seven major US accounting firms have also called for sweeping changes in generally accepted auditing standards (GAAS): "We [the public accounting profession] have an obligation to the public, our clients, and ourselves to devote our best professional efforts toward assuring the financial statements we audit maintain the relevance, reliability, and credibility necessary to assure their utility.

"Even if financial statements contain relevant and reliable data, their utility depends on whether users believe the data. This, in turn, depends on users' faith in the system of financial reporting and the competence and integrity of the auditor of a particular set of financial statements."

What will it take to preserve faith in the system? In addition to addressing the problems already discussed, the key will be greater cooperation and coordination -- at the provincial and national levels within the profession and between the private and public sectors. The price of failure will inevitably be more rules, less scope for professional judgment, and greater external regulation.

Stanley M. Beck, QC, is Chairman of the Ontario Securities Commission. Paul Cherry, CA, is the OSC's Chief Accountant.

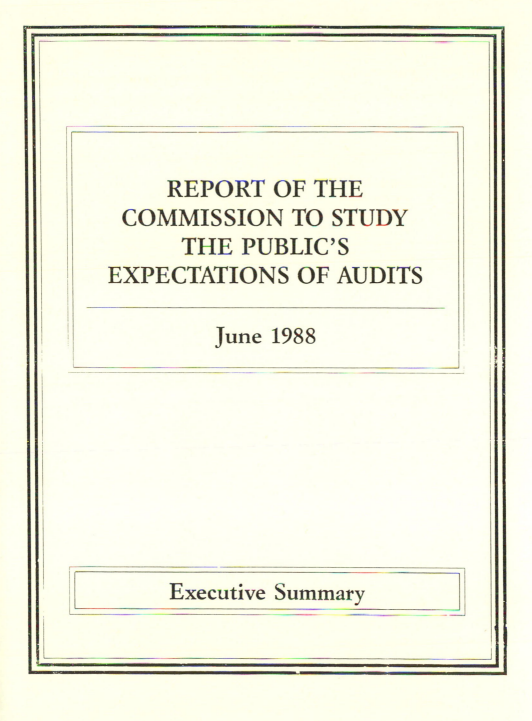

REPORT OF THE COMMISSION TO STUDY THE PUBLIC'S EXPECTATIONS OF AUDITS

June 1988

Executive Summary

INTRODUCTION

This Commission was established by the Board of Governors of the Canadian Institute of Chartered Accountants (CICA) with the following mandate:

The Commission is charged to study the public's expectations of audits. Where a gap exists between what the public expects or needs and what auditors can and should reasonably expect to accomplish, the Commission is charged to develop conclusions and recommendations to determine how the disparity should be resolved.

The members of the Commission are all volunteers, with varying backgrounds in accounting, business, banking, education, government, law, and public policy. The Commission was established as a body entirely independent of the CICA and received its full cooperation in maintaining that independence.

Our Report is addressed to the CICA Board of Governors, but its subject matter is clearly of general public interest. We have therefore assumed little knowledge of accounting or financial reporting on the part of the reader.

REASONS FOR THIS STUDY

In a free society, those entrusted with public responsibilities are accountable to the public for their actions. The concept of accountability is reflected in our political, economic, and social structures, and lies at the heart of our financial disclosure system.

A sound financial disclosure system is essential to a free economy and is clearly a matter of public interest. Every day, many individual economic decisions are made in reliance upon publicly available financial information. Good financial disclosure cannot undo poor economic performance, but it is basic to accountability and to the important decisions that allocate financial resources in our society. The public interest in financial disclosure is recognized in corporations and securities legislation, as well as statutes providing for the regulation of financial institutions.

Audited financial statements form the backbone of corporate financial disclosure. The legal responsibility for preparing and circulating financial statements is assigned to the directors of corporations. This responsibility is in practice shared by directors, audit committees, chief executive officers, and other management. Auditors are responsible for rendering an independent, professional opinion on the compliance of the financial statements with legal standards for financial reporting. In order to render this opinion, auditors must conduct an audit, in the form of an independent, professional examination of the financial statements and supporting evidence. The independence and professionalism of auditors add credibility to audited financial statements and are thus central to the public's expectations of audits.

In any relationship such as that existing between auditors and users of financial statements or other financial information, mutual satisfaction depends upon fairly close correspondence between what is expected and what is actually delivered. If that correspondence is not achieved, the relationship will be unstable, and changes may be imposed that are unsatisfactory to some, or even all, of the interested parties.

The establishment of this independent Commission by the CICA is important evidence of the profession's recognition that, in serving the public interest, it must be guided by public expectations. We believe that through hard work and dedication of purpose, the profession can meet those expectations and play a leading role in improving the performance of our financial disclosure system.

STUDY LOGIC AND PROCESS

We began our task with no preconceived notions, except a belief in the need for a free and independent accounting profession. Our inquiry focused primarily on audits of public corporations. We did not consider in any depth the public's expectations of audits of governments or government-controlled enterprises, although we did benefit from excellent submissions concerning legislative audits.

Our efforts were initially directed at ascertaining the nature of the public's expectations of audits and any expectation gaps that may exist. We then spent considerable time developing and considering the merits of recommendations directed at reducing or eliminating the gaps that we identified. We recognized that recommendations suggesting legislative change usually take time to achieve and sought other solutions wherever possible. We also recognized that, to be effective, recommendations would have to be practical and capable of reasonable implementation.

We gathered information from numerous sources, including:

- A major public opinion survey conducted by Decima Research Limited at our request.

- Focus group interviews with knowledgeable parties conducted by Decima.

- Public hearings held by the Commission in Montreal, Toronto, Winnipeg, Calgary, and Vancouver.

- Written submissions made to the Commission.

- Meetings and consultation with knowledgeable parties, including representatives of the accounting professions and financial regulators in the United States and England.

We are grateful for the time and effort expended by those who contributed to this process.

MAJOR FINDINGS

Our Report covers many topics, and accordingly includes a multitude of specific observations and conclusions. Our major observations and conclusions may be summarized broadly as follows:

- The public as a whole continues to have a high level of respect for auditors. However, the public is also largely ignorant of the extent of the responsibilities entrusted to auditors under our legal system and the limitations on what an audit can reasonably be expected to achieve. That being so, public trust in auditors could easily be shat-

tered by a few highly publicized instances of apparent audit failures.

- There exist a number of areas in which some of the most knowledgeable segments of the public feel that their expectations are not being fulfilled or may not be in future. The profession cannot afford to be complacent in the face of this trend. Vigorous actions are required to allay concerns about auditors' independence and professionalism and about the strength of the standards that govern financial disclosure with which auditors are associated.

- For the most part, the public's expectations of audits are reasonable and achievable. The public expects the auditor to be competent and independent, notwithstanding any commercial pressures. The public also assigns a high measure of responsibility to the auditor for the quality and adequacy of the financial information with which the auditor is associated.

- Inevitably, some expectation gaps stem from the public's limited knowledge of auditor responsibilities and what can reasonably be expected from an audit. Better communication of the respective roles of auditors and management can improve the public's understanding. It is unlikely, however, that any organized program of education would be effective. For the most part, expectation gaps will be narrowed only by the profession's acceptance of the need for change and improvement.

- The auditor faces significant challenges under our present system. The auditor's duty is to report on management's accounting, not to do the accounting. If not satisfied with management's financial report, an auditor's only recourse is to qualify the audit report. Such action can strain the auditor's relationship with management and may even damage the company itself. Hence, it will not be lightly undertaken. The auditor must also maintain the objectivity of his or her opinion, even though management has a strong influence on the audit appointment.

- The challenges to the auditor's independence and professionalism are unlikely to be relieved by any practical change to the present legal structure for financial reporting and audit. Measures to strengthen the audit environment, extend financial disclosure, and fortify the auditor's professionalism can be of significant assistance. In the end, however, the profession will stand or fall on the strength of the integrity and commitment of individual auditors and firms.

- There is a need for improved management of the relationships between the various parties responsible for financial reporting. The directors and management of companies, and, in the case of financial institutions, their regulators each have an important role and responsibility. It is not up to auditors alone to push for full and fair financial reports.

- The audit committee of the board should play a pivotal role in the management of these relationships. It should develop its own philosophy of good financial reporting, and it should be charged with a responsibility to oversee the company's financial disclosure, evaluate the effectiveness of the audit, and protect the independence of the auditor. An audit committee, however, is not a panacea. The auditor, when necessary, must be aggressive in seeing that each responsible party plays its part.

- Well-conceived accounting standards can greatly assist the auditor by reducing the scope for disagreement with management. Although the CICA standard-setting efforts are highly respected, improvements are needed in their completeness and timeliness, and in the elimination of alternative accounting methods not justified by substantial differences in circumstances.

- The profession faces challenges to its competence from the rapidly changing business and financial environment, and to its ability to maintain its economic well-being in the face of increasing competitive pressures. Some changes in standards of auditing and professional conduct should be helpful. What is most needed, however, is a determination by audit firms that the quality of the audit will not be compromised by commercial pressures. A dedication to professionalism is the best and only effective strategy for the long run.

- The public's satisfaction with auditors depends upon the scope as well as the reliability of financial disclosure with which the auditor is associated. Some public expectations of audits can only be met if the scope of financial disclosure is expanded. Above all, the public expects better information, in financial statements or in a "Management Discussion and Analysis," bearing on the risks to which a company is exposed. In particular, the public demands a warning of the possibility of imminent business failure.

- There appears to be a narrowly focused expectation gap concerning the auditor's responsibility with respect to fraud that may distort the financial statements of a company. It seems clear that the auditor must give more attention to the possibility of fraud in planning the audit program. There may also be some expectation that the auditor report to outside authorities on fraudulent or other illegal activities by a client. The auditor needs some better way to cope with this expectation, notwithstanding the normal rule that knowledge of a client's affairs is expected to be kept confidential.

- There are a limited number of occasions when the reasons for an auditor's resignation or dismissal ought to be disclosed in the public interest, and yet the present policy of the Canadian Securities Administrators will not elicit that disclosure. To allow for such situations, there ought to be much faster notification to securities commissions concerning an auditor's resignation or proposed replacement. Along with that notification the commissions should receive sufficient information from the auditor to make a judgment whether early public notification or some other action is required in the public interest.

- The public strongly believes that the auditor of a financial institution has a responsibility to act in the public interest as well as in the shareholders' interests. The best way to achieve this is to ensure that the government regulator is both able and required to participate in communications between the auditor, the audit committee, and management in all matters concerned with the financial well-being of the institution. The auditor should also be given a responsibility to report to the regulator on the design and functioning of internal control systems in such institutions.

SUMMARY OF RECOMMENDATIONS

Our recommendations for action are summarized below in the context of broad objectives and specific goals. In making these recommendations we have followed certain working principles. The recommendations should be effective in meeting their goals. They should not carry disadvantages that outweigh their advantages. Finally, they must take into account the reality of what cannot be changed.

Our recommendations have three broad objectives: (1) to strengthen the independence of the auditor, (2) to strengthen the professionalism of the auditor, and (3) to extend and improve financial disclosure. Coupled with these positive objectives is a defensive objective, namely, to lessen public misunderstanding.

Strengthening the Independence of the Auditor

We believe the independence of the auditor can be strengthened if three goals are achieved.

- The first goal follows logically from our conclusion that changes to the present legal structure of responsibility for financial reporting would not be workable. This being so, it is important to the public interest that each party bearing financial reporting responsibilities fulfil its role with maximum effectiveness. Our first goal, therefore, is to improve the management of the relationships between the responsible parties as a vital element in fulfilling public expectations. We believe that such effective management will materially strengthen the independence of the auditor, since the other responsible parties will need and should value the assistance of the auditor's impartial opinion and advice in performing their own roles.

- The second goal is to strengthen accounting standards. Given the division of responsibility for financial reporting, the auditor cannot control the quality of financial disclosure. The best that he or she can do is to influence it within the limits established under accounting standards. Since the auditor will always be deemed to have some responsibility when there is a perceived shortcoming in the quality of financial disclosure, these standards, in conjunction with the way in which the auditor manages relationships with other responsible parties, are central to the auditor's ability to meet public expectations. Indeed, we see accounting standards as essential bulwarks for the auditor's independence. Although business is far too complex to permit development of a specific accounting rule to cover every imaginable situation, well-reasoned, well-articulated, and timely standards should substantially reduce the scope for legitimate disagreement.

- The third goal is to strengthen the profession's code of conduct and its enforcement in those aspects that relate to the auditor's independence.

Management of the Relationships between Parties Responsible for Financial Reporting. Our view is that each party involved in financial reporting has its own role to play and its own problems in doing so, but the handling of the relationships between them is a problem they have in common. This means that no one party is entitled to ignore its own responsibility simply on the assumption that some other party is to be relied upon. We believe the public and the courts will expect each party to assume full responsibility for its own role. To discharge that responsibility fully, each party will be expected to satisfy itself that any reliance placed on other parties is justified.

Strengthening the communication among parties responsible for financial reporting should be a significant help to the performance of the auditor's responsibility. Establishing easy and active communication between directors and auditors is particularly important. Directors have responsibility for the final approval of the audited financial statements, but they lack the detailed knowledge of the company's activities necessary to ensure that the disclosure is the best possible. For this detailed knowledge they rely in the first instance upon management personnel. However, they should also not only welcome the independent viewpoint of the auditor but recognize they have an obligation to obtain it. For their part, auditors are able to perform their monitoring and

478

evaluation role much better if they are able to communicate easily with those who have the ultimate responsibility for the financial report. An effective audit committee has proved itself a valuable channel of communication between the auditor and the board. We believe it will become even more important in the future, and that the courts are likely to recognize this to an increasing degree when called upon to assess the performance and related responsibilities of auditors, audit committees, and directors in general.

We urge that auditors be aggressive in using this means of communication. Accordingly, we recommend that guidance be provided in the CICA Handbook concerning matters that auditors ought to raise with audit committees and how to conduct relations with them (Recommendation R-2). To facilitate this better liaison and performance, we recommend changes in the law as necessary to require that boards of public companies appoint audit committees composed entirely of outside directors (R-1). We also recommend that the law recognize the key role of audit committees by requiring that boards of directors make public the responsibilities assigned to their audit committees, that audit committees report annually to the shareholders on the performance of their mandate, and, specifically, that audit committees review interim financial statements as well as annual financial statements before publication (R-3).

We further recommend that auditors see that audit committees are fully informed about frauds that have, or could have had, a material effect on the financial statements and any significant weaknesses in internal controls, particularly those that are important to fraud prevention. Similarly, the auditor should see that the audit committee is fully informed about any significant infractions of the law committed in carrying on the business of the company of which the auditor is aware (R-33, 37).

A regulator of a financial institution is another party with a significant interest in its financial reporting. We believe that regulators are entitled to full disclosure of information in the possession of the management, directors, and auditors of a financial institution that is pertinent to the regulators' responsibilities. We also believe that regulators have a positive reciprocal obligation to disclose information to auditors and directors that may be important to the

institution's financial statements. We recommend that all financial institutions be required to have audit committees composed of outside directors (R-42). We suggest that model legal provisions be developed to facilitate communication between auditors, regulators, and directors of financial institutions (R-41). In addition, we recommend that, to cover the situation where legal obligations to communicate are absent or deficient, the provincial institutes of chartered accountants relax professional confidentiality requirements to enable the auditor to communicate matters of great moment to the regulator (with notice to the directors) if the institution itself fails to do so (R-43).

Finally, it must be recognized that there will be times when it proves impossible to achieve a strong relationship between the parties responsible for a company's financial reporting. There will even be occasions, fortunately rare, when an auditor feels compelled to resign because of loss of confidence in the trustworthiness of the managers and/or directors of a client, or for other reasons. It seems likely that on some, but not necessarily all, of these occasions the shareholders and public have a right to know why the auditor has resigned or has been replaced.

We think the auditor's existing responsibilities in connection with public notification of resignation or replacement should be modified. The present policy of the Canadian Securities Administrators requires public notification by the company of changes in auditors, accompanied by a description of "reportable disagreements" between the company and the auditor. A reportable disagreement, in essence, is a disagreement that led to a reservation of the auditor's opinion on financial disclosure of the company, or would have led to such reservation had the auditor completed the engagement. This policy should continue, but the definition of reportable disagreement should be strengthened (R-39).

A major amendment to the policy should also be made to cover the situation of auditor changes for reasons that are important—such as lack of trust by the auditor in the management of the client—but that do not fall under the definition of a reportable disagreement. We suggest that the present policy be expanded so that securities commissions would receive more timely notification from the auditor of the significant reasons he or she believes explain the auditor's resignation or dismissal. Upon receipt of this notification, the commissions should have the discretion to make further inquiries and require early public disclosure, or take such other action as may be decided is in the public interest (R-38).

We also recommend a change in the profession's codes of conduct for the protection of possible successor auditors of both public and private companies. We advocate a change in the codes so as to require an auditor who resigns or is displaced to disclose to a proposed successor auditor any knowledge of fraud or illegal activity by the company that the incumbent auditor believes was an important factor in the change of auditors (R-40). In general, we may note that securities regulators, like regulators of financial institutions, also have a significant responsibility for financial reporting of companies under their oversight. Better communication between them and auditors, and, where appropriate, audit committees, would be a desirable development.

Strengthening Accounting Standards. Although some criticisms of individual accounting standards have been expressed to us, we believe that, overall, the body of standards developed to date by the CICA is well regarded. At the same time, there is increasing dissatisfaction caused by holes in the coverage of accounting standards and by alternative methods of application which permit wide disparities in results reported in identical circumstances. In addition, there is marked dissatisfaction with the speed of the standard-setting process and its apparent inability to date to deal satisfactorily with fast-emerging accounting problems.

We have several recommendations. We believe the CICA Accounting Standards Committee should mount a special effort to identify and deal, in order of priority and urgency, with issues not satisfactorily covered in present accounting standards (R-4). There should also be a program to identify and eliminate so far as possible those alternative accounting methods that cannot be justified by differences in circumstances (R-7). Both these recommendations have particular application to financial institutions. There is a need to arrive at suitable accounting standards for banks that are consistent with accepted accounting theory. There is also a need for reduction of the alternatives found in accounting for other financial

institutions (R-44). If a regulator of a given type of financial institution desires financial statements that use artificial or unrealistically conservative valuations, we recommend that such statements be submitted as special-purpose reports and not be circulated in competition with financial statements prepared on the usual basis (R-45). We also see a need for a separate committee or task force to provide quick practical advice on new accounting issues (R-6).

Implementation of these recommendations will undoubtedly require an increase in the already substantial effort devoted to standard setting. We recommend a study how to expedite standard setting without sacrificing due process (R-5). We also suggest consideration of ways to increase output and obtain additional financial support for standard setting (R-9).

Auditor Independence and the Profession's Code of Conduct. In our view, the principal defence against pressures on the independence of auditors must lie in the integrity of individual auditors and audit firms. We have, however, some limited recommendations for actions by the provincial institutes to help ensure the auditor's independence. We suggest consideration of ways to limit overdependence upon a single client for revenue (R-28). We suggest a stronger warning in the profession's code of conduct that an auditor must not permit non-audit services performed for a client to affect the objectivity of the audit opinion (R-29). We also recommend that, when one firm is asked for an accounting opinion by the client of another firm, both firms should communicate fully with each other to establish the facts of the situation for which an opinion is requested and the bases of their separate opinions (R-30).

Strengthening the Professionalism of the Auditor

Strengthening the auditor's independence is essential to meeting public expectations but is not enough by itself. The services offered must also meet the public's needs and be performed with professional skill and judgment. We have identified several goals that, if achieved, should strengthen auditor professionalism and thereby help meet public expectations.

- The first goal is to increase the profession's responsiveness to public concerns. We suggest several specific changes in auditing standards to that end.

- The second goal is to achieve renewed recognition of the vital role of professional judgment in performing an audit. Coupled with this is an emphasis on the requirement for a professional level of skill.

- The third goal is to improve the profession's self-regulation.

Increasing the Responsiveness of Auditing Standards to Public Needs. Auditing standards provide general criteria for satisfactory performance and specific guidance to auditing procedures. The CICA Auditing Standards Committee is composed largely of chartered accountants engaged in the practice of auditing. Since much of the work is highly technical, its members need to be familiar with what an auditor does. At the same time, the decisions of the committee concerning the scope of the auditor's work and the form of the audit report are of broad public interest. We believe the public's views on these matters should be represented. We doubt, however, that direct lay representation on the Auditing Standards Committee would likely be effective in view of the largely technical nature of the committee's work. Our proposed answer is to form a small group of knowledgeable people drawn from business and government to advise the Auditing Standards Committee on such matters as public expectations for auditor performance, subjects that should be studied by the committee, and whether proposed auditing procedures are worth their cost (R-31).

We also recommend that auditing standards be modified and amplified in relation to the discovery of fraud. The auditor should give special attention to internal controls that guard against material employee fraud (R-32). Likewise, the auditor should give special attention to the possibility of fraud in view of the fact that attempts to cover up are likely to make discovery of management fraud by ordinary audit procedures less likely than discovery of error (R-34). Further, we recommend additional guidance with respect to the implications for the auditor's report and for financial disclosure of illegal acts by a client (R-35, R-36).

Finally, recent events in Canada and other countries have suggested that the traditional audited financial statements of financial institutions have not provided the degree of warning of financial difficulty that the public feels entitled to expect. Financial institutions are in the business of investing and lending at risk. Careful monitoring and control of that risk is vital to their continued well-being. That monitoring and control cannot be exercised without well-thought-out systems of management information and internal control. We believe that the time has come when the auditors of financial institutions should be asked to make a more complete review of those systems. The purpose would be to assist management, the directors, and the regulator by providing an independent assessment whether the systems meet criteria indicative of effective and prudent systems of record-keeping, control, and internal audit (R-49).

The Need for Professional Judgment. It is natural that auditors seek rules for their guidance and protection and that regulators and companies sometimes overemphasize literal adherence to rules. Certainly rules and detailed guidance are essential, and we have made several recommendations for their improvement. It would be misleading, however, to suggest that rules can replace the need for professional judgment and the auditor's stand-back assessment, exercised within the framework of reasonable expectations of shareholders and third parties and of the underlying character of accounting principles and standards. Courts are traditionally unwilling to interpret rules in a narrow and literal sense when the results of doing so appear to be unfair or out of keeping with overriding standards and objectives. The same can be assumed to be the case with the expectations of the public at large.

The profession, audit firms, and individual auditors need to bear these realities constantly in mind if public expectations are to be met and liability exposure minimized. Perhaps the biggest single risk and source of danger for the profession in terms of both public expectations and liability exposure, apart from failures of independence and impartiality, is too literal an approach or cast of mind. Neither the courts nor the public have such a cast of mind, so a literal approach to accounting and auditing rules and their application can readily lead auditors to a false sense of security.

There is no ultimate answer to this other than a sense of danger, a sensitivity to what shareholders and other third parties are reasonably entitled to expect, and good professional judgment based on a mature understanding of the possibilities and limits of accounting and auditing. However, we recommend amplification of existing auditing standards to re-emphasize and explain more specifically these matters of judgment: (1) the auditor must be satisfied that the client's choices of significant accounting policies are justified in the circumstances (R-18), (2) the auditor must make an independent assessment of the reasonableness of management's estimates (R-19), and (3) the auditor must be satisfied that the financial statements, resulting after incorporation of all management's judgmental decisions, are not misleading in their overall effect (R-20).

The auditor, of course, must be competent in technical matters as well as having good judgment. We advocate that auditing standards stress the need for the auditor to be knowledgeable about the client's business, especially when it is specialized in character (as are financial institutions, for example) (R-50).

Professional Self-Regulation. In the last analysis, maintenance of professional standards depends upon the behaviour of individual auditors and audit firms. They must maintain their competence and put service to the client ahead of their self-interest. We have also drawn attention to commercial practices that might not create problems in an ordinary business, but can do so for a profession operating within the structural arrangements we have described. To some extent auditors must control their commercial instincts. Or, perhaps more accurately, they must take full account of all factors important to their commercial well-being, including maintenance of reputation and avoidance of exposure to liability with consequent heavy insurance costs. They must be careful to accept and retain only clients with integrity. And, they must not price their services in such a way as to undermine their ability to attract qualified staff and perform work that meets professional standards on every engagement.

One of the principal functions of professional associations is to provide regulation to assist and encourage members to maintain professional standards. We have two observations to make about self-

regulatory provisions in the auditing profession. First, we think that professional discipline procedures are somewhat outdated in that they are taken against individual members only and ignore a larger unit of responsibility—the audit firm. The vast majority of audit reports are signed in a firm name, not that of an individual practitioner. In these cases the public relies on the reputation of the firm and usually is unaware of the identity of the individuals who have worked on the engagement. It is only logical, then, that discipline procedures should be directed to the firm, as well as to individuals who may be at fault (R-27).

A second matter of some concern is the fact that self-regulatory procedures are largely the responsibility of provincial institutes, while the public expects uniform standards nation-wide. We believe the profession would be wise to create a mechanism for achieving common and high standards in codes of professional conduct, practice review procedures, and professional discipline, much as it has done in the field of educational admission standards (R-26).

Extended and Improved Financial Disclosure

A direct way to reduce any public disappointment with the output of auditors is to improve and expand audited financial information so as to more nearly approach public expectations. This suggests two specific goals:

- Expansion of accounting standards so as to lead to better disclosure, both inside and outside financial statements, in line with public expectations.

- Assumption of greater responsibility by the auditor for financial disclosure not contained within the financial statements but associated with them because of its inclusion in the same document. This latter goal suggests broader consideration of the potential role for the auditor in connection with financial disclosure in general, whether or not the disclosure is associated with audited information.

Expansion of Accounting Standards. The evidence submitted to us on public expectations suggests a number of significant extensions of existing accounting standards.

- Additional guidance should be given to the accounting and disclosure to be provided by a company that has failed or is in danger of failing. Guidance is particularly needed to answer what is proper disclosure in the latter situation (R-10). Related to this, we recommend a change in auditing standards. The auditor should be required to call special attention, in an extra paragraph of the audit report, to the financial statements' disclosure of concerns about the company's ability to continue as a going concern (R-11).

- We also recommend an in-depth study, followed by *Handbook* standards, of the disclosure that should be made of the risks and uncertainties to which a company is exposed (R-12). Commitments by a business increase its potential risks and rewards. In view of the increase in the number of significant commitments undertaken by most businesses today, we recommend a comprehensive standard calling for more intensive disclosure of material commitments than is customary in today's practice (R-13). A separate study of risks and commitments in financial institutions is desirable because of their highly specialized nature (R-46).

- There is a risk that the increasing level of disclosure in financial statements could result in vital information being lost in routine, even if important, detail. We recommend consideration of ways to improve note disclosure so that matters of particular current importance will be highlighted (R-14).

- A number of representations were made to us concerning unsatisfactory asset valuations in current accounting. We are satisfied that clearer guidance is needed in accounting standards as to bases of writedowns of different types of assets in different circumstances (R-15). Such guidance is particularly needed for financial institutions (R-48). Consideration should also be given to the need for better disclosure of the bases of estimates and valuations generally (R-16).

- Study is also needed of the difficult problem of reporting information that is useful in assessing liquidity and liquidity trends in financial institutions (R-47).

- Finally, we believe present disclosure of accounting policies should be expanded to become a more comprehensive explanation of the basis for financial reporting, including explanation of management judgments required in the preparation of the financial statements (R-8, 23).

Many companies do provide considerable financial disclosure, in annual reports and elsewhere, over and above that in the audited financial statements. We did not discover a strong public demand for such financial information. We nevertheless believe that greater disclosure outside the financial statements could help public understanding of the significance of information inside the statements. We therefore recommend that the CICA assist and cooperate with securities commissions in developing standards for Management Discussion and Analysis to be presented in annual reports outside the audited financial statements (R-17).

Auditor Association with Financial Disclosure outside the Financial Statements. In view of the probable association of the auditor in the public mind with all financial disclosure in documents that contain audited financial statements, we recommend that auditors insist on the right to review any such information as a condition of accepting an engagement to report on the financial statements (R-21). Auditors may also be asked to take some responsibility for financial disclosure that is not provided in documents containing audited financial statements. Auditing standards should provide guidance to auditor review procedures and the form of reporting (if any) appropriate to the various types of information outside the financial statements (R-22).

Public Misunderstanding

Finally, our inquiries did disclose considerable confusion in the minds of some segments of the public concerning the work that an auditor actually performs and the extent of the auditor's responsibility for the financial information reported. A reduction of this confusion can only be beneficial in limiting expectation gaps. A specific goal, therefore, is to improve communication to the public of the extent of the auditor's responsibility, and that of other parties, for the financial information provided. We recommend two measures. First, a statement of management responsibility should be published in all documents that contain audited financial statements (R-24). Second, the standard audit report should be expanded to explain more fully the nature and extent of the auditor's work and the degree of assurance it provides (R-25). The audit committee's annual report to shareholders, which we have already mentioned, should also help reduce misunderstanding.

IMPLEMENTATION OF THIS REPORT

While this Report examines the public's expectations of audits, those expectations generally reflect the public's expectations of the financial disclosure system as a whole. In that sense, the Report contains messages for all parties who bear responsibility for good financial disclosure, including directors, audit committees, chief executive officers, management, auditors, and regulators. Each of these parties has its own role to play, but their roles should be mutually reinforcing. The public will hold each party to account if the financial disclosure system somehow fails to serve the public interest. In the real world, the public will measure the performance of responsible parties against its current expectations, rather than against fixed and predetermined standards that it is not equipped to understand.

We recognize that our observations and conclusions carry no legal weight. Our views are based on an assessment of public expectations, which in particular cases may exceed the legal duties presently imposed on auditors and other responsible parties. However, to the extent that the law evolves in response to changing times, we believe that all of the responsible parties would be wise to take appropriate action now, based on reasonable public expectations.

We suggest, for example, that as audit committees begin to perform more effectively, those committees that fail to meet established standards of performance will become increasingly exposed to legal liability. Audit committees will likely find the advice and information provided by independent auditors to be of invaluable assistance in meeting these standards.

We also believe that more will be expected of corporate directors in general. They, along with chief executive officers, are responsible for setting the overall tone for corporate behaviour, including the attitude toward financial disclosure. Directors and chief executive officers will both have an interest in, and a responsibility for, selecting audit committee members with suitable qualifications. Among the most important of these qualifications will be a keen sense of danger and an understanding of the importance of preserving the independence of the auditor.

If directors, audit committees, and chief executive officers are to meet their responsibilities, they must be supported by a management team that shares their philosophy of responsible financial disclosure. We believe that improved standards and guidelines for financial accounting and disclosure will assist management in reflecting this philosophy in corporate financial reporting. We also expect that management will be more accountable for failures to adhere to accounting standards if such standards are clear, comprehensive, and precise. Its responsibility will be explicit in the Statement of Management Responsibility that we advocate be included in the annual report.

We have emphasized that the public expects auditors to assist regulators to perform their role of monitoring the health of financial institutions overseen by them, and we have supported this expectation. In their turn, regulators must play their part by making clear what they expect by way of information from auditors, management, audit committees, and directors. We believe further that if communication is improved between regulators, auditors, directors, and audit committees, the public will find it unacceptable if any of these parties fails, in the course of their interaction, to inform the others of relevant financial information. In this sense, each of these parties will have a responsibility to assist the others in performing their roles.

Our recommendations to the CICA, provincial institutes, accounting firms, and individual auditors are stated explicitly in the Report. Each must take action in its sphere of responsibility, and each should be prepared to cooperate when joint action is required. The CICA has responsibility to act with respect to changes in accounting and auditing standards. The provincial institutes have responsibility for changes in codes of conduct and in self-regulatory matters generally. Accounting firms are responsible for appropriate professional behaviour with respect to matters that cannot be regulated in detail, such as their conduct when asked for opinions by clients of other auditors and their policy in competitive bidding situations.

We have one concluding observation. In striving to meet the public's expectations of audits, the profession can achieve an even broader objective. Through the energetic leadership of the CICA and the provincial institutes, and the professional dedication of individual auditors and firms, the profession can profoundly influence the performance of our financial disclosure system to the benefit of all.

Appendix

> The Report's formal Recommendations are reproduced below with paragraph numbers included for ease of reference. These Recommendations are broadly worded and are best understood in the context of the detailed discussion in the Report.

Listing of Recommendations

CHAPTER 4 — STRENGTHENING THE AUDIT ENVIRONMENT

Audit Committees

R-1 The CICA should enlist the support of provincial institutes and other interested bodies in seeking legislative amendments that would require all public companies to have audit committees composed entirely of outside directors. (4.28)

R-2 The CICA Auditing Standards Committee should provide guidance in the *CICA Handbook* to matters that should be raised by an auditor with an audit committee (or in the absence of an audit committee, with the board of directors) and to actions an auditor should take when not satisfied with the results of such communication. The guidance should stress the need for timeliness in communication. (4.28)

R-3 The CICA and provincial institutes of chartered accountants should press for changes in the law to require that (1) boards of directors draw up and publish to the shareholders a formal statement of responsibilities assigned to the audit committee, (2) audit committees report annually to the shareholders on the manner in which they have fulfilled their mandate, and that (3) audit committees review both interim financial statements and annual financial statements before publication. (4.28)

Accounting Standards

R-4 The CICA Accounting Standards Committee should make a comprehensive survey of the existing body of accounting theory, identify important issues for which accounting standards are unstated or unclear, determine priorities, and intensify its efforts to give guidance on those issues, all with a sense of real urgency. (4.35)

R-5 The CICA should move decisively so that the process for production of necessary standards is expedited without sacrificing due process. (4.39)

R-6 The CICA should sponsor a separate committee or task force to express considered opinions on new accounting issues that are likely to receive divergent or unsatisfactory accounting treatment in practice in the absence of some guidance. These opinions should be developed expeditiously and be given wide publicity so that members of the profession can give them due weight when dealing with the issues in question. (4.45)

R-7 The CICA Accounting Standards Committee should undertake a review of GAAP to identify situations in which alternative accounting methods are accepted under GAAP, and should make every effort to eliminate alternatives not justified by substantial differences in circumstances. When it is thought such justification exists, the criteria for selection of the appropriate policy should be stated clearly. (4.54)

R-8   If, in some individual area, support cannot be mustered for the elimination of alternatives not justified by substantial differences in circumstances, accounting standards should require disclosure that the choice of policies in this area is arbitrary. That disclosure should indicate the accounting result that would have been obtained by using the alternative. When disclosure of the result in quantitative terms would be impractical or excessively costly, the indication may be in approximate or general terms (at a minimum stating whether the alternative is more or less conservative than that actually adopted). (See also Recommendation R-23 in Chapter 5.) (4.54)

R-9   The CICA should study how to increase the output of its standard-setting activities. As part of this study, it should consider the possibility of obtaining additional financial support from sources other than membership fees without jeopardizing the independence of the standard-setting function. (4.58)

CHAPTER 5 — FINANCIAL REPORTING: CONTENT, COMMUNICATION, AND AUDIT CONTRIBUTION

Extensions of Financial Disclosure

R-10   The CICA Accounting Standards Committee should study the question of financial reporting when an enterprise is in financial difficulty and issue explicit standards giving guidance to:

- The basis of reporting appropriate for a company that has failed.

- The disclosure that should be made by management in financial statements when an enterprise is a going concern at the reporting date but there is significant danger that it may not be able to continue as such throughout the foreseeable future. Since every enterprise carries some risk of failure, the standard should be as clear as possible concerning (1) how serious the risk of failure must be to require special disclosure of that risk, (2) whether or how gradations in the degree of risk should be indicated in the disclosure, (3) the length of the period ahead for which the risk of failure must be evaluated, and (4) whether or to what extent there is a need for indication of the extent of changes that might be required in the figures reported in the event of business failure. (5.19)

R-11   The CICA Auditing Standards Committee should hold to its present position that qualification of the audit report is not required if financial statements give adequate warning of a serious risk of business failure. It should, however, issue a new standard requiring the auditor to highlight the risk by calling special attention, in an additional paragraph in the audit report, to the financial statement disclosure. (5.19)

R-12   The CICA should initiate and complete as soon as possible a study of risks and uncertainties leading to conclusions as to how they may best be disclosed in financial statements or elsewhere (e.g. in Management's Discussion and Analysis in the annual report). Such a study should:

- Describe the nature of uncertainties and risks in some depth.

- Attempt a classification of different types of uncertainties and risks and provide guidelines for assessing their significance, particularly in terms of magnitude and probabilities.

- Consider how each category might best be disclosed and provide guidance on the form of disclosure.

- Indicate how and when gains and losses should be recognized in the financial statements (along the lines of present recommendations with respect to contingencies).

Handbook recommendations based upon this study should be issued as soon as possible after its completion. (5.28)

R-13 *CICA Handbook* recommendations with respect to disclosure of commitments should be amplified so that material commitments, when not capitalized as assets and liabilities in the balance sheet, will be disclosed in fuller detail than is customary in today's practice. (5.32)

R-14 The CICA Accounting Standards Committee should consider how financial disclosure in notes supplementing the financial statements might be arranged so as to highlight matters of particular importance—including disclosure of risks and doubts as to going-concern status—and provide guidance in a standard on disclosure. (5.34)

Valuations and Estimates

R-15 The CICA Accounting Standards Committee should give priority to defining more precisely the bases for writedowns of assets below cost-based figures, particularly in relation to the assets of specialized industries where the valuation placed on specific classes of assets is highly material to the reported net equity of the enterprise. (5.42)

R-16 The Committee should also consider whether there is a need for better guidance with respect to disclosure of the bases used in making accounting estimates and the possible range in the valuation figures that could have resulted within the exercise of reasonable judgment. (5.42)

Disclosure Outside Financial Statements

R-17 The CICA should look favourably on additional financial disclosure of a softer, more subjective nature in a Management Discussion and Analysis section of the annual report. The CICA should assist and cooperate with securities commissions in the development of standards for information in the MD & A. (5.46)

Exercise of Auditor's Judgment

R-18 The general principle that the auditor should be satisfied that the client's accounting policies are appropriate should be continued. The CICA Auditing Standards Committee should amplify that standard to emphasize that:

- When an accounting standard is stated in general terms and judgment is required as to the accounting policy to be adopted for implementation, the auditor should be satisfied that the accounting policy used is a fair and reasonable interpretation of the spirit of the standard.

- When new accounting policies are adopted in response to new types of transactions or new kinds of assets or obligations, the auditor should be satisfied that the accounting policies adopted properly reflect the economic substance of the transaction, asset, or liability in accordance with the broad theory governing present-day financial reporting and the established concept of conservatism in the face of uncertainty.

- When the selection of an accounting policy is arbitrary in certain named areas, the auditor is not expected to object to the selection of an established alternative, notwithstanding that the auditor may have a personal preference for one of the possible alternatives. (5.53)

R-19 The CICA Auditing Standards Committee should amplify auditing standards to emphasize the auditor's responsibility to come to an independent opinion on the reasonableness of management's estimates. (5.55)

R-20 The CICA Auditing Standards Committee should amplify auditing standards to stress the auditor's responsibility to be satisfied that the end result of the client's application of accounting principles, judgment estimates, and disclosure is not materially misleading. (5.59)

Additional Auditor Responsibilities

R-21 Auditing standards or provincial codes of conduct, whichever is the more appropriate, should be amended so that auditors will accept an engagement to report on financial statements for public distribution only on the condition that they have a right to (1) review and comment on financial disclosure outside the financial statements that is intended to be included in the document in which the audited statements are to be published, and (2) refuse consent to publication of the audit report in association with that disclosure if the latter is seriously objectionable. (5.63)

R-22 The CICA Auditing Standards Committee should provide more guidance to appropriate procedures to be undertaken by the auditor, and the appropriate form of communication of the auditor's involvement and findings, with respect to all types of financial disclosure outside the traditional financial statements. This includes both information with which the auditor is required to be involved by auditing standards, and information with which the auditor may be involved by special engagement with a client. (5.67)

Clarification of Financial Reporting Responsibilities

R-23 The CICA Accounting Standards Committee should amplify the present standard requiring disclosure of accounting policies, so as to emphasize:

- The underlying theory of accounting being followed.

- The judgments made in the selection of accounting policies and the effect, if significant, of choosing one alternative from two or more acceptable policies (see Recommendation R-8 in Chapter 4).

- The judgments and estimates made in the valuation of assets and liabilities and the implementation of accounting policies, together with the evidence supporting such judgments.

Detailed disclosure of actual judgments and estimates made by management could be usefully integrated with the disclosure. (5.73)

R-24 The CICA should support a legal requirement that management clearly acknowledge its basic responsibility for the information in the audited financial statements. The management statement should be outside the financial statements themselves, but should be published in close association with them. (5.77)

R-25 The CICA Auditing Standards Committee should adopt an expanded standard audit report to explain more fully the nature and extent of the auditor's work, and the degree of assurance it provides. To the extent possible, the same wording should be used in the Canadian standard audit report as that used in other major industrial countries. (5.83)

490

CHAPTER 6 — PROFESSIONALISM

Professional Self-Regulation

R-26 The provincial institutes of chartered accountants should seek effective practical mechanisms to promote country-wide uniformity in self-regulatory functions that are designed to ensure a high quality of service to the public. An incidental objective should be to find ways to increase public awareness of the profession's self-discipline procedures. Three subjects suggested for priority action are coordination or harmonization of (1) the profession's code of conduct, (2) the profession's practice review procedures, and (3) the profession's disciplinary procedures. (6.21)

R-27 Provincial institutes of chartered accountants should study how to effectively bring audit firms as well as individual members within the ambit of disciplinary proceedings. (6.23)

R-28 Provincial institutes of chartered accountants should consider how to limit potential threats to the auditor's independent judgment caused by the fact that a significant percentage of revenue comes from one client or associated group of clients. (6.42)

R-29 The profession's codes of conduct or interpretations of the codes should be amplified to speak to the potential consequences if non-audit services are performed for an audit client. It should be stressed that the auditor has a professional obligation in assessing audit evidence to avoid any bias or predisposition that could result from advice given to the client in a consulting capacity. Independent advice from third parties may be helpful on occasion to ensure compliance. (6.50)

R-30 The profession's codes of conduct should be amended to require an accountant from whom advice is sought by the client of an incumbent auditor to communicate with that auditor before expressing any form of opinion. In the course of that communication, the accountant requested to advise should confirm the pertinent facts of the situation with the incumbent auditor. The auditor and the accountant consulted should each have an obligation to discuss fully the factors that lead them to the position they have taken or propose to take. (6.60)

Public Input to Auditing Standards

R-31 The CICA standard-setting structure should be broadened to provide a practical channel for effective advice on auditing standards from knowledgeable members of the lay public. (6.74)

CHAPTER 7 — FRAUD; ILLEGAL ACTS; CHANGE OF AUDITOR

Employee Fraud

R-32 The CICA Auditing Standards Committee should modify auditing standards to take greater account of the possibility of material undiscovered employee fraud. The auditor normally tests the functioning of internal controls only to the extent it is proposed to rely upon them in planning audit tests. In the auditor's initial review of internal controls, however, specific consideration should be given to the vulnerability of the enterprise to material employee fraud, and to the controls against such fraud. These controls should be tested even though some other parts of the internal control system are not tested. The need for extension of audit procedures should be considered if the controls against material employee fraud appear to be weak. (7.17)

R-33 The CICA Auditing Standards Committee should recommend that the auditor ensure that the audit committee (or board of directors if there is no audit committee) is adequately informed about material employee frauds that have occurred, and significant weaknesses in internal controls of which the auditor is aware, particularly those that are important to fraud prevention. (7.21)

Management Fraud

R-34 The CICA Auditing Standards Committee should extend its guidance to audit procedures related to the discovery of management fraud. Since normal audit procedures provide a lower level of assurance with respect to the discovery of management fraud than they do with respect to the discovery of simple errors, the auditor should extend his or her work to give specific consideration to the possibility that such fraud may have occurred. If that consideration raises any question in the auditor's mind about the validity of the traditional assumption of management honesty, additional audit procedures should be devised to provide additional assurance. (7.24)

Illegal Acts

R-35 The CICA Auditing Standards Committee should provide additional guidance to the implications for the auditor's report of illegal actions that have had or may have material financial consequences. (7.32)

R-36 The CICA Accounting Standards Committee should provide additional guidance to the implications for financial statement disclosure of illegal actions that have had or may have material financial consequences. (7.33)

R-37 The CICA Auditing Standards Committee should state specifically that the auditor should ensure that the audit committee (or board of directors if there is no audit committee) is fully informed about serious infractions of the law committed in carrying on the business of the company of which the auditor is aware. (7.34)

Changes of Auditors

R-38 Changes should be made to securities legislation or regulations with the objectives of (1) improving the timeliness of notification of auditor changes, (2) improving the ability of an auditor to make adequate disclosure of the reasons for the change in auditor, and (3) enabling proper and timely public disclosure of the reasons when, in the discretion of the securities commissions, the shareholders' and public's interests demand it. (7.45)

R-39 National Policy Statement No. 31 of the Canadian Securities Administrators, providing for disclosure upon resignation or replacement of an auditor, should be strengthened. The definition of a "reportable disagreement" should be revised so as to ensure disclosure of disagreements between an auditor and management that would have led to an audit qualification or comment had management not altered the financial information that was published. (7.45)

R-40 Provincial institutes of chartered accountants should amend their codes of conduct so that an auditor resigning or being replaced is obliged to inform a possible successor auditor if suspected fraud or other illegal activity by the client was an important factor in the resignation or in the client's decision to appoint a different auditor. (7.48)

CHAPTER 8 — REGULATED FINANCIAL INSTITUTIONS

Communication with Regulators

R-41 The CICA, together with representatives of provincial institutes of chartered accountants and regulators, should initiate a task force to study and recommend a model set of legal provisions to govern communications between auditors, regulators, management, and audit committees or directors of financial institutions. When completed, the CICA and the provincial institutes should actively support efforts to have the proposed provisions incorporated in appropriate legislation. The same task force should suggest a sample list of matters that a regulator might publish as matters to be communicated under present legislation. (8.17)

R-42 To facilitate the communication process, changes should also be made to certain laws so that all financial institutions are required to have audit committees made up of outside directors. (8.17)

R-43 Pending changes in the law, the provincial institutes of chartered accountants should immediately amend their codes of conduct to enable the auditor of a financial institution to communicate matters of great moment to the regulator (with notice to the directors) if the institution itself fails to do so. (8.19)

Accounting Standards for Financial Institutions

R-44 The CICA Accounting Standards Committee should continue its present efforts to define bank accounting standards that are both satisfactory to the industry and the federal Superintendent of Financial Institutions and can be considered in accordance with GAAP. The Accounting Standards Committee should also continue to give high priority to providing guidance with respect to the special accounting problems of other types of financial institutions. This would be an important part of the program recommended to eliminate holes in the coverage of accounting standards and reduce the number of alternative accounting practices that are not justified by differences in circumstances. The CICA should seek the cooperation of industry representatives and both federal and provincial regulators in this task and should continue to work with provincial institutes of chartered accountants to that end. If sufficient cooperation of all interested parties is not forthcoming, the CICA may have to consider more heroic measures to protect auditors and the public generally. (8.33)

R-45 A regulator of any type of financial institution for which GAAP have been established should be urged to treat any financial statement requested on an artificial or unrealistic basis of accounting as a special-purpose report and not as a substitute for statements prepared in accordance with GAAP. (8.34)

R-46 The CICA Task Force on Financial Institutions, in conjunction with regulators and representatives of financial institutions, should initiate a separate study similar to that proposed in Recommendation R-12 in Chapter 5, to determine the best manner of disclosing risks and uncertainties. (8.38)

R-47 The CICA Task Force on Financial Institutions, in conjunction with regulators and representatives of financial institutions, should study the best manner of presentation of information bearing on liquidity in the financial statements or annual reports of such institutions. (8.44)

R-48 The CICA Task Force on Financial Institutions, in conjunction with regulators and representatives of financial institutions, should study asset and liability valuation problems in financial institutions and furnish recommendations. Guidance should be provided with respect to the valuation of major categories of assets, actuarial liabilities, and loss provisions required for off-balance-sheet assets and liabilities, to the extent guidance is not already available. (8.49)

Auditor Reporting on Internal Control

R-49 The CICA should look favourably upon a request that the auditor report to the regulator on the design and functioning of internal control systems of financial institutions, provided satisfactory guidance is developed concerning the specific types of assurance that would be rendered in such a report. To this end, the CICA, in conjunction with regulators, auditors, and representatives of the various types of financial institutions, should develop criteria for effective and prudent systems of record-keeping, control, and internal audit for each type of institution. (8.56)

Auditor's Knowledge of the Business

R-50 The *CICA Handbook* should include a section dealing with the knowledge of the business required by auditors of companies in specialized industries. Particular emphasis should be given to the special requirements and characteristics of regulated financial institutions. The importance of an auditor's previous experience and commitment to ongoing professional development in the field should be stressed. (8.59)

Critical Perspectives on Accounting (1992) **3**, 000–000

INSTITUTIONAL RESPONSES TO BANK FAILURE: A COMPARATIVE CASE STUDY OF THE HOME BANK (1923) AND CANADIAN COMMERCIAL BANK (1985) FAILURES

BYRON LEW AND ALAN J. RICHARDSON

School of Business, Queen's University, Ontario

The circumstances surrounding the collapse of the Canadian Commercial Bank in 1985 and the Home Bank in 1923 bear many resemblances. There are similarities in the economic conditions which brought about the crashes, the extent to which financial reporting helped obscure worsening conditions in the banks and the role the government played in the crashes and subsequent investigations. We identify the three parties involved, the bankers, the auditors and the legislators, and examine their reactions. We highlight the role of the auditing profession and the legislators to determine their responsibilities and how they reacted to perceived breaches. Drawing on the work of O'Connor and Offe, we outline a model of regulatory demand, interpret these events and identify implications for the reform of financial regulation in Canada.

Introduction

This paper presents a theoretically informed, comparative case study of institutional responses to bank failures in Canada. The issues addressed in this analysis are of increasing concern in Canada as the federal government moves towards deregulation of financial services (e.g. Canada, 1985b, 1986; Hockin, 1986) and as the potential public liability due to bank failure becomes clear (e.g. as evidenced by the Savings and Loan crisis in the US, and warnings about default on loans by less developed countries). The analysis focuses on the way in which the institutional network surrounding the banking industry acts in times of crisis and on the way in which the accounting profession is implicated in the governance of financial institutions.

We examine the institutional responses to the Home Bank failure in 1923 and the Canadian Commercial Bank (CCB) failure in 1985. Although these incidents are separated by 62 years, they represent the two most recent bank failures in Canada. By using two incidents widely separated in time, and hence in different political and economic contexts, we intend to identify aspects of institutional responses to bank failures which may be regarded as structural features of the relationship between financial capital and the state. The analysis draws on O'Connor's (1973) model of *The Fiscal Crisis of the State* as a way of understanding the historic stability of the Canadian banking

Address for correspondence: Dr Alan Richardson, School of Business, Queen's University, Kinston, Ontario, Canada K7L 3N6.

Received December 1989; revised 25 January 1991; 6 November 1991; accepted 10 December 1991.

1

1045–2354/92/000000 + 00 $03.00/0

industry and of identifying the crisis tendencies which are imminent in this structure of institutional governance. In particular, we attempt to locate the role of financial disclosure and the audit profession in mediating the relationships between depositors, the banks and the state.

The article is organized as follows. In the next section we sketch O'Connor's (1973) model and more recent critical modifications to it by Offe (1984) and Piven and Friedland (1984) in order to identify specific characteristics and relationships which are crucial to understanding the cases we examine. We then describe the overall structure of the Canadian banking industry in terms of this model. This is followed by the case studies of the Home Bank and CCB failures and the institutional responses to those failures. Finally, we draw together the common elements in these incidents in order to assess the current process of bank deregulation and the enhanced disclosure and audit requirements which will accompany deregulation.

A Framework for the Analysis of Bank Failure and Regulation

Our analysis of institutional responses to bank failure in Canada draws on the pioneering work of O'Connor (1973) but with critical modifications suggested by the work of Offe (1984) and Piven and Friedland (1984). We adopt O'Connor's (1973) conception of the state as a semi-autonomous entity which acts to ensure its own survival by supporting profit-seeking (capital accumulation) activities which it can tax and by administering social assistance programs to maintain mass loyalty. These functional imperatives are mutually contradictory. Actions which increase the rate of capital accumulation (profit) in the economy reduce the payments to labour and result in capital investments which reduce the labour content of production. These consequences increase the demands for social services and transfer payments which can only be met through tax revenue. The diversion of funds into social services administered by the state reduces the funds available to the private sector and introduces non-market criteria into the allocation of resources both of which undermine the capital accumulation process.

O'Connor argues that the state's attempt to achieve both imperatives simultaneously will result in a fiscal crisis which will undermine the capitalist system. This conclusion downplays the state's ability to absorb or manage conflict and charts a deterministic course for capitalist societies. O'Connor (1981, p. 47) recognizes that his model does not accommodate historical contingencies nor does it allow for demands for social services independently on the increasing rate of capital accumulation. The model is also limited in that it projects an end-state but does not provide predictions about the short-run adjustments which the state makes in response to fiscal strains.

Offe's (1984) model is consistent with O'Connor's basic thesis but allows for a wider range of interim outcomes. Offe (1984, p. 162) theorizes that the state can be understood as an "institutionalized order of public authority" which is "the historical result of the will and the actions of individuals". The state is seen as an institution separate from, rather than merely an agent of, capital, but it is constrained by its position mediating between production and consumption. Like O'Connor, Offe argues that the state simultaneously supports capital accumulation to maintain a source of tax revenue while maintaining legitimacy through provision of an increasingly expanding social services sector. Unlike O'Connor, Offe (1984, p. 131) portrays the state's legitimation struggle as a continuous process of resolving dilemmas, of making policy to settle opposing demands. In this sense Offe's theory is similar to neo-pluralist theories of interest group competition and dominance (Held, 1987, p. 212). State policy is not interpreted as serving only capital but rather as serving to maintain legitimacy for the entire capitalist order, sometimes benefiting capital, sometimes labour. Given that power flows from more than just one source, changes over time in the institutional structure of the state can be accommodated within the model.

Piven and Friedland (1984) provide a similar analysis and suggest explicit hypotheses about the state's response to fiscal crises. They theorize how the state's institutional structure will be modified in reaction to fiscal crises by specifying how conflicts among competing elites are mediated. They identify the conflict inherent in a capitalist economy as conflicts between holders of property rights and holders of political rights (i.e. the vote). Both groups influence policy and the structure of the state with varying degrees of effectiveness in furthering their interests. Property rights holders act as an economic elite because they tend to have homogeneous interests relative to the interests of the holders of political rights. Property rights holders have command over resources necessary for the state to provide services and thereby exercise power by threatening to pull their resources out of particular jurisdictions. In contrast, voters have mainly diffuse voting power to control their representatives and must organize to gain any power.

Conflicts arise due to the entitlements and interests associated with each right. Property owners demand lower taxes; property-less voters demand increased social services. During booms, both groups will generally be supportive for policy favourable to investment. During economic slowdowns, however, conflicts become more intense. The state attempts to defuse conflict by structurally segregating agencies of government with potentially contradictory functions and assigning each differing degrees of power. Those agencies responding to political legitimacy—those that allocate social services—are generally accessible to the public but have little power over their source of funds; whereas agencies responsible for supporting capital accumulation tend to be insulated and secretive (Friedland et al., 1978). This institutionalization of conflict leads to fiscal crises as agencies responsible for economic growth are separated from agencies responsible for addressing the resultant externalities. Due to bureaucratic inertia institutions created in response to previous conflicts do not merely disappear as conditions change, thus over time control is increasingly fragmented.

There are a number of parallels between Offe's and Piven and Friedland's model. Both acknowledge that capital is a source of power, thereby accounting for the state's implicit bias in favour of capital accumulation (and differentiating these theories from pluralist models). Neither model assumes that the relationship between the state and interest groups achieves stability (differentiating these theories from corporatist models, e.g. Cooper et al., 1989). Both tacitly acknowledge that interests with other demands may at times have power and that the state must sustain legitimacy by enacting policy which favours these interests. Both recognize that addressing conflicting demands leads to fiscal strains. Whereas Piven and Friedland characterize how the institutional form of the state will respond to conflict and change, Offe seeks to differentiate "contradictions" from "dilemmas" to understand how certain crises ultimately undermine the preconditions for the continued existence of the state, irrespective of the form of institutional arrangement adopted (Offe, 1984, pp. 131–132). Whether evidence can be marshalled to demonstrate that a crisis exists is a matter of some scepticism (Held, 1987, pp. 237–238). On the other hand, the changing institutional structure of the state is readily visible. In this regard, Piven and Friedland's model is more useful in explaining short-run adjustments to fiscal strains. This basic framework can be extended to provide theoretical expectations about the structure of banking regulation. The next section develops the model in this direction.

The State and the Financial Sector

The nature of state intervention in banking is conditioned by the nature of profit seeking activity in that industry. The flow of deposits into banks requires confidence by depositors that their funds will be available upon demand and that they will receive some real return on their savings. Under a fractional reserve banking system, cash will only be available if the demand for funds is random. A "run" on the bank will quickly use the available cash resources and force the bank to deny further withdrawals. The coordinated loss of confidence among depositors, however, is only likely where evidence indicates that the loan portfolio held by the bank is insufficient to pay interest and realize sufficient cash to honour all deposit accounts. Since the bank's loan portfolio is risky, there will be a positive probability that some banks will face this situation and, ultimately, fail.

Although each bank will voluntarily take action to maintain depositor confidence, for example, by establishing monitoring and bonding mechanisms, the interdependence of banks and their centrality in the flow of resources in the economy has typically lead to some form of state intervention. O'Connor's (1973) model suggests that the form of this intervention will be such that the prerogative of banks to seek profit opportunities will be protected, while the costs of such actions will be absorbed by the state and thereby spread over all taxpayers. This has typically taken two forms. First, the state may provide barriers to entry to the banking industry through, for example, minimum capitalization requirements. This requirement assumes that the risks of failure decline as the size of the portfolio increases and that the risks borne by depositors decrease as the amount of equity capital at risk increases. Barriers to entry provide banks with a degree of monopoly power which allows them to earn higher than average rewards for their services and to restrict the supply of credit. These monopoly rents may be borne by depositors or borrowers depending on their access to alternative investment vehicles or sources of funding, respectively. More generally, a restriction of credit resulting from a monopolistic banking sector will also have a large impact on the rest of the economy.

Second, the state may absorb some of the risks of depositing by establishing government monitoring of bank activities, or further, by insuring deposits in case of bank failure. The costs under this scheme are covered by the tax base to benefit depositors and investors in monitored sectors. Both of these forms of intervention safeguard the banks' ability to seek profit while "socializing" some of the associated costs.

The crisis potential in this latter system of state intervention lies in the effects on bank and individual behaviour. For both parties in this relationship the cost of the bank's risky portfolio has been reduced. For the individual, deposit insurance and government monitoring reduces the individual's need for vigilance. Depositors may put faith, and money, in poorly managed financial institutions because they will not bear the consequences of that institution's inefficiencies. Bankers may be willing to accept a riskier portfolio of assets because part of the costs of failure are now borne by the state and, on average, a riskier portfolio will allow them to realize higher returns. Monopoly power within the industry may also allow continued inefficiencies, making banks more susceptible to failure in times of crisis and, in general, inhibiting a socially optimal distribution of resources.

The model sketched above does not predict a stable, equilibrium mode of regulation. The search for efficiency (profit) leaves open the possibility of bank failure and a crisis of confidence which will undermine the legitimacy of private banking. The attempt to maintain the legitimacy of financial institutions undermines the conditions for their efficient operation (Offe, 1984), and, ultimately, the costs of that inefficiency must be borne by society either directly due to the socialization of the costs of bank failure, or indirectly as a result of the misallocation of funds in the economy. The state's attempt to manage this contradiction is predicted, following Piven and Friedland (1984), to result in a fragmented system of controls. In particular, their model suggests that agencies responsible for monitoring banks and insuring deposits will be separate from and less efficient than agencies responsible for maintaining a profitable industry structure.

The Canadian Banking Industry and the Demand for Regulation

The current institutional structure of the Canadian banking regulation cannot be adequately explained outside its historical development. The first banks in Canada were established in the early nineteenth century to provide credit for local merchants within an export-based economy, and to provide a common medium of exchange prior to the establishment of a national currency.[1] The primary purpose of early banks was thus to accept the wide diversity of currency and promissory notes received by merchants and to provide bank notes for use in the local economy. Initial attempts by several banks to obtain monopolies on the issuance of bank notes were rejected by the colonial government. The concern expressed was that monopoly would allow a bank to "loot" the colony, accepting currency of real value for notes which might prove worthless.

The continuing crisis in banking in Canada has its origins in the contradictory relationship between monetary policy and the relatively large export sector of the Canadian economy. Because of its dependence on export of staple commodities, Canada's economy was both highly volatile and dependent on merchant credit. Canadian bankers' lending practices reinforced tendencies of the already volatile business cycle (Naylor, 1975, pp. 75–85). Bankers were willing to finance merchants' inventories and provide other short-term liquidity, but long-term fixed capital was always in short supply when needed (Marr and Paterson, 1980, p. 258).[2] Coupled with a lack of long-term capital was the tendency of banks further to restrict credit at the peak of business cycles in recognition of the reduced value of inventories during periods of over-production, thereby inducing more rapid decline. Economic instability exaggerated by the banks' own lending practices lead to growing monopolization of the financial sector as smaller banks with low capitalization and undiversified portfolios failed. The larger banks operating in the international market were more likely to survive and assume the failed banks' assets at discounted values, thereby growing larger.

Upon the establishment of an independent Canada in 1867, the government was immediately faced with failures in the bank sector. It established a precedent by intervening to guarantee the notes of all banks then in existence. The state's primary concern was to ensure stability in the bank sector as monetary policy could only be implemented indirectly through that sector, since the banks issued currency. The government's commitment to the stability of the banking sector was given force with the enactment of the Bank Act in 1871, which set minimum capitalization requirements and limited the scope of services which could be offered by the "Chartered" banks. The Act gave legislative authority to the emerging monopoly structure of the banking industry by setting a size restriction while limiting services, most notably lending on real estate, thereby ensuring that they would have to be national in scope to survive. These restrictions coupled with the thinness of the Canadian market lead to a stable oligarchic structure consisting of a small number of centrally organized and geographically dispersed branch banks. By the 1920s over 50% of banking assets were held by the three largest banks; three quarters by the largest nine (Neufeld, 1972, pp. 94, 99). This restructuring of the industry from many small to few large banks resulted in the transfer of the wealth from the depositors and shareholders of the failed or absorbed banks to those of the remaining banks. The loss of smaller, regional banks reinforced the perpetual undersupply of credit for local, smaller scale needs, particularly for western grain farming, and fuelled the animosity to federal economic policy from many non-merchant interests. Our first case study of the Home Bank thus focuses on the institutional responses to bank failure under a regulatory regime emphasizing the creation of monopoly in a restricted segment of the financial market.

The Institutional Context of the Home Bank Failure

Under the regulatory system in place since 1871, legislative control of banks has been the responsibility of the Federal Legislature, administered by the Minister of Finance and subject to review every 10 years (Perry, 1980, pp. 6–7). In the last Bank Act review prior to the Home Bank failure, a shareholders' audit requirement had been introduced. This was intended to respond both to failures in the industry and to the subsequently growing monopoly control of the remaining banks. At the time, shareholders' audits were gaining popularity as a means to incorporate shareholder interests into management's decisions. The state did not impose any restrictions on the qualifications of an auditor, except that the auditor be nominated by the Canadian Bankers' Association. Auditors were expected to treat a bank as they would any other business, with a few specific additional requirements such as reporting large, non-performing loans. Otherwise audits were at the discretion of auditors, though shareholders had the right to require additional disclosure.

The state had always maintained the final authority in monitoring banking operations. Banks were required to file reports with the Minister, who could then ask for further disclosure if needed. Suggestions for greater state involvement, however, had been repeatedly rejected. For example, government inspection of banks had been considered at every review of banking legislation, and was each time rejected on the ground that such an inspection would make the state liable to shareholders and depositors in the event of a failure (Canada, 1913, p. 108). The Canadian Bankers' Association was openly opposed to government inspection suggesting that state policy and industry interests were already allied. Again, in 1923, due to another bank failure, government bank inspection was suggested and again rejected in favour of the qualification that the auditor be a member of a professional body, recognized and authorized by the state. The state, trying to downplay its responsibility to monitor the industry, was only willing to regulate the monitors, i.e. the auditors. This amendment, however, had not yet been implemented when the Home Bank failed.

These amendments to the legislation regarding the shareholders' audit as a means of monitoring suggest the search for an independent and objective audit. However, critics had already observed the compromised relationships between the bank and its auditor (Patterson, 1987, p. 60). The auditor evaluates the operations of the firm for external parties but is paid by the firm. This conflict is exaggerated in banking since the auditor must trust the banker to represent the status of the assets. The state too faces a similar dilemma of monitoring the sector on which its source of revenue critically depends. The legitimacy of private banking relies on the state's monitoring activities, but the state also needs to maintain profitable and stable banking as the basis of continued economic prosperity, and, more directly, as a basis for maintaining state revenues. Given these two potentially conflicting demands, it is to be expected (following Piven and Friedland, 1984) that the state should seek to separate the two functions, monetary policy and small depositor banking services. It has tried this by separating those with the responsibility to monitor operations, auditors, from those responsible for monetary policy more generally, the Minister of Finance.

The Failure of the Home Bank

The Home Bank started operation as the Toronto Savings Bank in 1854. With the introduction of the Bank Act in 1871, it reorganized as the Home Savings and Loan Company. In 1903 it was granted chartered bank status. It operated throughout Canada, and established a western headquarters in Winnipeg which operated with a degree of autonomy from the main office in Toronto. The Bank closed on 17 August 1923. A chronology of the key events surrounding the collapse of the Home Bank is provided in Table 1.

The failure of the Home Bank was due to a combination of mismanagement and management corruption (Canada, 1924b). The Home Bank, at the time of its failure, was the third smallest of 17 chartered banks in Canada. The bank operated two separate divisions, a main office in the east and a division in the west. In 1916 and again in 1918, western directors filed complaints with the Minister of Finance charging that the bank had large non-performing loans to companies associated with the bank's management and was paying dividends out of uncollected interest. The Minister, in each case, called on the bank's auditor, under Section 56A of the Bank Act, to conduct an internal investigation but did not initiate an independent investigation, even though these reports had originated from within the bank itself and implicated bank management. The Minister later admitted that appointing an independent auditor might have brought about the failure of the bank, thereby destabilizing an already sensitive wartime economy. In each case he received a report from the bank·assuring him that the problems had been corrected. None of those events were made public. The bank, however, continued to recognize unpaid interest as profit and, on the basis of this profit, to pay dividends. The recession following a brief post-war boom eventually brought down the bank.

Table 1. Chronology of the Home Bank failure

1903	Home Bank granted chartered bank status
1913	Bank Act amended to require a shareholders' audit
1915	Home Bank western directors complain to the Minister of Finance, citing: (a) a lack of money available to western operations though the bank has a paid-up capitalization of $2 000 00.00, $500 000.00 in the west; (b) non-performing loans, including one particular account outstanding worth $1 780 00.00, $76 000 owed by the Bank's GM, and a loan to Prudential Trust re: the New Orleans & Grand Isle Railway Co. for $500 000; (c) non-arm's-length transactions, including loans to individuals and companies with connections to bank directors as well as an account of $394 000.00 for one bank director personally
	The Minister requests further information, first from the bank's president with regard to the specified outstanding loans and, second, a report from the bank's auditor. The directors assure him they will remedy the situation, though ultimately his instructions are ignored. No further communications are passed
1917	The bank recognizes a profit of $142 900, containing capitalized but uncollected interest of $205 000
1918	Further complaints are registered with the Minister of Finance. The Minister again inquires but is assured by the management that such accusations are unfounded and the bank is sound, having recovered from the irregularities of 1916, all contrary to the truth. The Minister does not follow up on these reports
1921	Post-war recession, particularly heavy in west with decline of grain prices. Farmers have difficulty obtaining financing
1923	The house amends the Bank Act to require an audit of banks by two auditors of different, recognized associations of accountants. On 17 August the Home Bank folds. Royal Commission of Inquiry called
1924	House adopts provision within the Bank Act limiting loans to directors and sets up Office of the Inspector General to inspect bank returns

Reactions the Home Bank Failure

As one immediate response, a Royal Commission was called to investigate the Home Bank failure, an acknowledgement that the collapse was an extraordinary crisis rather than an expected occurrence. The Commission determined that the bank was probably insolvent at the time of the complaints to the Minister of Finance in 1916 and that statements issued by management and attested to by the auditor did not fairly reflect the financial position of the bank. The president, vice-president, five directors and the bank accountant were all convicted of fraud.

The Royal Commission concluded that the state was not liable for events occurring after 1918 since no further complaints had been registered with the Minister, but depositors were given partial compensation for their losses as the state was found morally, if not legally, responsible for its inaction at the time of the 1916/1918 complaints against the bank. In essence, the Commission's indictment suggested that the state held a residual liability for the performance of the financial sector. In order to minimize this liability, the state was expected to exercise some degree of operational control of the banking industry.

The Home Bank failure caused a flurry of action in Parliament. Given the general public unease felt toward the banking sector, the government opened debate to all suggestions, even the more radical. These reforms are summarized in Table 2.

The proposals served to define changing public expectations of the state's role in ensuring a viable banking sector. An industry structure favouring large banks would damage investors and depositors in smaller and failing banks, and monopoly power would heighten consumer dissatisfaction. The state, unable to add legislative patches to the existing structure of monopolistic barriers to entry, moved towards active participatory regulation. Though up until the Home Bank failure, the state had merely reinforced the status quo regulatory structure through increasing provisions on auditor requirements; in its aftermath seemingly radical change was considered. In addition to the Royal Commission itself, suggestions were made for a deposit insurance system and/or a central bank. The state had already developed an insurance scheme for noteholders, therefore deposit insurance was within precedent. However, the long standing proposal for government bank inspection was finally adopted and the Office of the Inspector General of Banks (OIGB) was created.

These institutional changes introduced upon the collapse of the Home Bank can be partially interpreted as an attempt by the state to separate departments of government which bear conflicting demands (Friedland et al., 1978). The Ministry of Finance had been responsible both for general economic policy and monitoring banks. The Minister had been unwilling to investigate fully into the complaints of wrongdoings by the Home Bank's management given the implicit and conflicting demand by capital to maintain a stable economy, particularly during a potentially sensitive period such as war. The legitimacy crisis subsequent to that egregious lapse, coupled with other bank failures, resulted in institutional changes to bank monitoring; specifically the introduc-

10   B. Lew and A. J. Richardson

Table 2. Suggested regulatory measures in response to the Home Bank failure

---

1. Capital structure
    (a) Capital stock—reduction of capital requirement from $500 000 to $50 000
2. Financial reporting
    (a) Specification of income statement accounts
    (b) Government inspection and creation of OIGB (adopted)
    (c) Addition of appropriations, contingencies and undistributed profit accounts on balance sheet
3. Depositor/borrower security (asset/liability manipulation restrictions)
    (a) Deposit acceptance restricted to six times paid-up capital (none previous)
    (b) Issuance of bank notes:
        (i) Limited to half of paid up capital (previously had been 100%)
        (ii) Responsibility transferred from Bankers' Association and placed under the jurisdiction of
             the Department of Finance
    (c) Approval of loans to directors should require two-thirds majority of board of directors, not
        just half (adopted by committee, later rejected by the house)
    (d) No single loan can exceed 10% of paid up capital
    (e) Deposit insurance to be introduced on accounts in value less than $3000
    (f) Displayed notice of deposit and loans outstanding per branch
    (g) Displayed notice of government non-responsibility for deposits
4. Investor security
    (a) Elimination of government status as second creditor after noteholders of insolvent bank
    (b) Double liability of shareholder:
        (i) Removal of double liability clause
        (ii) Removal of clause allowing executive officers to avoid double liability
        (iii) Extension of shareholder's double liability from insolvency to a pro-rated liability in event
              of impairment of paid-up capital of bank
    (c) Contact for purchase of shares in bank can be voided if incomplete disclosure of conditions
        upon purchase is later discovered
5. Proposal for central reserve bank
6. Royal Commission investigation into collapse

---

tion of the government bank inspector. The transfer of the monitoring task from the Minister of Finance to a quasi-independent agency we interpret after Piven and Friedland (1984) as a means of legitimation by an attempt to separate structurally and bureaucratize a process which had been subject to excessive pressure from capital, or more specifically, bank and merchant interests. The Minister of Finance faced two contradictory pressures: a demand from small depositors for bank inspection to ensure safe banking, and a demand from the banking industry to continue profitable risk-taking.

The introduction of a state regulator, however, did not substantially increase the tendency towards fiscal strain. Piven and Friedland argue that fiscal strains result from competing demands for investment policy by capital and social expenditure by voters. There existed, however, no demand for social expenditure, beyond monitoring, and hence no political dilemma. If the state did not act, small depositors would simply withdraw their funds and the process of capital accumulation would be slowed to the detriment of both the state and the bank and merchant interest.

The solution adopted by the state attests to the relative power of the banking interest.[3] The introduction of a regulator would have little effect on the behaviour of large banks. The inspector's responsibilities did not differ greatly from those held previously by the Minister and he would have few staff, further limiting an expansion of authority through the office. The proposal was even well-received by the Canadian Bankers' Association. The introduction of the bank inspector could only support further the monopolistic industry structure by making it more difficult for newer, smaller and therefore riskier banks to enter the market. In contrast, proposals such as deposit insurance would make entry easier, thereby eroding the monopoly structure and drastically increase the state's potential liability. The state disclaimed any liability to depositors as a result of an inspection.

Ironically, the accounting profession, through the expert testimony of G. Edwards, defended the efficacy of private sector auditors, claiming that if the provisions of the 1923 Bank Act for professionally incorporated auditors had been in force, the Home Bank disaster would not have occurred. In his opinion, the Home Bank failure had been an example of the need for disclosure, and an objective auditor's report would have prevented such fraud from occurring (Canada, 1924a, pp. 7–8). His defence was moot, however, since the profession was without blemish as no recognized auditor had been involved. Sources in the profession cautioned that spelling out the duties of auditors in statutes would be equivalent to restricting their powers to those requirements, thereby reducing their professional judgment. Later, the profession's stand on auditor independence would be reversed completely after the failure of the CCB.

In summary, the protection of a stable banking monopoly to support state legitimacy in managing the economy had in the period considered involved greater and greater state involvement in regulating and monitoring the industry both to maintain consumer legitimacy eroded by misallocations resulting from monopoly and to prevent excessive bank risk-taking and thereby the threat of bank failure. In 1867 note insurance was provided to all banks, then in 1871 with the Bank Act, formal barriers to entry were erected. However, to deflect the growing potential financial liability or fiscal crisis facing the state in the event of bank failures, operational responsibility was gradually moved to "independent" agencies. First, an independent bank audit was instituted in 1910, upgraded to require a state-sanctioned professionally incorporated auditor in 1923, and finally in 1924 a state inspector was introduced.

Relevant Changes in the Financial Sector Since the Home Bank

The economic boom following World War Two and the consequent changes to the financial sector raised challenges to the legitimacy of the state's control over banking. First, consumers were beginning to vent concerns about the monopoly structure of the industry and the quality of service being provided, challenging the legitimacy of the "barriers to entry" regulation. Second, the growth of the consumer sector of the economy created a demand for consumer credit. As chartered banks faced restrictions on consumer lending, the mortgage and trust company sector grew rapidly, particularly in the mortgage market then prohibited to chartered banks and through retirement savings plans. In 1950 the chartered banking sector held over half of all financial assets, but by 1965 it had declined to only one third, due to growth in these competing sectors (Neufeld, 1972).

This alternate financial sector was still largely unregulated and many of its institutions were operating with higher risk and virtually no monitoring. Failures among these rapidly growing finance companies increased over time, causing losses to their depositors and reducing confidence in the country's financial sector as a whole. The sector had arisen as an unintended consequence of state restrictions which delineated acceptable services for the chartered banking sector and thereby created an unregulated sector for all other financial services. Its growth and instability, though a function of state regulation, was beginning to impinge on state legitimacy and the profitability of the regulated sector.

Regulatory changes in the financial sector in the post World War Two years were all part of the state's adoption of expansionary monetary policy, but institutional constraints adopted in the past prevented their rapid implementation. Such changes suggest a shift in relative power away from the bank and merchant interests towards industrial interests reflecting the changing economy. Incited by the refusal of the then governor of the Bank of Canada to expand the money supply as part of an employment policy, the government began to revise financial sector legislation to expand credit and, at the same time, to address the growing risk in the alternate financial sector that had arisen.

In 1967 a deposit insurance plan was introduced both as a direct response to the failure of one trust company, the Atlantic Acceptance Company, and the near failure of another, the British Mortgage and Housing Company; as well as a means of expanding the financial sector, insuring the small depositor now faced with a growing market for financial instruments, while maintaining control of financial institutions.[4] Being forced to recognize the broader impact of credit rationing by the monopolized banking sector on the expanding consumer population, the government allowed banks to expand their lending into real estate and lifted the then existing cap on interest rates. This allowed the large banks to enter into direct competition with trust and mortgage companies, while any costs of the inevitable industry shake-out would be absorbed, in part, by the public purse, acting as guarantor of the deposit insurance scheme. Deposit insurance is potentially a huge fiscal burden, and coupled with the private risk-taking behaviour of banks serves both to transfer risk and expense to the tax base for the benefit of those taking the risks, as well as to ameliorate the distributional inefficiencies for depositors of failed banks.

Following Piven and Friedland (1984), the introduction of deposit insurance can be interpreted as an expenditure in response to demand from small depositors. Its introduction resulted in two subtle changes. The role of the bank inspector shifted from that of protecting small depositors to protecting the state from liability caused by bank risk-taking. At the same time, however, risk-taking by banks was also encouraged. This was not a serious problem as long as the stable, oligarchic structure of the industry remained. Within this industry structure excessive risk-taking was not necessary to maintain profitability. As a consequence the shift in constituency which the monitor served would not yet be evident.

When the federal government granted a charter to the CCB in response to regional interests, an inherently risky bank was introduced into an otherwise conservative and stable sector. This created conflicting demands on the inspector. Either the inspector regulates the bank, making it more difficult for it to compete, risking alienating those interests for whom the bank was initially granted a charter, or the inspector allows risk-taking at the cost of potential state liability. Action taken on the part of the inspector which could have lead to closing the bank would not be in the interest of CCB's depositors and therefore not a proper course of action for the inspector as long as there was any chance for the bank's success.

At present there is further pressure from the chartered banks to deregulate financial markets in order to allow them to gain access to new opportunities, assuming that their size and organization, achieved under monopoly conditions, will now let them dominate over new entrants. In order to maintain political legitimacy in the face of this regulatory change, the state argues that competition will improve the quality of services and has increased the disclosure and inspection requirements of financial institutions. With the existing deposit insurance policies in place, however, it is clear that the increased competition and risks faced by financial institutions does create an increased public liability. In this, as in previous regulatory revisions, the state is faced with the contradictory demands of allowing the banks to maintain their profit opportunities while reassuring the public that they, at least individually, will not bear the costs of those actions. Our second case study of the Canadian Commercial Bank in 1983 thus focuses on institutional responses to bank failure under a regulatory regime emphasizing the socialization of the costs of risky bank portfolios and the consequent expansion of direct government monitoring of bank operations.

The Failure of the Canadian Commercial Bank

The second case study, the failure of the Canadian Commercial Bank (CCB), occurred in September 1985, over 60 years after the Home Bank failure, but the events surrounding the problematic disclosure leading up to its failure and the resultant legislative reforms further illustrate tendencies inherent in our model of state legislation. Table 3 provides a chronology of key events surrounding the bank's collapse.

The failure of the bank surprised both the public and the regulators. The government channelled up to $1 billion into the bank in the form of a bailout package when the bank was later realized to have been insolvent. Indeed, the bank's management had been virtually unaccountable to anyone, similar to the Home Bank's management, but this time with full knowledge of the auditors and a bank regulator. Though its eccentric accounting practices were known to both its auditors and to the government inspectors, the degree of its financial distress remained unknown.

The bank had been chartered in 1975 as a non-retail bank and the first bank in Canada headquartered in the west. It was to capture an unclaimed niche in the financial market and lend to medium-sized firms unable to obtain financing from regular banks and too small to issue equity. On the liability side, it intended to borrow on wholesale money markets, paying the higher

Table 3. Chronology of the CCB failure

1975	Charter granted to Canadian Commercial and Industrial Bank, renamed CCB in 1981
1977	Energy boom spurs growth of bank, opens offices in Los Angeles, Saskatoon, Montreal, Regina, Dallas and Toronto. The bulk of its loans were in Alberta and British Columbia, particularly in real estate and energy
1981	Acquires control of in Westlands Bank in Los Angeles
1982	Collapse of western economy. Some success at diversification, reducing concentration from 91% in Alberta and British Columbia in 1977 to 53% in 1981. 16% of loans classified as marginal and unsatisfactory (MUL). Bank switches to baseline valuation, with full knowledge of auditors and IG
1983	Seizure of Greymac, Crown and Seaway Trust by the Ontario Government in January prompts resignation of CCB CEO. Incoming CEO discovers poor lending practices of bank. Loss of public confidence in CCB, including withdrawals of large deposits. The Bank of Canada, the IG and the Big 5 Chartered Banks agree to provide liquidity support to CCB as the IG maintained the bank was solvent. This facility was allowed to lapse by June, no longer being needed. CCB ended up paying 15 to 25 basis points more for money because of scandal. Auditors thought bank was capitalizing suspect accounts' interest aggressively. Now 18% on loans classified as MUL and 31.5% as more than average risk
1984	CCB assumes full ownership of Westlands Bank and injects funds into the bank at request of FDIC who had issued a cease and desist order on the banks activity. This is perceived as contributing to the downfall of the CCB OIGB finds bank's performance deteriorating and classifies bank's condition as unsatisfactory
1985	February, CCB CEO informs OIGB of trouble. Later, FRB informs OIGB of trouble with CCB's US agency and potentially entire bank. Government ponders alternatives, attempts bailout. Press release on 25 March that government plans a support package to ensure viability of CCB. Those involved in bail-out: (a) the government—Minister of Finance, Deputy Minister, Minister of State (Finance), Governor of Bank of Canada, IG, Chairman of the CDIC, Province of Alberta (b) the private sector—the CEOs of the six largest Canadian banks Bank of Canada advances operating funds. As of April, OIGB still indicates bank is solvent. After inspections by: (1) the OIGB; (2) the bankers group involved in the bailout; (3) special appointees by the government consisting of TD and Royal Bank officials; and (4) a retired banker acting as a disinterested third party, the bank was declared insolvent September, Royal Commission recommends: (a) Consolidation of CDIC and OIGB (b) Closer contact between regulator, auditors and management (c) Review and additions to banking GAAP (d) Cease and refrain orders (as in Bill C-103) (e) Loan valuation powers suggested in C-103 not be included (f) Restrictions on loans to individuals, by regions/sectors Report of Standing Committee on Finance, Trade and Economic Affairs included proposals stemming from failure of banks (including the Northland Bank) including NFAA to be amalgamation of CDIC, OIGB and Department of Insurance, bank inspections to be similar to US system, including cease and desist orders and asset valuation, etc
1986	Minister of State (Finance) releases report recommending Superintendent of Financial Institutions to be amalgamation of Department of Insurance and OIGB
1987	Bill C-42 (29 June 1987): (a) Superintendent of Financial Institutions as above (b) Allows super to take control of bank when activities are viewed as unfavourable [s. 278–280] Bill C-56 (27 October 1987): (a) Appraisal of assets by superintendent in cases of conflict between super and auditors/management [s. 175(3.1)] (b) Directions of compliance "cease and desist" [s. 313.1–313.4] November: report of White Paper on Tax Reform; change to loan loss smoothing formula
1988	Bill C-108 (4 February 1988), loans to officers or employees [s. 50(1)(d)]. Release of Macdonald Commission report (expectations gap) including recommendations for banking GAAP.

rates by saving on retail banking costs. At the time of the incorporation of the CCB, the economy of western Canada was expanding due to growth in non-agricultural resources, oil and gas. A western-based chartered bank addressed western hostility to the centralized, monopolized bank sector seen as being allied with interests in Ontario to the detriment of the west.

The CCB exhibited particularly high growth in its early years up until 1982. Like the Home Bank, it held an undiversified portfolio. It built its portfolio in the west, particularly in the energy, real estate and construction sectors— sectors particularly vulnerable to business cycles—and later attempted to diversify, though with only moderate success. The bank had further tied up its assets by purchasing a bank in Los Angeles, the Westlands Bank, a bank whose operation would prove to be a substantial drain on the CCB's cash when US regulators demanded infusions to strengthen the Westland's declining portfolio (Estey, 1986, p. 82). It was not until the recession in the early 1980s, a recession of particular severity in western Canada and in the sectors of heavy investment by the CCB, that the dangerously undiversified asset portfolio began to prove problematic.

With the downturn in the western economy, the bank's loan default rate began increasing. The bank, keenly aware that a significant loss in earnings would result in increased borrowing rates on the money markets, began a series of asset restructuring programs intended to maintain reported earnings until the western economy could recover (Estey, 1986, pp. 83–84). To this end, it made a number of accounting changes. It chose to record loans not on current market values but on values which would be obtained on a recovered market, the "baseline" valuation method. As well, it reduced appropriations for contingencies, its bad loan buffer, and restructured terms of non-performing loans, a move which allowed the bank both to continue to accrue interest to earnings and to claim fees for such restructurings. The switch to these unorthodox accounting methods was known to auditors and the regulators yet neither group acknowledged any awareness of the intent behind these changes in accounting policy. The Home Bank had been able to provide fraudulent reports and maintain operations for almost 10 years. The CCB attempted to bend the rules of disclosure by adopting a non-standard basis upon which to value assets, hoping thereby to survive the recession. By 1985 the CCB was facing default and approached the government to obtain liquidity support. Undoubtedly aided by its overvalued books, the bank was able to stay afloat on government advances for a further 6 months. The bank was finally closed when it had drawn up to its $1 billion limit provided and was obviously only approaching the depths of its crisis.

Regulation and Chartered Banks

Reporting requirements contained in the Bank Act until the failure of the CCB have changed little in principle since the introduction of the OIGB in 1924. Specific disclosure requirements are outlined in the Bank Act (*Statutes of Canada*, 1980, s. 215) and auditors are required to follow generally accepted auditing principles [*Statutes of Canada*, 1980, s. 242(6)(a)]. Though the actions taken by both the auditors and the regulators respecting disclosure were apparently within the bounds of the legal system—there were no criminal convictions—the valuation and disclosure policies adopted by the bank were unique to it (and the Northland Bank). Waterhouse and Tims (1988) were able to demonstrate that by restating the bank's financial statements according to standard industry accounting policies, the problems with the bank were evident several years before the collapse. Estey, called to lead a Royal Commission investigation into the collapse, declared that there was a "lack of will to regulate the system", the regulators had relied on the auditors' judgment and the auditors insisted they were simply verifying what management told them and it was not within their responsibilities to revalue management's claims (Estey, 1986, p. 143). Neither the auditors nor the regulators had called into question the reasons behind the CCB's switch in accounting policy nor its implications.

Government Reaction

The failure occurred at a particularly bad time for a government planning to introduce changes to financial sector regulation. Therefore, when the news first broke of the bank's trouble, the government's reaction was rapid and two-pronged. To maintain legitimacy, depositors were immediately promised that all deposits, including uninsured deposits, would be insured. The state also announced its "Directions of Compliance", previously under discussion as a general financial institution reform (Little, 1985, p. B1). The "Directions of Compliance" spelled out further powers available to the Inspector General. The regulator would be able to direct a bank to undertake corrective actions when the bank was engaging in an "unsafe or unsound practice" (*Statutes of Canada*, 1980, s. 313.1), and could even take control of a bank for 7 days, or longer at the discretion of the Minister, in order to put right any perceived problems (*Statutes of Canada*, 1980, s. 279). As well, in the event of a disagreement between the inspector and management and their auditors over the value given a bank's asset, the inspector could adopt her/his value for the OIGB's books [*Statutes of Canada*, 1980, s. 175(3.1)].

The bank inspector had failed its first test because it proved to be less than fully independent for two reasons. First, given the relatively few resources available to the office of the inspector, its opinion was dependent upon and rendered in consultation with the bank's private sector auditors. Second, though the inspector could render opinions on bank health, only the Minister could act upon the inspector's opinions. Similar to the institutions of social expenditure within the Piven and Friedland model, the bank inspector had become powerless to correct the institutional source of the liability. The Directions of Compliance can be interpreted as an attempt to address this failing, specifically giving the regulator the ability, on behalf of the state, to order banks to "cease and desist". Unlike the Piven and Friedland model, the inspector was dependent on both the private sector auditors, themselves influenced by their clients, and the state. The inspector was thereby placed in the conflict for which the OIGB had been set up originally to relieve.

As in the failure of the Home Bank, a Royal Commission was called. The legislative changes and other actions considered are summarized in Table 4.

Table 4. Suggested regulatory measures in response to the CCB failure

(A) Government
   1. Delay of release of government documents Canadian Financial Institutions and Senate Report towards a more competitive financial environment after crash of banks, recommending that regulator have power to appoint one of two bank auditors
   2. Introduction of Bill C-103 in April 1986. Includes "directions of compliance" and asset appraisal override clause. Also gives Superintendent of Financial Institutions control over bank's assets in case of practice or state of affairs materially prejudicial to interests of depositors or creditors
   3. Bill C-56 in May 1987. Replacement of Office of Inspector General of Banks with Superintendent of Financial Institutions incorporating jurisdiction over insurance and banks. Alterations to Canada Deposit Insurance Corporation Act, including addition of risk premiums
   4. Royal Commission investigation into collapse—Estey
(B) CICA
   1. Studies
      (a) Expectations Gap—Macdonald Report
      (b) OIGB study by Coopers & Lybrand
      (c) Accounting Standards Steering Committee, re: banking GAAP

The Royal Commission's report under Judge Estey was particularly critical of the roles of the auditors and the Inspector General. Recognizing that legislative efficacy rests upon independent review or adequate monitoring, his suggestions included the addition of GAAP for banks in response to claims by auditors that they had no precedent with which to guide their judgments and were, therefore, unable to justify reporting practices to which common sense must have alerted them (Estey, 1986, pp. 300–304). After the failure of the Home Bank, the auditors argued that standards for bank reporting would be restrictive. As a result, discretion was left to the auditors and to the bank inspector, both bodies separate from the operating policy of the government. After the CCB, the lack of standards was ultimately the defence presented by both the auditors and the inspector and therefore the motivation for recommending their addition. However, equally clearly, the Home Bank failure illustrates that even when standards were unnecessary in order to detect fraud—the Minister was aware of fraudulent practices without needing to apply standards to financial data—the state had been unwilling to take any corrective action due to concerns about the resultant health of the financial sector and the overall economy. So too with the CCB, conflicts among constituencies rendered the state unwilling to act. This time the west, the region of strongest support for the government in power, would not have taken well to the government's folding a western bank, particularly during a recession. As well, the health of the financial sector more generally was potentially at risk if a government about to bring in financial sector deregulation was seen to be unable to maintain a solvent banking sector. Standards were not the problem, rather the link between the state and capital dictated the course of action.

The Auditors and the Expectations Gap

The profession's response to the CCB failure was to reformulate the problem and form its own commission to address the "expectation gap"—the gap between what the public perceives of the auditor's role and what the auditor is actually constrained to doing (CA Magazine, 1986; Neu and Wright, 1990). As far as the criticisms of the auditors of the bank, the CICA could "neither accept the validity of these criticisms nor disagree with them." (CA Magazine, 1986a). The issue of auditor negligence was not denied, rather, the CICA sought to inform the public of the role of the auditor in financial reporting; attempting to accentuate the limitations inherent in that role. The auditors, like the bank inspector, were caught in a contradictory position. Their response was to address the challenge to their legitimacy by redefining their role, a common reaction by auditors in situations where they bear some liability for failure (Fogarty *et al.*, 1991). The state addressed the same concerns by changing its role, its method of legitimation.

Discussion

Bank regulation in Canada has progressed from simple institutional barriers creating a stable monopoly to a system of state monitoring, propelled by internal contradictions and a changing environment, exaggerated by resulting crises of legitimacy. State intervention in banking arose to maintain stable capital accumulation before the state itself assumed currency issue. Intervention through barriers to entry provides temporary stability as long as the environment remains stable, but misallocates resources creating discontent among those disadvantaged. The monopolistic power of the bank sector was seen to inhibit growth and exaggerate business cycles through tight credit. Further, the consolidation of large banks within the industry made opportunities more scarce for the smaller remaining banks, driving them to seek riskier portfolios to compete, thereby causing the inevitable failures and depositor losses.

Since the state had provided the industry with protection, it shared the blame for the resultant inequities, whether they would have arisen due to the provision of monopoly power, or whether they would have arisen without any state involvement. Such involvement came initially in the form of enhanced monitoring. Monitoring members of a monopoly is reasonably simple as those obtaining the greatest advantage from their position have the greatest incentives to conform. Only those institutions not benefitting from cartelization will have incentive to deviate. Responses by the state to address the more risky institutions merely helped to consolidate further the monopolisitc position of those remaining. Historically, the state's choice of solutions to crises provide support to this conclusion.

The regulatory responses of the state have not always been clearly allied with the interests of capital, though they tend to evolve that way. The introduction of a bank regulator in response to the Home Bank failure could only have been a response to a loss of faith in the bank sector; it had not yet been established that the audit requirement recently introduced was itself insufficient. Responses to the CCB failure are much less clearly defined. To the extent that the regulator made it more difficult for smaller banks to compete with the larger, it can be interpreted as a move to support capital. On the other hand, the movement toward increased competition through the financial sector reforms then being proposed lead to the seemingly contradictory need for increased state involvement in the financial sector to support small investors (Clarke, 1986). Given that these reforms, including the response to the CCB failure, were part of a long time trend towards regulating the increasingly important non-bank sector of the financial market, a sector which had initially existed beyond the purview of the regulators, a far more complex picture is suggested in which different capital interests as well as public concerns over investor safety all played a part.

The state's involvement in the financial sector seems to be bound up with conflicting demands between, on one side, a stable sector for capital accumulation, and on the other, protection for consumers against risk-taking institutions and adequate provision of services. The conflict is mediated through monitoring and therefore the role of the monitor becomes the critical focus of the dilemma. Piven and Friedland (1984) suggest that conflict will be mediated by separating the state agencies addressing concerns of capital from those with legitimating functions which generate social expenditure. Rather than falling on either side, however, the role of the monitor straddles both sides in a contradictory position. In the short term, the monitor's responsibilities shift depending on the relative demand for increased competition or increased stability. In the long term, either reducing risk will lead to reduced competition or deposit insurance will shift risk to the state, simultaneously shifting the liability. A cycle alternating between increasing cost to depositors or increasing liability to the state is the outcome. However, as the cycle shifts towards the state bearing the burden, the more it will approach a crisis, and the more the public purse effectively subsidizes capital accumulation (O'Connor, 1973).

The problem facing the bank inspector is the same as that facing any auditor. The difference is that whereas the pressure facing the auditor comes from her/his relationship with the firm being audited, the inspector is an agent of the state and is thereby influenced by the same pressures which affect the state. When the interests of the state are too closely allied with the interests of the banks, the conflict facing the inspector will increase. The role of the bank inspector becomes the fulcrum upon which the conflicting tendencies of private profit and the public service rest. Actions taken by the state to increase pressure on it to support the financial sector, i.e. deposit insurance, made evident during downturns, becomes manifest as conflict facing the bank inspector, limiting the inspector from acting as intended.

An interesting outcome of this cycle is that the financial sector itself maintains relative autonomy as the crucial link between small depositors and capital in a capitalist economy. Given this relative stability, the outcome appears as a corporatist arrangement though the dynamics differ from the traditional explanation of hierarchically-mediated interests (Panitch, 1981; Streeck and Schmitter, 1985; Richardson, 1989). Though undoubtedly aided by the banks' relatively homogeneous interests, the arrangement whereby the banking sector remains relatively unencumbered by legislative changes emerges as a result of the state's contradictory attempt to maintain a stable sector and create conditions for small depositors to participate in the economy by deflecting the risk to which they are exposed. The stability of the sector is less than an equilibrial tendency than it is is a temporary calm in the midst of a storm.

Acknowledgements

An earlier version of this paper was presented at the Social and Behavioural Accounting Conference, Queen's University, August, 1989. The authors would like to acknowledge the comments of D. Cooper, J. Waterhouse, E. Neave, D. Heu, H. Ogden and the Journal's reviewers. The research for this paper was partially supported by a grant from the Social Sciences and Humanities Research Council of Canada.

References

CA Magazine, "CICA Responds to Estey Report", Vol. 119, No. 12, 1986, pp. 7–8. CA Magazine, "Macdonald Chairs CICA Commission on Audit Expectations Gap", Vol. 119, No. 2, 1986, p. 8.

Canada. Department of Finance. *Final Report of the Working Committee on the Canada Deposit Insurance Corporation* (1985a).

Canada. Department of Finance. *The Regulation of Canadian Financial Institutions: Proposals for Discussion* (1985b).

Canada Deposit Insurance Corporation Act (Minister of Supply and Services Canada, 1987).

Canada. House of Commons. Committee on Banking and Commerce. *Minutes of Proceedings, Evidence, etc.*, Appendix No. 2 to the Journals of the House of Commons (1913).

Canada. House of Commons. *Debates*, 25 June, 1924, p. 3616.

Canada. House of Commons. *Debates*, 7 July, 1966, p. 7315.

Canada. House of Commons. Select Standing Committee on Banking and Commerce. *Minutes of Proceedings, Evidence, etc.*, Appendix No. 1 to the Journals of the House of Commons, 1924a.

Canada. *Journals of the House of Commons*, Appendix No. 1, "Royal Commission re Home Bank, Interim Report", 1924b.

Canada. Senate. Standing Committee on Banking, Trade and Commerce, *Towards a More Competitive Financial Environment* (1986).

Canadian Bankers' Association, *Comments on Deposit Insurance Reform* (1984).

Clarke, M., *Regulating the City: Competition, Scandal and Reform* (Milton Keynes: Open University Press, 1986).

Cooper, D. *et al.*, "The Accounting Profession, Corporatism and the State", in W. Chua *et al.* (eds), *Critical Perspectives in Management Control*, pp. 245–270 (Houndmills: The MacMillan Press Ltd, 1989).

Estey, W. Z., *Report of the Inquiry Into the Collapse of the CCB and the Northland Bank* (Ottawa: Minister of Supply and Services Canada, 1986).

Fogarty, T. J. *et al.*, "The Rationality of Doing 'Nothing': Auditors' Responses to Legal Liability in an Institutionalized Environment", *Critical Perspectives on Accounting*, Vol. 2, No. 3, 1991, pp. 201–226.

Friedland, R. *et al.*, "Political Conflict, Urban Structure, and the Fiscal Crisis, "in D. Ashford (ed.), *Comparing Public Policies: New Concepts and Methods*, pp. 197–225 (Beverly Hills: Sage Publications Inc., 1978).

Held, D., *Models of Democracy* (Cambridge: Polity Press, 1987).

Hockin, T., *New Directions for the Financial Sector* (Ottawa: Department of Finance, 1986).

Little, B., "Bank Failures Prompting Tighter Rules", *Globe and Mail*, 3 September, 1985, p. B1.

Marr, W. & Paterson D., *Canada, An Economic History* (Toronto: Gage Publishing Ltd, 1980).

Naylor, T., *The History of Canadian Business 1867–1914. Vol. I, The Banks and Finance Capital* (Toronto: Lorimer, 1975).

Neu, D. & Wright, M., "Bank Failures, Stigma Management and the Canadian Public Accounting Profession", University of Calgary, April, 1990.

Neufeld, E. P., *The Financial System of Canada: Its Growth and Development* (MacMillan Company of Canada, 1972).

O'Connor, J., *The Fiscal Crisis of the State* (New York: St Martin's Press, 1973).

O'Connor, J., "The Fiscal Crisis of the State Revisited: A Look at Economic Crisis and Reagan's Budget Policy", *Kapitalistate*, Vol. 9, 1981, pp. 41–61.

Offe, C., in J. Keane (ed.) *Contradictions of the Welfare State*, (Cambridge, Massachusetts: MIT Press, 1984).

Panitch, L., "Recent Theorizations of Corporatism", *British Journal of Sociology*, Vol. 31, No. 2, 1980, pp. 159–187.

Patterson, R., "Bagehot on Banking", *The Canadian Banker and ICB Review*, Vol. 94. No. 5, 1987, pp. 58–62.

Perry, J. H., "The Legal Basis of Banking", *The Canadian Banker and ICB Review*, Vol. 87, No. 3, 1980, pp. 6–12.

Piven, F. F. & Friedland, R., "Public Choice and Private Power: A Theory of Fiscal Crisis", in A. Kirby *et al.* (eds) *Public Service Provision and Urban Development*, pp. 390–420 (Beckenham, Kent: Croom Helm Ltd, 1984).

Richardson, A. J., "Corporatism and Intraprofessional Hegemony: A Study of Regulation and Internal Social Order", *Accounting Organizations and Society*, Vol. 14, No. 5/6, 1989, pp. 415–431.

Richardson, A. J., "Accounting Knowledge and Professional Privilege", *Acounting Organizations and Society*, Vol. 14, 1988, pp. 381–396.

Statutes of Canada, 1980, 29 Eliz II, c. 40.

Streeck, W. & Schmitter, P. C., "Community, Market, State—and Associations? The Prospective Contribution of Interest Governance to Social Order in W. Streeck and P. C. Schmitter (eds), *Private Interest Government: Beyond Market and State*, pp. 1–29 (London: Sage, 1985).

Waterhouse, J. & Tims, D., "The GAAP in Bank Regulation", *Canadian Public Policy*, Vol. 14, No. 2, 1988, pp. 151–161.

Notes

1. A central bank and a federal currency were not established in Canada until 1935. Banks were required to hold a certain fraction of their cash reserves in Dominion notes issued by the government and backed by gold. These Dominion notes, however, rarely circulated.

2. The lack of farm credit had always been a source of contention between farmers and the financial sector and state policy. That this was significant is implied when, during a post-World War One recession following a spectacular wheat boom in western Canada, a Royal Commission was called to investigate the farm sector's financing difficulties.

3. It should be noted that, at that time, staple exports constituted a very large percentage of the Canadian economy and therefore short-term inventory financing was critical. The financial intermediators with the monopoly in trade financing, mostly large chartered banks, therefore had tremendous political influence. The prediction is consistent with Piven and Friedland's model.

4. Owing to the institutional constraints contained in the delimiting of powers between federal and provincial jurisdictions, the state was unable to regulate those finance companies that had been incorporated under provincial jurisdiction alone (Canada, 1966, p. 7315). Therefore, in order to entice all financial institutions to submit to federal monitoring, deposit insurance was made available to all institutions regardless of the authority under which the institution was incorporated. The mandatory participation of chartered banks was deemed necessary to ensure financial system stability and to provide a sufficient premium base to make the plan viable (Canadian Bankers' Association, 1984).

Section V: Chronologies

The Accounting Historians Journal
Vol. 13, No. 1
Spring 1986

George J. Murphy
UNIVERSITY OF SASKATCHEWAN

A CHRONOLOGY OF THE DEVELOPMENT OF CORPORATE FINANCIAL REPORTING IN CANADA: 1850 TO 1983

Abstract: A chronology of significant events in the development of corporate financial reporting standards and practices is presented. The introductory comments to
the various sections direct attention to some of the main patterns and trends in
that development and provide the framework in which the listing of events is to be
interpreted. The particularly significant domestic sources of influence are the legislative and professional activities in Ontario and, in more recent times, the activities of the Canadian Institute of Chartered Accountants. External influences have
been—not unexpectedly—the traditions of English Company law and the close
professional, institutional and economic relationships with the United States. Some
internationally significant developments unique to Canada are indicated.

INTRODUCTION

A few introductory comments to the chronology are useful in
suggesting some of the broad themes that characterize the whole
of the evolution of corporate financial reporting in Canada and in
providing a background or setting to aid interpretation. The
chronology itself has four divisions each of which in turn are
preceded by interpretive comments.

The evolution of financial reporting in Canada has developed
within the framework of both British and American influence. The
traditions of English law and, more particularly, the model of using
the Companies Acts to improve financial statement reporting practices have provided an ever-present guideline. Prior to the turn of
the century, actual legislated reporting requirements followed
the English statutes quite closely; since that time, the Canadian
requirements have generally been well in advance of those of

The author appreciates the helpful comment of P. H. Lyons of Deloitte Haskins
and Sells and R. D. Thomas of the Canadian Institute of Chartered Accountants;
the use of the libraries of the Ontario Archives, the Institute of Chartered Accountants of Ontario and the Ontario Legislature; and the financial assistance of the
Social Science and Humanities Research Council of Canada.

England. Since the 1920s and 1930s, Canadian reporting practices and standards have been much more significantly influenced by the United States. That influence has been felt through the importance, proximity and articulateness of the American accounting profession, the edicts of the Securities and Exchange Commission (SEC), the American parent-Canadian subsidiary relationships of many corporations, and the close ties amongst international public accounting firms.

Though Britain and the United States have been very important in this evolution, Canada has not been dominated by their influence. Indeed the virtually unrestricted government delegation of standard setting authority to the profession (i.e. to the Canadian Institute of Chartered Accountants (CICA)) sets Canada apart and speaks to the uniqueness and significance of the Canadian development. Of major importance in the tradition of this development was the early organization and leadership of the Institute of Chartered Accountants of Ontario (ICAO), the vigor and interest of the Office of the Provincial Secretary of Ontario, the untarnished prominence and strength of the CICA and the Canadian good fortune in having few corporate scandals—relative to the United States and Britain—that redounded to any enduring discredit of the accounting profession. Indeed, in light of this background this unrequested delegation of authority to the profession was not unpredictable.

As the chronology demonstrates, a great deal of required disclosure existed in the last third of the nineteenth century for such "regulated" enterprises as banks, insurance and savings companies, and railway and municipal corporations. Generally, however, it was not until the turn of the century that the various incorporating jurisdictions began to place exacting reporting demands on commercial, industrial and mining corporations. Most of these latter companies have sought federal rather than provincial incorporation from the earliest decades of the century and have therefore been subject to that jurisdiction's reporting requirements. In significant ways, however, for much of this century, and by virtue of the concentration of financial and industrial power in Ontario, and the leadership of the ICAO, Ontario has been in the vanguard of financial reporting improvements in matters relating to corporate legislation. For example, the financial statement disclosure requirements of the federal legislation of 1917 and 1964/65 were, respectively, virtual copies of the 1907 and 1953 Ontario Statutes. In turn, the Ontario legislation had followed directly from ICAO recommendations. The 1907 Ontario legislation is significant in the evolution of corporate disclosure because it is one of the earliest statutes in the English-speaking world to make detailed financial statements mandatory for commercial and manufacturing companies, and also because it is one of the earliest occasions in which an accounting organization has demonstrated its influence on disclosure legislation. Though, at the provincial level, the Association of Accountants in Montreal was the first accounting association organized in Canada or the United States, much of its energy in early times was devoted towards sorting out severe anglophone-francophone and Montreal-nonMontreal differences, rather than making improvements in financial reporting.

The overriding criteria for inclusion of events in the chronology is whether such events form part of (and support) the three major themes running through the evolution of Canadian financial reporting: firstly, the tradition over the whole period, of working for change within the framework of provincial and federal corporation laws; secondly, the recognition of the dominant influence of the ICAO and more recently the CICA in setting directly or indirectly the standards for corporate reporting practices; and thirdly, the acknowledgement, largely owing to public awareness, of serious concerns in the 1960s, that uniformity and consistency in reporting practices would be aided by the delegation of standard setting to the CICA. An integral part of the chronicle includes concern for the institutions around and within which corporate financial reporting has developed and the professional and academic writing which has influenced that development. Each of the CICA accounting and auditing Recommendations commencing in 1946 is listed in order to provide the record of standards that have been promulgated over the years and to provide a basis for international comparison. Those CICA Research Studies that have been most frequently cited or that have been the basis for standards are also included.

The chronology is usefully divided into the following periods and is preceded by interpretive comments:

Early public accountability and organization	1850 - 1885
Professional emergence	1885 - 1920
Consolidation of characteristic features	1920 - 1960
Delegation of standard setting	1960 - 1983

Early Public Accountability and Organization: 1850 - 1885

This period is distinguished by the emerging tradition for the widespread disclosure of the financial affairs of such "regulated" industries as banks, insurance and savings companies, railways and municipal corporations, and undoubtedly, this strong tradition provided an influencing background for the legislated disclosure requirements for general commercial and industrial companies that later took place in the early decades of the twentieth century. The stock exchanges and accounting associations which would later be so influential were formed during this period.

1850	The first general Companies Act permitted incorporation by registration with a County Registrar and the Provincial Secretary. The liability of shareholders was "joint and several" until total authorized capital had been paid in (altered in 1864) [Consolidated Statutes, Ch. 28, Sec. 11]. Manufacturing, mining, mechanical and chemical companies required to publish in newspapers a report stating "the amount of stock of the company, the proportion thereof then actually paid in, together with the amount of the existing debt of the company" [Consolidated Statutes, Ch. 28, Sec. 13]. Banks required to forward to the Inspector General "a full and clear statement of assets and liabilities," such statement to be published by the Inspector General "in such a manner as he thinks most conducive to the public good" [Consolidated Statutes, Ch. 21, Sec. 30].
1851	Railway companies required to file with the three branches of the Legislature "a detailed and particular account . . . of the moneys received and expended by the company" [Canada, Statutes, Sec. 22].
1855	An Act relating to the auditing of the public accounts required establishment of a Board of Audit composed of the Deputy Inspector General, the Commissioner of Customs and an appointed auditor to report on all government departments, banks and institutions funded by public moneys [Canada, Statutes, Secs. 1-6]. Municipalities with loans outstanding to send annually "a true account of all debts and liabilities" to the Board.
1864	General incorporation by letters-patent introduced with liability limited to amount payable on shares [Canada, Statutes, Secs. 1, 27 & 28].
1866	Municipal institutions of Upper Canada (later Ontario) required to appoint two independent auditors, and to prepare an abstract of receipts, expenditures, assets

and liabilities to be filed with the Municipal Clerk. Abstract to be open for inspection and published as Municipal Council directs. Municipal clerk to file detailed statement of transactions with Provincial Secretary [Province of Canada, Statutes, Secs., 156, 157 & 169].

1868 Life, Fire and Guaranty Insurance companies required to forward annual statement listing assets, liabilities, revenues and expenditures to Minister of Finance. Such statement to be published in the Canada Gazette and to be laid before Parliament. Exemptions provided for certain insurance companies established in the United Kingdom and which were not bound by the laws in force there to furnish or publish statements of its affairs [Canada, Statutes, Secs. 14 & 15].

1874 Montreal Stock Exchange incorporated [Quebec, Statutes].

1876 Ontario Building Societies Act required appointment of auditors and the forwarding annually of a "full and clear statement of assets and liabilities" to the Provincial Treasurer—the latter to publish "in such a manner as he thinks most conducive to the common good" [Ontario, Statutes, Secs. 18 & 19].

1877/ Canada Joint Stock Companies Act required "directors
1902   of every company to lay before its shareholders a full and clear printed statement of the affairs and financial position of the company at or before each general meeting" [Canada, Statutes, Sec. 87]. 1902 legislation required general meetings to be held annually [Canada, Statutes, Sec. 88].

1878 Toronto Stock Exchange incorporated [Ontario, Statutes]. Legislation established Office of the Auditor General of Canada [Canada, Statutes, Secs. 11-24].

1879/80 Organizing meeting of the Association of Accountants in Montreal held 11 June 1879 [Mann, p. 24]. Association incorporated 24 July 1880—the first formal organization of accountants in Canada and the United States [Quebec, Statutes, Ch. 88]. The Association later renamed the Institute of Chartered Accountants of Quebec in 1927 and since 1978, l' Ordre des comptables agréés du Québec [Collard, p. 71].

1879/83   Organizing meeting of the Institute of Accountants and Adjusters—later renamed the Institute of Chartered Accountants of Ontario (ICAO)—held November 11, 1879 [ICAO Minutes]. Institute incorporated in 1883. The incorporating statute specified the Institute as "an intellectual and education movement to raise the standard of accountancy" and empowered the Institute to "establish classes, lectures and examinations." This legislated mandate was very likely the stimulus for the subsequent energy and prominence of the ICAO [Ontario, Statutes].

1881   The leading financial journal, *The Monetary Times,* commenced tradition of reporting at length (often verbatim) on such ICAO activities as proceedings of annual meetings, questions and answers to exams, and papers delivered at regular meetings [ICAO Minutes: March 22, 1881; November 4, 1885; November 25, 1886; April 19, 1888].

Professional Emergence: 1885 - 1920

The activities and competence of the ICAO and its membership became very visible · during this period through educational programs and examinations, lobbying activities, text book writing and prominence as auditors of most major corporations. Honorary Fellowships in the Institute were awarded to the Provincial Secretary, the Assistant Provincial Secretary, the editor of the *Monetary Times* and to a prominent member of the Ontario legislature later to become the Lieutenant-Governor of the Province. The Office of the Ontario Provincial Secretary, which was in charge of corporate affairs, deferred to the Institute with regard to the pace-setting financial statement disclosure requirements of the provincial corporate legislation of 1907. The most influential personalities in this legislation, George Edwards, an ICAO President and Thomas Mulvey the Assistant Provincial Secretary, later installed equivalent disclosure requirements at the federal level in 1917.

Though there was some concern for financial statement disclosure in such regulated areas as insurance and banking (see 1907 and 1913), the general corporation disclosure requirements at the provincial Ontario level in 1907 and at the federal level in 1917 were more likely prompted by abuse in stock promotion rather than by concern over disclosure deficiencies. Influential in the tradition for high levels of disclosure were the Toronto Stock Exchange, which encouraged the publishing of annual compilations of all listed corporate financial statements, and the financial press itself.

This period also saw the establishment of the prominence of the ICAO and of the use of the vehicle of the Companies Act to improve corporate reporting practices.

1886   Incorporation of the Institute of Chartered Accountants of Manitoba [Manitoba, Statutes]. (Other provincial Institutes of Chartered Accountants organized and incorporated in early part of twentieth century).

1888/   ICAO commenced tradition of submitting briefs and
90/1902   making representations to legislative bodies—in 1888 to the Provincial Secretary relating to municipal accounting [ICAO Minutes, April 19]; in 1890 to the federal Finance Minister relating to the duties and qualifications of bank auditors [ICAO Minutes, March 21]; and in 1902 to the Secretary of State relating to the Dominion Companies Act [Ontario Archives, RG8 1-1-D File 3240].

1892   Ontario Insurance Act required appointment of auditors to furnish statements of assets, liabilities, income and expenditures to members and to Provincial Registrar [Ontario, Statutes, Sec. 29].

1892/   Publication of several widely-used Canadian accounting
1907   texts, some through several editions: *Expert Book-keeping*, C. A. Fleming [1892]; *Manual for Accountants*, W. C. Eddis [1899]; *Canadian Accountant*, S. C. Beatty and J .W. Johnson [1908]; *Canadian Standard Bookkeeping*, J. W. Westervelt, and *Municipal Accounting*, F. H. Macpherson; [as indicated in ICAO Yearbook 1898, p. 20]; *Bookkeeping For Joint Stock Companies*, D. Hoskins [1901]; *Joint Stock Company Accounts*, D. Hoskins [1907].

1893   ICAO sought out and accredited various colleges and schools in Ontario to provide introductory level of public accounting competency. Ontario Business College, Belleville; Kingston Business College, Kingston; Northern Business College, Owen Sound; St. Thomas Business College, St. Thomas; Pickering College, Pickering; Upper Canada College, Toronto; and British

American Business College, Toronto [ICAO Minutes and ICAO Yearbook, 1989, p. 33].

1894   Senate Debates emphasized the importance of the public's right to have greater information about the financial affairs of the large commercial and manufacturing firms [Canada, Senate Debates, June 13, pp. 523-524].

1894/   J. D. Warde an employee of (and with the support of) the
1907   Ontario Provincial Secretary's Office authored through seven editions *The Shareholders' and Directors' Manual* which recommended full disclosure in financial statement presentation and put forward as a model the balance sheet format prescribed by Table A of the 1862 U.K. Companies Act [Warde].

1897   Fellows of the ICAO recognized in provincial legislation as being suitable for municipal audit work [Ontario, Statutes, Ch. 48, Sec. 1].

Companies Act of Province of Ontario required directors to present to annual general meeting a statement of income and expenditure. Inspection provisions on shareholders' request and with approval of courts instituted [Ontario, Statutes, Ch. 28, Sec. 75]. Provisions in draft bill of 1896 relating to mandatory audit and revenue and expenditure statement and balance sheet in form prescribed by Table A of 1862 English Companies Act dropped in 1897 legislation [Ontario, Bills, Sec. 89], because such provisions would be too onerous for smaller firms [Ontario Archives, RG8 1-1-D].

1900/   ICAO standards recommended by the *Monetary Times*
02/07   for all public accountants [*Monetary Times,* Sept. 14, 1900, p. 841]. ICAO Presidents proclaimed the Institute to be the "leading and recognized head of the accounting profession on the continent" [ICAO Minutes, July 18, 1902] and after returning from meetings of the American Association of Public Accountants, that the "Ontario Institute is certainly far in advance of any of the State Associations" [ICAO Minutes, July 1907].

1900-40   Publication of annual anthology—*The Annual Financial Review, Canadian*—of financial statements of corporations listed on the Toronto Stock Exchange by the long-time Assistant-Secretary of the Exchange, W. R. Houston [1901-1941]. This anthology provided widespread publicity of corporate financial statements. Though the Exchange likely encouraged such publication, its listing provisions as late as 1970 required only that annual corporate financial statements be disclosed "in customary form" [Toronto Stock Exchange, 1960, By-law 63].

1902　Incorporation of the Dominion Association of Chartered Accountants (DACA) [Canada, Statutes, Ch. 58]—later renamed the Canadian Institute of Chartered Accountants (CICA).

1904/10　Companies Act of the province of British Columbia 1904, required annual audit and submission to shareholders' meeting of detailed income and expenditure statement and balance sheet. The form and contents for income and balance sheet disclosure identical to the optional clauses of Table A of the 1862 U.K. Companies Act [British Columbia, Statutes]. This detailed financial statement disclosure reduced in the 1910 Act to conform to the 1907 U.K. Act requirement of "a summary of capital, liabilities and assets giving such particulars as will disclose the general nature of those liabilities and assets and how the values of the fixed assets have been arrived at" [British Columbia, Statutes].

1904　Appointment of T. Mulvey as Assistant Provincial Secretary in Ontario. Held position until 1909 when he became the Under Secretary of State in the federal government. Influential in promoting the 1907 Ontario and 1917 Canadian Companies Acts and the financial statement disclosure requirements therein.

1905　Election of Premier J. P. Whitney's Conservative but "progressive" and reform-minded government in Ontario heralded significant changes in legislation relating to health and education, workmen's compensation, hydroelectric utilities, and mining, commercial and manufacturing companies [Humphries, 1966].

1905/12　Toronto Stock Exchange Regulations called for "a full statement of the affairs of the company" upon listing application [Toronto Stock Exchange By-laws, 1905, 1912, Rule 26].

1906/07　ICAO under the leadership of George Edwards made recommendations with respect to financial statement disclosure to the Provincial Secretary [ICAO Minutes,

February 8, 1906]. Provincial Secretary and Assistant
Provincial Secretary of Ontario Government attend Institute meeting to solicit and receive comments on draft
companies act legislation [ICAO Minutes, January 18,
1907].

1906/11   Rash of seven bank failures provokes concern for independent compulsory audits [Bank Audit . . . , 1911, p. 24].
Journal of Accountancy acknowledges competence and
ability of Canadian profession to undertake such audits
[Bank Examinations . . . , 1909, pp. 41-42]. (In the
United States in 1902, the Report of the Industrial Commission had indicated "that no independent group of
technically qualified professionals was available to
perform the necessary audits (of large corporations)
[Previts, p. 135].)

1907   Royal Commission on Insurance alerted financial community to abuses in accounting practices of Insurance
companies [Canada, Royal Commission on Life Insur-
ance]. However, more generally, the *Financial Post*
praised Canadian corporate disclosure—"nearly all the
most important companies have adopted a straight forward policy of publicity of earnings and condition"
[Financial Post, February 16, p. 1].

Ontario legislation levied 3% tax on mining company income in excess of $10,000 [Ontario, Statutes, Ch. 9,
Sec. 6(1)].

Companies Act of the Province of Ontario required, for
presentation to shareholders at annual general meeting, a revenue and expenditure statement and balance
sheet—the latter required the distinguishing of various
asset, liability and equity accounts. Mandatory balance
sheet (not income statement!) audit and prospectus
provisions also legislated. Financial statement disclosure provisions were direct copies of ICAO recommendations and were well in advance of comparable
statutes in Britain and the United States. This legislation reflected one of the earliest occasions in which
an accounting association was so directly influential
[Ontario, Statutes, Ch. 34, Secs. 36, 97, & 123].

1908/10   Wave of industrial mergers took place forming the basis
of many of the existing large Canadian corporations
[Skelton, pp. 259-261].

1908/ 13/21	The Certified General Accountants' Association founded in Montreal in 1908 and chapter formed in Toronto in 1921; federally incorporated in 1913 [CGA—Quebec, p. 50].
1909/10	Jurisdictional disagreements resolved between provincial institutes of Chartered Accountants and Dominion Association of Chartered Accountants with membership in DACA now automatic for, and restricted to, members of provincial institutes [Creighton, pp. 62-65].
1911	*The Canadian Chartered Accountant* first published. Name later changed to *CA Magazine* in 1973.
1913	Following a series of bank failures, the Bank Act prescribed mandatory balance sheet and income statement audits [Canada, Statutes, Sec. 56].
1914/17	Agreement reached that graduates of École des Hautes Études Commerciales de Montréal who had passed a special Licentiate examination would be admitted to membership in the Association of Accountants in Montreal. In 1917, the Association made arrangements to have their students taught in evening courses at McGill University [Collard, pp. 109, 116].
1916/17	Canadian legislation initiated taxes on Income and business profits [Canada, Statutes, 1916 and 1917]. Depreciation based on historical cost accepted for tax purposes [Breadner, p. 108]. This practice tended to officially recognize what had become accepted accounting practice.
1917	The Federal Reserve Board's "Uniform Accounting" was reprinted in *The Canadian Chartered Accountant* and recommended as a guide for Canadian usage [*Uniform Accounting,* July 1917, p. 49].
	Model set of financial statements with comments proposed by leading ICAO member, George Edwards, in *Dominion Company Law* by Thomas Mulvey [pp. 54-56], with elaborate emphasis on income statement components of sales, cost of sales, interest, taxes, depreciation and management, selling and general expenses.
1917/20	Canadian Companies Act required prospectus, financial statement and auditor provisions similar to those of the 1907 Ontario legislation [Canada, Statutes, 1917, Sec. 105]. Identical financial statement and auditor

provisions introduced in Quebec legislation of 1920 [Quebec, Statutes, Secs. 6024-6024a].

Consolidation of Characteristic Features: 1920 - 1960

The inter-war and post-war years saw the resolution of problems in corporate reporting handled through the now-established traditions of Companies Act legislation and ICAO/CICA leadership. Relatively modest changes in financial statement disclosure requirements accompanied provisions circumscribing the indigenous corporate stock promotion and capitalization abuses of the late 1920s in the Companies Acts legislation of 1934 and 1935. Similarly, growing concerns in the immediate post-war years for improved disclosure led to the introduction of the first CICA standards. The important Ontario disclosure legislation of 1953 was not prompted by any corporate scandals or widespread discontent but simply reflected a raising of former legislated minimums (of 1907) to the new CICA promulgated standards. The 1964-65 federal Companies Act was almost a direct copy of this provincial legislation.

It was during this period that American influence on the setting of Canadian practices began to assume important proportions.[1]

1920   Queen's University offered program of courses for the ICAO and began long-standing relationship in supplying academic support to the educational goals of the Ontario Institute and the CICA—most notable of which was the Queen's correspondence and lecture note program which many students across Canada used for over four decades [Creighton, pp. 101-112].

The Canadian Society of Cost Accountants (later the Society of Management Accountants) incorporated by representatives of provincial Institutes of Chartered Accountants [Special Issue, p. 20].

1926   Canadian Society of Cost Accountants began monthly journal *Cost and Management.*

1926/33   Publication of widely used and long-lived Canadian texts: *Accounting Principles and Practice* by R. G. H. Smails and C. E. Walker [1926]; and *Auditing* by R. G. H. Smails [1933].

1928/29   Concern raised that amendments to the Companies Act should correct "illegitimate promotions, flagrant stock watering, over-capitalization and misrepresentation" that attend the speculative boom [Mackintosh, p. 407].

1929   The Federal Reserve Board's "Verification of Financial Statements" was reprinted in *The Canadian Chartered Accountant* and recommended as a standard for good reporting [Clapperton p. 10].

1929/30   The Royal Mail Steam Packet Case in Britain which was concerned with the undisclosed use of secret reserves to bolster current profits was followed avidly in professional and financial journals in Canada. Canadian legislation of 1934 was said to have contemplated the prevention of such an occurrence [Smails, Students' Department, 1934, p. 283].

1931/33   Professor R. G. H. Smails [1931, pp. 101-103] and a study group of Queen's University professors called for improved financial statement disclosure relating particularly to the need for greater detail in the income statement and the need to provide the basis of asset valuations. [Members of Department . . . Queens, pp. 274-77].

1931/34   CICA commenced tradition of submitting briefs and making representations to legislating bodies—in 1931 a proposal for uniform legislation relating to financial statements [Editorial Comment 1934, p. 73] and in 1934 and 1935, briefs respecting the anticipated Companies Act revisions [General Notes, 1934, p. 327; Dominion Year Book, 1935-36, p. 234]. CICA claimed to be influential in securing increased financial statement disclosure requirements in Statutes of the provinces of Saskatchewan in 1933 and Manitoba in 1932 [Dominion Year Book, 1934-35, p. 222].

1932/34   Conference of Commissioners on Uniformity of Legislation recommended increased and uniform financial statement disclosure amongst all incorporating jurisdictions. The draft legislation of the Commissioners provided the immediate stimulus for the 1934 Companies Act legislation [Canada, Senate Debates, 1934, p. 452].

1933   The financial press regularly listed shortcomings in disclosure in financial statements [*Financial Post*, January 21, p. 11; June 24, p. 12; December 16, p. 11; May 6, p. 11].

           Members of the Department of Political and Economic Science at Queen's University concerned with abuses in corporate promotion and capitalization relating to the failure of prospectus provisions, allocation of proceeds of no par value shares, transfers of capital surplus to distributable surplus and lack of information regarding the proceeds from an underwriter [Members of Department . . . , pp. 274-277]. The financial press also raises similar issues [*Financial Post,* December 16, p. 11; June 24, p. 12; June 10, p. 11; and June 17, p. 3].

1934   House of Commons Debates [May 29, pp. 3454-58; and Ralston, p. 87] emphasized the importance of discouraging the abuses of stock promotion and capitalization in the 1934 legislation.

1934/35   Federal Companies Act legislation specified much increased disclosure in financial statements particularly with regard to greater detail in the income statement and the basis of valuation for inventories and fixed assets as well as the requirement to disclose a reconciliation of surplus accounts items. Consolidated financial statements, a long-standing practice, now permitted in the legislation. Auditors required to certify financial statements in prospectuses. This legislation was inspired by concerns and factors in Canada comparable to those that motivated the American Securities legislation of 1933-34 [Canada, Statutes, 1934 & 1935]. The legislation was well ahead of earlier counterpart legislation in Britain [Great Britain, Statutes, 1928, Secs. 39-40], but much less demanding than SEC Accounting Series Release No. 7 [Securities Exchange Commission].

1938   CICA's first publication: *Accounting Terminology for Canadian Practice.*
          The Royal Commission on the Textile Industry (The Turgeon Report) noted inadequacies in the financial statement disclosure provisions of the 1934 Companies Act [Canada, Royal Commission, p. 127].

1939   Gap between the 1934 Companies Act disclosure requirements and the standards necessary for good reporting emerged [Capon, pp. 380-381]. Undertakings made by CICA with Queen's University to develop a series of research studies [General Notes, 1939, p. 288] aborted by war.

1943   Accounting Research Committee of CICA provided recommendations relating to the refundable portion of Excess Profits Tax [Refundable Portion, p. 140].

1946   Province of Quebec restricted the practice of "public accounting" to chartered accountants [Quebec, Statutes].

Initiation of CICA recommendations *on authority of the Accounting and Auditing Research Committee.* Bulletin #1 concerned with standards of disclosure for mercantile and manufacturing companies. Authorship attributed to the Committee on Accounting and Auditing of the ICAO [Wilson]. (Recommendations become enforceable when provincial Institutes require adherence in their rules of professional conduct—required first in 1973 in Ontario).

1947   CICA issued Bulletin #2 on the minimum standards of audit and disclosure in respect of prospectuses.

1948   CICA issued Bulletin #3 on the accounting treatment of the loss "carry-forward" and "carry-back" provisions, the tax liability of prior years and refundable taxes.

1948/ 62/80   Chapters of the American based Financial Executive Institute formed in 1948; received federal incorporation in 1962 and single district Canadian status in 1980. Institute interested in the quality of corporate reporting through briefs to, and representations on, various influential organizations and committees.[2]

1949/54   Depreciation provisions of the 1949 Income Tax Act radically altered to promote government fiscal policy and to simplify calculation. Generous diminishing-balance rates of depreciation applied to asset pools introduced [Canada, Statutes, Secs. 7 & 8]. Requirement that depreciation taken for tax purposes ("capital cost allowance") must not exceed the amount recorded on the taxpayers' books rescinded, after much protest, in 1954 [Comment and Opinion, pp. 1-2].

1950   CICA issued Bulletins: #4 relating to accounting for bad debt losses; and #5 on inventory costs.

1951   The *Financial Post* initiated the sponsorship of annual awards for accounting content and design of financial statements.

CICA issued Bulletins: #6 relating to the standard form of auditor's report; and #7 relating to auditor's responsibility for validity of the inventory figure.

1952   CICA issued Bulletin #8 on depreciation for deferred tax purposes, emphasizing the distinction between the determination of income for tax purposes and for financial statement presentation purposes.

1953   Ontario Companies Act required income statement audit and increased disclosure in income statements, balance sheets and footnotes [Ontario, Statutes, Secs. 82-93]. Disclosure requirements based on the 1946 CICA Bulletin #1. The income statement audit had become a commonly accepted practice in the preceding decade.

Initiation of CICA's biannual compendium of the accounting practices of approximately 300 corporations, *Financial Reporting in Canada.*

CICA issued Bulletin #9 on the use of the term "Reserve" and accounting for reserves.

1954   CICA issued Bulletin #10 recommending the "deferred credit" basis of tax allocation but permitting the "taxes payable" or "flow through" method for the tax treatment of differences arising from depreciation for tax purposes (capital cost allowance) and depreciation for accounting purposes. 1954 marked the beginning of the increasing and sizeable appearances of deferred taxes accounts on Canadian corporate balance sheets. The CICA also issued Supplement to Bulletin #6 to reflect the change in Ontario legislation requiring the opinion section of the Auditor's report to use "presents fairly" rather than gives a "true and correct view."

1955   CICA issued Bulletin #11 on definition and appropriate use of the term "surplus."

1956   CICA issued Bulletin #12 on loss carry-over tax credits (superseding Bulletin #3).

1957   *The Royal Commission on Canada's Economic Prospects —Final Report* (The Gordon Report) indicated that very little is known about the financial activity of a significant portion of the economy owing to the financial statement disclosure exemptions for private corporations [Canada, Governor-General, p. 393].

CICA Issued Bulletins: #13 on unaudited financial statements; and #14 on standards of disclosure in financial statements (revising Bulletin #1).

1958   CICA issued Bulletin #15 on confirmation of accounts receivable.

1959   CICA issued Bulletins: #16 on auditor's responsibility for the validity of the inventory figure (superseding Bulletin #7); and #17 on the auditor's standard report (superseding Bulletin #6 and its Supplement).

Delegation of Standard Setting: 1960 - 1983

The 1960 period reflected a significant measure of dissatisfaction with corporate reporting practices. Much of the controversy, reflected in the financial press and in variously appointed committees of inquiry, was centered on the wide diversity in accounting principles. A rash of bankruptcies and corporate failures, highlighted by the collapse of the Atlantic Acceptance Corporation, aggravated the situation [Murphy, pp. 18-20]. Additional disclosure requirements were added in provincial and federal legislation throughout the period. However, the concerns for requiring minimum disclosure and uniformity in accounting principles through amendments to companies acts were largely set aside by the momentous and unrequested—but not unexpected—designation of the *CICA Handbook* recommendations as mandatory standards by the Canadian Securities Administrators in 1972, the Canada Business Corporations Act in 1975 and the Ontario Securities Act in 1978. The ~~1981~~ 1971 recommendations of Dickerson, Howard & Getz [pp. 108-109] that minimum required contents of financial statements be dealt with by Regulation rather than by statutory provisions and the subsequent initiatives of the Department of Consumer and Corporate Affairs to have these Regulations defer to the *CICA Handbook* were formative in this regard.

Of great significance was the designation in 1966 of the Ontario Securities Commission (OSC) by the Ontario Securities Act to oversee the Toronto Stock Exchange with powers not unlike those of the SEC [Ontario Statutes, 1966, Ch. 142, Sec. 139]. This Act took much of its inspiration from the SEC legislation and though the Commission has not set up extensive review procedures for annual reporting, it has—and increasingly so—added an American-style dimension to the standard setting process in its prodding of the CICA to direct its attention to particular areas of concern. No instances exist of the OSC countermanding standards set by the CICA.

1960   CICA issued Bulletin #18 on qualifications in the auditor's
           report.

1961   CICA initiated its series of Research Studies as prepara-
           tory background for the eventual issuance of Bulletins
           [Thomas, p. 93].
           CICA issued Bulletin #19 on financial statements of un-
           incorporated businesses.

1962   The Corporations and Labour Unions Returns Act
           (CALURA) required of unions and public and private
           companies (annual sales of more than $500,000 or
           assets of more than $250,000) the annual filing with
           the Minister of Industry, Trade and Commerce, of
           annual financial statements and returns detailing man-
           agement, share structure, ownership and foreign con-
           trol [Canada, Statutes].
           ICAO merged with Certified Public Accountants Associ-
           ation of Ontario [Creighton, pp. 235-246].
           Governmental regulation of public accounting in Ontario
           restricted the practice of "public accounting" essen-
           tially to chartered accountants [Ontario, Statutes, 1961-
           62].

1963   Publication of CICA Study *Accounting for Costs of Pen-
           sion Plans* by W. B. Coutts and R. B. Dale-Harris.
           CICA issued Supplement to Bulletin #17 requiring use of
           standard auditor's report for prospectuses.

1964   *Report of the Royal Commission on Banking and Finance*
           (The Porter Report) noted that corporate disclosure
           standards in federal corporations acts are inadequate
           [Canada, Royal Commission, pp. 350, 560-561].
           CICA issued Bulletin #20 on standards of disclosure in
           financial statements (superseding Bulletin #14).

1964/65   Canadian Companies Act legislation required financial
           statement disclosure provisions similar to 1953 Ontario
           Act [Canada, Statutes]; roughly the same lag in time
           as the 1907 Ontario and the 1917 Federal legisation!

1965   *Report of the Attorney General's Committee on Securities
           Legislation in Ontario* (the Kimber Report) recom-
           mended improved financial statement disclosure
           [Ontario, Attorney General, p. 29].
           A financial scandal of international dimensions, the failure
           of Atlantic Acceptance Corporation, provoked broad
           interest in narrowing the range of acceptable account-

ing practices; in defining more closely the extent to which a parent-company auditor may rely on the work of the subsidiary-company auditor; and in promoting interest in the requirement of audit committees of boards of directors [Ontario, Royal Commission . . . Atlantic Acceptance . . .].

CICA issued Bulletins: #21 on accounting for pension plan costs; and #22 on reliance on other auditors in reporting on consolidated financial statements.

1966	Ontario Securities Act required that the auditor's report shall not contain any qualification where it is reasonably practicable to revise the financial statement presentation with respect to the matter that would otherwise be the subject of a qualification [Ontario, Statutes, Ch. 142, Sec. 46(4)].

Following the Kimber Report of 1965, which found much of its inspiration in the model of the American SEC, the Ontario Securities Act gave on-going surveillance of Canada's chief exchange, the Toronto Stock Exchange, to the Ontario Securities Commission (OSC) [Ontario, Statutes, Ch. 142]. The OSC has much the same powers as the SEC, but has not set up intensive procedures to review annual financial statements.

Ontario Companies Act Amendments required increased disclosure relating, *inter alia,* to funds statements, the provision of comparative figures and gross revenues [Ontario, Statutes, Ch. 28].

Publication of CICA Study *Accountants and the Law of Negligence* by R. W. V. Dickerson.

CICA issued Bulletin #23 on standards of financial reporting applicable to prospectuses (superseding Bulletin #2).

1966/69	Publication by Howard Ross, one of the most prominent of Canada's practitioners and educators, of two influential books advocating adoption of current valuations methods: *The Elusive Art of Accounting,* 1966 and *Financial Statements—A Crusade for Current Values,* 1969 [*Ross*].
1967	CICA issued Bulletins: #24 on accounting for government grants for fixed assets; #25 on the auditor's standard report (replacing Bulletin #17 and its Supplement); and #26 delineating the usage of "deferred" and

"accrual" methods of tax allocation (superseding Bulletins #10 and #12).

1967/   *Interim Report of the Select Committee on Company Law*
70/75   (The Lawrence Report) indicated that "no need for amendments of major significance to the financial disclosure provisions of the Ontario Act" appear to exist [Ontario, Interim Report . . . , par. 10.1.4]. The Committee did recommend establishment of audit committees and these were first reflected in Ontario in 1970 [Ontario, Statutes, Secs. 171, 182] and later in federal legislation in 1975 [Canada, Statutes, Sec. 165].

1967/76 Organizational meeting and first annual conference held of the Canadian Regional Group of the American Accounting Association. Successor organization, the Canadian Academic Accounting Association, formed in 1976 [News, 1977, p. 15].

1968   Introduction of *CICA Handbook,* replacing the Bulletins on Accounting and Auditing Practices published since 1946. Dissents of Committee members no longer to be published. Loose-leaf handbook format is subject-indexed and cross-referenced and permits greater flexibilit in revision and updating of Recommendations. Accounting Research Committee called for disclosure of departures from its Recommendations.

Watkins Report on *Foreign Ownership and the Structure of Canadian Industry* detailed *inter alia* extent to which there is a lack of public disclosure of financial affairs of private Canadian companies [Canada, Privy Council, p. 214].

CICA Handbook Recommendations relating to: disclosure of departure from Recommendations in notes to financial statements and auditor's report; and amendments to extraordinary items, prior period adjustments, capital transactions and unaudited statements.

1969   Unprecedented issuance of an accounting policy statement on the handling of profits for land development companies by the Ontario Securities Commission [Ontario Securities Commission]. Issuance prompted CICA to set up a liaison committee with securities commissions and stock exchanges [News and Events, 1970, p. 8].

Toronto Stock Exchange required quarterly financial statements of listed companies [By-law 208, Sec. 1908].

CICA Handbook Recommendations relating to: standards of financial reporting applicable to prospectuses; and the classification of current assets and liabilities.

1970   Federal Companies Act legislation adopted additional disclosure requirements of Ontario Companies Act amendments of 1966 and abolished the financial statement disclosure exemptions for private companies [Canada, Statutes, 1969-70].

Publication of CICA study in cooperation with the University of Western Ontario on *Business Combinations in the '60s: A Canadian Profile* by S. Martin.

CICA Handbook Recommendations relating to: the reporting and calculation of earnings per share; and the auditor's report.

1971   Publication of *Proposals for a New Business Corporations Law for Canada* with recommendations that minimum required contents of financial statements be dealt with by regulation rather than by statutory provisions [Dickerson, pp. 108-109].

CICA Handbook Recommendations relating to: the financial reporting of diversified operations; interim financial reporting; amendments respecting extraordinary items, prior period adjustments, capital transactions and share capital; and unaudited financial statements.

1972   Publication of CICA studies on *Accounting Principles: A Canadian Viewpoint* by R. M. Skinner and *Current Value Accounting and Price-Level Restatements* by L. S. Rosen.

CICA Handbook Recommendations relating to long-term corporate investments.

National Policy Statement No. 27 of the Canadian Securities Administrators required financial statements to be drawn up to conform to the GAAP as reflected in the CICA Handbook [Canadian Securities Commission pp. 54-864]. This Statement, though not having the force of law, was the harbinger of the federally legislated delegation of standard setting authority to the CICA in 1975.

1972/73   CICA Accounting and Auditing Research Committee divided into two groups—the Accounting Research

Committee (ARC) and the Auditing Standards Committee (ASC). Membership in the ARC to be broadened by representation from other occupational and institutional backgrounds; but no fewer than two-thirds of twenty-two ARC committee members to be CA's. All sixteen members of ASC to be CA's. Research staff of CICA expanded and a separate research studies section established [Mulcahy, pp. 69-70].

1973 ICAO required members to qualify audit reports in respect to financial statements not drawn up in accordance with the *CICA Handbook* [ICAO Rules].

Formation of International Accounting Standards Committee (IASC) of which Canada was a founding member [News and Events, p. 9].

CICA Handbook Recommendations relating to: refundable taxes, earned depletion allowance and tax rate reductions; expansion of treatment of tax losses and carryovers; and to business combinations.

1973/74 Publication of CICA Studies: *Financial Reporting for Life Insurance Companies and Financial Reporting for Property and Casualty Insurers.*

Province of Quebec legislated Quebec "Professional Code" which established the Office des professions du Québec whose mandate was to supervise and control the operations of the various professions within the Province. The membership of the Office was to be determined by the Government and the independent Conseil Interprofessional du Québec. The office to have representation on the governing bodies of each of the professions [Quebec, Statutes].

1974 Initiation of CICA procedure to have ARC and ASC periodically publish "Guidelines" as "interim-positions," or as clarifications of Handbook Recommendations. Guidelines do not have authority of Recommendations. Guideline issued on "Accounting for the Effects of Changes in the Purchasing Power of Money."

CICA Handbook recommendations relating to: the statement of changes in financial position (funds statements); and the disclosure of accounting policies.

1975 The recommendations of *The Report of the Independent Review Committee on the Office of the Auditor General of Canada* (the Wilson Report) on government accounts related to the "value for money" concept, the reporting of changes in financial position statement, and independence of the Auditor General [Auditor General].

Canada Business Corporations Act abolished par value shares, expanded directors' liability, transferred financial statement content requirements to the (more easily altered) Regulations Section and modified auditor and established audit committee provisions. Most significantly, the Act required financial statements be drawn up to conform to the GAAP and generally accepted auditing standards (GAAS) as reflected in the *CICA Handbook* [Canada . . . Regulations, p. 189]. This requirement gave virtual unrestricted delegation of accounting authority in Canada to the CICA.

CICA Handbook Recommendations relating to: consolidated financial statements and the equity method of accounting; accounting for government assistance grants; generally accepted auditing standards; and conformity with or deviations from International Accounting Standards (IASC).

1973/76   Accounting Research Committee of the CICA issued Exposure Draft cn "Accounting for Changes in the Purchasing Power of Money." Withdrawn in 1976 as considerations of current value accounting assumed importance.

1976   Accounting Research Committee of the CICA published Discussion Paper on "Current Value Accounting."

CICA Accounting and Auditing Guidelines issued relating to recent "Federal Anti-Inflation Legislation."

CICA Handbook Recommendations relating to: unaudited financial statements; and the auditor's standard report, wherein the financial statements are viewed to "present fairly" by virtue of their conformity with GAAP.

1977   International Federation of Accountants (IFAC) formed with the Certified General Accountants' Association of Canada, the Society of Management Accountants and the Canadian Institute of Chartered Accountants as charter members [IFAC, p. 13].

Federal government creation of a Comptroller General of Canada to be the chief financial administrator of the federal Public Service [Ottawa Report, p. 18].

Province of Ontario commissioned *Report of the Ontario*

Committee on Inflation Accounting recommended inclusion of effect of inflation in financial statements
[News, September, p. 8].

CICA Guidelines issued relating to: federal budget 3%
inventory allowance; and term-preferred shares.

CICA Handbook Recommendations relating to: internal
control; investment in joint ventures; and audit evidence.

1978   Ontario Securities Act required financial statements be
drawn up to conform to the GAAP as reflected in the
CICA Handbook [Ontario Gazette].

Ontario Securities Commission proposed regulation requiring public companies in Ontario to file information
which is otherwise requested from other jursdictions—
effective as of 1979. The general intention of the regulation is to secure any required filings for the SEC
which are not otherwise required by the Commission
[Information Begins . . . , p. 12].

Issuance of CICA *Report of the Special Committee to
Examine the Role of the Auditor* (the Adams Report).
Recommendations extended to the auditor's role,
enterprises subject to audit, the detection of fraud,
illegal acts, the standard report, independence, regulation of the profession and education [The Adams
Report].

CICA Guidelines issued relating to: audit of candidates
under Election Acts; frontier exploration allowance;
and financial reporting by Property and Casualty Insurance companies.

CICA Handbook Recommendations relating to communication with law firms regarding claims and possible
claims; foreign currency translation; research and
development costs; contingencies; subsequent events;
long-term investments; unaudited interim financial information; and leases.

1979   Publication of CICA Exposure Draft on "Current Cost
Accounting."

Public companies subject to the Ontario Securities Act
are required to prepare quarterly financial statements
for shareholders and Ontario Securities Commission
[Quarterly Reporting, pp. 20-21].

The (Staff) Report of the Professional Organizations Committee, *Professional Regulation,* commissioned by the Ontario Government recommended establishment of a new Public Accounting Licensing Admissions Board and the rescinding of the limiting of the practice of public accounting to chartered accountants.

CICA Handbook's 1978 Recommendations on foreign currency translation suspended pending further study. (Reissued in 1983.)

CICA Handbook Recommendations relating to: segmented information; disclosure considerations—related party transactions; auditing aspects of knowledge of the client's business, documentation, planning and supervision and special reports; and revisions of former Recommendation on subsequent events.

1980   Publication of CICA Study *Corporate Reporting: Its Future Evolution* by Prof. Edward Stamp.

Formation of Canadian Comprehensive Auditing Foundation to increase accountability in public sector [Canadian Comprehensive Auditing, pp. 14-15].

Office des professions du Québec recommended that practice of auditing no longer be exclusive responsibility of chartered accountants [Quebec May Open . . . p. 16].

Proposed Accounting Guideline on presentation and disclosure of forecast data in prospectuses and auditor's involvement therein issued by CICA. (Issued in final form in 1983.)

Publication by Canadian Academic Accounting Association of *University Accounting Programs in Canada: Inventory and Analysis* by Tom Beechy; and by CICA of *Accounting for Pension Costs and Liabilities* by Ross Archibald.

CICA Handbook Recommendations relating to: reservations in auditor's reports and the reporting of inconsistencies; accounting changes and prior period adjustments; and international auditing guidelines.

1981   Proposal by the Certified General Accountants Association of Canada to establish the Accounting Standards Authority of Canada. The Authority would promulgate GAAP thereby hoping to replace the CICA's Accounting Research Committee which authors the statutorily recognized *CICA Handbook.* (It has not succeeded in doing so as of 1983.) Member composition of Authority to have broader representation than the ARC [Accounting Standards Authority of Canada].

CICA Report of the Special Committee on Standard Setting (SCOSS) recommends *inter alia* that the *CICA Handbook* should be written in terms of general principles rather than detailed rules, that the number of persons on ARC should be reduced, and that the percentage of non-CICA nominees be doubled. (ARC composition unaltered as of 1983) [Scoss Highlights].

Formation of a new CICA committee, the Public Sector Accounting and Auditing Committee (PSAAC), to offer guidance and establish accounting and auditing standards for national and provincial levels of government.

Publication of a joint study of the CICA and the Financial Executive Institute, *The Management Report in the Annual Report,* suggesting inclusion of a management accountability report in corporate annual reports.

Corporations and Labour Union Returns Act (CALURA) amended raising reporting thresholds of the private companies to $10 million in assets and $15 million in gross revenues—effective as of 1983 [Canada Statutes, 1981].

CICA Guideline issued on auditing in an EDP environment.

CICA Handbook Recommendations relating to: reliance on other auditors; audit of financial statements; fraud and error; auditor's report on non-consolidated financial statements in specified circumstances; and using the work of a specialist.

1982   *CICA Handbook* called for "supplementary information" disclosure of the effects of changing prices in annual reports of larger public corporations. Information to consist of income and balance sheet items related to inventories, fixed assets and monetary gains or losses.

CICA Guidelines issued: Canada-United States Reporting Conflict with Respect to Contingencies and Going-Concern Considerations; extension of GAAP to financial reporting by Property and Casualty Insurance Companies; and Accounting for the Petroleum Incentives Program and Petroleum Gas Revenue Tax. This latter Guideline conflicted with the accounting treatment

federal government desired, occasioning the first notable tension between the CICA standard setting body
and the government. The Ontario Securities Commission supported the CICA Guideline by requiring companies with reservations in their audit reports to appear
before the Commission [Crandall, p. 59].

1983   Establishment of a Canadian accounting journal, *Contemporary Accounting Research* by the Canadian
Academic Accounting Association with publication to
commence in 1984.

CICA Guidelines issued relating to the presentation and
disclosure of financial forecasts.

CICA Handbook Recommendations relating to: foreign
currency translation; and disclosure of variations in
the effective income tax rate.

FOOTNOTES

[1]See reasons therefor previously indicated in the second paragraph of the introduction.

[2]From discussion with Mr. K. Smith former President and Mr. D. Simpson current Executive Director of the Financial Executive Institute of Canada.

REFERENCES

A list of references relating to the Canadian evolution follow together with references to chronologies relating to Great Britain and the United States of America.

Canadian

Collard, E. A., *First in North America, One Hundred Years in the Life of the Ordre
Des Comptables Agréé du Québec* (l'ordre des Comptables Agréés du Québec,
1980).

Creighton, Philip, *A Sum of Yesterdays: Being a History of the First One Hundred
Years of the Institute of Chartered Accountants of Ontario* (The Institute of Chartered Accountants of Ontario, 1984).

Mann, Harvey, *The Evolution of Accounting in Canada* (Touche Ross & Co., 1972).

_____, "CAs in Canada . . . the First Hundred Years," *CA Magazine* (De-
cember, 1979), pp. 26-30.

Murphy, George J., *The Evolution of Selected Annual Corporate Financial Reporting Practices in Canada: 1900-1970*, (unpublished doctoral thesis, Michigan State
University, 1970).

_____, "The Influence of Taxation on Canadian Corporate Depreciating
Practices," *Canadian Tax Journal* (May/June, 1972), pp. 233-239.

_____, "The Evolution of Corporate Reporting Practices in Canada," *The
Academy of Accounting Historians*, (Working Paper Series #20, 1976), pp. 1-35.

_____, "Some Aspects of Auditing Evolution in Canada," *The Accounting
Historians Journal* (Fall, 1980), pp. 45-61.

_____, "Financial Statement Disclosure and Corporate Law: The Canadian Experience," *The International Journal of Accounting* (Spring, 1980), pp. 87-99.

_____, "Early Canadian Financial Statement Disclosure Legislation," *The Accounting Historians Journal* (Fall, 1984), pp. 38-59.

Zeff, Stephen A., "Forging Accounting Principles in Canada," *The Canadian Chartered Accountant* (May, 1971), pp. 324-330 and (June, 1971), pp. 396-402.

Chronologies of the United States and Great Britain

Knight, C. L., Previts, G. J., and Ratcliffe, T. A., *A Reference Chronology of Events Significant to the Development of Accountancy in the United States,* Monograph No. 1 (The Academy of Accounting Historians, 1976).

Nobes, C. W., and Parker, R. H., "The Development of Company Financial Reporting in Great Britain 1844-1977," Lee, T. A. and Parker, R. H., eds., *The Evolution of Corporate Financial Reporting* (Thomas Nelson & Sons, 1979), pp. 197-207.

Zeff, S. A., "Chronology—Significant Developments in the Establishment of Accounting Principles in the United States, 1926–1978," Lee, T. A. and Parker, R. H., eds., *The Evolution of Corporate Financial Reporting,* (Thomas Nelson & Sons, 1979), pp. 208-221.

_____, *Forging Accounting Principles in Five Countries* (Stipes Publishing Company, 1972).

Other References

"Accounting Standards Authority of Canada" (CGA Canada, undated).

"The Adams Report," *CA Magazine* (April, 1978), pp. 35-70.

Auditor General of Canada, *Report of the Independent Review Committee* (Auditor General of Canada, 1975).

"Bank Audit or Inspection Compulsary from Outside: Is it Justifiable and Expedient?," *The Canadian Chartered Accountant* (July, 1911).

"Bank Examinations in Canada," *The Journal of Accountancy* (May 1909).

Beatty, S. G. and Johnson, J. W., *Canadian Accountant,* Seventeenth edition (Ontario Business College, 1908).

Breadner, R. W., "The Business Profits and Income War Tax Acts," *The Canadian Chartered Accountant* (October, 1918).

British Columbia, "An Act to Amend the Companies Act," 1903-04, 3-4 Edw. VII, Ch. 12.

_____, Statutes, "An Act to Revise and Consolidate the Companies Act, 1897 and Amending Acts," 1910, 10 Edw. VII, Ch. 7.

Canada, "Canada Business Corporations Act Regulations" (Richard DeBoo, 1976).

_____, Consolidated Statutes, 1850, "An Act to Provide for the Formation of Incorporating Joint Stock Companies for Manufacturing, Mining, Mechanical or Chemical Purposes," 13-14 Vict., Ch. 28.

_____, Consolidated Statutes, 1850, "An Act Respecting Banks and Freedom of Banking," 13-14 Vict., Ch. 21.

_____, Governor-General in Council, *Royal Commission on Canada's Economic Prospects—Final Report* (Queen's Printer, 1957).

_____, Privy Council Office, *Foreign Ownership and the Structure of Canadian Industry* (Queen's Printer, 1968).

_____, *Report of the Royal Commission on Banking and Finance* (Queen's Printer, 1964).

——————————, *Royal Commission on Life Insurance* (King's Printer, 1907).

——————————, *Royal Commission on the Textile Industry* (King's Printer, 1938).

——————————, Senate Debates.

——————————, Statutes, 1851, "The Railway Act," 14-15 Vict., Ch. 51.

——————————, Statutes, 1855, "An Act to Secure the More Efficient Auditing of the Public Accounts," 17-18 Vict., Ch. 78.

——————————, Statutes, 1864, "An Act to Authorize the Granting of Charters of Incorporation to Manufacturing, Mining and other Companies," 27-28 Vict., Ch. 23.

——————————, Statutes, 1868, "An Act Respecting Insurance Companies," 31 Vict., Ch. 48.

——————————, Statutes, 1877, "The Canada Joint Stock Companies Act 1877," 40 Vict., Ch. 43.

——————————, Statutes, 1878, "An Act to Provide for the Better Auditing of the Public Accounts," 41 Vict., Ch. 7.

——————————, Statutes, 1902, "An Act to Incorporate the Dominion Association of Chartered Accountants," 2 Edw. VII, Ch. 58.

——————————, Statutes, 1902, "The Companies Act 1902," 2 Edw. VII, Ch. 15, Sec. 88.

——————————, Statutes, 1913, "The Bank Act," 3-4 Geo. V, Ch. 9.

——————————, Statutes, 1916, "Business Profits War Tax Act, 1916," 6-7 Geo. V, Ch. 11.

——————————, Statutes, 1917, "The Companies Act Amendment Act, 1917," 8 Geo. V, Ch. 25.

——————————, Statutes, 1917, "The Income War Tax Act," 8 Geo. V, Ch. 28.

——————————, Statutes, 1934, "The Companies Act, 1934," 24-25 Geo. V, Ch. 33.

——————————, Statutes, 1935, "The Companies Act, 1935," 25-26 Geo. V, Ch. 33.

——————————, Statutes, 1949, "An Act to Amend the Income Tax Act and the Income War Tax Act," 13 Geo. VI, Ch. 25.

——————————, Statutes, 1962, "Corporation and Labour Union Returns Act," 10-11 Eliz. II, Ch. 26.

——————————, Statutes, 1964-65, "Canada Corporations Act," 13-14 Eliz. II, Ch. 52.

——————————, Statutes, 1969-70, "Canada Corporations Act," 18-19 Eliz. II, Ch. 70.

——————————, Statutes, 1975, "Canada Business Corporations Act," 23 Eliz. II, Ch. 33.

——————————, Statutes, 1981, "An Act to Amend the Corporations and Labour Union Returns Act," 29-30 Eliz. II, Ch. 79.

"Canadian Comprehensive Auditing Foundation," *CA Magazine* (May, 1980).

Canadian Securities Commissions, *National Policy No. 27, Generally Accepted Accounting Principles* (CCH, 1972).

Capon, F. S., "Financial Statement Reform," *The Canadian Chartered Accountant* (December, 1943).

"CGA-Quebec Celebrates," *CGA Magazine* (March, 1984).

Clapperton, C. A., "The Balance Sheet," *Cost and Managment* (July, 1927).

Collard, Andrew, *First in North America, One Hundred Years in the Life of the Ordre Des Comptables Agréés Du Québec* (Ordre des comptables Agree du Québec, 1980).

"Comment and Opinion," *The Canadian Chartered Accountant* (January, 1954).

Crandall, Robert H., "Government Intervention—The Pip Grant Accounting Controversy," *Cost and Management* (September-October, 1983).

Creighton, Philip, *A Sum of Yesterdays: Being a History of the First One Hundred Years of the Institute of Chartered Accountants of Ontario* (The Institute of Chartered Accountants of Ontario, 1984).

Dickerson, R. W. V., Howard, J. L., Getz, L., *Proposals for a New Corporation Law for Canada* (Queen's Printer, 1971).

Dominion Year Book (The Dominion Association of Chartered Accountants).

Eddis, W. C., *Manual for Accountants* (Wilton C. Eddis, 1899).

"Editorial Comment," *The Canadian Chartered Accountant,* 1934 (July, 1934).

The Financial Post.

Fleming, C. A., *Expert Bookkeeping* (Northern Business College Steam Press, 1892).

"General Notes," *The Canadian Chartered Accountant* (April, 1934).

"General Notes," *The Canadian Chartered Accountant* (March, 1939).

Great Britain, Statutes, 1928, "The Companies Act," 18 & 19 Geo. V, Ch. 45.

Hoskins, David, *Bookkeeping for Joint Stock Companies* (Warwick Bros., and Rutter, 1901).

_____, *Joint Stock Company Accounts* (The Shaw Correspondence School, 1907).

House of Commons Debates.

Houston, W. R., *The Annual Financial Review, Canadian* (Houston's Standard Publications, 1901-1941).

Humphries, C. W., "The Political Career of Sir James P. Whitney," Unpublished doctoral thesis (University of Toronto, 1966).

"Information Begins at Home," *CA Magazine* (April, 1978).

Institute of Chartered Accountants of Ontario (ICAO), *Yearbook* (ICAO, 1898).

_____, *Rules of Professional Conduct,* 1973, Rule 206.

_____, Minutes of Council.

"IFAC Moves Closer to Reality," *CA Magazine* (April, 1977).

Mackintosh, W. A., "Economics and Accountancy," *The Canadian Chartered Accountant* (December, 1932).

Manitoba, Statutes, 1886, "The Chartered Accountants' Association Act," 49 Vict., Ch. 66.

Manitoba, Statutes, 1932, "An Act Respecting Joint Stock Companies and Other Corporations," 22 Geo. V, Ch. 5, Secs. 91-94.

Mann, Harvey, *The Evolution of Accounting in Canada* (Touche Ross & Co., 1972).

Members of the Department of Political and Economic Science at Queen's University, "Financial Manipulation: A Project of Reform," *Queen's Quarterly* (May, 1933).

Monetary Times.

Mulcahy, G., "Restructuring the CICA Research Program," *The Canadian Chartered Accountant* (May, 1973).

Mulvey, Thomas, *Dominion Company Law* (The Ontario Publishing Co., 1920).

Murphy, George J., "The Evolution of Corporate Reporting Practices in Canada," *The Academy of Accounting Historians* (Working Paper Series #20, 1976), pp. 1-35.

"News," *CA Magazine* (March, 1977).

_____, *CA Magazine* (September, 1977).

"News and Events," *The Canadian Chartered Accountant* (January, 1970).

_____, *The Canadian Chartered Accountant* (May, 1973).

"Notes and Comments," *The Canadian Chartered Accountant* (July, 1966).

Ontario Archives.

Ontario, Attorney General, *Report of the Attorney General's Committee on Securities Legislation in Ontario* (Queen's Printer, 1965).
_____, Bills, 1896 "Bill 199," 59 Vict.
Ontario Gazette, "Publications Under the Regulations Act," Part II (28 July 1979).
Ontario, *Interim Report of the Select Committee on Company Law—1967* (Queen's Printer, 1967).
_____, Lieutenant Governor in Council, *Report of the Royal Commission Appointed to Enquire into the Failure of Atlantic Acceptance Company* (Queen's Printer, 1969), Four volumes.
Ontario Securities Commission, *Recognition of Profits in Real Estate Transactions,* Bulletin (Ontario Securities Commission, 1969).
Ontario Statutes, 1876, "Building Societies Act," 39 Vict., Ch. 32.
_____, Statutes, 1878, "An Act to Incorporate the Toronto Stock Exchange," 41 Vict., Ch. 65.
_____, Statutes, 1883, "An Act to Incorporate the Institute of Chartered Accountants of Ontario," 46 Vict., Ch. 64.
_____, Statutes, 1892, "The Insurance Corporations Act, 1892," 55 Vict., Ch. 39.
_____, Statutes, 1897, "The Ontario Companies Act, 1897," 60 Vict., Ch. 28.
_____, Statutes, 1897, "An Act to Make Better Provision for Keeping and Auditing Municipal and School Accounts," 60 Vict., Ch. 48.
_____, Statutes, 1907, "The Ontario Companies Act, 1907," 7 Edw. VII, Ch. 34.
_____, Statutes, 1907, "The Supplementary Revenue Act, 1907," 7 Edw. VII, Ch. 9.
_____, Statutes, 1953, "The Corporations Act," 1 Eliz. II, Ch. 19.
_____, Ontario, Statutes, 1961-62, "The Public Accountancy Amendment Act," 10-11 Eliz. II, Ch. 113.
_____, Statutes, 1966, "The Securities Act," 14-15 Eliz. II, Ch. 142.
_____, Statutes, 1966, "An Act to Amend the Corporations Act," 14-15 Eliz. II, Ch. 28.
_____, Statutes, 1970, "Ontario Business Corporations Act," 19 Eliz. II, Ch. 25.
"Ottawa Report," *CA Magazine* (June, 1977).
Previts, G. J., and Merino, B. D., *A History of Accounting in America* (Ronald Press, 1979).
Province of Canada, Statutes, 1866, "An Act Respecting Municipal Institutions of Upper Canada," 29-30 Vict., Ch. 51.
"Quarterly Reporting for Ontario Companies," *CA Magazine* (November, 1979).
"Quebec May Open up Public Accounting," *CA Magazine* (August, 1980).
Quebec Statutes, 1874, "An Act to Incorporate the Montreal Stock Exchange," 37 Vict., Ch. 54.
_____, Statutes, 1880, "An Act to Incorporate the Association of Accountants in Montreal," 43-44 Vict., Ch. 88.
_____, Statutes, 1920, "An Act Respecting Certain Companies and Corporations," 10 Geo. V, Ch. 72.
_____, Statutes, 1946, "An Act to Regulate the Practice of Accountancy and Auditing," 10 Geo. VI, Ch. 47.
_____, Statutes, 1973, "Professional Code," Ch. 43.
_____, Statutes, 1974, "An Act to Amend the Professional Code and Other Legislative Provisions," Ch. 65.

Ralston, J. L., "Discussions on Dominion Companies Act," *The Canadian Chartered Accountant* (February, 1935).

"Refundable Portion of Excess Profits Tax," *The Canadian Chartered Accountant* (Feb., 1943).

Ross, H., *The Elusive Art of Accounting* (Ronald Press, 1966).

——————————, *Financial Statements—A Crusade for Current Values* (Sir Isaac Pitman, 1969).

"Scoss Highlights," *CA Magazine* (June, 1981), pp. 35-49.

Securities Exchange Commission, Accounting Series Release No. 7, "Analysis of Deficiencies Commonly Cited by Commission in Connection with Financial Statements," May 1938, reprinted in *Federal Securities Law Reports* (Commerce Clearing House).

Skelton, O. D., *General Economic History of the Dominion 1867-1912* (The Publishers Association of Canada, 1913).

Smalls, R. G. H., "Directors' Reports—A Criticism and Suggestion," *The Canadian Chartered Accountant* (September, 1931).

——————————, *Auditing* (The Commercial Text Book, 1933).

——————————, "Students' Department," *The Canadian Chartered Accountant* (September, 1934).

—————————— and Walker, C. E., *Accounting Principles and Practice* (Ryerson Press, 1926).

"Special Issue 50th Anniversary of The Society of Industrial Accountants of Canada," *Cost and Management* (May-June, 1970), Vol. 44, No. 3.

Thomas, R. D., "The Value of Accounting Research," *The Canadian Chartered Accountant* (July, 1961).

Toronto Stock Exchange, *Annual Reports of Listed Companies,* By-Laws.

"Uniform Accounting," *The Canadian Chartered Accountant* (July, 1917).

Warde, J. D., *The Shareholders' and Directors' Manual* (The Canada Railway News Co., Limited, 1907).

Wilson, J. R. M., Correspondence with author, May 8, 1970.

An Interpretative Chronology of the
Development of Accounting Associations in Canada:
1879 - 1979

Alan J. Richardson
School of Business
Queen's University
Kingston, Ontario.

Funding was provided by: various sources within Queen's University including the Research Program of the School of Business; the Advisory Research Committee and Principal's Development Fund; the School of Business and School of Graduate Studies and Research; the Clarkson Gordon Foundation (through Bob Crandall, Queen's University); SSHRCC (through a Doctoral Fellowship); and, the Centre for the Advancement of Professional Accounting Education and the Department of Accounting, University of Alberta. This support is gratefully acknowledged.

This project would not have been possible without the cooperation of accounting associations and individuals across Canada. Their help in providing published materials and access to their files is greatly appreciated.

The comments of George Murphy and Harvey Mann have been instrumental in focusing and improving this chronology. I am particularly grateful to George Murphy for his constant encouragement of this project. I would also like to acknowledge Denis Goodale and Phil Creighton for their comments and inputs; to Bob Leong in providing an unpublished history of the Society of Management Accountants of Alberta; to Gerry Gerard for his assistance in securing materials from the CICA library; to Helen Cutherburton for her aid with materials in the Canadian Society of Management Accounts library; and to W.A. Atkinson for providing archival material assembled for his history of the Society of Management Accountants of British Columbia. The assistance of Gordon Stewart, Byron Lew and Donna Egglestone (at the University of Alberta) and Kathy Klass and Kristi Ludig (at Queen's University) during the latter stages of the project is also acknowledged. The author retains full responsibility for the contents of this chronology.

'The nature of things is much more easily conceived when they are beheld coming gradually into existence, than when they are only considered as produced once in a finished and perfect state.'   René Descartes

INTRODUCTION

The Canadian accounting profession is predated only by the accounting associations of Scotland and England. The first accounting organizations in Canada appeared in 1879 only twenty years or so after the first associations in Great Britain and three years ahead of the first accounting association in the United States (eight years before the forerunners of associations which have survived to the present). In spite of the long history of the accounting profession in Canada, and the contributions which the profession has made to the economic life of this country, there is surprisingly little published work on its history.

Part of the difficulty in researching the history of the accounting profession in Canada is that the profession is organized on a provincial basis such that the relevant records are scattered across the country. Within each province, moreover, the profession is organized as a number of independent accounting associations. The difficulties in gaining access to records is further exacerbated by the lack of records on the early years of many associations, particularly those which have merged with other associations or simply disappeared.

This chronology represents a selection of events from the history of accounting associations. The focus of the chronology is the institutional structure of accounting, in particular, the development of standards of entry and training (i.e. professionalization), the emergence of a division of labour among accounting associations and related occupations, and the development of the profession's role with respect to the conduct of private enterprise. It is, therefore, complementary to the work of Murphy (1970, 1972, 1976, 1980, 1984, 1986) who focuses on the evolution of corporate financial disclosure in Canada and to the work of Richardson and Williams (1988) on the development of management accounting practice in

553

Canada.   This chronology is not intended to detail the evolution of accounting practices or standards.

The construction of a chronology such as this inevitably involves choices about which events are "significant" in the history of the profession. The events chosen are intended to include all incidents which affect the way in which the profession is organized. Events in the early years of the profession have been over-reported relative to events in later years in order to provide coverage of those events for which fewer public sources exist. Some events reported, for example, name changes of accounting associations, may not affect the organization of the profession directly but are reflections of processes within the profession which shape the domains and roles of particular associations. These events are the empirical outcroppings of aspects of the profession's development which require further research to identify the forces at work.

In constructing this chronology I have drawn on journals and internal documents of various associations, commissioned histories, newspaper accounts, interviews and a small number of brief academic papers on the history of the profession. These are listed in the bibliography. For each event included in the chronology, a primary reference is provided. These references have been chosen to be as close as possible to the event while also being publically available. Where possible, source documents have been used to verify the events described and/or multiple, independent citations have been sought. In the event of conflicting citations, the event is recorded based on my judgment of the credibility of sources, however, details of alternate reports of the event are also given. In some cases, single references to an event, particularly with regard to smaller associations, have been used. This chronology, therefore, must remain as work in process and corrections, additions or deletions, with verifiable sources, would be welcome from any user of this chronology.

The chronology has been divided into five sections as shown below. Each section is preceded by brief interpretative comments.

The emergence of Chartered Accountancy ......1879 - 1908

The birth of competing associations ......1908 - 1920

A division of labour in accountancy ......1920 - 1945

Regulating public accountancy ......1945 - 1962

Consolidation and 'rationalization' ......1962 - 1979

A major part of this chronology involves the constant changes in the constitution and organization of associations within the profession. In order to aid the readers' understanding of the relationships among accounting associations, Figure 1 provides a schematic overview of the births, mergers, divisions and name changes of accounting associations in Canada (revised from Richardson, 1985b). Only those associations which have a direct connection to current designation granting bodies have been included. The Key to Figure 1 provides the abbreviations which are used in that Figure. Appendix A provides a complete listing of abbreviations used in the text.

KEY TO FIGURE 1

Associations are listed in order of founding

ABBREVIATION FULL NAME

AAM	Accountants and Auditors in Montreal
IAAO	Institute of Accountants and Adjusters of Ontario
ICAO	Institute of Chartered Accountants of Ontario
ICAM	Institute of Chartered Accountants of Montreal
ICANS	Institute of Chartered Accountants of Nova Scotia
DACA	Dominion Association of Chartered Accountants
ICABC	Institute of Chartered Accountants of British Columbia
ICAS	Institute of Chartered Accountants of Saskatchewan
CAA	Canadian Accountants Association
SIPABC	Society of Independent Public Accountants of B.C.
IAM	Independent Accountants of Montreal
GAA	General Accountants Association
CSCA	Canadian Society of Cost Accountants
IAAPQ	Inst. of Acct's and Auditors of the Province of Quebec
AA	Accountants Association
CPAPQ	Certified Public Accountants of the Province of Quebec
SIAAE	Society of Independent Acct's and Auditors of Edmonton
UAA	United Accountants and Auditors
AAAO	Accountants and Auditors Association of Ontario
CSCAIE	Canadian Society of Cost Acct's and Industrial Engineers
CI	Controllers' Institute
FEI	Financial Executives Institute
IPA	Independent Public Accountants*
IAEC	International Accountants and Executives Corporation
APA	Accredited Public Accountants
CPAAO	Certified Public Accountants Association of Ontario
SICAC	Society of Industrial and Cost Accountants in Canada
IPAA	Independent Public Accountants Association*
GA	Guild of Accountants
CICPA	Canadian Institute of Certified Public Accountants
IAPA	Institute of Accredited Public Accountants
GICIA	Guild of Institutional Commercial and Industrial Acct's
SIAC	Society of Industrial Accountants of Canada
IPA	Independent Public Accountants*
SMAC	Society of Management Accountants of Canada

* Although these groups used similar names, there is little or no overlap in membership.

FIGURE 1: THE EVOLUTION OF THE CANADIAN ACCOUNTING
PROFESSION: 1880 to 1985*

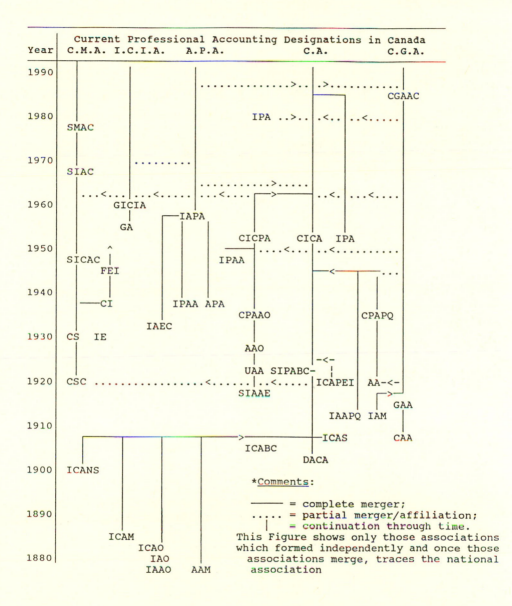

The Emergence of Chartered Accountancy: 1879 - 1908

The emergence of professional accounting associations in 1879 followed the growing demand for accounting services during the industrial revolution, reflected in the formation of public accounting firms in Montreal and Toronto in the 1840's (Hyde, 1904), and the rise of accounting associations in Scotland (1853) and England (1870) (Brown, 1905: 253). Several causes of the increased demand for accounting services may be cited such as the increasing complexity of manufacturing operations and the separation of ownership from control but the profession, in its early years, appears to have been concerned most with bankruptcy (Thompson, 1939: 171; Mann, 1975b). The majority of accounting firms developed as liquidators, assignees and trustees in bankruptcy and only began to concentrate on accounting per se as the economy stabilized. These various accounting roles were institutionalized in early legislation notably the Insolvent Act, S.C. 1862 (Second Session) c.17, s.2-3, the Railway Act, S.C. 1867-68, c.68, s.9 and the Bank Act, S.C. 1867, c.11. The emergence of accounting associations in Canada may also have been a response to the formation of associations in England and concern that these associations may attempt to control accounting throughout the Commonwealth (Edwards, 1915: 335; Johnson and Caygill, 1971; Allan, 1982). The Canadian profession, as an organized body of practitioners, thus emerged to control and exploit the opportunities provided by industrialization in the face of global competition for financial service roles.

The first accounting associations in Canada arose within weeks of each other, although apparently independently, in the commercial centers of Montreal and Toronto. Each association took the name Chartered Accountant (CA) which had been established as a mark of competence in accountancy in Great Britain (see CCA V17, 1927: 40-44, for a contrary argument by

R.R.Thompson). Although adopting the same designation, these associations differed markedly in their entrance requirements and initially operated as rivals. The Montreal CAs in the first decade of the twentieth century backed the creation of a Federal organization which engaged in various legislative battles with CAs in Ontario. By the end of this period, Institutes of CAs had been established in six Provinces and a major step had been taken towards reforming the Federal association as a federation of the provincial institutes.

1879

The first meeting of the Association of Accountants of Montreal (AAM) [currently the Ordre des comptables agrees du Quebec (OCAQ)] is held on June 11 in the Mechanics Institute of Montreal (Collard, 1980: 18; Brown, 1905: 253, records this as June 18, 1879; A.F. Riddell, on the 25th anniversary of the Institute, on authority as the last surviving founding member, put the date as Dec. 5, 1879, CCA V19, 1929: 254; Creighton, 1984: 4, claims June 13, 1879 to be the date). The exact date is important as a matter of pride for the right to claim to be the oldest accounting association in Canada. The ICAO had claimed this honour, e.g. CCA V20, 1930: 61, but it appears settled now in favour of the AAM). The purpose and structure of the association were probably borrowed from the Institute of CAs of Edinburgh to which some of the founding members had ties (Thompson, 1939: 172; Mann, 1976: 24; Collard, 1983: 39-40).

The first meeting of the Institute of Accountants and Adjusters of Canada [currently the Institute of CAs of Ontario (ICAO)] is held on November 11 in the offices of Robins Myles and Co., Toronto (Creighton, 1984:1). The officers of the Institute were directed to 'frame the rules, as far as possible, on the model of the Institute of CAs of Great Britain (Edwards, 1954: 356). It may be noted that at least one of the incorporators, W.H. Cross, had received his accounting training in England (Little, 1964: 15).

The "Toronto Committee of Accountants" contacts the AAM suggesting the creation of an Institute of Accountants of Canada (Hyde, 1904:84, Collard, 1980:56; Mann, 1975b: 26). Further initiatives by the ICAO followed in 1881, 1886 (Mann, 1975b:26), 1887 and 1899 (Collard, 1980:56) but in each case were rebuffed.

1880

The Charter of the Association of Accountants of Montreal (AAM) receives Royal Assent (S.Q. 1880 (3rd Session), c.88), becoming the first formal accounting organization in North America and the fifth in the world (CCA v16, 1927: 215). The Act received some opposition from independent accountants fearing the growth of regulation in accountancy but the Act was passed substantially unaltered. The Act prohibits members from working for a salary or in any other occupation. This meant that members were limited to full time public accountants which lead the AAM to consider themselves the "creme-de-la-creme" (Mann, 1975b) of accounting associations in Canada. The association was not active for the first 15 years of its life, for example, at the annual meeting of 1894 only one member was present. It was not until competing associations emerged that the association took an active role in the development of the profession (Collard,1980: 56).

1882

The ICAO's first attempt to gain a Charter is rejected resulting in a change in the structure of the association (from a voluntary organization to an educational movement) and its executive (electing individuals with political experience and connections to the government through the Anglican Church and Masonic Order) to make it more politically acceptable. During this period the Institute operated under the name of the Institute of Accountants of Ontario (Creighton, 1984: 11-12).

1883

The Charter of The Institute of Accountants of Ontario (CA) is given Royal Assent (S.O. 1883, c.62).

1884

The ICAO establishes its entrance and certification criteria. Three classes of membership are created: "member" requiring a majority vote of those present at a regular meeting of the Institute; "associate" awarded on successful completion of a written examination on bookkeeping, law, penmanship, English and business arithmetic; and, "Fellow" awarded after passing further examinations in auditing, arbitration and awards, adjusting and expert accountancy, and on successful defense of a thesis (Creighton, 1984: 15-17, 33).

1885

The ICAO elects Mrs. M.L. Rattray, Principal of Shaw Business School in Hamilton, as their first woman member. The ICAO allowed any educational institution affiliated with a CA member to train candidates for their primary examination (Creighton, 1984: 20). There is no record of the Shaw Business School in the Hamilton city directories of this time period. Moreland (1977) lists a Mrs. Rattery as owner of the Brantford Business College between 1890 and 1900 (when it was purchased by the Canadian Business College, later the Shaw Bussiness College, of Hamilton). It is possible that these references are to the same woman.

1886

The Association of CAs in Manitoba is formed. The structure of the organization was explicitly patterned after the ICAO although none of the originators were CAs (Neville, 1986: 6). They drafted legislation calling for a monopoly on the practice of accounting in Manitoba and the right to set minimum fees. The Bill was supported by the Attorney General (who was also the Mayor of Winnipeg). The provincial legislature rejected both of these clauses (Hoole, 1963: 5).

The Charter of the CAs Association of Manitoba (ICAM) receives Royal Assent (S.M. 1886, c.66). Charter members were required to pay a fee of $25 which would allow them to become members without examination. Applicants to the Institute subsequent to incorporation would be required to write examinations to qualify for membership. The Association changed its name to the Institute of CAs of Manitoba on Feb. 15, 1913 in order to bring uniformity of title among the provincial associations (Hoole, 1963: 5; Affleck, 1980: 1-2).

1887

The ICAM decides against setting examinations, admitting new members, or holding lectures until their charter could be amended to provided greater incentives for members (Hoole, 1963: 6). The following year they vote to suspend activities indefinitely. No further activities are recorded until 1902.

1888

The ICAO makes their first attempt to influence the legislative process, lobbying with regard to the Municipal Act and the Bank Act (Creighton, 1984: 21).

The ICAO holds their first written examinations for the right to use their designation (Creighton, 1984: 33).

1890

The Confederation Life Case: this was the first formal disciplinary case heard by the ICAO. The case affirmed the importance of auditor independence but created a rift among senior members. The following year Clarkson and Cross resigned from the council, their names are prominent among incorporators of the Dominion Association of CAs (DACA) in 1902 (Creighton, 1984: 23-27; Richardson, 1990a).

1891

The ICAO passes by-laws prohibiting members from describing themselves as CAs unless they had passed examinations set by the Institute or were members at the time of the Institute's founding. This results in the resignation of many members in industry who could see no benefit in preparing for such an examination (Thompson, 1938: 175; Edwards, 1954: 359; CCA V16, 1927: 217). These changes were described as changing from the Scottish model to the English model of chartered accountancy (CCA V18, 1928: 302).

1892

The ICAO expels its first member (Creighton, 1984: 28).

1895

Faced with declining membership, the ICAO restructures its council (reducing the size of the council from 21 to 15) and its examination process. The new process requires four levels of examination: primary, intermediate, final and an additional examination for fellowship. The primary examination was delegated to proprietary schools whose 'masters' were ICAO members (Edwards, 1954: 359). The intermediate examination tested mercantile arithmetic, negotiable instruments, bookkeeping, auditing, shareholders' and partners' accounts and insolvency. The final examination tested bookkeeping, accounting for joint-stock companies, partnerships, auditing and mercantile law. Students who passed the intermediate examination were given a certificate of competence as a bookkeeper (Creighton, 1984: 38-40).

1896

The ICAO votes to ban women from membership (Creighton, 1984: 44-47). The Institute had granted an associate membership to Julia Manning who 'came close' to passing their examination in 1894 but decided against allowing women into membership as increasing numbers of women began applying. The rational for the decision was that 'the employment of women clerks was detrimental to the value of male labour' (Edwards, 1954: 358).

The AAM makes its first use of its disciplinary powers by expelling a member for fraud (Collard, 1980:186).

The AAM attempts to gain legislation conferring the right of privileged communication with clients and a minimum tariff. This bill is rejected by the private Bills Committee (Hyde, 1904:86). The Attorney General, however, agreed to support a bill allowing a minimum tariff to be established.

1897

The Ontario Municipal Act (S.O. 1897,c.228, s.2; see also S.O. 1897, c.48, s.1) is revised to require municipal auditors to be FCAs or "other expert accountant". Note that the CA designation, which had been granted without examination was insufficient. This was the first legislation to specify a particular accounting association to fill a mandated role (Creighton, 1984: 131).

1899

The ICAO forms a student society (Edwards, 1915: 339; Brown, 1905: 256 reports this as 1900).

1900

The AAM holds its first examinations for membership (Collard, 1980: 104). The subjects tested were bookkeeping and accounting, insolvent law, arithmetic and algebra (Brown, 1905: 254). Each applicant had to be at least 21 years old, have been in practice for one year or have served as an apprentice for three years with a member of the association (Thompson, 1938: 173).

The Institute of CAs of Nova Scotia (ICANS) is incorporated (S.N.S. 1900, c.154). Candidates for membership, at the discretion of council, may be required to write three examinations. The primary examination is a test of general knowledge. The secondary examination tests bookkeeping, accounting and law. The final examination tests the ability to classify accounts, open the books of a new business, detect bookkeeping errors and audit (Brown, 1905: 257).

1901

A Federal bill to incorporate the Institute of CAs, Actuaries and Finance receives second reading but is quashed by the Senate due to opposition from existing accounting bodies (Bill O, Senate of Canada, 1st session, 9th Parliament I Edward VII, 1901; Creighton, 1984: 52). This attempt finally convinced some members of the existing accounting associations of the need for a federal body, if only to pre-empt others (Collard, 1980: 57; Mann, 1975b: 26-27). These members were also concerned with the trend towards allowing inexperienced accountants into the Institutes. They, therefore, set out to create a national body limited to practicing accountants (Edwards, 1915: 338; see also CCA V11, 1921: 316-319).

1902

Edwards Morgan becomes the first accounting firm to open branch offices (Creighton, 1984). This becomes an important factor in the creation of CA Institutes in other provinces most notably in Alberta and British Columbia.

The ICAM resumes operations in order to oppose the creation of Federal bodies claiming the right to use the CA designation across Canada (Hoole, 1963: 7). There is some ambiguity in Hoole's account. The group he describes as the one which the ICAM opposed matches the Institute of CAs, Actuaries and Finance but the dates given are after this bill had been successfully blocked. Creighton (1984: 52) speaks of the Manitoba association being "shaken awake" by a partner of Edwards Morgan to oppose the DACA (see also Neville, 1986: 9). This is more consistent with the time pattern cited.

In spite of opposition from the provincial associations (excluding the AAM), the Dominion Association of CAs receives its Charter (S.C. 1902 (Second Session), c.58). The approval of this Charter reflects the ability of the DACA to gain support from the AAM (by virtue of their policy of accepting only established practitioners as members, in contrast with the emphasis on training and universal membership criteria of other Institutes), and the presence of several prominent accountants, notably Clarkson and Cross who had resigned from the ICAO in 1890

(Creighton, 1984: 51-52). Collard (1980: 58) presents a markedly different view of these events, suggesting that the provincial Institutes were active participants in the DACA from the outset. Edwards (1954: 359) indicates that the provincial Institutes may have expected, as a result of negotiations leading to the withdrawal of their objections, that they would be Charter members but found that only members with experience in public practice were accorded this privilege. This, of course, would apply to all members of the AAM but not to all members of other associations.

It may be noted that the scope of this Act was less than at least one incorporator had intended. Among papers belonging to E.R.C. Clarkson was a draft bill entitled 'An Act to Incorporate the Institute of CAs of North America' (Little, 1964: 53).

1903

The Institute of CAs of British Columbia (ICABC) is formed in response to the creation of the DACA (Affleck, 1980: 1). A key member of this group was J.B. McKilligan who had served as the first President of the ICAM and had moved to B.C. in 1902 as Surveyor of Taxes for the provincial government (Hoole, 1963: 4).

The ICAM holds its first examinations for membership. Prior to this time admission had been by a secret vote of the membership. If an applicant received five "blackballs" he was rejected. Later, the number of "blackballs" required for rejection was reduced to three in order to tighten admission standards (Hoole, 1963: 8). The ICAM conducts an active membership campaign in this year for fear of losing the CA designation to the DACA due to "non-usage", and to prevent the DACA from gaining members in Manitoba (Neville, 1986: 18).

1905

The Institute of Accountants of Newfoundland is incorporated with the right to offer the FCA designation (S.N. 1905, c.16).

The AAM agrees to allow the formation of a student society and provides a library for their use (Mann, 1975b: 29).

The Institute of CAs of British Columbia receives a provincial Charter (S.B.C. 1905, c.59). It was originally proposed to follow the system used in Manitoba where all charter members were allowed to use the CA designation without examination. Opposition to the bill by established bodies, however, forced an amendment which gave this right only to accountants who were members of other bodies and were resident in the province. All others would have to pass an examination set initially by members of established associations and ultimately by a committee of members. The incorporators of the ICABC, therefore, immediately wrote examinations set by CAs from England and the ICAO. Only four of the twelve incorporators passed this examination and these four, along with a small number of members of other associations who had joined the ICABC, constituted the continuing membership of the Institute (Affleck, 1980: 2). This procedure was subsequently used to qualify the founding members of the ICAA and ICAS (Edwards, 1915: 336-337).

1906

The Act incorporating the Institute of Accountants of Newfoundland is revised rescinding the right to offer the FCA designation (S.N. 1906, c.29).

The ICAM forms a student society, the President of the Society is appointed at the pleasure of the ICAM council (Hoole, 1963: 8).

1908

The Institute of CAs of Saskatchewan (ICAS) is incorporated (S.S. 1908, c.55). The founding members were subject to examinations for membership conducted by the established Institutes (Edwards, 1915: 337). The impetus for the founding of the ICAS came from contacts with the ICAM (Neville, 1986: 13).

The ICAO Charter is amended to give the Institute exclusive right to the CA designation in Ontario (S.O. 1908, c.42). Although the Act was declared ultra vires by the Federal courts, it marks the beginning of Ontario's legislative pressure on the DACA and the beginning of reserve title legislation for accountants in Canada (Creighton, 1984: 62-63). Edwards (1954: 360) suggests that this and subsequent events concerning the right to use the CA designation precipitated the reconciliation of the ICAO and DACA.

The Canadian Accountants Association (currently the Certified General Accountants Association of Canada, CGA) is formed under the sponsorship of John Leslie, Assistant Comptroller, Canadian Pacific Railways. The association was created due to difficulties which industrial accountants had in meeting apprenticeship requirements for admittance to the CA Institutes. It was created primarily as an alternative vehicle for the professional advancement of industrial accountants (Bentley, 1938: 5). The association would allow entry by examination only but avoided the apprenticeship requirements of the CAs. Willis (no date) reports that the founders of the association set the first examinations and then resigned. Two founding members were never able to pass the association's examinations in order to qualify for examination.

The executives of the DACA and ICAO meet at the American Association of Public Accountants Convention in Atlantic City and, under the chairmanship of Harry L. Price, President of the Society of Incorporated Accountants and Auditors of England, discuss the rationalization of the profession (Creighton, 1984: 63-64; Collard, 1980: 60).

The Birth of Competing Associations: 1908 - 1920

The emerging Institutes of CAs adopted selection and training procedures which excluded certain groups from membership. In particular, women, accountants in industry and senior practicing public accountants found access to the Institutes was blocked. As the Institutes gained in public esteem and legal privileges, non-members could perceive a degradation of their own position. To reverse this trend, a number of associations were established with different entrance and training requirements, and these associations began to compete with the Institutes for the key professional roles. This competition forced each association to reassess its structure and operations. During this period, the accounting associations adopted many of the attributes of traditional professions, perhaps most important of which was the development of university affiliations (Richardson, 1986a,b). There were also legislative changes which began to establish roles for accountants and to specify certain groups of accountants to fill these roles. Notable among these changes are the introduction of income taxes to support the war effort.

Another major development is the rise of public concern over the development of cost accounting techniques and, as a corollary, cost accounting associations. The professional journals suggest three sources for this concern which are discussed below. First, the Russian revolution and labour unrest in Canada resulted in calls for manufacturers to demonstrate that they were earning only a fair return and for educators to inform the "masses" about the nature of costs. Second, the needs of the state during wartime created a demand for products which allowed firms to earn "excess" profits. The development of costing technologies was needed for wartime contracting between private enterprise and the state, and in order to implement the taxation systems developed to finance the war. Third, the high rate of bankruptcies due to "ruinous competition" was creating concern to both the state and organized manufacturing interests. The solution proposed was to develop an understanding of the "full" cost of products to ensure that pricing strategies would not undercut this amount (e.g. Bennett, 1917). By the end of the period Canada had followed the lead of the U.K. and U.S.A. and established a separate association of managment accountants.

1909

The provincial Institutes of CAs (excluding Quebec), following the suggestion of the ICAM and meetings held at the American Institute of Accountants in St. Paul in 1907, form the Federation of CAs of Canada to challenge the DACA. The Federation existed for only a year and does not appear to have acted as a professional body in any way (Creighton, 1984: 64; Hoole, 1963: 10-13; Neville, 1986:12).

The ICAM introduces a 1 year articling requirement to be served between writing the intermediate and final examinations. The decision was made on the basis of concerns for the training needs of students and the economic benefits to the firms (Neville, 1986: 14; Hoole, 1963: 14-15, places this event in 1910).

The ICAM passes a resolution calling for members to restrict themselves to "conservative" advertising (Hoole, 1963: 12).

In December the DACA is restructured as a federation of Provincial Institutes. Members of the provincial Institutes will still be known as CA's of particular provinces, members of the DACA who were not members of a provincial Institute would be known as members at large (Mann, 1976: 27).

1910

The CAA begins an education program consisting of lectures on retail, bank and department store accounting, claims and collecting debts. A library is also started (Stuart, 1988:17).

The first by-laws of the DACA come into force empowering the association:
(1)   to secure the incorporation of provincial societies in provinces of the Dominion where none existed;
(2)   to assist provincial societies in securing uniform legislation for the better protection and regulation of local professional interests;
(3)   to secure the adoption by provincial societies of uniform standards of examination and membership;
(4)   to arrange for reciprocal privileges between provincial societies for the benefit of their members;
(5)   to consider questions of ethics;
(6)   to secure harmony of action in all matters affecting the common interest and generally to act in an advisory capacity to provincial societies. (Edwards, 1915:

340)

The Charter of the Institute of CAs of Alberta (ICAA) receives Royal Assent (S.A. 1910, c.43). The founding members were all accredited practitioners of existing Institutes (Edwards, 1915: 337).

1911

The English Colonial Office intercedes in discussions of reserved title legislation for CAs in Ontario to ensure that English CAs retain their right to use their designation in Canada. The CAs respond by creating a list of societies whose members would be accepted as Ontario CAs upon application. This marks the beginning of attempts to gain reciprocal recognition among Canadian provincial societies and, thus, the standardization of qualifications (Creighton, 1984: 67-69).

The Charter of the ICAO is rewritten to give the Institute exclusive right to use the CA designation in Ontario (S.O. 1911, c.48). At the same time, the composition of the Board was changed to require that two-thirds of its members be in public practice. This move signals the increasing specialization of the Institute in public accounting.

Due to continued poor showings on the final examination, the ICAM Board of Examiners recommends that the period of apprenticeship be extended to two or three years (Neville, 1986: 16).

The ICAA succeeds in having its members appointed to the list of official auditors. The Act was passed in 1909 (S.A. 1909, c.10).

The first issue of the Canadian Chartered Accountant is produced. The Journal is published quarterly until 1920, bi-monthly until 1932 and monthly since that date. There were prior attempts to develop a means of communication among members of the ICAO including two pages per issue of Institute news in Business (a Toronto magazine) during 1895 and the publication of some Canadian material in Accountics (published in New York) during 1897 - 1899 (Creighton, 1984: 69-70). The secretary to the ICAO is appointed editor for the new Journal.

1912

The ICAS student society forms (CCA V2 1911/1912: 220).

The first interprovincial agreements for reciprocity of membership in Institutes of CAs are reached (Pontifex, 1913: 37).

The ICABC begins indenturing students under a contract of articles (Affleck, 1980: 49).

The ICAO opens their library (Creighton, 1984: 72, puts this in 1913).

The CAA meets to consider the benefits of incorporation and the advisability of issuing certificates of competence to members. It was decided that such a step was desireable (Bentley, 1938: 9).

The ICAM admits nine senior members of international accounting firms practicing in Manitoba without examination in two meetings on October 29 and December 7. This was necessary to overcome these firms' opposition to the amendments to the CA Act (Hoole, 1963: 17, reports this as February 3, 1913). Other demands from failed students and a Charter member who claimed that his initial involvement entitled him to membership for life without paying fees, were rejected (Neville, 1986: 19

The Institute of Accountants and Auditors of the Province of Quebec (L'Institut des compatables et auditeurs de la province de Quebec) (IAAPQ) is incorporated (S.Q. 1912, c.94). Although the AAM objected to the bill, the Institute was supported by government on the grounds that there were too few francophone names on the CA membership list and due to their intent to expand audit requirements (CCA V3 1913/1914: 119). The bill was amended, however, to prevent the use of the title 'compatible licencie' which was used as the french translation of Chartered Accountant (Collard, 1980: 28).

The by-laws of the ICABC are amended to require five years of practice as a public accountant, two years of which must have been in B.C., or two years employment in the office of a CA in good standing with a recognized society, prior to writing the final examination. The Institute had adopted the three-stage examination process in use in Ontario (Affleck, 1980: 5).

1913

The ICABC student society is formed (CCA V2 1912/1913: 212).

The ICABC requires four years of service with a member before granting the CA designation (CCA V3 1913/1914: 199).

The ICAS negotiates successfully with the University of Saskatchewan to introduce an accountancy degree (CCA V3 1913/1914: 50). The Institute had been using the University to supervise examinations since 1910. Classes began in 1917 and the first degree in accountancy was granted in 1923 (King, 1959: 47).

The AAM is consulted by McGill to ensure that McGill's accountancy courses conform with CA requirements (CCA V3 1913/1914: 44).

The DACA annual conference in Winnipeg addresses technical issues for the first time (CCA V3 1913/1914: 67).

The ICAM opens its library (CCA V3 1913/1914: 123).

The Association of CAs of Manitoba is renamed the Institute of CAs of Manitoba (S.M. 1913, c.1). The Act also allows the Institute to create classes of membership, set a minimum tariff of fees, set conditions of entry for members of other associations, and gives the Institute exclusive rights to the CA designation in Manitoba (Hoole, 1963: 16). The new Act also allows voting by mail ballots and represents a change from a private to a public Act (Neville, 1986: 18).

The Federal Charter of the General Accountants Association (formerly CAA) receives Royal Assent (S.C. 1913, c.116). The Charter was patterned after the DACA's charter which had gained legislative approval. The bill was opposed by the CAs who succeeded in having the Association's name changed to prevent the use of initials similar to the CA designation. This period resulted in the first discussion of the distinction between public and cost or management accounting. The CGAs provided informal assurance to the DACA, through George Edwards, that they were concerned with the standards of practice of management accountants and had no desire to set standards for public accountants (Creighton, 1984: 76-77; Bentley, 1938: 2).

The GAA adopts a system of examinations (pre-admission, intermediate and final) for membership suggested by the Principal of the Shaw Business School in Toronto (Stuart, 1988:23).

The ICABC votes to ban women (Affleck, 1980: 7).

John Sutcliffe raises the issue of admitting women to the Institutes of Chartered Accountancy at the annual meeting of the DACA held in August (CCA V3 1913/1914: 80-81). Although a committee is struck to consider the issue, the onset of war prevents any action being taken. (CCA V4 1914/1915: 281 notes that at the annual meeting of 1914 the report on this was requested but had not been prepared).

The GAA convenes its first Board of Examiners who set the subjects for Preliminary and Final examinations and draw up a list of texts (Bentley, 1938: 10). The final examination covered commercial arithmetic, advanced bookkeeping, commercial and statute law, the companies, banking and Bills of Exchange Acts, cost accounting theory, auditing and office routine (Stuart, 1988:23).

The ICAM meets to discuss the need for a code of ethics. It is decided that "the precepts of professional conduct should be worked into our daily practice rather than injected into our by-laws" (Hoole, 1963: 19-20). A paper by Joplan (published in CCA 1914) was distributed to illustrate the "precepts".

1914

The IAAPQ reached an agreement with the Ecole des Hautes Etudes Commerciales de Montreal to admit graduates of their three year accounting program to membership provided they were over twenty-one, passed a special examination and had one year's experience in public accounting (S.Q. 1914, c.27). Collard (1980: 116) incorrectly reports this as the AAM. The

AAM made similar arrangements in 1918.

The ICABC announces that almost all (7) members of the "Incorporated Society" were admitted to membership during the year (CCA V4 1914/1915: 162).

The ICAM passes a by-law prohibiting auditors from operating as limited liability companies (Hoole, 1963: 21).

The ICAS votes in favour of women members (CCA V4 1914/1915: 167).

The ICAS establishes the FCA as a reward for service (CCA V4 1913/1914: 289).

The first candidate passes the GAA Preliminary examination (Bentley, 1938: 9).

The ICAM defeats a proposal to include a code of ethics in their yearbook (CCA V4 1913/1914: 284).

The B.C. CAs Act is amended to give the ICABC exclusive rights to the CA designation in that province (Affleck, 1980: 6).

The General Accountants Association holds their first Final examinations and begins granting the CGA designation (Bentley, 1938: 10). The ICAO disputes the right to use this designation (Stuart, 1988: 25).

A university Board of Examiners is created for the ICAS (CCA V4 1914/1915: 66).

The ICAA votes to ban women from membership (ICAA, 1985, No.1).

The ICAM votes against a resolution to ban women from membership (Hoole, 1963: 40). The argument in favour of the resolution was that women could not be assigned to certain classes of businesses due to objections from clients, and, therefore, could not gain the breadth of experience expected of a CA (Neville, 1986: 23).

The ICAA and the University of Alberta sign an affiliation agreement which gives the U. of A. complete responsibility for the primary examination, and joint responsibility for the intermediate and final examinations (ICAA, 1985: No. 1). The arrangement for the primary examination is regarded as being consistent with "that required of candidates entering upon the study of law, medicine, dentistry and other professions" (CCA V4 1914/1915: 258).

1915

The ICAS adopts a by-law concerning unprofessional conduct which prohibits solicitation, advertising, price competition and criticism of peers (CCA V5, 1915: 66). This is the first formal code of ethics adopted by the CAs. The President of the DACA, while commending the

ICAS, suggests that the definition of misconduct should simply be 'conduct unbecoming a gentleman' (CCA v5, 1916: 178).

The ICAS elects their first fellows (CCA V5 1915/1916: 67).

The ICAM considers making their student society lectures mandatory (CCA V5 1915/1916: 61).

The AAM arranges a series of lectures on "higher accountancy and finance" given through the McGill School of Commerce by David S. Kerr CA (CCA V5 1915/1916: 152).

The ICAA membership is appointed "en mass" as "official auditors". This gives them the right to act as an auditor in respect of any Act in Alberta which requires audited statements.

1916

The ICAA student society makes arrangements with the Institute of Technology, Calgary, to provide a series of lectures (CCA V6 1916/1917: 232).

The ICAS is forced by the Provincial government, in light of wartime conditions, to suspend their service requirements. This requirement is reinstated in 1919 (CCA 1919: 101).

The ICAM passes a new by-law concerning ethical conduct (CCA V6, 1916: 50). This issue arose when George Edwards filed a complaint against a fellow member but lost. Edwards offered his resignation but reconsidered when council changed the by-law consistent with Edwards position on the case (Neville, 1986).

The ICABC forms a library (CCA V5, 1916: 225).

The ICABC passes a by-law allowing transference of time spent as an apprentice with one CA to another CA provided the former master gives his consent (CCA V6, 1916: 141). This represented the first step toward registration of students directly with the Institutes.

The AAM and IAAPQ approach the Quebec Premier suggesting legislation regulating the profession. Their suggestion is rejected as too politically sensitive (Collard, 1980: 30).

The Charter of the Institute of CAs of New Brunswick (ICANB) receives Royal Assent (S.N.B. 1916, c.53). The Act was originally sought by nine petitioners, only one of whom was a CA. The lack of CAs and applications by other accountants to be included in the Act caused the government to disallow all names on the petition. The Government, through the Committee on Corporations, then appointed three people, two CA's from Nova Scotia, including R.A. McIntyre who served as President of the ICANS in 1906 - 1907, and the comptroller-general of the Province of New Brunswick, to carry out the charter. These three advertised and conducted examinations for membership which resulted in two additional members (CCA V6, 1916: 227-228). The Act allows any member of any incorporated society in the British Empire or

United States to refer to themselves as a CA in New Brunswick. The ICANB was formed with the explicit intention of affiliating with the DACA and initially used the ICAO examination papers (Hudson, 1966: 13-17). The ICANB becomes affiliated with the DACA on Sept. 18, 1918.

The ICAO forms a committee on taxation consisting of one member of each of the nine major firms in Toronto (Creighton, 1984: 79).

The ICAM arranges with the University of Manitoba to conduct examinations for the Institute (Hoole, 1963: 23). This is endorsed by the membership at the Annual Meeting of June 27, 1917 (CCA V7, 1917: 54-55) The ICAM subsequently co-operates in establishing accounting courses at the university (CCA V7, 1917: 241).

1917

A uniform final examination for CA's is suggested following the unification of CPA associations in the U.S.A. and their acceptance of uniform examinations (CCA V6, 1916/1917: 311).

The University of McGill begins a series of evening lectures in accounting which the AAM "recommends" to its students (Collard, 1980: 109).

The ICAM fee tariff is set for the last time (Hoole, 1963: 23; CCA V7, 1917: 329).

The ICAM negotiates the transfer of their examinations to the University of Manitoba. The new University Act explicitly allows for this type of arrangement (CCA V7 1917/1918: 55). The intent of the arrangement of the University's part appears to have been to develop a school of business (CCA V7, 1917/1918: 241).

The ICAA and AAM restrict membership to British subjects (CCA V7, 1917: 52).

The ICAA passes a by-law requiring that two-thirds of its council be practicing public accountants (CCA V7, 1917: 245; CCA V8 1918/1919: 64).

The ICABC amends their by-laws to allow members to article three instead of two clerks in order to speed the return of servicemen into the profession (CCA V7, 1917/1918: 58).

The GAA advertises examinations in public accounting. This expands the domain of the CGAs into territory claimed by the CAs and begins a series of disputes which continue to the present (Creighton, 1984: 76-77). A search of the major newspapers in Toronto and Montreal for the years surrounding this date failed to produce an example of advertisements by the GAA with one exception in the Montreal Gazette, April 2, 1917, p.11. This advertisement announces a meeting "at which the plans of the Association will be announced" and is hardly inflammatory. The GAA, however, did prepare pamphlets which call for a broader role for the GAA than simply cost accounting.

The ICAO accepts N.L. Martin and J.L.Thorne, senior practicing accountants, into membership after closed door 'special examinations' (Creighton, 1984: 75).

1918

An advertisement for A.P. Gibbon I.A. (member of International Accountants Society of America) appears in the Hamilton City Directory. This is the only known reference to this group.

The ICANB and IAAPQ apply for membership in the DACA (CCA V8, 1918: 100). The ICANB is accepted (CCA V8, 1918: 169) but a decision on the IAAPQ is deferred pending the outcome of legislative action in Quebec to close the profession.

The ICAS turns its examinations over to a University Board of examiners (CCA V8, 1918: 62).

The Quebec government passes Acts (S.Q. 1918, 2nd session, c.43; S.Q. 1918, 2nd session, c.44) allowing Bachelors of Commerce of L'Universite de Montreal and McGill University the right to write examinations in accounting and auditing leading to membership in either the AAM or IAAPQ. This was later extended to include the CPAPQ (Thompson, 1938: 175, 185).

The ICAA in co-operation with its student societies establishes libraries in Calgary and Edmonton (CCA V8, 1918/1919: 64).

The ICABC sets and publishes a minimum tariff of fees. Public and practitioner criticism of the tariff ensures that the exercise is not repeated (Affleck, 1980: 7-8).

1919

The CAs are explicitly named as auditors in Ontario's Trust Company Act (S.O. 1919, c.42). Although the Ontario government had suggested that the list of auditors be limited to members of the ICAO this was rejected by the Institute fearing that this would create pressures to accept as members individuals currently acting as Trust Company auditors who did not have the qualifications for membership in the Institute (Creighton, 1984: 80-81). The Act, therefore, allows auditors to be "any member of the Institute of CAs of Ontario or any person approved by the Dominion Mortgage and Investments Association and the Land Mortgage Companies Association of the Province of Ontario" (CCA V8, 1919: 245).

The ICAM adopts a four tier membership structure: (A) Principals of Big Eight Firms or individuals practicing in the province; (B) members in the employment of CA's; (C) non-resident members and resident members not in the employ of CA's; (D) honorary members (CCA V9, 1919/1920: 95).

The ICAS reinstates a requirement of three years service with a practicing CA before admission to membership. Due to University regulations this is not implemented until 1920 (CCA V9 1919:

101).

The ICAS adopts a new, higher tariff of fees (CCA V8 1919: 256).

The ICAS adopts a by-law requiring three years service in the office of a "practicing" Chartered Accountant prior to admission to membership. Six months remission of service is allowed if the candidate has received "approved instruction" (CCA, V9 1919: 101). This requirement had been suspended in 1916 at the request of government due to the manpower shortage created by the war.

The Society of Incorporated Accountants and Auditors is formed (CCA, 1920, V10: 81). Creigton (1984) based on the oral history of the CGAAO and George Cathercole's memoirs of Chester Walters suggests that this group was latter associated with the Accountants Association of Ontario (AAO) and the Certified Public Accountants Association of Ontario (CPAAO). This can not be verified in the records, for example, the incorporators of the Society do not appear to be prominent members of these latter groups (see Canada Gazette, Dec. 13, 1919, p. 1783, and Canada Gazette, May 29, 1920, p. 4140).

The ICABC, by a vote of the membership, decides to accept women members and one woman is registered as an articling clerk (CCA V9 1919: 99; Affleck, 1980: 9).

The AAM offers membership to any members of the Institut des comptables et auditeurs (IAAPQ) in an attempt to balance their membership between anglophone and francophone members, and, thereby, secure legislation to close the profession. The AAM (CAs) attempted to gain legislation requiring that all public accountants in the Province be CAs in 1916, 1918, and 1919. Only the 1919 attempt made it to the legislature, the earlier attempts were quashed during informal discussions (Collard, 1980: 30; CCA V8, 1919: 341).

The ICAO notes that their student society had been unable to mount a lecture series in the past year due to lack of funds. It is resolved that the Institute should provide some support (CCA V9, 1919/1920: 138).

Queen's University approaches the ICAO seeking a reduction in entry requirements for graduates of their degree program. Exemptions from the primary examination and one year of apprenticeship are granted (Creighton, 1984: 101).

The ICABC passes a by-law allowing 1 years remission of articles for candidates holding a degree from a recognized university within the British Empire (CCA V9 1919: 99; Affleck, 1980: 9).

The Independent Accountants of Montreal (25 members) merge with the GAA (Bentley, 1938:11).

<u>1920</u>

The DACA committee on Uniformity of Standards report is published which recommends that: (1) each Institute have a sequence of three examinations of increasing difficulty; (2) candidates must have attained, at least, Arts matriculation (high school graduation); (3) candidates for the intermediate examination must be at least 19 years old, and must be 21 years old before writing the final examination and be a resident of the province in which they are writing; (4) candidates should have one years service before writing the intermediate examination and three years service before writing the final examination with any member of any registered society. The ICABC registered society list is recommended to all provinces (<u>CCA</u> V10, 1920: 96-101).

The Society of Incorporated Accountants and Auditors of Edmonton applies for Federal incorporation but, due to the similarity of this title and that of an English society, the society is renamed the United Accountants and Auditors in Canada (UAA) (<u>CCA</u>, 1920, V10:81; Canada Gazette, Dec 13, 1919: 1783; May 29, 1920: 4140). This change was brought about as a result of opposition by the CAs. John Hyde of the DACA was awarded an honorary membership in the Incorporated Society of Accountants and Auditors of England in recognition of this service (<u>CCA</u> v10, 1920: 277). News of the existence of this group caught the ICAA by surprise (<u>CCA</u> V9, 1920: 212). Members of the UAA also held membership in the GAA and unsuccessfully attempted to gain control of its charter in 1920 (Creighton, 1984: 124). They subsequently incorporated as the AAO.

The AAM lobbies against the incorporation of a company wishing to practice under the title "Comptables Experts Incorpores" (<u>CCA</u> V9, 1920: 207).

The AAM splits their final examinations into practical (bookkeeping, accountancy and auditing) and theoretical (company, law, partnership, trustees, banking, political, economy and insolvency [sic]) and allows candidates failing the theoretical component to rewrite this section alone (<u>CCA</u> 1920: 207).

The ICANS grants Diplomas of Accountancy to members in addition to membership certificates. This provision is incorporated into the revised by-laws of the Institute approved by government in 1921 (<u>CCA</u> V9, 1920: 209).

The ICANS adopts minimum age requirements of 17 for the primary, 19 for the intermediate and 21 for the final examination (<u>CCA</u> V9, 1920: 209).

The ICAM increases its terms of service (apprenticeship) from three to four years (<u>CCA</u> V10 1920: 87; Hoole, 1963: 26, reports this as a five year requirement). The five year apprenticeship requirement was introduced in 1922.

The Society of Independent Public Accountants of British Columbia is formed (Affleck, 1980: 10).

The CGAs in public practice in Quebec gain provincial incorporation as the Accountants Association (AA) (S.Q. 1920, c.118) using the L.A., Licenciate in Accounting, designation [later the Corporation of Public Accountants of the Province of Quebec (CPAPQ) which merged with the CAs in 1946] (CCA V9 1920: 279, 285; Bentley, 1938: 11). They had sought incorporation as the GAA of the Province of Quebec with the right to offer the Certified Public Accountant designation, CPA, but changed their name due to the opposition of the AAM (CCA, V10 1920: 82).

The Canadian Society of Cost Accountants (CSCA) is incorporated Federally. The president of the DACA contacted each provincial Institute to suggest the need for such a body and the first board of the Society consisted of the provincial presidents of the eight member Institutes of the DACA (CCA v10, 1920: 31-34; CCA V10 1920: 116-119). The CCA is expanded to a monthly publication and increases its coverage of cost accounting topics. George Edwards is elected the Society's first president. The Society was designed to allow accountants in industry to exchange of technical information and interact socially but it was explicitly not intended as a professional body. It would not offer training nor offer a certificate of competence or designation (CCA, 1920: 31,45; Mann, 1975b: 36). Allan (1982: 4), in the official history of the Society, suggests that the formation of the Society was independent of other accounting bodies. This is inconsistent with the evidence.

A Division of Labour in Accountancy: 1920 - 1945

The emergence of competing associations and the general increase in the scope of accounting services led to the specialization of accounting associations in particular domains. In particular, public and management accounting were recognized as complementary aspects of the accounting task. The Institutes of CAs began increasing their emphasis on public accounting while encouraging other associations to restrict their activities to the management accounting field. This commitment is signified by the Institutes' sponsorship of the creation of the Society of Management Accountants. Competition for public accounting roles among associations continued, however, and the period ends with demands for the regulation of public accounting in several jurisdictions.

The period also witnessed the recognition of the equality of men and women under the law. This was reflected in the formal acceptance of women into accounting associations. The rate of entry of women to the profession, however, would remain low until the 1970's.

1921

The General Accountants Association by a vote of 17 to 14 (Stuart, 1988: 30 reports the vote as 44 to 3), with many abstentions, decides against accepting women as members (CCA, V10 1921: 276-277).

The Institute of CAs of Prince Edward Island (ICAPEI) gains a provincial Charter (S.P.E.I. 1921, c.25). This occurred without the knowledge or consent of the existing CAs and the ICAPEI was not accepted into the DACA for two years (CCA V11, 1921: 142-143). Hudson (1966: 19-20) records that this group also sought membership in the ICANB but was rejected. Furthermore, the ICANB took legal action to prevent the PEI group from using their CA designations in New Brunswick. The ICAPEI and ICANB finally recognized each other's designations in 1926.

The ICABC arranges for candidates for the primary examination to write the University of British Columbia junior matriculation instead of the Institute's own examinations (CCA V11, 1921: 167; CCA V10 1921: 209).

The by-laws of the DACA and provincial Institutes are altered to allow non-resident accountants into membership. This results in a jump in membership from 570 to 724 members (CCA V11, 1921: 139-140).

The ICABC attempts to amend its act to prevent the use of any designation other than the CA as a mark of competence in accounting. The bill was opposed by at least six (unnamed) accounting associations and to placate these interests the ICABC was forced to allow some "grandfathering". Therefore, the ICABC absorbed 13 members of the Society of Independent Public Accountants and 15 other experienced public accountants without examination or articles. This action required an amendment to the CAs Act removing the clause, inserted in 1905, that limited entry to those who passed an examination (S.B.C. 1921 (2nd Session), c.53). This clause was reintroduced in 1924.

Sixteen other people were rejected by the ICABC and three of these eventually took their case to the supreme court of B.C.. Among these was a woman accountant, Mercy Crehan, wife of a former ICABC president. The Supreme Court of British Columbia ordered the ICABC to accept her as a member. The ICABC had, thus, gained its first woman member (Affleck, 1980: 10).

The ICAO encountered difficulty in negotiations with Shaw Correspondence Schools over the content of their accounting curriculum (Edwards, 1954: 361). On January 10, 1921, therefore, the ICAO voted to take control of their own educational program. In this endeavour they turned to O.D. Skelton, Dean of the Faculty of Arts, Queen's University, primarily for advice on running a correspondence course as he had successfully presented the Canadian Bankers' Course since 1914 (Gibson, 1983: 37). Skelton and W.C. Clark presented a proposal for Queen's to take over the ICAO education program. The proposal would leave the Institute with substantial control over the content of the program but would free it from the administrative burden (Creighton, 1984: 106-108). The change was announced in Jan., 1921 (CCA V10, 1921: 184) to take effect Sept. 1, 1921. The first syllabus was published in CCA V11, 1921: 251-260). Smails (1951:7) suggests that these events reflect Skelton's strategy of building the Commerce program on the backs of extension courses.

The ICAO plan requiring students to take the Queen's University correspondence course in recommended to all provinces by the President of the DACA as a means of achieving uniformity of standards (CCA V11, 1921: 140). A paper by George Edwards specifies the principles of the program (i.e.: offered by correspondence, based on texts prepared by Canadian or British authors, following a programmed course of instruction without optional courses, to be considered as a post-graduate program obligatory for CA membership).

1922

The ICAM admits an American CPA to membership without examination. The procedures and information used by the ICAM in this case were shared with the DACA who subsequently negotiated a reciprocal agreement with the American Institute in 1924. This agreement lasted until 1939 when the AICPA introduced a citizenship requirement (Neville, 1986: 39).

The University of Alberta begins a four year B.Comm. program (the first year was taken in Arts) which entitles graduates to exemptions from the CA primary and intermediate examinations and a reduction in apprenticeship from four to two years (CCA V11, 1921: 196; CCA V15 1925: 61).

DACA forms a committee on the uniformity of provincial standards under the Chairmanship of George Edwards.

The DACA sends George Edwards to help the ICAPEI to establish policies and procedures (CCA V12, 1922: 137). The ICAPEI was seeking affiliation with the DACA at this time (CCA V12, 1922: 153) but no action was taken (CCA V14, 1924: 134).

The ICAM increases its apprenticeship requirements to five years prior to writing the final examination (CCA V13, 1923: 80), and begins the use of a formal registration agreement between students and employers (CCA V12, 1921/1922: 157). This policy continues in force until the university degree requirements is introduced in 1970.

The ICAS accepts its first woman member, Mrs. Irene Lynn Patterson (Fairclough, 1966: 469-471); this name does not appear in the ICAS membership lists published in CCA for 1923-1924.

The ICAO revises their rules of professional conduct. The major change is a complete ban on advertising by members. The advisability of auditors investing in their clients was also raised by the ICAO, but a proposal to ban such practices was rejected by the Board (see also the Atlantic Acceptance case of 1965)(Creighton, 1984: 115-116; CCA V12, 1922: 158).

The AAM considers the need for "rules of personal conduct" (CCA V12, 1921/1922: 156).

The CSCA signs an affiliation agreement with the U.S.-based National Association of Costs Accountants (Allan, 1982: 9; see also CCA V11, 1922: 384-385).

Miss Florence Eualie Herkins passes the final examinations of the ICANS (CCA V12, 1921/1922). Her name, however, does not appear on subsequent membership lists.

A provincial CGA branch is formed in Montreal (Bentley, 1938: 11).

1923

The CGAs attempt to organize in Saskatchewan, but the ICAS convinces potential members to organize as a social rather than professional group. All CAs in Saskatchewan were urged to join this group to ensure that it developed in an appropriate direction (CCA, 1923: 70).

The ICABC encourages students to gain their training through commercial correspondence schools. This continued until 1927 at which time the Queen's Correspondence Course is adopted (Affleck, 1980: 15).

The GAA produces a newsletter, The General Accountant, through their Toronto branch (Bentley, 1931: 14). This continues until 1941 when it is transferred to the Vancouver branch and produced as a magazine. The magazine returned to Toronto in 1967.

A branch of the CSCA is opened in Toronto (Allan, 1982: 11). The branch structure of the CSCA became particularly important during the provincial incorporation drive of the 1940's. The CSCA, however, did not exercise control over the formation of chapters and many failed due to inadequate membership bases (CCA V13, 1923: 255, 258-260).

1924

The ICAM arranges with the University of Manitoba to provide all non-professional courses for their students (CCA V14, 1924: 147). A passing grade in these subjects (english, arithmetic and law) is required before writing the Institute's examinations. Professional subjects are taught through the Queen's University program. The examinations are now restricted to accounting and auditing subjects (Hoole, 1963: 29).

The ICAPEI is admitted to the DACA (CCA V14, 1924: 192).

The GAA begins printing and selling old examinations as a guide to candidates (Stuart, 1988: 33).

The Quebec government establishes a Board of Accountants to audit municipal finances. The government rejected lobbying by the AAM, IAAPQ and AA to restrict membership on this Board to their members (CCA V14, 1924: 140-141).

The Charter of the ICABC is amended to reinstate the requirement that all applicants for membership undergo a series of examinations (Affleck, 1980: 13).

A CSCA branch is opened in Montreal (Allan, 1982: 11).

The GAA expels its first member for unprofessional conduct (Stuart, 1988: 36). The meaning of "unprofessional conduct" was not codified within the GAA at this time.

The by-laws of the CSCA are revised to allow a "junior membership classification" (student) (Allan, 1982: 14).

1925

The ICABC increases its period of apprenticeship from four to five years (Affleck, 1980: 13) and reduces the number of students that may be articled to each member from three to two (CCA V15, 1925: 145).

The ICAA gives the provincial auditor, provided he is a CA, the right to article students (CCA V15, 1925: 61).

The ICAPEI places its examinations under the control of the ICANS who provides and grades the examination papers (CCA V14, 1925: 330).

The ICAS adopts a by-law allowing experienced practitioners to be admitted to membership on a vote of council (CCA V15, 1925: 147).

The ICANS adds the ICAPEI to its list of registered societies (CCA V15, 1925: 62). This is followed by the ICAO and AAM in 1926 (CCA V15, 1926: 334).

The DACA establishes a code of ethics and a standing committee on professional ethics to provide interpretations (CCA V15, 1925: 166-169).

A motion for reciprocal recognition among all members of the DACA is brought forward at the AAM Annual Meeting. The motion is defeated due to the existence of members who had entered the profession without examination in some Institutes (CCA V15, 1925: 173-174).

The need for a university degree to be considered a profession is raised at the DACA conference; it is agreed that candidates with degrees may be exempt from other requirements, but in no case may there be fewer than 3 years service required (CCA V15, 1925: 183).

In recognition that the CCA had become a public document, it is decided that editorial policy should be set by the DACA council (CCA V15, 1925: 184).

The ICABC adopts a code of ethics (Affleck, 1980: 14).

The CSCA passes a motion removing the right of provincial CA Institutes to appoint CSCA board members. This followed several years in which provincial Institutes failed to nominate the representative to which they were entitled (Allan, 1982: 14).

1926

The ICAO extends its apprenticeship, for those with only high school educations, from 4 to 5 years (Creighton, 1984: 150).

The AAM votes against the adoption of the DACA uniform code of ethics (CCA V16, 1926: 143-44).

An editorial suggests that a university degree would improve examination performance (CCA V16, 1926: 51).

The ICAO by-laws are amended to grant university graduates 2 years remission of service (from 5 years to 3) and exemption from the primary examination.

The AAM adopts a by-law allowing mail voting (CCA V16, 1926: 143).

The Association of Accountants and Auditors of Ontario (AAAO) are incorporated using the LA, Licentiate in Accounting, designation (later CPA's)(S.O. 1926, c.42; CCA V16, 1926: 56). The association required entry by examination. Their charter called for three levels of examination and specified the subjects to be tested at each level. The association's charter and designation follow that of the Accountants Association of Quebec. There was a significant overlap between the Boards of the CGAAO and the AAAO including F. Sudbury, C. Walters and three others. Walters, who is credited as the founder of the AAAO, was on the CGAAO Board from 1926 to 1928. Creighton (1984: 126-128) suggests that this group had been in existence since the early 1920's as the UAA (unsupported by other documents).

An early woman accountant, Jean B. McBride, was among the incorporators of the AAAO and, when this body became the CPAAO in 1936, rose to the position of Vice-President (Canada Almanac, 1937).

The ICAM adopts a formal code of ethics drafted at the DACA conference in 1925 (Hoole, 1963: 29).

In May, the U.S.-based NACA proposes a merger between them and the CSCA in response to a CSCA request for access to NACA materials at more favorable rates. The suggestion is not well received (Allan, 1982: 13). In August, the CSCA dissolves its association with the U.S.-based NACA (Allan, 1982: 13). Jamieson (1948: 96) attributes the break up to differences in the "maturity" of the US and Canadian economies and, therefore, the different interests of cost accountants in each country.

The CSCA publishes the first issue of Cost and Management. CSCA president John Craig published the first issue out of his own finances and on his own initiative. The Board did not consider the matter until their meeting of Oct. 21, 1926 (Allan, 1982: 17). The CSCA changes the format of the Journal from a magazine to a monthly bulletin and transfers legal title from John Criag to the CSCA (Allan, 1982: 18).

The AAAO produces the first issue of the Licentiate in Accounting. It was published until July, 1930, when it was discontinued due to the lack of quality material to publish. The journal was reinstituted under the title Canadian Journal of Accountancy in 1951, and continued until 1962 (Creighton, 1984: 128).

1927

The Associated Public Accountants of Ontario is formed (Canada Almanac, 1927).

The AAM is renamed the Society of CAs of the Province of Quebec (SCAQ) (S.Q. 1927, c.101). The Act also gives the SCAQ greater disciplinary powers and control of the CA designation. The AAM had attempted to use the word "Institute" to achieve compatibility with other provinces, but the IAAPQ already had that word as part of their title (Collard, 1980: 27).

The GAA allows graduates of the Commercial Academy of Quebec, L'Ecole des Hautes Etudes Commerciale and Mount St. Louis College the right to write the CGA final examination without writing the preliminary or intermediate examination (Stuart, 1988: 33).

The ICANS requires 1 year service or 3 years practice prior to writing its intermediate examination, and 3 years service or 5 years practice prior to writing its final examination (CCA V17, 1927: 121).

It is suggested that the examination procedures of all CA Institutes be standardized (CCA V17, 1927: 174-184).

The SCAPQ votes to admit women to membership. They request an amendment to their charter so that "person" is interpreted as either male or female, but the bill is rejected by the legislature in 1928 and 1929. The question is settled in 1930, when the Imperial Privy Council in England rules that the words "he" and "person" in the BNA Act refer equally to both sexes (Collard, 1980: 69).

The ICAA adopts the DACA uniform code of ethics (CCA V17, 1927: 141).

The Accountants Association changes their name to the Corporation of Public Accountants of the Province of Quebec and their designation from LA to CPA (S.Q. 1927, c.61).

The ICABC requires all students to complete the Queen's University correspondence course prior to writing their final examination. This requirement is discontinued in 1934, due to the depression, and reinstated in 1939 (Affleck, 1980: 15).

The CSCA adopts a proposal by Colonel R.R. Thompson of McGill University to begin examinations leading to a "certificate of efficiency". In structuring the educational policy of the Society, the CSCA was lead by the example of the Institute of Cost and Works Accountants in Great Britain. The content of their examinations, however, followed the US example and was more concerned with financial control than production/operations management (Allan, 1982: 21).

The ICAA votes to accept women members (ICAA, 1985, No. 2) and registers their first woman member in 1928 (Mann, 1975b: 34).

1928

The ICAA adopts a modified version of the ICAO code of ethics (ICAA, 1985, No. 2).

The GAA produces its first year book indicating a total membership of 254 (Bentley, 1938: 12; Stuart, 1988: 35 reports this as 1930).

The ICABC forms a student society. Weekly study sessions are organized in 1931 and in 1936 a formal program was instituted (Affleck, 1980: 15).

1929

The ICABC attempts, unsuccessfully, to have the B.C. Companies Act amended to have "accountant" mean CA (Affleck, 1980: 16).

The ICAA votes in favour of proposals to standardize examinations in the Western provinces (CCA V19, 1929: 62; Neville, 1986: 45-47).

The CSCA, in consultation with the Montreal Board of Trade and Chartered Institute of Secretaries (CIS), establishes a 3-year program of lectures given by staff of McGill University. The first 2 years of the program prepares students for the intermediate examination of the CIS and the primary examination of the CSCA. It also qualified the student for the Board of Trade's "Commercial Education" diploma. The third year of the program prepared students for the final examinations of the CIS and the CSCA (Allan, 1982: 22). Stuart (1988: 34) suggests that the GAA was part of this arrangement.

1930

The ICANB amends its charter to gain exclusive rights to the CA designation in New Brunswick (S.N.B. 1930, c.51; Hudson, 1966: 25).

The ICAM amends its registered society by-law to remove a requirement that registered societies give reciprocal recognition allowing the Institute to accept English CAs as members without examination (Hoole, 1963: 33).

The ICAA expels a member for fraudulent practices marking the first use of disciplinary powers by the ICAA (ICAA, 1985, No. 2). The proceedings highlighted weaknesses in the disciplinary powers of the Institute and amendments to the Act were undertaken (CCA V20, 1930: 545; ICAA, 1985, No.3).

The Canadian Society of Cost Accountants becomes the Canadian Society of Cost Accountants and Industrial Engineers (CSCAIE)(Allan, 1982: 44).

The GAA accepts its first woman member, Ivy A. Cox of Toronto. The acceptance of women was seen as a "radical change" in policy (Bentley, 1938: 12). The event received wide press coverage. The GAA was forced to correct one item which suggested that Miss Cox had been allowed to write her examination based on experience in a business office. She had actually served in a public accountants office.

The first women (Charlotte N. Howell, SCAQ; Helen Burpee, ICAO) gain their CAs through training and examination. Women had gained a CA prior to this time by proclamation (e.g. ICAO, 1895) or through court action (e.g. ICABC, 1921), but Howell and Burpee are generally regarded as the first women CAs. It may be noted that Howell completed the requirements for the CA in May 1929, but was not awarded the designation until women achieved the status of "person" under the B.N.A. Act in September, 1930 (Collard, 1980: 68-69). The ICAO had reported female candidates writing examinations in 1919 and 1920 (CCA V10, 1920: 84).

1931

The ICAO relaxes its requirement for continuous time in articles in recognition of the extent of unemployment during the depression (CCA V21, 1931: 204-5), but increases its apprenticeship period from 2 to 3 years prior to writing the intermediate examinations (CCA V20, 1931: 303).

The CGAAO forms a study group and arranges a lecture series.

The AAAO attempts to use the CPA designation. Due to the opposition of the ICAO, this legislation is amended giving the AAAO the IPA, Incorporated Public Accountant, designation (S.O. 1931, c.143).

The GAA board decides to register the CGA designation as a trademark in each province (Stuart, 1988: 40).

1932

The International Accountants and Executives Corporation (IAEC) is established Federally (Sievers, 1977: 18). Members used the designations SFAE, FAE and AAE (Canada Almanac 1934 and 1940).

The Canadian Chartered Accountant begins to publish monthly (CCA V21, 1932: 350).

The ICAM seek legal council to clarify the CGAs right to use that designation in Manitoba and put pressure on several members who operate accounting schools to stop advertising that they can prepare candidates for the CGA examinations (Neville, 1986: 51).

The Quebec Municipal Commission grants CGAs residing in Quebec a general permit to audit municipal and school corporations (Bentley, 1938: 12).

1933

The ICAO board approves a special examination to facilitate the admittance of four senior accountants, all members of the AAAO, to membership. The membership, however, forced a general meeting which rejected the procedure (Creighton, 1984: 143-146).

The ICABC amends its fellowship requirements, removing the fee and re-emphasizing the intent that the fellowship should be used to honour those who have contributed to the profession (Affleck, 1980: 17).

1934

The ICAM delegates its 5-year training program to the University of Manitoba (Hoole, 1963: 35); this is known as the Manitoba Course of Studies (Neville, 1986: 52).

The ICAS revises its charter to explicitly provide disciplinary powers (S.S. 1934).

The SCAPQ votes against adopting written codes of ethics as unbecoming an association of their stature. On September 11, the issue is reopened on the grounds that the SCAQ is the only CA Institute without a code of ethics. The first rules of professional ethics were drafted and came into force in 1935. The code was enforced by Council with rights of appeal to a special meeting of the membership (Collard, 1980: 177-179, 183).

1935

The DACA calls for the creation of practice advisors following the lead of the ICAEW (CCA V26, 1935: 6).

The ICAA makes the Queen's correspondence program mandatory and expands the terms of articles from 4 to 5 years (ICAA, 1985, No. 3).

The Queen's accounting program is expanded from 4 to 5 years following the change in the ICAO apprenticeship requirements (Creighton, 1984: 150).

The charter of the ICANB is amended (S.N.B. 1935, c.45) to provide greater disciplinary powers to the Institute including a requirement that non-resident CAs practising in New Brunswick register with the ICANB and comply with their regulations (Hudson, 1966: 31).

The SCAPQ approves revised by-laws which include rules of professional conduct and a 5 year apprenticeship requirement (Collard, 1980: 90).

1936

The GAA adopts entrance examinations covering history, grammar and composition, commercial geography and a choice of chemistry, physics or agriculture (Stuart, 1988: 34).

The AAAO gains the rights to the CPA designation and becomes the CPAs Association of Ontario (S.O. 1936, c.68). The Association offers its training through the University of Toronto (Creighton, 1984: 147).

A motion to require that the majority of council members for the ICAM be in public practice is defeated on grounds that the governing bodies of Medicine, Law and Engineering include non-practising members (Neville, 1986: 57).

The GAA initiates the FCGA designation for service to the profession (Stuart, 1988: 38).

1937

A bill to incorporate the Public Accountants Association of British Columbia is introduced in the legislature, but is withdrawn before coming to a vote (Affleck, 1980: 18). This group may have been CGAs under the leadership of Ron Leavitt (Stuart, 1988: 56).

1938

The Institute of Accredited Public Accountants (IAPA) is founded in Winnipeg (Mann, 1975b: 38).

The ICAO forms a committee of past presidents to consider the need for uniformity in audit procedures and reports. The committee recommends against such action (Creighton, 1984: 174-179).

Representatives of the CA Institute meet in Winnipeg to consider the need for uniform examinations. It is agreed that the DACA will provide uniform examinations which each province may use and co-ordinate a Board of Examiners to mark the examinations (Hoole, 1963: 37). The issue had been raised in 1927 without success (Collard, 1980: 124).

1939

The General Accountant is renamed The Bulletin (Stuart, 1988: 37).

The DACA forms the Accounting and Auditing Research Committee and consults with academics at Queen's University on the development of a series of research studies (CCA 1939, V34: 288).

The DACA advises provincial Institutes that The Institute of Accredited Public Accountants, operated by the International Society of Commerce Ltd. of Winnipeg, was attempting to gain provincial incorporations (Affleck, 1980: 18).

The CSCAIE votes to create a designation to be granted on examination of competence as a cost accountant. Candidates for the examination had to be older than 25, have 10 years experience as a cost accountant and have been a member of a Canadian accounting association for 5 years. This commits the CSCAIE to seeking provincial incorporations as education is a provincial responsibility under the BNA Act. This move led to a split among members over whether the Society should be management oriented, i.e. focusing on the interpretation of cost information, or should be training oriented, i.e. focusing on the preparation of cost information. Many of those holding the former view resigned the Society after this point and, in 1948, formed the Controllers Institute (now the Financial Executives Institute)(Allan, 1982: 29).

The CAs begin Uniform Intermediate Examinations in all provinces (Hoole, 1963: 37). The first Uniform Final Examinations were held in 1941 (Collard, 1980: 126). The SCAPQ maintained separate examinations, largely due to their agreements with the Universities, until 1954 (Mann, 1975b: 29).

1940

The IAEC begins using University of Toronto extension courses to qualify for their designation (Canada Almanac, 1940).

A private bill is introduced in the Ontario legislature to incorporate the Society of Industrial and Cost Accountants of Ontario with the right to offer the Certified Industrial Accountant (CIA) designation. The bill was rejected in committee (Allan, 1982: 31).

The ICAO restricts apprenticeships to the offices of CA members which are capable of offering a wide diversity of experience (Creighton, 1984: 155-156).

1941

The Ontario Municipal Act gives the Department of Municipal Affairs the right to licence accountants to conduct municipal audits (CCA, 1941: 69).

The GAA begins publishing their journal, The General Accountant, replacing a newsletter which had been produced since 1923. The Journal is produced by the association's head office in Vancouver.

The Quebec chapter of the CSCAIE incorporates as the Cost and Management Institute using the Licentiate of the Cost and Management Institute, LCMI, designation (S.Q. 1941, c.95)(Allan, 1982: 31).

The Ontario chapter of the CSCAIE incorporates using the Registered Industrial Accountant, RIA, designation (S.O. 1941, c.77). The first President reaffirmed the Society's commitment to the CAs not to use their designation as a standard of qualification in public accounting (Allan, 1982: 31).

The provincial and national Societies of Cost Accountants and Industrial Engineers meet to establish the terms of their affiliation. It is agreed that there would be uniform national examinations and reciprocal recognition of members. The national body was given responsibility for co-ordinating provincial programs. A formal affiliation agreement was signed on June 20: 1942 (Allan, 1982: 32-33, 131-135).

The SCAPQ's agreement to allow university graduates to write their final examination is extended to include L'Ecole Superieure de Commerce de Quebec of Laval University (Mann, 1975b: 30).

1942

The SCAPQ adopts an expanded code of ethics (Collard, 1980: 180).

The CSCAIE begins a correspondence program through Queen's University and the University of Toronto. Lecture programs are operated through McGill, the University of Montreal, McMaster and Sir George Williams University. the curriculum includes bookkeeping, accounting, cost accounting, industrial organization and management, advanced cost accounting, industrial legislation and culminated with the preparation of a thesis (Allan, 1982: 35).

The CPAAO adopts its first formal rules of professional conduct after a legal opinion that they had no power to discipline their members (Creighton, 1984: 186-188).

1943

The ICABC Rehabilitation Committee is formed to facilitate re-entry of servicemen into the profession. Liaison between this committee and the University of British Columbia results in the development of a university based training program (Affleck, 1980: 21).

The ICABC moves that henceforth women would be "welcomed" into articles (Affleck, 1980: 20). This motion was seen as necessary even though the ICABC had voted in 1919 to allow women to become members.

1944

The ICAM passes a by-law restricting to three the number of students that a member can supervise and establishing minimum standards for offices accepting students (Hoole, 1963: 40; Neville, 1986: 69).

The SCAPQ passes a by-law requiring offices supervising students to be investigated to ensure that the diversity and quality of experience received by students was appropriate (Collard, 1980: 120).

The Canadian Bar Association and DACA begin a joint committee on taxation (CCA, 1944: 338-343).

The Society of Management Accountants of British Columbia (SMABC) applies for incorporation in B.C., but is denied due to the small number of members and an opposition from the ICABC (Atkinson, 1985: 2).

The CPAAO requires 3 years of supervised practice prior to writing their final examinations. Although it was first proposed to limit eligible experience to public practice, this was opposed by Chester Walters and subsequently amended (Creighton, 1984: 159).

An unsuccessful attempt is made to incorporate the Society of CAs of the Yukon. The intent of this group was to seek affiliation with the ICABC and, thus, gain membership (Affleck, 1980: 21).

The RIAs incorporate in Alberta as the Society of Industrial Accountants. The term "cost" was dropped to better reflect the business environment in Alberta (S.A. 1944, c.79). The incorporation was supported by many individual CAs, including F. Winspear, head of the Department of Accounting at the University of Alberta, but opposed by the ICAA until a clause was inserted in the Act to prohibit the use of the RIA in public practice. This clause was repealed in 1971 following the adoption of a university degree requirement for CAs (ICAA/SMAA proposal, 1981; Allan, 1982: 35-36).

The ICABC revises its examination process to require a primary examination, intermediate law, intermediate uniform accounting and auditing, final law and final uniform accounting and auditing (Affleck, 1980: 21).

1945

The DACA publishes their first standards written by A.W. Gilmour of the SCAPQ. Two previous editions had been published by the provincial institute under the title of "Income Tax Handbook" (CCA 1945: 65).

The RIAs incorporate in British Columbia (S.B.C. 1945, c.81). In other provinces the RIAs were supported by the CAs; in British Columbia, the CAs resisted the RIA bill. The difference was that in British Columbia the incorporators were not CAs, rather they were CGAs or independent accountants. The RIA bill finally gained approval with amendments which restricted the RIA designation to members who were also CAs. Others could join the Society as general members without the right to use the designation. The RIAs initially used correspondence courses from Queen's University and the University of Toronto, but switched after 1950 to courses developed through the University of British Columbia (Atkinson, 1985: 5; Allan, 1982: 39-40).

The ICAM gains its first woman member. Marion Cathie McTaggart was also the Gold Medalist on the final exam of that year (Neville, 1986: 54, 55, 67).

The SCAPQ begins a correspondence course to facilitate the re-entry of servicemen into the profession. By 1949, the course is being phased out in centers with university accounting courses available and it is eliminated in 1953. Students still requiring correspondence courses after that date were referred to the Queen's University course (Collard, 1980: 114).

The DACA forms a committee to review auditing and accounting theory and issue pronouncements (Englebert, 1962: 150).

The CPAs in Quebec approach the SCAPQ to develop joint legislation to regulate the profession. After brief talks the CPAs withdrew and drafted independent legislation. On the advice of government, the SCAPQ drafted legislation and circulated it to the CPAs and IAAPQ. This draft received favorable responses and was presented to the legislature (Collard, 1980: 37-39).

Women attend the GAA annual conference for the first time (Stuart, 1988: 46).

The SIAA accepts 48 established accountants as RIAs without examination (Allan, 1981: 12-13).

The CSCAIE votes to seek a uniform name for their provincial bodies in order to establish a strong public identity (Allan, 1982: 41).

The ICABC increases its minimum requirements for applicants to their training program from grade 12 to grade 13 (Affleck, 1980: 22).

Regulating Public Accountancy: 1945 - 1962

The move to regulate public accountancy began in Quebec in the early 1940's and rapidly had an impact on other provinces. Associations of accountants developed and attempted to establish their legal status across Canada in anticipation of legislation which would restrict access to the field of public accounting. There is also a rash of merger activities as associations attempt to establish dominant positions in the profession. The merger of the CAs and CPAs finally brings this period to a close. The activities of this period established a movement towards the separation of public and management accounting into distinct professional associations but, as will become clear in this last section of this chronology, this has yet to be realized.

1946

The CGAs incorporate in Ontario and Quebec.

The Institute of Accredited Public Accountants gains Federal incorporation (Mann, 1975b: 38). An attempt to gain provincial incorporation in Alberta is blocked by the ICAA (ICAA, 1985: No. 5).

A resolution is passed calling for a change in the name of the CSCAIE to the Canadian Society of Industrial and Cost Accountants (CM V20, 1946, N7: 229-30).

The Quebec CGAs incorporate as a defensive manoeuvre in the face of the provinces plan to close the profession (Stuart, 1988: 52).

Quebec passes legislation closing the public accounting profession (S.Q. 1946, c.47). All existing public accountants are merged into one body to be known as CAs. Exceptions are the International Society of Commerce Ltd. using the APA designation who may continue to practice under that designation, but may not accept new members and the International Accountants and Executives Corporation of Canada who may continue under the FAE designation. In addition, auditors of schools, municipalities, co-operatives and certain other corporations are exempted from the Act. The SCAPQ is renamed the Institute of CAs of Quebec. The Act adopts the pattern of education established in 1914 by the IAAPQ and Ecole des Hautes Etudes Commerciales de Montreal and provides the Institute with strong disciplinary powers. The Act stimulated Ontario accounting associations to consider rationalization in their jurisdiction (Collard, 1980: 42-43, 184). The Act protects the right of the CSCAIE to practice as management accountants and to use the LCMI designation (Allan, 1982: 42-43). The Act, therefore, also establishes a division of labour in accountancy.

The past presidents committee of the ICAO, in light of legislation in Quebec, recommends that the ICAO seek legislation controlling accountancy in Ontario in co-operation with the CPAAO. Representatives of the ICAO and CPAAO meet in the summer of 1946 to discuss the proposal (Creighton, 1984: 196-197).

Bulletin No. 1 of the Accounting Research Committee (a statement of standards of disclosure in annual financial statements of manufacturing and mercantile companies) is published in the CCA. The statement recommended the best current practices. Further Bulletins followed at the rate of approximately 1 per year (Creighton, 1984: 179-180). Bulletin No. 26, issued in 1967, is the first to go beyond current practice. Bulletin No. 6, issued in 1951, was the first attempt to create auditing standards. The committee consisted of 12 practising accountants and 2 academics (Cooper, 1973).

The CSCAIE revises its courses to include mathematics, two courses in cost accounting, industrial organization and management, two courses in accounting and a thesis in cost accounting (Allan, 1981: 14-15). Course notes are commissioned directly from authors and are the property of the Society. This is a unique aspect of the Society's education program (Allan, 1982: 44-45).

1947

The IAEC incorporates in Ontario (Sievers, 1977: 18).

The Independent Accountants Association forms in Ontario as a bargaining agent for unaffiliated accountants during negotiations leading to the creation of regulatory legislation (Creighton, 1984: 200).

The APAs incorporate in New Brunswick (S.N.B. 1947, c.166; Hudson, 1966: 51).

The SICABC begins a lecture series - Accounting 1 & 2, Business Math, and fundamentals of cost accounting - through the Department of Extension, University of British Columbia. The SICAM similarly arranges classes in Business Math and Accounting 1 through the University of Manitoba (CM 1947, V21, N11: 393).

The CAs Act of Manitoba is amended, without notice to the Institute, to allow appeal of disciplinary rulings to the provincial courts. The amendment followed the decision to suspend a member for 3 years for preparing misleading statements. The change allowed the suspended member to appeal. Mr. Justice J.T. Beaubien reversed Council's decision on the grounds that the processes of gathering information and deciding on disciplinary action were conducted by the same people, thereby rendering a fair hearing impossible (Neville, 1986: 77; Hoole, 1963: 42-43, puts this event in 1948).

The RIAs incorporate in Manitoba (S.M. 1947, c.101; CM 1947, V21, N5: 161-2). The Society sought and received the ICAM's endorsement (Allan, 1982: 46).

The DACA adopts a national Code of Ethics (Houle, 1963: 43 puts this in 1949).

The CSCAIE is renamed the Society of Industrial and Cost Accountants of Canada (SICAC) and calls on a provincial associations to change their names to establish a uniform identity across the country (Allan, 1982: 45; CM 1948, V22, N4: 132). The change in name was significant to several provinces: Quebec wanted a managerial emphasis; Ontario did not want the word "cost" removed because of fears that this would allow encroachment by others; and, the prairie provinces did not see the relevance of the word "cost" to their business environments (Allan, 1981: 19-20).

1948

The Cost and Management Institute in Quebec changes their designation from LCMI to RIA (S.Q. 1948, c.95; CM 1948, V22, N4: 132).

The RIAs incorporate in Saskatchewan (S.S. 1948, c.74; CM 1948, V22, N4: 132). Although there was no Society chapters in Saskatchewan, the Society was able to organize and incorporate over a period of only eighteen months. The first chapter in Saskatchewan was organized in Saskatoon in September, 1948 (CM 1948, V22, N9: 326). The initial members included academics, CAs and practising cost accountants (Allan, 1982: 48).

The SIAA changes its name to the Society of Industrial and Cost Accountants of Alberta (SICAA) (Allan, 1981: 20; CM 1948, V22, N4: 132).

The SICAC takes charge of the education program developed by the Ontario Society (Allan, 1982: 48).

The Controllers Institute is incorporated in Ontario and Quebec (Allan, 1982).

1949

The SICAA begins offering courses through the University of Alberta (Allan, 1981: 24).

The ICABC proposes legislation to close the profession, but fails to win legislative approval. The bill required the merger of the ICABC and CGAABC and would allow other public accountants to continue under the Registered Public Accountant designation. New entrants to the profession would be required to complete the ICABC training program (Affleck, 1980: 24).

The ICANB accepts its first woman member, Emma Morrison, who had previously been a member of the ICAPEI and ICANS (Hudson, 1966: 56).

The ICAM adopts the Queen's Correspondence course for non-resident students unable to attend the University of Manitoba (Hoole, 1963: 43; Neville, 1986: 82).

The CAs incorporate in Newfoundland (S.N. 1949, c.30).

The DACA starts the Tax Review Journal in co-operation with the Canadian Bar Association.

The ICAA admits its first woman member (ICAA, 1985:No. 5).

The ICAO and CPAAO successfully block an attempt to incorporate by the Accredited Public Accountants of Ontario (Creighton, 1984: 201).

The ICANB proposes a merger with the APAANB and CGAANB but a bill fails to gain approval (Hudson, 1966: 51).

Legislation is passed in Prince Edward Island limiting the right to practice as a public accountant to members of the ICAPEI (S.P.E.I. 1949, c.52). The Act also gives the Institute exclusive rights to the CA designation.

The CPAAO proposes a merger with the CGAAO. The CGAAO surrenders their charter in 1950 and most CGAs become CPAs, but the Toronto branch refuses to join. The CGAs and the CPAs in Manitoba merge the following year (Creighton, 1984: 210; Stuart, 1988: 55). Some CGAs in B.C. also join the CPAs and attempt to incorporate the CPAs Association of British Columbia. The bill dies in committee (Affleck, 1980: 24).

The ICAO, CPAAO, CGAAO and SIAO discuss legislation regulating the profession in Ontario (Allan, 1982: 53).

The SICAC accepts Mrs. Anne Marie Boyer of Montreal as the first woman RIA (Allan, 1982: 52).

1950

The CPAs incorporate in Newfoundland (S.N. 1950, c.35).

The CPAs incorporate in Manitoba (S.M. 1950, c.103).

The Manitoba CPAs and CGAs discuss a merger (Stuart, 1988: 55).

The APAs incorporate in Manitoba (S.M. 1950, c.100).

The RIAs incorporate in Nova Scotia (S.N.S. 1950, c.95) and New Brunswick (S.N.B. 1950, c.55). The creation of these societies came at a time when the SICAC was under financial restraint. The decision to pursue incorporation was motivated by ongoing attempts by other associations to incorporate in the maritimes and a fear that legislation may soon be imposed which would preclude future incorporations. In New Brunswick the Act was supported by the CAs, but in Nova Scotia, due to the acrimony among associations, the CAs approved of but did not publicly support the Society's application (Allan, 1982: 50-52; CM 1950, V24, N5: 142).

The Government of Alberta adopts a policy requiring one professional association in each field with examinations under university control. Applicants with unusual qualifications were to be assessed by a university council. Under this policy applications for incorporation by new associations were denied and applicants directed to either the RIAs or CAs (ICAA/SMAA proposal, 1981).

The Board of the SICAC is reformed allowing proportional representation of provincial societies. Over time this leads to a Board with over a hundred members (Allan, 1982: 54). A Co-ordinating Executive is formed "to formulate policies of the Society and to deal with such matters as in a general way related to the operations of the affiliated provincial societies and the relationship to the society and to each other". The committee consists of the executive of the national society and 2 directors of each of the affiliated provincial societies (CM V24, N9: 286-7).

The Independent Public Accountants Association is absorbed by the CPAAO (Creighton, 1984: 210).

Ontario passes the Public Accountancy Act (S.O. 1950, c.60) giving the CAs and CPAs the power to regulate entry to practice through the Public Accountants Council. Membership on the Council was based on the proportion of public accountants in each association, however after all public accountants had registered it was apparent that independent accountants had been under-represented (Richardson, 1990b). The independents had 2 out of 15 seats on the Council, but constituted almost half of the population of public accountants (see Toronto Daily Star, Jan. 28, 1950).

1951

The CICA releases Bulletin No.6 of the Accounting and Auditing Research Committee containing the first recommendations on audit practice.

The DACA is renamed the Canadian Institute of CAs (CICA).

The CPAs incorporate in New Brunswick (S.N.B. 1951, c.41).

The SICAS arranges with the Department of Extension, University of Saskatchewan, to offer introductory and intermediate subjects (CM 1951, V25 N8: 275).

The CSICA establishes two grades of membership: Associate member for those qualified as cost accountants and Fellow for those qualified as management accountants (CM 1951, V25 N9: 315).

The RIAs incorporate in Prince Edward Island (S.P.E.I. 1951. c.34). This Act differed from previous Acts incorporating the Society by not allowing general members, i.e., members who would not complete the program of study and examination leading to the RIA designation (Allan, 1982: 55; CM 1951, V25 N4: 118).

The Canadian Institute of CPAs (CICPA) gains Federal incorporation

The CGAs incorporate in British Columbia (S.B.C. 1951, c.2). Concurrently the CAs Act is amended and both Acts ban the use of the CPA designation in B.C. (Affleck, 1980: 25).

The CGA/UBC program of studies is initiated (Stuart, 1988: 63).

The RIAs incorporate in Newfoundland (S.N. 1951, c.69) with the right to use the RIA designation (Allan, 1982: 55-56; CM 1951, V25 N7: 234-5).

1952

An attempt to incorporate the CPAs in Saskatchewan fails due to opposition from CAs and American CPAs (CJA 1952, V1: 45).

An attempt to incorporate the CPAs in Alberta fails.

The Securities Act of Newfoundland requires that brokers' auditors be a member of any Institute or association incorporated with the legislature (S.N. 1952, c.61). This is the first specification of an accounting association in Newfoundland legislation.

The ICANS introduces a Bill requiring all accountants in public practice in the province to register. This is enacted as the Public Accountants Act which creates a Board to approve applications to practice as a public accountant. Accountants registered with the Board could refer to themselves as Public Accountants (no abbreviation is allowed) (S.N.S. 1952, c.14).

The ICANB introduces a bill to regulate the practice of public accounting and auditing. The bill creates the Public Accounting Board to certify qualified public accountants (Hudson, 1966: 53).

The ICAA amend their Act to allow experience and education to be considered in modifying the requirements for granting the CA. This represents a strategy to restore the supply of accountants following WWII (ICAA, 1985: No. 6). Horne (1956:46) suggests that this amendment resulted from attempts by the CPA's and CGA's to gain formal recognition in Alberta.

An analysis of ICAO final examination results reveals a significantly higher pass rate for university graduates than for high school graduates. Public criticism of the pass rates on CA exams gave this finding particular significance and it significantly influenced future education decisions (Creighton, 1984: 225).

The Society of Accredited Public Accountants of British Columbia is registered under the Societies Act (Affleck, 1980: 25).

The first edition of the Canadian Journal of Accountancy is published by the CICPA.

CPAs in Nova Scotia incorporate but only with a name change to the Registered Public Accountants Association (S.N.S. 1952, c.128). The CPAs were supported in this application by the CGAs and APAs and opposed by the CAs and American CPAs (CJA 1952, V1: 45).

In May, the membership of the CPAAO votes against a proposal by their Board to admit members of the Accredited Public Accountants Association and International Accountants and Executives Corporation (Creighton, 1984: 215-216).

The Toronto branch of the CGAAO approves a merger with CPAAO in October (GA 1952, V11 N6: 18). This represents the culmination of four to five years of negotiations between the two groups (GA 1952, V11 N6: 4).

The University of Alberta requests the SICAA's permission to adopt their courses as part of a Bachelor of Commerce degree program (Allan, 1981).

1953

The Ontario RIAs begin a progam of continuing education. Responsibility for the program was transferred to the national body in 1956 and became available across Canada (Allan, 1982: 58, 66-67).

The CPAs Association of Saskatchewan is incorporated (S.S. 1953, c.84; S.S. 1954, c.72).

The ICAM approves the Queen's Correspondence course for all its students, becoming the last province to join this program (Neville, 1986: 82).

The SICAC creates an educational Foundation to administer their education program (Allan, 1982: 58, 137-139; CM 1953, V27 N6: 235-6).

The ICABC approves a joint B.Comm./CA program at the University of British Columbia (Affleck, 1980: 26). This was put in place in 1955 (Horne, 1956: 48).

1954

The SICAC decides to encourage the enrollment of General Members (Allan, 1982: 68-69).

The SICAC revises its final cost accounting course to emphasize cost analysis and cost control (subjects include standard costs, budgetary control and forecasting, distribution costing, break-even analysis, etc.)(CM 1954, V29 N10: 354-5).

The ICANB adopts the CICA uniform final examination (Hudson, 1966: 55).

The Toronto Branch of the CGAAO approves formation of an Ontario Council composed of 5 representatives from Toronto and 2 representatives from Ottawa to seek incorporation and to arrange for the University of British Columbia CGA course of instruction to be given through an Ontario university (Jenkins, 1962: 2).

The name Certified General Accountants Association of Ontario is officially adopted by the Toronto CGA group (Jenkins, 1962: 2).

1955

The CGAAS and CPAAS merge (letter from J.Rhodes, Sec.Treas., to the Directors of GAA, dated May 24, 1955 in CGAO archives).

The ICAM bylaws are rewritten, incorporating their code of ethics (Hoole, 1963: 46).

The SICAC course is revised to include business mathematics (or grade 12 mathematics), three courses in accounting, two courses in cost accounting, industrial legislation, industrial organization and management, managerial statistics, report writing and a thesis (Allan, 1982: 64). This curriculum was implemented in 1957-58 (Allan, 1981: 38-39).

The CAs and RIAs organize a conference attended by 19 universities to consider the common educational requirements of public and management accountants. In June, 1956, a second conference was held but it emerged that the CAs did not support the development of joint education programs (Allan, 1982: 64).

1956

The Tax Executives Institute, Inc. is formed. This is the Canadian branch of the US Institute formed in 1944. (CM 1959:62).

The CGAs training program is offered nationally (CGA document dated Aug., 1976).

The CGAs in Manitoba are absorbed by the ICAM (CGA Magazine, February 1977: 4).

The Guild of Accountants, now the Guild of Industrial, Commercial and Institutional Accountants (GICIA), is formed in association with the International Accountants Society and Lasalle Extension University (both correspondence schools) to provide a designation and association for non-university qualified accountants. Branches are formed in Montreal and Toronto, and the Guild begins publishing a newsletter, later a Journal, quarterly (Ross and Brown, 1978: 2).

1957

The APAs incorporate in Ontario (Sievers, 1977).

The SICAC committee on Publications and Technical services recommends changes in their journal (implemented in 1958), publication of special studies (implemented in 1960) and creation of a research program (implemented in 1967) (Allan, 1982: 70-71).

The CGAs incorporate (again) in Ontario with the right to offer an educational program. They also petition to be named as a qualifying body under the Public Accountants Act but are denied.

The GAA creates the Co-ordinating Council on Education to control the delivery of the CGA program across Canada (CGAAO News Bulletin, 1957, V1 N3).

1958

The APAs and CPAs merge in New Brunswick (Swinburne, 1978).

The APAs and IAEC merge in Ontario (Sievers, 1977: 18).

The ICAQ rules that CAs can engage in management consulting if it is distinct from their public accounting practice. For example, the management accounting branch could not bear the same name as the public accounting branch. In 1966 this was relaxed to require that the distinction be self-evident (Collard, 1980: 80-81).

The ICABC, SMABC and CGAABC begin negotiations to develop legislation to regulate the profession of accountancy in B.C. (Affleck, 1980: 40).

The SICAC introduces new course: Accounting 3 (focusing on accounting systems and internal control), Managerial Statistics and Report Writing (CM 1959, V33 N3: 89-90).

The ICABC begins an appraisal program for offices employing students to ensure that students receive diverse and high quality training (Affleck, 1980: 40).

1959

The ICABC transfers the first 3 years of its training program to the University of British Columbia (Affleck, 1980: 44).

Bulletin No.17 of the CICA Accounting and Auditing Committee is released changing the phrase "exhibits a true and correct view" to "presents fairly" in the audit opinion and including the phrase "in accordance with generally accepted accounting principles applied on a basis consistent with that of the previous year". This wording was included in the Companies Act of 1964.

1960

The GAA discontinues its examination procedures in favour of the UBC program (Stuart, 1988: 64).

The SICAC publishes their first special study "An appraisal of capital expenditures" by C.G.

Edge (Allan, 1982: 71).

The ICANB establishes a committee to negotiate with other accounting bodies on the regulation of the profession. The committee reported in 1963 and in 1964 a commission, composed of academics, was established to consider the appropriate qualifications for public accountants. The CPAANB and APAANB agreed to support this commission, the CGAANB declined. (Hudson, 1966: 64-65).

The CPA attempt to incorporate in Alberta (Journal of Accountancy V10 N1: 43).

The ICAA holds its first continuing education courses (ICAA, 1986, N8: 1).

The councils of the ICAO and CPAAO agree on terms for a merger (Creighton, 1984: 240-244).

The ICABC begins setting their own primary examinations, departing from the tradition of using the ICAO primary examinations (Affleck, 1980: 44).

The ICABC revises its by-laws to update its rules of professional conduct and to allow for the adoption of uniform codes of ethics (Affleck, 1980: 41).

1961

The GAA establishes a Committee of Examiners to oversee its national education program. D. Blazouske becomes the first chairman of the committee (Stuart, 1988: 64).

The CICA establishes the "Committee on Regulatory Legislation and Relations with Other Bodies" to keep the provinces aware of legislative challenges from the CPAs and CGAs (ICAA, 1986, N8: 3).

The Alberta RIAs vote to replace the thesis requirement with two comprehensive cases. This is the first breach of provincial uniformity of standards among the RIA societies (Allan, 1982: 78). The use of a final examination instead of a thesis requirement became national practice in 1965 (Allan, 1981: 41).

The CGAAO petition to be named as a qualifying body under the Public Accountants Act but are denied. As part of the CPA/CA merger, CGAs in public practice are invited to become CAs and 25 accept this offer.

The ICAQ delegates its disciplinary function from Council to a Disciplinary Committee and an Investigations Committee (Collard, 1980: 185).

The CGAs incorporate under the Societies Act in Alberta (Stuart, 1988: 68).

The CGAs incorporate in New Brunswick (S.N.B. 1961-62, c.93).

An attempt to gain Federal incorporation the Guild of Accountants is unsuccessful. The application is resubmitted as the Guild of Industrial, Commercial and Institutional Accountants and is accepted. The Federal incorporation provides no rights to train or grant a designation (Ross and Brown, 1978: 4-5).

The membership of the ICAO rejects a proposed merger with the CPAAO 475 to 422. The vote reflected the fears of small firms that the merger would dilute the value of their "CA" in public esteem and would increase competition. In 1962, voting procedures were changed to allow proxies and the argument for merger was made strongly behind the scenes (Creighton, 1984: 244-246).

1962

The CICA committee on accounting and auditing research establishes a Research Studies Program.

The ICAA establishes a practice inspection program for firms employing students (ICAA, 1986, N8: 3).

The ICAA allows CPAs in Alberta to join the Institute without examination (ICAA, 1986, N8: 3).

The ICAO votes to merge with the CPAAO.

The ICABC proposes legislation to close the profession but this fails to receive approval (Affleck, 1980).

The SICAC creates a register of qualified RIAs allowing members to move between provinces without requalifying for their designation (CM 1962, V36 N7: 331).

The SICAC revises Accounting 1 and 2, and the course in industrial legislation, to provide greater emphasis on the analytic and control functions of accounting. Accounting 4 is added, dealing with taxation, finance, capital investment, data processing and accounting systems (CM 1962, V36 N9: 425).

The Ontario CPAs vote 782 to 7 to merge with the ICAO. As the Ontario CPA association was the largest in Canada and provided all national services, this also means the demise of other CPA associations. The CPA's 5-year training program is taken over by the SICAC and all students subsequently graduating from it were to become RIA's. Creighton (1986, personal communication) suggests that many students transferred to the CGA program and contributed to the Renaissance of the CGAAO. The Public Accountancy Act is subsequently amended to name the ICAO as the sole qualifying body (Creighton, 1984: 316-318). The merger also creates pressures for the SICAC and CGAAC and their provincial bodies to merge. Although negotiations are opened, no serious proposals to merge result (Allan, 1982: 80).

The Ontario Public Accountancy Act is amended (S.O. 1961-62, c.113) giving the ICAO 12 seats on the Council and "others" 3 seats. The CPAs are no longer listed as a qualifying body. CGAs can apply under this act for licencing as a public accountant. (For an example of opposition to the Bill see Globe and Mail, Feb. 28, 1962).

Consolidation and 'Rationalization': 1962 - 1979

The merger of the CAs and CPAs, and related merger activity, resulted in the consolidation of the accounting profession into a small number of associations specializing in either public or management accounting. In the aftermath of these activities there was pressure to complete this process and a long process of negotiations began. Each association, meanwhile, turned their efforts to internal issues associated with their new size and diversity of memberships. The apparent "rationalization" of the profession, however, fails to hold and the CGAs resume their efforts to develop expertise in the public accounting field.

1963

A new National curriculum is introduced by the SICAC (Atkinson, 1985: 60). A course in internal auditing is added and the accounting courses revised to reflect the RIAs increasing presence in the public and non-manufacturing sectors (CM 1963, V37 N7: 330).

The APAs in Ontario gain supplementary letters patent allowing them to use the APA designation in Ontario but limiting their members to current licencees under the Public Accountancy Act and prohibiting them from accepting new members implying that the APA in Ontario would die with its current members (Sievers, 1977).

The ICAQ takes a central role in organizing the Canadian Association of Management Consultants (Collard, 1980: 82-83).

Legislation is proposed in B.C. which would merge all public accountants into the ICABC and regulate public accounting. A legislative committee rejects the bill on the grounds that it would restrict access to accounting service in outlying areas. In 1964 the bill was submitted with special licencing provisions for remote areas but the bill was rejected (Affleck, 1980: 40).

The SICAC begins a graduate studies program for accountants with professional designations.

This runs for two years but is discontinued due to funding constraints (Allan, 1982: 76-78).

1964

The CGAs apply for incorporation in Newfoundland against the opposition of the ICANF, CPAANF and SICANF.

The ICAA discontinues the practice of articling students and begins registering students directly with the Institute. The new system allows students to move freely among firms (ICAA, 1986, N8: 1).

The Queen's University Correspondence course is abandoned as a part of the training of CAs. The ICAA and ICABC were among the first provinces to take this step, followed quickly by others (ICAA, 1986, N8: 1). The ICAO replaced this system of training with a summer school program.

The RIA program is revised to include auditing, all other components remain the same (Allan, 1982: 87; CM 1964 V38 N5: 233, 237-8).

The SICAC adopts a policy of bilingualism for all publications and promotional material (CM 1963, V37 N7: 333; CM 1964, V38 N9: 425).

The ICABC suspends new enrollments to the B.Comm/CA program. The ICABC and ICAA cooperate in the development of a 5 year training program drawing on the expertise of the University of British Columbia and the University of Alberta. In 1966, the ICAS and ICAM joined this effort to form the CAs Course of Instruction (Western Provinces) (Affleck, 1980: 47-48).

The Treasury Board and the SICAC begin to train Treasury Board personnel to RIA standards through Carleton University in response to the Glassco Commission Report call for greater budgetary control in government (Allan, 1981: 51; CM 1964, V38 N10: 473).

1965

The CGA/UBC course is removed from provincial jurisdiction and placed under GAA control (Stuart, 1988: 64).

The ICANF and CPAANF propose regulatory legislation for auditing in Newfoundland.

The ICAO implements more formal disciplinary procedures (Creighton, 1984: 257-263).

The ICANB adopts SICAC courses as first year courses for their students while retaining the Queen's University correspondence course for senior levels (Hudson, 1966: 67).

The RIAs adopt comprehensive cases instead of a thesis requirement as the capstone of their training program. This format was initiated in Alberta but was now accepted nationally (Allan, 1982: 78). The course sequence was also overhauled (CM 1965, V39 N9: 425).

Atkinson (1985: 10) suggests that this was necessary in order to stem the flow of students to the CGAs.

The SICAC forms a standing committee on research with a mandate to explore possibilities for collaboration with other accounting bodies (CM 1965, V39 N6: 281-2).

A proposal to merge the ICAM and the CPAM is defeated at the ICAM general meeting (Neville, 1986: 104).

1966

The Accountant's International Study Group is formed by Canadian, British and American accountants (CGA Magazine, Jan. 1988: 35).

The ICANS, ICANB and ICAPEI form the Atlantic Provinces Association of CAs to facilitate the education of CA students. In 1969 they developed a correspondence course and summer school program which replaced the Queen's University program (Mann, 1975b: 31).

The SICAC publishes its annual report in both French and English for the first time (Allan, 1982: 84).

The Ontario Securities Act (S.O. 1966 c.142 s143) creates a Financial Disclosure Advisory Board to advise the Ontario Securities Commission on disclosure issues.

The CICA Accounting and Auditing Research Committee is expanded from 14 to 21 members including 2 members from industry; three regional work groups are established with a steering committee to handle administrative details; and, the system of releasing numbered bulletins is replaced with a handbook (Cooper, 1973).

The Report of the Commission for the Investigation of Public Accountancy in New Brunswick recommends that accountants in the province should join the ICANB (if in public practice) or the SICANB (if in industry) (CM 1966, V40 N6: 282).

The ICAM and CPAAM merge. CA designations are granted, without, examination, to 122 CPAs (Neville, 1986: 105).

The SICAC creates a committee on Accounting Principles and Practice.

The SICAC changes its name to the Society of Industrial Accountants (SIAC) (Atkinson, 1985: 50; CM 1966 V40 N4: 185). It was felt that the term "cost" excluded the financial management function which was of growing importance (CM 1968, V42 N4: 49).

The CGAAO Long Range Educational Planning Committee calls for (1) expanded access to CGA courses through the universities; (2) raising entrance requirements from Grade 12 to Grade 13 graduation; and (3) the creation of a post-graduate designation MCGA.

1967

The SICAO is renamed the Society of Industrial Accountants of Ontario (S.O. 1967, c.129).

The CICA releases the Handbook as a looseleaf binder to be updated with Bulletins.

The IAPAO brief to the McRuer Royal Commission on Civil Rights claims that the dominance of the ICAO prevents APAs from practicing in public accounting and violates their civil rights. No action was taken on this brief.

The ICANF and CPAANF merge continuing as the ICANF and retaining rights to the CPA designation (S.N. 1966-67, c.42).

The Newfoundland Public Accountancy Act (S.N. 1966-67, c.45) is passed creating a licencing board to regulate entry to public accounting. The Board is composed of 1 lawyer (as Chairman), 5 CAs and 1 'other' accountant (ICAA/SMAA Proposal, 1981).

The ICAA abandons the Queen's correspondence course in favour of the Western Canada CA Course of Instruction developed jointly with the ICABC.

The ICAM and the University of Manitoba agree to hire a Professor of Accountancy as a Department Chairman. One-third of the incumbents time would be spent on Institute affairs (Neville, 1986: 105).

The SICAC passes a motion to limit their research to areas complementary to that undertaken by other accounting bodies unless such research is undertaken as a joint venture (Allan, 1982: 96-97).

The CICA releases Bulletin 26, Accounting for Corporate Income Taxes, and for the first time goes beyond current practices in setting accounting standards.

1968

The CGAs approve in principle a Research Foundation (Stuart, 1988: 73).

The CGAs incorporate in Prince Edward Island (S.P.E.I. 1968, c.64; CGA Magazine, April, 1982: 45).

The RIAs in Nova Scotia amend their Act to change their name from the Society of Industrial and Cost Accountants to the Society of Industrial Accountants (S.N.S. 1968, c.124).

The SICAC changes its name to the Society of Industrial Accountants of Canada (SIAC) (Allan, 1982: 99).

The SICANB changes its name to the Society of Industrial Accountants of New Brunswick (N.B. Royal Gazette, V. 125, p. 112, Mar. 6, 1968).

1969

York and other universities recognize RIA courses for credit towards a BA degree (CM 1969 V43 N6: 59).

The Ontario Securities Commission, at the request of the SEC to review the reporting practices of Revenue Properties, issues a policy statement on accounting disclosure. The CICA establishes a liaison committee to prevent such 'surprises' in the future. This is the first time that a government/government agency, has set accounting policies for non-regulated companies which exceed professional pronouncements (Murphy, 1970: 157).

A Manitoba government committee is established to examine the ability of the professions to define and enforce ethical conduct. No action is taken but the ICAM takes this as a signal that formal rules of conduct are needed (Neville, 1986: 103).

The University of British Columbia creates a Licentiate in Accounting program (Affleck, 1980: 49).

The SIAC adopts a national code of ethics (Allan, 1982: 100).

1970

The ICABC ends the practice of indenturing students under contract of articles (Affleck, 1980: 49).

The CAs require candidates to hold a university degree. Ontario defeated a proposal to adopt the university degree requirement in 1970 in a vote taken in 1967 but approved the change in 1968 consequently they switched to this standard in 1972 (Creighton, 1984: 281-292). It was not until 1974, however, that this requirement was adopted from coast to coast (Collard, 1980: 135).

The ICAM charter is amended to allow the FCA designation to be granted to individuals without public practice experience (Neville, 1986: 106).

The SIAC adopts a 5-year plan which sets out the Society's objectives, the role for RIAs and the body of knowledge necessary for management accountants. The knowledge base includes the preparation of financial statements, integration of accounting and information systems, internal control, introductory programming, mathematics and statistics, and introductory courses in behavioural sciences (CM 1970, V44 N3: 42-4,61).

The ICAQ appoints a Professional Practice Advisor who could be consulted by members (Collard, 1980: 135).

The ICAM adopts a formal code of ethics (a slightly amended version of the CICA code) (Neville, 1986: 111).

1971

The ICAM, in co-operation with the SIAC, introduces professional development courses (Neville, 1986: 117).

The CGAAO calls on the SIAO to discuss the possibility of merger (Allan, 1982: 116).

The Society of Industrial Accountants of Alberta repeals its by-law prohibiting the use of the RIA designation in public practice. The adoption of a university degree requirement by the CAs effectively prohibited many RIAs, with ambitions to open a public practice, from gaining a CA.

The SIAC adopts a new curriculum consisting of accounting, economics, report writing, law, organizational behaviour, quantitative methods, financial management, auditing, informations systems and management processes (Allan, 1981: 58-59).

The Yukon Area Organization of the Society of Industrial Engineers is formed with the intention of seeking incorporation as the Society of Industrial Accountants (CM 1971, V45 N6: 57).

1972

Quebec Bill 250 proposes a professional code to regulate all professions.

The B.C. CAs Act is amended to allow a lay member on the ICABC Council (Affleck, 1980: 50).

The GAA form an accounting standards committee.

The ICAQ disciplines two members for failure to adhere to "generally accepted standards" in the audit of Trizec with regard to accounting for deferred taxes. As a result of this case the Provincial Securities Commissions requested a benchmark for GAAP from the CICA which in turn lead to the acceptance of the CICA Handbook as GAAP (Elliot, 1974).

1973

The International Accounting Standards Committee (IASC) is formed by 9 countries (CGA Magazine, Jan. 1988: 35).

The CICA divides the activities of its Research Department into the Accounting Research Committee and the Auditing Standards Committee. Representatives of other accounting associations are invited to sit on the Accounting Research Committee only (Cooper, 1973).

A new companies Act in British Columbia creates the Auditors Certification Board and recognizes CAs and CGAs as equally qualified to conduct audits (S.B.C. 1973, c.18, s.203, 205). The Board began certifying auditors in 1975 (Atkinson, 1985: 53).

The CGAABC proposes a merger with the ICABC. This results in the formation of a committee to consider the rationalization of accountancy.

The RIAs pass a motion requiring four years of experience prior to qualifying for their designation. Although this had been the nominal policy of the provincial associations, it was not consistently enforced (Allan, 1982: 115).

The GICIA gains the right to issue certificates to Accredited Members who may use the ICIA designation (Ross and Brown, 1978: 6).

The CGAs incorporate in Manitoba (S.M. 1973, c.38). This group did not affiliate with the national body until 1978. They also adopted a continuing education requirement (Stuart, 1988: 68).

The CAs adopt a national code of ethics (Creighton, 1984: 277).

The Provincial Securities Commission releases Policy Statement #27 accepting the CICA Handbook as the sole source of accounting standards for publically traded companies in Canada (Lafranconi, 1981).

The SIAC promotes General membership in the Society (CM 1973, V47 N3: 57).

A joint meeting of the SIAC and GAAC discusses the possibility of a national merger. This results in the creation of Provincial Joint Committees on Unification in each province. Although initially promising, the discussions ended in Oct. 1974 without developing a proposal (Allan, 1982: 116-117).

Following the ICAA, the ICABC establishes a professional practice advisor (Affleck, 1980: 51).

1974

The maritime CGA association forms an Atlantic Regional Board (Stuart, 1988: 68).

The SIAC and General Accountants Association of Canada (GAA) create a national steering committee to consider merging the two groups (Atkinson, 1985: 55).

The GAA approves a National Code of Ethics (Stuart, 1988: 73).

The ICABC, CGABC and SMABC form an Ad Hoc committee to consider 'rationalizing' the profession in B.C. (Atkinson, 1985: 56).

The President of the SIAC presents a report on the Status of Unification of the Accounting profession which indicates that unification is desireable but not feasible at this time (CM 1974, V48 N6: 58).

The CGAAO petitions the Ontario government for the right to act as a qualifying body under the Public Accountants Act.

Quebec's Professional Code comes into effect requiring mandatory practice inspection and major readjustments of the CAs education and examination program. A new CAs Act is also enacted which required the ICAQ to be renamed the Order of CAs of Quebec. All students hence forth would also have to have a working knowledge of french. On July 1, 1978 the English version was outlawed and the Quebec CAs became known as the Ordre des comptables agrees du Quebec. This legislation also created pressure to rationalize the remaining associations in Quebec but this has not been realized (Collard, 1980: 219-222).The SIAQ is renamed the Professional Corporation of Industrial Accountants of Quebec (CM 1974, V48 N3: 59).

1975

The Society of Industrial Accountants of the Yukon gains a charter with the right to offer the RIA designation (S.Y.T. 1975, c.2).

The ICABC adopts the CICA uniform code of professional conduct (Affleck, 1980: 53).

1976

The Accountant's International Study Group is disbanded (CGA Magazine, Jan. 1988: 35).

The ICAA requires that students complete Institute courses in audit procedures, taxation, audit techniques and financial accounting subsequent to completing the university course requirements (ICAA, 1986, N10: 4).

The Canada Business Corporations Act, S.C. 1974-76, c.33, s.149 (and regulations), accepts the CICA Handbook as GAAP (Lafranconi, 1981).

The ICABC, on the basis of a report by D.C. Selman, withdraws from merger discussions with the SMABC and CGAABC (Affleck, 1980: 54).

The CGAM attempt to have a reference to the CICA Handbook as GAAP deleted from the Manitoba Corporations Act. This is blocked by the ICAM (Neville, 1986: 124).

The ICAM students club is disbanded. The university degree requirement had eliminated many of the purposes served by the club (Neville, 1986: 120).

The ICAM replaces their code of ethics with rules of professional conduct, providing greater emphasis on enforcement by the Institute (Neville, 1986: 115).

The Institute of CAs of the Yukon gains a charter with the rights to the CA designation (S.Y.T. 1976, c.2).

The SICAA provides services to accountants in the Northwest Territories. Although the Legislative Council of the NWT suggestes that there are too few accountants to warrant separate legislation, and proposed a single accounting association, this was rejected by all three accounting associations (Allan, 1981).

The CGAs in Quebec accept lay members on their Board as a result of government interference (Stuart, 1988: 70).

The SIAC is renamed the Society of Management Accountants of Canada (SMAC) and their designation is changed from RIA to CMA (Certified Management Accountant) (CM 1977, V51 N6: 54-55). The change allows the same designation to be used in French and English, and is consistent with developments in Great Britain and the United States (Allan, 1982: 119-120).

The Canadian Academic Accounting Association is incorporated as a charitable foundation. The CAAA replaced the Canadian Region of the American Accounting Association. The Canadian Region had been holding separate conferences since 1966.

The ICABC establishes a system of monitored professional development (Affleck, 1980: 54).

1977

The International Federation of Accountants (IFAC) is formed (CGA Magazine, Jan. 1988: 35).

The Society of Industrial and Cost Accountants of Prince Edward Island are renamed the Society of Management Accountants of Prince Edward Island (S.P.E.I. 1977, c.52).

The Society of Industrial Accountants of Newfoundland are renamed the Society of Management Accountants and the RIA designation is amended to Registered Management Accountant (S.N. 1977, c.9).

The Society of Industrial and Cost Accountants of New Brunswick become the Society of Management Accountants of New Brunswick (S.N.B. 1977, c.62).

The Society of Industrial Accountants of the Yukon are renamed the Society of Management Accountants (S.Y.T. 1977, c.9).

A merger is proposed among CAs, CMAs and CGAs in Quebec which would leave the Order of CAs in control of public accounting and the Corporation of Management Accountants representing all other accountants. The CGAs reject the plan (CM 1977 V51 N6: 54-56).

The national curriculum of the CMAs is revised to include economics, taxation and data processing (Atkinson, 1985: 13).

The Accredited Public Accountants are incorporated in Saskatchewan (S.S. 1976-77, c.1).

The Ontario Attorney General's office forms the Professional Organizations Committee to consider, among other things, the organization of public accounting.

The CGA Association of the Northwest Territories is incorporated (CGA Magazine March, 1978: 3).

The Society of Industrial Accountants of British Columbia change their name to the Society of Management Accountants (S.B.C. 1977, c.84).

1978

The SMANF Act is amended to give the Society the right to use the RIA designation (S.N. 1978, c.62).

The GAA creates a National Research Committee (CGA Magazine, Oct. 1978).

The CGAs in Manitoba sign an affiliation agreement with the GAA (Stuart, 1988: 68).

The SMAC adopts a monitored voluntary professional development program (Atkinson, 1985: 43).

The Society of Industrial Accountants of Nova Scotia changes their name to the Society of Management Accountants of Nova Scotia (S.N.S. 1977, c.129).

The ICAM establishes a committee to consider the concept of practice reviews (Neville, 1986: 126).

The CICA releases the Report of the Special Committee to Examine the Role of the Auditor (Johnson et al, 1980).

The Society of Industrial Accountants of Alberta changes its name to the Society of Management Accountants of Alberta (ICAA/SMAA Proposal, 1981).

The Government of Alberta adopts a policy statement on professions calling for a single body in each field, the separation of the bargaining and licensing functions, clear boundaries around occupational domains, strict codes of ethics and disciplinary procedures, and legislative accountability of self-regulated professions (Government of Alberta Policy Paper, 1981).

The SIAS changes their name to the Society of Management Accountants of Saskatchewan (S.S. 1978, c.28).

The CGA incorporate in Saskatchewan (S.S. 1978, c.6)(CGA Magazine Sept. 1978: 2).

1979

The SIAC approves in principle a motion to require professional entrance examinations at the end of the CMA program (CM 1979, V53, N3: 68).

The CGAAO begins mandatory professional development.

The ICAA replaces a program of monitored voluntary professional development with a mandatory office review program (ICAA, 1986, N12: 2).

The Certified General Accountants of the Northwest Territories gains a charter with the right to offer the CGA designation (S.N.W.T. 1979, c.16).

The Newfoundland Municipalities Act (S.N. 1979, c.33) is amended to require municipalities to be audited by CAs. This is the first Newfoundland legislation to specify a particular association as auditors.

BIBLIOGRAPHY

The following bibliographical lists secondary source material on the history of the accounting profession in Canada. This biography includes all material cited in the chronology above as well as selected additional references.

Affleck, E.L. 1980 Seventy Fifth Anniversary Commemorative History of the Institute of CAs of British Columbia Vancouver: ICABC.

Allan, J.N. 1981 A History of the Society of Management Accountants of Alberta, mimeo, (undated) 98 pgs.

Allan, J.N. 1982 History of the Society of Management Accountants of Canada Hamilton: SMAC.

Atkinson, W.A. 1985 History of the Society of Management Accountants of British Columbia 1945-1985 Vancouver: SMABC.

Bennett, R.J. 1917 "The Vital Importance of Knowing Costs" Canadian Chartered Accountant V7: 34-42.

Bentley, W. 1938 History of the Association Montreal: General Accountants Association.

Brown, R. 1968 [1905] A History of Accounting and Accountants New York: Kelley.

Canadian Institute of Chartered Accountants Handbook.

CCA - The Canadian Chartered Accountant published by the Dominion (now Canadian) Institute of Chartered Accountants.

CJA - The Canadian Journal of Accountancy published by the Canadian Association of Certified Public Accountants.

CM - Cost and Management published by the Canadian Society of Management Accountants 1926.

Collard, E.A. 1980 First in North America Montreal: Ordre des Comptables Agrees du Quebec.

Collard, E.A. 1983 Stories About 125 Years at Touche Ross Montreal: Touche Ross.

Cooper, D.A. 1973 "Canada: Reshaping Research" The Accountants Magazine (Edinburgh) V77: 430-431.

Cooper Brothers and Co. A History of Cooper Brothers and Co. 1854-1954 London: Coopers

Brothers and Co. 1954.

Crate, H.E. 1970 Thorne Gunn Helliwell & Christenson: A History 1880-1970 Toronto: Thorne Gunn Helliwell & Christenson.

Creighton, P. 1984 A Sum of Yesterdays Toronto: ICAO.

Desrochers, A. (Executive Director, OCAQ) 1986 Personal Communication.

Dobell, S.H. 1934 "The Chartered Accountant -- His Widening Horizon" CCA V24: 314-321.

Edwards, G. 1915 "Accountancy in Canada" Journal of Accountancy November: 334-348.

Edwards, G. 1921 "The Educational Responsibilities of the Chartered Accountant Societies" Canadian Chartered Accountant V11: 150-159.

Edwards, H.P. 1940 "Three Score Years" Canadian Chartered Accountant V36: 76-93.

Edwards, H.P. 1954 "After Three Score Years and Ten" Canadian Chartered Accountant V64: 356-363.

Elliot, S. 1974 "Accounting and Canada" Arthur Anderson Chronicle V34: 78-82.

Englebert, R. 1962 "A Diamond Jubilee Progress of the Profession in Canada" Canadian Chartered Accountant V81 N2: 147-152

Fairclough, E (1966)"Women as CA's" CA Magazine pp. 469-471.

GA - General Accountant published by the General Accountants' Association 1923-1939, 1941-1967.

Gibson, F.W. 1983 To Serve and Yet Be Free: Queen's University 1917-1961 McGill-Queen's Press: Kingston.

Goodman, M. 1917 "The CAs of the Dominion" Canadian Chartered Accountant V7: 44-46.

Gordon, H.D.L. 1961 "Fifty Years Ago" Canadian Chartered Accountant V79: 96-98.

Gorelik, G. 1973 "The Professional Accountant Today and Tomorrow" CGA Magazine January.

Haskins and Sells Haskins and Sells: Our First Seventy Five Years New York: Haskins & Sells 1970.

Henderson, M. 1984 Plain Talk! Memoirs of an Auditor General Toronto: McClelland and

Stewart.

Hoole, A.H. 1963 <u>A Brief History of the Institute of CAs of Manitoba</u> Winnipeg: ICAM.

Horne, G.R. 1956 "Professional Training for Accountancy in Canada" <u>Accounting Review</u> V31: 43-49.

Hudson, G.W. 1966 <u>A History of the New Brunswick Institute of CAs</u> Saint John: ICANB.

Hurdman, F.B. "Accountancy in the United States and Canada" <u>The Journal of Accountancy</u> Nov. 1928.

Hyde, J. "Address to the Congress of Accountants Federation of Societies of Public Accountants, Saint Louis, U.S.A. September 1904" pp. 83-91.

Institute of CAs of Alberta 1985 "CA 75 Years ... And <u>Still</u> Accounting" <u>Perspectives</u> (12 issues).

Johnson, D.J.; Lemon, W.M. and Neumann, F.L. 1980 "The Canadian Study of the Role of the Auditor" <u>Journal of Accounting, Auditing and Finance</u> V3 Spring: 251-63.

Johnson, T. and Caygill, M. 1971, "The Development of Accountancy Links in teh Commonwealth" <u>Accounting and Business Research</u> pp. 135-173.

King, C. "<u>The First Fifty: Teaching, Research and Public Service at the University of Saskatchewan</u>. Toronto: McClelland and Stewart, 1959.

Lanfranconi, C.P. 1981 "The Establishment of Financial Accounting in Canada: The Power and the Responsibility" <u>Cost and Management</u> January/February.

Lazar, F., Sievers, J.M. and Thronton D.B. 1978 "Analysis of the Practice of Public Accounting in Ontario" Working Paper, Professional Organizations Committee, Attorney General of Ontario.

Leach, C.W. 1976 <u>Coopers & Lybrand in Canada</u> Montreal: Coopers & Lybrand.

Lew, B. 1987 "A Tale of Two Banks: The Failures of the Home and Canadian Commercial Banks" MBA Project, University of Alberta.

Little, A.J. 1964 <u>The Story of the Firm</u> Toronto: Clarkson Gordon.

MacDonald, W.J. 1933 "The Student Body as a Factor in the Profession" <u>CCA</u> V23: 16-26.

MacKenzie, D.C. 1989 <u>The Clarkson Gordon Story</u> Toronto:University of Toronto Press.

Mann, H. 1975a "The Eleventh of June" American Accounting Association Proceedings Tuscon, Arizona, August.

Mann, H. 1975b The Evolution of Accounting in Canada Montreal: Touche Ross.

Mann, H. 1979 "CAs in Canada ... The First Hundred Years" CA Magazine Dec.:26-30.

McKeen, C. and Richardson, A. 1988 "Women, Accounting Education and the Profession in Canada" Canadian Academic Accountants Association Education Conference, Montreal Nov. 1988.

McLeod, J.A. 1933 "Historical Outline of Banking Legislation in Canada" Journal of the Canadian Bankers Association V41 N1: 15-30.

Moreland, P.a. 1977 A History of Business Education Toronto: Pitman.

Mulvey, T. 1920 Dominion Company Law Toronto: The Ontario Publishing Co.

Murphy, G.J. 1972 "The Influence of Taxation on Canadian Corporate Depreciation Practices" Canadian Tax Journal V20 N3: 233-239.

---- 1976 "The Evolution of Corporate Reporting Practices in Canada" Working Paper 20, The Academy of Accounting Historians.

---- 1980a "Financial Statement Disclosure and Corporate Law: The Canadian Experience" International Journal of Accounting V15 N2: 87-99.

---- 1980b "Some Aspects of Auditing Evolution in Canada" Accounting Historians Journal Fall: 45-61.

---- 1984 "Early Canadian Financial Statement Disclosure Legislation" Accounting Historians Journal V11 N2: 39-59.

---- 1986 "A Chronology of the Development of Corporate Financial Reporting in Canada: 1850-1983" Accounting Historians Journal V13 N1: 1-49.

---- 1988 "Corporate Financial Reporting Practices in Canada 1900-1970" New York : Garland Publishing 1988, pp. 221.

Neville, W.A. 1986 Raising the Standards Winnipeg: Institute of CAs of Manitoba.

Parton, J. 1961 "Fifty Years Ago" Canadian Chartered Accountant V79.

Pontifex, B. 1913 "Evolution of Accountancy in Canada" Monetary Times V50 (January): 37.

Richardson, A.J. 1984 "Professionalization and Intraprofessional Competition: The Canadian Accounting Profession 1880 to 1940" Proceedings of the <u>Administrative Sciences Association of Canada</u> Guelph, May.

---- 1985a "Legitimation, Professionalization and Intraprofessional competition" unpublished doctoral dissertation, Queen's University, Canada.

---- 1985b "The Professionalization of Accountancy in Canada" Proceedings of the <u>Canadian Academic Accounting Association</u> Montreal, May.

---- 1986a "Homage to Santa Rosalia or Why are There So Many Kinds of Accounting Associations" Proceedings of the <u>Canadian Academic Accounting Association</u> Winnipeg, May.

----1986b "The Role of Educational Policy in the Legitimation of Professional Status: A Case History of Accountancy in Ontario" <u>Canadian History of Education Association</u>, Halifax, October.

---- 1986c "Professionalization and Intraprofessional Competition in the Canadian Accounting Profession" <u>Work and Occupations</u> V14, N4 (1987): 591-615.

---- 1986d "The Production of Institutional Behaviour" <u>Canadian Journal of Administrative Sciences</u> V3 N2 (1986): 304-316.

---- 1989 "Canada's Accounting Elite: 1880-1930" <u>The Accounting Historians' Journal</u> V16 N1:1-21.

---- 1990 "The Confederation Life Case" (Parts A,B,C) in Gardner, E. (Ed.) Cases in Financial Accounting: Fundamentals Toronto: John Wiley

Richardson, A.J. and McKeen, C. 1988 "Women Pioneers in Accounting in Canada" Working Paper, Queen's University.

Richardson, A.J. and Williams, J.J. 1988 "The Evolution of Management Accounting in Canada: 1911-1961" Fifth World Congress of Accounting Historians, Sydney Australia, August.

Ross, H. and Brown, G., 1978 <u>History of the Guild of Industrial, Commercial and Institutional Accountants</u> mimeo, Toronto: GICIA.

Ross, H.T. 1927 "The Evolution of the Bank Act Since 1867" <u>Journal of the Canadian Bankers Association</u> V34 N4: 394-405.

Sievers, J.M. 1977 "The Regulation of the Practice of Accounting in Ontario" unpublished paper prepared for the Professional Organizations Committee, Attorney General of Ontario.

Smails, R.G.H. 1951 "The Story of Commerce at Queen's" Commerceman V6 N1: 6-10, 33-35 (reprinted with substantial editorial revisions in Queen's Review V28 1953: 180-185).

Smyth, J.E. 1953 'Notes on the Development of the Accounting Profession (Part II)' The Canadian Chartered Accountant.

Stuart, R.C. 1988 The First Seventy-Five Years: A History of the Certified General Accountants' Association of Canada Vancouver: CGAC.

Sutherland, J.B. 1925 'Presidential Address' Canadian Chartered Accountant V15:138-140.

Thompson,R.R. 1939 'The Development of the Profession of Accounting in Canada' Canadian Chartered Accountant V34:171-186.

Watt, M.L. 1982 The First Seventy Five Years Montreal: Price Waterhouse.

Wilson, D.A. 1988 Public Accountancy in Ontario: Modernization and Reform Toronto: Institute of Chartered Accountants.

Worthington, B. 1895 Professional Accountants: An Historical Sketch London: Gee (pp.102-3 recognizes the existence of Canadian associations, no other data).

Zeff, S. 1970 'Forging Accounting Principles in Canada - A Summary of Recent Trends' Working Paper 34, Tulane University.

LEGISLATION CITED

Federal

The Insolvent Act of 1864, S.C. 1864 (2nd Session), c.17
The Railways Act, 1868, S.C. 1867-1868, c.68
An Act Respecting Banks, S.C. 1867, c.11
An Act to incorporate the Dominion Association of Chartered
     Accountants, S.C. 1902 (2nd Session), c.58
An Act to amend the Bank Act, S.C. 1911, c.4
An Act to incorporate the General Accountants Association, S.C.
     1913, c.116
The Business Profits War Tax Act, 1916, S.C. 1916, c.11
The Companies Act amendment Act, 1917, S.C. 1917, c.25
The Income War Tax Act, 1917, S.C. 1917, c.28
The Bankruptcy Act, S.C. 1919, c.36
The Bank Audit Act, 1923, S.C. 1923, c.30
The Bank Act, S.C. 1923, c.32
The Board of Audit Act, 1925, S.C. 1925, c.32
The Companies Act, 1934, S.C. 1934, c.33
The Excess Profits Tax Act, 1940, S.C. 1940, c.32
An Act to amend the Excess Profits Tax Act, 1940, S.C. 1940-41, c.15
The Unemployment Insurance Act, 1940, S.C. 1940, c.44
An Act to amend the Companies Act, S.C. 1964-65, c.52
Canada Business Corporations Act, S.C. 1974-75-76, c.33

Alberta

An Act to incorporate "The Institute of CAs of Alberta", S.A. 1910 (2nd Session), c.43
The Society of Industrial Accountants of Alberta Act, 1944, S.A. 1944, c.79
An Act respecting Official Auditors, S.A. 1909, c.10
Certified General Accountants Act, S.A. 1984, c.C-3.5

British Columbia

CAs Act, S.B.C. 1905, c.59
CAs Act, S.B.C. 1921 (2nd Session), c.53
Society of Industrial Accountants of British Columbia Act, S.B.C. 1945, c.81
Certified General Accountants Act, S.B.C. 1951, c.2
Companies Act, S.B.C. 1973, c.18
Society of Industrial Accountants of British Columbia Amendment Act, S.B.C. 1977, c.84

Manitoba

The CAs' Association Act, S.M. 1886, c.66
The CAs' Act, S.M. 1913, c.1
The Society of Industrial and Cost Accountants Act, S.M. 1947, c.101
The CPAs Act, S.M. 1950, c.103
The Manitoba Accredited Public Accountants Act, S.M. 1950, c.100
An Act to incorporate the Certified General Accountants Association of Manitoba, S.M. 1973, c.38

New Brunswick

CAs Act, S.N.B. 1916, c.53
An Act to amend an Act to incorporate The New Brunswick Institute of CAs, S.N.B. 1930, c.51
An Act to Amend Chapter 53 of the Acts of 6 George V (1916) "The CAs' Act", S.N.B. 1935, c.45
The New Brunswick Accredited Public Accountants Act, 1947, S.N.B. 1947, c.166
The Industrial and Cost Accountants Act, 1950, S.N.B. 1950, c.55
The CPAs Association of New Brunswick Act, S.N.B. 1951, c.41
Certified General Accountants' Act, S.N.B. 1961-62, c.93
Municipalities Act, S.N.B. 1966, c.20
An Act to amend an Act to Incorporate the Society of Industrial and Cost Accountants of New Brunswick, S.N.B. 1977, c.62

Newfoundland

An Act to incorporate the Institute of Accountants of Newfoundland, S.N. 1905, c.16
An Act to amend 5 Edward VII, Chap. 16, entitled "An Act to incorporate the Institute of Accountants of Newfoundland, S.N. 1906, c.29
CAs Act, 1949, S.N. 1949, c.30
The CPAs Act, 1950, S.N. 1950, c.35
The Industrial and Cost Accountants Act, 1951, S.N. 1951, c.69
The Securities Act, 1952, S.N. 1952, c.61
The CAs and CPAs (Merger) Act, 1966-67, S.N. 1966-67, c.42
The Public Accountancy Act, 1966-67, S.N. 1966-67, c.45
An Act to Change the Corporate Name of the Society of Industrial Accountants of Newfoundland, S.N. 1977, c.9
An Act to Amend the Management Accountants Act, S.N. 1978, c.62
The Municipalities Act, S.N. 1979, c.33

Northwest Territories

Certified General Accountants' Association Ordinance, S.N.W.T. 1979, c.14
Institute of CAs Ordinance, S.N.W.T. 1979, c.16
Society of Management Accountants Ordinance, S.N.W.T. 1982 (3rd Session), c.17

Nova Scotia

An Act to Incorporate the Institute of CAs of Nova Scotia, S.N.S. 1900, c.154
An Act to amend Chapter 154, Acts of 1900, entitled, An Act to Incorporate the Institute of CAs of Nova Scotia, S.N.S. 1913, c.154
An Act regarding the Auditing of Provincial Accountants, S.N.S. 1926, c.1
The Security Frauds Prevention Act, S.N.S. 1930, c.3
The Securities Act, S.N.S. 1945, c.8
Society of Industrial and Cost Accountants of Nova Scotia Act, S.N.S. 1950, c.95
The Registered Public Accountants' Act, S.N.S. 1952, c.128
Public Accountants' Act, S.N.S. 1952, c.14
An Act to Amend Chapter 95 of the Acts of 1950, The Society of Industrial and Cost Accountants of Nova Scotia Act S.N.S. 1958, c.124
Society of Management Accountants of Nova Scotia Act, S.N.S. 1977, c.129
An Act to Amend Chapter 95 of the Acts of 1950, The Society of Management Accountants of Nova Scotia Act, S.N.S. 1983, c.95

Ontario

An Act to incorporate the Institute of Accountants of Ontario, S.O. 1882-83, c.62
An Act to make better provision for keeping and auditing Municipal and School accounts, S.O. 1897, c.48
The Ontario Companies Act, S.O. 1907, c.34
An Act to revise and amend the CAs Act, S.O. 1908, c.42
The CAs Act New S.O. 1911, c.48
An Act to amend the Loan and Trust Companies Act, S.O. 1919, c.42
The Association of Accountants and Auditors Act, 1926, S.O. c.124
The Association of Accountants and Auditors Act. S.O. 1931, c.143
The CPAs Act, 1936, S.O. 1936, c.68
The Society of Industrial and Cost Accountants of Ontario Act, 1941, S.O. 1941, c.77
The Public Accountancy Act, 1950, S.O. 1950, c.60
The Corporations Act, 1953, S.O. 1953, c.19
The Public Accountancy Amendment Act, 1961-62, S.O. 1961-62, c.113
An Act to Amend the Companies Act S.O. 1964 c.10
The Securities Act S.O. 1966 c.142
The Society of Industrial Accountants of Ontario Act, 1967, S.O. 1967, c.129
An Act respecting the Society of Management Accountants of Ontario, S.O. 1981, c.100

Certified General Accountants Association of Ontario Act, 1983, S.O. 1983, c.Pr6

Prince Edward Island

An Act to incorporate the Institute of CAs of Prince Edward Island, S.P.E.I. 1921, c.25
An Act to regulate the practice of public accountancy and auditing in the Province of Prince Edward Island, S.P.E.I. 1949, c.52
An Act to incorporate the Society of Industrial and Cost Accountants of Prince Edward Island, S.P.E.I. 1951, c.34
Prince Edward Island Certified General Accountants Act, S.P.E.I. 1951, c.64
An Act to amend an Act to incorporate the Industrial Accounts of Prince Edward Island, S.P.E.I. 1977, c.52

Quebec

An Act to incorporate the Association of Accountants in Montreal, S.Q. 1880 (3rd Session), c.88
An Act to Incorporate the Institute of Accountants and Auditors of the Province of Quebec, S.Q. 1912, c.94
An Act to amend the act to incorporate the school for higher commercial studies at Montreal, S.Q. 1914, c.27
An Act respecting certain diplomas from the School of Commercial Studies of McGill University, Montreal, S.Q. 1918 (2nd session), c.43
An Act to amend the Act to incorporate the school for higher commercial studies at Montreal, S.Q. 1918 (2nd session), c.44
An Act to incorporate the Accountants Association, S.Q. 1920, c.118
An Act to amend the Accountants Act, S.Q. 1927, c.61
An Act to amend the Charter of the Association of Accountants in Montreal, S.Q. 1927, c.101
The Cost and Management Institute Act, S.Q. 1941, c.95
An Act to regulate the practice of accounting and auditing, S.Q. 1946, c.47
An Act to amend the charter of the Cost and Management Institute, S.Q. 1948, c.95

Saskatchewan

An Act to Incorporate the Institute of CAs of Saskatchewan, S.S. 1908, c.55
The CAs Act, 1934 The Industrial and Cost Accountants Act, 1948, S.S. 1948, c.74
The CPAs Act, 1953, S.S. 1953, c.84
An Act to Amend the CPAs Act, S.S. 1954, c.72
The Accredited Public Accountants Act, 1977, S.S. 1976-1977, c.1
The Certified General Accountants Act, 1978, S.S. 1978, c.6
An Act to Amend the Industrial Accountants Act, S.S. 1978, c.26

Yukon

Legal Profession Accounts Ordinance, S.Y.T. 1965 (1st Session), c.1
Society of Industrial Accountants Ordinance, S.Y.T. 1975 (2nd Session), c.2
Institute of CAs Ordinance, S.Y.T. 1976 (3rd Session), c.2
An Ordinance to amend the Society of Industrial Accountants Ordinance, S.Y.T. 1977 (2nd Session), c.3
Certified General Accountants Act, S.Y.T. 1983, c.14
An Act to amend the Society of Management Accountants Act, S.Y.T. 1983, c.28

APPENDIX A: ABBREVIATIONS USED IN THE TEXT

AA	Accountants Association
AAAO	Association of Accountants and Auditors in Ontario
AAM	Association of Accountants of Montreal
AAO	Accountants Association of Ontario
AEFA	Accounting Education Foundation of Alberta
APA	Accredited Public Accountant (designation)
APAANB	Accredited Public Accountants Association of New Brunswick
BNA	British North America
CA	Chartered Accountant (designation)
CAA	Canadian Accountants Association
CAAA	Canadian Academic Accountants Association
CCA	Canadian Chartered Accountant (Magazine)
CI	Controllers Institute
CIA	Certified Industrial Accountant (designated)
CICA	Canadian Institute of CAs
CICPA	Canadian Institute of CPAs
CIS	Chartered Institute of Secretaries
CGA	Certified General Accountant (designated)
CGAABC	Certified General Accountants Association of British Columbia
CGAAC	Certified General Accountants Association of Canada
CGAAM	Certified General Accountants Association of Manitoba
CGAANB	Certified General Accountants Association of New Brunswick
CGAANS	Certified General Accountants Association of Nova Scotia
CGAAO	Certified General Accountants Association of Ontario
CGAAPEI	Certified General Accountants Association of Prince Edward Island
CGAAS	Certified General Accounts Association of Saskatchewan
CJA	Canadian Journal of Accountancy
CM	Cost and Management (Magazine)
CMA	Certified Management Accountant (designated)
CPA	Certified Public Accountant
CPAAM	Certified Public Accountants Association of Manitoba
CPAANB	Certified Public Accountants Association of New Brunswick
CPAANF	Certified Public Accountants Association of Newfoundland
CPAAO	CPAs Association of Ontario
CPAAS	Certified Public Accountas Association of Saskatchewan
CPAPQ	Corporation of Public Accountants of the Province of Quebec
CSCA	Canadian Society of Cost Accountants
CSCAIE	Canadian Society of Cost Accountants and Industrial Engineers
DACA	Dominion Association of CAs
FCA	Fellow, Chartered Accountant
FCGA	Fellow, Certified General Accountant
FEI	Financial Executives Institute

GA		Guild of Accountants
GA		General Accountant (Magazine)
GAA		General Accountants Association
GICIA		Guild of Industrial, Commercial and Institutional Accountants
IAAO		Institute of Accountants and Adjusters of Ontario
IAAPQ		Institute of Accountants and Auditors of the Province of Quebec
IAEC		International Accountants and Executives Corporation
IAM		Independent Accountants of Montreal
IAPA		Institute of Accredited Public Accountants
IAPAO		Institute of Accredited Public Accountants of Ontario
ICAA		Institute of CAs of Alberta
ICABC		Institute of CAs of British Columbia
ICAM		Institute of CAs of Manitoba
ICANB		Institute of CAs of New Brunswick
ICANF		Institute of CAs of New Foundland
ICANS		Institute of CAs of Nova Scotia
ICAO		Institute of CAs of Ontario
ICAPEI		Institute of CAs of Prince Edward Island
ICAQ		Institute of CAs of Quebec
ICAS		Institute of CAs of Saskatchewan
ICIA		Industrial Commercial and Institutional Accountant
IPA		Independent Public Accountant
IPA		Incorporated Public Accountant
IPAAO		Independent Public Accountants Association of Ontario
LA		Licentiate in Accounting (designation)
LCMI		Licentiate of the Cost and Management Institute (designation)
NAA		National Association of (Cost) Accountants
OCAQ		Ordre des Comptables agrees du Quebec
RIA		Registered Industrial Accountant (designation)
RPA		Registered Public Accountant (designation)
SCAPQ		Society of CAs of the Province of Quebec
SIAA		Society of Industrial Accountants of Alberta
SIAAE		Society of Independent Accountants of British Columbia
SIAC		Society of Industrial Accountans of Canada
SIAO		Society of Industrial Accountants of Ontario
SIAS		Society of Industrial Accountants of Saskatchewan
SICAA		Society of Industrial and Cost Accountants of Alberta
SICABC		Society of Industrial and Cost Accountants of British Columbia
SICAS		Society of Industrial and Cost Accountants of Saskatchewan
SICANB		Society of Industrial and Cost Accountants of New Brunswick
SIPABC		Society of Independent Public Accountants of British Columbia
SMAA		Society of Management Accountants of Alberta
SMABC		Society of Management Accountants of British Columbia
SPABC		Society of Public Accountants of British Columbia

SIAC		Society of Industrial Accountants of Canada
SICAC		Society of Industrial and Cost Accountants of Canada
SMABC		Society of Management Accountants of British Columbia
SMAC		Society of Management Accountants of Canada
UAA		United Accountants and Auditors in Canada
UBC		University of British Columbia

A

Abbott, Harry, I,4,p.21
Accounts receivable, confirmation of, II,2,p.97
Accountability, IV,5,p.3
Accountants and Auditors of Ontario, II,8,p.17
Accountics, II,6,p.56-57
Accounting
    associations, rights of, II,7,p.597
    information and social choice, III,4,p.100-102
    elite in Canada, II,9,p.6-15
    nature of, III,5,p.5-7; III,6,p.8,10
    objectives of, III,5,p.3-4; III,6,p.15
    users of information, III,5,p.7-8, III,6,p.14-17,19
Accounting Principles Board, or APB, (see also: FASB)
    III,3,p.284,288-289,293; III,4,p.101
Accounting profession, (see also: Professionalism)
    foreign influences, III,3,p.273-274
    history of in Canada, III,3,p.269-275
Accounting research, III,4,p.127-128,138-139,144,148,150
Accredited Public Accountants, or APAs, II,7,p.597,599; II,8,p.4
Accounting Research Association, or ARA, III,3,p.275
Accounting Standards,
    for financial institutions, IV,5,p.21
    recommendations to revise, IV,5,p.15-16
    setting, III,4,p.96-97
Accrual accounting, early examples of, I,2,p.270-271; I,4,p.54
Acheson, T.W., II,9,p.19
Acts of Parliament, I,4,p.8
Affleck, E.L., V,2,p.62
Aitken, Hugh G.J., I,2,p.276; I,4,p.21
Aitken, Max, I,4,p.18
Allan, J.N., II,7,p.612; II,8,p.34;II,9,p.19; V,2,p.62
Allen, Sir Hugh, I,4,p.11,15
Amernic, Joel H., III,6,p.5
American Association of Public Accountants, II,6,p.48; II,8,p.8;
    V,1,p.38; V,2,p.13
American Institute of Certified Public Accountants, or AICPA,
    II,8,p.34; III,3,p.276,299; III,5,p.1; IV,4,p.8
American system of accounting, I,4,p.58-59,62; V,1,p.31
Anderson, Rod, II,5,p.205,209-210,213
Anderson, Wm., II,3.p.76-77,79,82
Angus, Richard R. I,4,p.11
Aranya, Nissim, III,6,p.5
Archer, John H., I,2,p.276
Archibald, Ross, III,4,p.136; V,1,p.55
Armour, Robert, I,4,p.13
Armstrong, C., II,6,p.55,57
Armstrong, D., II,7,p.612; II,8,p.34
Armstrong, P., II,8,p.34
Arrow, K.J., III,4,p.129

Arthur Anderson & Co., IV,3,p.58
Ashley, C.A., II,9,p.19
Association of Accountants and Auditors (see also: Certified
    Public Accountants) II,8,p.10
Association of Accountants in Montreal, see Institute of
    Chartered Accountants of the Province of Québec
Atkinson, W.A., V,2,p.62
Atlantic Acceptance Company, IV,1,p.96; IV,6,p.12; V,1,p.47-48
Atlantic Provinces Association of CAs, V,2,p.53
Audits,
    "balance sheet", II,5,p.199,205
    bulletins, III,3,p.280
    "current", II,5,p.199,205
    early examples of, III,2,p.198-199
    early experiences in Western Canada, II,1,p.94-96
    exclusive rights for Cas, II,7,p.608-609
    "failures", IV,4,p.1-2
    in Canada in the 1930s, II,5,p.199
    public misunderstanding of, IV,5,p.11-12
    required for banks, II,1,p.95; IV,6,p.7
    required by Canada Corporations Act, I,4,p.8
    required for insurance companies, V,1,p.35
    required for municipalities, V,1,p.35,38; V,2,p.61
    required for various Companies Acts, II,6,p.40,49;
    III,3,p.271 III,2,p.198; IV,1,p.88-89; IV,2,p.104
    required in England, IV,1,p.89
    standard report, III,2,p.199; III,3,p.280
    tax law, III,3,p.272
    test basis, II,5,p.200,205
Audit Committees, IV,5,p.7,12,15; V,1,p.50
Auditors,
    and fraud, IV,5,p.9,19
    and illegal acts, IV,5,p.20
    as general business consultant, IV,2,p.106
    association with financial disclosure outside the Financial
    Statements, IV,5,p.11,17
    change of, IV,5,p.20
    duties of, IV,2,p.105-106; IV,5,p.3,6-7
    failure to discharge professional responsibility, IV,4,p.1-2
    knowledge of the business, IV,5,p.22
    report of,
        requirement to provide, (see also: audits) III,1,p.1
        qualification of, III,3,p.294-295; IV,3,p.57;
        V,1,p.48,52
    report on internal control, IV,5,p.22
    resignation of, IV,5,p.7-8
    role of, IV,4,p.2-3
    parent auditors' responsibility with respect to subsidiary
    auditor, IV,1,p.96
    qualifications of, II,6,p.47
Auerbach, J.S., II,7,p.612

B
Bachrach, P., II,9,p.19
Balance Sheet, (see also: Financial Statements)
      arrangement and order of assets and liabilities,
      III,2,p.194-197; IV,2,p.104
      early examples of, I,2,p.272-275; III,2,p.200-203
      limitations of, IV,2,p.101-102
      prepared from existing source documents, I,1,p.65,72-7
      required classes of assets and liabilities, III,1,p.1;
      III,7,p.107; IV,1,p.89-90
      required disclosure, IV,1,p.91,93
      requirement to provide, II,6,p.40-41; III,1,p.1; IV,1,p.88;
      IV,2,p.100,104
      valuation of assets, IV,2,p.104
Bank Act, I,4,p.14,58; II,4,p.4; IV,6,p.6,11,15; V,1,p.41;
      V,2,p.6,9
Bank failures, IV,6,p.1-20; V,1,p.40-41
Bank of Montreal, I,4,p.8,12-14; I,4,p.54-59,77
Banks,
      establishment in Canada, IV,6,p.5-6
Barber, B., II,7,p.612
Baxter, William T., I,2,p.270-271,276
Beatty, S.G., II,6,p.46; V,1,p.37
Beechy, T., V,1,p.55
Begun, J.W., II,7,p.612
Bell,
      Alexander Graham, I,4,p.8,21
      Alexander Melville, I,4,p.8-10
      National Telephone Company of Boston, I,4,p.9
      Telephone Company of Canada, I,4,p.7-10,21,62-63
Bell, Mathew, I,1,p.73
Belli, R.D., III,3,p.273
Bendix, R., II,9,p.19
Bennett, R.J., V,2,p.62
Bentley, W., II,7,p.612; II,8,p.34; V,2,p.62
Berlant, J.L., II,7,p.612; II,8,p.34
Bill of Exchange, use of, I,3,p.13
Blackburn, R.M., II,9,p.20
Bliss, M., II,6,p.43,55,57
Board of Audit, V,1,p.34
Boland, R.J., II,7,p.612
Bonar, James Charles, I,4,p.21
Bothwell, R., II,9,p.19
Bourdieu, P., II,8,p.34
Bowering, Ian, I,2,p.263,276
Boyd, M., II,9,p.19
Brewers Association of Canada, I,2,p.262,276
British Accounting Standards Committee, III,5,p.2
British Columbia Statutes, V,1,p.58
British Mortgage and Housing Company, IV,6,p.12
British North America Act, I,4,p.8
British system of accounting, I,4,p.53-54,58,62; V,1,p.31

Brown, G., II,7,p.614; II,8,p.36; V,2,p.65,66
Brown, R., II,7,p.612; II,8,p.34; V,2,p.62
Brown, R.C., II,6,p.55,57; II,9,p.19
Brown, R. Gene, I,4,p.77
Bucher, R., II,7,p.612; II,8,p.34
Budgets,
    capital budgets, I,1,p.66-67,74-78
    cash budgets, I,1,p.69-71
    operating budgets, I,1,p.67-69,78-80
Burchell, S., II,8,p.34
Burpee, Helen, II,3,p.85; V,2,p.33
Bush, John, I,4,p.13
Buttar, William I,2,p.262-265

<u>C</u>
Campbell, Sharp, IV,3,p.58
Canada Business Corporations Act, III,4,p.96; IV,1,p.97;
    IV,3,p.56-59; V,1,p.47,53
Canada Corporations Act, I,4,p.8-9; II,7,p.598; II,8,p.6;
    III,3,p.300; IV,1,p.95
Canada Deposit Insurance Act, IV,6,p.20
Canada Gazette, II,6,p.57
Canada, House of Commons, IV,6,p.20; V,1,p.44
Canada Joint Stock Companies Act, V,1,p.35
Canada Securities Commission, IV,1,p.98
Canada, Senate Debates, II,6,p.56-57
Canada Statutes, II,6,p.55,57; IV,1,p.88,90-91; IV,6,p.21;
    V,1,p.58-59
Canadian Academic Accounting Association, V,1,p.50,55; V,2,p.59
Canadian Accountants' Association, see General Accountants'
    Association
Canadian Bankers' Association, IV,6,p.7,10
Canadian Chartered Accountant, II,3,p.90; II,4,p.4;
    III,3,p.271,275-276,279,284,294; IV,1,p.91,94; V,1,p.41;
    V,2,p.16,34
Canadian Commercial Bank, IV,4,p.1; IV,6,p.1-2,13-20
Canadian Comprehensive Auditing Foundation, V,1,p.55
Canadian Corporate Secretary; the Canadian Division of the
    Chartered Institute of Secretaries, I,4,p.8,20
Canadian Institute of Chartered Accountants or CICA, (see also:
    Dominion Association of Chartered Accountants)
    Accounting and Auditing Research Committee, also Accounting
    Research Committee,
        emergence and structure of, III,3,p.275-278;
        III,4,p.96; III,4,p.102-104,127-128; V,1,p.45,52;
        V,2,p.40-41
        impact of, III,4,p.150-151 III,5,p.11; III,6,p.4
        secrecy of, III,4,p.136-138,142-145,
        monitoring of financial statements, III,3,p.295;
        V,1,p.45,50
        redesign of, III,3,p.304; V,1,p.56; V,2,p.53,57
        role of, III,4,p.140-142

      subcommittee on liaison with securities commissions and
      stock exchanges, III,3,p.302
Accounting Research Advisory Board, III,4,p.103
Accounting Research Steering Committee, III,4,p.103
Accounting Standards Committee, or AsSC, III,6,p.10-11;
  IV,3,p.55-59; IV,5,p.8-9,15-19
Accounting Standards Financial Institutions Task Force,
  IV,4,p.5
admission of women, V,2,p.18
Auditing Standards Committee, IV,3,p.58; IV,5,p.16-18;
  V,1,p.52
bulletins, III,3,p.279-284; V,1,p.44-62; V,2,p.40-61
Committee on Co-operation with Stock Exchanges, III,3,p.277
Committee on Terminology, III,3,p.276,279
Committee to Enquire into the Effect of the Changing Value
      of the Dollar on Financial Statements, III,3,p.282
cost of handbook and research programs, III,3,p.296-299
disciplinary procedure, IV,4,p.5-6
exposure draft process, III,3,p.294;
III,4,p.102,104,115,136-137
formation of, III,3,p.269-270; V,1,p.39; V,2,p.11
founding members, V,2,p.9
guidelines, V,1,p.52-62
legal status of standards issued, III,4,p.98-100; III,6,p.4;
  IV,1,p.97-99; IV,3,p.55; V,1,p.32
Handbook, II,7,p.598; II,8,p.6; III,3,p.293;
III,4,p.104,138; IV,4,p.3-5,7; V,1,p.47,50-62; V,2,p.62
historical highlights, V,2,p.7-61
membership in IFAC, V,1,p.53
organization and membership, III,3,p.269,291-292; V,1,p.41;
  V,2,p.15
Public Sector Accounting and Auditing Committee, V,1,p.56
research studies, III,3,p.286-291; V,1,p.44-62
Special Committee on Standard Setting, III,4,p.142; V,1,p.56
standard setting procedure, III,4,p.102-105,126-128;
  IV,1,p.98-99; IV,4,p.5
survey of ARC committee members regarding the standard
  setting procedure, III,4,p.105-115,130-134
survey of respondents to a sample of exposure drafts,
  III,4,p.115-125
Canadian Institute of Public Real Estate Companies, or CIPREC,
  III,3,p.303
Canadian Manufacturers' Association, II,6,p.43
Canadian Men and Women of the Time, II,9,p.5
Canadian Pacific Railway Company,
     early financial statements, I,4,p.59,62
     incorporation and growth I,4,p.7-8,10-12,15,21,
Canadian Securities Administrators, IV,1,p.97; V,1,p.47
Canadian Society of Cost Accountants, or CSCA, (see also:
     Certified Management Accountants) II,4,p.4; II,8,p.16;
     II,9,p.6; V,1,p.42; V,2,p.25,33,36

Canadian Society of Cost Accountants and Industrial Engineers,
    see Canadian Society of Cost Accountants
Canadian Who's Who, II,9,p.5
Capital Budgets; see Budgets
Capital Cost Allowance, V,1,p.45
Capon, F.S., V,1,p.59
Cappell, C.L., II,7,p.613
Carr, Austin H., II,3,p.90
Carr-Saunders, A.M., II,7,p.612; II,8,p.34
Carscallen, Morley, III,4,p.136; III,5,p.3
Cash-Flow Statement, I,4,p.59
Cash Budgets; see Budgets
Caygill, M., II,7,p.613; II,8,p.35; V,2,p.64
Certified General Accountants, or CGAs, also (see also: General
    Accountants Association)
    challenge the Public Accountancy Act, II,7,p.609; II,8,p.22
    designation, II,7,p.597; II,8,p.4
    education in British Columbia, II,7,p.603
    formation of, II,7,p.599; V,1,p.41; V,2,p.13,40
    historical highlights, II,8,p.16,18; V,1,p.53; V,2,p.18-61
    in management accounting, II,7,p.607
    origins as Canadian Accountants Association, II,8,p.9
    participation in standard setting, II,8,p.6;
    III,4,p.103,116,125
    proposal to create the Accounting Standards Authority of
    Canada, V,1,p.55
    status of, II,7,p.597-598,602, II,8,p.6-7
Certified Management Accountants, or CMAs
    assumption of the CPAs training program, II,8,p.19
    designation, II,7,p.597; II,8,p.4
    formation of, II,7,p.599
    historical highlights, V,1,p.53; V,2,p.10-61
    participation in standard setting, II,8,p.6;
    III,4,p.103,116,125
    status of, II,7,p.597-598,604; II,8,p.6-7
Certified Public Accountants, or CPAs,
    challenge to the CAs, II,7,p.602
    challenge to the CGAs, II,8,p.17
    designation, II,7,p.599; II,8,p.4,10-11
    historical highlights, II,8,p.10-11; V,2,p.23; V,2,p.10-61
    origins as the Society of Independent Accountants and
    Auditors, (also called the United Accountants and Auditors
    in Canada)II,8,p.9,17
    merger with the CAs, II,7,p.606,609; II,8,p.17-19; V,1,p.48
    status, II,9,p.6
Chatfield, Michael, I,2,p.271,276
Charge and discharge accounting, I,2,p.272
Chartered Accountants Act, II,4,p.3; II,7,p.607
Chartered Accountants, or CAs,
    apprenticeship requirements, II,7,p.602-603
    code of ethics, V,2,p.57

education, (see also Queen's course) II,7,p.603; II,9,p.13;
III,6,p.5-6
designation, II,7,p.605; II,8,p.4
granted exclusive right to audit in Ontario, II,7,p.609
granted exclusive right to practice public accountancy in
Ontario, V,1,p.48
granted exclusive right to practice public accountancy in
Québec, V,1,p.45
mandatory examinations, II,7,p.601-602
merger with the CPAs, II,7,p.606,609; II,8,p.17-19; V,1,p.48
status, II,7,p.597-598; II,8,p.6-7; II,9,p.6
university degree requirement, II,7,p.604; II,8,p.20;
V,2,p.55
Child, J., II,7,p.612
Church, J.R., III,3,p.286
Clapperton, C.A., IV,1,p.93; V,1,p.59
Clark, M., IV,6,p.20
Clark, W.C., V,2,p.26-27
Clarkson & Gordon, II,4,p.6; II,5,p.197-201; II,9,p.7; IV,3,p.58
Clarkson, Gordon & Dilworth, II,2,p.97; II,5,p.197
Clarkson, E.R.C., II,2,p.97; II,3,p.76-77,79; II,4,p.1; II,9,p.6;
V,2,p.9,12
Clements, W., II,9,p.19
Clubb, C., II,8,p.34
Collard, E.A., II,7,p.612; V,1,p.57,59; V,2,p.62
Collins, Barrow/Maheu, Noiseux, IV,3,p.58
Commission des valeurs mobilières du Québec, IV,4,p.7-8
Commission to Study the Public's Expectations of Audits, also
known as the Macdonald Commission
findings, IV,5,p.4-6
implementation of, IV,5,p.12-13
mandate, IV,4,p.3; IV,5,p.3
recommendations, IV,5,p.6-22
study logic and process, IV,5,p.3-4
Companies Act,
English (or British), II,4,p.1; II,6,p.40,47,52,54:
III,3,p.271,300-301; IV,1,p.89,92-94; IV,2,p.104; V,1,p.31
Federal, I,4,p.18; III,2,p.193,198; III,3,p.271,300,
IV,1,p.88-90,93; IV,2,p.100,103; V,1,p.37,39,41-44,48,51
general, 1850, V,1,p.34
Ontario, II,4,p,2; II.6,p.40-54; III,1,p.1-4; III,3,p.300;
IV,1,p.88-90,93-94; V,1,p.38-40,46,48-49
other provinces, III,3,p.300; V,1,p.39; V,2,p.57
Trust and Loan, II,4,p.3; III,3,p.271
Conceptual Framework
FASB, II,5,p.216; III,4,p.101; III,5,p.2,11-12; III,6,p.1-
2,5-6,10-17,21-22
in Canada, III,4,p.96,101; III,5,p.11-16; III,6,p.1-22
in England, III,5,p.2
Confederation Life Case, V,2,p.9
Conservatism, I,4,p.54; III,7,p.103

Consistency and comparability, III,2,p.193; III,7,p.103;
     IV,2,p.104; V,1,p.33
Contemporary Accounting Research, establishment of, V,1,p.57
Contingent Liabilities, I,4,p.63
Cook, R., II,6,p.55,57; II,9,p.19
Cooke, Jay, I,4,p.10
Cooper, D.A., IV,6,p.20; V,2,p.62
Cooper Brothers and Co., V,2,p.62
Coopers & Lybrand, IV,3,p.58
Corporation of Public Accountants of the Province of Quebec, or
     CPAPQ, II,9,p.13; V,2,p.32
Corporate Reporting: Its Future Evolution, III,5,p.1-16;
     III,6,p.1,8,16; V,1,p.55
Corry, J.A., II,7,p.614
Cornud, Michel, I,2,p.263
Cost Accounting; see Management Accounting
Coulter, J., II,7,p.613
Coutts, W.B., III,3,p.287; V,1,p.48
Cox, Ivy A., V,2,p.33
Crandall, Robert H., V,1,p.59
Crate, H.E., V,2,p.63
Creighton, P., II,4,p.1; II,7,p.613; II,8,p.34; II,9,p.19;
     V,1,p.57,60; V,2,p.63

Cross, Alexander, I,4,p.15
Cross, W.H., V,2,p.7,9
Cugnet, François-Etienne, I,1,p.65-66,68-73
Culver, Dennis, IV,3,p.58
Cuvillier, Austin, I,4,p.13

D
Dale-Harris, R.B., III,3,p.287; V,1,p.48
Davis, J.D., I,1,p.71,81
Davis, John P., I,1,p.81
Day, P., II,7,p.614
Datini, Marco and Company, I,4,p.54
Debit and credit,
     use of, I,2,p.265; I,3,p.3-8,11-12
Deferred taxes, appearance of, V,1,p.46
De Francheville,
     François Poulin I,1,p.64-65
     Mrs. François Poulin I,1,p.69
Dell, H.C., II,5,p.201
Deloitte Haskins & Sells, IV,3,p.58
Demski, J.S., III,4,p.129
Denison, Merrill, I,2,p.262-263,276; I,4,p.21
Denman, J. III,4,p.136
Depreciation, I,4,p.54; III,2,p.197
De Reinack, Baron J., I,4,p.11
De Roover, Raymond, I,4,p.54,77
De Santis, G., II,7,p.613
Desrochers, A., V,2,p.63

De Valmur, Bricault, I,1,p.65
Dictionary of Canadian Biography, I,2,p.263,276
Dickerson, R. W. V., V,1,p.60
Dicksee, Lawrence R., II,2,p.97
Dilworth, J., II,2,p.96-97
Directors' Report to the Shareholders,
    requirement to provide, IV,1,p.88; IV,2,p.100
    content, IV,2,p.100-106
    president's message, IV,2,p.101,104
Disclosure, see Financial Statements
Dividends, III,2,p.197-198
Dobell, S.H., V,2,p.63
Dominion Association of Chartered Accountants, (see also:
    Canadian Institute of Chartered Accountants) II,3,p.87-88;
    II,4,p.3-4; II,6,p.42-43,47; II,7,p.599,605; II,8,p.8-9;
    III,3,p.270
Dominion Textile Company Limited,
    founding members, I,4,p.15
    incorporation and growth, I,4,p.8,16-17
Donovan, Kenneth, I,2,p.262,276
Dopuch, J.S., III,4,p.129; III,6,p.15
Double entry accounting,
    early use of, I,2,p.271-272,276
    primer, I,3,p.1-17
Douglas, W.A., II,3,p.79,81
Dowling, J.B., II,8,p.35
Drummond, I., II,9,p.19
Dunwoody and Company, IV,3,p.58
Dupre, J.S., II,7,p.614

E
Easterbrook, W.T., I,2,p.276; I,4,p.21
Eccles, W.J., I,1,p.81
Economic reality, III,5,p.4-5; III,6,p.8
Eddis, H.W., II,3,p.76-77,79
Eddis, Wilton C., II,3,p.88; II,6,p.44; V,1,p.37,60
Edey, H.C., I,4,p.77; IV,1,p.89
Edwards, George, II,4,p.1-6; II,6,p.48-49,53,55-57; II,8,p.35;
    II,9,p.5; III,3,p.270; IV,6,p.11; V,1,p.39,41; V,2,p.18-
    61,63
Edwards, H. Percy, II,4,p.5; V,2,p.63
Edwards Morgan, V,2,p.11
Edwards, Oswald, II,4,p.5
Educational programs, (see also: Queen's course) II,7,p.600
Efficient Market Hypothesis, III,5,p.9; III,6,p.9
Elliot, S., V,2,p.63
Englebert, R., II,7,p.613; V,2,p.63
English, J., II,9,p.19
English Royal Mail Steam Packet Scandal, IV,1,p.92
Ermatinger,
    Frederick William I,2,p.263
    Charles Oakes I,2,p.263

Ernst & Whinney, IV,3,p.58
Estey, Mr. Justice Willard Z., IV,4,p.1-3,8; IV,6,p.15-17,20
Estey Report, IV,4,p.2-3
Eudy, Kimberly Ham, III,6,p.6-7
Excess Profits Act, II,5,p.198
Expectations gap, IV,6,p.17
Extra Provincial Corporations Act, II,6,p.42

F
Factorage accounts, I,3,p.16
Fairclough, E., V,2,p.63
Federal Combines Investigations Act, II,8,p.23
Federation of CAs of Canada, V,2,p.15
Feldman, R.D., II,7,p.612
Fellow of the Chartered Accountant, or FCA, II,8,p.13
Ferris, K.R., II,7,p.613
Fielding, A., II,7,p.614; II,8,p.36
Financial Accounting Standards Board, or FASB,
      conceptual framework, see Conceptual Framework
      Emerging Issues Task Force, IV,4,p.5
      exposure draft process, III,4,p.116,119,124-125,
      formation, III,5,p.1
      standards, III,4,p.129; IV,1,p.98-99
      standard setting, III,4,p.101,104,141,143-144,150
Financial Analysts,
      Canadian Council of Financial Analysts, III,4,p.103,116
      Montreal Society of, III,3,p.302
      Toronto Society of, III,3,p.302
Financial Executives Institute of Canada, or FEIC, II,8,p.6;
      III,3,p.302; III,4,p.103,116; III,5,p.13; V,1,p.45
Financial Reporting in Canada, III,3,p.275,295; V,1,p.46
Financial Reporting, objectives of, III,6,p.9 ,21-22
Financial Statements, (see also: Balance Sheet, Income
      Statement, Statement of Retained Earnings)
      Consolidated,
            legal status in Canada, III,3,p.272; IV,1,p.91
            research study, III,3,p.294
      disclosure requirements, II,6,p.43,45,54; III,3,p.272,301;
            IV,1,p.88-89,92-93; IV,5,p.11-12,16-17; V,1,p.33,38-
            39,44,46,48,53
      disclosure requirements of regulated companies, II,6,p.43-
            44; V,1,p.32,34
      early examples of, I,2,p.269-271,276; V,1,p.41
      elements of, III,7,p.107
      evolution in Canada I,4,p.53-63
      filed with Provincial or Federal Secretaries, II,6,p.52
      measurement, III,7,p.109
      objective of financial statements, III,7,p.101
      role of, III,4,p.99
      Segmented information, III,4,p.115,120-121; IV,4,p.7-8
      sufficiency of disclosure, III,2,p.193
      valuation of assets, IV,2,p.104; IV,5,p.11,17

        voluntary disclosure, II,6,p.53-54
Financial Statement Concepts, CICA Handbook Section 1000,
        benefit versus cost constraint, III,7,p.103
        elements of financial statements, III,7,p.107
        generally accepted accounting principles, III,7,p.110-111
        materiality, III,7,p.103
        measurement, III,7,p.109
        objective of financial statements, III,7,p.101-102
        purpose and scope, III,7,p.101
        qualitative characteristics, III,7,p.103-105
        recognition criteria, III,7,p.108
Financial Times of Canada, III,3,p.303
Financial World (US), III,3,p.303
Findlay, W.F., II,3,p.78
Fleming C.A., V,1,p.37,60
Fogarty, T.J., IV,6,p.20
Fowler, Gordon C., III,6,p.3
Fleming, C.A., II,6,p.46
Freidlin, J.N., III,3,p.273
Freidson, E., II,7,p.613; II,8,p.35
Friedland, R., IV,6,p.20-21
Fulk, J., II,7,p.612

G
Gale, Samuel, I,2,p.263
Galbraith, J.K., III,3,p.274
Gambino, Anthony J., I,2 p.270-272,276
Gamelin, Ignace I,1,p.65,68,71-73
Garden, George, I,4,p.13
Garner, S. Paul, II,6,p.46,56-57
Garnsey, Sir Gilbert, IV,2,p.101
Gates, Horatio, I,4,p.13
Gault, A.F., I,4,p.15
Generally Accepted Accounting Principles, or GAAP, II,5,p.211-
        217; III,3,p.281,289; III,4,p.99-100; III,6,p.5,15;
        III,7,p.110-111; IV,3,p.58; IV,4,p.4-5; IV,5,p.15,21;
        IV,6,p.17; V,1,p.51
Generally Accepted Auditing Standards, or GAAS, IV,4,p.8
General Accountants' Association, also the Canadian Accountants
        Association, II,7,p.606; II,8,p.9; V,2,p.15-61
General Road Companies Act, II,6,p.44
George II, King, I,2,p.264
Gerstl, J.E., II,7,p.613-614
Gibbon, A.P., V,2,p.22
Gibson, F.W., V,2,p.63
Gibson, J.M., II,6,p.47,57
Giddens, A., II,8,p.35; II,9,p.19
Gilb, C.L., II,7,p.613; II,9,p.19
Glassco, J. Grant, II,5,p.198,203-204; IV,1,p.93,95
Goode, W.J., II,7,p.613
Goodman, M., V,2,p.63
Goodwill, III,2,p.197

Gordon & Dilworth, II,2,p.96
Gordon, Col. H.D. Lockhart, II,2,p.94,96; II,4,p.6;
     II,5,p.198,200; V,2,p.63
Gordon, Walter, II,4,p.198,203-204
Gordon, William, I,1,p.81; I,4,p.53,77
Gorelik, G., V,2,p.63
Goyder, J., II,9,p.19
Grady, Paul, II,5,p.213; III,3,p.289
Gramsci, A., II,8,p.35
Gray, Edward William, I,2,p.263
Grenfell, Pasco du P., I,4,p.11
Guild of Industrial, Commercial and Institutional Accounts, or
     GICIAs, II,7,p.597; II,8,p.4; V,2,p.47-61
Gurnham, C., I,4,p.16,22
Guy, Paul, IV,4,p.8

H
Hagerman, R.I., III,4,p.129
Hall, R., II,7,p.613
Halliday, T.C., II,7,p.613
Hamilton, Alexander, I,4,p.20
Hanna, W.J., II,6,p.51
Haring, John R., III,4,p.130
Harman, S.B., II,3,p.80,89; II,6,p.47; II,9,p.6
Harris, E.C., IV,1,p.96
Hartley, E.N., I,1,p.81
Hart-Smith, Alexander, II,4,p.1
Haslam, D.F., III,3,p.290
Haskins and Sells, V,2,p.63
Hastings, A., II,7,p.613
Hatfield, Henry Rand, III,3,p.276; IV,1,p.89
Heap, J., II,9,p.19
Hegemonic perspective on accounting, II,8,p.2-31
Heinz, J.P., II,7,p.6
Held, D., IV,6,p.20
Henderson, M. V,2,p.63
Herkins, Miss Florence Eualie, V,2,p.28
Hill, James J., I,4,p.11
Hinings, C.R., II,7,p.613
Historical Statistics of Canada, IV,1,p.90
Historical Statistics of the United States, I,1,p.81
Hockin, T., IV,6,p.20
Hocquart, Gilles, I,1,p.64-66
Hodge, M.N., II,7,p.615
Hoffer, Eric, I,4,p.7,20
Holder, William W., III,6,p.6-7
Home Bank, IV,6,p.1-2,6-19
Hoole, A.H., II,7,p.613; V,2,p.64
Hopkins, W., III,4,p.146-149
Hopwood, A., II,8,p.34
Horack, F.E., II,6,p.51,57
Horne, G.R., V,2,p.64

Hoskins, D., II,6,p.44; V,1,p.37,60
Houston, W.R., V,1,p.38
Howell, Charlotte N., V,2,p.33
Hudson, G.W., V,2,p.64
Hudson's Bay Company, I,4,p.8,11,13
Huer, J., II,7,p.613
Humphries, C.W., II,6,p.55,57; V,1,p.60
Hurdman, F.B., V,2,p.64
Hutchison, T.A.M., III,3,p.286
Hutton, S.P., II,7,p.613
Hyde, John, II,9,p.6; IV,1,p.91; V,2,p.64

I
Ijiri, Y., III,4,p.130
Income Measurement,
     early examples of, I,2,p.271; I,4,p.14; I,4,p.54-55
Income Statement (see also: Financial Statements)
     early examples, III,2,p.198,204-206
     required disclosure, IV,1,p.91,93; V,1,p.44
     requirement to audit, V,1,p.46
     requirement to provide, II,6,p.40-41; III,1,p.1;
     IV,1,p.88,92; IV,2,p.100
Income tax,
     introduction of, II,1,p.96; II,2,p.98; IV,1,p.90
Independence, III,6,p.5; IV,5,p.6-8; V,2,p.9
Independent Accountants Association of Ontario, II,8,p.10;
     V,2,p.41
Independent Public Accountants Association, or IPAA, II,8,p.4
Insolvency Act, V,2,p.6
Institute of Accountants and Adjusters of Canada, see Institute
     of Chartered Accountants of Ontario, or ICAO
Institute of Accountants and Auditors of the Province of Québec
     II,7,p.599; V,1,p.33,35,41; V,2,p.7,10-61
Institute of Accountants of Great Britain, II,3,p.76,79;
     V,2,p.1,7
Institute of Accredited Public Accountants, V,2,p.35,40
Institute of Chartered Accountants, Actuaries and Finance,
     V,2,p.11
Institute of Chartered Accountants of Alberta, V,2,p.11,16-61,64
Institute of Chartered Accountants of British Columbia, V,2,p.11-
     12,16-61
Institute of Chartered Accountants of England and Wales,
     III,3,p.278; V,2,p.6
Institute of Chartered Accountants of Manitoba, V,1,p.37;
     V,2,p.8-61
Institute of Chartered Accountants of Montreal, see Institute of
     Chartered Accountants of the Province of Québec
Institute of Chartered Accountants of New Brunswick, V,2,p.20-61
Institute of Chartered Accountants of Newfoundland, V,2,p.12-61
Institute of Chartered Accountants of Nova Scotia, V,2,p.11-61
Institute of Chartered Accountants of Ontario, or ICAO,
     admission of women, II,3,p.84-85; II,8,p.8; V,2,p.8-10

admission standards, V,2,p.8
association with the CICA, III,3,p.269
Board of Instruction, members of, II,3,p.91
Committee on Accounting and Auditing, IV,1,p.94
challenge to exclusive rights to audit, II,8,p.23-28
education,(see also: Queen's course) II,8,p.14; V,2,p.8-61
examination process, V,2,p.9-61
exclusive right to practice public accounting, IV,1,p.98;
    V,2,p.10
exclusive right to use CA designation, V,2,p.13,16
first Council of, II,3,p.77
founding meeting, V,1,p.36; V,2,p.7
founding members, II,3,p.76
historical highlights, II,3,p.76-93; II,6,p.39,42-43,45-
    48,53-54; II,8,p.7-15; IV,1,p.88-90; V,1,p.32-57; V,2,p.7-61
incorporation, II,1,p.95; II,3,p.76,81; II,7,p.598;
    II,8,p.8; V,2,p.8
influence of, V,1,p.33; V,2,p.9
minutes, II,6,p.55-56,58
participation in standard setting, IV,1,p.93
qualifying examinations, II,3,p.82-83; II,6,p.45;
    II,7,p.601; II,8,p.10
Rules of Professional Conduct, IV,1,p.97; V,1,p.60
students' association, II,3,p.86,89; II,6,p.45; V,2,p.10
yearbook, V,1,p.60
Institute of Chartered Accountants of Prince Edward Island,
    V,2,p.26
Institute of Chartered Accountants of Saskatchewan, V,2,p.13,16-
    61
Insurances, I,3,p.15
Internal Control, evaluation of, II,5,p.205-210
International Accountants and Executives Corporation, or IAEC,
    II,8,p.4; V,2,p.34
International Accountants Society of America, V,2,p.22
International Accounting Standards Committee, V,2,p.57
International Federation of Accountants, or IFAC, V,1,p.53;
    V,2,p.59
Inventory,
    physical counts, II,2,p.97
    reporting of, III,2,p.197
Italian method of book-keeping, I,3,p.2

J
Jacobs-Ermatinger Estate Papers, I,2,p.276
Jacobs, Samuel, I,2,p.263,270
Jamieson, A.B., I,4,p.21
Jamous, H., II,7,p.613
Jewell, George, II,4,p.1
Johnson, D.J., V,2,p.64
Johnson, Hans V., I,2,p.263,277
Johnson, J.W., II,3,p.78-79,89; II,6,p.46; V,1,p.37
Johnson, T., II,7,p.613; II,8,p.35; V,2,p.64

Johnston, Kenneth S. I,4,p.77
Jones, E., II,9,p.19
Jones, F.E., II,9,p.19
Jones, Haydn, I,2,p.272,277
Jones, Thomas, I,2,p.271
Journal, use of, I,3,p.3

K
Kaelble, H., II,9,p.19
Kennedy, John S. I,4,p.11
Kilbourn, William, I,4,p.18,22
Kimber, J.R., Kimber Committee, Kimber Report, IV,1,p.95-96
King, C.L., III,3,p.277; V,2,p.64
Kitson, Norman, I,4,p.11
Klegon, D., II,7,p.613
Knight, C.L., V,1,p.58
Knowles, Henry, IV,3,p.59
Kreiser, Larry, I,2,p.271,277
Kronus, C.L., II,7,p.614
Kuhn, A.K., II,6,p.51,57,58
Kylsant, Lord, trial of, IV,2,p.100

L
Laiken, S.N., III,3,p.290
Lalonde, Marc, IV,3,p.58
Lanfranconi, C.P., V,2,p.64
Larson, M.S., II,7,p.614; II,8,p.35; II,9,p.19
Laumann, E.O., II,7,p.613
Lavine, S. IV,1,p.94
Lazar, F., V,2,p.64
Leach, C.W., V,2,p.64
Leal, H.A., II,7,p.614; II,8,p.35
Leases, III,4,p.115,122-123
Leavitt, Ron, V,2,p.35
Ledger, use of, I,3,p.3
Lemon, W.M., V,2,p.64
Leslie, Don, II,5,p.205,210
Leslie, James, I,4,p.13
Leslie, John, V,2,p.13
Lew, B., V,2,p.64
Licentiate in Accounting, or LA designation, see CPA
Light, D.W., II,7,p.614
Limited liability, V,1,p.34
Lipset, S., II,9,p.19
Liquidity, III,2,p.194; IV,5,p.11
Little, A.J., V,2,p.64
Little, B., IV,6,p.20
Littleton, A.C., I,2,p.271-272,277; III,6,p.12
Loan and Trust Companies Act, II,8,p.9
Loft, A., II,8,p.35
London Public Records Office, I,2,p.264,277
Louisbourg, accounting in, I,2,p.265-276

Lowden, Steve, II,5,p.209

M
Ma, Ronald, II,6,p.57-58
Macdonald Commission, see the *Commission to Study the Public's Expectations of Audits*
MacDonald, K.M., II,9,p.19
MacDonald, W.J., V,2,p.64
Macdonnell, J.J., II,5,p.215
MacGillivray & Co., IV,3,p.58
MacInnes, C., II,6,p.55,58
Macintosh, W.A., IV,1,p.92
Mackenzie, Alexander, I,2,p.263-270,276
MacKenzie, D.C., V,2,p.64
Mackintosh, W.A., V,1,p.60
Macpherson, F.H., II,6,p.44; V,1,p.37
MacMillan, David S., I,2,p.263-264,269,277
Mair, John, I,2,p.271,277
Malcolm, Alexander, I,2,p.265,271,277
Management Discussion and Analysis of Financial Condition and Results of Operations, or MD&A, IV,4,p.7-8; IV,5,p.16
Managerial Accounting
    use in New France I,1,p.64
Mann, Harvey, I,2,p.263,276; II,7,p.614; II,8,p.36; V,1,p.57,60; V,2,p.65
Martin, N.L., V,2,p.22
Martin, S.A., III,3,p.290; V,1,p.51
Mason, J.J., II,3,p.78,82; II,6,p.47
Materiality, III,7,p.103; IV,4,p.6
May, George O., II,5,p.199
May, Robert G., III,4,p.130
Mayer, J.W., II,7,p.614
McDougall, D.M., II,9,p.19
McIntyre, Duncan, I,4,p.11
McKeen, C.A., II,9,p.20; V,2,p.65,66
McKilligan, J.B., V,2,p.12
McLeod, J.A., V,2,p.65
McRoberts, H.A., II,9,p.19
McTaggart, Marion Cathie, V,2,p.39
Measurement, see Financial Statements
Mepham, Michael J., I,2,p.264,277
Merino, B.D., II,6,p.48,56,58; II,7,p.614; II,8,p.37; V,1,p.61
Michels, R., II,9,p.19
Milburn, Alex, III,4,p.140
Miller, Harry, I,1,p.81
Millie, I.E., II,8,p.36
Mills, C.W., II,9,p.19,20
Miranti, P.J., II,9,p.20
Moffatt, George, I,4,p.13
Moffet, H.S., III,3,p.287
Molson, John, I,2,p.262
Montagna, P.D., II,7,p.614

644

Montgomery's *Auditing*, II,5,p.199,205
Montreal Cotton Company,
early financial statements, I,4,p.59-61
founding members, I,4,p.15
incorporation and growth, I,4,p.8,14-16
Montreal Stock Exchange, V,1,p.35
Moore, Christopher, I,2,p.262,277
Moore, J.T., II,3,p.79
Moore, Underhill, III,3,p.276
Moreland, P.A., V,2,p.65
Morgan, Henry James, II,9,p.5
Morgan, William Pomeroy, II,4,p.2
Morris, Richard, II,6,p.57-58
Mouffe, C., II,8,p.36
Moyser, G., II,9,p.20
Mulcahy, Gertrude, III,3,p.287,289-290; III,4,p.130;
IV,1,p.97,99; V,1,p.60
Mulvey, Thomas, II,6,p.40,42,49,51-54,58; IV,1,p.88-90;
V,1,p.39,41,60; V,2,p.65
Mumford, M.J., II,6,p.57-58
Municipal Act, V,2,p.9
Murphy, George, I,2,p.271,277; III,3,p.272; V,1,p.57-58;
V,1,p.60; V,2,p.65

N
Naphapiet, J., II,8,p.34
National Association of Cost Accountants (USA), II,9,p.6;
V,2,p.30-31
National Association of Accountants (USA), III,3,p.303
National Energy Program, or NEP, IV,3,p.55-58
National Policy in Canada, effects of, I,4,p.15,18
Naylor, T., IV,6,p.20
Neimark, M.D., II,8,p.37
Nelles, H.W., II,6,p.55,57
Neu, D., IV,6,p.20
Neufeld, E.P., IV,6,p.20
Neumann, F.L., V,2,p.64
Neville, W.A., V,2,p.65
Nish, Cameron, I,1,p.81
Nobes, C.W., V,1,p.58
Nonprofit accounting, II,5,p.212
Norman, H.G., III,3,p.273,277
Northcote, Henry Stafford, I,4,p.11
Northern Electric Manufacturing Company, I,4,p.10
Northland Bank, IV,4,p.1; IV,6,p.16
North West Company, I,4,p.13

O
O'Connor, J., IV,6,p.20
Offe, C., IV,6,p.20
Office of the Inspector General of Banks, IV,6,p.9; V,1,p.34
Olivier de Vézain, Pierre, I,1,p.66,68,71-73

Olsen, D., II,9,p.20
Ontario, Archives, II,6,p.56-58
Ontario Bills, II,6,p.58
Ontario Building Societies Act, V,1,p.35
Ontario Companies Act, see Companies Act
Ontario Corporations Act, IV,1,p.97
Ontario Insurance Act, V,1,p.37
Ontario Municipal Act, V,2,p.10,36-37
Ontario Public Accountancy Act, V,2,p.51
Ontario Securities Act, IV,1,p.95,97; V,1,p.49,54; V,2,p.53
Ontario Securities Commission, or OSC, III,3,p.301; IV,1,p.95,98;
     IV,3,p.55,59; IV,4,p.3,5,7; V,1,p.47,50,54; V,2,p.55
Ontario *Sessional Papers*, II,6,p.58
Ontario Statutes, II,6,p.54-59; IV, 1,p.88,95,97-98; V,1,p.32,61
Ontario Trust Companies Act, V,2,p.22
Operating Account - see Income Statement
Operating budgets; see Budgets
Organization for Economic Cooperation and Development; III,5,p.2

P
Paciolo, I,4,p.53-54,77
Pahl, R.E., II,9,p.20
Palmer, John R., I,2,p.270-272,276
Panitch, L., IV,6,p.20
Panitpakdi, Prot, IV,1,p.89
Parker, R.H., II,8,p.36; V,1,p.58
Parkin, F., II,9,p.20
Parsons, T., II,8,p.36
Partnership agreements, I,1,p.71-73
Parton, John, II,1,p.94; IV,1,p.90; V,2,p.65
Passeron, J.C., II,8,p.34
Paterson, A., II,7,p.614
Paton, W.A., III,6,p.12
Patterson, R., IV,6,p.20
Peasnel, K.V., III,6,p.4
Peliolle, B., II,7,p.613
Perrucci, R., II,7,p.614
Perry, J.H., IV,6,p.20
Petroleum and Gas Revenue Tax, or PGRT, III,4,p.137; IV,3,p.55-56
Petroleum Incentive(s) Program, or PIP,
     accounting for, III,4,p.137; III,6,p.4; IV,3,p.55-57
Pettigrew, A.M., II,7,p.614
Pfeffer, J., II,8,p.35
Pineo, P.C., II,9,p.19
Pitt, William, I,2,p.264
Piven, F.F., IV,6,p.21
Podmore, D., II,7,p.614
Pollins, Harold, I,4,p.62,77
Pontifex B., V,2,p.65
Porter, J., II,9,p.19; II,9,p.20
Portwood, D., II,7,p.614; II,8,p.36
Positive accounting theory, III,6,p.13,16

Poulin, Pierre I,1,p.65
Powell, M., II,7,p.614
Prandy, K., II,9,p.20
Previts, G.J., II,7,p.614; V,1,p.58,61
Prewitt, K., II,9,p.20
Price, Harry L., V,2,p.13
Price Waterhouse, IV,3,p.58
Professional Code of Conduct, IV,5,p.8,18,19
Professional discipline, IV,5,p.10
Professional judgement, IV,4,p.6,9; IV,5,p.9-10,17
Professional Organizations Committee, II,8,p.21-28; V,2,p.60
Professional segmentation, II,7,p.592-597,610-611
Profit; see Income Measurement
Profit and loss account, (see also: Income Statement)
      early examples of,I,2,p.267,272; I,4,p.53; III,2,p.202,206;
      contents of, III,2,p.197-198, IV,2,p.104-105
      requirement to provide, IV,1,p.88; IV,2,p.100-101,104
Prospectus,
      criticism of, V,1,p.44
      issuance of stock without, II,6,p.51
      requirements to file, II,6,p.40,44,49,51-52
      requirement to use standard auditor's report, V,1,p.48
      segmented information included in, IV,4,p.7
Provincial Institutes of Chartered Accountants,
      Alberta, II,1,p.95; II,3,p.90
      British Columbia, II,1,p.95; II,3,p.90; II,7,p.601
      duties and responsibilities, III,3,p.271
      Manitoba, II,1,p.95; II,3,p.90; II,7,p.599
      New Brunswick, II,3,p.90
      Nova Scotia, II,3,p.90; II,7,p.599
      Ontario, see Institute of Chartered Accountants of
      Prince Edward Island, II,3,p.90
      Quebec, II,1,p.95; II,3,p.90; II,7,p.598; III,3,p.269
      Saskatchewan, II,1,p.95; II,3,p.90
Public Accountancy Act, or Public Accountants Act,
      creation, II,7,p.609; II,8,p.12,18
      challenged by CGAs, II,7,p.609
Public Accountancy Amendment Act of Ontario, IV,1,p.98
Public Accountants Association of British Columbia, V,2,p.35
Public Accounting, regulation of, II,7,p.598; II,8,p.4
Public Accounting Board, II,8,p.4,31
Public Archives of Canada, I,2,p.263,265,277

Q
Québec Securities Commission, IV,4,p.8
Québec Statutes, V,1,p.61
Queen's course, II,3,p.91; II,4,p.4; II,5,p.198; II,7,p.603;
      II,9,p.13,16; V,1,p.42; V,2,p.23,26-27,35,52-53

R
Railways Acts, I,4,p.12,59,62
Ralston, J.L., V,1,p.62

Ratcliffe, T.A., V,1,p.58
Ratio analysis, IV,2,p.105
Rattray, Mrs. M.L., II,8,p.8; V,2,p.8
Raymond, Chabot, Martin, Paré & Associés, IV,3,p.58
Raynauld, A., IV,1,p.90
Recognition criteria, III,7,p.108
Registered Industrial Accountants, or RIA, II,7,p.606; V,2,p.38-61
Relevance, III,7,p.103
Reliability, III,7,p.103
Re London and General Bank, IV,2,p.106
Report of the Attorney General's committee on Securities Legislation in Ontario, (The Kimber Report), V,1,p.48-49
Report of the Special Committee to Examine the Role of the Auditor, also known as *The Adams Report*, III,5,p.12-13; V,1,p.58; V,1,p.54
Research and development costs, III,4,p.115,119-120
Responsibility of the profession to the public, II,9,1-2
Richardson, A.J., II,7,p.614; II,8,p.36; II,9,p.20; IV,6,p.21; V,2,p.65,66
Richardson, George, II,5,p.203
Richardson, John, I,4,p.13
Roberts, Sir Charles George Douglas, II,9,p.5
Robertson, Charles, II,3,p.77,82
Robinson, Chris, IV,3,p.57
Rose, Charles D. I,4,p.11
Rosen, L.S., V,1,p.51
Rosenberg, D., II,7,p.614
Ross, H., II,7,p.614; II,8,p.36; IV,1,p.95; V,1,p.49,62; V,2,p.65,66
Ross, J.W.., III,3,p.304
Rothman, R.A., II,7,p.614
Rothstein, W.G., II,7,p.614
Rowan, B., II,7,p.614
Royal Commission on Banking and Finance, Report of,(The Porter Report) V,1,p.48
Royal Commission on Canada's Economic Prospects, (The Gordon Report) V,1,p.46
Royal Commission on Insurance, in Canada, II,6,p.44,55,57; IV,1,p.90; V,1,p.40
Royal Commission on the Textile Industry (The Turgeon Report) V,1,p.44
Royal Mail Steam Packet Case, V,1,p.43
Rutherford, Robert, IV,3,p.57

S
Saint-Maurice, les forges de, I,1,p.63; I,4,p.7
Santayana, George, I,4,p.53,77
Saunders, Thomas H., III,3,p.276
Scheutze, Walter P., III,6,p.3,5-6
Schmitter, P.C., IV,6,p.21
Securities Act, IV,4,p.5

Segmented information, see Financial Statements
Select Committee on Company Law, IV,1,p.94
Seventh Census of Canada, I,1,p.82
Shaughnessy, Thomas George, I,4,p.11
Sheldahl, T.K., I,2,p.271,277
Siegel, G.H., II,7,p.615
Sievers, J.M., V,2,p.64,66
Simonnet, Jacques I,1,p.66,68,71-72
Single entry accounting,
    use in 18th century, I,2,p.270
Sinotte, G., II,7,p.615
Sise, Charles Fleetford, I,4,p.9
Skelton, O.D., IV,1,p.90; V,1,p.62; V,2,p.26-27
Skinner, Ross, II,5,p.197-217; III,3,p.287; III,4,p.136
Smails R.G.H., *Auditing*, II,5,p.199; V,1,p.42
Smails, R.G.H., II,8,p.36; III,3,p.272; IV,1,p.91-93; V,1,p.42-
    43,62; V,2,p.67
Smith, Donald A. I,4,p.11
Smith, H.L., II,7,p.615
Smith, St.Elmo V., III,3,p.287
Smithers, C.F., I,4,p.58,77
Smyth, J.E., III,3,p.272; V,2,p.67
Society of Incorporated Accountants and Auditors, IV,2,p.103;
    V,2,p.22
Society of Incorporated Accountants and Auditors of England,
    V,2,p.13
Society of Independent Accountants and Auditors, see CPAs
Society of Independent Public Accountants of British Columbia,
    V,2,p.24
Society of Industrial Accountants of Canada, III,3,p.304
Society of Industrial and Cost Accountants of Canada, V,2,p.10-
    61
Society of Industrial and Cost Accountants of Ontario, V,2,p.10-
    61
Society of Management Accountants, see Certified Management
    Accountants
Solomons, David, III,6,p.4
Sorokin, P., II,7,p.615
Stacey, N.A.H., II,7,p.615
Stamp, E., III,4,p.130; III,6,p.8; V,1,p.55
Starr, P., II,7,p.615
Standard and Poor's, II,5,p.203
Standing Committee on Energy Legislation, House of Commons,
    IV,3,p.59
Statement of Retained Earnings,
    (see also: Financial Statements) I,4,p.58
    early examples of, combined with profit and loss account,
    III,2,p.201-202, 206
    required disclosure, IV,1,p.93
Steel Company of Canada, I,4,p.8,18-19
Stephen, George, I,4,p.11
Sterett, J.E., II,6,p.51,57,59

Sterling, R.R., III,6,p.12
Stevens, R., II,7,p.615
Stewart, A., II,9,p.20
Stewart, Ian, IV,3,p.56
Stone, A., II,9,p.20
Stone, Henry, I,4,p.14
Strauss, A., II,7,p.612; II,8,p.34
Streeck, W., IV,6,p.21
Stuart, R.C., V,2,p.67
Sullivan, Jerry, IV,4,p.8
Sundem, Gary L., III,4,p.130
Sunder, Shyam, III,4,p.129; III,6,p.15
Sutcliffe, John, V,2,p.18
Sutherland, J.B., V,2,p.67
Swinburne, F., II,7,p.615; II,8,p.36

T
T-accounts
     early use, I,2,p.265; I,4,p.59
Talon, Jean, I,2,p.262
Taschereau, Thomas Jacques I,1,p.71-72
Teitlebaum, Albert, II,5,p.210
Tims, D., IV,6,p.21
Tindall, W.B., II,6,p.44
Tinker, S., II,8,p.37
The Accountant, IV,2,p.106
The Adams Report, see *The Report of the Special Committee to
Examine the Role of the Auditor*
The Annual Financial Review, Canadian, II,6,p.55,59; II,7,p.612;
     V,1,p.38
The Financial Post, II,6,p.44,55,59; III,3,p.272,303; IV,1,p.91;
     IV,3,p.57,59; V,1,p.40,45
The Globe and Mail, II,6,p.57,59; III,3,p.303
The Monetary Times, II,6,p.55-57,59; V,1,p.36
Thomas, R.D., III,3,p.269,286; III,4,p.130; IV,3,p.57; V,1,p.62
Thompson, R.R., III,3,p.271; V,2,p.67
Thomson, H.W., I,4,p.77
Thorne, J.L., V,2,p.22
Thorne Riddell, IV,3,p.58
Thronton, D.B., V,2,p.64
Tomlinson, R.H., II,3,p.81
Tonkins, C., II,7,p.614
Toronto Stock Exchange, II,6,p.45,52-53,55,59; III,3,p.287,301-
     302; IV,1,p.95; V,1,p.62; V,1,p.35,38-39,47,49
Touche Ross & Co., IV,3,p.58
Transport Act, I,4,p.63
Trebilcock, M.J., II,8,p.37
Tremain, D.J., II,7,p.615; II,8,p.37
Trial Balance, I,4,p.53,55
Treasury of the Navy, I,1,p.71,73
Tuohy, C.J., II,8,p.37
Tunnel, Alfred Leonard, II,9,p.5

Tupper, Sir Charles, I,4,p.77
Turgeon, Hon. Mr. Justice W.F.A., Report of, I,4,p.17,20,22
Turner, C., II,7,p.615
Turner, Thomas, I,4,p.13

U
Understandability, III,7,p.103
Uniform Accounting, IV,1,p.92; V,1,p.41
Uniform final examinations, V,2,p.21,36
Uniform intermediate examinations, V,2,p.36
Uniformity, V,1,p.33,43
United Accountants and Auditors in Canada, V,2,p.24
United Nations, III,5,p.2
University of Western Ontario study for the CICA, III,3,p.290-291
Urban Development Institute (Ontario), III,3,p.303

V
Valleau, W.J., II,3,p.90
Valuation of assets, see Financial Statements
Van Horne, William Cornelius, I,4,p.11
Verification of Financial Statements, IV,1,p.92
Voke, Albert F., I,2,p.270,277

W
Wagstaffe, M., II,9,p.20
Walker, C.E., II,5,p.199; V,1,p.42
Walker, J.K., III,3,p.287
Walters, Chester, II,8,p.9
Ward, D., III,4,p.146-149; IV,3,p.57
Warde, J.D., II,6,p.49,56,59; V,1,p.38,62
Waste Book, I,3,p.2-3
Waterhouse, J.H., III,4,p.135-139,142-144,151; IV,6,p.21
Watkins, M.H., III,3,p.273
Watt, M.L., V,2,p.67
Watts, R.L., II,6,p.57,59; III,4,p.130; III,6,p.7,13
Weaver, J.C., II,9,p.20
Westervelt J.W., II,6,p.44; V,1,p.37
Whitney, J.P., II,6,p.43,51-52,54; IV,1,p.90; V,1,p.39
Who's who in Canada, II,9,p.5
Wilcox, C.S. I,4,p.18
Williams, J.J., V,2,p.66
Willmott, H., II,7,p.615; II,8,p.37
Wilson, D.A., V,2,p.67
Wilson, J.R.M., II,5,p.198,201-202,204,209; IV,1,p.94; V,1,p.62
Wilson, P.A., II,7,p.612; II,8,p.34
Winkler, J.T., II,9,p.20
Wolfson, A.D., II,8,p.37
Wood, E.R. I,4,p.18
Wood, William, I,2,p.262,277
Women chartered accountants, II,8,p.8; V,2,p.8,19,26,28,31,33,38-
    39
Worthington, B., V,2,p.67